Oracle9*i* Performance Tuning:

Optimizing Database Productivity

VIEW 2 DIAG BUFFER CACHE • V$SYSSTAT

VALID SGA GANUALS • 4M

LIBRARY CACHE MISS → HARD PARSE MEMOR

DEFINE LATCHES → C PROTECT RAM

PGA COMPONENT → PRIVATE SQL AREA

50 V$ DISPATCHER → RECONNECT

By Hassan A. Afyouni

THOMSON

COURSE TECHNOLOGY ™

Australia • Canada • Mexico • Singapore • Spain • United Kingdom • United States

THOMSON
————————— ™
COURSE TECHNOLOGY

Oracle9i Performance Tuning: Optimizing Database Productivity
By Hassan A. Afyouni

Senior Product Manager: Tricia Boyle	**Editorial Assistant:** Amanda Piantedosi	**Cover Designer:** Betsy Young
Executive Editor: Mac Mendelsohn	**Marketing Manager:** Amy Yarnevich	**Cover Artist:** Rakefet Kenaan
Development Editor: Betsey Henkels	**Production Editor:** Anne Valsangiacomo	**Compositor:** Gex Publishing Services
Associate Product Manager: Mirella Misiaszek		**Manufacturing Coordinator:** Laura Burns

BRIEF
Contents

TABLE OF
Contents

CHAPTER 3

Tuning the Redo Log Buffer   91

CHAPTER 4

Tuning the Shared Pool Memory   129

CHAPTER 5

Working with the Program Global Area   **201**

CHAPTER 7

CHAPTER 8

CHAPTER 10

CHAPTER 11

CHAPTER 14

CHAPTER 15

Tuning Workshop and Statistic Collector Project   921

APPENDIX A

Oracle Architecture Overview   937

APPENDIX B

Diagnostics Queries Collection   943

Glossary   955

Index   961

Preface

This textbook is a detailed guide to Oracle9*i* performance and tuning. The database administrator (DBA) can use concepts, methodologies, and techniques demonstrated in the book to configure and diagnose the database for optimal performance. The book can be categorized as both an introductory and intermediate level guide to performance tuning because it covers most of the diagnosis, troubleshooting, and tuning tasks that every DBA faces, and it omits more advanced performance tuning topics such as Real Application Clusters.

Intended Audience

This book presents topics from both a practical point of view as well as from a conceptual perspective to benefit database administrators, database modelers, and database developers regardless of their experience. This book is intended to support individuals in database courses covering performance tuning using the Oracle9*i* database. It is also intended to support individuals who are preparing for the Oracle9*i* Performance and Tuning exam that is required for certification as an Oracle Certified Professional (OCP).

To benefit from this book, prior knowledge of general database administration is required. In addition, the reader should have basic knowledge of SQL (Structured Query Language). While it is preferable that the reader know Oracle9*i*'s SQL, a reader's experience using SQL on other databases, such as SQLServer, is sufficient. The reader should be able to write SQL commands for querying, inserting, updating, and deleting data in relational tables.

Oracle Certification Program (OCP)

This textbook covers the objectives of *Exam 1Z0-033, Oracle9i Performance Tuning*. This is the final exam required for individuals seeking certification as an Oracle Certified Professional (OCP). Information about registering for these exams can be found at *www.oracle.com/education/certification*.

Approach

The concepts introduced in this textbook are presented in business scenarios. A unique feature of this book is the presentation at the start of each chapter of an actual performance problem. Readers are asked to keep the problem in mind as they read the chapter and are asked to solve the problem in the end of chapter sections. Concepts are introduced and examples of real-life uses for the concept are discussed. Then students follow along with hands-on practices to drive home the concepts in every chapter. The case project at the end of each chapter works within the context of a hypothetical real world business: a startup reseller company named Acme Company. The case studies use data provided in this book to simulate practical examples. Each chapter builds on the concepts of the previous chapter, and the case study adds details to the database analysis. By the end of the book, the student has established a full comprehensive understanding of performance tuning tasks. The student also solves performance problems to cover as many real-life scenarios as possible. This allows students to not only learn how to deal with such problems, but also to apply this knowledge in daily diagnosis routines.

To organize topics in a logical manner, the book is divided into six parts. The Part 1 includes Chapter 1 and gives an overview of performance tuning concepts, goals, and methodology. Part 2, which includes Chapters 2, 3, 4, and 5, focuses on how to optimally configure memory to maintain database performance and efficiency. Part 3 includes Chapters 6, 7, and 8 and covers another important tuning subject—data storage. In these chapters, discussion and implementation of how to optimize the smallest to the largest data unit is presented with details outlining important storage techniques that help optimize the performance of the database. Part 4 of the book includes Chapters 9, 10 and 11 and discusses advanced performance topics to add another layer of performance tuning knowledge to the repertoire of the DBA. Part 5 of the book includes Chapter 12, which presents to the reader the most commonly used diagnostic and tuning tools that are available in Oracle. Finally, Part 6 includes Chapters 13, 14, and 15, which are dedicated to application tuning and which outline methods and guides on how to tune SQL queries, performance advantages of tables and indexes, and characteristics of different types of applications.

To reinforce the material presented, each chapter includes a chapter summary. In addition, at the end of each chapter, groups of activities are presented that test students' knowledge and challenge them to apply that knowledge to solving business problems.

Overview of This Book

The examples, projects, and cases in this book will help students to achieve the following objectives:

- Understand key components of the Oracle9*i* performance tuning concepts.
- Optimally configure logical and physical data storage units: Oracle block, extents, segments, data files, and tablespaces.
- Optimize undo segments to support rollback operations, read-consistency, and data recovery.
- Diagnose and prevent lock contention as well as detect dead locks.
- Learn the performance advantages and disadvantages of dedicated and shared servers.

- Understand how Oracle background processes work and how to prevent performance degradation of these processes.
- Understand the role of the operating system and how to monitor system performance.
- Learn how to use Oracle tools to diagnose, troubleshoot, and tune the database.
- Learn how to tune a SQL query.
- Use Data Dictionary views to monitor database structures and activities.

The contents of each chapter build on the concepts of previous chapters. **Chapter 1** describes the overview of performance tuning objectives and methodologies. **Chapter 2** shows DBAs the importance of buffer cache memory, one of the main components of the System Global Area. Chapter 2 also explains how to configure the buffer cache memory properly. **Chapter 3** presents guidelines and steps on how to tune the redo log buffer, which is another important component of Oracle memory. **Chapter 4** details how to tune each structure of the shared pool memory as well as other memory parts such as the Java pool and large pool. **Chapter 5** discusses sort operations, causes of sort operations, and how to perform most sort operations in memory. **Chapter 6** discusses the smallest data unit in Oracle, which is a data block. It presents guidelines and tips on how to configure the size of the block based on the type of application. **Chapter 7** describes the logical and physical structure of Oracle storage. It discusses each logical and physical entity within a comprehensive methodology and demonstrates how to configure storage optimally taking advantages of Oracle9*i* features. **Chapter 8** explains how to tune undo segments to enhance performance of application transactions. **Chapter 9** illustrates how to prevent lock contention and detect deadlocks. **Chapter 10** demonstrates the advantages and disadvantages of dedicated and shared servers as well as how to detect shared server performance problems. **Chapter 11** presents a concise coverage of the main Oracle background processes and how to optimize and regulate each process. It also presents operating system performance issues and considerations. **Chapter 12** details how to use most of Oracle diagnostic and tuning tools. **Chapter 13** describes how to tune a SQL query—the most important task in performance tuning. **Chapter 14** presents performance advantages of different types of tables and indexes explaining the concepts for each type. **Chapter 15** presents two workshops to enforce all the topics covered in the book.

Features

To enhance students' learning experience, each chapter in this book includes the following elements:

- **Chapter Objectives:** Each chapter begins with a list of the concepts to be mastered by the chapter's conclusion. This list provides a quick overview of chapter contents as well as a useful study aid.

- **Performance Problem:** Each chapter displays a performance problem after the Chapter Objectives. The performance problem is designed to present a real-life scenario that the DBA might be confronted with. The chapter discusses topics and concepts that are relevant to the problem and at the end of the chapter the student is asked to solve the problem.

NOTE

- **Note:** These explanations, designated by the *Note* icon, provide further information about concepts or a syntax structures.

- **Visual Diagrams:** Numerous diagrams and tables throughout the text illustrate difficult concepts.

- **Chapter Summaries:** As a helpful recap, each chapter concludes with a summary of chapter concepts.

- **Review Questions:** End-of-chapter assessment begins with a set of approximately 20 review questions that reinforce the main ideas introduced in each chapter. These questions ensure that students have mastered the concepts and understand the information presented.

- **Exam Review Questions:** Approximately 15 certification-type questions are included to prepare students for the type of questions that can be expected on the certification exam, as well as to measure the students' level of understanding.

- **Hands-on Projects:** Along with conceptual explanations and examples, each chapter provides a number of hands-on projects related to the chapter's contents. The purpose of these projects is to provide students with practical experience.

- **Case Projects:** Case projects are also presented at the end of each chapter. These cases are designed to help students apply what they have learned to real-world situations.

- **Glossary:** For easy reference, a glossary at the end of the book lists the key terms in alphabetical order along with definitions.

The Course Technology Kit for Oracle9i Software, available when purchased as a bundle with this book, provides the Oracle database software on CDs, so users can install on their own computers all the software needed to complete the in-chapter examples, Hands-on Projects, and Case Projects. The software included in the kit can be used with Microsoft Windows NT, 2000, or XP operating systems. The installation instructions for Oracle9i and the log in procedures are available at *www.course.com/cdkit* on the Web page for this books' title.

Boson Software and Course Technology have partnered to extend Students' Oracle learning experience. We have created a powerful multimedia practice test engine to help students prepare for Oracle certification exams. The CD containing an extended demo of this tool is located in the back of the book. This self-assessment tool demo includes 50 interactive questions, much like the questions on Oracle Certification Exam 1Z0-033,

Oracle9i Performance Tuning. If students would like to obtain additional questions, they may upgrade from the demo to a more robust version of the tool for a fee. This engine offers approximately 150 additional exam practice questions. To upgrade, visit the Boson Web site at www.boson.com.

Teaching Tools

The following supplemental materials are available when this book is used in a classroom setting. All teaching tools available with this book are provided to the instructor on a single CD-ROM.

- **Electronic Instructor's Manual:** The Instructor's Manual that accompanies this textbook includes additional instructional material to assist in class preparation, such as suggestions for lecture topics.

- **ExamView®:** This textbook is accompanied by ExamView, a powerful testing software package that allows instructors to create and administer printed, computer (LAN-based), and Internet exams. ExamView includes hundreds of questions that correspond to the topics covered in this text, enabling students to generate detailed study guides that include page references for further review. These computer-based and Internet testing components allow students to take exams at their computers, and save the instructor time because each exam is graded automatically.

- **PowerPoint Presentations:** Microsoft PowerPoint slides are included for each chapter. Instructors might use the slides in three ways: As teaching aids during classroom presentations, as printed handouts for classroom distribution, or as network-accessible resources for chapter review. Instructors can add their own slides for additional topics introduced to the class.

- **Distance Learning:** Course Technology is proud to present online courses in WebCT and Blackboard to provide the most complete and dynamic learning experience possible. When you add online content to one of your courses, you're providing a gateway to the 21st century's most important information resource. We hope you will make the most of your course, both online and offline. For more information on how to bring distance learning to your course, contact your local Course Technology sales representative

- **Data Files:** The script file necessary to insert data into the TUNER schema tables is provided through the Course Technology Web site at *www.course.com*, and is also available on the Teaching Tools CD-ROM. Additional script files needed for use in specific chapters are also available through the Web site.

- **Solution Files:** Solutions to the end of chapter material are provided on the Teaching Tools CD-ROM. Solutions may also be found on the Course Technology Web site at *www.course.com*. The solutions are password protected.

ACKNOWLEDGMENTS

I dedicate this book to my beautiful and patient wife Rouba for her everlasting love and support. I devote every single letter in this book to my angels Aya, Wissam, and Sammy for every moment I missed being with them when I was writing this book. To my brothers, Omar and Maan, to my sisters Amal and Sammar. Finally, this book could not happen without the prayers and blessings of my parents who gave me love and strength. I love you all.

Special thanks to the Course Technology development team, headed up by Tricia Boyle and Betsey Henkels. Also thanks to Anne Valsangiacomo and her Production team, as well as Serge Palladino and Chris Scriver of the Quality Assurance team. Also, thanks to Bill Larkin, Acquisitions Editor, for giving me the chance to become an education contributor.

The following reviewers also provided helpful suggestions and insight into the development of this textbook:

John W. Fendrich – Spoon River College

Gary Hackbarth – Iowa State University

James Hager - Pierce College

Norma Hall – Manor College

Ensie McGathey - University of New Mexico

Samiaji Sarosa - Atma Jaya Yogyakarta University, Indonesia

Mark Smith – Trident Technical College

Peter Wolcott – University of Nebraska at Omaha

Read This Before You Begin

TO THE USER

Data Files

Much of the practice you do in the chapters of this book involves creating, modifying and then dropping a database structure (such as a table, index, or user). Most of the practices in the chapters and the hands-on exercises at the end of the chapters can be done without running any data files. At certain points in the book, however, you will need to load data files created for this book. Your instructor will provide you with those data files, or you can obtain them electronically from the Course Technology Web site by accessing *www.course.com* and then searching for this book's title. When you reach a point in the book where a data file is needed, the book gives you instructions on how to run each data file. The data files provide you with the same tables and data shown in the chapter examples, so you can have hands-on practice re-creating the practice commands. It is highly recommended that you work through all the examples to re-enforce your learning.

The script files for Chapters 2 through 14 are found in the **Data** folder under their respective chapter folders (for example **Chapter02** and **Chapter15**) on your data disk and have the file names that correspond with the instructions in the chapter. If the computer in your school lab—or your own computer—has Oracle9*i* database software installed, you can work through the chapter examples and complete the hands-on assignments and case projects. At a minimum, you will need the Oracle9*i* Release 2, Personal Edition of the software to complete the examples and assignments in this textbook.

Using Your Own Computer

To use your own computer in working through the chapter examples and completing the hands-on assignments and case projects, you will need the following:

- **Hardware:** A computer capable of using the Microsoft Windows NT, 2000 Professional, or XP Professional operating system. You should have at least 256MB of RAM and between 2.75GB and 4.75GB of hard disk space available before installing the software.

- **Software:** Oracle9*i* Release 2 Enterprise Edition, or, at a minimum, Oracle9*i* Release 2 Personal Edition. The Course Technology Kit for Oracle9*i* Software contains the database software necessary to perform all the tasks shown in this textbook. Detailed installation, configuration, and logon information are provided at *www.course.com/cdkit* on the Web page for this title. *Note: when prompted for the Database Identification, type **ORACLASS** in the Global Database Name box and in the SID box.*

■ **Data files:** You will not be able to use your own computer to work through the chapter examples and complete the projects in this book unless you have the data files. You can get the data files from your instructor, or you can obtain the data files electronically by accessing the Course Technology Web site at *www.course.com* and then searching for this book's title.

When you download the data files, they should be stored in a directory separate from any other files on your hard drive or diskette. You will need to remember the path or folder containing the files, because you'll have to locate the file while in SQL*Plus Worksheet in order to execute it. (The SQL*Plus Worksheet is the interface tool you will use to interact with the database.)

When you install the Oracle9*i* software, you will be prompted to supply the database name for the default database being created. Use the name "ORACLASS" to match the name used in the book. If you prefer a different name, remember that anywhere the book instructs you to type in ORACLASS, you should type in your database name instead. You will be prompted to change the password for the SYS and SYSTEM user accounts. Make certain that you record the names and passwords of the accounts because you will need to log in to the database with one or both of these administrative accounts in some chapters. After you install Oracle9*i*, you will be required to enter a user name and password to access the software. Chapter 2 data scripts provided in this book create a user called TUNER and password TUNER and load data, which is used throughout the book. Chapter 15 data scripts create a user WKSHP and password WKSHP and load data to use for all tasks presented in the first part of the chapter. If you have installed the Personal Edition of Oracle9*i*, you will not need to enter a connect string during the log in process. As previously mentioned, full instructions for installing and logging in to Oracle9*i*, Release 2, are provided on the Web site for this textbook at *www.course.com*.

Visit Our World Wide Web Site

Additional materials designed especially for you might be available on the World Wide Web. Go to *www.course.com* periodically and search this site for more details.

To The Instructor

To complete the chapters in this book, your students must have access to a set of data files. These files are included in the Instructor's Resource Kit. They may also be obtained electronically by accessing the Course Technology Web site at *www.course.com* and then searching for this book's title.

The set of data files consists of script files that are executed either at the beginning of the chapter or before starting the hands-on exercises. After the files are copied, you should instruct your students in how to copy the files to their own computers or workstations. Maintain the directory structure found in the original data files: Data\Chapter01, Data\Chapter02 and so on.

You will need to provide your students with this information, which is used in several chapters:

- The passwords for the SYSTEM and SYS users on their workstation.
- The database name, which is assumed to be ORACLASS. If the database name is not ORACLASS, inform the students that they should substitute the correct name whenever the text tells them to enter ORACLASS.
- The full path for the ORACLE_BASE and ORACLE_HOME directories on their workstations. ORACLE_BASE is a variable name used in Oracle documentation and in this book to refer to the root directory of the Oracle database installation. ORACLE_HOME is the root directory of the Oracle software. In Windows, ORACLE_BASE is typically **C:\oracle** and ORACLE_HOME is typically **C:\oracle\ora92**.
- The computer name of the workstation.
- The full path names for directories where the students can create additional directories and files. The directories must be on the hard drive (not removable media, such as floppy disks). The approximate data storage requirement is about 5GB. Note that you may drop any data objects created which is not part of ACME Company schema after the chapter is completed.

The chapters and projects in this book were tested using the Microsoft Windows 2000 Professional operating system with Oracle9*i* Release 2 Enterprise Edition and the Microsoft Windows XP Professional operating system with Oracle9*i* Personal Edition, Release 2 (9.2.0.1.0).

Course Technology Data Files

You are granted a license to copy the data files to any computer or computer network used by individuals who have purchased this book.

Tuning Fundamentals

PERFORMANCE TUNING OVERVIEW

In this chapter you will:

♦ Learn general concepts of database tuning

♦ Review the System Development Life Cycle

♦ Identify tuning goals and measurements

♦ Describe and understand performance problems

♦ Learn the steps of the tuning process

♦ Use a database tuning checklist

♦ Understand the roles and responsibilities of the database administrator (DBA)

♦ Learn about Oracle tuning tools

In this day and age, data has become the most valuable asset of a company. Managers and employees rely on this data to be highly accurate and quickly accessible. As guardians of data and facilitators of data access and retrieval, database administrators (DBAs) are themselves resources essential to the effectiveness of an organization. Performance tuning is one of the most important database administration responsibilities, and database administrators are often called forward to resolve and prevent performance problems whenever they arise. To effectively carry out their responsibilities, database administrators should have a firm grasp of all the concepts and tools necessary to prevent performance problems and should proactively monitor and troubleshoot the database before problems occur.

One of the challenging tasks a DBA encounters is the tuning of a database that is performing poorly. It is not easy to optimize database performance because many factors and components contribute to performance optimization. This chapter presents a high-level overview of performance issues and tuning methodology that later chapters flesh out with technical material and details. Using material presented in this chapter, you learn the scope of your responsibilities as a DBA, and you are introduced to the process of tuning a database as well.

DATABASE-TUNING OVERVIEW

Database tuning is an ongoing process to optimize the operation of the database configuration based on attainable tuning goals. Most DBA experts label tuning "an art and a science" rather than strictly a science, because there are no quick formulas or specific methods for tuning a database. So how is it done? This is not a simple question that can be answered in one or two or even three sentences. This chapter explores the answer by presenting a methodology—a basic framework—that DBAs should use to tune their databases.

Consider the following scenario. Suppose there are several highway routes leading to the city and there are many cars running optimally and moving synchronously towards the city. If you were the traffic reporter in a helicopter, you would report to your audience that the roads are free of traffic jams. However, say that two or three of the cars develop problems and stall or have to stop, or suppose there's a multiple-car accident on one of the routes or it is snowing and visibility is low. Suddenly, you, the traffic reporter, are reporting traffic jams and problems. And as more and more cars set out on these routes and begin to exceed the highway system's "bandwidth," traffic jams begin to definitely occur.

Now put this into a database perspective. A query is like a car: a good car runs well and an optimized query runs fast. But an optimized query cannot run fast if there is a "traffic jam" caused by another query that is consuming most of the resources. A traffic accident involving two cars is like two transactions colliding, resulting in one blocking the other. Snow and low visibility are similar to poor database configuration, and as such, occur less frequently than traffic jams caused simply by heavy traffic. The point is, if you create a database and let it run without following any specific methodology, your database becomes like these highways with numerous traffic jams because the databases are not optimal and scalable, and they suffer from poor design.

To return to the art and science label, performance tuning is definitely an art, but it uses scientific measures and means. It is an art because it depends on your creativity to develop good designs and on your artistic skills for troubleshooting and analyzing problems. Tuning uses scientific measures and means—technical tools to detect problems before they occur—and you are always working to achieve the realistic tuning goals that are set by business requirements. For example, one typical tuning goal is to shorten the average response time for a query or transaction, and this must be set by understanding the business goals of an organization as well as the technical resources it owns. **Response time** is defined as the time the database spends responding to a query that is submitted by a user.

This book focuses on optimizing database operations and preventing performance problems that may increase frustration, decrease user satisfaction, and ultimately affect productivity. However, before you jump into learning all the performance technical material and techniques, you should learn how to accomplish your goals. To facilitate this process you will be introduced in this chapter to a tuning methodology.

Before learning this methodology, you need to review the **System Development Life Cycle (SDLC)** process, which is a structured methodology for building software application systems. Since most application systems employ a database system to store data, you need to understand your role and responsibilities within the SDLC process. In the next section, you learn just that.

SYSTEM DEVELOPMENT LIFE CYCLE (SDLC)

Ken is an expert DBA who joined a large credit collection agency to administer a new database, which was being developed to replace a legacy system. Ken was very excited when he learned during the interview that he would be administering this new database.

As the first week went by, Ken saw no documentation about the new database that he was supposed to administer, and the database manager did not say anything about the status and progress of the new application. Ken was assigned to work with a couple of developers to write migration scripts to transfer data from the legacy system to the new database, which was in the works, but Ken felt he needed to learn about the new application. He wanted to be involved in all stages and did not want to inherit a database application without knowing the ins and outs, which would help him make the right design decisions.

The second week, during a meeting with his manager, Ken asked about the new database and wanted information on the development timeline. His manager told him that the application was in the analysis phase, that it wouldn't go into production for another six months, and that it was too early for him to be involved. Ken asked to be invited to all the analysis and review meetings, but his manager replied, "What for? When the time comes for the application to go into production, I'll get you involved." Ken lost control and told his manager that he should review all database designs to avoid database problems before the application was implemented. To this his manager replied with sarcasm, "But you're a DBA. What does it have to do with you?"

It may be helpful to place the topic of tuning in a context with which you are familiar, such as the SDLC. Every information system is developed through a life cycle of defined phases, in which each phase outlines specific tasks and deliverables. Many methodologies can be adopted depending on the type of the application and implementation paradigm to be used. The following is a list of the major system development methodologies:

- Structured analysis and design

- Object-oriented analysis and design

- Rapid application development

- Prototyping development

- Joint application development

When implemented properly, each of these software-engineering methodologies serves the following purposes:

- Establishes a consistent framework for development

- Provides a solution to solve a problem

- Delivers the application design and code that has been reviewed and signed off by technical leads

Short cutting any of the phases often increases the cost of development through problems such as undelivered user requirements, dysfunctional modules, bad design, or inefficient code. You may wonder how this is related to the performance issues that are the subject of this book. Simply put, by conducting design and code reviews, design deficiencies and code problems can be identified early in the software development process, so that fewer performance problems occur when an application goes into production. In general, the SDLC process outlines what performance issues DBAs should be aware of and where to focus their efforts in each phase.

It is important to highlight that most performance problems stem from inferior design, poor system architecture, and inefficient application code. It should be noted that the most expensive phases in an SDLC are the analysis and design. Design and analysis are equally important because one of the deliverables of these phases is the blueprint of the application. Poor design leads to poor performance, which leads to lower user productivity.

Regardless of which methodology you use, it is likely to include all of the phases illustrated in Figure 1-1.

System Development Life Cycle (SDLC)   7

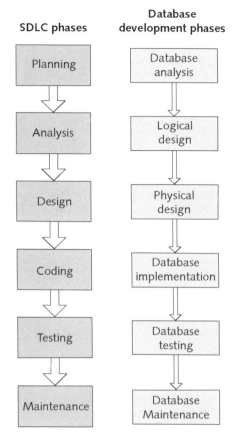

Figure 1-1   System Development Life Cycle with a database design perspective

As you see, for each phase of the SDLC shown on the left, there is a corresponding database phase shown on the right, which is specific to database analysis, design, development, and implementation. The following outlines DBA tasks for each of the database phases:

- **Database analysis phase:**
    - Identify new resources and capacities that are required for the new system.
    - Analyze the business functions of the new system to determine database features and functions.
    - Identify database performance goals and objectives.

- **Logical design phase:**
    - Identify the type of database application.
    - Gather data from existing system and business requirements.
    - Analyze data and identify all entities.
    - Identify relationships between entities.

- Create a conceptual data model.
- Identify degrees of relationships and cardinalities.
- Identify all attributes for each entity.
- Create a logical data model.
- Identify domains for each attribute.
- Create a data dictionary.
- Identify data constraints and validation techniques.
- Normalize data model.

- **Physical design phase:**
  - Decide which database management system will be employed.
  - Examine the features of the database management system to be used.
  - Create a storage capacity plan.
  - Analyze initial data and growth.
  - Design database procedures to implement business rules.
  - Identify data migration procedures.
  - Identify and create backup and recovery strategies.

- **Database implementation phase:**
  - Create the database by using a template configuration.
  - Create application users and roles and grant privileges.
  - Create application schema.
  - Create and code all database procedures and scripts.
  - Create data migration procedures and scripts.
  - Create necessary data feeds and/or loads.
  - Document database configuration.
  - Implement a backup strategy for testing.

- **Database testing phase:**
  - Test database connections.
  - Identify problematic queries.
  - Gather database statistics and analyze results to determine whether performance goals are met.
  - Test all database procedures and scripts.

- Identify database configuration problems.

- Document database maintenance procedures and administration tasks.

- Test backup and recovery strategies.

- **Database maintenance phase:**

   - Create a production database.

   - Migrate data to the production database.

   - Use tools to monitor the database and install scripts.

   - Tune and improve database performance as required.

   - Verify backups and perform random recovery testing.

This list includes high-level and generic tasks to give you an idea of the range of tasks you need to perform as you progress through the SDLC process. It is important to point out that a DBA must be involved in all phases of the SDLC; the earlier your involvement, the more prepared you are to inherit the administration of the database. Also, it is worth noting that one of the high-level features of Oracle9*i* is its automatic management capability. This is a boon to you as a DBA because it eliminates the routine tasks that otherwise consume much of your time and enables you to concentrate on more complicated tasks that significantly impact performance. Many Oracle experts have labeled Oracle9*i* "the DBA-less version," which means that it enables you to spend less time on simple routines and instead focus on complex database management features, planning, strategic direction, and long-term goals.

In Figure 1-1, you can see that most of the DBA groundwork and tasks are accomplished in the analysis and design phases of the SDLC. In some companies, these tasks are assigned to a person who holds the title of Application DBA. The Application DBA works with issues that are closely related to the application database design, performance analysis, query optimization, tablespace, tables sizing, and so on.

Whether or not you're familiar with the SDLC and have worked on projects that used the process, you were probably surprised that the DBA should be involved from the beginning. The best database managers and development managers realize and capitalize on the fact that the DBA's involvement adds tremendous value and prevents major performance problems when the application goes in production.

Once you work through your role in the SDLC, what do you face when you tune a database? How do you know where to start? To answer those questions, you need to set some goals that are realistic and achievable. The next section presents an overview of tuning goals to help you better understand your responsibilities when it comes to database tuning.

TUNING GOALS

Khalil is a database architect who had been working for a local bank for 15 years when a nationwide bank bought the local bank. Khalil was transferred to a new group and was assigned to an existing application used nationwide. His new manager, Jana, called him to her office on his first day of work and said that he would be taking over her responsibilities and that the application he was responsible for would now have added functionality, as well as a group of new customers and users added to its existing pool. Jana asked Khalil to survey the current architecture, review the new business requirements, and write a report to assess the application. Khalil agreed to do his best to have a report ready in one week.

A week passed and Khalil was busy interviewing business analysts, developers, and main users to learn more about the application. Almost everyone believed that there were performance issues that needed to be dealt with. However, the most interesting meeting he had was with the DBA, who said, "Just between you and me, the whole database architecture is flawed. We're having performance problems right now and I am working hard to keep it under control. But the real problem will be when we add the new functionality with the new pool of users. I think we are going to have a disaster." Khalil asked the DBA where he could find the business requirements for the following:

- Response time for an average transaction

- Response time for application reports

- Requirements for the new functionality

The DBA shook his head and told Khalil that the company's VP expected that the performance of the revised application should be at least as good as its current performance.

This scenario presents a database architect in hot soup. His goals and the goals of management were askew. The best DBAs are proactive rather than reactive. Preventing performance problems reduces time spent on troubleshooting and explaining to users and managers why the system is behaving badly. To be proactive, you need to make sure that the design, code, and configuration of the database meet the realistic performance goals set by a business committee. Performance goals must be realistic and feasible. For example, suppose management wants summary reports to be generated on demand within a few seconds from a table that holds millions of rows. Even with query optimization and high-performance hardware, this goal may not be possible because such a report requires resources and time to process data. Performance-tuning goals must be measured by the following criteria:

Database response time: It is important that users experience no performance problems when working with the database. Both query response time and application response time should be optimal. To ensure fast response time, all queries submitted to the database must be tuned.

Database availability: Although this factor is not directly related to tuning, it is recommended that DBAs keep a close eye on long-running processes that consume high levels of resources. These processes must be tuned or scheduled at a time that does not interfere with the availability of the database. Resource-intensive processes have a big impact on availability and response time.

Database statistics and ratios: DBAs rely heavily on indicators that tell how the database is behaving. **Database statistics** measure database operations, such as how fast a database reads data from a disk, to determine if database operations are optimal. All indicators have thresholds that assist in determining if tuning is needed or not. You should never respond to any indicator from one reading only. You must have several readings to see a trend. These indicators are called hit ratios and are computed from statistics collected during database operations.

CPU utilization: Database or application processes should be monitored to identify those that are heavily consuming CPU resources in order to tune them or eliminate them. The number of CPU-intensive processes should be minimized.

Memory utilization: Caching data or queries in memory always enhances the performance of the database. Identify queries that unnecessarily use memory and thereby take resources from other processes. Overallocating memory also takes memory resources from the operating system that is needed for other applications.

Disk thrashing or paging: This could cause considerable database performance degradation. Most often, thrashing or paging results from poor database or instance configuration or from problematic queries that require sorting or reading huge amounts of data. Measurement of the amount of thrashing or paging should be minimized.

Excessive I/O (caused by reads and writes): Similar to disk thrashing or paging, excessive I/O is usually caused by unwise tablespace or table allocation, an improper setting for the Oracle block size, a bad memory configuration, or poorly written queries. Most database experts agree on the average response times presented in Table 1-1, which can serve as a guideline for acceptable response times for different types of applications.

Table 1-1   Average application response time

Average query for application type	Response time
Web application (WEB)	Within 3 seconds
Online transactional application (OLTP)	Within 1 second
Combination of OLTP and decision support system (DSS) (Hybrid)	Within 30 seconds
Decision support system (DSS): Data warehouse, reporting, and batch processing	Within 60 seconds

At this point in the chapter, you have looked at tuning goals and had a glimpse of what your database objectives should be. To put another piece of the performance puzzle in place, turn now to an examination of the kinds of performance problems that may occur.

PERFORMANCE PROBLEMS

Most database applications experience performance problems ranging from minor annoyances to serious delays. There is no escape from this harsh reality. Performance problems are bound to occur because of oversights in design, queries that were not optimized, and improperly configured database parameters.

It is important that all involved parties, such as system analysts, designers, developers, database administrator, and system administrators, cooperate proactively to identify or at least minimize problems before they occur in production. Understanding what can be done to minimize performance issues is a key task for all of these involved parties to ensure that the user does not experience unpleasant and frustrating slow downs of the system. Believe it or not, you as a DBA should be customer oriented no matter how experienced and technical you are. When all is said and done, you are providing a service to the user by keeping the database available and accessible during business hours.

Performance problems stem from many causes that can be prevented. These problems are classified as follows:

Contention problems: Caused by improper system design, resource configuration, or system specification, these problems contribute to performance degradation. **Contention** can be defined as the competition between or among two or more processes for the same resources. There are four kinds of contention:

- Input

- Output

- File

- Locks and Latches

Resource consumption problems: Caused by inefficient code, which consumes most or all of the resources of the system memory or CPU. Most performance problems are caused by problematic queries that are submitted to the database.

Scalability problems: Caused by system architecture that is not designed to scale up as the workload increases. **Scalability** can be defined as the capability of a system to increase or decrease in size in response to the utilization load without impacting the performance of the system. This a serious problem for everyone involved with the application. An application that can't scale up degrades system performance and eventually slows database performance to a crawl.

Architectural problems: Caused by flawed system design or data model design. These problems definitely lead to costly performance issues. Overnormalization of the data model can also decrease performance.

1

Application problems: Problematic queries that consume resources degrade the performance of the system. Other application problems may stem from a poorly designed user interface, inefficient batch-processing activity, improper implementation of the business rules, improper data validation, or other improper implementation that produces inconsistent data.

Network problems: Caused by heavy network traffic generated by the system or insufficient bandwidth that is not capable of handling normal traffic demands. Network configuration and methods can significantly impact performance and network availability. It should be noted that most network problems are bandwidth and traffic bound. In other words, you must make sure that the network can handle expected network traffic.

Sorting problems: Caused by issuing queries that require extensive sorting. The query should perform the sort in memory rather than using temporary disk space. Because I/O trips are very expensive, adequate memory must be allocated for most expected sorting tasks.

Connection problems: Performance problems can arise from improper connection management. An example of this is when database applications constantly disconnect and reconnect rather than maintaining one continuous connection until the application terminates. Another example is an application that uses a middle tier that manages all user connections, but manages the connections incorrectly by keeping a pool of connections open, waiting to handle client's requests.

Allocation problems: The database administrator must be aware that misallocation of tablespaces and improper sizing of tables leads to serious I/O contention and excessive reads/writes of the disks that could be expensive to the database operation and performance. Using Optimal Flexible Architecture, known as OFA, and disk configuration with Redundant Arrays of Inexpensive Disk (RAID) improves or prevents I/O performance problems.

Full Table Scan (FTS) problems: An **FTS** occurs when the database server scans through an entire table to retrieve rows. FTS degrades the performance of the system when trying to retrieve rows from a large table without using indexes. FTS on small tables does not negatively impact performance.

Parsing problems: Parsing problems are due to improper sizing of memory that results in insufficient space to cache the most frequently used queries. Other reasons include improper use of bind variables, improper setting of instance parameters, and lack of development standards that would ensure consistent code.

Index problems: In general, indexes are created to enhance the performance of queries. Indexes are mechanisms for retrieving data quickly. If an index is missing on a column that is used in a WHERE clause, the database may perform a full-table scan (FTS). However, depending on the size of the table, the type of application, and the type of index, creating an index can be a performance liability.

Storage parameters problems: When creating objects in Oracle, it is highly recommended to specify storage parameters to configure optimal space allocation for an object. This specification reduces overallocation, which results in storage waste or under-allocation, and ultimately to performance problems.

At this point, you have learned about tuning goals and seen most performance problems that may occur, so what's next? You need to acquire a methodology for tuning databases. To optimize database operations, it is highly recommended that you adopt the tuning process described in the following section.

TUNING PROCESSES AND STEPS

Users are the ultimate judge of system success. The users' point of view differs from yours on productivity in general and system performance, specifically. When you are developing a system or building a database, you need to follow specific steps to prevent performance problems that could result in an unpleasant experience for users. There is one proven and tested approach to prevent these problems. Table 1-2 outlines the ten steps of this tuning approach. A **tuning approach** is a step-by-step process to optimize database performance. You can apply this approach to any database regardless of whether it is in the design phase, analysis phase, or any other phase. For example, if users are experiencing performance problems using a database that is already in production, you can follow these steps as a methodology to detect and tune the database.

Table 1-2 Steps of the tuning approach

Tuning step	Type	Primary person responsible
1. Identify performance goals	Business requirements	Business analyst
2. Optimize application design	Application	System architect and analyst
3. Tune application code	Application	Developer
4. Configure optimal hardware specification	Hardware	System architect and analyst
5. Configure disks: disk striping and controller striping (see Figure 1-2)	Hardware	System architect and system administrator
6. Properly allocate data files and file structure according to OFA guidelines (You can view Oracle OFA guidelines on the Oracle Technology Network at *otn.oracle.com*)	Database	Database administrator
7. Develop optimal memory configuration	Database	Database administrator
8. Tune I/O	Database	Database administrator
9. Prevent and reduce contention	Database	Database administrator
10. Configure optimal setup of the operating system	Operating system	System administrator

Based on many surveys conducted by various companies and organizations, including Oracle, it has been concluded that about 70 percent of performance problems are due to design and coding. The survey results emphasize the importance of tuning steps #2 and #3 (Table 1-2). Too often architects and developers are pressured to cut short the tuning process by paying inadequate attention to performance issues because of time constraints, lack of experience, or both. This always results in trying to tune the database too late in the application development process to accommodate design deficiencies and problematic code. In this situation, no matter what magical or ingenious tricks you apply to the database to improve performance, you never achieve the performance goals.

Consider the following situation in which a module of an application was designed to meet an auditing requirement. For every data record change of a table, the record is saved in an audit table. Developers have decided not to use table triggers, so for every data change that occurred on a row they followed these procedures:

1. Save the data temporarily in a placeholder. If a record is new, save it.

2. Use UPDATE or DELETE or INSERT for the change.

3. Get the new ID for the change generated by a sequence.

4. INSERT the row before the change occurs in the audit table.

This design degrades the performance of the database regardless of how optimal its configuration is. Here are the issues with this design:

- Inserting a new record should not be included as part of the auditing process because auditing creates an historical record of what happened and who did it. Don't forget that if the table is one million records large, you are storing in the audit table one million records that are duplicates. This not only creates data redundancies, it requires more storage space to be allocated for the database.

- By using a table trigger that fires on INSERT or UPDATE, you could reduce the number of operations from four steps performed at the application level to one step performed at the application level, and another step at the database level.

The degree of performance necessary to eliminate or improve performance issues is illustrated in Figure 1-2. Each pyramid represents the relative effort needed for tuning during and after system development. Each pyramid is divided into several levels. The fact that level one at the base is the largest section of the pyramid indicates that this is where the effort to tune is greatest and where it most strongly affects performance, either positively or negatively. The amount of effort needed to improve performance at the top level is the smallest and has the smallest effect on performance.

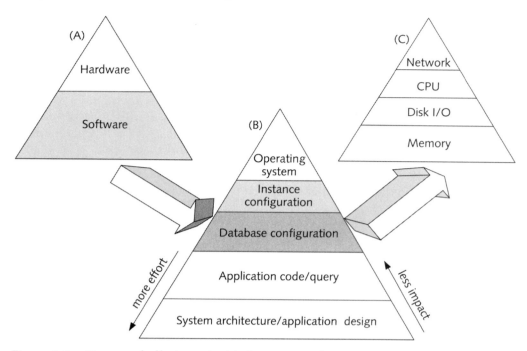

Figure 1-2   Degree of effort required to improve performance

Pyramid A shows the two main components of a system that can be tuned, software and hardware. The software area of Pyramid A is greater than the hardware area because tuning is performed more intensively on software than hardware. This is contrary to many opposing opinions that favor solving performance issues by throwing hardware at the problem, and there is no denying that hardware definitely contributes to improved performance of applications.

Pyramid B is an expansion of the shaded area of Pyramid A (software). Pyramid B shows all the components of software that can be tuned. The size of each component reflects the amount of tuning required. For example, the lowest level of Pyramid B, System architecture and application design, is larger than the next level up, Application code and query, because more tuning effort is required for design. The effort and impact arrows on the sides of Pyramid B indicate that the DBA should put more effort into the lower sections of the pyramid to make the most impact on performance. The shaded sections of Pyramid B are expanded in Pyramid C.

Problem Scenario

Now that you have been presented with an overview of some tuning concepts, it is time to put these ideas into practice. Consider the following situation. An OLTP Web application was deployed recently in production. During the first few weeks in production the performance of the database was reasonably good. Suddenly the application performance slowed down considerably and customer complaints about the Web site started to increase by the hour. Your manager assigned you to investigate the problem, assess the situation, and provide recommendations in a short report. Outline the steps you would take to perform tasks assigned by your manager. What types of user actions could be causing the problem?

Problem Investigation and Solution

Investigation Steps: The following steps should be adopted to investigate the problem:

- Since the database application is already in production, you should look at the queries the application is submitting to the database. Identify any problematic query that is consuming significant CPU resources, that is I/O excessive, or parse intensive.

- Quickly check the health of the database by identifying any bad configurations. Although one health check reading does not represent a solid statistical trend, it should provide some general indication of database performance. **Statistical trend** is defined here as a plot of several database measurements that shows the behavior of various database operations. Checking the health of the database should include:

  - Top sessions: Identify sessions that are top consumers of resources, memory, or other criterion.

  - Top queries: Identify top queries that are consuming the most CPU resources, causing the most I/O activities or performing excessive parsing.

  - CPU utilization: Monitors CPU consumption by database, users, and other applications.

  - Memory configuration: Determines if memory is configured optimally.

  - I/O activities: Identifies transactions that are causing high levels of I/O activities.

- Take an operating system reading of the CPU, I/O, and the network.

Situation Assessment: The following is a list of possible issues that could cause the performance problem presented in this scenario:

- Database application code:

  - Queries are not optimized causing full-table scans to be performed.

  - Columns in the WHERE predicates in queries are indexed.

  - Application is not using any coding standards or conventions, which could lead to excessive parsing.

  - Application is not using bind variables in queries. This situation could also lead to excessive parsing.

  - Application does not take advantage of using stored procedures that improve parsing.

  - Application is retrieving a huge amount of data all at once. The design could be better if the application retrieves a number of rows (say 20) at a time as they are needed

- Memory could be configured improperly which could lead to excessive reads from disks rather than reading data from memory cache

- Excessive I/O could be caused by poor storage allocation, disk configuration, or memory configuration

Recommendation: The following is a list of items that you should consider when recommending a solution:

- As a DBA, you should be objective in your assessment and recommendation, pointing out the problems uncovered by your findings and proposing solutions that are qualified by success factors as well as failure factors.

- You should be aware of all the factors contributing to the performance degradation.

- You should be aware of the fact that solving performance problems caused by design or application code might not be feasible as a short-term solution.

- For every proposed solution you should outline tasks to be performed and their impact on the application.

Since you are responsible to tune the database, you should employ any tool that can facilitate this process, be it software procedures or manual processes. In this section you learned about the tuning process that you can adopt to be consistent in detecting and preventing performance issues and problems. The next section presents a tuning checklist to use for putting these processes into action.

USING THE DATABASE TUNING CHECKLIST

The expression "Every penny counts" applies to performance tuning. Every performance tip or hint counts, because it can bail you out when you think you're sinking. Table 1-3 is a checklist of issues to consider when tuning the database. Note that some of the terms presented in this checklist are explained later in this book; this list is meant to merely introduce you to the issues.

Table 1-3 Sample database-tuning checklist

Analysis completed	Database issue
	Number of users connecting to the database
	Type of application interface
√	Network bandwidth and speed
√	Amount of historical and current data required to be online
√	Type of users
√	Software languages and tools
	Operating system
√	Service hours
	Amount of data queried
	Project deadlines
√	Budgeting issues
	Collecting statistics
√	Statistical trends
√	Hardware configuration

The following list elaborates on the checklist issues presented in Table 1–3:

- **Number of users connecting to the database:** Knowing in advance how many users will be concurrently connecting assists the DBA in configuring memory and other resources properly.

- **Type of application interface (Web, Windows-based, batch processing, or text-based):** How the DBA configures the Oracle Optimizer mode depends on the type of user interface. (Optimizer mode is a mechanism, or algorithm, that Oracle uses to determine the best path to retrieve data.)

- **Network bandwidth and speed:** As discussed earlier in the chapter, network bandwidth may affect performance. Based on the bandwidth, you should choose the connection method that best prevents performance problems.

- **Amount of historical and current data required to be online:** Knowing ahead of time how much data should be available online, especially historical data, can influence the physical table design.

- **Type of users:** It is important for the DBA to know the end users, their level of expertise with the application, and their job titles. Knowing your users enables you to focus on their issues.

- **Software languages and tools:** Before developing an application, developers select a language or tools to use for development. Although the selection of software languages, middle tiers, and tools (reporting and data mining, for example) does not have a significant effect on performance, analysts, developers, and DBAs should always decide wisely.

- **Operating system:** The selection of an operating system can often be a sore issue because of divergent preferences for platforms. Some DBAs prefer UNIX over Windows and vice versa. Regardless of your preference, you should make the selection based on which operating system can enhance or degrade the performance of the application.

- **Service hours:** Database availability is one of the measurements of database performance. Therefore, it is an important factor for the DBA to keep this in mind when scheduling jobs or performing database maintenance, backups, and other tasks to ensure availability with high performance.

- **Amount of data queried:** Knowing the amount of data to be queried for an average application's operation helps you decide on the best retrieval method, optimizer mode, and type of index.

- **Project deadlines:** Tight software development deadlines are the most frequent cause of dysfunctional applications. In general, an aggressive schedule is likely to result in bad database performance. A schedule that is too lax is likely to result in overengineering of the application. Schedules should be set based on previous projects and experience.

- **Budgeting issues:** Another factor that influences application development, which in turn influences performance, is the budget. A low budget leads to overworked and burnt-out staff, which in turn leads to shortcuts in design and code. A high budget leads to hiring too many unnecessary staff (too many cooks with their spoons in the broth).

- **Collecting statistics:** Statistics are useful for monitoring database and system performance. It is highly recommended that some form of statistics gathering be implemented. The DBA should decide before the application goes to production which statistics to collect. Table 1-4 lists different statistical tools available with Oracle for the UNIX and Windows operating systems.

Table 1-4   Tools for collecting statistics

Environment	Available tools
Oracle	STATSPACK, Oracle Enterprise Manager, UTLBSTAT/UTLESTAT, or Custom scripts (See Chapter 15 for the Performance Statistics Collector Project)
UNIX	sar, vmstat, mpstat, iostat, netstat
Windows	Performance Monitoring Tool

Statistical trends: Analyzing statistics collected for a database is a good method for identifying performance trends. Therefore, as a DBA, you should consider methods to respond to tuning issues that were detected using statistical analysis.

Hardware configuration: Hardware can directly improve performance. However, you should remember two things: first, hardware should be scaleable; and second, hardware may enhance performance, but may not solve every issue.

DBA ROLES AND RESPONSIBILITIES

A team of two DBAs, Leo and Brad, were working for a small retail company administering around 20 databases. These two DBAs had nothing in common except their database work. Leo had more experience in Oracle databases, but was not willing to do anything outside Oracle. Brad's experience could not measure up to Leo's, but his diversified experience and personality superseded Leo's. Brad believed that a DBA should be very involved and that everyone involved with the database operation, from users to customers to managers, were all his customers and all of equal importance. Unlike Brad, Leo thought of himself as a resource of central importance to the organization.

Everyone in the company knew about these two DBAs. Any employee who needed assistance or had a database issue went straight to Brad. Brad would help anyone with any issue related to databases. He was not unwilling to say, "I don't know, but I'll try to come up with an answer," and most of the time he came through. Leo lived in his own world, his database world, that is. If people approached him for help about a query, he would help them, but make them feel so uncomfortable and inferior that they never returned. This situation became a huge problem for their manager whose actions were limited by the scarcity of DBAs. With a downturn in the economy, the manager was asked to reduce his staff to one DBA. He had no choice: he had to layoff one of them, and it was Leo, even though he was more technically proficient than Brad.

As a DBA, you have many responsibilities that revolve around the database you are managing or maintaining. You usually interact with most of the database application business personnel—business managers, users, business analysts—and you interact with technical staff—developers, analysts, and designers. Figure 1-4 illustrates DBA interactions and activities with other persons involved in a database application.

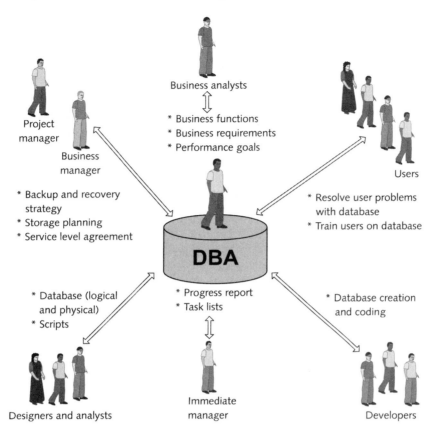

Figure 1-3   DBA interactions with different groups

As a successful, experienced DBA you will find yourself working with all the groups shown in Figure 1-4 to make sure that you are aware of any business or technical decisions that affect the database you are administering. The DBA must be aware of architectural changes to the system and the implications of the change on the database. With any design decision you must take into account the impact on database performance; therefore, you must ensure that all code changes are optimized. In respect to database performance tuning, your role as DBA should be focused on the following activities:

- Be involved in all SDLC phases.

- Recommend best practices in data modeling and database designs.

- Educate developers on how to optimize their code (queries).

- Work with designers and developers on transaction controls.

- Recommend to developers SQL tuning tools.

- Monitor database performance.

- Collect and analyze database statistics.

- Educate users on best practices for working with database applications.

At this point, you have a general understanding of your role as a DBA within the organization and how you relate to various groups. Now take a quick look at your specific responsibilities. Table 1-5 defines typical DBA responsibilities, which include database architecture, development support, general database support, and production support. Note that the tasks in the list are not prioritized.

Table 1-5 DBA responsibilities

Function type	Responsibilities
Oracle	■ Install Oracle database and application products ■ Research and evaluate advanced database functionality ■ Evaluate and perform Oracle upgrades and patches ■ Manage Oracle licenses and contracts ■ Set up and maintain Oracle infrastructure ■ Provide expertise on best use of Oracle functionality
Administration	■ Lead and assist with database projects and issues ■ Evaluate new database software, for example, data-modeling tools ■ Set up production database and schema ■ Troubleshoot and resolve all production issues ■ Develop database configuration standards ■ Participate in database infrastructure projects ■ Manage allocation of machine resources among production databases ■ Participate in knowledge transfer from and to other DBAs ■ Create a database implementation task list ■ Create and maintain database support documentation ■ Set up users, roles, privileges, and other resources ■ Assist with the design of application security and other database architectures
Tuning	■ Evaluate corporate data model implications and integration ■ Lead or participate in the design of database server architecture ■ Work with developers and analysts to build database development standards ■ Work with architects and designers to create data modeling and database standards ■ Lead and assist in capacity planning ■ Gather and analyze database statistics ■ Monitor database space storage ■ Monitor and tune production databases ■ Assist in the design, development, and review of SQL ■ Assist the application team with resolving performance issues ■ Review physical database design ■ Performance test and tune SQL

Function type	Responsibilities
Backup and recovery	■ Set up and monitor database backups and archive logs ■ Perform database recovery if necessary ■ Participate in backup and recovery strategizing ■ Design application database backup and recovery process ■ Set up and verify database backup and recovery process
Applications	■ Apply application database changes and upgrades ■ Create and configure development databases ■ Set up and monitor development schema exports ■ Export and import test data ■ Create and alter schema objects as needed ■ Collect data and transaction volume information ■ Participate as a dedicated member of the application team ■ Migrate PL/SQL packages and compile into database

ORACLE TUNING TOOLS

This last section in the chapter gives you a brief introduction to the Oracle performance tools, utilities, PL/SQL stored packages, and commands included with the Oracle9i product. This list is not meant to overwhelm you with new terminology, so even if the terms are unfamiliar, look at the list as a set of tools you will eventually understand and stash in your pocket to be handy when needed. Most of the tools are presented in future chapters in more detail, so you will be learning to use them to perform your database application tuning responsibilities.

Oracle Tools and Utilities

- **Performance Views (V$ Views):** Dynamic views of performance with metrics that are continuously changing while the database is up and running

- **Data dictionary views:** Static views containing metadata

- **Oracle Optimizer:** A logical component of Oracle that determines the optimal way to process and execute SQL statements

- **Oracle Optimizer Hints:** A method for influencing the Optimizer to execute an SQL statement in a specific way

- **Explain Plan Statement:** A statement that displays the execution plan of an SQL statement

- **SQL Trace:** A utility that traces sessions to generate performance statistics

- **Autotrace settings:** SQL*Plus settings that can generate, execute, and plan statistics for all submitted SQL statements in SQL*Plus

- **Tkprof:** A performance tool that formats the output generated by SQL Trace

- **Outlines:** A stored execution plan generated for a specific SQL statement

- **UTLBSTAT.SQL and UTLESTAT.SQL:** SQL scripts used to generate database statistical reports for a specific time frame

- **Statspack package:** An Oracle-supplied package that creates a statistics repository, collects database statistics, and generates statistical reports for specific time frames

Oracle Manager Tools

- **Oracle Enterprise Manager:** A graphical user interface administration tool used at Central Command Control to perform various database administrative tasks, backup and recovery, data management, and tuning

- **Diagnostic Pack:** Is a collection of tools used to diagnose and troubleshoot a database

  - **Lock Monitor:** Monitors table lock and memory latches

  - **Performance Manager:** Displays performance statistics of Real Application Clusters

  - **Performance Overview:** Provides overall performance assessments

  - **Top Sessions:** Displays top sessions that are utilizing various resources

  - **Top SQL:** Displays the most problematic SQL statements submitted to the database

  - **Trace Data Viewer:** Analyzes and traces contents of a trace file

- **Tuning Pack:** Is a collection of tools used to assist and facilitate database administration in tuning specific areas of the database

  - **Oracle Expert:** A tool that provides full performance analysis and tuning recommendations

  - **Outline Management:** A tool that stores and maintains outlines

  - **SQL Analyze:** A wizard used to analyze objects in the database

  - **Tablespace Map:** A tool that displays tablespace data block mapping

CHAPTER SUMMARY

- The System Development Life Cycle provides a consistent methodology for solving business problems.
- A DBA should be involved in most SDLC phases.
- Performance tuning is one of the most challenging tasks of a DBA.
- DBAs should focus their efforts on database design and code.
- Most performance problems stem from bad design and inefficient code.

- To provide optimal service, DBAs should know their users' tasks and responsibilities.
- DBAs should implement a mechanism to collect statistics and analyze these statistics to determine performance trends.
- The Oracle9*i* product provides DBAs with a number of tools that assist with performance tuning.
- Knowing who should perform tuning tasks and what should be tuned is essential for allocating resources to performance problems.
- Hardware, network, and operating system configuration can enhance or degrade performance but are not the major causes of performance problems.
- Knowing the type and cause of performance problems expedites the performance-tuning process.
- DBAs should follow the tuning approach outlined in this chapter to help focus their efforts on performance issues.
- The design phase of the SDLC outlines how an application should perform. Faulty design leads to poor performance.
- Problematic queries can consume system resources resulting in degraded performance.
- Reducing contention (memory, I/O) enhances application performance.
- Performance measurements, such as response time, should be set realistically and should be documented in the user requirements or the functional specification.
- When tuning a database, a DBA should use a checklist of performance considerations.
- DBAs play important roles in organizations because of their interaction with many different departments.

REVIEW QUESTIONS

1. DBAs must be involved in the database design to ensure that all functional specification requirements are met. (True/False)

2. Tuning I/O is the first thing a DBA should tackle after all application design and code is tuned. (True/False)

3. A DBA constantly monitors response time measurements. (True/False)

4. VMSTAT is an Oracle tool that collects database statistics. (True/False)

5. Reading data from data files improves read consistency and has little performance impact. (True/False)

6. The task of disk striping is performed by the DBA. (True/False)

7. Problematic queries impact performance by causing high CPU utilization. (True/False)

8. List five tasks that a DBA is responsible for when tuning a database.

9. List five tuning considerations of which the DBA should be aware.

10. List five performance problems that may occur.

11. Outline what aspects of the database should be tuned by each person involved in the SDLC process. Emphasize the role of the DBA in this process.

12. List the different areas of expertise and skills that a database performance expert should have.

13. Explain why historical statistics are needed for improving performance.

14. How can you tell if your database is performing in an optimal way?

15. When should you start tuning?

16. What phase of the SDLC is most important for performance? Outline your responsibilities as DBA in that phase.

17. As a DBA, do you believe you should demand from developers a list of all queries submitted to the database to review? Why or why not?

18. As a DBA, should you learn about applications, their functions, and users from a business point of view? Why or why not?

19. What is the difference in responsibilities between a system DBA and application DBA with respect to performance tuning and performance problems?

20. Outline the steps you would take to tune a performance problem in production.

EXAM REVIEW QUESTIONS: ORACLE9i PERFORMANCE TUNING (#1Z0-033)

1. After analyzing the database, you determine that some queries are excessively consuming database resources. What should you do?

    a. Do nothing, since no users have complained about any performance issues.

    b. Analyze those queries further to determine if corrective action is needed.

    c. Inform developers about the problem queries and wait for their response.

    d. Modify the database configuration so the queries run more efficiently.

2. After the database application is tuned, what should be tuned next?

    a. Design

    b. Queries

    c. Contention

    d. Operating system

    e. Memory

3. When tuning the database, which of the following is considered the most important?

    a. Operating system

    b. Application design

    c. Application code

    d. Database configuration

    e. Input/output throughput

    f. Network bandwidth

4. When tuning the database, which of the following is considered the least important?

    a. Operating system

    b. Application design

    c. Application code

    d. Database configuration

    e. Input/output throughput

    f. Network bandwidth

5. A new design support system application is currently being tested. You were not involved in the earlier phases of the System Development Life Cycle. What can you do at this stage to ensure that performance problems are prevented?

    a. Configure the database with high parameters settings.

    b. Analyze all queries submitted during testing.

    c. Analyze the design of the database.

    d. Ensure that hardware is configured with a large amount of memory and a fast CPU.

6. For an OLTP application, what should your tuning goal be?

    a. Fast response time

    b. High database availability

    c. Efficient memory and CPU utilization

    d. Statistics collection

    e. Reduction of excessive I/O operations

1

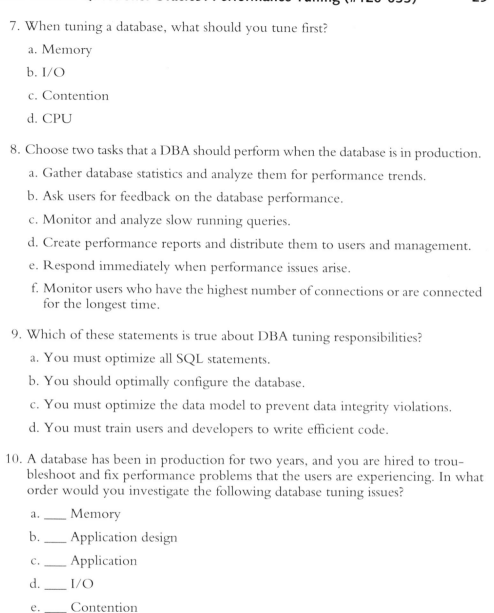

7. When tuning a database, what should you tune first?

   a. Memory

   b. I/O

   c. Contention

   d. CPU

8. Choose two tasks that a DBA should perform when the database is in production.

   a. Gather database statistics and analyze them for performance trends.

   b. Ask users for feedback on the database performance.

   c. Monitor and analyze slow running queries.

   d. Create performance reports and distribute them to users and management.

   e. Respond immediately when performance issues arise.

   f. Monitor users who have the highest number of connections or are connected for the longest time.

9. Which of these statements is true about DBA tuning responsibilities?

   a. You must optimize all SQL statements.

   b. You should optimally configure the database.

   c. You must optimize the data model to prevent data integrity violations.

   d. You must train users and developers to write efficient code.

10. A database has been in production for two years, and you are hired to troubleshoot and fix performance problems that the users are experiencing. In what order would you investigate the following database tuning issues?

    a. ____ Memory

    b. ____ Application design

    c. ____ Application

    d. ____ I/O

    e. ____ Contention

    f. ____ Operating system

11. For the same scenario described in Question 10, list the following database-tuning issues in the order you would fix them.

    a. ____ Memory

    b. ____ Application design

    c. ____ Application

    d. ____ I/O

    e. ____ Contention

HANDS-ON PROJECTS

**HANDS-ON
PROJECTS**

Please complete the projects provided below.

1. Users are experiencing long waits every time they run summary reports for an online transactional processing (OLTP) application that tracks purchase orders submitted to the department. Architects designed the system as a transactional system. Identify the steps you would take to determine the cause of the problem.

2. A new accounting application is on the horizon for the Accounting Department of ABC Company. Outline the role the DBA should assume to minimize performance issues.

3. You receive a call from a business manager complaining about the current performance degradation of the database. You have a collection of performance queries that you use to get the status of several database hit ratios. (Hit ratios are explained in Chapter 2. For now, you need only this definition: the buffer cache hit ratio is a useful indicator, which provides a percentage of how often data was found in buffer memory compared to how often data was retrieved from disk.) The reading that you take with these queries indicates that there are some long running queries and memory ratios that are significantly below the level of their acceptable performance thresholds. Explain what you should do to fix and prevent this problem.

4. A production DBA is asked to implement a last minute database change that will add a new table with millions of rows of data needed for new reports and inquiries. The DBA implements the change in production and a few hours later everyone experiences low response times. Explain what went wrong and how you can prevent this from occurring again.

5. Management asks you, the DBA, to attend a design review meeting for a new application. On reviewing the proposed logical data model, you discover that the data model is denormalized. After inquiring about denormalization, you are told that the data model was denormalized to access some of the data quickly. You know that in some situations denormalization enhances the performance of the system, but you have concerns about the denormalization process. Outline these concerns.

1

6. A customer calls ABC Company customer service inquiring about an order he placed. The customer service representative (CSR) asks the customer for an account number, but the customer does not have it, so the CSR asks for the customer's phone number. The customer provides the phone number and the CSR asks the customer to wait and enters the query to retrieve the customer's account record. A minute goes by with no results, so the CSR apologizes to the customer by saying that the system is slow. How would you respond if you were the customer calling? How would you feel if you were the CSR? How would you respond and feel if you were the DBA administering the database?

7. Suppose that you are administering a database that was recently pushed into production. You don't have any monitoring tools or scripts installed, and you have not received any performance complaints and issues. Explain in detail the consequences and issues that might arise from current conditions. Also indicate what you would do to rectify any problems that exist.

8. During your routine checkup of the production database, you notice that a long query is consuming much of the CPU resources. After further investigation you determine that the query is optimal. What would you do to solve this problem? Justify your answer.

9. As a DBA, you notice that an application is frequently connecting and disconnecting to and from the database. Should you be concerned? Explain.

10. Should you tune the database for an application while it is in development? If so, what would you tune? If not, why not?

11. You are hired as a DBA consultant to conduct a performance survey of a database in production. Outline in detail the steps you would take to perform this task.

12. Figure 1-3 illustrates the performance effort a DBA should spend on various aspects of an application. For each layer in pyramid B, list three items: (1) one performance issue; (2) one issue the DBA may confront; and (3) one performance item that the DBA would tune.

CASE PROJECTS

CASE PROJECTS

Performance Problem Prevention Plan

Consider the following application specifications for a computer time-tracking system:

1. It is a three-tiered Web application.

2. The data model contains 30 tables used for transactions and data retrieval and 10 tables used to store historical data.

3. The application code is a combination of Java code and SQL.

4. All business rules are implemented at the application level.

5. The application is a hybrid of OLTP and DSS.

6. The host machine of the database is shared with three other applications.

7. The business requirements include fast response time for users.

Build a plan and outline a process to prevent performance issues. Your plan should include person(s) involved and their responsibilities.

PART

II

Tuning Memory

2

TUNING THE BUFFER CACHE

In this chapter you will:

- Understand how the buffer cache works
- Learn how to configure the buffer cache
- Learn how to configure a database with one or multiple database block sizes
- Dynamically allocate SGA memory
- Configure a buffer cache with multiple buffer pools
- Understand how automatic table caching works
- Learn how to use the new Buffer Cache Size Advice
- Diagnose buffer cache configuration
- Look inside the buffer cache

Chapter 1 presented at a high level a methodology for database tuning and explained the role of the DBA in understanding and correcting performance problems. This chapter describes how to tune the buffer cache. You learned in previous courses that a buffer cache is a high-speed memory used to cache data that is being sent and received to and from the database. Information is cached in the buffer cache to locate it closer to the user, thus making it more readily and speedily accessible. Understanding how to work with the buffer cache is key to becoming an effective DBA. To prepare you for this role, this chapter gives you an overview of the buffer cache memory structure, steps you through creating a buffer cache, and shows you how to adjust the size of the buffer cache and how to diagnose and resolve buffer cache problems.

Figure 2-1 represents the Oracle instance and database architecture and highlights the buffer cache as one of the major memory structures of the System Global Area (SGA) within an Oracle instance. The buffer cache configuration is a major piece of the database configuration and significantly affects, either positively or negatively, the performance of the database. In this chapter, you learn how to configure the buffer cache optimally and monitor its performance using an Oracle-provided advisor and queries.

Performance Problem

This section outlines an actual performance problem. As you look it over, imagine yourself as the DBA who reported it and keep it in mind as you proceed through the chapter. The chapter presents concepts relevant to the problem. In the first Hands-on Assignment at the end of the chapter, you are asked to use the concepts you have learned to provide a solution, or partial solution, to this performance problem.

From: Joe Doe <mail to: doe@cachebuffer.com>

Dates: 13-Feb-02 15:27

Subject: Buffer Cache Problem

I have a large table (500 MB+ and growing), which is being constantly read by the application as part of a data load validation process.

My buffer cache is 1.2 GB, and total SGA is 1.7 GB.

When I start the instance and begin loading data from a third-party application, I get a 100% buffer cache hit ratio, even though the large table in question is constantly queried and updated.

However, when I begin running queries using other tables including V$VIEW, the buffer cache hit ratio drops to 50–60%. It seems that when I run queries, other tables are loaded into buffer cache and push out my large production tables.

Is there any way I can keep these tables from being aged out (I understand BUFFER_POOL KEEP should be used for small lookup tables only)? The only solution that has worked for now is to bounce the instance.

Thanks in advance for your help,

Joe D.

BUFFER CACHE OVERVIEW

As you already know, the Oracle architecture is composed of a logical structure known as the instance, and a physical structure known as the database. The Oracle instance consists of background processes and the System Global Area (see Appendix A for an overview of Oracle architecture). The **System Global Area (SGA)** is the memory structure in which Oracle caches data that is retrieved for access, updates, submitted SQL statements, executed PL/SQL blocks, data dictionary definitions, and other cache mechanisms. The major purpose of this memory structure is to enhance data retrieval by placing the most frequently used data in memory rather than retrieving it from a disk each time it is requested. Reducing retrieval from a disk is important, because excessive disk I/O can degrade system performance tremendously. Figure 2-1 illustrates Oracle architecture and the five major memory structures of the SGA:

- **Buffer cache:** Stores the most frequently accessed and modified data blocks for fast retrieval

- **Redo log buffers:** Temporarily stores all transaction entries submitted to the database

- **Shared pool memory:** Stores the most frequently submitted SQL statements and PL/SQL blocks to expedite the parsing process

- **Large pool:** Is used for parallel query, the Recovery Manager (RMAN), and the shared server

- **Java pool:** Stores Java code used by user sessions

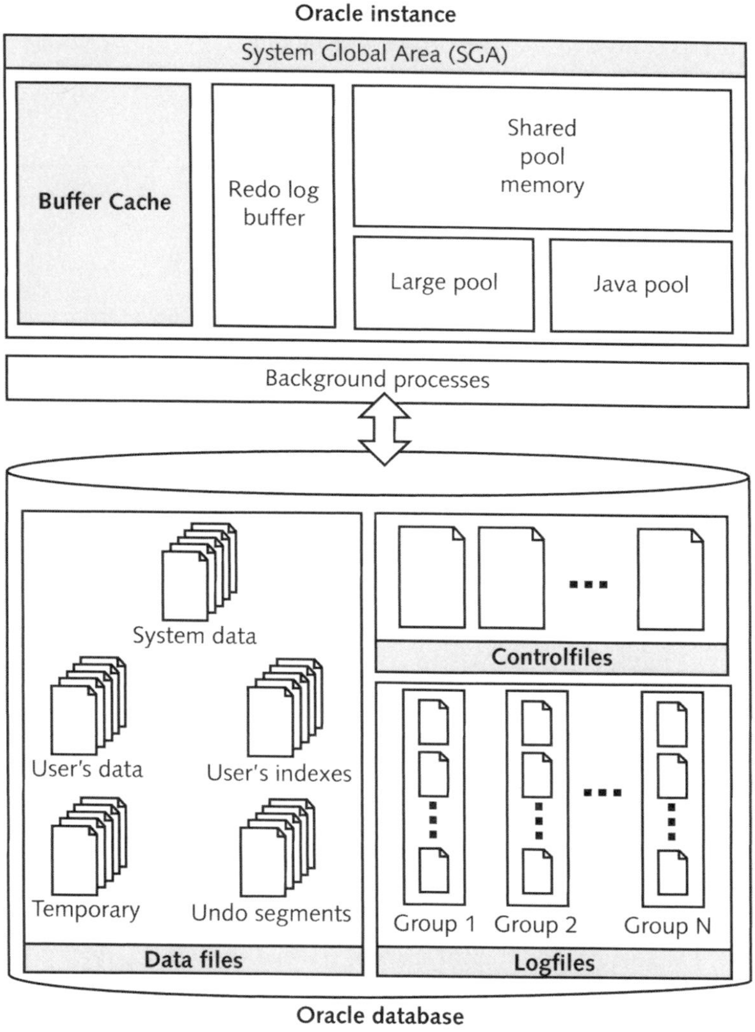

2

Figure 2-1   System Global Area (SGA) structure of Oracle architecture

As stated previously, the **buffer cache** stores the most frequently accessed Oracle data blocks. These blocks are cached temporarily until space is needed for other blocks that are being accessed. Oracle uses the **Least Recent Used (LRU)** structure and algorithm to determine which block is being used the least and flushes that block to release the memory it occupies. Again, the major purpose of the buffer cache is to reduce disk I/O. Oracle maintains two lists of data for that purpose: the LRU list and the write list. The LRU list is a listing of free blocks, and the write list is a listing of dirty block buffers. Figure 2-2 illustrates the data-caching process.

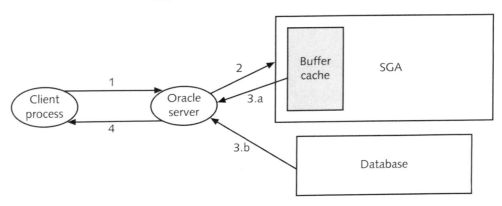

Figure 2-2   Data-caching process

The four data-caching steps shown in Figure 2-2 are detailed as follows:

1. The client issues a SQL statement.

2. The Oracle server parses the statement to make sure it is valid, determines if the user is authorized to see the data, and determines the execution plan.

3. The Oracle server checks to see if the requested data already exists in the buffer cache.

   a. If data is cached, the Oracle server sends back the data requested without returning to the data files (this is known as a **cache hit**).

   b. If data is not cached, the Oracle server fetches the data from data files in the database based on the execution plan determined in Step 2 (this is known as a **cache miss**).

4. The client receives the requested data, and presents the data to the user.

If the same data is requested repeatedly, the Oracle server does not have to fetch the data files from database. Data stays cached until space is needed for other requested data.

Figure 2-3 delves into this example in more detail by illustrating the internal structure of the buffer cache. You can configure the buffer cache into three main buffer pools, each with a specific function as follows:

1. **Default buffer pool:** Used when data is not assigned to any specific pool (Keep or Recycle)

2. **Keep buffer pool:** Used for data blocks that should be retained as long as possible. This pool is also subject to the LRU process for flushing data blocks when space is needed. (This buffer pool is optional.)

3. **Recycle buffer pool:** Used for data blocks that have lower priority for being kept in memory than Default and Keep. (This buffer pool is optional.)

You can configure other optional default buffer pools that are used specifically when you have tablespaces with different block sizes than the default set by using the DB_BLOCK_SIZE parameter. Notice that Figure 2-3 shows that the Default buffer pool is using a 4 KB block buffer that is set by DB_BLOCK_SIZE, and that other default pools are set for 2 KB, 8 KB, 16 KB, and 32 KB block buffers to be used by tablespaces that are configured with a corresponding block size. For example, if you create a tablespace with a block size of 16 KB, you must configure a Default buffer pool of 16 KB.

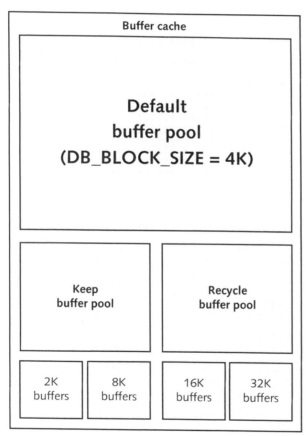

Figure 2-3　Buffer cache internal structure

CONFIGURING THE BUFFER CACHE

A DBA consultant joined a large team of database administrators for a large telecommunication company. He was assigned to a new database application for which he had to create new databases for development, QA, and later for production. He obtained from business analysts and developers all the information he needed about the application, and decided to build the new database using the same configuration as another database application in production because it was generally similar to the new database.

After he created the database for development and QA, he monitored the database memory, and specifically, the database block buffers. He determined that he had overallocated, but did not do anything since the database was not in production, and therefore the database application went into production with the same memory configuration. He kept an eye on the database performance, especially the memory configuration. When he noticed that memory was being hit hard, he recorded it and observed it more closely to make sure it was not just a spike. Eventually, he adjusted the database buffer configuration, but it took him one month to reach optimal settings.

When creating a new database, you as the DBA must configure the buffer cache. Most database administrators initially configure memory based on best estimates of the usage of similar existing databases and the applications that use them.

When the database is up and running, you must take performance readings to make sure that the memory configuration is not a performance bottleneck. This process is typically applied to all memory structures.

To configure the buffer cache size, you can use the initialization parameter file of DB_CACHE_SIZE, or the old parameter DB_BLOCK_BUFFERS (this parameter has been deprecated in Oracle9*i* and is kept for backward compatibility). DB_BLOCK_BUFFERS can still be used, although Oracle9*i* does not allow dynamic changes to it.

NOTE

The initialization parameter file goes by a number of names including the following: init.ora file ("init dot ora"), PFILE, parameter file, initialization file, server parameter file, and SPFILE.

To change the buffer cache size, you must change the parameter in the initialization parameter file and bounce (shutdown and start) the database. The new parameter, DB_CACHE_SIZE, enables you to allocate and deallocate memory dynamically as needed. Another advantage to using the DB_CACHE_SIZE parameter is that it enables you to use a new feature of Oracle9i, Buffer Cache Size Advice, which is a mechanism that projects the impact of reducing or increasing the buffer cache. When configuring the buffer cache, you should consider the following:

1. What is the estimated maximum size that the SGA will ever need to be? Normally when configuring the SGA, you allocate memory according to guidelines and experience. If you determine later that the SGA configuration is not proper, you can increase it. If the SGA_MAX_SIZE parameter is not configured or not large enough, you are not allowed to increase the SGA configuration.

2. Will you need to dynamically resize memory? For example, if your application is functioning properly without performance problems and was recently upgraded to Oracle9i, you should not reconfigure the instance or the database.

3. Will your database employ different database block sizes? Some applications require tablespaces with different database block sizes, as usually determined by database designers/architects and DBAs. If so, you should configure your memory to accommodate it.

TIP

It is highly recommended that you evaluate and assess each Oracle feature specifically for your database application. Not every new feature that Oracle introduces applies to your database, is beneficial to implement, or delivers what it promises. Many experts negatively compare the capabilities of Buffer Cache Size Advice with its advertised benefits.

Oracle9i supports multiple database block sizes, which can be useful when the database application benefits from large database block sizes that accommodate large tables that are queried often for reporting purposes. The database application can also benefit from having small database block sizes for tables that have frequently used data manipulation language (DML) statements.

DATABASE WITH ONE DATABASE BLOCK SIZE

The size of the buffer cache is set initially by adding the following lines to the initialization parameter file to configure the database for dynamic allocation using the Buffer Cache Advisor feature and a maximum SGA size and block size of 4 KB.

TIP

Once a tablespace is created with a default block size set by the DB_BLOCK_SIZE parameter, you may not be able to change it.

```
#############################################
# Cache and I/O
#############################################
db_block_size=4096
db_cache_size=33554432
db_cache_advice=ON


#############################################
# SGA
#############################################
sga_max_size = 200000000
```

NOTE   DB_CACHE_ADVICE can be dynamically set to ON or OFF using an ALTER SYSTEM statement, but SGA_MAX_SIZE cannot be changed while the database is up and running. You must shut down the database and restart it to change the SGA_MAX_SIZE parameter.

After the instance is started, you can verify SGA allocation by querying the VSGA, VSGASTAT, and V$PARAMETER views. Notice that the first three queries set out here display similar results using different methods. Also notice that the total size of the SGA is set to 202142048, which is configured by the SGA_MAX_SIZE parameter as the maximum size to which the SGA can grow. Now compare this value to the results of the second query presented here. You find that the SGA reserved is actually the sum of DB_CACHE_SIZE, SHARED_POOL_SIZE, LARGE_POOL_SIZE, and JAVA_POOL_SIZE. The result of the last query is the sum of all the bytes in V$SGASTAT that are used by all memory structures in the SGA.

```
SQL> select * from v$sga;

NAME                      VALUE
--------------------      ----------
Fixed size                  282976
Variable size            163577856
Database buffers          37748736
Redo buffers                532480
```

```
SQL> show sga

Total System Global Area  202142048 bytes
Fixed size                   282976 bytes
Variable size             163577856 bytes
Database buffers           37748736 bytes
Redo buffers                 532480 bytes
```

```
SQL> column name format a20
SQL> column value format a20
SQL> select name, value
  2     from v$parameter
  3     where name in ('db_cache_size',
                       'db_cache_advice',
                        'db_8k_cache_size',
                         'sga_max_size');

NAME                 VALUE
-------------------- --------------------
sga_max_size         202142048
db_8k_cache_size     4194304
db_cache_size        33554432
db_cache_advice      ON
```

NOTE

Fixed Size and Variable Size are memory allocated by other memory pools and other structures.

```
SQL> select sum(bytes) from v$sgastat;

SUM(BYTES)
----------
 118247776
```

DATABASE WITH MULTIPLE BLOCK SIZES

The phone rang when Tim was checking his e-mail Monday morning. "Hello Tim, we have a design question and we need your help. Do you have time to join us in a meeting now?" Tim joined the meeting and discovered that his colleagues were discussing the design of a hybrid application and, specifically, the design of several tables used for reporting. These tables would be refreshed once a month and would be queried most of the time. One of the database designers suggested table partitioning and others suggested different types of tables. Their main concern was that there would be frequent full-table scans. One of the developers popped a question to Tim: "What do you think we should do?" Tim thought for a second and said that they could adopt table partitioning as part of the solution, but to improve full-table scans, they needed to use a properly sized database block. This application would most likely use 4 KB, but for the reporting tables it would use 16 KB or 32 KB. Everyone looked at Tim and wondered, "Is this possible?"

Sometimes databases are required to support multiple database block sizes. For example, you may have an online transaction processing (OLTP) application in which the 4 KB default block size is efficient except when dealing with a few tables that are used for reporting purposes. In this situation, the tables would be more efficient if they resided on a tablespace with a large database block size, such as 16 KB. Oracle9*i* allows you to configure the buffer cache for each block size using the following initialization parameters. These parameters can be set or changed dynamically:

- DB_2K_CACHE_SIZE

- DB_4K_CACHE_SIZE

- DB_8K_CACHE_SIZE

- DB_16K_CACHE_SIZE

- DB_32K_CACHE_SIZE

NOTE The maximum block size can that can be set is determined by the operating system platform.

You can use the following steps to configure the database for the preceding scenario.

1. Set DB_16K_CACHE_SIZE to 8 MB by issuing the following statement:

```
SQL> ALTER SYSTEM SET DB_16K_CACHE_SIZE = 8M;
System altered.

SQL> SHOW PARAMETER DB_16K

NAME                                TYPE        VALUE
----------------------------------- ----------- ------------------
db_16k_cache_size                   big integer 8388608

SQL> SHOW PARAMETER BLOCK_SIZE

NAME                                TYPE        VALUE
----------------------------------- ----------- ------------------
db_block_size                           integer    4096
```

NOTE If you encounter Oracle ORA-02097 followed by ORA-00384 it means that there is not enough memory for the SGA to accommodate the memory modification.

Or, you can set the parameters in the initialization file as follows:

```
#########################################
# Cache and I/O

#########################################

db_block_size=4096

db_cache_size=16000000

db_cache_advice=ON

db_16k_cache_size=8000000
#########################################
# SGA
#########################################
sga_max_size = 200000000
```

TIP   When changing any parameter dynamically, set the parameter only while the database is up and running. Once the database is down, the setting change is gone. If you want the setting to always be in effect, you need to change it in the initialization file.

2. Create a tablespace that uses a 16 KB block size as follows:

```
SQL> CREATE TABLESPACE TEST_DATA_16K
  2      LOGGING
  3      DATAFILE 'C:\ORACLE\ORADATA\SAM\TEST_DATA_16K.ORA' SIZE 100M
  4      BLOCKSIZE 16384
  5      EXTENT MANAGEMENT LOCAL
  6  /

Tablespace created.

SQL> SELECT TABLESPACE_NAME, BLOCK_SIZE
  2    FROM DBA_TABLESPACES;

TABLESPACE_NAME                     BLOCK_SIZE
--------------------------------   ----------
SYSTEM                                   4096   <=== DEFAULT BLOCK SIZE
UNDOTBS                                  4096
CWMLITE                                  4096
DRSYS                                    4096
EXAMPLE                                  4096
INDX                                     4096
TEMP                                     4096
TOOLS                                    4096
USERS                                    4096
TEST_DATA_16K                           16384   <=== 16k BLOCK SIZE
```

3. Create a table that resides in the TEST_DATA_16K block size and populate it with data:

```
SQL> CREATE TABLE TEST_16K
  2  (  NUM      NUMBER,
  3     TEXT     VARCHAR2(80)
  4  )
  5  TABLESPACE TEST_DATA_16K
  6  /

Table created.

SQL> BEGIN
  2      FOR I IN 1..20000 LOOP
  3          INSERT INTO TEST_16K
  4              VALUES(I, 'THIS IS A SAMPLE TEST DATA FOR TABLE
RESIDING IN 16K BLOCK SIZE #'||I);
  5      END LOOP;
  6      COMMIT;
  7  END;
  8  /

PL/SQL procedure successfully completed.
```

NOTE   The fact that the preceding PL/SQL block is committing at the end of the block requires large UNDO segments. It is better to commit more frequently within the FOR loop and thus reduce the amount of UNDO segment space. However, frequent commits within the loop will slow down the performance of the PL/SQL block significantly. You can introduce code to commit once every 200 INSERTS, like so:

```
SQL> BEGIN
  2      FOR I IN 1..20000 LOOP
  3          INSERT INTO TEST_16K
  4              VALUES(I, 'THIS IS A SAMPLE TEST DATA FOR TABLE
  5              RESIDING IN 16K BLOCK SIZE #'||I);
  6          IF MOD(I, 200) = 199 THEN
  7              COMMIT;
  8          END IF;
  9      END LOOP;
 10  END;
 11  /
```

4. Now, every time you issue a DML statement operating on this table, data will be residing in the 16 KB buffer cache that was allocated for it. Later in this chapter, you learn to detect whether or not the size allocated is properly configured.

DYNAMIC SGA ALLOCATION

"The database will be shutdown at 8:00 pm for maintenance." That's what Ken read in an e-mail from the DBA. Ken is the database manager for a group of DBAs. He was curious why the database was being shutdown, especially when Oracle9*i*'s claim to fame is avoiding database disruption for maintenance issues. So he replied to the e-mail in this way: "Hi, can you explain what maintenance you are planning to do?" The DBA replied, "I am planning on increasing memory!"

Some circumstances require adjusting the size of allocated SGA memory without shutting down the database. For example, the buffer cache could have been incorrectly configured or the buffer pools may require configuration. As a DBA, you can adjust the size of the allocated SGA memory without shutting down the database by adjusting the size of any of the five main SGA memory structures shown in Figure 2-4. Figure 2-4 presents the same five memory structures with corresponding configuration initialization parameters. However, it should be noted that the initialization parameter of SGA_MAX_SIZE indicates the maximum memory allocation that can be configured for the SGA. The default value of the SGA_MAX_SIZE is equal to the sum of the values of all initialization parameters displayed in Figure 2-4.

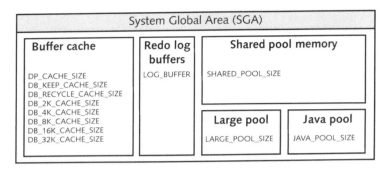

Figure 2-4   SGA initialization parameters

If the value of the SGA_MAX_SIZE is set to a value less than the sum of the size of the five memory structures, Oracle ignores the SGA_MAX_SIZE value.

NOTE

If you anticipate the need to increase the SGA allocated memory, you can set SGA_MAX_SIZE to a value larger than the default size. When you are adjusting the size of any memory structure in the SGA, it is decremented or incremented in granules (a **granule** in Oracle9i is a memory unit) based on the size of the SGA as shown in Table 2-1. For instance, if you decide to change the setting of the DB_CACHE_SIZE from 32 MB to 23 MB, Oracle rounds up to the next granule increment, which is 24 MB.

Table 2-1   SGA granules

SGA size	Granule
Less than 128 MB	4 MB
Greater or equal to 128 MB	16 MB

Oracle provides a view called V$SGA_DYNAMIC_COMPONENTS, which contains information about the size of the major memory structures in the SGA. Table 2-2 presents the structure of this view.

Table 2-2   V$SGA_DYNAMIC_COMPONENTS

Component	SGA memory structure name
CURRENT_SIZE	Current size of memory structure
MIN_SIZE	Minimum size of memory structure since the instance started
MAX_SIZE	Maximum size of memory structure since the instance started
OPER_COUNT	Number of operations on memory structure since the instance started
LAST_OPER_TYPE	Type of last operation on memory structure; there are two possible values: **GROW**: operation on memory structure was to increase its size **SHRINK**: operation on memory structure was to decrease its size
LAST_OPER_MODE	**MANUAL**: memory structure was operated on manually by the DBA **AUTO**: memory structure was operated on automatically by Oracle

Component	SGA memory structure name
LAST_OPER_TIME	Time when the operation on memory structure occurred
GRANULE_SIZE	Size of the increment or decrement unit

The information in this table is derived from the online documentation that Oracle provides at the Oracle Technology Network site: *www.otn.oracle.com.*

Now that you understand the structure of the V$SGA_DYNAMIC_COMPONENTS view, you can examine an example of the contents of the V$SGA_DYNAMIC_COMPO-NENTS view, as shown in the following code sample. As you can see, the granule size value is 8 MB, which does not comply with the granule size criteria. According to Table 2-1, granule size should be 16 MB, because the SGA_MAX_SIZE is set to a value greater than 128 MB (this is a known Oracle bug).

```
SQL> SHOW PARAMETER SIZE

NAME                                        TYPE         VALUE
------------------------------------------- ------------ ----------
sga_max_size                                big integer  319364076
...

SQL> SELECT * FROM V$SGA_DYNAMIC_COMPONENTS;

COMPONENT       CURRENT_SIZE   MIN_SIZE    MAX_SIZE OPER_COUNT LAST_O LAST_O LAST_OPER GRANULE_SIZE
--------------- ------------ ---------- ----------- ---------- ------ ------ --------- ------------
shared pool        25165824   25165824    25165824          0                                8388608
large pool                0          0           0          0                                8388608
buffer cache       33554432    8388608    33554432          3 GROW   MANUAL 21-DEC-02         8388608
```

CONFIGURING MULTIPLE BUFFER POOLS

Figure 2-3 illustrates the internal structure of the buffer cache memory component of the SGA. As mentioned earlier in this chapter, there are three major pools that can be configured for different purposes.

For example, suppose you are administering a decision support system (DSS) database application that generates daily business reports which perform full-table scans on large tables. This implies that the data will be loaded into the default buffer cache, a process that could consume a major portion of its space. To improve performance, you could place this large amount of data in the Recycle buffer pool, which will age out (flush) the data as soon as it is used and the freed buffer can be used for other operations.

As another example, suppose that an OLTP database application is constantly referencing a small lookup table. If the data for the table is cached in the default buffers, there is a chance that when these buffers are needed for other operations, this table data will be flushed out causing additional I/O when it is referenced again. The additional I/O could degrade the performance of the application. You can solve this problem by caching the table in a higher priority buffer called the Keep buffer pool.

Oracle9*i* has two initialization parameters to configure the buffer cache pools:

- **DB_KEEP_CACHE_SIZE:** Configures memory allocation for the Keep buffer pool in the buffer cache

- **DB_RECYCLE_CACHE_SIZE:** Configures memory allocation for the Recycle buffer pool in the buffer cache

NOTE For the Oracle Real Application Cluster referenced as RAC instances, buffer pools can be set with the same or different size pool for each instance. You should tune the configuration of each instance based on the application type and requirements.

The total memory size of the buffer cache can be determined by summing all values of the following buffer cache parameters:

- DB_CACHE_SIZE

- DB_KEEP_CACHE_SIZE

- DB_RECYCLE_CACHE_SIZE

- DB_2K_CACHE_SIZE

- DB_4K_CACHE_SIZE

- DB_8K_CACHE_SIZE

- DB_16K_CACHE_SIZE

- DB_32K_CACHE_SIZE

The following statements show the total memory size allocated for the buffer cache. Notice that the SHOW SGA command shows that the database buffer cache allocated is 44 MB, which is the same as the results of the preceding query.

```
SQL> SHOW SGA

Total System Global Area   114061244 bytes
Fixed Size                    282556 bytes
Variable Size               67108864 bytes
Database Buffers            46137344 bytes
Redo Buffers                  532480 bytes

SQL> SELECT SUM(VALUE)/(1024*1024)
  2    FROM V$PARAMETER
  3   WHERE NAME IN('db_cache_size','db_keep_cache_size',
  4                 'db_recycle_cache_size', 'db_2k_cache_size',
  5                 'db_4k_cache_size', 'db_8k_cache_size',
  6                 'db_16k_cache_size', 'db_32K_cache_size')
  7  /

SUM(VALUE)/(1024*1024)
----------------------
                    44
```

Oracle9*i* allows you to cache a table in buffer cache memory for fast retrieval and to prioritize the table using different buffer pools. There are two methods for caching a table.

Method 1: You can cache a table in a specified buffer pool using the BUFFER_POOL storage parameter of the CREATE TABLE or ALTER TABLE statements, which can be set when creating the table, or set later with an ALTER statement. To cache a table in the Keep buffer pool, follow the steps shown in the code that follows:

```
SQL> ALTER TABLE DEPARTMENTS
  2      STORAGE ( BUFFER_POOL KEEP)
  3  /

Table altered.

SQL> ALTER TABLE DEPARTMENTS CACHE;

Table altered.

SQL> SELECT TABLE_NAME, CACHE, BUFFER_POOL
  2    FROM USER_TABLES
  3   ORDER BY TABLE_NAME
  4  /
```

```
TABLE_NAME                          CACHE BUFFER_POOL
----------------------------------  ----- -------
CATEGORIES                          N DEFAULT
CUSTOMERS                           N DEFAULT
DEPARTMENTS                         Y KEEP
EMPLOYEES                           N DEFAULT
EMPLOYEE_RANKS                      N DEFAULT
JOBS                                N DEFAULT
ORDERS                              N DEFAULT
ORDER_LINES                         N DEFAULT
PAYMENT_METHOD                      N DEFAULT
PRODUCTS                            N DEFAULT
PRODUCT_INVENTORY                   N DEFAULT
PRODUCT_PRICES                      N DEFAULT
PRODUCT_SUPPLIER                    N DEFAULT
PROMOTIONS                          N DEFAULT
SALES_COMMISSION                    N DEFAULT
SHIPMENT_METHOD                     N DEFAULT
SUPPLIERS                           N DEFAULT
```

To uncache a table, issue the following statement:

```
SQL> ALTER TABLE DEPARTMENTS NOCACHE;

Table altered.
```

Method 2: You can use an optimizer **hint** when issuing a SELECT statement. This hint instructs Oracle to place the data block for the table to be cached in the buffers.

NOTE

The **Optimizer** is a logical component of Oracle that determines how to execute SQL statements in the most optimal manner. A hint can influence how the Oracle Optimizer executes a SQL statement. More details on Oracle Optimizer hints are found in Chapter 13.

```
SQL> SELECT /*+ CACHE(CATEGORIES) */ *
        FROM CATEGORIES
     /
```

To uncache a table using hints, issue the following statement:

```
SQL> SELECT /*+ NOCACHE(CATEGORIES) */ *
        FROM CATEGORIES
     /
```

Tables that were created using the BUFFER_POOL KEEP storage option are not affected by the NOCACHE clause.

AUTOMATIC TABLE CACHING

Oracle9i Release 2 has introduced the automatic caching of small tables based on the size of the table. A table is considered small if it is less than 20 blocks or two percent of the total cached blocks. A table is considered medium-sized if it is more than 20 blocks and less than 10 percent of the total cached blocks. Automatic table caching is based on these criteria, caching statistics, and table scan frequency. These criteria do not apply to any table that has the CACHE option enabled.

BUFFER CACHE SIZE ADVICE

Oracle9i employs a handy feature called the Buffer Cache Size Advice (also called the Cache Advice or Cache Size Advice), which enables you to determine at any time whether the cache size is properly sized for the database application. You can compare different cache sizes and decide whether there is a significant benefit to increasing or reducing the cache size. To take advantage of this feature, you must turn on the DB_CACHE_ADVICE by setting the DB_CACHE_ADVICE parameter in the initialization file to ON. The DB_CACHE_ADVICE parameter can have one of the settings shown in Table 2-3.

Table 2-3   DB_CACHE_ADVICE parameter settings

Setting	Allocate memory	Collect data	Explanation
ON	√	√	Memory is allocated in a shared pool memory and advisory data is collected
READY	√	x	Memory is allocated in a shared pool memory, but advisory data is not collected; this option is used in anticipation of collecting advisory data
OFF	x	x	Memory is not allocated, and advisory data is not collected

It is recommended that the DB_CACHE_ADVICE parameter *not* be set to ON all the time. Turn it on whenever performance problems are suspected or when collecting memory statistics. When turned on or in a ready state, memory is allocated and advisory data is recorded that may increase CPU utilization. This increased CPU utilization may not be noticeable by users, but with other accumulated CPU usages or performance issues, there is a slight possibility that the user could experience some performance degradation.

After the DB_CACHE_ADVICE parameter is turned on, Oracle collects data statistics that you can examine at any time by using the V$DB_CACHE_ADVICE dynamic performance view. The contents of the view includes physical reads, and factor forecasts for the physical reads for each block size and for each Buffer Cache Size increment starting with smallest memory granule of 4 MB or 16 MB. Table 2-4 presents column descriptions of the V$DB_CACHE_ADVICE view.

NOTE Every time you change Buffer Cache Size allocation, the DB_CACHE_SIZE parameter is switched off automatically. This means that if you want to continue to collect Buffer Cache Size Advice data, you must turn it on again.

Table 2-4   V$DB_CACHE_ADVICE view definition

Column	Description
ID	Identification number of the buffer pool type
NAME	Name of the buffer pool type
BLOCK_SIZE	Block size of the buffer pool used to cache data residing in tablespaces with the same block size; buffer pool block size possible values are 2048, 4096, 8192, 16384, or 32768
ADVICE_STATUS	Indication of whether the advisory data is being collected for this buffer pool or not; possible values are ON or OFF
SIZE_FOR_ESTIMATE	Estimated size of the cache size for this buffer pool; values are expressed in megabytes
BUFFERS_FOR_ESTIMATES	Estimated number of buffers for this buffer pool
ESTD_PHYSICAL_READ_FACTOR	Percentage of the estimated physical reads to the number of reads for the buffer pool cache
ESTD_PHYSICAL_READS	Estimated number of physical reads for this buffer pool

The information in this table is derived from the online documentation that Oracle provides at the Oracle Technology Network site: *www.otn.oracle.com*.

The following query displays the estimated physical reads for each database block size cache for each buffer pool:

2

```
SQL> SELECT  BLOCK_SIZE,
  2            NAME,
  3            SIZE_FOR_ESTIMATE CACHE_SIZE,
  4            BUFFERS_FOR_ESTIMATE,
  5       ESTD_PHYSICAL_READ_FACTOR,
  6       ESTD_PHYSICAL_READS
  7        FROM V$DB_CACHE_ADVICE
  8       WHERE ADVICE_STATUS = 'ON'
  9       ORDER BY 1, 2, 3
 10   /
```

BLOCK_SIZE	NAME	CACHE_SIZE	BUFFERS_FOR_ESTIMATE	ESTD_PHYSICAL_READ_FACTOR	ESTD_PHYSICAL_READS
4096	DEFAULT	.7656	196	1.0567	1691
4096	DEFAULT	1.5313	392	1.0435	1670
4096	DEFAULT	2.2969	588	1.0428	1668
4096	DEFAULT	3.0625	784	1.0424	1668
4096	DEFAULT	3.8281	980	1.0013	1602
4096	DEFAULT	4.5938	1176	1.001	1602
4096	DEFAULT	5.3594	1372	1.001	1602
4096	DEFAULT	6.125	1568	1.0008	1601
4096	DEFAULT	6.8906	1764	1.0006	1601
4096	DEFAULT	7.6563	1960	1	1600
4096	DEFAULT	8.4219	2156	.9999	1600
4096	DEFAULT	9.1875	2352	.9999	1600
4096	DEFAULT	9.9531	2548	.9998	1600
4096	DEFAULT	10.7188	2744	.9992	1599
4096	DEFAULT	11.4844	2940	.9989	1598
4096	DEFAULT	12.25	3136	.9989	1598
4096	DEFAULT	13.0156	3332	.9988	1598
4096	DEFAULT	13.7813	3528	.9987	1598
4096	DEFAULT	14.5469	3724	.9975	1596
4096	DEFAULT	15.3125	3920	.9974	1596
4096	KEEP	.7656	196	1	27
4096	KEEP	1.5313	392	1	27
4096	KEEP	2.2969	588	1	27
4096	KEEP	3.0625	784	1	27
4096	KEEP	3.8281	980	1	27
4096	KEEP	4.5938	1176	1	27
4096	KEEP	5.3594	1372	1	27
4096	KEEP	6.125	1568	1	27
4096	KEEP	6.8906	1764	1	27
4096	KEEP	7.6563	1960	1	27
4096	KEEP	8.4219	2156	1	27
4096	KEEP	9.1875	2352	1	27
4096	KEEP	9.9531	2548	1	27
4096	KEEP	10.7188	2744	1	27
4096	KEEP	11.4844	2940	1	27
4096	KEEP	12.25	3136	1	27
4096	KEEP	13.0156	3332	1	27
4096	KEEP	13.7813	3528	1	27
4096	KEEP	14.5469	3724	1	27
4096	KEEP	15.3125	3920	1	27
16384	DEFAULT	.7813	50	24.9561	374
16384	DEFAULT	1.5625	100	24.7456	371
16384	DEFAULT	2.3438	150	1	15
16384	DEFAULT	3.125	200	1	15
16384	DEFAULT	3.9063	250	1	15
16384	DEFAULT	4.6875	300	1	15
16384	DEFAULT	5.4688	350	1	15
16384	DEFAULT	6.25	400	1	15
16384	DEFAULT	7.0313	450	1	15

16384 DEFAULT	7.8125	500	1	15
16384 DEFAULT	8.5938	550	1	15
16384 DEFAULT	9.375	600	1	15
16384 DEFAULT	10.1563	650	1	15
16384 DEFAULT	10.9375	700	1	15
16384 DEFAULT	11.7188	750	1	15
16384 DEFAULT	12.5	800	1	15
16384 DEFAULT	13.2813	850	1	15
16384 DEFAULT	14.0625	900	1	15
16384 DEFAULT	14.8438	950	1	15
16384 DEFAULT	15.625	1000	1	15

The preceding results show that estimated physical reads are not reduced if the default cache size is increased, and that more physical reads will occur if you decrease the cache size.

Oracle9i comes with an enhanced Oracle Enterprise Manager Console and includes helpful tools and options for viewing, configuring, and diagnosing the database. Figures 2-5 and 2-6 present snapshots of screens from Oracle Enterprise Manager (OEM) pertaining to Buffer Cache Size Advice.

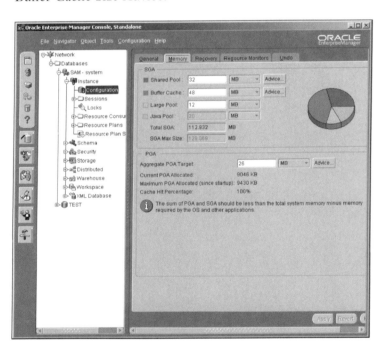

Figure 2-5   Oracle Enterprise Manager main screen showing instance configuration

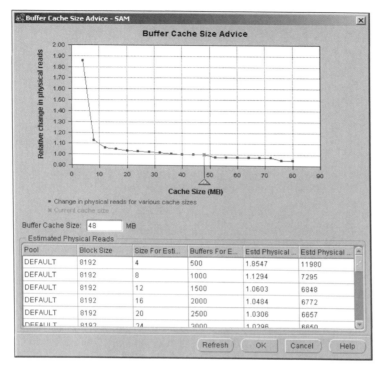

Figure 2-6   Buffer Cache Size Advice chart

Follow these steps to view instance and database configuration using OEM:

1. Click Start, click Programs, click Oracle–OraHome, click Enterprise Manager Console.

2. Click the Databases folder and select the database you want.

3. At login screen, enter SYS or SYSTEM. Use the standalone option if you did not set up the OEM repository.

4. Click the Instance node and select the Configuration node under it. Several tabs are displayed on the right panel.

5. Click on the Memory tab that is shown in Figure 2-5.

6. Click the Buffer Cache Advice button. Figure 2-6 is displayed. This is the contents of V$DB_CACHE_ADVICE view.

Using this view, you can issue the following query to determine if the Default buffer size for the default database block size is optimal or not.

```
SQL> SELECT   DECODE(SIZE_FACTOR,
               1, '==>', null) " ",
            SIZE_FOR_ESTIMATE CSIZE ,
              TRUNC(SIZE_FACTOR*100)||'%' PERCENT,
            BUFFERS_FOR_ESTIMATE BUFFERS_EST,
              ESTD_PHYSICAL_READ_FACTOR E_PHY_READ_FACTOR,
              ESTD_PHYSICAL_READS E_PHY_READS
       FROM V$DB_CACHE_ADVICE
      WHERE NAME = 'DEFAULT'
        AND ADVICE_STATUS = 'ON'
        AND BLOCK_SIZE = (SELECT VALUE
                            FROM V$PARAMETER
                           WHERE NAME = 'db_block_size');
```

	CACHE SIZE	PERCENT	BUFFERS_EST	E_PHY_READ_FACTOR	E_PHY_READS
	4	33%	500	2.1007	6084420
	8	66%	1000	1.3393	3879163
==>	12	100%	1500	1	2896319
	16	133%	2000	0.8335	2414111
	20	166%	2500	0.7709	2232899
	24	200%	3000	0.7646	2214471
	28	233%	3500	0.755	2186828
	32	266%	4000	0.7444	2156114
	36	300%	4500	0.72	2085473
	40	333%	5000	0.72	2085473
	44	366%	5500	0.72	2085473
	48	400%	6000	0.72	2085473
	52	433%	6500	0.72	2085473
	56	466%	7000	0.72	2085473
	60	500%	7500	0.72	2085473
	64	533%	8000	0.72	2085473
	68	566%	8500	0.72	2085473
	72	600%	9000	0.72	2085473
	76	633%	9500	0.72	2085473
	80	666%	10000	0.72	2085473

The results of this query indicate that if you decrease the size for the default cache buffers from its current value of 12 MB to 8 MB, physical reads (disk reads) will increase from 2896319 to 3879163, an estimated increase in physical reads of 33%. If you reduce the default cache buffers further to 4 MB, the performance will be impacted tremendously with twice the number of the current physical reads. What about increasing the size of the default cache buffers? The query results show that if you add 4 MB to the cache buffers, the performance will improve by only 17%, and if you add 4 MB more it will improve by only 6% more. The more you add to the buffer cache size, the smaller improvement achieved. Figure 2-7 illustrates this concept. The graph demonstrates that, in the beginning, adding more memory noticeably influences physical reads, but as you add more and more, the physical reads are minimally affected.

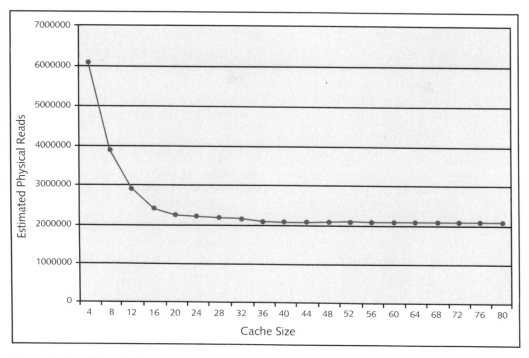

Figure 2-7 Plot of V$DB_CACHE_ADVICE view showing Buffer Cache Size Advice graph

BUFFER CACHE DIAGNOSIS

"Everyone is complaining about how slow the database is," said the business manager for the application in an urgent conference meeting with the DBA and all others involved, from the development team to the operation team.

Ziena joined a countrywide car dealership chain as a DBA. The first month at work, she expressed her concerns verbally to her manager, telling him that the machine housing two databases did not have enough memory to add more database block buffers to one of the databases that needed it urgently. Ziena spent two weeks closely diagnosing memory for the two databases, especially the database block buffers. She collected 30 measurements to determine a trend in the database buffer cache hit ratios, and after a quick analysis, she determined that one of the databases was overallocated with database block buffers, and the database with a problem was underallocated. When Ziena told her manager about her findings, he said that he would take her concerns into consideration and talk to the lead DBA, John. Even though Ziena was not as experienced as John, she stood up for her opinion. After the database manager consulted with John, he told Ziena that John felt her findings were a little off.

John said to everyone in the meeting: "The problem is that the machine needs more memory in order to allocate more buffers to the database." The operation manager said that the machine had been upgraded to the fullest and that it is not possible to add more memory without getting another machine. Ziena said that she thought that even though John disagreed with her, they could deallocate buffers from the other database for the database having the problem, and monitor both for a couple of weeks to see if that reallocation would rectify the solution. John said he didn't think this would lead anywhere. Somehow Ziena's idea struck with the majority of the meeting participants who agreed to try it while exploring other ideas in the meantime and to meet again in a week. Also, the business manager agreed to tell the users that the problem was being worked on and to be a little more understanding.

Ziena deallocated 20 percent of the allocated database buffers and gave it to the other database, and kept monitoring both databases. She performed another round of 20 percent deallocation because the trend was showing no impact on performance on the database being deallocated. Finally, after seven days, she told her manager that everything should be fine.

They met again, and the business manager immediately expressed his gratitude to Ziena, saying, "All users noticed improved performance during the last three days. Whatever you did is working."

Although the Buffer Cache Size Advice introduced in Oracle9*i* is a useful mechanism for predicting the impact of changing the memory allocation of the buffer cache, you can also diagnose the size of the buffer cache by looking at statistics collected by the system. The buffer cache hit ratio is a useful indicator; it is a percentage of how often data is found in buffer memory compared to how often data is retrieved from disk. This ratio is obtained by issuing a query against the database using the V$SYSSTAT view. This hit ratio is computed using the following formula that calculates the overall buffer cache hit ratio percentage:

```
Hit Ratio = Percentage of (Physical Reads/Logical Reads)

Buffer cache hit ratio = 1 - (physical reads/(block gets +
consistent gets))/100
```

Where:

- **Physical reads:** Total number of data blocks accessed from disk
- **Block gets:** Total number of buffers that are obtained for update (this means that the data block was read for update)
- **Consistent gets:** Total number of buffers that are obtained in consistent read (this means that the data block that was accessed used the System Change Number (SCN) to determine that the data block being read did not change since the query was submitted)

The V$SYSSTAT dynamic performance view contains full statistics of the database. You can use this view to issue the following query:

```
SQL> DESC V$SYSSTAT
 Name                                       Null?    Type
 ------------------------------------       --------  -------------------
  STATISTIC#                                          NUMBER
  NAME                                                VARCHAR2(64)
  CLASS                                               NUMBER
  VALUE                                               NUMBER


SQL> COLUMN RATIO HEADING "Buffer Cache Hit ratio" FORMAT A30
SQL> SELECT ROUND( (1 - (PHY.VALUE/(CUR.VALUE + CON.VALUE)))*100,
1)||'%' ratio
  2     FROM V$SYSSTAT PHY, V$SYSSTAT CUR, V$SYSSTAT CON
  3    WHERE PHY.NAME = 'physical reads'
  4      AND CUR.NAME = 'db block gets'
  5      AND CON.NAME = 'consistent gets';

Buffer Cache Hit ratio
------------------------------
97.7%
```

The results of the preceding query indicate that the hit ratio is 97.7 percent, which means that the data was found in the buffer almost all the time. The performance threshold for this ratio is 90 percent. A lower hit ratio indicates that the buffer cache may benefit from increasing the cache size. Figure 2-8 presents the buffer cache hit ratio threshold.

 NOTE You should respond to hit ratio readings only if they are consistent. Also, having a high hit ratio (above 95%) means that the buffer cache might be too big. A large buffer cache may influence the Oracle Optimizer to load the whole table in memory because it has the space and hence causes access to data using full-table scans.

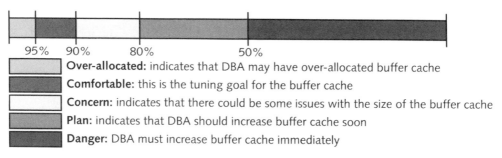

Over-allocated: indicates that DBA may have over-allocated buffer cache
Comfortable: this is the tuning goal for the buffer cache
Concern: indicates that there could be some issues with the size of the buffer cache
Plan: indicates that DBA should increase buffer cache soon
Danger: DBA must increase buffer cache immediately

Figure 2-8   Buffer cache hit ratio indicator ranges

 TIP Getting a negative buffer cache hit ratio means that the buffer cache is too small. Objects are being aged out of the buffer cache and reloaded to be used again even before they are used initially.

As an alternative, you can use V$SESSTAT, V$STATNAME and V$SESSION to get the buffer hit ratio per session, by issuing the following query:

```
SQL> SELECT PHY.SID,
  2          S.USERNAME,
  3          1 - (PHY.VALUE)/(CUR.VALUE + CON.VALUE) "BUFFER_HIT_RATIO"
  4     FROM V$SESSTAT PHY, V$SESSTAT CUR, V$SESSTAT CON,
  5          V$STATNAME S1, V$STATNAME S2, V$STATNAME S3,
  6          V$SESSION S
  7    WHERE S1.NAME = 'physical reads'
  8      AND S2.NAME = 'db block gets'
  9      AND S3.NAME = 'consistent gets'
 10      AND PHY.STATISTIC# = S1.STATISTIC#
 11      AND CUR.STATISTIC# = S2.STATISTIC#
 12      AND CON.STATISTIC# = S3.STATISTIC#
 13      AND CUR.VALUE <> 0
 14      AND CON.VALUE <> 0
 15      AND PHY.SID = CUR.SID
 16      AND PHY.SID = CON.SID
 17      AND PHY.SID = S.SID
 18  /

       SID USERNAME                              BUFFER_HIT RATIO
---------- ------------------------------------ ----------------
         5                                             .709053008
         8                                             .994878234
         9 SYSTEM                                       .93513701
        12 SYSTEM                                      .882637629

        10 TUNER                                       .999418751
```

Now that you understand the concepts, take a look at some practical examples. Suppose that you placed in the Keep buffer pool some database objects, such as a small table that is frequently accessed by the database, and some other objects that are infrequently accessed in the Recycle buffer pool. Objects could be moved between these buffers based on usage and changes to the size of the object. You may want to see the individual buffer pool hit ratios. In this case, you can use V$BUFFER_POOL_STATISTICS which contains statistical values for each pool. The same formula mentioned earlier could be used in the query you submit:

```
SQL> DESC V$BUFFER_POOL_STATISTICS
 Name                                     Null?    Type
 ---------------------------------------- -------- ----------------------------
 ID                                                NUMBER
 NAME                                              VARCHAR2(20)
 BLOCK_SIZE                                        NUMBER
 SET_MSIZE                                         NUMBER
 CNUM_REPL                                         NUMBER
 CNUM_WRITE                                        NUMBER
 CNUM_SET                                          NUMBER
 BUF_GOT                                           NUMBER
 SUM_WRITE                                         NUMBER
 SUM_SCAN                                          NUMBER
 FREE_BUFFER_WAIT                                  NUMBER
 WRITE_COMPLETE_WAIT                               NUMBER
 BUFFER_BUSY_WAIT                                  NUMBER
 FREE_BUFFER_INSPECTED                             NUMBER
 DIRTY_BUFFERS_INSPECTED                           NUMBER
 DB_BLOCK_CHANGE                                   NUMBER
 DB_BLOCK_GETS                                     NUMBER
 CONSISTENT_GETS                                   NUMBER
 PHYSICAL_READS                                    NUMBER
 PHYSICAL_WRITES                                   NUMBER
```

```
SQL> COLUMN RATIO HEADING "Buffer Cache Hit ratio" FORMAT A30 SQL> COLUMN
NAME HEADING 'Buffer Pool' FORMAT A15
SQL> COLUMN BLOCK_SIZE HEADING "Block Size"
SQL> SELECT NAME,
  2          BLOCK_SIZE,
  3          ROUND( (1 - (PHYSICAL_READS/
  4          (DB_BLOCK_GETS + CONSISTENT_GETS)))*100) || '%' ratio
  5    FROM V$BUFFER_POOL_STATISTICS
  6    WHERE (DB_BLOCK_GETS + CONSISTENT_GETS) > 0
  7  /

Buffer Pool     Block Size Buffer Cache Hit ratio
--------------- ---------- ------------------------------
KEEP                  8192 70%
RECYCLE               8192 74%
DEFAULT               8192 98%
```

For the overall hit ratios of the buffer pools, you can issue the following query:

```
SQL> SELECT BLOCK_SIZE,
  2          ROUND( (1 - AVG((PHYSICAL_READS/(DB_BLOCK_GETS +
CONSISTENT_GETS))))*100) || '%' ratio
  3    FROM V$BUFFER_POOL_STATISTICS
  4    GROUP BY BLOCK_SIZE
  5  /


Block Size Buffer Cache Hit ratio
---------- -----------------------------
      8192 81%
```

Oracle Enterprise Manager Console provides a tool called **Performance Overview**. You can get to this tool by clicking the Diagnostics Pack icon on the left of the screen as shown in Figure 2-9.

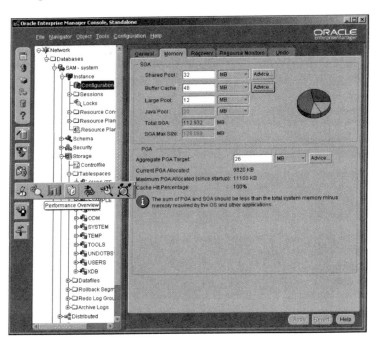

Figure 2-9   Oracle Enterprise Manager showing session information entry screen

When you click the Performance Overview icon, Figure 2-10 is displayed, which is the main screen for this tool. Notice that the buffer cache hit ratio was 59.29% at the instant this screen was accessed. This tool provides a database Health Overview. If this value for the buffer cache hit ratio stays consistently low, you should be concerned.

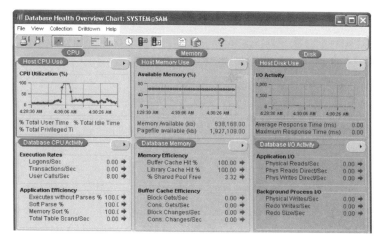

Figure 2-10   Oracle performance overview

You may click any right-arrow button to drill down for advice on this tool. Advice in a Help screen appears similar to that shown in Figure 2-11.

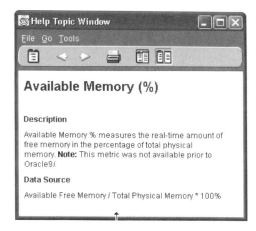

Figure 2-11   Oracle Enterprise Manager Help

You can also use the Memory at a Glance option which is shown in Figure 2-12, to drill down and look at the memory. To reach this option, click the **right arrow** in the Host Memory Use chart, and then click **Available Memory % > Memory at a Glance**.

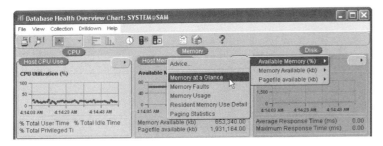

Figure 2-12   Performance overview—available memory

Figures 2-13 and 2-14 display screens that present an overview of memory usage.

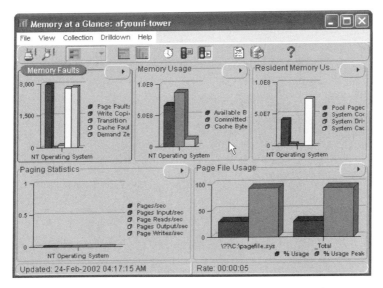

Figure 2-13   Performance overview—Memory at a Glance

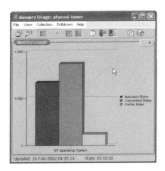

Figure 2-14   Performance overview—Memory Usage

Of course, this tool offers a number of options and functions. For additional functional definition and details on how to interpret these readings, you may want to consult the Oracle Enterprise Manager documentation.

INSIDE THE BUFFER CACHE

So far, this chapter has discussed the internal architecture of the buffer cache, but has not looked inside the buffers. A dynamic performance view enables you to peek into the buffers to see what data objects reside there and how much of the buffer is occupied by them. You can do so by using the V$BH view, which serves the following additional purposes:

1. You can query the view for a list of data objects residing in the buffers and the number of data blocks in use. Use this query to generate a report. Any object that consumes more than 20 percent of the buffer cache should be examined more closely to determine if there is any impact on the buffer hit ratio.

```
SQL> SELECT O.OWNER,
  2          O.OBJECT_TYPE,
  3          O.OBJECT_NAME,
  4          COUNT(*) buffers,
  5          ROUND((COUNT(*)/(SELECT COUNT(*)
  6                           FROM V$BH))
  7                 *100) BUFFER_PERCENT
  8     FROM DBA_OBJECTS O, V$BH B
  9    WHERE O.OBJECT_ID = B.OBJD
 10      AND O.OWNER NOT IN ('SYS','SYSTEM')
 11    GROUP BY O.OWNER, O.OBJECT_TYPE, O.OBJECT_NAME
 12    ORDER BY 1, 2 DESC
 13  /


OWNER     OBJECT_TYPE  OBJECT_NAME        BUFFERS    BUFFER_PERCENT
-------   -----------  ----------------   ---------  --------------
DEMO      TABLE        CUSTOMER                1          0
TUNER     TABLE        CUSTOMERS             229          5
TUNER     TABLE        DEPARTMENTS             2          0
TUNER     TABLE        EMPLOYEES               9          0
TUNER     TABLE        ORDERS                100          2
TUNER     TABLE        PRODUCTS               95          2
TUNER     INDEX        PK_PRO_PRODUCT_ID      28          1
TUNER     INDEX        SYS_C002798             2          0
TUNER     INDEX        XIF13ORDER_LINES       65          1
```

2. You can use this view to get buffer counts for the different usage and types of the cache. The following query produces a display of how many free buffers exist and how many are locked and shared for a consistent read:

```
SQL> SELECT DECODE(STATUS, 'free', 'Free: not currently in use',
  2                         'xcur', 'Locked: exclusive',
  3                         'scur', 'Locked: shared',
  4                         'cr',   'Consistent Read',
  5                         'read', 'Being read from disk',
  6                         'mrec', 'In media recovery mode',
  7                         'irec', 'In instance recovery mode',
  8                         'Total Buffers') STATUS,
  9         COUNT(*) BUFFERS
 10    FROM V$BH
 11    GROUP BY ROLLUP(STATUS)
 12  /

STATUS                            BUFFERS
------------------------------- ----------
Consistent Read                       394
Free: not currently in use           1739
Locked: exclusive                    2307
Total Buffers                        4440
```

3. Use the following query to determine how many blocks are modified (**dirty**) and how many are free or read:

```
SQL> SELECT DECODE(DIRTY, 'Y', 'DIRTY BLOCK',
  2                        'N', 'READ OR FREE',
  3                        'TOTAL BUFFERS') STATUS,
  4         COUNT(*) BUFFERS
  5    FROM V$BH
  6    GROUP BY ROLLUP(DIRTY)
  7  /

STATUS          BUFFERS
------------- ----------
READ OR FREE       4285
DIRTY BLOCK         155
TOTAL BUFFERS      4440
```

4. You can use V$BH view to inspect blocks that have been rewritten and reread in an Oracle Real Application Cluster configuration.

5. Use this view to find out more about which data files or tablespaces are being accessed most often and how many buffers they use:

2

```
SQL> SELECT FILE_NAME,
  2         COUNT(*) BUFFERS
  3    FROM V$BH B, DBA_DATA_FILES F
  4   WHERE B.FILE#=F.FILE_ID
  5   GROUP BY FILE_NAME
  6   /

FILE_NAME                                    BUFFERS
-------------------------------------------- ----------
C:\ORACLE\ORADATA\SAM\CWMLITE01.DBF                1
C:\ORACLE\ORADATA\SAM\DRSYS01.DBF                  1
C:\ORACLE\ORADATA\SAM\EXAMPLE01.DBF                1
C:\ORACLE\ORADATA\SAM\INDX01.DBF                   1
C:\ORACLE\ORADATA\SAM\SYSTEM01.DBF              1357
C:\ORACLE\ORADATA\SAM\TEST_DATA_16K.ORA          506
C:\ORACLE\ORADATA\SAM\TOOLS01.DBF                  1
C:\ORACLE\ORADATA\SAM\UNDOTBS01.DBF              302
C:\ORACLE\ORADATA\SAM\USERS01.DBF                532


SQL> SELECT T.NAME TABLESPACE_NAME,
  2         COUNT(*) BUFFERS
  3    FROM V$BH B, V$TABLESPACE T
  4   WHERE B.TS#=T.TS#
  5   GROUP BY T.NAME
  6   /

TABLESPACE_NAME                BUFFERS
------------------------------ ----------
CWMLITE                              1
DRSYS                                1
EXAMPLE                              1
INDX                                 1
SYSTEM                            3105
TEST_DATA_16K                      506
TOOLS                                1
UNDOTBS                            292
USERS                              532
```

CHAPTER SUMMARY

- The buffer cache is a memory structure of the SGA.
- The buffer cache facilitates faster access to data, because when data is retrieved from a disk, the cost to performance is high.
- The Least Recent Used algorithm ages out the least retrieved and changed blocks of data from the buffer.
- The buffer cache consists of three major internal structures: the Default buffer pool, Keep buffer pool, and Recycle buffer pool.
- The DB_CACHE_SIZE parameter configures the size of the buffer cache.
- DB_CACHE_SIZE can be allocated dynamically.
- The buffer cache can be configured to support tablespaces with one or multiple block sizes.
- The size of the buffer cache is computed by adding all parameter values with a name containing "CACHE_SIZE."
- The true size of the SGA is computed by adding all values in the BYTES column in V$SGASTAT.
- SGA_MAX_SIZE is a parameter that is used to set the maximum memory size to which the SGA is allowed to grow.
- The SGA_MAX_SIZE parameter cannot be set dynamically.
- 4 MB granules are used when the actual SGA size is less than 128 MB; otherwise, 16 MB granules are used.
- When allocating memory for any of the major SGA structures, memory structures size are rounded up to the next granule.
- The DBA can use the DB_CACHE_ADVICE parameter to turn on the Buffer Cache Size Advice in Oracle9i.
- V$DB_CACHE_ADVICE is a dynamic performance view that contains estimated physical reads for each different cache size and block size.
- Use the BUFFER_POOL storage parameter to specify where a table object should be cached in the buffers.
- The results of the Buffer Cache Size Advice view can be plotted in a graph to view the estimated impact of reducing or increasing the cache on physical reads.
- The buffer hit ratio is a percentage of physical reads to total reads from buffers.
- The buffer cache hit ratio formula is: 1 - (physical reads/(block gets + consistent gets))/100.
- DBAs can use V$SYSSTAT to compute the buffer cache hit ratio.
- The buffer cache hit ratio threshold is 90%, and a consistently low hit ratio value indicates that the cache is not large enough.
- Use the V$BUFFER_POOL_STATISTICS dynamic performance view to get an individual pool hit ratio.

2

❏ Use the V$BH dynamic performance view to look inside the buffer cache.

❏ Initialization parameters presented in this chapter include the following:

- DB_16K_CACHE_SIZE

- DB_2K_CACHE_SIZE

- DB_32K_CACHE_SIZE

- DB_4K_CACHE_SIZE

- DB_8K_CACHE_SIZE

- DB_BLOCK_BUFFERS

- DB_BLOCK_SIZE

- DB_CACHE_ADVICE

- DB_CACHE_SIZE

- DB_KEEP_CACHE_SIZE

- DB_RECYCLE_CACHE_SIZE

- JAVA_POOL_SIZE

- LARGE_POOL_SIZE

- LOG_BUFFER

- SGA_MAX_SIZE

- SHARED_POOL_SIZE

❏ Views used in this chapter include the following:

- DBA_TABLES

- DBA_TABLESPACES

- V$BH

- V$BUFFER_POOL

- V$BUFFER_POOL_STATISTICS

- V$DB_CACHE_ADVICE

- V$PARAMETER

- V$SESSION

- V$SESSTAT

- V$SGA

- V$SGA_DYNAMIC_COMPONENTS
- V$SGASTAT
- V$STATNAME
- V$SYSSTAT

REVIEW QUESTIONS

1. You can use a formula to configure the size of the buffer cache. (True/False)

2. The buffer cache does not support tablespaces with multiple data block sizes. (True/False)

3. Dynamic allocation is not allowed on the default cache size of the same DB_nK_CACHE_SIZE (where n is 2, 4, 8, 16, or 32). (True/False)

4. The Keep buffer pool is used to store all data objects as long as they are used. (True/False)

5. You need to shut down the database when you decide to change the SGA_MAX_SIZE parameter. (True/False)

6. Explain briefly the role of the buffer cache in Oracle9i architecture, and why it is important to configure the cache size properly.

7. Describe the internal structure of the buffer cache.

8. What are the two dynamic performance views you would use to compute the buffer cache hit ratio and individual buffer pool?

9. What is the buffer cache hit ratio threshold? Explain what you would do if it is 70%.

10. What is the purpose of the Buffer Cache Size Advice?

11. Define the purpose of the V$BH dynamic performance view.

12. What is implied when you set the Buffer Cache Size Advice to a ready state?

13. Define the purpose of DB_nK_CACHE_SIZE (where n is 2, 4, 8, 16, or 32).

14. How can you determine the impact of reducing the buffer cache?

15. Write three statements that can be run to determine the size of the SGA.

16. Explain the impact of setting the SGA_MAX_SIZE parameter.

17. Write a query to compute how much buffer cache is allocated.

18. How do you cache a table in the Recycle buffer pool?

19. Why would you need to look inside the buffer cache?

20. How do you configure the buffer cache to have multiple buffer pools?

EXAM REVIEW QUESTIONS: ORACLE9*i* PERFORMANCE TUNING (#1Z0-033)

2

1. Which dynamic performance view would you use to see what objects are present in the cache buffer?

    a. V$BUFFER_STATISTICS

    b. V$BUFFER_POOL

    c. V$BH

    d. V$BUFFER_OBJECTS

2. Which dynamic performance view would you query to get the buffer cache hit ratio?

    a. V$SYSSTAT

    b. V$SGASTAT

    c. V$SYSTEM_STATISTICS

    d. V$CACHE_STATISTICS

3. What happens after issuing the statement, ALTER TABLE EMPLOYEE CACHE?

    a. If the buffer pool storage parameter is set to KEEP, it has a high priority for being kept in the Default buffer pool.

    b. Data of the employee table is cached in the buffer cache and is retained in the Keep buffer pool.

    c. If the buffer pool storage parameter is set to KEEP, it is cached in the Keep buffer pool.

    d. Data of the employee table is kept in the buffer and is retained in the Keep buffer pool as long it is being used.

    e. If data is too large, it resides in the Default buffer pool, and if it is too small it is retained in the Keep buffer pool

4. After performing a database health check, you find that the buffer cache hit ratio is 46%. What is the buffer cache hit ratio threshold?

  a. 100%

  b. 90%

  c. 10%

  d. 0%

  e. 80%

  f. 5%

5. What would you do if the Keep buffer hit ratio is not high enough?

  a. Decrease the number of buffers.

  b. Increase the Keep cache size.

  c. Decrease the Keep cache size.

  d. Increase the number of Keep buffers.

  e. No action is required.

6. The Recycle buffer pool stores data of:

  a. Small tables that are accessed frequently

  b. Large tables that are accessed infrequently with full-table scans

  c. Large tables that are accessed infrequently

  d. Small tables that are accessed infrequently

7. What dynamic performance view would you use to determine if the buffer cache is properly allocated?

  a. V$DB_CACHE_ADVICE

  b. V$CACHE_ADVICE

  c. V$BUFFER_ADVICE

  d. DB_CACHE_ADVICE

  e. DBA_CAHCE_ADVICE

8. Which statement is true about the buffer cache?

   a. The Buffer Cache Size Advice determines the appropriate size of the buffer cache.

   b. The buffer cache size can be dynamically changed only if the Buffer Cache Size Advice is turned on.

   c. The buffer cache size can be dynamically changed, but this change is limited by the maximum SGA size value.

   d. The cache size for 8 KB block size must be a multiple of 8 KB.

9. Select the columns you use to compute the buffer pool hit ratio. (Choose three.)

   a. DB_BLOCK_GETS

   b. BUFFER_BUSY_WAIT

   c. CONSISTENT_GETS

   d. PHYSICAL_READS

   e. PHYSICAL_WRITES

   f. DB_BLOCK_CHANGE

10. Which parameter does not impact the size of the buffer cache?

   a. DB_BLOCK_BUFFERS

   b. DB_BLOCK_SIZE

   c. DB_CACHE_SIZE

   d. DB_2K_CACHE_SIZE

11. Which value would you set for the Buffer Cache Size Advice parameter to turn it on and collect data?

   a. TRUE

   b. ON

   c. READY

   d. GO

   e. RUN

12. If the SGA size is 256 MB, what would be the size of a memory granule?

   a. 4 MB

   b. 8 MB

   c. 16 MB

   d. 32 MB

13. What two statements are used to cache data in the buffers?

    a. ALTER TABLE ... CACHE

    b. SELECT /*+CACHE*/ ...

    c. CACHE TABLE ...

    d. ANALYZE TABLE ... CACHE

    e. SELECT ... CACHE

14. When reading the output of the Buffer Cache Size Advice, what are you looking for?

    a. The impact on physical reads if you reduce or increase the buffer cache

    b. The impact on physical reads if you reduce or increase the SGA

    c. The buffer cache hit ratio for each block size

    d. The hit ratio for each type of the buffer pool

15. Why would you want to look in the buffer cache?

    a. To examine the number of blocks consumed by each data object

    b. To predict the number of buffers needed for optimal performance

    c. To see if you can cache more data objects in the buffer cache

    d. To examine the type of data in each buffer pool

16. Which statement is true?

    a. All DB_nK_CACHE_SIZE (where n is 2, 4, 8, 16, or 32) parameters must be configured when the database is created.

    b. If the DB_BLOCK_SIZE is set to 8 KB, the DB_8K_CACHE_SIZE cannot be set.

    c. All DB_nK_CACHE_SIZE (where n is 2, 4, 8, 16, or 32) parameters must be configured before starting the database.

    d. You may set DB_8K_CACHE_SIZE if DB_BLOCK_SIZE is set to 8 KB.

HANDS-ON PROJECTS

Please complete the projects provided below.

2

1. After re-examining the performance problem set out at the start of the chapter, answer the following questions:

   a. Define Joe Doe's problem in your own words.

   b. What does he mean by the term BUFFER_POOL KEEP?

   c. Do you think bouncing the database is an acceptable method of solving the problem?

   d. What would you recommend as a solution?

2. Write a query that displays a list of all dynamic performance views and initialization parameters that are related to the buffer cache. This list should resemble the two lists presented in the Chapter Summary.

3. Write a report that lists each object in the buffer cache and its owner.

4. Write two queries that display the following:

   a. The number of buffers and size for each type of Keep buffer pool

   b. The hit ratio for each buffer pool

5. Suppose you were asked by a colleague to assist in writing a query that shows the buffer cache hit ratio for a session. Write down the query that you would issue.

6. Your manager just read an article about looking inside buffers. He calls you over to his office and asks you to write a daily report and to collect statistics on what data objects are in memory and how many buffer blocks they are consuming. Write down the query you need to issue to generate this report as well as the approach to take to store this statistical data.

7. After you did so well in collecting statistical data for Project 6, your manager asked you to draw observations from the data. Describe how you would analyze the data and whether it is beneficial or not to keep running this process. Explain your answer in detail and include an analysis and queries.

8. Interpret the following output that resulted from running a query against $DB_CACHE_ADVICE. What would the graph look like if you plot the values of ESTD_PHYSICAL_READS against CACHE_SIZE?

	CACHE_SIZE	PERCENT	BUFFERS_FOR_ESTIMATE	ESTD_PHYSICAL_READ_FACTOR	ESTD_PHYSICAL_READS
	4	33%	500	5.7617	908838
	8	66%	1000	1.4044	221529
==>	12	100%	1500	1	157739
	16	133%	2000	.8984	141709
	20	166%	2500	.7019	110723
	24	200%	3000	.5285	83373
	28	233%	3500	.3929	61972
	32	266%	4000	.3614	57014
	36	300%	4500	.3143	49577
	40	333%	5000	.3117	49164
	44	366%	5500	.3106	48999
	48	400%	6000	.3101	48916
	52	433%	6500	.308	48586
	56	466%	7000	.308	48586
	60	500%	7500	.308	48586
	64	533%	8000	.308	48586
	68	566%	8500	.308	48586
	72	600%	9000	.308	48586
	76	633%	9500	.3075	48503
	80	666%	10000	.3075	48503

9. You just took over a database that was administered by another DBA. As part of your routine tasks, you ran a query to get the buffer cache hit ratio and found that it was 45%. Answer the following:

   a. What query did you submit to get the hit ratio?

   b. What other query would you issue to investigate the problem?

   c. What other analysis or steps would you perform to decide on corrective action?

   d. If corrective action is necessary, what would you do after your investigation and analysis, and when?

10. You were hired as a DBA consultant to assist the DBA team in administering all databases in production. While you were becoming familiar with the database, you came across a table that is too large to be placed in the Keep buffer pool. Answer the following:

    a. What is your observation about the finding?

    b. What would you do about it?

    c. Suppose that another DBA asked you to fix the situation so that the table could be placed in the Keep buffer pool. Write down the steps you would take to perform the task.

    d. Suppose that you decided to unkeep the table and cache it only in the default buffers. Write down the steps you would take to perform this task.

11. You are asked to recommend a database block size for a new, large table that will be used mainly for reporting purposes. You have decided that it would be best if you place it on a tablespace with a 16 KB block size or higher. After checking with the system administrator, you determine that the operating system platform limitation for the maximum block size is 16 KB. Write the steps for creating the tablespace on which the table can reside and for allocating memory for this task. Use the following table definition:

```
Name                              Null?      Type
--------------------------    --------   --------
INVOICE_ITEM_ID               NOT NULL   NUMBER
INVOICE_ID                               NUMBER
AMOUNT                        NOT NULL   NUMBER(12,2)
DESCRIPTION                   NOT NULL   VARCHAR2(255)
```

12. The developer for an OLTP database application that went to production about six months ago told you that there is a reference table that is constantly queried and that the developers would like to cache it in memory. Write down the steps for each of the following items:

a. Determine the number of buffer blocks that the table would take.

b. Allocate memory for the Keep buffer pool by adding enough buffers to hold the new table. If they are not configured, set the Keep buffers. If the Keep buffers are set too low, add buffers.

c. Cache the table in the Keep buffers.

13. Use the following script to create the table and populate it with data:

```
SQL> CREATE TABLE KEEP_DATA_REF
  2  (
  3    CODE          NUMBER(4),
  4    DESCRIPTION VARCHAR2(80)
  5* )
SQL> /
SQL> BEGIN
  2      FOR I IN 1..1000 LOOP
  3          INSERT INTO KEEP_DATA_REF VALUES
  4              (I, 'THIS IS DESCRIPTION TEXT ' || I);
  5      END LOOP;
  6  END;
  7  /
```

Perform the following steps:

a. Turn the Buffer Cache Advice feature on. If it was already on, turn it off and then on.

b. Look at the collected statistics.

c. Having completed Step a and Step b, what do you observe when you perform Step c and Step d?

d. Increase or reduce the cache buffer size.

e. Check the DB_CACHE_ADVICE parameter value.

What conclusion would you draw from all the steps you performed in this project?

CASE PROJECTS

Your manager summons you to the office to inform you that you have been doing a *great* job administering all the production databases. The manager described a new database application that the department is taking over as follows: "This is a small database that keeps customer orders and a list of the products they purchased. It is a sensitive application, and I can't trust anyone but you. Here is the documentation I got from the senior vice president of operations." Presented here is the documentation you received from your manager. This application will be used throughout the book.

Application Description

CASE PROJECTS

The application maintains all customer transactions of orders purchased from the Acme Company. The application records all the products the company sells and all the suppliers the company deals with. A diagram of the Acme order system is shown in Figure 2-15.

Application E-R Diagram

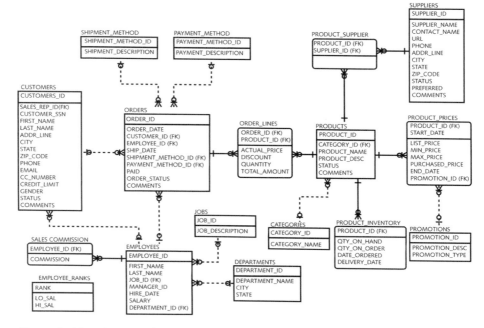

Figure 2-15   Acme order system E-R diagram

Table Structure

```
Table Name          Column Name           Null?     Type
----------------    --------------------  --------  ---------------
CATEGORIES          CATEGORY_ID           NOT NULL  NUMBER(2)
                    CATEGORY_NAME                   VARCHAR2(80)
```

```
Table Name          Column Name           Null?     Type
----------------    --------------------  --------  ---------------
CUSTOMERS           CUSTOMER_ID           NOT NULL  NUMBER(8)
                    SALES_REP_ID                    NUMBER(4)
                    CUSTOMER_SSN                    VARCHAR2(9)
                    FIRST_NAME                      VARCHAR2(20)
                    LAST_NAME                       VARCHAR2(20)
                    ADDR_LINE                       VARCHAR2(80)
                    CITY                            VARCHAR2(30)
                    STATE                           VARCHAR2(30)
                    ZIP_CODE                        VARCHAR2(9)
                    PHONE                           VARCHAR2(15)
                    EMAIL                           VARCHAR2(80)
                    CC_NUMBER                       VARCHAR2(20)
                    CREDIT_LIMIT                    NUMBER
                    GENDER                          CHAR
                    STATUS                          CHAR
                    COMMENTS                        VARCHAR2(1024)
```

```
Table Name          Column Name           Null?     Type
----------------    --------------------  --------  ---------------
DEPARTMENTS         DEPARTMENT_ID         NOT NULL  NUMBER(2)
                    DEPARTMENT_NAME                 VARCHAR2(20)
                    CITY                            VARCHAR2(30)
                    STATE                           CHAR
```

```
Table Name          Column Name           Null?     Type
----------------    --------------------  --------  ---------------
EMPLOYEES           EMPLOYEE_ID           NOT NULL  NUMBER(4)
                    FIRST_NAME                      VARCHAR2(20)
                    LAST_NAME                       VARCHAR2(20)
                    JOB_ID                          NUMBER(2)
                    MANAGER_ID                      NUMBER(4)
                    HIRE_DATE                       DATE
                    SALARY                          NUMBER
                    DEPARTMENT_ID                   NUMBER(2)
```

2

Table Name	Column Name	Null?	Type
EMPLOYEE_RANKS	RANK	NOT NULL	NUMBER(2)
	LO_SAL		NUMBER
	HI_SAL		NUMBER

Table Name	Column Name	Null?	Type
JOBS	JOB_ID	NOT NULL	NUMBER(2)
	JOB_DESCRIPTION		VARCHAR2(80)

Table Name	Column Name	Null?	Type
ORDERS	ORDER_ID	NOT NULL	NUMBER(5)
	ORDER_DATE		DATE
	CUSTOMER_ID		NUMBER(8)
	EMPLOYEE_ID		NUMBER(4)
	SHIP_DATE		DATE
	SHIPMENT_METHOD_ID		NUMBER(2)
	PAYMENT_METHOD_ID		NUMBER(2)
	PAID		CHAR
	ORDER_STATUS		CHAR
	COMMENTS		VARCHAR2(1024)

Table Name	Column Name	Null?	Type
ORDER_LINES	ORDER_ID	NOT NULL	NUMBER(5)
	PRODUCT_ID	NOT NULL	NUMBER(4)
	ACTUAL_PRICE		NUMBER
	DISCOUNT		NUMBER
	QUANTITY		NUMBER
	TOTAL_AMOUNT		NUMBER

Table Name	Column Name	Null?	Type
PAYMENT_METHOD	PAYMENT_METHOD_ID	NOT NULL	NUMBER(2)
	PAYMENT_DESCRIPTION		VARCHAR2(80)

```
Table Name         Column Name           Null?     Type
----------------   --------------------  --------  ---------------
PRODUCTS           PRODUCT_ID            NOT NULL  NUMBER(4)
                   CATEGORY_ID                     NUMBER(2)
                   PRODUCT_NAME                    VARCHAR2(80)
                   PRODUCT_DESC                    VARCHAR2(512)
                   STATUS                          CHAR
                   COMMENTS                        VARCHAR2(1024)
```

```
Table Name         Column Name           Null?     Type
----------------   --------------------  --------  ---------------
PRODUCT_INVENTORY  PRODUCT_ID            NOT NULL  NUMBER(4)
                   QTY_ON_HAND                     NUMBER
                   QTY_ON_ORDER                    NUMBER
                   DATE_ORDERED                    DATE
                   DELIVERY_DATE                   DATE
```

```
Table Name         Column Name           Null?     Type
----------------   --------------------  --------  ---------------
PRODUCT_PRICES     PRODUCT_ID            NOT NULL  NUMBER(4)
                   START_DATE            NOT NULL  DATE
                   LIST_PRICE                      NUMBER
                   MIN_PRICE                       NUMBER
                   MAX_PRICE                       NUMBER
                   PURCHASED_PRICE                 NUMBER
                   END_DATE                        DATE
                   PROMOTION_ID                    NUMBER(2)
```

```
Table Name         Column Name           Null?     Type
----------------   --------------------  --------  ---------------
PRODUCT_SUPPLIER   PRODUCT_ID            NOT NULL  NUMBER(4)
                   SUPPLIER_ID           NOT NULL  NUMBER(4)
```

```
Table Name         Column Name           Null?     Type
----------------   --------------------  --------  ---------------
PROMOTIONS         PROMOTION_ID          NOT NULL  NUMBER(2)
                   PROMOTION_DESC                  VARCHAR2(80)
                   PROMOTION_TYPE                  VARCHAR2(20)
```

2

```
Table Name            Column Name            Null?      Type
-----------------     -------------------    --------   ---------------
SALES_COMMISSION      EMPLOYEE_ID            NOT NULL   NUMBER(4)
                      COMMISSION                        NUMBER
```

```
Table Name            Column Name            Null?      Type
-----------------     -------------------    --------   ---------------
SHIPMENT_METHOD       SHIPMENT_METHOD_ID     NOT NULL   NUMBER(2)
                      SHIPMENT_DESCRIPTION              VARCHAR2(80)
```

```
Table Name            Column Name            Null?      Type
-----------------     -------------------    --------   ---------------
SUPPLIERS             SUPPLIER_ID            NOT NULL   NUMBER(4)
                      SUPPLIER_NAME                     VARCHAR2(80)
                      CONTACT_NAME                      VARCHAR2(30)
                      URL                               VARCHAR2(255)
                      PHONE                             VARCHAR2(15)
                      ADDR_LINE                         VARCHAR2(80)
                      CITY                              VARCHAR2(30)
                      STATE                             VARCHAR2(30)
                      ZIP_CODE                          VARCHAR2(9)
                      STATUS                            CHAR
                      PREFERRED                         CHAR
                      COMMENTS                          VARCHAR2(1024)
```

Data Scripts

Script name	Function
Tuning_create_user.sql	Creates application user TUNER password TUNER
Tuning_create_tables.sql	Creates application tables
Tuning_create_sequences.sql	Create application sequences
Tuning_insert_data.sql	Populates application data, this script calls the following scripts: tuning_categories.sql tuning_departments.sql tuning_jobs.sql tuning_employee_ranks.sql tuning_payment_methods.sql tuning_promotions.sql tuning_shippment_method.sql tuning_employees.sql tuning_sales_commision.sql tuning_customers.sql tuning_products.sql tuning_suppliers.sql tuning_product_prices.sql tuning_product_inventory.sql tuning_product_supplier.sql tuning_orders.sql tuning_order_lines.sql
tuning_setup.sql	This will run all preceding scripts. You should run this script to create schema and populate data. Note that this script will drop user TUNER and its objects if it already exists.

Data Statistics

Table name	Max Row Length	Row count
CATEGORIES	82	18
CUSTOMERS	1347	4000
DEPARTMENTS	54	90
EMPLOYEES	57	294
EMPLOYEE_RANKS	2	10
JOBS	82	99
ORDERS	1056	9916
ORDER_LINES	7	108038
PAYMENT_METHOD	82	9
PRODUCTS	1622	5001
PRODUCT_INVENTORY	17	5001
PRODUCT_PRICES	19	7739
PRODUCT_SUPPLIER	6	5001
PROMOTIONS	102	27
SALES_COMMISSION	3	9
SHIPMENT_METHOD	82	11
SUPPLIERS	1558	1000

Case Questions

1. Create a copy of the initialization file and save it as a backup of the original.

2. Configure the SGA according to the following settings in the PFILE:

   a. Shared pool memory = 20 MB

   b. Large pool memory = 0 MB

   c. Java pool memory = 20 MB

   d. Buffer cache = 4 MB

   There should be no other buffer cache settings or SGA-related setting, such as SGA_MAX_SIZE. If they exist, remove all buffer configurations from the PFILE.

3. Shut down the database and open the database with new settings.

4. Verify the settings in Step 2 and compute the size of the SGA and buffers.

5. Display the maximum size of the SGA and determine the SGA size granule.

6. Dynamically adjust the size of SGA_MAX_SIZE and explain what happens.

7. Shut down the database and set SGA_MAX_SIZE to a value three times the size of the SGA that was obtained in Step 4. Then open the database.

8. Determine the SGA size granule.

9. Open another session as TUNER and run the following query:

   SELECT SHIPMENT_METHOD.SHIPMENT_DESCRIPTION, COUNT(*)

   FROM ORDERS, SHIPMENT_METHOD

   WHERE ORDERS.PAYMENT_METHOD_ID = SHIPMENT_METHOD.SHIPMENT_METHOD_ID

   AND ORDERS.CUSTOMER_ID IN (SELECT CUSTOMER_ID

   FROM CUSTOMERS WHERE STATE = 'SD')

   GROUP BY SHIPMENT_METHOD.SHIPMENT_DESCRIPTION

10. List all TUNER objects, including the type of each object and the number of buffer blocks used by each object that is residing in the buffer.

11. Explain the results of the query.

12. From these results, determine if the whole or a partial object is in the buffer cache.

13. Turn on the Buffer Cache Size Advice.

14. View the Buffer Cache Size Advice using a query and using the Oracle Enterprise Manager Console. Explain the results.

15. Take a reading of the buffer cache hit ratio and record it here.

```
Reading #1:
```

16. Download dbSessions tools to simulate multiple sessions. Documentation on how to use the tool is included with the setup procedures for the tool. The URL for downloading the tool is *dba-cyberspace.com/docs/dbSessions_book.zip*.

17. After the tool is installed, use dbSessions to establish 20 sessions and run the tool with the parameters listed in Figure 2-16. (These settings will run for about 45 minutes. If you need more time, adjust the interval value to ten seconds. It is not recommended to reduce the time interval value to less than three seconds.)

2

Figure 2-16   dbSessions Session Info dialog box

18. While dbSessions is running, take another reading of the buffer cache hit ratio and record it here:

Reading #1:

19. While dbSessions is running, view the Buffer Cache Size Advice statistics to see if there are any changes in the data or the graph. Describe what will happen if more buffers are added. Will memory efficiency and database performance improve?

20. Take another reading of the buffer cache hit ratio

Reading #2:

21. When dbSessions has completed, take a final reading of the buffer cache hit ratio and record it here:

Reading #3:

22. Analyze the results from the buffer cache hit ratio readings.

23. Increase the buffer cache size by one granule and verify the new size.

24. Check the Buffer Cache Size Advice value and explain what happened.

25. Determine the object that has the average number of blocks and cache it in the Keep buffer.

26. Verify how many Keep buffer blocks are consumed by Step 25.

3

TUNING THE REDO LOG BUFFER

In this chapter you will:

♦ Learn to describe the redo log buffer at an overview level

♦ Use guidelines to size the redo log buffer

♦ Describe the relationship between the redo log buffer and the log writer (LGWR)

♦ Diagnose redo log buffer problems

♦ Optimize redo log buffer operations

In the previous chapter, you learned how to tune one memory sector of the Oracle SGA buffer cache. In this chapter, you work with another memory sector, the redo log buffer, which is pictured in Figure 3-1. Although the redo log is a major part of the SGA, it is usually one of the smallest memory structures. (To refresh your memory, the other memory structures are the buffer cache, Shared Pool Memory, large pool, and Java pool.) This chapter presents guidelines for sizing, diagnosing, and tuning the redo log buffer. Because the redo log size typically impacts the user by causing increased I/O and waits which degrade performance, it is important for you as a DBA to understand how it works and how to manage it.

Performance Problem

This section outlines an actual performance problem. As you look it over, imagine yourself as the DBA who reported it, and keep it in mind as you proceed through the chapter. The chapter presents concepts relevant to the problem. In the first Hands-on Project at the end of the chapter, you are asked to use the concepts you have learned to provide a solution, or partial solution, to this performance problem.

From: DBA

Date: 05-Sep-01 14:04

Subject: Log Buffer Problem

Hi,

I have a 9i database and I am getting log switches every minute or even more often. I have three redo log groups with two files each of 3 MB. I have set my LOG_BUFFER to 163840 which is the default, LOG_CHECKPOINT_INTERVAL=10000, LOG_CHECKPOINT_TIMEOUT=1800.

Also, I have noticed that REDO LOG SPACE REQUESTS=76 when I query select name value from v$sysstat where the name='redo log space requests'.

Please advise if all the settings are correct. I think I have to increase LOG_BUFFER setting. Is it okay to be getting log switches so often?

Redo Log Buffer Overview

Before learning the specifics of how to manage the redo log buffer, it is important to understand just what it is and how it works. This section explains what the redo log buffer contains, where it resides, what processes it runs, and what functions it performs.

Purpose and Function

The **redo log buffer** is a memory structure that contains all the database transactions entered by the user. You have seen Figure 3-1 before (in Chapter 2), but it is repeated here to remind you where the redo log buffer resides in relation to the other SGA memory structures. The purpose of the redo log buffer is to provide the capability of redoing transactions when needed, in other words, redoing all changes made by the user to the database.

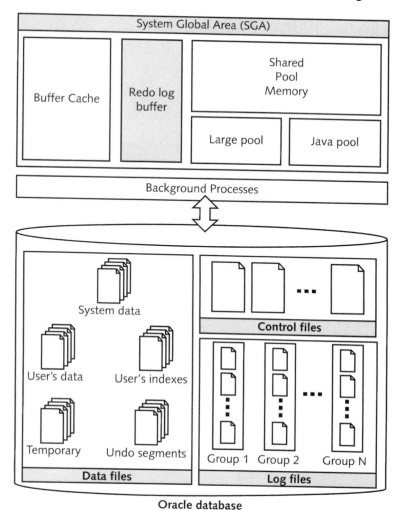

Figure 3-1   System Global Area (SGA) structure of Oracle architecture

Transactions

As stated previously, the redo log buffer is a memory space used to temporarily store transactions entered by users. These transactions consists of DML and DDL statements as follows:

- **DML statements:** INSERT, DELETE, and UPDATE

- **DDL statements:** CREATE, ALTER, DROP, and RENAME

Flushing the Redo Log Buffer

Statements stored in the log buffer are called redo entries. All transaction entries are saved sequentially in continuous log buffer space, and they remain in the log buffer until one of the events outlined in Table 3-1 occurs. Any one of these events causes the log writer (LGWR) to flush the redo log buffer.

Table 3-1   Redo log buffer flush criteria

Criteria for flushing the redo log buffer
1. A COMMIT or ROLLBACK is issued.
2. The log buffer becomes one-third full.
3. The log writer (LGWR) background process is instructed by the database writer (DBWR) background process to flush the log buffer.

The information in this table is derived from the online documentation that Oracle provides at the Oracle Technology Network site: *www.otn.oracle.com*.

Processes

Figure 3-2 illustrates the redo log process for recording transaction entries entered by users. The steps shown in Figure 3-2 are outlined as follows:

- **Step 1:** The user issues a DML or DDL statement.

- **Step 2:** The Oracle server takes the DML or DDL statement and constructs it in the log buffer.

- **Step 3:** The log buffer is flushed by the log writer (LGWR) background process. This process takes all entries in the log buffer and writes them to the redo logfiles. The LGWR is instructed to do this based on the conditions listed in Table 3-1.

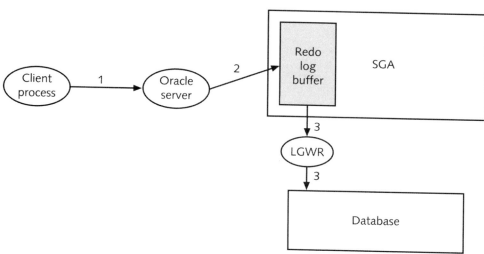

Figure 3-2   Redo log buffer process

Figure 3–3 is an illustration of how the log buffer is written to and flushed.

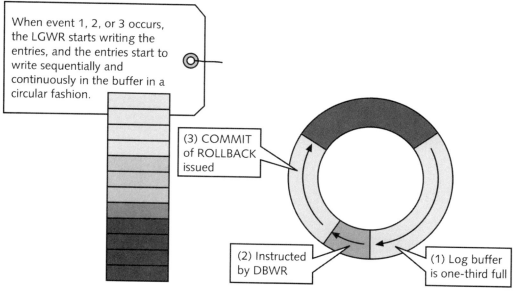

Figure 3-3   Redo log buffer flushing process

As illustrated in Figure 3–3, the redo log entries generated from user transactions are written to the redo log buffer sequentially in a circular fashion, and the buffer is flushed when any of the events outlined in Table 3–1 occurs. Now that you understand what the redo log buffer is and how it functions, you are ready to examine how to size it.

REDO LOG BUFFER SIZING

The size of the redo log buffer can influence database performance. Although there is no formula for sizing the log buffer, this section presents you with clear guidelines on how to configure the log buffer optimally.

Setting the Initialization Parameter

The size of the redo log buffer can be configured by setting the initialization parameter, LOG_BUFFER. This parameter cannot be set or changed dynamically while the database is in an open state, but can be set in the initialization file at the creation of the database or at a later time. The default size of the redo log buffer depends on the operating system and the number of server CPUs. Oracle uses the following algorithm to determine the default value if it is not set in the initialization file:

```
Maximum of {512 KB or (128 KB * CPU Count)}
```

NOTE The log buffer is set to a multiple of the operating system block size.

Regardless of the default value, there are two important factors that you should keep in mind when setting the LOG_BUFFER initialization parameter:

1. The smaller the default value, the more negative the impact on database performance.
2. The higher the default value, the less positive the impact on database performance.

Size Impacting Performance

"A larger redo buffer is not necessarily better." That's what Joe read in a prominent information technology magazine. Joe is a junior DBA who works for a pharmaceutical startup company. He was hired to assist a senior database administrator in the daily database administration tasks. After reading the magazine article, he went straight to his mentor, Larry, and said, "Can you believe what this author is saying about redo log buffer?" and handed the magazine to him.

Larry quickly read the article and replied that the statement was absolutely true and he could give an example. He explained that last year they had hired a contractor to take care of their prescription database that is hosted by a machine that hosts five other databases. A quick survey of the database was conducted and a few readings taken. From these, the consultant decided to modify the settings of the LOG_BUFFER to 50 MB from a 1 MB value. She modified the setting of the LOG_BUFFER for all other databases on the same machine. Before long, they began to receive complaints about the performance of operations that required more memory than normal operations. They spent a few hours investigating the problems and then examined the rationale for selecting 50 MB, not 2 MB or 5 MB.

The rationale was that readings from some of the indicators showed that there was redo log buffer contention. The consultant had wanted to improve it by a factor of 50 times, so she multiplied the current value by 50. Joe then asked if they had eliminated redo log buffer contention. Larry replied that contention had been eliminated when they reduced the log buffer memory from 50 MB back to 2 MB, and after that there were no complaints. Reducing the log buffer for all databases releases all memory taken by the redo log buffer and makes it available to those database operations that need it.

When you set the size of the redo log buffer, you must always keep in mind how its size impacts the performance of the database. Figure 3-4 illustrates the relationship between the redo log buffer size and the impact on performance. This illustration is based on statistics collected for the redo log buffer performance of ten different production databases. It shows that when the redo log buffer is increased in size to more than 2 MB, the performance gain is insignificant and not beneficial compared to the memory taken from other resources. Even when setting the LOG_BUFFER to a very small value such as 1 KB, Oracle ignores the setting of this parameter and allocates the redo log buffer based on the formula presented earlier. The graph presented in Figure 3-4 illustrates that real performance gain is obtained when the redo log buffer is set to a value in the range of 500 KB to 2 MB. Note that the y-axis performance percentage represents performance gain. For example, when the redo log buffer is set to a value between 1 KB and 256 KB, performance is 30 percent of its optimal level.

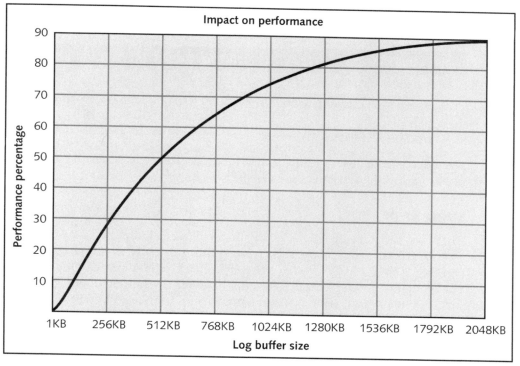

Figure 3-4   Impact of redo log buffer size on performance

Figure 3-4 shows you that determining the log buffer size can be tricky. The next section, therefore, gives you some guidelines for sizing.

Sizing Guidelines

A DBA student told her instructor that she was very confused about the numbers for configuring the memory structure of the SGA. She asked if there was an easy way to remember what values to use. The instructor told her to write down guidelines for every memory structure and use them as a starting point when necessary. For example, if you are creating a new database and you need to configure the redo log buffer and do not have a similar database in production, you can use the guidelines to configure the log buffer. At the same time, you need to monitor performance to adjust configuration when needed. The instructor told the student to develop guidelines from Oracle documentation, textbooks, articles, Web sites, and DBA experts. The key point is to establish a reasonable value for any configuration as a starting point and to keep monitoring, because there is no set formula for configuring any parameter. In general, most companies provide a good framework by establishing their own specific guidelines for all development projects and database configurations. These guidelines are compiled from technical documentation, technical experts, and previous and existing projects. Developing guidelines is an ongoing process, and you are encouraged to revise and modify guidelines whenever necessary. The guidelines for sizing the redo log buffer that are presented in Table 3-2 come from surveying several databases for different applications.

Table 3-2   Guidelines for sizing the redo log buffer

Application type	Redo log buffer size	Bytes
Online transaction processing (OLTP)	LARGE	1 MB–2 MB
DSS, reporting, or data warehouse	SMALL	50 KB–250 KB
Hybrid or general	MEDIUM	250 KB–1 MB

Now that you understand how to determine the optimal size for the redo log buffer, you need to learn the actual steps for sizing.

Sizing Steps

The following steps are used to configure the redo log buffer for a new database supporting a hybrid database application, such as an inventory system that produces reports. As a DBA, you should always adopt good practices. Here are two examples of good practices: 1) When you are shutting down a database, verify that you are shutting down the correct database; and 2) after you have made a configuration change to an initialization parameter, verify that the change was made.

NOTE

In the code segment that follows, the SQL command contains "*db_name.*" On your system, the name of your database will replace "*db_name.*"

Modify or add Init.ora to add the LOG_BUFFER parameter

```
##########################################
# Redo Log and Recovery
##########################################
log_buffer=1048576
```

1. Open the database

```
SQL> SHUTDOWN
Database closed.
Database dismounted.
ORACLE instance shut down.
SQL> startup PFILE=C:\ORACLE\ORA92\ADMIN\db_name\PFILE\INIT.ORA
ORACLE instance started.

Total System Global Area    64559648 bytes
Fixed Size                    453152 bytes
Variable Size               58720256 bytes
Database Buffers             4194304 bytes
Redo Buffers                 1191936 bytes
Database mounted.
Database opened.
```

2. Verify the setting using one of these methods.

Method 1:
```
SQL> SHOW PARAMETER LOG_BUFFER

NAME                                 TYPE         VALUE
------------------------------------ ----------- --------------------
log_buffer                           integer      1048576
```

Method 2:
```
SQL> SELECT * FROM V$SGASTAT
  2   WHERE NAME = 'log_buffer';

POOL         NAME                         BYTES
----------- --------------------------- ----------
            log_buffer                   1180672
```

Method 3:
```
SQL> SHOW SGA

Total System Global Area    64559648 bytes
Fixed Size                    453152 bytes
Variable Size               58720256 bytes
Database Buffers             4194304 bytes
Redo Buffers                 1191936 bytes
```

Method 4:
Use the Oracle Enterprise Console>Instance >Configuration>All Initialization Parameters button, shown in Figure 3-5. This screen displays all initialization parameters for the current Oracle instance.

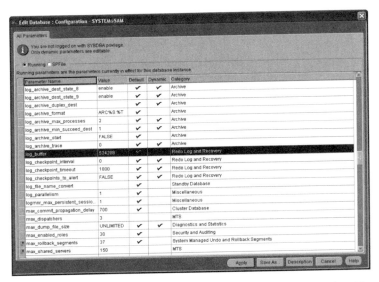

Figure 3-5 Configuration option for the Oracle Enterprise Manager

Note in the previous example that Methods 1 and 4 display the log buffer value exactly as it is set in the parameter file, but Methods 2 and 3 each display a different value for the log buffer size and neither is the same value that is derived from Methods 1 or 4. Do not be alarmed when you observe this in the database you are administering, because it is normal. Oracle reserves memory set through the parameter LOG_BUFFER and surrounds this memory with guard pages to protect it. That is the reason the reported sizes differ.

A log buffer that is sized above 2 MB does not yield significant additional benefits.

TIP

There is another measurement for estimating how large the log buffer should be. This measurement should be taken when the database application is operating at peak transaction volume; otherwise, the measurement is misleading, because at off-hours, for example, there are fewer transactions. This results in the generation of fewer redo entries so that contention might not exist. The following steps show you how to estimate the optimum size of the log buffer:

1. Select a time frame when the volume of transactions is at a maximum.

2. Issue the following query to get the average size of the redo entries; this value is expressed in number of bytes.

```
SQL> SELECT R.VALUE/E.VALUE "Average Size of Redo Entries"
  2     FROM V$SYSSTAT R, V$SYSSTAT E
  3    WHERE R.NAME = 'redo size'
  4      AND E.NAME = 'redo entries'
  5  /

Average Size of Redo Entries
----------------------------
                   214.653707
```

3. Record the number of concurrent transactions during this time frame.

```
SQL> SELECT COUNT(*) "Concurrent Transactions"
  2     FROM V$TRANSACTION
  3  /

Concurrent Transactions
-----------------------
                     51
```

4. Compute the estimated redo log buffer size; note that you are adding 10 percent as a fudge factor.

```
Concurrent Transactions * Average Size of Redo Entries * 1.10
```

Using numbers that you obtained from Steps 2 and 3, you get 12042.07.

5. Round this value up to the next multiple value of operating system block size using the following formula:

```
CEIL(Est. Redo Log Buffer Size/OS Block Size) *  OS Block Size
```

If you suppose that the OS block size is 2 KB, you get 12288 (12 KB) as an estimate for the initial log buffer size.

As you can see from this result, a 12 KB redo log buffer size would be sufficient to handle the observed transaction volume of entries. But if you follow the guidelines indicated in Table 3-2, the smallest size of the redo log buffer should be 50 KB. This means that if you size the redo log buffer to 512 KB per the guideline, you can handle up to 240 concurrent transactions based on 214 average-sized redo entries.

Now that you have learned about how to configure the log buffer properly or at least how to configure it as a starting point, you need to understand the other dependencies that exist before you learn how to diagnose and monitor the configuration of the redo log buffer. In the next section, you learn these dependencies and how to work with them.

Log Buffer and Log Writer (LGWR)

When you are sizing the redo log buffer, you must also consider the log writer. There is a dependent relationship between the log buffer and the log writer (LGWR) background process. The LGWR manages the redo log buffer, and the LGWR's performance depends on the size of the redo log buffer. Also, contention for the services of the redo log buffer can result from decreased LGWR speed. The following section details the dependent relationship between the log buffer and the log writer.

Log Writer and LGWR Dependencies

As you know, the LGWR process writes all the entries registered in the log buffer to the redo logfiles. The LGWR background process is triggered by the criteria outlined in Table 3-1, which states that the database writer (DBWR) background process instructs the LGWR to flush the log buffer. If the log buffer is too small, the LGWR writes to the redo log more frequently than usual, which in turn generates more I/O trips to the disk. Another impact of a small log buffer is that more requests for log buffer space forces the LGWR to flush the buffer more often than is necessary.

Another important relationship between the redo log buffer and the LGWR relates to log buffer contention that could be the result of reduced LGWR speed. If the LGWR is delayed, for example, by waiting for the ARCH background process to finish writing to the archive logs, the server process must wait for space, and if there are many synchronous requests, this situation could result in additional contention.

TIP   For OLTP applications in which many transactions are being submitted to the database, a large log buffer reduces I/O and could thus result in *less* performance degradation. In other words, a small log buffer has less space for redo entries and this forces LGWR to flush it more frequently and causes more frequent I/O.

Log Switches

Another effect worth noting is the inverse relationship between the log buffer and the redo logfiles. The size of the redo logfiles can influence the frequency of log switches. When a **log switch** occurs, the recording of information is switched from one logfile to another. As mentioned previously, increased log switches result in a busier LGWR and can cause log buffer contention. Decreased log switches can enhance the speed of the log buffer, which reduces I/O; however, you may run the risk of losing transaction entries or experience a longer recovery time in the case of database failure.

Checkpoints

A logfile switch occurs when the redo logfile is filled or when an ALTER SYSTEM SWITCH LOGFILE is issued. Log switching can be controlled by managing the number of blocks written and the checkpoint frequency. A **checkpoint** is a method to commit data to the data file and timestamp it with time, date, and SCN. The SCN (System Change

3

Number) is associated with transaction entries in the redo log and recorded in the control file as well as in the header of each data file. SCN is used for data file synchronization and recovery purposes. Two parameters regulate checkpoints:

- **LOG_CHECKPOINT_TIMEOUT:** Based on the number of seconds that have passed since the last checkpoint occurred. For example, if this parameter is set to five seconds, a checkpoint occurs after five seconds of idle time.

- **LOG_CHECKPOINT_INTERVAL:** Based on the number of OS blocks that have been written to the redo logfiles.

NOTE These two parameters can be set dynamically (using ALTER SYSTEM), and they are mutually exclusive. This means that the parameters should not be configured at the same time. You should set the parameter you don't want to use to 0 and the other to the desired value.

For example, suppose you want to trigger a checkpoint every time the checkpoint is idle for 10 minutes. To do so, you issue the following statement:

```
SQL> ALTER SYSTEM SET LOG_CHECKPOINT_TIMEOUT = 600;

System altered.
```

Similarly, you can set the LOG_CHECKPOINT_INTERVAL to 10 KB by issuing the following statement that establishes a checkpoint when LGWR has written 10 KB of entries to the redo logfiles.

```
SQL> ALTER SYSTEM SET LOG_CHECKPOINT_INTERVAL = 10240;

System altered.
```

NOTE If you want to record the time when a checkpoint occurs to the ALERT.LOG file, set the parameter LOG_CHECKPOINTS_TO_ALERT to the value TRUE.

This chapter has given you guidelines for setting the size of the redo log buffer, and the next step is to learn the Oracle performance views and statistics to diagnose the redo log configuration.

LOG BUFFER DIAGNOSIS

Omar is a senior DBA and has been working as an Oracle DBA for a long time. He has perfected his skills by diligently staying on top of things. He has automated most of his routine tasks, and monitors database performances, specifically memory, from two aspects—the database and the operating system. Omar creates a biweekly chart of memory and storage to perform trend analysis and thereby identify configuration problems. He maintains a proactive stance when statistical threshold values are consistently nearing the red zone. Many DBAs would be surprised that Omar does not use any fancy, third-party graphical tools, and in fact his manager offered to purchase these tools for him, but he declined the offer. Omar's secret to success is that he is simply using performance dynamic views supplied by Oracle.

Oracle provides many performance dynamic views to give you indicators on how well the database is performing and how optimally the database is configured, especially the memory structure. Listed below are eight dynamic views that you can use to obtain specific redo log buffer statistics and ratios:

- **V$SYSSTAT dynamic performance view:** System statistics

- **V$SESSTAT dynamic performance view:** Session statistics

- **V$STAT_NAME dynamic performance view:** Statistics names

- **V$SYSTEM_EVENT dynamic performance view:** System events waits

- **V$SESSION_EVENT dynamic performance view:** Session events for the current session

- **V$SESSION_WAIT dynamic performance view:** Event waits for the current session

- **V$EVENT_NAME performance view:** A list of all events that could occur

- **V$WAITSTAT dynamic performance view:** A summary of all waits for the system since it was started

"Waits" is an Oracle statistical term. It means the number of times or the length of time a process or event suspends action until resources are available.

NOTE

In the following steps you use these performance views to understand how they provide indicators about the redo log buffer configuration, which you can use to prevent contention. Use the steps listed here to experience a redo log tuning process that you could use:

1. Size the redo log buffer according to the guidelines presented in this chapter.

2. Monitor redo log statistics and wait events. Adjust the size of the redo log buffer when necessary until it is stable.

3. Monitor how fast the LGWR is freeing the redo log buffers. Then adjust the size of the redo logfiles and adjust the checkpoint frequency.

Issue the following statement to get a list of all statistics related to the redo log buffer from V$SYSSTAT:

3

```
SQL> SELECT NAME, VALUE
  2    FROM V$SYSSTAT
  3    WHERE NAME LIKE '%redo%'
  4  /

NAME                                                      VALUE
-----------------------------------------------------  ----------
redo synch writes                                              2
redo synch time                                                2
redo entries                                              296592
redo size                                               63406964
redo buffer allocation retries                                 2
redo wastage                                             4757572
redo writer latching time                                     31
redo writes                                                19961
redo blocks written                                       137471
redo write time                                             5502
redo log space requests                                        2
redo log space wait time                                      52
redo log switch interrupts                                     0
redo ordering marks                                            0
```

Issue the following statement to get a list of all event waits related to redo log buffer from V$SYSTEM_EVENT. Note that all times are expressed in hundredths of a second:

```
SQL> SELECT EVENT, TOTAL_WAITS, TIME_WAITED, AVERAGE_WAIT
  2    FROM V$SYSTEM_EVENT
  3    WHERE EVENT LIKE '%log%';

EVENT                       TOTAL_WAITS TIME_WAITED AVERAGE_WAIT
--------------------------- ----------- ----------- ------------
logfile sequential read               6           6            1
logfile single write                  6           0            0
logfile parallel write            20036         922            0
logfile switch completion             2          52           26
logfile sync                          2           2            1
log buffer space                     17           5           16
```

TIP It is best to turn on the TIMED_STATISTICS parameter only during statistics collection. The TIMED_STATISTICS parameter tells Oracle whether or not to collect timing statistics. If set to TRUE, Oracle requests timing statistics from the operating system, and this may cause slight performance degradation. If set to FALSE, no time-related statistics are collected, and this may produce less accurate statistics for some operations.

Using this view, you can issue the following queries to get the following ratios:

- **Redo buffer allocation retries statistic:** This statistic indicates the number of times a user process had to wait for redo log buffer space. Issue the following query to get this value:

```
SQL> SELECT NAME, VALUE
  2    FROM V$SYSSTAT
  3    WHERE NAME = 'redo buffer allocation retries';

NAME                                                          VALUE
------------------------------------------------------ ----------
redo buffer allocation retries                                    0
```

This value must be close to zero, and if it is consistently above zero, it indicates that the log buffer needs to be increased or the checkpoint process needs to be regulated.

- **Redo log space requests statistic:** This statistic value indicates the number of times that the server processes had to wait for redo log files space. Issue the following statement to get this value:

```
SQL> SELECT NAME, VALUE
  2    FROM V$SYSSTAT
  3    WHERE NAME = 'redo log space requests';

NAME                                                          VALUE
------------------------------------------------------ ----------
redo log space requests                                           0
```

If this value is consistently above zero, you should regulate checkpoints or increase the size of redo logfiles.

- **Redo log space wait time statistic:** This value indicates the amount of time the LGWR/server processes waited for the redo log space requests and is expressed in multiples of 10 milliseconds. Issue the following query to display this value:

```
SQL> SELECT NAME, VALUE
  2    FROM V$SYSSTAT
  3    WHERE NAME = 'redo log space wait time'
  4  /

NAME                                                          VALUE
------------------------------------------------------ ----------
redo log space wait time                                          0
```

As with the redo log space requests statistics, a consistent value above zero indicates that the server processes are waiting for the LGWR process to complete writing.

- **Log buffer space wait event:** This value indicates the number of times the server processes are waiting for free space in the log buffer. Issue the following statement to get this statistic:

```
SQL> SELECT EVENT, TOTAL_WAITS
  2     FROM V$SYSTEM_EVENT
  3    WHERE EVENT LIKE '%log%'
  4   /

EVENT                        TOTAL_WAITS
------------------------     -----------
log buffer space                 17
```

3

Performance tuning experts differ on the interpretation of the log buffer space wait event value. Some believe that if the value is above zero, you should automatically increase the log buffer. Other experts say that if the value is above zero for 15 minutes, the log buffer is too small. The best interpretation is the middle of the road. If the value is consistently above zero compared to a previous reading, an increase in the size of the log buffer *may* help. Remember that if the log buffer is already large and you are still getting high numbers, the most likely conclusion is that the LGWR is not writing fast enough, but this could be caused by I/O contention or too frequent checkpoints.

- **Log buffer Requests and Entries Ratio**: This ratio provides the percentage of redo log requests to the number of entries. The ratio threshold should be very close to zero. Issue the following statement to compute this ratio. If the ratio is consistently above zero, increase the log buffer size. Notice that you are allowing one request for 5000 entries:

```
SQL> SELECT (R.VALUE*5000)/E.VALUE "Redo Requests/Entries Ratio"
  2     FROM V$SYSSTAT R, V$SYSSTAT E
  3    WHERE R.NAME = 'redo log space requests'
  4      AND E.NAME = 'redo entries'
  5   /

Redo Requests/Entries Ratio
---------------------------
                          0
```

- **Log buffer Retries and Entries Ratio:** This ratio compares the total number of retries for space in the log buffer to the actual number of redo entries. If this ratio is high, the LGWR is probably not writing fast enough to free space in the log buffer. Issue the following query to compute this ratio:

```
SQL> SELECT R.VALUE/E.VALUE "Redo Retries/Entries Ratio"
  2     FROM V$SYSSTAT R, V$SYSSTAT E
  3    WHERE R.NAME = 'redo buffer allocation retries'
  4      AND E.NAME = 'redo entries'
  5  /

Redo Retries/Entries Ratio
--------------------------
                         0
```

The threshold of this ratio is one percent. A consistent value above one percent indicates either that the log buffer is too small or that the redo log file is too small. Both circumstances cause the LGRW to wait.

Table 3-3 presents statistics related to redoing the log buffer and Table 3-4 presents events related to the log buffer.

Table 3-3 Log buffer statistics

Statistics	Description
Redo synch writes	Number of times the content of the log buffer must be written to log files because a COMMIT was issued
Redo synch time	Time in tens of milliseconds spent to perform "redo synch writes"
Redo entries	Count of redo entries copied into the log buffer
Redo size	Number of bytes of generated redo entries
Redo buffer allocation retries	Number of times Oracle retried to allocate space in the redo log buffer
Redo wastage	Number of bytes wasted from redo log buffer blocks because they were written to redo log file before they were filled
Redo writer latching time	Time in tens of milliseconds that the LGWR spent to get and release copy latch
Redo writes	Number of times LGWR wrote to redo log files
Redo blocks written	Total number of redo entry blocks written to redo log files
Redo write time	Time in tens of milliseconds spent to write entries in the log buffer to current redo log file
Redo log space requests	Number of times Oracle waited for disk space to be allocated for redo entries while a log switch is performed
Redo log space wait time	Time in tens of milliseconds that the LGWR waited for redo log space; these are known as "redo log space requests"
Redo log switch interrupts	Number of times an instance requested another instance to switch the log file
Redo ordering marks	Number of times a SCN was allocated for a redo record with a SNC number higher than the SCN number generated by another process for the same block

The information in this table is derived from the online documentation that Oracle provides at the Oracle Technology Network site: *www.otn.oracle.com*.

Table 3-4 Log buffer events

Event name	Description of what the event is waiting for
Log buffer space	Space in the log buffer while the LGWR is writing to a log file
Log file parallel write	All parallel processes to complete writing all redo records in the log buffer to the log file
Log file sequential read	LGWR to complete reading redo records from the current log file
Log file single write	LGWR to complete writing to the header of the log file due to the increment of the redo log sequence number or addition of a new log file member
Log file switch (archiving needed)	ARCH to complete archiving the log file to which the LGWR is switching
Log file switch (checkpoint incomplete)	A checkpoint to complete in order for the LGWR to switch to the next log file
Log file switch (clearing log file)	A switch from the active log file to the next log file to complete because a request was made to clear the active log file. The request can be made explicitly using the CLEAR LOGFILE command or implicitly executed during recovery.
Log file switch completion	A switch from the active log file to the next log file to complete
Log file sync	LGWR to complete writing redo entries in the log buffer to the log file for a session that issued an implicit or explicit COMMIT
Log switch/archive	The current log file to be archived when the ALTER SYSTEM LOG CHANGE SCN statement is issued
Redo wait	Not used by Oracle

The information in this table is derived from the online documentation that Oracle provides at the Oracle Technology Network site: *www.otn.oracle.com*.

Using the Oracle Enterprise Manager Console

Oracle has provided a graphical tool for almost every configuration of the database. This tool is Oracle Enterprise Manager, which you can use to administer and diagnose your database. This section explains how to use the Database Health Overview Chart of the Oracle Enterprise Manager Console to get all the statistics presented in this section. Use the following steps to accomplish this task:

1. Open the Oracle Enterprise Manager console.

2. Select **Performance Overview** from the Diagnostics Pack (see Figure 3-6). The Database Health Overview Chart opens (see Figure 3-7).

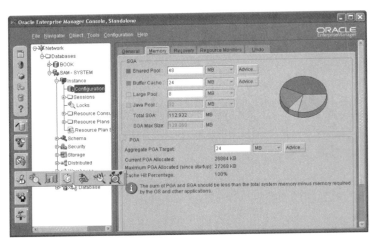

Figure 3-6   Selecting Performance Overview from the Diagnostic Pack

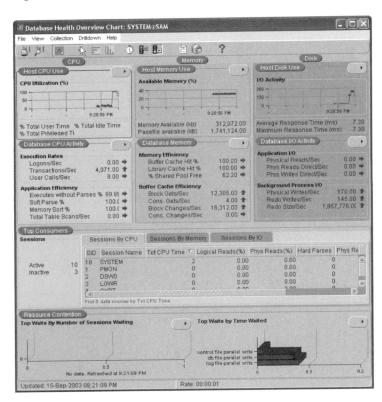

Figure 3-7   Performance Overview utility

3. Click the **right-arrow** for Database I/O Activity as shown in Figure 3–8 and point to **Redo Size/Sec**. Then select the **Redo Analysis** option.

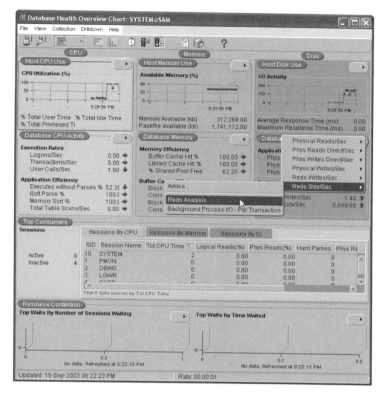

Figure 3-8   Performance Overview redo analysis option

   4. The Redo Analysis window presents four charts that display most of the important
      Redo Log Buffer Statistics as shown in Figure 3-9.

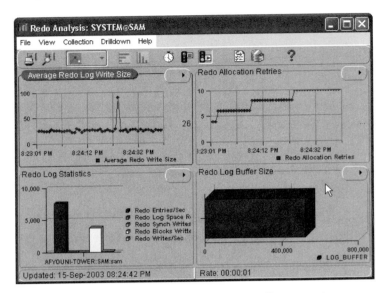

Figure 3-9 Charts displaying Redo Log Buffer Statistics

In Figure 3-9, the top-left chart illustrates that the Average Redo Log Write Size is holding steady at 25 blocks except for one spike in which the Redo Write Size went up to 90 blocks, which suggests that there were more transaction activities than usual. The top-right chart indicates that the Redo Allocation Retries is consistently low, which indicates that there is no log buffer contention. The bottom-left chart presents Redo Log Statistics that indicate that the Redo Log Space Request is very close to 0, which is excellent. Lastly, the bottom-right chart shows that the size of the Redo Log Buffer is 10 KB. Overall, analysis of this diagram indicates that there are no performance problems with the current redo log buffer configuration.

5. You can view advice and Help for any chart at any time by clicking on the arrow in the upper-right corner of the chart. Figures 3-10 and 3-11 are examples of screens that open when you press the arrow.

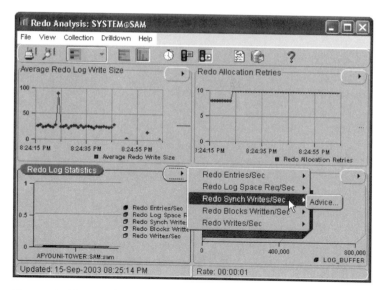

Figure 3-10   Redo Analysis advice option

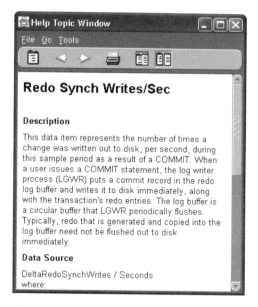

Figure 3-11   Help screen on Redo Allocation Retries

OPTIMIZING REDO OPERATIONS

A developer called a DBA for help on a critical feed that needed to be loaded within five minutes. Bob, the developer, described this feed as taking about nine minutes, which was not acceptable and would never pass user acceptance. The DBA asked how Bob was loading this data. Bob replied that he was using a Java module with JDBC. The DBA asked if he had tried the SQL*Loader for loading the data since it is a fast tool for loading data. Bob said that he would try it.

A day later, the DBA received another call from Bob, who reported that the SQL*Loader improved the data load from nine minutes to six minutes which represented an improvement, but was still not acceptable. Bob asked what could be done on the database to speed up the load, and whether he should add more memory. The DBA smiled at Bob's suggestion and asked Bob to send him the SQL*Loader instruction for examination. The DBA investigated the instruction and added an option to it and sent it back to Bob. The next day the DBA received another call from Bob thanking him and telling the DBA that the feed was only taking two minutes to load.

As you already know, DDL and DML operations issued by users generate redo entries. There are situations in which you can reduce the number of redo entries without compromising the functionality of the application and at the same time enhance the performance of these statements. Table 3-5 outlines methods for doing so.

Table 3-5 Optimizing redo operations

Option/mode	Use with tool/statement
NOLOGGING	- Most CREATE and ALTER statements - Oracle SQL*Loader utility
DIRECT PATH	- Oracle EXP/IMP utility - DIRECT INSERT - Oracle SQL*Loader utility

The information in this table is derived from the online documentation that Oracle provides at the Oracle Technology Network site: *www.otn.oracle.com*.

 The NOLOGGING option impacts only DDL statements; DML statements are not affected.

NOTE

Oracle provides two methods for loading data when importing with the IMP utility: loading using the SQL*Loader utility and inserting data using the INSERT statement. These two methods are numbered in Figure 3-12 and described as follows:

1. **Conventional path method:** A **conventional path method** is the normal method of issuing DML statements.

2. **Direct path method:** A **direct path method** bypasses the buffer cache and loads data directly into the data file.

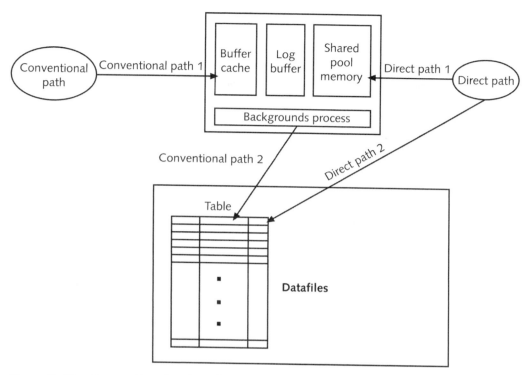

Figure 3-12   Conventional path and direct path processes

NOLOGGING Examples

Using the NOLOGGING option in CREATE TABLE and ALTER TABLE statements reduces the number of generated redo entries, but does not eliminate them. Oracle keeps generating redo entries only for system-related operations (these operation are generated by Oracle) that result from the following DMLs and DDLs issued against the table:

```
CREATE TABLE ... NOLOGGING
ALTER TABLE ... NOLOGGING
```

SQL*LOADER Example

Here is an example of how you could use the DIRECT PATH option when loading data with the Oracle SQL*Loader utility:

```
sqlldr USERID=tuner CONTROL=customers.ctl LOG=customers.log
DIRECT=true
```

EXP/IMP Example

Here is an example of how you could export a table using the DIRECT PATH option:

```
exp tuner file=customers.dmp tables=customers rows=yes direct=yes
```

If you do not choose the DIRECT option at the time of export, you cannot import using the DIRECT option. Use the following command to import the table from the preceding export:

```
imp tuner file=customers.dmp tables=customers rows=yes
```

DIRECT INSERT Example

You can insert data into the table using the DIRECT PATH option when using the DIRECT INSERT method. To use this method, you add the APPEND hint to the insert statement as shown in this example:

```
INSERT /*+APPEND */ INTO CUSTOMERS_BACKUP
    SELECT * FROM CUSTOMERS;

OR

INSERT INTO CUSTOMERS_BACKUP
    SELECT / * + APPEND * / * FROM CUSTOMERS;

OR

INSERT INTO CUSTOMERS_BACKUP
    NOLOGGING
    SELECT / * + APPEND * / * FROM CUSTOMERS;
```

CHAPTER SUMMARY

- ❏ The log buffer is one of the major memory structures of the SGA.
- ❏ The log buffer is used to temporarily store all redo entries generated by DDL and DML statements.
- ❏ The LOG_BUFFER parameter is used to size the log buffer.
- ❏ The log buffer is managed by the LGWR.
- ❏ The Log buffer is flushed when it is one-third full, a COMMIT statement is issued, or it is instructed to do so by other processes.
- ❏ A log buffer size of over 2 MB has minimal impact on enhancing performance.
- ❏ The performance of the log buffer is closely related to and affected by the size of the log buffer.
- ❏ Use V$SYSSTAT and V$SYSTEM_EVENT performance dynamic views to diagnose whether the log buffer is properly configured or not.
- ❏ Use the NOLOGGING option to reduce generated redo log statements.
- ❏ Use the DIRECT PATH option to enhance performance when loading data.
- ❏ Initialization parameters presented in this chapter include:
  - ■ LOG_BUFFER

- LOG_CHECKPOINT_INTERVAL
- LOG_CHECKPOINT_TIMEOUT
- LOG_CHECKPOINTS_TO_ALERT
- TIMED_STATISTICS

3

❐ Views used in this chapter include:

- V$EVENT_NAME
- V$PARAMETER
- V$SESSION_EVENT
- V$SESSION_WAIT
- V$SESSTAT
- V$SGASTAT
- V$STAT_NAME
- V$SYSSTAT
- V$SYSTEM_EVENT
- V$TRANSACTION
- V$WAITSTAT

REVIEW QUESTIONS

1. The LOG_BUFFER parameter can be set dynamically using an ALTER SYSTEM statement. (True/False)

2. The higher the default LOG_BUFFER value, the stronger an impact on database performance. (True/False)

3. You can set the LOG_CHECKPOINT_INTERVAL parameter to adjust the frequency of the checkpoints. (True/False)

4. You can set the LOG_CHECKPOINT_TIMING parameter to adjust the frequency of the checkpoints. (True/False)

5. Redo entries are DML and DDL statements issued by users. (True/False)

6. The smaller the default value for LOG_BUFFER, the weaker the impact on database performance. (True/False)

7. The size of the redo log file does not impact the performance of the log buffer size. (True/False)

8. The LGWR background process manages the redo log buffer. (True/False)

9. Log Buffer size = OS Block Size * Number of Concurrent Transactions. (True/False)

10. What is the default size for the redo log buffer?

11. Define the log buffer space wait event.

12. Describe the redo buffer allocation retries statistic.

13. Write a query that lists all wait events for the redo log buffer.

14. Write a query that shows the value of the redo log space requests.

15. Write a query that displays the average size of redo log entries.

16. Write a query that gets the percentage of redo retries to redo entries.

17. In Oracle documentation, look up the description of the redo sync writes statistic, and then write a query to look up its value in your database.

18. List the three steps you would take to tune the redo log buffer.

19. When does log buffer contention occur?

20. What is the impact of a small redo log buffer and small redo logfiles?

21. What is the ideal size of a redo log buffer for a DSS application? What happens if you double it?

22. What is the effect of frequent commits on the redo log buffer and database performance?

EXAM REVIEW QUESTIONS: ORACLE 9i PERFORMANCE TUNING (#1Z0-003)

1. Which statement about the redo log buffer is true?

   a. Tuning the redo log buffer does not significantly increase database performance.

   b. The smaller the size of the redo log buffer, the better the database performance.

   c. The larger the size of the redo log buffer, the worse the database performance.

   d. The redo log buffer size may influence database performance if it is set improperly.

2. The redo log buffer hit ratio threshold is:

   a. 0

   b. one percent

   c. 90 percent

   d. 95 percent

   e. None of the above

3. With which statement would you use NOLOGGING mode to reduce redo operations?

   a. INSERT

   b. UPDATE

   c. ALTER

   d. DELETE

   e. ANALYZE

4. Suppose you took a reading from V$SESSION_WAIT, and it showed that the session waited for a long time for log space. What should you do?

   a. Increase the size of the redo log file for the session.

   b. Increase the size of the redo log buffer.

   c. Increase the size of the redo log file for the system.

   d. Do nothing and keep monitoring system wait events.

5. Which dynamic performance view would you query to get the number of times the server processes waited for free space in the log buffer?

   a. V$SESSTAT

   b. V$SYSSTAT

   c. V$WAITSTAT

   d. V$SYSTEM_EVENT

   e. V$WAIT_EVENTS

6. Which value indicates redo log buffer contention when it is above zero?

   a. Redo buffer allocation retries statistic

   b. Redo buffer allocation entries statistic

   c. Log buffer space retries wait event

   d. Log buffer allocation request wait event

7. What would you do if the redo log space wait time statistic is consistently above zero?

   a. Nothing

   b. Increase the size of the log buffer.

   c. Decrease the size of the redo log buffer.

   d. Increase the size of the redo log file.

   e. Decrease the size of the redo log file.

8. Which two initialization parameters would you use to regulate the frequency of checkpoints?

   a. LOG_ARCHIVE_BUFFER

   b. LOG_BUFFER

   c. LOG_CHECKPOINT_TIMEOUT

   d. LOG_CHECKPOINT_BUFFER

   e. LOG_CHECKPOINT_INTERVAL

   f. LOG_CHECKPOINT_SIZE

   g. LOG_BUFFER_SIZE

9. Which view would you use to determine the ratio of the number of retries to the number of entries?

   a. V$SYSTEM_EVENT

   b. V$WAITSTAT

   c. V$SYSSTAT

   d. V$WAIT_EVENTS

10. Which parameter cannot be altered while the database is running?

    a. LOG_CHECKPOINT_SIZE

    b. LOG_CHECKPOINT_INTERVAL

    c. LOG_BUFFER

    d. LOG_BUFFER_SIZE

    e. LOG_CHECKPOINT_TIMEOUT

11. What is the optimal value of the redo log space requests statistic?

    a. Below 1

    b. Near 0

    c. Above 1

    d. Equal to 0

    e. Between –1 and 1

12. Which event does not cause the LGWR to flush the log buffer?

    a. COMMIT statement

    b. ROLLBACK statement

    c. When the log buffer is two-thirds full

    d. When LGWR is instructed by the DBWR

    e. All of the above

    f. None of the above

13. Suppose you had created an index with the NOLOGGING option, and it became damaged, so you decided to rebuild the index. Which statement is true?

    a. Oracle will not generate redo log entries when you rebuild the index.

    b. Oracle will generate redo log entries when you rebuild the index.

    c. The NOLOGGING option is dropped when you rebuild the index.

    d. The NOLOGGING option is stored in the data dictionary even after you drop the index, and it is used again when you recreate the index.

HANDS-ON PROJECTS

Please complete the projects provided below.

HANDS-ON
PROJECTS

1. Reread the Performance Problem at the start of the chapter. Think of it in terms of the concepts you have learned in this chapter and answer the DBA's question about the log buffer.

2. From this chapter you know that the result of the following query should be a very small value.
   ```
   SELECT 'Redo Log Buffer Contention', VALUE
      FROM  V$SYSSTAT
     WHERE NAME = 'redo log space wait time'
   ```

    a. What is considered a small value?

    b. What is considered a high value?

    c. When would you stop increasing the redo log buffer if the result is still too high?

3. Consider the following configuration of initialization parameters and statistics obtained from a general-purpose database application:

```
log_buffer                 524288
db_block_size              8192
log_checkpoint_interval 0
log_checkpoint_timeout  1800


NAME                                    VALUE
------------------------------   ----------
redo synch writes                       39300
redo synch time                         50135
redo entries                          3674420
redo size                           895116128
redo buffer allocation retries             22
redo wastage                         59092372
redo writer latching time                585
redo writes                            223008
redo blocks written                  1924719
redo write time                        203398
redo log space requests                   26
redo log space wait time               1059
redo log switch interrupts                 0
redo ordering marks                       16
```

Analyze these statistics to determine if a problem exists. Explain your analysis.

4. Consider the following statistics and wait events. Analyze these numbers and state if the redo log buffer is sized properly, and if not, recommend an action. Note that all times are expressed in hundredths of a second

```
EVENT                        TOTAL_WAITS TIME_WAITED AVERAGE_WAIT
-------------------------    ----------- ----------- ------------
logfile sequential read         218620      28439    .130084164
logfile single write                34         13    .382352941
logfile parallel write          717957      87662    .122099234
log buffer space                   521       2207    4.23608445
logfile switch completion           23        167    7.26086957
logfile sync                    589069     156134    .265052142


NAME                              VALUE
-------------------------     ----------
redo synch writes                590528
redo synch time                  159354
redo entries                   23028295
redo size                    6622101904
redo buffer allocation retries      545
redo wastage                  200083676
redo writer latching time          6361
redo writes                      718277
redo blocks written            13759151
redo write time                  138478
redo log space requests              24
redo log space wait time            167
redo log switch interrupts            0
redo ordering marks                 157
```

5. You are asked to assess the redo log buffer for a database application in production. State the steps you would take to tune the redo log buffer, and write the query you issue for each step.

6. Suppose you ran the following queries on a database in production:

```
SQL> select name, value
  2    from v$sysstat
  3    where name like '%redo%'
SQL> /

NAME                                               VALUE
-------------------------------------------------- ----------
redo synch writes                                     648249
redo synch time                                       221202
redo entries                                        24215605
redo size                                         6934086804
redo buffer allocation retries                           551
redo wastage                                       217079636
redo writer latching time                               6646
redo writes                                           778885
redo blocks written                                 14422666
redo write time                                       157181
redo log space requests                                   31
redo log space wait time                                 219
redo log switch interrupts                                 0
redo ordering marks                                      186

SQL> select count(*) from v$transaction;

  COUNT(*)
----------
         5

SQL> show parameter log_buffer

NAME                                TYPE        VALUE
----------------------------------- ----------- --------
log_buffer                          integer     163840
```

a. Compute the average size of the redo log size.

b. Compute the estimated size of the log buffer.

c. Is the log buffer sized properly?

d. Do you have any concerns about the statistics presented above?

7. Analyze statistics obtained from the Oracle Enterprise Manager Performance Overview window presented in Figure 3-13.

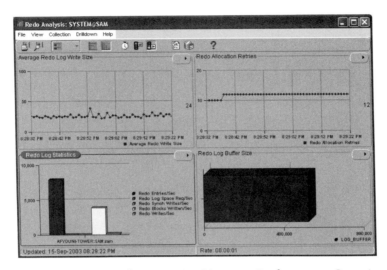

Figure 3-13   Oracle Enterprise Manager Performance Overview

8. Suppose you are monitoring a database for an OLTP Web application. You are taking a reading every day at 6:00 a.m. of the Redo Log Space Requests statistic. Table 3-6 shows readings for the last five days. The average number of concurrent transactions is 30.

Table 3-6   Daily statistics

Day	Redo log space requests	Redo entries	Redo size
1	12	216050	5345464
2	25	221300	5357096
3	23	240040	5371028
4	30	257030	5376036
5	35	264021	5377096

Analyze these readings to conclude if you should be alarmed or not. Explain your conclusion.

9. Having read this chapter, someone could conclude that the best way to configure the redo log buffer is by setting it to 1 MB regardless of the type of application using the database. Do you agree with this statement? Explain why or why not.

10. Suppose your database is receiving a feed of data. You have sized the redo log buffer to 512 KB.

   a. What method would you recommend to load this data, and what options would you use?

   b. Is the size of the redo log buffer sufficient for this operation?

11. Suppose you are trying to delete millions of records from a large table. While the statement is executing, you take a reading of wait events for that session. The results are shown here:

```
SQL> select * from v$session_event where sid = 13 order by time_waited desc;

SID EVENT                           TOTAL_WAITS TOTAL_TIMEOUTS TIME_WAITED AVERAGE_WAIT
--- ------------------------        ----------- -------------- ----------- ------------
13  db file sequential read           4774208              0    10975798   2.29897776
13  log buffer space                    35484            572     1061939   29.927263
13  latch free                         525321         525319      569661   1.08440553
13  free buffer waits                    5062           1035      228744   45.1884631
13  buffer busy waits                   18142             75       67459   3.71838827
13  logfile switch completion            713            208       40266   56.4740533
13  logfile sync                         617            118       29308   47.5008104
13  write complete waits                 192             21        8825   45.9635417
```

Analyze these numbers and draw a conclusion for this operation. What would you recommend?

CASE PROJECTS

Redo Test

Two DBAs were discussing log buffer configuration. One of them was insisting that more memory does not really improve performance of the log buffer. So he asked the other DBA to perform the following tasks to prove this point. Perform the following steps:

1. Create a new table called REDO_TEST by using the following statement:

```
CREATE TABLE REDO_TEST
(
    NUM NUMBER,
    TEXT VARCHAR2(80)
);
```

Make sure that you have at least 75 MB of space on the default tablespace.

2. Shut down the database.

3. Edit the INIT.ORA file and set the redo log buffer to 5 KB.

4. Open the database, verify the size of the log buffer, and explain any errors or observations you have.

5. Populate the REDO_TEST table with data using the following script:

```
BEGIN
    FOR I IN 1..100000 LOOP
        INSERT INTO REDO_TEST VALUES (I, 'TEXT LINE ' || I);
        COMMIT;
    END LOOP;
END;
/
```

 This may take some time depending on the speed of your CPU.

NOTE

6. In another session, get the following statistics and wait events and save them as reading #1:

   a. Log buffer entries and request ratio

   b. Log buffer retries and entries ratio

   c. Log buffer space wait event

7. Repeat Steps 2, 3, 4, and 5, but this time set the redo log buffer to 100 KB.

8. Get all statistics and wait events, and save them as reading #2.

9. Repeat Steps 2, 3, 4, and 5, but this time set the redo log buffer to 500 KB.

10. Get all statistics and wait events, and save them as reading #3.

11. Repeat Steps 2, 3, 4, and 5, but this time set the redo log buffer to 1000 KB.

12. Get all statistics and wait events, and save them as reading #4.

13. After analyzing readings 1, 2, 3 and 4, answer the following questions:

   a. What setting for the redo log buffer would be best for this scenario?

   b. What is the trend of the buffer allocation retries statistic?

   c. What do you conclude from this scenario about the redo log buffer?

TUNING THE SHARED POOL MEMORY

In this chapter you will:

♦ Understand the role of the Shared Pool Memory

♦ Learn Shared Pool Advice terms

♦ Learn Shared Pool Memory performance terms

♦ Learn terms for the internal structures of the Shared Pool Memory

♦ Learn the role of the library cache and data dictionary cache

♦ Configure the Shared Pool Memory

♦ Use the Shared Pool Size Advice feature

♦ Diagnose the Shared Pool Memory configuration

♦ Look inside the Shared Pool Memory using performance dynamic views

♦ Flush the Shared Pool Memory

♦ Pin objects in Shared Pool Memory

♦ Configure initialization parameters related to Shared Pool Memory

♦ Understand and configure the Large Pool

♦ Understand and configure Java Pool

Memory is a fundamental component of the logical structure of an Oracle instance. It is used as temporary storage to enhance performance. In a previous chapter, you learned the importance of the buffer cache and redo log buffer to performance and how improper configuration of these structures can impact the performance of the database. In this chapter, you learn how to tune another major SGA (System Global Area) structure, the Shared Pool Memory. To fully understand tuning, you need to learn the role of the shared pool and the internal components of this memory structure. This chapter presents guidelines for properly configuring the shared pool and presents you with steps for its diagnosis. This chapter also demonstrates how to peek into the Shared Pool Memory to determine what SQL statements are hampering performance. Finally, the chapter presents a brief overview of the large pool memory and Java pool memory.

Performance Problem

This section outlines an actual performance problem. As you look it over, imagine yourself as the DBA who reported it and keep it in mind as you proceed through the chapter. The chapter presents concepts relevant to the problem. In the first Hands-on Project at the end of the chapter, you are asked to use the concepts you have learned to provide a solution, or partial solution, to this performance problem.

From: Joe Moe
Date: 22-Sep-99 17:13
Subject: Library Cache

Hello Gurus,

I have increased shared_pool_size to 210 MB, and I still get PINHITRATIO (pinhits/pins) on V$LIBRARYCACHE at around 72 percent, but HITRATIO (pins/(pins+reloads)) is over 99 percent.

This is a small database, less than 210 MB, and it's used only by the inventory system. Judging from the operating system, we are already short of memory. Do I conclude that this software inventory system is poorly written in SQL, or is my shared_pool_size too small? (I tried setting SHARED_POOL_SIZE=425 MB, and still got a PINHITRATIO just above 80 percent.)

SHARED POOL MEMORY OVERVIEW

This section presents an overview of the functionality and purpose of Shared Pool Memory, which is an important structure of the SGA. It is used to cache SQL statements, PL/SQL blocks, and other memory objects to reduce CPU consumption and I/O trips to data files. You, as the DBA, should carefully configure this memory structure to prevent performance problems. Figure 4–1 displays the Oracle architecture highlighting the Shared Pool Memory and two other independent memory structures, which are presented later in this chapter, the Large pool and the Java pool.

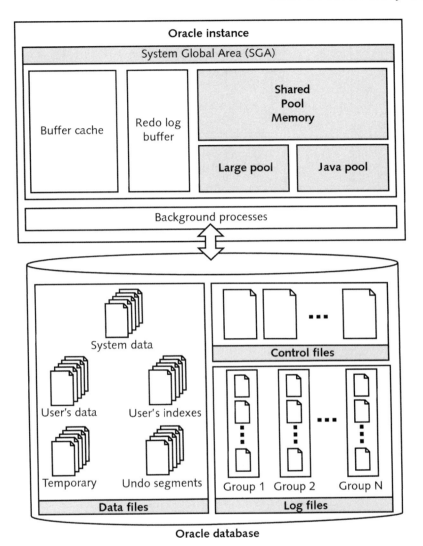

Figure 4-1   System Global Area structure of Oracle architecture

As you know, memory is used to cache data for faster access. There are six classifications for this data, each with a specific memory area and a specific method for its management. Figure 4-2 shows the six classifications.

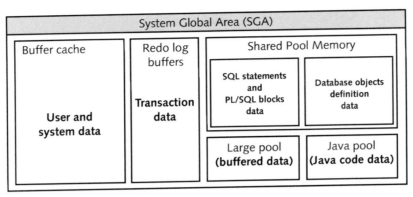

Figure 4-2   Types of data cached in the System Global Area

- **User and system data:** Stored and retrieved in a data file and cached in the buffer cache

- **Transaction data:** Consists of all the DMLs and DDLs issued against the database. Data is cached in the log buffer and ultimately stored in the redo log files.

- **SQL statements and PL/SQL blocks data:** Consists of the SQL and PL/SQL code issued against the database. It is cached in Shared Pool Memory.

- **Database objects definition data:** Retrieved from system data files and cached in the shared pool. Database objects definition data contains metadata about the database object structures and privileges.

- **Java code data:** Consists of Java-related code, which is loaded and executed by different sessions. It is cached in the Java pool.

- **Buffered data:** Can be from any of the above classifications, but is buffered in the large pool

Notice that the Shared Pool Memory has two types of data, code and database object definitions. In the next section you examine how this data is cached and why it is cached. You begin by looking at how a SQL statement or PL/SQL block is processed.

Processing SQL Statements

SQL statements are processed in three steps. When a user submits a SQL statement, it is first parsed for syntax validity, user privileges are verified, and a plan for retrieving data is created. Second, the plan created in the first step is executed. Last, the data is retrieved and submitted to the user. Figure 4-3 illustrates this process in detail.

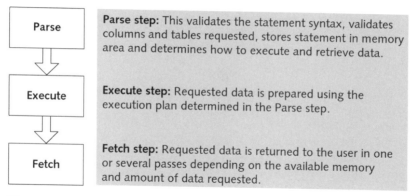

Parse step: This validates the statement syntax, validates columns and tables requested, stores statement in memory area and determines how to execute and retrieve data.

Execute step: Requested data is prepared using the execution plan determined in the Parse step.

Fetch step: Requested data is returned to the user in one or several passes depending on the available memory and amount of data requested.

Figure 4-3   Processing a SQL statement

In this process, the Parse step is the most expensive, because it consumes more CPU and I/O resources than the other processing stages.

Processing PL/SQL Blocks

When a PL/SQL block is submitted or called for execution, it is processed in the same steps shown in Figure 4-3, except there are specific steps only for PL/SQL, as shown in Figure 4-4.

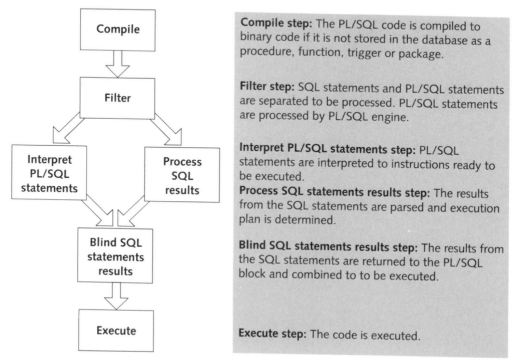

Compile step: The PL/SQL code is compiled to binary code if it is not stored in the database as a procedure, function, trigger or package.

Filter step: SQL statements and PL/SQL statements are separated to be processed. PL/SQL statements are processed by PL/SQL engine.

Interpret PL/SQL statements step: PL/SQL statements are interpreted to instructions ready to be executed.
Process SQL statements results step: The results from the SQL statements are parsed and execution plan is determined.

Blind SQL statements results step: The results from the SQL statements are returned to the PL/SQL block and combined to to be executed.

Execute step: The code is executed.

Figure 4-4   Processing a PL/SQL block

As you can see from this process, if the code is not compiled, an extra compilation step is executed. For this reason, DBA experts recommend the use of stored procedures, functions, and packages because code is already compiled. You should also note that SQL statements are processed as shown in Figure 4-3.

Now that you have a theoretical understanding of the processing of SQL statements and PL/SQL blocks, you can examine a situation you might typically face as a DBA. Suppose you had an application that called a SQL statement frequently. That statement is parsed only once because it is found in memory for all subsequent calls; how do you think this affects the performance of the application? If you guessed that performance would be enhanced, you're right. Instead of being parsed every time it is called, the Oracle server uses the processed statement found in memory. You might be wondering how Oracle recognizes if the submitted statement is already parsed and can be found in memory. Oracle has a hash function algorithm that is called when a user submits a SQL statement. This function takes the SQL text as input and generates a hash value as output as shown in Figure 4-5.

Figure 4-5   Hash function process

If Oracle finds the hash value in memory, this means that the SQL statement is already in memory. Next, Oracle compares the SQL text to the text in memory to ensure that it is identical. If the two statements are identical, Oracle uses the statement in memory. In this case, the term "identical" means that the two statements must have the same pattern of characters and the same number of white spaces. (A white space is a blank, tab, or new line). If the two statements are not the same, the submitted SQL statement is parsed.

Figure 4-6 outlines the detailed process executed when a SELECT statement is submitted. Again, the most expensive step in this process is the Parse statement step; because this step requires many tasks for completion, it consumes CPU resources. These tasks are presented in the next section.

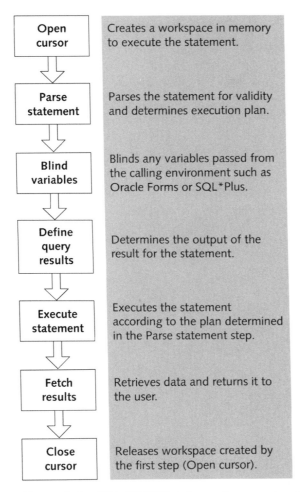

Figure 4-6   SQL SELECT statement processing tasks

Parsing Process

The parsing process comprises six main tasks, and each is performed every time a statement is parsed. These tasks ensure the validity of the statement as well as the validity of the selected columns, and determine the best method to retrieve the data. Finally, the parsed statement is submitted and the parsing details are cached in the Shared Pool Memory. Figure 4-7 illustrates this process.

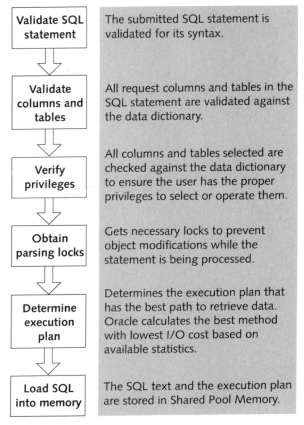

Validate SQL statement	The submitted SQL statement is validated for its syntax.
Validate columns and tables	All request columns and tables in the SQL statement are validated against the data dictionary.
Verify privileges	All columns and tables selected are checked against the data dictionary to ensure the user has the proper privileges to select or operate them.
Obtain parsing locks	Gets necessary locks to prevent object modifications while the statement is being processed.
Determine execution plan	Determines the execution plan that has the best path to retrieve data. Oracle calculates the best method with lowest I/O cost based on available statistics.
Load SQL into memory	The SQL text and the execution plan are stored in Shared Pool Memory.

Figure 4-7   Parsing process steps

SHARED POOL MEMORY PERFORMANCE TERMS

This section presents the common terminology found in Oracle documentation that you need to understand to interpret the results of Shared Pool Memory performance statistics.

- **Hard parse:** The parsing process outlined in Figure 4-7. When a statement is submitted and is not found in memory, a hard parse is performed. Hard parses use considerably more resources than soft parses.

- **Soft parse:** Occurs when a SQL statement is found in memory and can be reused. Obviously, the ideal situation is to have the most frequently submitted statements parsed once and cached in memory.

- **Execute call:** A call to execute a SQL statement. If the statement is already parsed, a soft parse occurs, but if the statement has been aged out from memory, a hard parse occurs.

- **Parse call:** A call to parse a SQL statement because it was not found in memory

- **Bind variable:** The process of passing a variable from the calling environment such as SQL*Plus, Oracle Forms, Oracle Reports, and other Oracle development tools

- **Hash function:** An algorithm used to convert the submitted SQL statement to a hash value, which can be compared to hash values stored in memory to determine if the statement is already in memory

- **Reloads:** The number of times a cached SQL statement was reloaded or reparsed because the statement was aged out

- **Invalidations:** The number of times a cached SQL statement became invalid and could not be shared because there was a modification to the database objects used by the statement

- **Library cache hit:** Synonymous with soft parse

- **Library cache miss:** Synonymous with hard parse

TERMS FOR INTERNAL STRUCTURES OF THE SHARED POOL MEMORY

The Shared Pool Memory is partitioned into different memory structures, each serving a specific purpose, as shown in Figure 4–8. The structures are defined in the following list:

- **Library cache:** One of the major memory spaces of the shared pool memory. It is used to cache SQL statements, PL/SQL blocks, and other object code used by the application.

- **Data dictionary cache:** Another major memory space of the shared pool memory. It is used to store database object definitions temporarily.

- **Character set structure:** A space in memory used to store the character set used by the Oracle instance

- **Locks structures:** Data structures used to synchronize and coordinate access to database objects

- **Latches structures:** Data structures used as mechanisms to protect memory while it is in use

- **Enqueues structures:** Data structures used for serial access to the database in a Real Application Cluster (RAC) or in a standalone instance

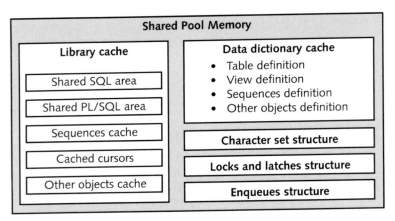

Figure 4-8   Shared Pool Memory internal structures

LIBRARY CACHE

The library cache is a major structure of the Shared Pool Memory. It is used to store application code that is in use. In this context, code is SQL statements that include the following: anonymous or stored PL/SQL blocks (procedures, functions, triggers, and packages), cursors, sequences, objects, and other codes. The library cache contains all parsed memory objects for future executions. When a statement is called and is found in the library cache, it is considered a GETHIT and a soft parse is performed.

The Oracle instance controls and allocates the library cache memory depending on database activities. Oracle takes memory from the shared pool memory and gives it to the library cache based on demand. You cannot allocate memory directly to the library cache. If you want to increase the library cache, you must allocate more memory to the Shared Pool Memory.

The library cache is divided into pieces of memory structures called namespaces. A **namespace** is an area or section of the library cache used to hold specific data types such as SQL statements, triggers, and data as listed in the following query results. You can look at the library cache namespaces by displaying the contents of the **V$LIBRARYCACHE** performance dynamic view. The following query displays all namespaces in the database with statistics for each structure. Interpretation of the result is presented later in this chapter.

```
SQL> SELECT NAMESPACE, GETS, GETHITS, GETHITRATIO
  2     FROM V$LIBRARYCACHE
  3  /

NAMESPACE            GETS    GETHITS GETHITRATIO
--------------- ---------- ---------- -----------
SQL AREA            18125      17956 .990675862
TABLE/PROCEDURE     18920      18701 .988424947
BODY                    2          0          0
TRIGGER                 3          0          0
INDEX                5897       5855 .992877734
CLUSTER               159        152 .955974843
OBJECT                  0          0          1
PIPE                    0          0          1
JAVA SOURCE             0          0          1
JAVA RESOURCE           0          0          1
JAVA DATA               0          0          1
```

Oracle provides another performance dynamic view called V$LIBRARY_CACHE_MEMORY. The contents of this view are aggregated summaries of the cached objects in the library cache for each object type. Table 4-1 presents the structure of the view.

Table 4-1 V$LIBRARY_CACHE_MEMORY

Column	Description
LC_NAMESPACE	Library cache namespace
LC_INUSE_MEMORY_OBJECTS	Number of objects currently in use in the library cache
LC_INUSE_MEMORY_SIZE	Size of objects in use in library cache; value is expressed in MB
LC_FREEABLE_MEMORY_OBJECTS	Number of objects in the library cache that can be freed
LC_FREEABLE_MEMORY_SIZE	Size of objects that can be freed from library cache, value is expressed in MB

NOTE Use the V$FIXED_VIEW_DEFINITION view to get the view definition (QUERY) for any performance dynamic view as follows:

```
SQL> SELECT VIEW_DEFINITION
  2     FROM V$FIXED_VIEW_DEFINITION
  3   WHERE VIEW_NAME=UPPER('&view_name')
  4  /
```

You can use V$SESSION_OBJECT_CACHE to get a full statistics report on cached objects for the current session. The following code segment displays the contents of this query. For example, the results of this query show (in the highlighted row) that there are about 66

SQL statements that are cached in the library cache consuming less than 1 MB, and that there are about 896 SQL statements that could be freed from the library cache; they are not used as frequently by the Oracle server because it is using the Least Recent Used (LRU) algorithm. These statements that can be freed are consuming about 5 MB. The results in the code segment that follows show all cached objects in memory and identify the number of objects and memory consumed for each namespace:

```
SQL> SELECT LC_NAMESPACE,
  2          LC_INUSE_MEMORY_OBJECTS INUSE_OBJECTS,
  3          LC_INUSE_MEMORY_SIZE INUSE_SIZE,
  4          LC_FREEABLE_MEMORY_OBJECTS FREEABLE_OBJECTS,
  5          LC_FREEABLE_MEMORY_SIZE FREEABLE_SIZE
  6     FROM V$LIBRARY_CACHE_MEMORY
  7  /
```

LC_NAMESPACE	INUSE_OBJECTS	INUSE_SIZE	FREEABLE_OBJECTS	FREEABLE_SIZE
BODY	2	0	26	0
CLUSTER	13	0	2	0
INDEX	8	0	7	0
JAVA DATA	0	0	0	0
JAVA RESOURCE	0	0	0	0
JAVA SOURCE	0	0	0	0
OBJECT	0	0	0	0
OTHER/SYSTEM	0	0	15	0
PIPE	0	0	0	0
SQL AREA	66	0	896	5
TABLE/PROCEDURE	59	0	817	1
TRIGGER	0	0	18	0

DATA DICTIONARY CACHE

The data dictionary is also a part of memory in the Shared Pool Memory. Like the library cache, this structure cannot be controlled and sized directly. You indirectly control memory allocated to it by configuring the total memory allocated to the Shared Pool Memory.

This structure plays an important role in storing data definitions of database objects. For example, if you submit a query to retrieve data from the CUSTOMERS table, Oracle retrieves the structure definition from the system data file and stores it in the data dictionary cache if it has not been retrieved before. The next time a query retrieves data from this table, Oracle uses the definition stored in memory. This process reduces I/O trips to retrieve this metadata from system data files.

Similar to the library cache, the data dictionary cache is divided into several memory structures for the different types of database objects. You can use the V$ROWCACHE dynamic performance view to list these structures along with their statistics as shown in the following code segment:

```
SQL> SELECT PARAMETER, COUNT, USAGE, FIXED
  2     FROM V$ROWCACHE
  3     ORDER BY 1
  4  /

PARAMETER                            COUNT      USAGE      FIXED
--------------------------------  ----------  ----------  ----------
dc_app_role                            0          0          0
dc_constraints                         0          0          0
dc_database_links                      0          0          0
dc_encrypted_objects                   0          0          0
dc_encryption_profiles                 0          0          0
dc_files                               0          0          0
dc_free_extents                        0          0          0
dc_global_oids                         6          6          0
dc_histogram_data                      0          0          0
dc_histogram_data_values               0          0          0
dc_histogram_defs                     24         24          0
dc_object_ids                        220        220         55
dc_objects                           223        223         55
dc_outlines                            0          0          0
dc_partition_scns                      0          0          0
dc_profiles                            1          1          0
dc_qmc_cache_entries                   0          0          0
dc_rollback_segments                  22         22          1
dc_segments                          185        185          0
dc_sequences                           1          1          0
dc_table_scns                          0          0          0
dc_tablespace_quotas                   0          0          0
dc_tablespaces                         3          3          0
dc_used_extents                        0          0          0
dc_user_grants                        16         16          0
dc_usernames                          10         10          0
dc_users                              26         26          0
dc_users                               0          0          0
```

These definitions may increase your understanding of the previous code segment:

- dc stands for data dictionary.
- Parameter column is the memory structure within the data dictionary.
- Count column is the number of objects within the memory structure.
- Usage column is the number of valid objects that can be used.
- Fixed column number is the number of objects that are permanent in the data dictionary area.

As you can see from the results in this code segment, there is a row for each structure within the data dictionary. For example, the highlighted row in the results shows the dc_segments structure, which stores definitions of tables used in SQL statements.

CONFIGURING THE SHARED POOL MEMORY

Shared Pool Memory is configured by setting the SHARED_POOL_SIZE parameter. This parameter can be set in the initialization file when the database is started, or it can be set dynamically while the database is open. The default value of the SHARED_POOL_SIZE is 50 MB. Proper configuration of the Shared Pool Memory prevents many performance problems.

 Use this guideline: Shared Pool Memory should be 30 percent to 40 percent of the total memory of the SGA.

TIP

As with other memory structures, you can size the Shared Pool Memory when creating a new database, based on existing databases. For databases already in operation, you can diagnose the Shared Pool Memory as explained later in this chapter. Use the following statement to set the Shared Pool Memory to 40 MB.

```
SQL> ALTER SYSTEM SET SHARED_POOL_SIZE = 40
  /
```

For a new database that you are creating manually, you can add this statement SHARED_POOL_MEMORY = 40M SHARED_POOL_SIZE in the initialization file. Or you can set the Shared Pool Memory option to 40 MB if you are using the Database Configuration Assistant as shown in Figure 4-9.

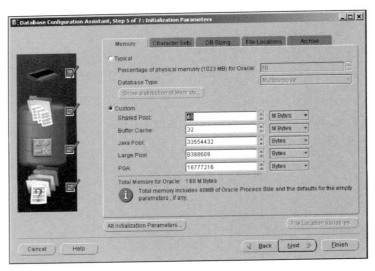

Figure 4-9   Using the Database Configuration Assistant

Configuring the Shared Pool Memory

NOTE

Shared Pool Memory size is rounded to the next SGA granule, as is the buffer cache.

You can change the size of the Shared Pool Memory dynamically by issuing the following statement:

```
SQL> ALTER SYSTEM SET SHARED_POOL_SIZE = 8M
  2  /

System altered.

SQL> SHOW PARAMETER SHARED_POOL_SIZE

NAME                                    TYPE        VALUE
------------------------------------    ----------- ---------
shared_pool_size                        big integer 8388608
```

You can also issue the following statement to list all the different structures and their corresponding sizes in the Shared Pool Memory, specifically the library cache and data dictionary cache:

```
SQL> SELECT * FROM V$SGASTAT
  2   WHERE POOL = 'shared pool'
  3  /

POOL         NAME                             BYTES
-----------  --------------------------  ----------
shared pool  enqueue                         171860
shared pool  KGK heap                          3756
shared pool  KQR M PO                        260628
shared pool  KQR S PO                         57344
shared pool  KQR S SO                          4096
shared pool  sessions                        410720
shared pool  sql area                       1362872
shared pool  1M buffer                      2098176
shared pool  KGLS heap                       598048
shared pool  processes                       144000
shared pool  parameters                        1044
shared pool  free memory                    4900420
shared pool  PL/SQL DIANA                    389472
shared pool  FileOpenBlock                   695504
shared pool  PL/SQL MPCODE                    31460
shared pool  library cache                  2074324
shared pool  miscellaneous                  3859380
shared pool  MTTR advisory                     8456
shared pool  PLS non-lib hp                    3296
shared pool  joxs heap init                    4220
shared pool  kgl simulator                   564060
shared pool  sim memory hea                   21164
shared pool  table definiti                     168
shared pool  trigger defini                    1700
shared pool  trigger inform                    1076
shared pool  trigger source                     352
shared pool  Checkpoint queue                282304
shared pool  VIRTUAL CIRCUITS                265160
shared pool  dictionary cache               1610880
shared pool  ksm_file2sga region             148652
shared pool  KSXR receive buffers           1033000
shared pool  character set object            274508
shared pool  FileIdentificatonBlock          323292
shared pool  KSXR large reply queue          166104
shared pool  message pool freequeue          834752
shared pool  KSXR pending messages que       841036
shared pool  event statistics per sess      1718360
shared pool  fixed allocation callback          180
```

The following query shows the total size of shared pool memory in use:

```
SQL> SELECT SUM(BYTES)/1024/1024 TOTAL_SIZE_IN_MB
  2    FROM V$SGASTAT
  3    WHERE POOL = 'shared pool'
  4  /

TOTAL_SIZE_IN_MB
----------------
              24
```

4

Memory objects cached in Shared Pool Memory, whether they are in library cache or data dictionary cache, are subject to the Least Recent Used (LRU) mechanism to determine which object to age out from the Shared Pool Memory when space is needed. An object that is used more often has a better chance of staying in memory. Therefore, if the Shared Pool Memory is sized too small for a database that is highly active, memory objects in cache are aged out sooner, and therefore more parsing and more I/O trips occur.

Reserved Shared Pool Memory

Sometimes there might be instances in which your application requires you to load and cache a very large stored procedure in contiguous Shared Pool Memory. You can set aside a percentage of the Shared Pool Memory for this purpose by setting the SHARED_POOL_RESERVED_SIZE parameter. If this parameter is not specified in the SPFILE or initialization file, it is set to the default, which is usually five percent of the Shared Pool Memory size, as shown in the following code segment:

```
SQL> SHOW PARAMETER SHARED_POOL

NAME                                 TYPE         VALUE
------------------------------------ ------------ -------
shared_pool_reserved_size            big integer  419430
shared_pool_size                     big integer  8388608
```

NOTE

SHARED_POOL_RESERVED_SIZE cannot be changed dynamically.

The maximum size for reserved Shared Pool Memory is 10 percent of the Shared Pool Memory size. Follow these steps for a quick demonstration of how the maximum size is retained:

Step 1: Determine the size of Shared Pool Memory.

```
SQL> SELECT VALUE
  2    FROM V$PARAMETER
  3    WHERE NAME = 'shared_pool_size'
  4  /
```

Step 2: Allocate more than half of the Shared Pool Memory to the reserved pool by using the following statement:

```
SQL> ALTER SYSTEM
  2    SET SHARED_POOL_RESERVED_SIZE=6M SCOPE=SPFILE
  3  /
```

Step 3: Stop the database.

```
SQL> SHUTDOWN IMMEDIATE
```

Step 4: Start the database.

```
SQL> STARTUP
```

You receive the following error:

```
ORA-00093: shared_pool_reserved_size must be between 5000 and
4194304 <4194304 is 50% of 8388608, shared_pool_size?>
<< is 5000 a min?>
```

TIP

To restart the database after making the change to shared_pool_reserved_size, use the following: SQL>startup pfile=C:\Oracle\admin*dbname*\pfile\init.ora.

Oracle provides a dynamic performance view called V$SHARED_POOL_RESERVED, which contains statistics about the reserved Shared Pool Memory. It is used to obtain general values about the number of objects cached, free space, used space, and other statistical values about the memory objects cached in this memory. Three indicators inform you whether or not the reserved Shared Pool Memory requires more space or less space. Table 4–2 presents these indicators with their thresholds:

Table 4-2 Shared Pool Memory reserved pool indicators

Indicator	Threshold	Action
FREE_SPACE	Consistently greater than 50 percent	Decrease the size of SHARED_POOL_RESERVED _SIZE
REQUEST_FAILURES column value	Consistently greater than 0	Increase the size of the Shared Pool Memory, because it is too small.
REQUEST_MISSES Column value	Consistently less than or equal to 0	Decrease the size of the Shared Pool Memory.

4

SHARED POOL SIZE ADVICE

A DBA was being interviewed for a position at a large financial company. After meeting several people on the team, he met a person who introduced himself as the principal DBA of the team and who then pulled out a piece of a paper with ten questions. The interviewer asked the interviewee one question after another until he reached the last question. At this point, the interviewer announced that, so far, the interviewee had answered all questions correctly, and the last question was crucial. The interviewer said, "Suppose the database is performing poorly and you know that you tuned every SQL statement that the application is using and submitting to the database. You have allocated enough memory for all SGA functions. What would you do next?"

Without hesitation, the interviewee responded that memory is an important resource and using it wisely and efficiently is even more important. Therefore, he would investigate further, and he would use the new feature of Oracle9*i*—Shared Pool Size Advice—to guide him. If everything checked out, he would diagnose other areas.

Even though the interviewer was expecting a different answer—one more in the line of the tuning process—he was impressed to learn about the new Oracle9*i* feature.

Like the Buffer Cache Size Advice feature presented in Chapter 2, Oracle's Shared Pool Size Advice feature provides advisory statistics for the Shared Pool Memory, specifically for its library cache portion. As stated by the interviewee in the preceding scenario, memory is an asset that should be used wisely and efficiently. Despite the low cost of memory compared to ten or twenty years ago, memory resources should not be wasted. Some database administrators inadvertently overallocate memory to structures of the Oracle SGA thinking that more memory yields better performance, or at least will not impact performance negatively. Because of this myth, you should take advantage of any tool, such as the Shared Pool Size Advice feature, which can enhance your ability to configure memory to an optimal state.

NOTE You should always keep 50 percent of the server memory free for the operating system and other applications. The other 50 percent can be allocated to the Oracle instance(s).

Although you have to turn on the Buffer Cache Size Advice, you do not need to turn on the Shared Pool Size Advice. These advisory statistics are always collected and can be viewed two ways: by using either Oracle Enterprise Manager, or by using the dynamic performance view V$SHARED_POOL_ADVICE. Table 4-3 presents the structure definition of this view.

Table 4-3   V$SHARED_POOL_ADVICE view

Column	Description
SHARED_POOL_SIZE_FOR_ESTIMATE	Shared pool memory size for estimating in MB
SHARED_POOL_SIZE_FACTOR	Size factor compared to current size of the shared pool memory. Factor 1 indicates current size
ESTD_LC_SIZE	Estimated library cache size
ESTD_LC_MEMORY_OBJECTS	Estimated number of objects that are in the library cache
ESTD_LC_TIME_SAVED	Estimated parse time savings in seconds because it was found in the library cache
ESTD_LC_TIME_SAVED_FACTOR	Estimated parse time factor compared to Shared Pool Memory current size
ESTD_LC_MEMORY_OBJECT_HITS	Estimated number of times an object was found in the library cache

These advisory statistics are based on database activities and can be interpreted to forecast time savings when parsing SQL statements if the size of the Shared Pool Memory is increased or decreased. You can retrieve this advisory data at any time from V$SHARED_POOL_ADVICE by issuing the following query:

```
SQL> SELECT SHARED_POOL_SIZE_FOR_ESTIMATE ESTD_SIZE,
  2         SHARED_POOL_SIZE_FACTOR SIZE_FACTOR,
  3         ESTD_LC_SIZE LC_SIZE,
  4         ESTD_LC_MEMORY_OBJECTS OBJECTS,
  5         ESTD_LC_TIME_SAVED TIME_SAVED,
  6         ESTD_LC_TIME_SAVED_FACTOR TIME_SAVED_FACTOR,
  7         ESTD_LC_MEMORY_OBJECT_HITS OBJS_HITS
  8    FROM V$SHARED_POOL_ADVICE
  9  /


ESTD_SIZE SIZE_FACTOR   LC_SIZE    OBJECTS TIME_SAVED TIME_SAVED_FACTOR OBJS_HITS
--------- ----------- --------- ---------- ---------- ----------------- ---------
        4          .5         4       2080       2732             .9964    607732
        8           1         7       3517       2742                 1    609336
       12         1.5        10       5789       2752            1.0036    611250
       16           2        13       7493       2756            1.0051    612000
```

Looking at the ESTD_LC_TIME_SAVED_FACTOR column in the results of this query tells you that increasing the Shared Pool Memory from its current size of 8 MB to 12 MB saves parse time only slightly and therefore yields little enhancement in database performance.

Also, if you reduce the Shared Pool Memory from its current size to 4 MB, the impact on parse time alters performance only a little. You should remember that this view provides an estimated parse time savings and has to be consistent before you take any action.

From the Oracle Enterprise Manager console>Instance>Configuration>Memory option, you can click on the Advice button next to the Shared Pool text box to display the Shared Pool. See Figures 4-10 and 4-11.

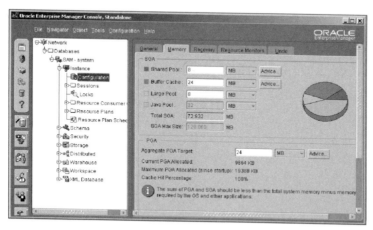

Figure 4-10   Oracle Enterprise Manager console instance configuration option

Figure 4-11 shows that an incremental increase in the Shared Pool Memory size only slightly affects the parsed time savings. For example, if the Shared Pool Memory is increased from the current value of 8 MB to 12 MB, the time saved factor for parsing is enhanced only by 0.01 percent, which is not significant.

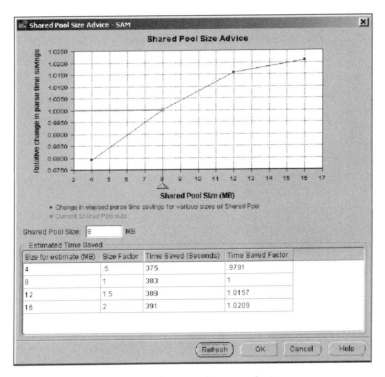

Figure 4-11   Shared Pool Size Advice analysis

DIAGNOSING SHARED POOL MEMORY

Judy attended an Oracle9*i* seminar about diagnosing and tuning memory. She came out of the meeting energized by the speaker and thinking of his analogy that the Oracle engine is like a car engine and the performance dynamic views and other tuning tools are like the car dashboard that has indicators giving hints of how the car is performing. The speaker had emphasized the importance of not over-allocating or under-allocating memory to prevent performance problems and avoid memory wastage. At the same time, he challenged the audience to take diagnosis and monitoring as serious performance measures.

Diagnosing SGA configuration cannot be done as one step, but it is possible to diagnose each part of the SGA. In previous chapters, you learned how to diagnose the buffer cache and redo log buffer. In this chapter you learn how to diagnose the Shared Pool Memory and to diagnose sectors of the Shared Pool Memory, the library cache, and data dictionary. Although there is no particular ratio for the entire Shared Pool Memory to determine whether or not it is sized properly, there are many useful indirect ratios. These ratios indicate precisely the Shared Pool Memory configuration.

Diagnosing Library Cache

As stated earlier in this chapter, the library cache is a major portion of the Shared Pool Memory. This section explains the library cache view and then shows you how to obtain various indicators and ratios.

The library cache hit ratio is one of the indicators used to diagnose the Shared Pool Memory configuration. This ratio is obtained from the dynamic performance view V$LIBRARYCACHE. This view provides statistical data about each namespace of the library cache. The most frequently used columns of V$LIBRARYCACHE are defined in Table 4-4.

4

Table 4-4 Most frequently used columns of V$LIBRARYCACHE view

Column	Description
NAMESPACE	Name of memory area within the library cache
GETS	Number of object requests for this namespace
GETHITS	Number of object requests for this namespace found in memory
GETHITRATIO	Ratio of GETHITS over GETS
PINS	Number of times objects of this namespace were executed or requested from memory
PINHITS	Number of times objects of this namespace to be executed were found in memory
PINHITRATIO	Ratio of PINHITS over PINS
RELOADS	Number of times objects of this namespace were reloaded into memory because objects were flushed
INVALIDATIONS	Number of times objects were invalidated because it was not efficient or safe to reuse the object

Using this view, you can get the following indicators and ratios:

1. **GETHITRATIO value:** This has a threshold of 90 percent. A consistent value that is greater than 90 percent indicates that objects within the library cache are being aged out, possibly because the Shared Pool Memory is not large enough. Use the following query to get this ratio:

```
SQL> SELECT NAMESPACE, GETHITRATIO
  2     FROM V$LIBRARYCACHE
  3  /

NAMESPACE          GETHITRATIO
---------------    -----------
SQL AREA            .998418306
TABLE/PROCEDURE     .997928182
BODY                .727272727
TRIGGER             .727272727
INDEX               .998939448
CLUSTER             .955696203
OBJECT                       1
PIPE                         1
JAVA SOURCE                  1
JAVA RESOURCE                1
JAVA DATA                    1
```

This query caused the display of the GETHITRATIO for each namespace. However, you could use the following query to display the GETHITRATIO for the whole library cache. This query, in some instances, may display a misleading ratio, especially if there are no objects in the namespace:

```
SQL> SELECT SUM(GETHITS)/SUM(GETS) LIBRARYCACHE_HIT_RATIO
  2     FROM V$LIBRARYCACHE
  3  /

LIBRARYCACHE_GETHITRATIO
------------------------
               .998255542
```

2. **PINHITRATIO value:** This has a threshold of 90 percent. A consistent value less than 90 percent indicates that objects that were executed were not found in memory. This is an effect of an undersized Shared Pool Memory. Use the two following queries to get this ratio for each namespace and for the whole library cache:

```
SQL> SELECT NAMESPACE, PINHITRATIO
  2     FROM V$LIBRARYCACHE
  3  /

NAMESPACE          PINHITRATIO
---------------    -----------
SQL AREA           .998924937
TABLE/PROCEDURE    .997247247
BODY                       .8
TRIGGER            .727272727
INDEX              .998959958
CLUSTER            .962962963
OBJECT                      1
PIPE                        1
JAVA SOURCE                 1
JAVA RESOURCE               1
JAVA DATA                   1
```

4

```
SQL> SELECT SUM(PINHITS)/SUM(PINS) LIBRARYCACHE_HIT_RATIO
  2     FROM V$LIBRARYCACHE
  3  /

LIVRARCACHE_PINS_HIT_RATIO
--------------------------
                .998486288
```

3. **RELOADS Ratio:** This has a threshold of five percent of the reloads over the number of cached objects in the library cache. A consistently large number of reloads indicates that the objects were reloaded because the objects were flushed. The flushing could be caused by infrequent use of the object or in inadequate size of the shared pool. Use the following query to determine this ratio:

```
SQL> SELECT (RELOAD_COUNT/OBJECT_COUNT)*100 RELOADS_RATIO
  2     FROM (SELECT SUM(RELOADS) RELOAD_COUNT
  3              FROM V$LIBRARYCACHE
  4          ),
  5          (SELECT COUNT(*) OBJECT_COUNT
  6              FROM V$DB_OBJECT_CACHE
  7          )
  8  /
RELOADS_RATIO
--------------------------
         1.1111111
```

4. **INVALIDATIONS Ratio:** This has a threshold of one percent of the invalidations to the number of cached objects. A consistently large number of

invalidations indicates that the objects were invalidated due to a change in the database object or privileges. Use the following query to get this ratio:

```
SQL> SELECT (INVALIDATION_COUNT/OBJECT_COUNT)*100 INVALIDATION_RATIO
  2     FROM (SELECT SUM(RELOADS) INVALIDATION_COUNT
  3              FROM V$LIBRARYCACHE
  4          ),
  5          (SELECT COUNT(*) OBJECT_COUNT
  6              FROM V$DB_OBJECT_CACHE
  7          )
  8  /

INVALIDATION_RATIO
------------------
        0.38504155
```

5. **RELOADS to PINS Ratio:** This has a threshold of one percent of the number of pins to the number of reloads. A consistently high ratio indicates that the Shared Pool Memory is not large enough. Use this query to get the ratio shown in the following code segment:

```
SQL> SELECT SUM(RELOADS)/SUM(PINS)*100 RELOADS_PINS_RATIO
  2     FROM V$LIBRARYCACHE
  3  /

RELAODS_PINS_RATIO
------------------
        .001846378
```

Diagnosing Data Dictionary Cache

Like the library cache, the data dictionary can be diagnosed to determine if the Shared Pool Memory is adequately configured or not. This section explains the elements of a dynamic performance view and how to use it for data dictionary cache diagnosis. A diagnosis of the data dictionary cache can be made by using the dynamic performance view V$ROW CACHE. Table 4-5 presents definitions for the most frequently used columns of this view:

Table 4-5 Definition of the most frequently used columns of V$ROWCACHE view

Column	Description
PARAMETER	Name of the dictionary object type cache
COUNT	Number of objects cached for this parameter
USAGE	Number of used objects that are cached in the data dictionary cache for this parameter
FIXED	Number of objects that are permanent in the data dictionary cache for this parameter

Column	Description
GETS	Number of requests for this parameter
GETMISSES	Number of requests for this parameter that were not found in memory
MODIFICATIONS	Number of changes to cached database objects
FLUSHES	Number of cached objects flushed from memory

4

From the V$ROWCACHE view you can issue the following query to display data dictionary statistics for each data dictionary object. The result of this query shows the number of times a request was issued for an object of each parameter type and the number of times a request was not found in data dictionary cache:

```
SQL> SELECT PARAMETER, GETS, GETMISSES
  2     FROM V$ROWCACHE
  3  /

PARAMETER                              GETS   GETMISSES
------------------------------   ----------  ----------
dc_free_extents                           0           0
dc_used_extents                           0           0
dc_segments                         4685060     3136577
dc_tablespaces                          178          62
dc_tablespace_quotas                      0           0
dc_files                                  0           0
dc_users                             384833      178242
dc_rollback_segments                  38881          21
dc_objects                          8787654     3473497
dc_global_oids                           16           6
dc_constraints                            0           0
dc_object_ids                      21323015     5525919
dc_sequences                              7           7
dc_usernames                        1833706      720836
dc_database_links                         0           0
dc_histogram_defs                       114         103
dc_table_scns                             0           0
dc_outlines                               0           0
dc_profiles                               7           7
dc_encrypted_objects                      0           0
dc_encryption_profiles                    0           0
dc_qmc_cache_entries                      0           0
dc_users                                  0           0
dc_histogram_data                         0           0
dc_histogram_data_values                  0           0
dc_partition_scns                         0           0
dc_user_grants                         7582         162
dc_app_role                               0           0
```

Based on this query, you can determine the percentage of requests that missed. The following query displays the GETMISSESS ratio for each dictionary parameter type. The threshold of this ratio is 15 percent. If this value is consistently higher than 15 percent, you should consider increasing the Shared Pool Memory:

```
SQL> SELECT parameter,
  2          (SUM(GETMISSES)/SUM(GETS))*100 GETMISSES_RATIO
  3     FROM V$ROWCACHE
  4    WHERE gets > 0
  5    GROUP BY parameter
  6  /

PARAMETER                              GETMISSES_RATIO
-------------------------------------- ---------------
dc_constraints                                    53.8
dc_free_extents                                   10.4
dc_histogram_defs                                   .7
dc_object_ids                                       .1
dc_objects                                          .5
dc_profiles                                         .0
dc_rollback_segments                                .0
dc_segments                                         .7
dc_sequence_grants                                 4.3
dc_sequences                                        .4
dc_synonyms                                         .6
dc_tablespace_quotas                               4.9
dc_tablespaces                                      .0
dc_used_extents                                   38.8
dc_user_grants                                      .0
dc_usernames                                        .0
dc_users                                            .0
```

You can get the data dictionary GETMISSES ratio for the whole structure by issuing the following query:

```
SQL> SELECT (SUM(GETMISSES)/SUM(GETS))*100 GETMISSES_RATIO
  2     FROM V$ROWCACHE
  3    WHERE gets > 0
  4  /

GETMISSES_RATIO
---------------
             .1
```

Also, you can derive the corollary to the GETMISSES ratio, which is called the GETHIT ratio, using this query:

```
SQL> SELECT (SUM(GETS - GETMISSES - FIXED))/SUM(GETS)*100 GETHIT_RATIO
  2    FROM V$ROWCACHE
  3  /

GETHIT_RATIO
------------
  90.2921525
```

Diagnosing Shared Pool Memory Usage

There is another ratio you can use to determine if the memory allocated to the shared pool is being used efficiently the shared pool usage ratio. Although this ratio is not a precise indicator, it presents the amount of memory used compared to the total amount of memory assigned. Figure 4-12 illustrates different zones of Shared Pool Memory usage with percentages. A consistently high ratio indicates that the Shared Pool Memory is underallocated, as shown in the band furthest to the left in Figure 4-12. A consistently low ratio indicates that the Shared Pool Memory is overallocated, as shown in the band furthest to the right. If neither is consistently high nor low, the Shared Pool usage ratio indicates that the Shared Pool Memory size is properly configured.

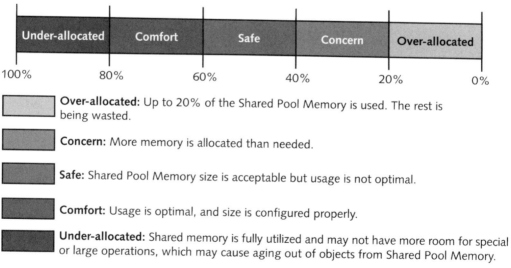

Figure 4-12   Shared Pool Memory usage percentages

You can use the following query to determine the Shared Pool Memory usage ratio:

```
SQL> SELECT (USED/VALUE)*100 SHARED_POOL_USAGE_RATIO
  2    FROM V$PARAMETER P,
  3         (SELECT SUM(BYTES) USED
  4            FROM V$SGASTAT
  5           WHERE POOL = 'shared pool'
  6             AND NAME <> 'free memory'
  7         )
  8   WHERE P.NAME = 'shared_pool_size'
  9  /

SHARED_POOL_USAGE_RATIO
-----------------------
              41.5184577
```

Diagnosing Shared Pool Free Memory

In the previous section, you looked at the shared pool usage ratio. Similarly, you can determine how much free memory in the shared pool is available at any time compared to the amount of memory allocated to it. See Figure 4-13 for an interpretation of this ratio:

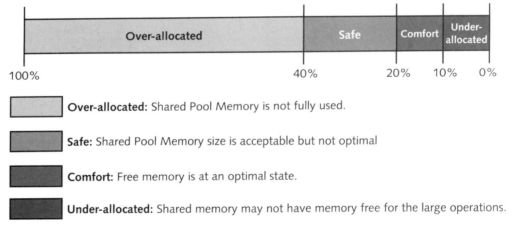

Over-allocated: Shared Pool Memory is not fully used.

Safe: Shared Pool Memory size is acceptable but not optimal

Comfort: Free memory is at an optimal state.

Under-allocated: Shared memory may not have memory free for the large operations.

Figure 4-13   Shared Pool free memory diagnosis—Part 1

Use the following query to get the shared pool free ratio:

```
SQL> SELECT (S.BYTES/P.VALUE)*100 SHARED_POOL_FREE_RATIO
  2    FROM V$PARAMETER P, V$SGASTAT S
  3   WHERE S.POOL = 'shared pool'
  4     AND S.NAME = 'free memory'
  5     AND P.NAME = 'shared_pool_size'
  6  /

SHARED_POOL_FREE_RATIO
----------------------
             91.7314529
```

After looking at Shared Pool Memory usage and the free ratio, you can derive another ratio that determines the percentage of free memory to the memory in use in the shared pool. The optimal value of this ratio is 20 percent. See Figure 4-14 for an interpretation. Issue the following query to get this ratio:

```
SQL> SELECT (S.BYTES/USED)*100 SHARED_POOL_USAGE_FREE_RATIO
  2      FROM V$SGASTAT S,
  3          (SELECT SUM(BYTES) USED
  4            FROM V$SGASTAT
  5           WHERE POOL = 'shared pool'
  6             AND NAME <> 'free memory'
  7          )
  8    WHERE S.POOL = 'shared pool'
  9      AND S.NAME = 'free memory'
 10  /

SHARED_POOL_USAGE_FREE_RATIO
----------------------------
                  218.941441
```

As you can see, the results of this query indicate that the Shared Pool Memory is overallocated and most likely that the memory assigned to the shared pool is wasted.

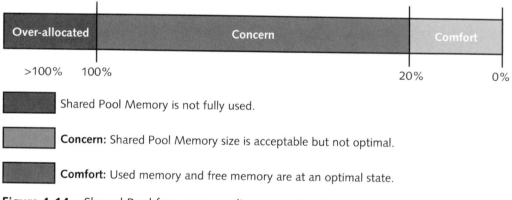

Figure 4-14   Shared Pool free memory diagnosis—Part 2

Diagnosing the Shared Pool Using Oracle Enterprise Manager

The Oracle Enterprise Manager (OEM) console has functions that can assist you in administering, maintaining, and troubleshooting databases. As described in previous chapters, the OEM diagnostics pack offers a Performance Overview tool, which delivers a quick snapshot of the database status. The following eight screen shots are related to the Shared Pool Memory.

Figure 4-15 is the Database Health Overview Chart showing memory usage.

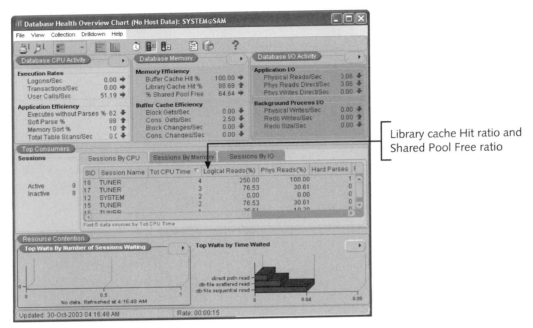

Figure 4-15   Oracle Enterprise Manager presentation of the Database Health Overview Chart

Figure 4–16 shows another portion of the Database Health Overview Chart—sessions that consume the most resources. Figure 4–16 shows that the TUNER session is the top consumer of CPU time.

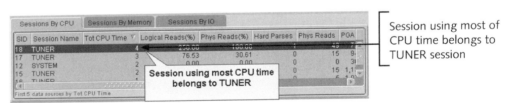

Figure 4-16   Database Health Overview Chart showing the top resource consumers

Figure 4–17 shows the Memory at a Glance window, which is obtained by selecting the following menu options: Host Memory Use>Available Memory (%)> Memory at a Glance.

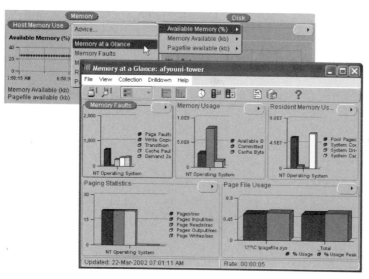

Figure 4-17   Memory at a Glance window showing detailed statistics on memory usage

Figure 4–18 shows the SGA usage screen obtained by highlighting the following menu options: Database Memory >% Shared Pool Free>SGA Overview.

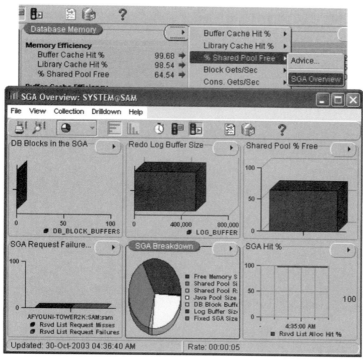

Figure 4-18   SGA Overview option screen showing statistics for all SGA structures

Figure 4-19 shows the Help advice that is available at any time from the Performance Overview.

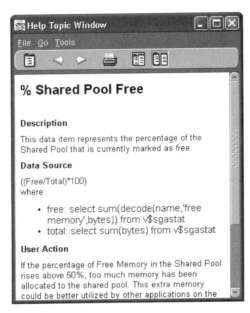

Figure 4-19   Help advice window

Figure 4–20 shows another tool provided by the OEM console. This tool, called TopSQL, displays the SQL statement that consumes the most resources.

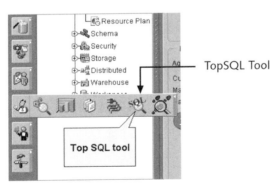

Figure 4-20   Oracle Enterprise Manager navigation bar showing TopSQL tool

Figures 4-21 and 4-22 display TopSQL showing a horizontal view of SQL sessions and a detailed view of the current SQL session.

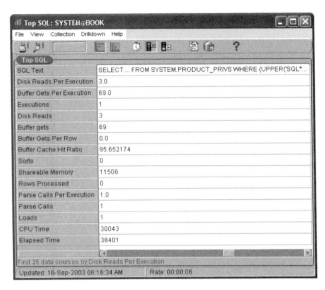

Figure 4-21   Horizontal view of TopSQL main screen

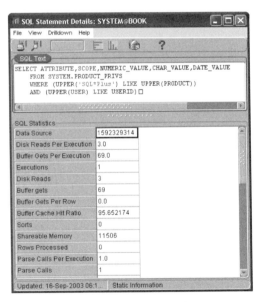

Figure 4-22   Detailed view of current session of TopSQL

LOOKING INSIDE SHARED POOL MEMORY

A fourteen-year-old girl looked over her dad's shoulder at 9:06 p.m. and said, "They beeped you again, didn't they?" Her father said, "Yes, it looks as if there is a runaway query." The girl laughed and asked if that was like a kid running away from home. Her father told her the runs were similar, and both were serious.

When the father solved the problem at hand, he explained to his daughter what happened, why it was serious, and how he figured it out. A developer was asked to write a quick report on production for a business manager. He wrote the query and submitted it to the database. Usually a query returns results quickly, but this one was taking hours, so the developer was worried about impacting the database and decided to call the data center to stop the query. That action started the father's beeper. First, the father gathered information including the username and the commands issued by the developer. Then he queried the database to see all queries submitted and to find out more about the query: how long it had been running, its demand on resources, and other indicators. But that was not enough. He had to kill the session and then analyze it. Most important was stopping the query to gather statistics about it.

As you know, the Shared Pool Memory has many structures containing different types of cache data. Not all cached data in the Shared Pool Memory is of interest to you, as the DBA. This section is focused on examining certain parts of the Shared Pool Memory, particularly in the library cache. The library cache structures hold important data that shows you what application code is being submitted to the databases. Application code can be SQL statements, PL/SQL blocks, Java code, or other commands. First, you examine one of the most important data types cached in the library cache, application code.

Oracle offers many variations of dynamic performance views. Each is provided for specific purposes. Here are several views that enable looking inside the library cache.

V$DB_OBJECT_CACHE

This view contains data about each memory object residing in the library cache. Table 4-6 displays column descriptions of this view.

Table 4-6   V$DB_OBJECT_CACHE view

Column	Description
OWNER	Owner of the object cached in library cache
NAME	Name of the object cached in library cache
DB_LINK	Database link name
NAMESPACE	Library cache namespace
TYPE	Type of library cache
SHARABLE_MEM	Memory used by the object in library cache
LOADS	Number of times the object was loaded because it was invalidated
EXECUTIONS	Not used
LOCKS	Number of users currently locking this object
PINS	Number of users currently using the object
KEPT	Whether or not the object is kept permanently in library cache using DBMS_SHARED_POOL package
CHILD_LATCH	Child latch number protecting the object

The following query displays all cached memory objects in the library cache for the TUNER user:

```
SQL> SELECT NAME,
  2          TYPE OBJECT_TYPE,
  3          NAMESPACE,
  4          SHARABLE_MEM MEMORY,
  5          LOADS,
  6          KEPT
  7     FROM V$DB_OBJECT_CACHE
  8    WHERE OWNER = 'TUNER'
  9    ORDER BY TYPE
 10    /

NAME                OBJECT_TYPE NAMESPACE            MEMORY     LOADS KEPT
----------------    ----------- ----------------    --------   ----- ----
DBA_TAB_COLUMNS     NOT LOADED  TABLE/PROCEDURE          0         1 NO
TUNER               NOT LOADED  PUB_SUB                  0         2 NO
DBA_CONS_COLUMNS    NOT LOADED  TABLE/PROCEDURE          0         1 NO
DBA_CONSTRAINTS     NOT LOADED  TABLE/PROCEDURE          0         1 NO
CATEGORIES          NOT LOADED  TABLE/PROCEDURE          0         2 NO
CUSTOMERS           TABLE       TABLE/PROCEDURE       1479         1 NO
PRODUCTS            TABLE       TABLE/PROCEDURE       1430         1 NO
ORDERS              TABLE       TABLE/PROCEDURE       2188         1 NO
ORDER_LINES         TABLE       TABLE/PROCEDURE       2089         1 NO
```

These results tell you that the CUSTOMERS table is cached and was loaded once in the TABLE/PROCEDURE namespace occupying 1479 bytes, but it is not pinned in memory (PINNED means that the object is KEPT in memory). The LOADS column indicates the number of times an object was loaded in memory because it was invalidated. For example, the CATEGORIES table was loaded twice in memory because it was invalidated possibly due to data updates or structural changes.

V$OBJECT_USAGE

This view provides information about indexes used at least once by a statement submitted to the database. This view has the following columns:

```
SQL> DESC V$OBJECT_USAGE
 Name                                      Null?    Type
 --------------------------------------    -------- -----------
 INDEX_NAME                                NOT NULL VARCHAR2(30)
 TABLE_NAME                                NOT NULL VARCHAR2(30)
 MONITORING                                         VARCHAR2(3)
 USED                                               VARCHAR2(3)
 START_MONITORING                                   VARCHAR2(19)
 END_MONITORING                                     VARCHAR2(19)
```

V$SQL

This view contains SQL statements and the statistical data for all statements without a GROUP BY clause. These SQL statements and statistical data are stored in the SQL area of the library cache. This view contains only the first 1000 characters of the statement.

V$SQLAREA

This view contains all SQL statements and the statistical data for all statements stored in the SQL area of the library cache. This view contains only the first 1000 characters of the statement. Table 4-7 contains descriptions of the most frequently used columns from this view.

Table 4-7   Useful columns of V$SQLAREA view

Column	Description
SQL_TEXT	Text of the SQL statement (First 1000 characters)
SHARABLE_MEM	Number of bytes used by the statement from the library cache memory
SORTS	Number of sorts performed for this statement
USERS_OPENING	Number of users executing this statement
EXECUTIONS	Number of times this statement was executed
USERS_EXECUTING	Number of users who executed this statement
LOADS	Number of times this statement was loaded or reloaded into the library cache
FIRST_LOAD_TIME	Time when the statement was first loaded into library cache
INVALIDATIONS	Number of times this statement was invalidated due to a change of the used database objects
PARSE_CALLS	Number of times a parse call was made for this statement
DISK_READS	Number of disk reads that occurred for this statement
BUFFER_GETS	Number of times that the statement was found in the buffer
ROWS_PROCESSED	Number of rows processed for this statement
OPTIMIZER_MODE	Optimizer mode used to perform this statement
PARSING_SCHEMA_ID	User ID of the schema that parsed this statement
KEPT_VERSIONS	Indication of whether the statement is pinned in the library cache using DBMS_SHARED_POOL package
ADDRESS	Memory address of this statement in the library cache
HASH_VALUE	Hash value of this statement
CPU_TIME	CPU time consumed, in microseconds, to parse and execute this statement and fetch results of this statement
ELAPSED_TIME	Time in microseconds spent to parse and execute this statement and fetch results of this statement

The following query is issued to display all statements submitted by the TUNER user:

```
SQL> SELECT SUBSTR(SQL_TEXT, 1, 40) SQL_TEXT,
  2           SHARABLE_MEM MEMORY,
  3           LOADS,
  4           EXECUTIONS EXEC,
  5           ROWS_PROCESSED ROWS,
  6           CPU_TIME CPU
  7    FROM V$SQLAREA
  8   WHERE PARSING_SCHEMA_ID = (SELECT USER_ID
  9                                FROM DBA_USERS
 10                               WHERE USERNAME = 'TUNER')
 11  /

  SQL_TEXT                                    MEMORY LOADS EXEC ROWS   CPU
  --------------------------------------      ------ ----- ---- ---- -----
    SELECT rowid, "TUNER"."CATEGORIES".* FRO    3639     1    2   36     0
  ❶select First_name, last_name    from cust    7423     1    2  182     0
  ❷select First_name, last_name    from cust    7547     1    2  182 15625
  ❸select first_name, last_name    from cust    7371     1    6  546 31250
```

As you see in the preceding results, the last three rows are logically identical, but appear as different statements to the optimizer/compiler because they do not have the same pattern, although they do produce the same results. Statements ❶ and ❷ are almost identical except that statement ❶ has an extra space before the FROM clause. Statements ❶ and ❸ are almost identical except that "first_name" in statement ❸ is a different pattern than in statement ❶ with its a single uppercase character.

To put this in perspective, suppose there are three modules in an application issuing the three statements, ❶, ❷, and ❸. The impact on performance is this: rather than parsing one statement, it parses three statements, because these statements were not issued in an identical pattern. This problem can be eliminated in three ways: using stored procedures, using coding standards, or using formatting tools and editors, which standardize statement formats.

Another benefit of the V$SQLAREA view is to perform TopSQL time analysis which shows the statements that are consuming the most CPU time, parse time, I/O, or any performance criteria. For example, if you are interested in the top 10 SQL statements that use CPU time, you can issue the following query:

```
SQL> SELECT USERNAME, SUBSTR(SQL_TEXT, 1, 30) SQL_TEXT, CPU_TIME
  2    FROM V$SQLAREA, DBA_USERS
  3   WHERE PARSING_SCHEMA_ID = USER_ID
  4     AND ROWNUM <= 10
  5   ORDER BY CPU_TIME DESC
  6  /
```

Also, you could issue the following statement to find out what SQL statement each session executed or is executing:

```
SQL> SELECT USERNAME,
  2         SID,
  3         SERIAL#,
  4         OSUSER,
  5         TERMINAL,
  6         SUBSTR(SQL_TEXT, 1, 25) SQL_TEXT
  7    FROM V$SESSION, V$SQLAREA
  8   WHERE USERNAME NOT IN ('SYS', 'SYSTEM')
  9     AND USERNAME IS NOT NULL
 10     AND (SQL_ADDRESS = ADDRESS OR PREV_SQL_ADDR = ADDRESS)
 11  /

USERNAME SID SERIAL# OSUSER                      TERMINAL     SQL_TEXT
-------- --- ------- --------------------------- ------------ -------------------------
QUEST      9    1054 AFYOUNI-TOWER\Administrator AFYOUNI_XP   select * from user_ca
SCOTT     10    7157 SYSTEM                      AFYOUNI-TOWER select * from emp
DEMO      15      30 AFYOUNI-TOWER\Administrator AFYOUNI-MARS select first_name, last_n
TUNER     14      36 AFYOUNI-TOWER\Administrator AFYOUNI-TOWER select* from customers
```

V$SQLTEXT

This view contains the full statement text for all statements stored in the SQL area of the library cache. Statements are cut into pieces of 64 characters. Table 4-8 presents column descriptions of this V$SQLTEXT view:

Table 4-8   Column descriptions of V$SQLTEXT view

Column	Description
ADDRESS	Memory address of the statement in the library cache
HASH_VALUE	Hash value of the statement
COMMAND_TYPE	Command type code of the statement. Codes for the most common commands: 2 = INSERT 3 = SELECT 6 = UPDATE 7 = DELETE 47 = PL/SQL Block 44 = COMMIT 45 = ROLLBACK 35 = ALTER DATABASE 42 = ALTER SESSION
PIECE	Piece number of the statement; the first piece is number 0
SQL_TEXT	64-character pieces of the statement text

The query that follows displays all statements cached in the library cache for the TUNER user. Notice that the first statement is two pieces (two lines): the first piece is the first 64 characters of the statement, and the second line is only the closing single quote character:

```
SQL> SELECT SQL_TEXT
  2     FROM V$SQLTEXT
  3   WHERE ADDRESS IN (SELECT ADDRESS
  4                       FROM V$SQLAREA, DBA_USERS
  5                        WHERE PARSING_SCHEMA_ID = USER_ID
  6                          AND USERNAME = 'TUNER')
  7   ORDER BY ADDRESS, PIECE
  8  /

SQL_TEXT
----------------------------------------------------------------
select first_name, last_name   from customers  where state = 'MA
'
select First_name, last_name   from  customers  where state = 'MA '
select First_name, last_name   from customers  where state = 'MA
'
SELECT rowid, "TUNER"."CATEGORIES".* FROM TUNER."CATEGORIES"
```

V$SQLTEXT_WITH_NEWLINES

This view is the same as V$SQLTEXT except that it preserves original white spaces. The query below illustrates how white space is preserved and displayed in the results of the query:

```
SQL> SELECT SQL_TEXT
  2    FROM V$SQLTEXT_WITH_NEWLINES
  3    WHERE ADDRESS IN (SELECT ADDRESS
  4                      FROM V$SQLAREA, DBA_USERS
  5                      WHERE PARSING_SCHEMA_ID = USER_ID
  6                      AND USERNAME = 'TUNER'
  7                      AND UPPER(SQL_TEXT) LIKE '%SELECT%')
  8    ORDER BY ADDRESS, PIECE
  9  /

SQL_TEXT
-----------------------------------------------------------------
select first_name, last_name
  from customers
 where state = 'MA'


select First_name, last_name
  from  customers
 where state = 'MA'


select First_name, last_name
  from customers
 where state = 'MA'


SELECT rowid, "TUNER"."CATEGORIES".* FROM TUNER."CATEGORIES"
```

FLUSHING THE SHARED POOL MEMORY

In this scenario, a DBA called her instructor for help, saying that she thought the main reason to flush the Shared Pool Memory was to clear out the library cache especially when an application does not use bind variables. She told the instructor she had heard that flushing the Shared Pool Memory frequently improves the performance of the system and decreases the amount of fragmentation. She was confused

The instructor replied with a smile on his face "Welcome to the real world of Oracle! Both statements are right, because there are situations in which the Shared Pool Memory is fragmented and you need to have contiguous memory for large objects. There are also situations in which the Shared Pool Memory is cluttered with objects that are not used often and have not aged out, so you clear the Shared Pool Memory." But the instructor warned the student that flushing the Shared Pool Memory frequently affects performance adversely because it leads to excessive parsing, especially if the application is properly using bind variables.

In some circumstances, you may need to free up (flush) the Shared Pool Memory to load big objects into a contiguous piece of memory. In this case, issue the following ALTER statement:

```
SQL> ALTER SYSTEM FLUSH SHARED_POOL
/

System altered.
```

PINNING OBJECTS

In this scenario, a DBA wrote to one of the Oracle forums about a problem with sequences as follows:

Dear Sir/Madame:

We have an application that uses sequences. Because this is an OLTP application, I created all sequences using the CACHE option to cache in advance 500 numbers. I have noticed lately that some of our numbers are skipping and they are skipping exactly by 500. Is this related to the CACHE option and is there something I can do?

Yours truly,

Samantha, DBA

The response Samantha received from the forum was as follows:

Dear Samantha:

Your problem is a common one. You need to understand how sequences are cached—they function just as all objects do. Sequences are cached in Shared Pool Memory and kept like other objects and aged out for the following two reasons: 1) the object is not accessed frequently; and 2) space is needed.

When the sequence is aged out, it skips. So, from what I see, one of these two criteria is are being met. If the sequence is not used frequently, you should not cache it. But if it is used frequently, most likely you did not allocate enough memory to the Shared Pool Memory. However, you can solve this problem by pinning the sequence in memory.

Danny

In the previous section, you looked inside the Shared Pool Memory to determine which SQL statements are executed most frequently and which statements are consuming the most CPU time. You also learned that because parsing is expensive, you should reduce parsing as much as possible. One way to reduce parsing is to cache the most frequently used statements in Shared Pool Memory to prevent the object from being aged out. The following steps guide you through the process of caching (pinning) an object using the Oracle-supplied package called DBMS_SHARED_POOL.

Step 1: You must first determine if the DBMS_SHARED_POOL package is already installed. To do so, issue the following command as SYS user:

```
SQL> DESC DBMS_SHARED_POOL

PROCEDURE ABORTED_REQUEST_THRESHOLD
 Argument Name            Type                             In/Out Default?
 ----------------------   ----------------------------     ------ --------
 THRESHOLD_SIZE           NUMBER                           IN

PROCEDURE KEEP
 Argument Name            Type                             In/Out Default?
 ----------------------   ----------------------------     ------ --------
 NAME                     VARCHAR2                         IN
 FLAG                     CHAR                             IN     DEFAULT

PROCEDURE SIZES
 Argument Name            Type                             In/Out Default?
 ----------------------   ----------------------------     ------ --------
 MINSIZE                  NUMBER                           IN

PROCEDURE UNKEEP
 Argument Name            Type                             In/Out Default?
 ----------------------   ----------------------------     ------ --------
 NAME                     VARCHAR2                         IN
 FLAG                     CHAR                             IN     DEFAULT
```

NOTE

If you issue the DESCRIBE command in SQL*Plus and you do not get a result similar to that shown in the previous segment, then the package has not been installed.

Of the four procedures in the DBMS_SHARED_POOL package, you are interested only in the following two procedures:

- **KEEP procedure:** Used to pin objects in Shared Pool Memory

- **UNKEEP procedure:** Used to unpin objects from Shared Pool Memory

For more details on DBMS packages, consult the following documentation: Oracle9i-Supplied PL/SQL Packages and Types Reference Release 2 (9.2) Part Number A96612-01.

If the DBMS_SHARED_POOL package is not installed, you should install it using the Oracle-supplied script stored in the RDBMS/ADMIN folder under ORACLE_HOME.

Step 2: Use the following command to install the package:

```
SQL> @C:\ORACLE\ORA92\RDBMS\ADMIN\DBMSPOOL.SQL

Package created.


Grant succeeded.


View created.


Package body created.
```

4

Step 3: Continuing with the pinning example, create the following stored procedure as TUNER:

```
CREATE OR REPLACE PROCEDURE DISPLAY_CUSTOMER_INFO(
                                          P_CUSTOMER NUMBER
                                        ) IS


    V_CUSTREC      CUSTOMERS%ROWTYPE;
    V_SALES_REP    VARCHAR2(255);
    V_ORDERS_CNT   NUMBER(6);
    V_ORDERS_AMT   NUMBER;

BEGIN

    BEGIN
       SELECT *
         INTO V_CUSTREC
         FROM CUSTOMERS
        WHERE CUSTOMER_ID = P_CUSTOMER;
    EXCEPTION
       WHEN NO_DATA_FOUND THEN
          RAISE_APPLICATION_ERROR(-20000, 'CUSTOMER DOES NOT EXIST');
    END;

    SELECT FIRST_NAME || ' ' || LAST_NAME
      INTO V_SALES_REP
      FROM EMPLOYEES
     WHERE EMPLOYEE_ID = V_CUSTREC.SALES_REP_ID;

    SELECT COUNT(*)
      INTO V_ORDERS_CNT
      FROM ORDERS
     WHERE CUSTOMER_ID = P_CUSTOMER;

    SELECT SUM(TOTAL_AMOUNT)
      INTO V_ORDERS_AMT
      FROM ORDER_LINES
     WHERE ORDER_ID IN (SELECT ORDER_ID
                          FROM ORDERS
                         WHERE CUSTOMER_ID = P_CUSTOMER);

    DBMS_OUTPUT.PUT_LINE('Customer Name:   ' ||
                         V_CUSTREC.FIRST_NAME||' '||
                         V_CUSTREC.LAST_NAME);
    DBMS_OUTPUT.PUT_LINE('Customer Phone:  ' || V_CUSTREC.PHONE);
    DBMS_OUTPUT.PUT_LINE('Customer Status: ' || V_CUSTREC.STATUS);
    DBMS_OUTPUT.PUT_LINE('Number of orders:' || V_ORDERS_CNT);
    DBMS_OUTPUT.PUT_LINE('Orders Amount:   ' || V_ORDERS_AMT);
END;
/
```

Step 4: Execute this procedure for three different customers, as follows:

```
SQL> SET SERVEROUTPUT ON SIZE 1000000
SQL> EXEC DISPLAY_CUSTOMER_INFO(301862);
Customer Name:    Valeri Borges
Customer Phone:  9621882418
Customer Status: X
Number of orders:0
Orders Amount:

PL/SQL procedure successfully completed.

SQL> EXEC DISPLAY_CUSTOMER_INFO(801907);
Customer Name:    Hugh Walsh
Customer Phone:  4918873431
Customer Status: A
Number of orders:3
Orders Amount:    2661985.41

PL/SQL procedure successfully completed.

SQL> EXEC DISPLAY_CUSTOMER_INFO(401890);
Customer Name:    Demetrius Johnsen
Customer Phone:  3803307199
Customer Status: I
Number of orders:3
Orders Amount:    2934736.67

PL/SQL procedure successfully completed.
```

4

Step 5: Look inside the SQL area to determine the number of executions for this procedure. (To do this, you need another session open as SYS or SYSTEM.)

```
SQL> COLUMN SQL_TEXT FORMAT A50
SQL> SELECT SQL_TEXT, SHARABLE_MEM, EXECUTIONS, CPU_TIME
  2     FROM V$SQLAREA
  3    WHERE SQL_TEXT LIKE UPPER('%DISPLAY%')
  4    /

SQL_TEXT                                           SHARABLE_MEM EXECUTIONS CPU_TIME
-------------------------------------------------- ------------ ---------- ----------
BEGIN DISPLAY_CUSTOMER_INFO(301862); END;                10493          2    1341930
BEGIN DISPLAY_CUSTOMER_INFO(401890); END;                11081          1     660950
BEGIN DISPLAY_CUSTOMER_INFO(801907); END;                10533          1     670965
SELECT SQL_TEXT, SHARABLE_MEM, EXECUTIONS, CPU_TIM       46166          4     320460
E   FROM V$SQLAREA  WHERE SQL_TEXT LIKE UPPER('%DI
SPLAY%')

SELECT SQL_TEXT, SHARABLE_MEM, EXECUTIONS, CPU_TIM       44794          1     110159
E   FROM V$SQLAREA  WHERE SQL_TEXT LIKE UPPER('%DI
SPLAY5')
```

Step 6: Look again inside the Shared Pool Memory to determine if the stored procedure is pinned (kept) in memory. Use the following statement as SYS or SYSTEM user. Note that KEPT is equal to NO, which indicates that this stored procedure is not pinned:

```
SQL> SELECT TYPE, NAMESPACE, EXECUTIONS, KEPT
  2    FROM V$DB_OBJECT_CACHE
  3   WHERE OWNER = 'TUNER'
  4     AND NAME = 'DISPLAY_CUSTOMER_INFO'
  5  /

TYPE                            NAMESPACE                   EXECUTIONS KEPT
------------------------------  --------------------------- ---------- ----
PROCEDURE                       TABLE/PROCEDURE                      4 NO
```

Step 7: As SYS or SYSTEM user, pin this procedure in Shared Pool Memory using the procedure KEEP in the DBMS_SHARED_POOL package:

```
SQL> EXEC DBMS_SHARED_POOL.KEEP('TUNER.DISPLAY_CUSTOMER_INFO');

PL/SQL procedure successfully completed.
```

Step 8: Verify that the procedure is pinned in Shared Pool Memory. Notice from the result of the query that follows that KEPT is YES, which indicates the object is now pinned in memory:

```
SQL> SELECT TYPE, NAMESPACE, EXECUTIONS, KEPT
  2    FROM V$DB_OBJECT_CACHE
  3   WHERE OWNER = 'TUNER'
  4     AND NAME = 'DISPLAY_CUSTOMER_INFO'
  5  /

TYPE                            NAMESPACE             ..  EXECUTIONS KEPT
------------------------------  --------------------------- ---------- ----
PROCEDURE                       TABLE/PROCEDURE                      4 YES
```

Step 9: Unpin the stored object:

```
SQL> EXEC DBMS_SHARED_POOL.UNKEEP('TUNER.DISPLAY_CUSTOMER_INFO');

PL/SQL procedure successfully completed.
```

In some circumstances, you want to pin objects in memory that are both large and frequently used. The following query displays all statements that are consuming more than 100,000 bytes:

```
SQL> SELECT SUBSTR(SQL_TEXT,1,50) SQL_TEXT,
  2           COUNT(*) STMT_COUNT,
  3           SUM(SHARABLE_MEM) MEMORY_USED,
  4           SUM(EXECUTIONS) EXECUTIONS
  5      FROM V$SQLAREA
  6    GROUP BY SUBSTR(SQL_TEXT,1,50)
  7   HAVING SUM(SHARABLE_MEM) > 100000
  8   /

SQL_TEXT                                           STMT_COUNT MEMORY_USED EXECUTIONS
-------------------------------------------------- ---------- ----------- ----------
INSERT INTO ORDER_LINES ( ORDER_ID, PRODUCT_ID, AC       3609     5656071          0
select q_name, state, delay, expiration, rowid, ms         16      248790      18781
select substr(sql_text,1,40) stmt, count(*), sum(s          3      143386          3
```

To summarize this section on pinning objects: the main two criteria for pinning objects in the Shared Pool Memory are that the object must be used frequently, and it is not large.

CURSOR_SHARING Parameter

In this scenario, a newly hired DBA consultant was first asked to tune all SQL statements submitted to the database. As soon as he started this task, he found one major problem: about 70 percent of the SQL statements submitted to the database were similar and were parsed every single time. The queries were similar in that they all differed in the literals used in the WHERE clauses. An example of two queries that are similar is as follows:

```
SELECT *
  FROM CUSTOMERS
 WHERE CUSTOMER_ID = 123;

SELECT *
  FROM CUSTOMERS
 WHERE CUSTOMER_ID = 423;
```

The consultant went to the development manager and explained that instead of using bind variables, the application was using literals that caused each statement to be parsed and resulted in performance degradation. After a long talk, the development manager and her team leaders explained that there was no possibility of changing the code at that stage and they asked the DBA to explore another way to resolve this problem. The DBA consultant agreed to try, but said he could make no promises.

It is useful at this point to look into some of the issues faced by the consultant in the preceding scenario. As outlined earlier in this chapter, the parsing process performs many tasks that consume CPU and I/O resources. You should take advantage of any opportunity to reduce parsing, especially when a SQL statement used in an application is frequently executed with a different literal. For example, suppose that an application is constantly retrieving different customer information. During the course of a day in which 4000 customers call with inquiries, the application issues 4000 queries that are literally different but logically perform the same query. Therefore, these 4000 queries are parsed, which means performance eventually degrades. Examine the example queries in the following code segment:

```
SELECT FIRST_NAME, LAST_NAME
  FROM CUSTOMERS
 WHERE CUSTOMER_ID = 801627;

SELECT FIRST_NAME, LAST_NAME
  FROM CUSTOMERS
 WHERE CUSTOMER_ID = 101672;
              .
              .
              .
SELECT FIRST_NAME, LAST_NAME
  FROM CUSTOMERS
 WHERE CUSTOMER_ID = 901574;
```

In the situation represented by the preceding code segment, Oracle enables you to reduce parsing by configuring a parameter called CURSOR_SHARING. Table 4-9 presents three values and descriptions for valid settings of this parameter.

Table 4-9 CURSOR_SHARING parameter values

Value	Description
EXACT	Is the default value. Tells Oracle to share SQL statements only if the pattern of the submitted statement is exactly the same as that cached in memory.
FORCE	Tells Oracle to share SQL statements if they are literals. This option forces the Optimizer to use the same execution plan.
SIMILAR	Tells Oracle to share SQL statements if they are literals. This option tells Oracle to share the same execution plan only if it is optimal.

This parameter can be set dynamically while the database is open by using the ALTER SYSTEM statement as shown in the following code segment:

```
SQL> ALTER SYSTEM SET CURSOR_SHARING=SIMILAR
  2  /

System altered.
```

Now look at a scenario in which the CURSOR_SHARING parameter was set to EXACT. TUNER, the user, issued three statements that differ only in the literal. The user then looks at SQL area to see how these statements are represented. The outcome is illustrated in the following code segment:

```
SQL> SELECT SUBSTR(SQL_TEXT, 1, 80) SQL_TEXT,
  2          EXECUTIONS EXECS
  3      FROM V$SQLAREA
  4      WHERE PARSING_SCHEMA_ID = (SELECT USER_ID
  5                                    FROM DBA_USERS
  6                                    WHERE USERNAME='TUNER')
  7      ORDER BY 2 DESC
  8 /

SQL_TEXT                                                                  EXECS
----------------------------------------------------------------------- --------
SELECT FIRST_NAME, LAST_NAME   FROM CUSTOMERS   WHERE CUSTOMER_ID = 801627      4
SELECT FIRST_NAME, LAST_NAME   FROM CUSTOMERS   WHERE CUSTOMER_ID = 101672      1
SELECT FIRST_NAME, LAST_NAME   FROM CUSTOMERS   WHERE CUSTOMER_ID = 901574      1
```

After looking at the SQL area, as a DBA, you set CURSOR _SHARING to SIMILAR, and TUNER issues similar statements for different customers. Notice that the statements submitted with a similar pattern are no longer parsed but are shared instead:

```
SQL_TEXT                                                                  EXECS
----------------------------------------------------------------------- -----
SELECT FIRST_NAME, LAST_NAME   FROM CUSTOMERS   WHERE CUSTOMER_ID = 801627      4
SELECT FIRST_NAME, LAST_NAME   FROM CUSTOMERS   WHERE CUSTOMER_ID = :"SYS_B_0"  3
SELECT FIRST_NAME, LAST_NAME   FROM CUSTOMERS   WHERE CUSTOMER_ID = 101672      1
SELECT FIRST_NAME, LAST_NAME   FROM CUSTOMERS   WHERE CUSTOMER_ID = 901574      1
```

Because the SIMILAR value performs so well, why don't you use this setting all the time? The answer lies in the execution plan: this parameter influences Oracle to make a decision to use the same execution plan regardless of the situation. The Oracle Optimizer has determined that every statement will be shared even when it is not optimal. This could impact performance in a negative way, especially if the application is of a DSS type. The SIMILAR value is used most frequently for OLTP type of applications.

CURSOR_SPACE_FOR_TIME Parameter

Another parameter that Oracle provides to improve execution of a SQL statement is CURSOR_SPACE_FOR_TIME. This parameter can take two values as shown in Table 4-10. You are always encouraged to use any parameter that enhances performance as long as you are aware of the side effects of using the parameter. For instance, if this parameter is set to FALSE, the side effect is that Shared Pool Memory must be configured to be as large as possible to ensure that statements are not deallocated due to lack of memory space.

Table 4-10   CURSOR_SPACE_FOR_TIME parameter

Value	Description	Library cache misses	Advantages and disadvantages
TRUE	Indicates that a statement cannot be aged out of library cache if it is in use.	0	Enhances execution efficiency because Oracle does not have to wait for space in the library cache until the cursor for a statement is closed.
FALSE	Is the default value. Indicates that a statement is subject to deallocation when space is needed regardless of whether it is used or not.	> 0	Does not impact performance if Shared Pool Memory is configured properly. Using the value of TRUE requires a large Shared Pool Memory.

LARGE POOL MEMORY

The large pool memory is an optional structure of the SGA. Refer back to Figure 4-2 to review how large pool memory fits into the overall structure of the SGA. It is used as a temporary placeholder for special programs and functionality as follows:

1. Recovery Manager (RMAN)

2. Shared server, formerly known as Multithreaded server (MTS)

3. PARALLEL_AUTOMATIC_TUNING option

4. Parallel query

Large pool memory is configured by setting the initialization parameter, LARGE_POOL_SIZE. As with the Shared Pool Memory, this parameter can be set dynamically by issuing the following statements:

```
SQL>  ALTER SYSTEM SET LARGE_POOL_SIZE = 4M;

System altered.

SQL> SELECT NVL(POOL, 'Buffer Cache and log buffer') POOL,
  2           ROUND(SUM(BYTES)/1024/1024) SIZE_IN_MB
  3      FROM V$SGASTAT
  4      GROUP BY POOL
  5  /

POOL                      SIZE_IN_MB
--------------------      ----------
java pool                         32
large pool                         4
shared pool                       24
Buffer cache and log buffer       25
```

When you increase the size of the large pool dynamically, you receive an error if the new size exceeds the SGA_MAX_SIZE, as shown in the following statement:

```
SQL>  ALTER SYSTEM SET LARGE_POOL_SIZE = 10M;
 ALTER SYSTEM SET LARGE_POOL_SIZE = 10M
 *
ERROR at line 1:
ORA-02097: parameter cannot be modified because specified value is invalid
ORA-04033: Insufficient memory to grow pool
```

4

JAVA POOL

Java pool memory is another optional structure of the SGA. Refer back to Figure 4-2 to review how Java pool memory fits into the overall structure of the SGA. Java pool memory is used to cache executed Java programs, Java classes, and other Java–related objects. This memory is shared among all users in either dedicated server mode or shared server mode. The Java pool structure is configured using the initialization parameter, JAVA_POOL_SIZE. The Java pool does not have the same mechanism as the shared pool to age out objects. It is simply memory space used for caching Java code when it is available. The default value of this parameter is 30 MB. However, if your application does not use Java, you should set it to 0. This parameter can be modified dynamically while the database is up and running, but you must shut down and restart the database to make the change effective. You can modify this parameter directly in the initialization parameter file as shown in the following steps:

Step 1: Assign a new value to JAVA_POOL_SIZE parameter.

```
SQL> ALTER SYSTEM SET JAVA_POOL_SIZE = 0 SCOPE = SPFILE;
```

Step 2: Shut down the database.

```
SQL> SHUTDOWN IMMEDIATE
Database closed.
Database dismounted.
ORACLE instance shut down.
```

Step 3: Start up the database.

```
SQL> STARTUP
ORACLE instance started.

Total System Global Area    59841036 bytes
Fixed Size                    453132 bytes
Variable Size               33554432 bytes
Database Buffers            25165824 bytes
Redo Buffers                  667648 bytes
Database mounted.
Database opened.
```

Step 4: Verify parameter settings.

```
SQL> SHOW PARAMETER JAVA_POOL_SIZE
NAME                            TYPE        VALUE
------------------------------- ----------- ---------------
java_pool_size                  big integer 0
```

Step 5: Verify memory allocation.

```
SQL> SELECT * FROM V$SGASTAT
  2    WHERE POOL LIKE '%java%'
  3  /

no rows selected
```

TIP

When you flush Shared Pool Memory, the Java pool is also flushed.

Unlike other SGA structures, Java pool memory has no indicator or dynamic performance view to assist you in tuning it. Normally, if you are using Java within the database, a value for this parameter between 30 MB and 50 MB is adequate. You would not know if you overallocated memory for Java pool, but you would get an error if you allocated less memory than is needed. In this case, you receive an **ORA-04031** error when either compiling or loading Java code.

There are three Java-related parameters shown in the following code segment. These parameters are defined in Table 4-11:

```
SQL> SHOW PARAMETER JAVA

NAME                                 TYPE        VALUE
------------------------------------ ----------- ----------
java_max_sessionspace_size           integer     0
java_pool_size                       big integer 33554432
java_soft_sessionspace_limit         integer     0
```

Table 4-11 Java pool parameters

Column	Description
JAVA_MAX_SESSIONSPACE_SIZE	Configures the hard limit on the amount of space from the Java pool that is available to a user session. Set this parameter very high if you want to bypass it.
JAVA_POOL_SIZE	Configures the size of the Java pool memory.
JAVA_SOFT_SESSIONSPACE_LIMIT	Configures the soft limit memory for each session. A warning is generated to the trace file when the session exceeds this parameter value. This parameter does not impact the execution of the application; it is merely a warning.

CHAPTER SUMMARY

- The Shared Pool Memory is an important structure of the SGA used to cache SQL statements, PL/SQL blocks, and other memory objects to reduce CPU consumption and I/O trips to data files.
- SQL statements are processed in three steps: 1) The statements are parsed for syntax validity, user privileges are verified, and a plan for retrieving data is created; 2) the plan created in the first step is executed; and 3) the data is retrieved and submitted to the user.
- The parsing process comprises six main tasks that ensure the validity of the statement as well as the validity of the selected columns, and determines the best method for retrieving the data.
- The library cache is a major structure of the Shared Pool Memory and is used to store application code that is in use.
- The library cache is divided into pieces of memory structures called namespaces.
- You can look at the library cache namespaces by displaying the contents of the V$LIBRARYCACHE performance dynamic view.
- You can use V$SESSION_OBJECT_CACHE to get a full statistics report on cached objects for the current session.

❏ The data dictionary is a part of memory in the shared pool, and it cannot be controlled and sized directly.

❏ The data dictionary structure is used to store data definitions of database objects.

❏ Shared Pool Memory is configured by setting the SHARED_POOL_SIZE parameter.

❏ Memory objects cached in Shared Pool Memory are subject to the Least Recent Used (LRU) algorithm to determine which object to age out from the shared pool when space is needed.

❏ You can set aside a percentage of the Shared Pool Memory to load and cache a very large stored procedure in contiguous Shared Pool Memory. This is done by setting the SHARED_POOL_RESERVED_SIZE parameter.

❏ Oracle provides advisory statistics for the Shared Pool Memory, specifically for its Library Cache portion. This feature is called Shared Pool Size Advice.

❏ You do not need to turn on the Shared Pool Size Advice because the advisory statistics are collected at all times.

❏ You can retrieve this advisory data at any time from V$SHARED_POOL_ADVICE performance dynamic view.

❏ V$LIBRARYCACHE performance dynamic view provides statistical data about each namespace of the library cache.

❏ The Library Cache GETHITRATIO has a threshold of 90 percent.

❏ The Library Cache PINHITRATIO has a threshold of 90 percent.

❏ The Library Cache RELOADS ratio has a threshold of five percent.

❏ The Library Cache INVALIDATIONS ratio has a threshold of one percent.

❏ You can use V$ROWCACHE performance dynamic view to display data dictionary statistics.

❏ The data dictionary GETMISSESS ratio has a threshold of 15 percent.

❏ The optimal Shared Pool Memory usage and the free memory ratio is 20 percent.

❏ The OEM Diagnostics pack offers a Performance Overview tool, which delivers a quick snapshot of the database health status.

❏ The V$DB_OBJECT_CACHE performance dynamic view contains data about each memory object residing in the library cache.

❏ The V$OBJECT_USAGE performance dynamic view provides information about indexes used at least once by a statement submitted to the database.

❏ The V$SQL performance dynamic view contains SQL statements and the statistical data for all statements without a GROUP BY clause.

❏ The V$SQLAREA performance dynamic view contains all SQL statements and the statistical data for all statements stored in the SQL area of the library cache.

❏ The V$SQLTEXT performance dynamic view contains the full statement text for all statements stored in the SQL area of the library cache.

❏ The V$SQLTEXT_WITH_NEWLINES performance dynamic view is the same as V$SQLTEXT except that it preserves original white spaces.

❏ Use ALTER SYSTEM FLUSH SHARED_POOL to flush the Shared Pool Memory.

❏ Use the Oracle-supplied package known as DBMS_SHARED_POOL to pin objects in Shared Pool Memory.

❏ The large pool memory is an optional structure of the SGA. It is used as a temporary placeholder for special programs and functionality.

❏ Java pool memory is another optional structure of the SGA used for caching Java code.

❏ Use the CURSOR_SHARING initialization parameter to reduce parsing.

❏ Use the CURSOR_SPACE_FOR_TIME initialization parameter to improve execution of a SQL statement.

4

❏ Initialization parameters presented in this chapter include the following:

- CURSOR_SHARING
- SHARED_POOL_SIZE
- SHARED_POOL_RESERVED_SIZE
- LARGE_POOL_SIZE
- JAVA_POOL_SIZE
- JAVA_MAX_SESSIONSPACE_SIZE
- JAVA_SOFT_SESSIONSPACE_LIMIT
- CURSOR_SPACE_FOR_TIME

❏ Views used in this chapter include the following:

- DBA_USERS
- V$DB_OBJECT_CACHE
- V$FIXED_VIEW_DEFINITION
- V$LIBRARY_CACHE_MEMORY
- V$LIBRARYCACHE
- V$OBJECT_USAGE
- V$PARAMETER
- V$ROWCACHE
- V$SESSION
- V$SESSION_OBJECT_CACHE
- V$SGASTAT
- V$SHARED_POOL_ADVICE
- V$SHARED_POOL_RESERVED
- V$SQL
- V$SQLAREA

- V$SQLTEXT
- V$SQLTEXT_WITH_NEWLINES

REVIEW QUESTIONS

1. Match the definition with each term.

   a. Hard parse

   b. Executions

   c. Pins

   d. Hit ratio

   e. Miss ratio

   f. Reloads

   g. Gets

   h. Library cache

   i. Data dictionary cache

   j. Parsing process

   k. SQL Area

   ___H___ A structure of the Shared Pool Memory used to store application code

   ___D___ The percentage of time an object was found in memory

   ___J___ A process that validates the SQL statement and determines an execution plan for the statement

   ___K___ A piece of the library cache

   _____ The number of times a call to the statement was made

   ___F___ The number of times that a statement was reparsed

   ___I___ A structure of the Shared Pool Memory used to store database object definitions

   ___E___ The number of times a request for an object was not found in memory

   ___A___ The event that occurs when a statement is parsed because it was not found in memory

   ___C___ The number of times an object was executed from memory

   ___G___ The number of requests for an object

2. Shared Pool Memory stores data that is retrieved from data files. (True/False)

3. You cannot control the size of the library cache directly. (True/False)

4. The library cache miss ratio should be less than 15 percent. (True/False)

5. The Library Cache Advice feature provides a way to determine if an increase in memory will improve performance or not. (True/False)

6. A Java pool is a component of the shared pool. (True/False)

7. You can use V$ROWCACHE to look at all database object definitions cached in the data dictionary cache. (True/False)

8. Write a query that displays all statements and the time the statements were submitted by the user, TUNER.

9. From the results obtained in Question 8, choose one statement and write a query that displays the complete query from V$SQLTEXT.

10. Suppose your manager asked you to determine if the Shared Pool Memory is properly sized. Write down the step(s) you would take to determine your answer.

11. Suppose you issued a query to determine the amount of free memory in the shared pool and the result was 30 percent.

   a. Write the query that you issued.

   b. What is your interpretation of the result?

12. Log on as TUNER and issue the following query:
```
SQL> SELECT * FROM CUSTOMERS
```

   a. How can you improve the performance of this statement?

   b. Write a query that displays statistical details of queries submitted by TUNER in the current session.

13. When would you use large pool memory and how would you configure it?

14. Suppose you took a reading of the library cache hit ratio and found it very low. Is this a problem? If you need to solve the problem, describe the steps that you would take to rectify the problem.

15. Write a statement that you would issue to change the shared pool to half its size. Provide reasons for why and when you would do this.

16. As you learned in this chapter, the hit ratio for data dictionary cache should be less than 15 percent. You submitted a query to display the contents of V$ROWCACHE and you received the following the results:

```
PARAMETER                    GETHIT RATIO
-----------------------      ------------
dc_sequence_grant            16.2536119
dc_constraints               45.1459606
dc_used_extents              50.5747126
dc_user_grants                0.002162125
dc_usernames                  0.021606272
dc_users                      0.003081016
```

a. How do you explain that some of these ratios are above 15 percent?

b. Should you be concerned about the results?

17. List the criteria to pin an object in Shared Pool Memory. What are the benefits of pinning the object in Shared Pool Memory?

18. Write a query that displays the total size of the Shared Pool Memory.

19. Given the following criteria for a database, what are the initialization parameters explained in this chapter that you would use for this database?

a. New database

b. OLTP application

c. A database that uses Java code and large objects of stored PL/SQL procedures

d. A database that uses RMAN to perform backup and recovery

20. When would you use V$SQLAREA and V$SQLTEXT? Provide an example.

EXAM REVIEW QUESTIONS: ORACLE9i PERFORMANCE TUNING (#1Z0-033)

1. Which statement is true about the library cache?

a. When a statement is submitted, it is automatically cached in the library cache.

b. The hash function determines whether or not the submitted statement needs to be cached in library cache.

c. You cannot see what is in the library cache, but you can see what is inside the data dictionary cache.

d. All statements in library cache are usually pinned when the same statement is executed more than once.

2. Like data in the buffer cache, which statement about the Least Recent Used (LRU) algorithm is true? The LRU is:

a. Applicable to the buffer cache only

b. Not applicable to the Shared Pool Memory

c. Applicable to the Shared Pool Memory, but not to the large pool and not to the Java pool

d. Applicable to the Shared Pool Memory and large pool

e. Applicable to the Shared Pool Memory, large pool, and Java pool

3. What dynamic performance view would you query to view the advisory data for the Shared Pool Memory?

a. V$SHARED_ADVICE

b. V$POOL_ADVICE

c. V$SHARED_POOL_ADVICE

d. V$DB_SHARED_ADVICE

e. V$DB_POOL_ADVICE

4. What is the dynamic performance view V$SHARED_POOL_RESERVED used for?

a. Contains all objects that are cached in the reserved pool

b. Is used to determine whether or not the reserved pool is adequately sized

c. Contains data about all components of the shared and reserved pool memory

d. Contains statistical data about the reserved pool

5. What dynamic performance view would you use to get statistical data about queries submitted to the database?

a. V$DB_OBJECT_CACHE

b. V$SQLTEXT

c. V$SQLAREA

d. V$DB_SQL_CACHE

6. What view would you use to determine if an object is pinned in the Shared Pool Memory?

a. V$ROWCACHE

b. V$LIBRARYCACHE

c. V$DB_OBJECT_CACHE

d. V$LIBRARY_CACHE_MEMORY

7. Which value is not valid for the CURSOR_SHARING parameter?

   a. FORCE

   b. VALIDATE

   c. EXACT

   d. SIMILAR

8. Which statement is true about the Shared Pool Size Advice feature?

   a. No parameters have to be set to turn on this feature.

   b. You must turn this feature on using SHARED_POOL_ADVICE parameter.

   c. SHARED_POOL_ADVICE can be dynamically set while the database is open.

9. What is the data dictionary hit ratio threshold?

   a. 15 percent

   b. 85 percent

   c. 95 percent

   d. 5 percent

10. The hit ratio threshold for which of the following is 90 percent?

    a. Data dictionary cache

    b. Library cache

    c. Shared Pool Memory

    d. Free shared memory

    e. Large pool

    f. Java pool

11. Which Oracle-supplied package do you use to pin an object in the Shared Pool Memory?

    a. DBMS_POOL

    b. DBMS_SHARED

    c. DBMS_SHARED_POOL

    d. DBMS_POOL_KEEP

    e. DBMS_SHARED_KEEP

    f. None of the above. You use an ALTER SYSTEM command.

12. Which function is a justification to use the large pool?

   a. Parallel query option

   b. Distributed Lock Manager

   c. Real Applications Cluster

   d. Dedicated server

13. Which task is not performed by the parsing process?

   a. Determines an execution plan for the statement

   b. Validates the syntax of the statement

   c. Verifies columns are valid

   d. Executes the statement

14. What percent would result in an error if you tried to allocate reserved pool memory from the Shared Pool Memory?

   a. 10 percent

   b. 25 percent

   c. 50 percent

   d. 75 percent

   e. 90 percent

15. Which statement(s) is true about the Shared Pool Memory?

   a. Proper sizing of Shared Pool Memory increases I/O.

   b. It helps speed up statement execution by flushing similar statements.

   c. Proper configuration of the shared pool causes cached memory objects to age out quickly and therefore improves performance.

   d. It improves performance, because Shared Pool Memory facilitates the SQL statement process.

HANDS-ON PROJECTS

Please complete the projects provided below.

1. Reread the Performance Problem at the start of the chapter. Think of it in terms of the concepts you have learned in this chapter and answer the following questions:

   a. Define the problem facing Joe Moe.

   b. What actions would you recommend to Joe Moe? If queries are necessary, present them all. Explain how to carry out your recommendations.

2. Write a query to display the five queries that were executed most frequently in an application.

3. Analyze the result of the following query and explain what action, if any, you would recommend.

```
SQL> SELECT PARAMETER, COUNT, USAGE, FIXED, GETS, GETMISSES
  2      FROM V$ROWCACHE
  3  /
```

PARAMETER	COUNT	USAGE	FIXED	GETS	GETMISSES
dc_free_extents	278	264	0	32951	3460
dc_used_extents	154	149	0	1458	562
dc_segments	881	864	0	520079	3472
dc_tablespaces	23	19	0	12452015	38
dc_tablespace_quotas	17	12	0	445	22
dc_files	1	0	0	0	0
dc_users	61	50	0	4637927	132
dc_rollback_segments	62	55	1	913766	54
dc_objects	1429	1423	52	1071254	5583
dc_global_oids	1	0	0	0	0
dc_constraints	4	3	0	26	14
dc_object_ids	924	914	52	5724688	3638
dc_synonyms	282	280	0	185369	1179
dc_sequences	58	48	0	38154	171
dc_usernames	40	29	0	1389991	44
dc_database_links	1	0	0	0	0
dc_histogram_defs	1944	1941	0	891726	6608
dc_outlines	1	0	0	0	0
dc_profiles	6	4	0	843616	4
ifs_acl_cache_entries	1	0	0	0	0
dc_users	1	0	0	0	0
dc_sequence_grants	98	97	0	8405	370
dc_histogram_data	1	0	0	0	0
dc_histogram_data_values	1	0	0	0	0
dc_user_grants	57	48	0	2804060	97

4. Log on as TUNER and select from different tables to issue different queries. Write a query to display all cached objects in the Shared Pool Memory for the TUNER user.

5. Connect to the database using three different user accounts and issue a query for each session. Write a query that displays the username, machine name, how long the user has been connected, and the query submitted from each session.

6. Perform the following steps:

   a. Create a public synonym for TUNER.CATEGORIES.

   b. Log on as TUNER.

   c. Grant read access on CATEGORIES to DEMO user. (If the DEMO user account is not set up, you can run this Oracle-supplied script: %ORACLE_ HOME%\RDBMS\ADMIN\DEMO.SQL.

   d. Log on as DEMO with a new session (at this point, you should have two sessions, one for TUNER and one for DEMO) .

   e. As TUNER, issue the following query:

   ```
   SELECT CATEGORY_ID, CATEGORY_NAME
     FROM CATEGORIES;
   ```

   f. As DEMO, issue exactly the same query three times.

   g. What do you predict will happen?

   h. Get the number of executions of the two queries submitted by TUNER and DEMO.

   i. What do you conclude from this problem?

7. Perform the following steps and explain what happened.

   a. Take a reading of the total number of statements in the SQL area and record the result here. _____

   b. Flush the Shared Pool Memory.

   c. Take another reading of the total number of statements in the SQL area and record the result here. _____

8. This is a partial report from an Oracle utility called Statspack (this tool is covered in Chapter 13). Analyze this report and draw a conclusion. Explain what necessary actions you would take.

```
STATSPACK report for

DB Name  DB Id      Instance      Inst Num  Release      OPS  Host
------   -------    ------------  -------   -----------  ---  ------------
INP      85696763   INP                1    9.2.0        NO   pluto

              Snap Id  Snap Time           Sessions
              -------  ----------------    --------
Begin Snap:      8276  02-Jan-02 00:00:15     213
End Snap:        8306  02-Jan-02 23:00:02     213
Elapsed:     1,379.78 (mins)

Cache Sizes
~~~~~~~~~~
           db_block_buffers:     150000       log_buffer:      163840
             db_block_size:       8192    shared_pool_size:  700000000

Load Profile
~~~~~~~~~~~
                                   Per Second      Per Transaction
                                   ----------      ---------------
                    Redo size:      71,280.99            1,984.12
                Logical reads:      12,178.97              339.00
                Block changes:         563.92               15.70
               Physical reads:       1,245.50               34.67
              Physical writes:         163.42                4.55
                   User calls:         745.13               20.74
                       Parses:          80.49                2.24
                  Hard parses:           0.32                0.01
                        Sorts:          36.62                1.02
                       Logons:           2.45                0.07
                     Executes:         275.93                7.68
                 Transactions:          35.93

    % Blocks changed per Read:    4.63   Recursive Call %:    26.32
  Rollback per transaction %:    84.99     Rows per Sort:     92.69

Instance Efficiency Percentages (Target 100%) ------------------------------
              Buffer Nowait %:   99.90     Redo NoWait %:    100.00
              Buffer  Hit  %:    89.77   In-memory Sort %:   100.00
              Library Hit  %:    99.71      Soft Parse %:     99.60
            Execute to Parse %:  70.83       Latch Hit %:     99.73
    Parse CPU to Parse Elapsd %: 65.85   % Non-Parse CPU:    100.00

Shared Pool Statistics            Begin   End
                                  ------  ------
               Memory Usage %:    42.01   62.90
       % SQL with executions>1:   16.50   20.29
      % Memory for SQL w/exec>1:  19.02   20.65
```

9. Follow the steps below:

a. Submit the following statement as TUNER user:
```
SELECT FIRST_NAME, LAST_NAME, SALARY
  FROM EMPLOYEES
  WHERE EMPLOYEE_ID = 7878
  /
```

b. Get all the statistics from V$SQLAREA for the query you just submitted.

c. Resubmit the same query four more times.

d. Change one character in the same query from uppercase to lowercase.

e. Submit the new query.

f. Get a full statistical report using V$SQLAREA for both queries.

g. What do you observe from the results?

10. Suppose your database has the following parameter setting:
```
shared_pool_size = 30M
```

With those parameter settings, you ran a query to get the data dictionary hit ratio, which produced the result below:
```
Data Dictionary Hit Ratio
--------------------------
        82.21235
```

Since the Data Dictionary hit ratio is less the 90 percent, you decided to increase the Shared Pool Memory to 80 MB. Then you shut down the database and reran the query to get the new data dictionary hit ratio. You got the following result:
```
Data Dictionary Hit Ratio
--------------------------
 70.243135
```

Answer the following questions:

a. Write the query that will produce the data dictionary hit ratio.

b. Explain why the data dictionary hit ratio dropped, even though the Shared Pool Memory increased.

c. Is the increase of Shared Pool Memory necessary?

d. What do you recommend?

11. Write the steps you need to take to perform the following tasks:

   a. Pin the following function in Shared Pool Memory.

   b. Write statement(s) to verify that the object is pinned.

   c. Unpin the object from Shared Pool Memory

```
CREATE OR REPLACE FUNCTION EMPLOYEE_SALES(
                                    P_EMPID    NUMBER
                                 ) RETURN NUMBER IS

   V_AMT NUMBER;

BEGIN

   SELECT COUNT(*)
     INTO V_AMT
     FROM EMPLOYEES
        WHERE EMPLOYEE_ID = P_EMPID;

   IF V_AMT = 0 THEN
      RETURN -1;
   END IF;

   SELECT SUM(ORDER_LINES.TOTAL_AMOUNT)
     INTO V_AMT
     FROM ORDER_LINES
        WHERE ORDER_LINES.ORDER_ID IN (SELECT ORDER_ID
                                         FROM ORDERS
                                            WHERE EMPLOYEE_ID = P_EMPID);


   RETURN V_AMT;

EXCEPTION
   WHEN NO_DATA_FOUND THEN
      RETURN -2;

   WHEN OTHERS THEN
      RETURN -3;

END;
/
```

12. Analyze the output of Shared Pool Size Advice from Oracle Enterprise Manager. See Figure 4-23.

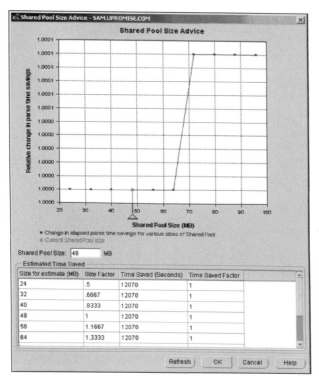

Figure 4-23   Shared Pool Size Advice analysis

CASE PROJECTS

Cache Diagnosis Case Project

On your first day at work, you are asked to analyze the new database applications that were commissioned into production three weeks ago. A sheet of tasks was handed to you by the senior DBA in your team with the following tasks:

1. Log on as SYS or SYSTEM and flush Shared Pool Memory.

2. Set the size of Shared Pool Memory to 8 MB.

3. Take a reading of the library cache hit ratio and data dictionary miss ratio. Record results here.

   Library cache:_____ Dictionary cache:_____

4. Start dbSessions and load DbSessions_chapter04a.qry (note that the contents of this file contains two statements only). Run 20 sessions using this file.

5. As the dbSessions run, get all queries and statistics submitted by TUNER% users.

6. How many distinct queries are there?

7. Using statistics obtained in Step 5, record your observations.

8. Are any SQL statement(s) shared?

9. Take a reading of the library cache hit ratio and data dictionary miss ratio. Record results here.

   Library cache: _____ Dictionary cache:_____

10. Is there any difference from the readings obtained in Step 3? Explain why or why not.

11. Display the number of cached objects.

12. Display how much Shared Pool Memory is available.

13. Explain the results obtained in Step 12.

14. Write a simple stored function that takes an order number and returns the total amount of the order as TUNER.

15. Set your CURSOR_SHARING parameter to EXACT.

16. Log on as TUNER using three different sessions.

17. For each TUNER session, execute the function created in Step 15 three times using different order numbers.

18. Get full statistics from the SQL area to determine if the code cached is being shared.

19. Record your observations on the results of Step 18.

20. Flush the Shared Pool Memory.

21. Change CURSOR_SHARING to SIMILAR and repeat Steps 17 through 19.

22. Take a reading of the Library cache hit ratio and data dictionary miss ratio. Record results here.

   Library cache: _____ Dictionary cache:_____

23. Record your observations. Is the size of the shared pool adequate? What would you recommend?

24. Suppose the ACME Order System frequently uses the stored function created earlier. What would you recommend to facilitate database performance? Present your answer in an explanation or list of action steps.

25. Using dbSessions, load DbSessions_chapter04b.qry. Then run 20 sessions. (The CHANGE option changes the pattern of some of the statements in QRY file.)

26. Display the Shared Pool Size Advice using Oracle Enterprise Manager or dynamic performance view and analyze results.

27. Take a final reading of the library cache hit ratio and data dictionary miss ratio. Record results here.

    Library cache: _____ Dictionary cache:_____

28. Record your observations. Is there any problem with shared pool performance? Explain why or why not?

29. Get the Shared Pool Memory usage ratio and determine if the results from this ratio provide a similar analysis as the library cache and dictionary cache ratios.

30. If you were to collect statistics for future analysis, outline what data you would gather. How would you collect it? How does it assist you as a DBA to determine if performance is at an acceptable level or not?

4

CHAPTER

5

WORKING WITH THE PROGRAM GLOBAL AREA

In this chapter you will:

♦ Learn about the Program Global Area (PGA) components, their uses, and their impact on performance

♦ Configure the PGA for dedicated and shared servers

♦ Learn how to use the PGA Advice feature

♦ Diagnose the PGA by using dynamic performance views

♦ Tune PGA sort operations

♦ Create temporary tablespaces

In previous chapters, you learned the importance of each memory component of the SGA and how to best configure, diagnose, and tune each one. This chapter explains the final memory structure of the Oracle instance to be considered. This memory structure is called the Program Global Area (PGA). The PGA is not part of the SGA, but it is important because it is the area of memory exercised by the user sessions.

This chapter is divided into two parts and follows the general order of all chapters in this book: overview, configuration, diagnosis, and then tuning. In the first part of this chapter you are introduced to the Program Global Area concept and its functions. Then you are shown how to configure the PGA and are presented with features and how they are adjusted.

The second part of the chapter deals with tuning the most important area of the Program Global Area structure—the sort area. That section presents tips on how to prevent and avoid queries that cause sort operations, and how to optimize sort operations when they are unavoidable.

Performance Problem

This section outlines an actual performance problem. As you look it over, imagine yourself as the DBA who reported it and keep it in mind as you proceed through the chapter. The chapter presents concepts relevant to the problem. In the first Hands-on Project at the end of the chapter, you are asked to use the concepts you have learned to provide a solution, or partial solution, to this performance problem.

From: W PROB EMAIL: prob@or.com

DATE: 17-Jul-02 15:52

SUBJECT: Which should be set on 9i, PGA_AGGREGATE_TARGET or SORT_AREA_SIZE?

Hi,

I am confused about whether to set PGA_AGGREGATE_TARGET or SORT_AREA_SIZE. Whichever you recommend, what is the proper value for the continuous running of multiple applications for a database that is sized between 6GB and 10GB? If you recommend using the SORT_AREA_SIZE, what is a proper value for the corresponding SORT_AREA_RETAINED_SIZE?

Currently my system is set to values as follows: sort_area_size : 346640 bytes sort_area_retained_size : 97312 Your help is much appreciated.

PROGRAM GLOBAL AREA

This scenario is based on actual events that happened to a senior-level DBA named Jay. Jay joined a local Internet provider to administer an existing customer service database that had been recently migrated to Oracle9i. Jay had his hands full doing all sorts of routine tasks and database enhancements. One day he got a call from the customer service manager complaining about specific queries that took a long time to run. Jay immediately started investigating the problem and looking at the queries. He found no apparent problems with the way they were written. He performed a quick health check of the database memory configuration and data file configuration; again he found nothing. Then he looked at each table and index that the queries were using and found that two of the indexes being used were unbalanced because of a high number of deletions. He looked at the size of the two indexes and found them large—in fact they were in the range of tens of gigabytes. Jay met with the customer service manager and his team and explained that because the possible cause of the problem were the indexes, he needed to schedule a rebuild of the indexes on the weekend. His manager gave him the go ahead.

The weekend came and Jay started the job. Among other preparatory tasks, he created a huge temporary space and then issued the statement to rebuild the indexes. The job took approximately 24 hours for both indexes. On Monday, he told his boss how much time it had taken to complete the task. She was astonished and asked him if there was a way to speed up the process. Jay said that additional memory was needed, and that there was hardly enough memory on the machine to handle the normal load. He said that he could not add memory from the current pool of RAM to the rebuild process without impacting users.

Jay said that because memory is cheap and the machine needed to be upgraded anyway, they should submit a formal request for more memory. His manager replied that she was not sure that more memory would speed up the process.

After a long bureaucratic process was completed to approve the requisition of memory for the machine, the extra memory was added, and Jay was scheduled to rebuild the indexes the next weekend. The following Monday he reported to his boss that the task of rebuilding both indexes had been reduced by seven hours.

After reading this scenario, you may be wondering if there was another way to speed up rebuilding the index. The answer to that question is "Yes." But Jay's goal was to kill two birds with one stone: improve the performance of the index rebuilding process, and obtain more memory for the machine to benefit all databases residing on it.

5

This first section of this chapter describes the Program Global Area and explains its use. The overview outlines the purposes of the PGA, the PGA components, and the impact of the PGA on database performance.

If you have never been exposed to this topic before, you may be asking yourself what the Program Global Area is and why you should study it. The PGA is the memory allocated from RAM (random access memory) on the host machine where Oracle resides. The PGA is added to the SGA memory when you are using a dedicated server and is part of the SGA when you are using a shared server. (The dedicated server and shared server are explained in detail in Chapter 11). Subsequent sections explain how to configure, diagnose, and tune the PGA.

As you can see in Figure 5-1, the PGA memory is a component allocated when a user establishes a connection to an Oracle server. The PGA serves two purposes: first, it holds user connection information, such as session properties, bind variables, cursor state, and other user-related data; and second, it is used to provide a temporary place to perform sorting operations for statements issued by the user. PGA memory is deallocated automatically when the user process is gracefully terminated. If the user process is terminated abnormally, the PMON (Process Monitor) Oracle background process cleans up the PGA memory allocated to the terminated user process.

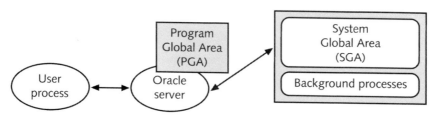

Figure 5-1   Program Global Area and an Oracle instance

Some textbooks and DBAs refer to the PGA as process global area, which is the same as Program Global Area.

TIP

Components of the PGA

PGA memory consists of three main components, as illustrated in Figure 5-2.

- **SQL workareas**: Are areas in which different operations that require temporary memory space are performed. These areas and operations are presented in Table 5-1.

- **Session data**: Holds user's session information such as username, password, user's machine name, user's terminal name, and other session-related data

- **Private SQL area**: Holds information about and the status of the cursor for the most recent statement submitted by the user and the bind variables used by the cursor. There are two areas in the private SQL area (as listed in Table 5-3): the runtime area and the persistent area.

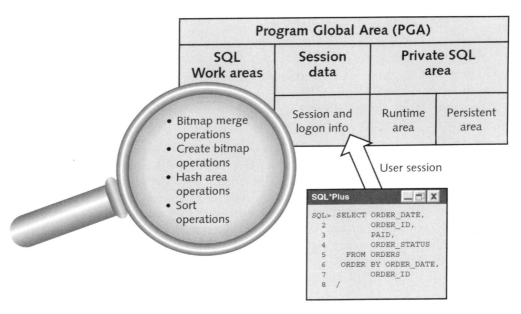

Figure 5-2   PGA components

As described in the preceding list, the SQL workareas within the PGA are used for sorting and other operations that require temporary memory. Table 5-1 outlines the operations conducted in these four different workareas.

Table 5-1   SQL workarea operations

SQL workareas	Operation type
Bitmap merge area	The bitmap merge operation results from a statement that is retrieving the **rowid** from two bitmap indexes that are merged into one. (Rowid stands for "row identification" and is the physical address of the row.)
Create bitmap area	The create bitmap area operation results from a CREATE BITMAP INDEX statement.

SQL workareas	Operation type
Hash area	The hash-join operation is the joining of a small- to medium-sized table to a large table in memory.
Sort area	The sort operation is caused by a statement that contains ORDER BY, DISTINCT, GROUP BY clauses, or other statements that require sorting.

As noted in Table 5-1, the SQL workareas are essential workspace used to hold data temporarily for the completion of the SQL statement process. Table 5-2 presents descriptions of the data held in the session area.

Table 5-2 Session data area

Session data	Description
User data	This data includes username, password, roles granted to the user, default role, and other related logon information.
Connection data	This data includes the name of the machine from which the session is connected, the name of the terminal from which the user is connected, the IP address of the machine, network protocol, time logged on, and other related information.

You may have noticed that most of the information held in the session data area can be obtained by querying the V$SESSION dynamic performance view which contains all session information for all connected users. Similarly, Table 5-3 presents descriptions of the data held in the private SQL area.

Table 5-3 Private SQL data area

Private SQL area	Description
Runtime area	Contains information about the submitted SQL statement. This information stays in memory while the statement is being executed.
Persistent area	Contains bind variable information and cursor status that stays in memory until the cursor is closed.

Impact of PGA on Performance

As you know, Oracle parses, executes, and fetches the required data. Just before Oracle is ready to send back the result set to you, the data must be sorted in the columns specified in the ORDER BY clause.

```
SQL> SELECT ORDER_DATE, ORDER_ID, PAID, ORDER_STATUS
  2    FROM ORDERS
  3    ORDER BY ORDER_DATE, ORDER_ID
  4  /
```

Figure 5-3 illustrates the process of sorting these rows. For simplicity, suppose the sort area in PGA has space for only 100,000 rows. Examine the figure as you read the explanation of the steps that follow.

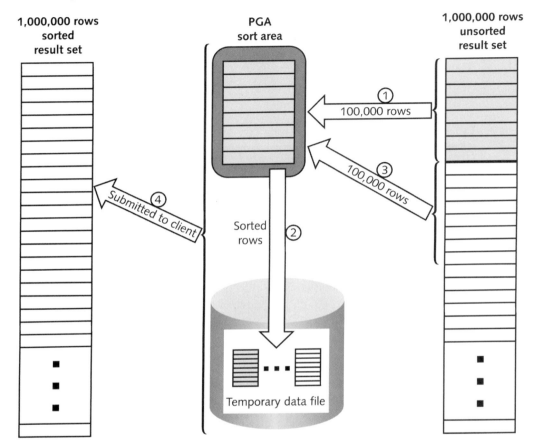

Figure 5-3   Sorting process

1. 100,000 rows of the result set are placed temporarily in PGA for sorting.

2. When the sorting is completed on the first 100,000 rows in the PGA, the sorted result set is moved to the temporary data file resulting in a disk write (One I/O).

3. Steps 1 and 2 are repeated until all 1,000,000 rows are sorted, and this process results in at least ten disk writes, if the rows were already sorted.

4. After all the rows are sorted and placed in the temporary data file, the result set must be retrieved, prepared and sent back to you, which results in at least ten disk reads.

Therefore, this simple statement has already caused at least over 20 I/O operations, just to sort the result. Remember also that parsing and the I/O generated to place data in the Buffer Cache have not been accounted for. Now, suppose that your PGA has space to hold 200,000 instead of 100,000 rows. This means that the number of I/O trips to temporary space on disk is reduced by at least half from 10 to five disk trips and thereby reduces I/O trips yielding improved performance.

As you observed in the preceding process, data that must be sorted requires temporary space, preferably in memory, rather than on a disk. The PGA is the memory that is used for this type of operation. When the PGA is too small, sort operations use both memory and temporary disk space to perform the operation. So, as you can see, PGA has a significant role in database performance, and its configuration clearly impacts performance, either positively or negatively. In the next section, you learn how to configure the PGA.

PGA CONFIGURATION

As a DBA, one of your primary objectives is to optimally configure databases for efficient throughput. Sometimes you use settings based on past experience, such as the existing database configuration, and at other times you use Oracle or database experts' guidelines. Configuring the PGA is no different. This section covers the configuration of the PGA for the following circumstances: dedicated server, shared server, auto setting, and manual setting.

PGA configuration depends on the database configuration of the Oracle server—whether it is a dedicated or a shared server—and whether the PGA is set manually or automatically. When PGA is set automatically, Oracle manages workareas for each connecting user session and allocates more or less PGA memory as it sees fit. As you work through the configuration, you may find it useful to structure the process based on the PGA configuration decision path shown in Figure 5-4.

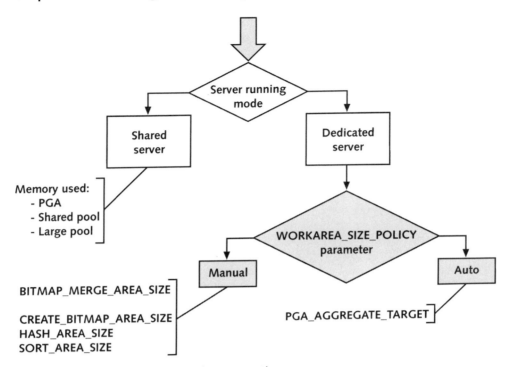

Figure 5-4   PGA configuration decision path

Before you delve into PGA configuration, it may be helpful to quickly review the following summary of differences between dedicated server and shared server modes:

- Dedicated server mode: This mode has the Oracle database server dedicated to serve requests for one user process. This is the default server mode.

- Shared server mode: Formerly known as multithreaded server (MTS), this mode has an Oracle database server or servers that handles requests for all user processes on a network.

PGA Configuration for Dedicated Servers

In a dedicated server mode configuration, the PGA memory management can be set in two ways. If PGA memory management is set to manual mode, you, as the DBA, set and monitor allocated memory for all areas of the PGA. If the PGA memory management is set to automatic mode, Oracle manages the PGA automatically based on criteria you set. Use the WORKAREA_SIZE_POLICY parameter to set Oracle to either manual or automatic PGA memory management mode. Table 5-4 presents more details on the WORKAREA_SIZE_POLICY parameter:

Table 5-4 WORKAREA_SIZE_POLICY parameter

Value	Description
MANUAL	Indicates that you manage PGA memory allocation by setting the following parameters: SORT_AREA_SIZE CREATE_BITMAP_AREA_SIZE BITMAP_MERGE_AREA_SIZE HASH_AREA_SIZE
AUTO	Indicates that Oracle manages PGA memory allocation. All parameter settings related to PGA area are ignored. Oracle recommends the use of AUTO management because PGA memory can be adjusted by increasing or reducing memory as needed.

NOTE

The WORKAREA_SIZE_POLICY parameter is a dynamic parameter that can be set or changed while the database is open.

You can set this parameter by issuing the following statement:

```
SQL> ALTER SYSTEM SET WORKAREA_SIZE_POLICY = AUTO
  2  /

System altered.
```

Or you can set this parameter in the initialization parameter file with an ALTER statement using the SCOPE option:

```
SQL> ALTER SYSTEM SET WORKAREA_SIZE_POLICY = AUTO SCOPE = SPFILE
  2  /

System altered.
```

What are the ramifications of setting this parameter to AUTO management? The next section explores this question.

AUTO Setting

Although the AUTO setting indicates automatic memory management, Oracle allows you to limit the total memory used for all user processes by configuring the PGA_AGGRE-GATE_TARGET parameter. Table 5-5 outlines the values for this parameter.

Table 5-5 PGA_AGGREGATE_TARGET parameter

Value	Description
0 Default value	Indicates that PGA memory management is set to MANUAL
10 MB to (4096 GB -1)	Indicates that Oracle attempts to keep the total memory allocated for all user connections below this value

Now that you know what the values for the PGA_AGGREGATE_TARGET parameter indicate, you need to understand how to set the initial value for this parameter. The initial value of this parameter usually depends on the four factors listed here, in order of priority:

1. Available RAM memory on the host machine

2. SGA memory allocation (maximum is 50 percent of the available memory)

3. Free memory for use by the operating system (normally 20 percent to 25 percent of available memory)

4. Type of application (for example OLTP or DSS)

To bring these criteria into a real-world context, consider the following scenario, which is depicted in Figure 5-5. Your database is residing on a machine with 4 GB of RAM. Oracle experts recommend that the total SGA not exceed 50 percent of the available RAM. So you have configured the total SGA to be 2 GB. You decide to keep 1 GB free. In this case, the PGA_AGGREGATE_TARGET is set to a value that is 25 percent of the total RAM memory available on the system. This leaves you with 1 GB for the PGA, which is 25 percent of the memory, and 1 GB for the PGA is appropriate because Oracle experts recommend that 20 to 25 percent of RAM be kept available on the host machine for operating system tasks and other programs. You can use this as an initial value for RAM allocation. With this setting, Oracle allocates up to 1 GB of memory for user connections that are performing operations requiring temporary space.

NOTE

You must remember that when needed for an operation, a user process may take up all PGA memory allocated, but it also releases it immediately when the operation is completed.

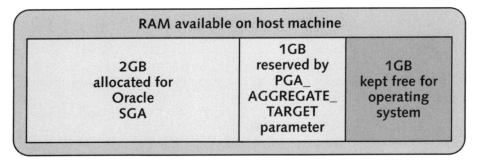

Figure 5-5   RAM allocation

Figure 5-6 is a screen shot of the configuration option in instance node. It displays a reminder note about the PGA.

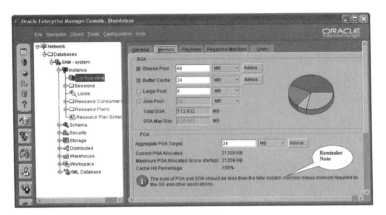

Figure 5-6   Oracle Enterprise Manager—Reminder Note

Manual Setting

Some DBAs prefer to control all aspects of the database configuration because they do not trust Oracle automatic management or because the type of application requires specific settings. This section shows you how to manually manage the PGA by setting the workarea parameters listed in Table 5-6. Of all parameters listed in Table 5-6, the SORT_AREA_SIZE parameter is most useful for tuning.

Table 5-6   Workarea parameters

Parameter	Default value	Description
SORT_AREA_SIZE	64 KB	Total memory that can be allocated for sort operations
CREATE_BITMAP_AREA_SIZE	1 MB	Total memory that can be allocated for create bitmap operations. Used if your application incorporates bitmap indexes
BITMAP_MERGE_AREA_SIZE	8 MB	Total memory that can be allocated for bitmap merge operations. Used when applications use bitmap indexes.
HASH_AREA_SIZE	2 * SORT_AREA_SIZE	Total memory that can be allocated for hash-join operations

When you use the automatic memory management of the PGA, you can adjust the aggregate target value dynamically as needed.

TIP

When you configure the PGA manually, use Figure 5-7 to guide you through the configuration steps.

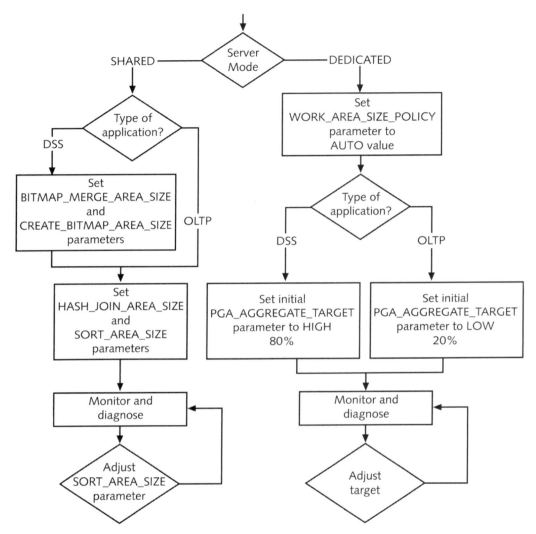

Figure 5-7 PGA configuration process

As you can see, for a dedicated server, it is best to use automatic memory management for the PGA. The target should be set to 80 percent of the available free memory for DSS and 20 percent for OLTP. The shared server mode is outlined in the next section.

To understand these concepts more fully, imagine yourself as a DBA working with a dedicated server. In this situation, you have 8 GB of RAM available on your system, and you are creating a new DSS application database. After analysis, you have determined that you need 1 GB for the SGA. Your new database is sharing the system with another database or other applications consuming a total 2 GB of memory including the PGA. Follow these steps to determine how you should set the PGA target of the new database:

1. Determine the available free memory:

   8 GB available—2 GB used by existing database equals 6 GB free

2. From free memory, determine how much is available after allocating the SGA for the new database and allocating 20 percent for the operating system:

   6 GB available—1 GB for the SGA—(20 percent for the operating system)

   In the following calculation, the result implies that 3.4 GB is available to allocate to the PGA from RAM.

   6 GB - 1 GB - 1.6 GB = 3.4 GB

3. Now, using the guidelines presented previously for a DSS application, you can set the target for up to 80 percent of available memory, which is:

   3.4 GB * 0.8 = 2.72 GB, or about 3 GB for the PGA

PGA Configuration for Shared Servers

As you observed in Figure 5-7, the only parameter that should be adjusted is the SORT_AREA_SIZE. The others are set according to the guidelines in Table 5-7.

Table 5-7   Guidelines for setting workareas

Parameter	OLTP	DSS	HYBRID
SORT_AREA_SIZE	1 MB	256 MB	128 MB
CREATE_BITMAP_AREA_SIZE	0	8 MB	8 MB
BITMAP_MERGE_AREA_SIZE	0	1 MB	1 MB
HASH_JOIN_AREA_SIZE	2 MB	512 MB	256 MB

You should always remember that these guidelines are considered best practice, but may not be applicable to all situations. In addition, monitoring and diagnosing should be part of the routine tasks you perform, and these tasks indicate whether your settings are proper or not. The following command shows the current setting for all the workareas:

```
SQL> SHOW PARAMETER AREA

NAME                                 TYPE         VALUE
------------------------------------ ------------ --------
bitmap_merge_area_size               integer      1048576
create_bitmap_area_size              integer      8388608
hash_area_size                       integer      1048576
sort_area_retained_size              integer      0
sort_area_size                       integer      524288
workarea_size_policy                 string       AUTO
```

Now that you have worked through the configuration of the PGA for dedicated and shared servers, it will be helpful to understand how to use the PGA Advice feature to support such work. The next section explains this.

PGA Advice Feature

Jenny joined an accounting firm as a junior DBA to administer an Oracle financial application for the firm. Jenny was a career changer and had been an accountant in her professional life. This was her first position as a DBA, and she started with the jitters like everyone else, but was even more nervous about messing up the database than most new hires. As she had learned to do in college, she did a quick survey of the database to see if any of the new Oracle9*i* features were being used. She was specifically eager to employ any feature that would reduce the routine tasks or make it easier to configure the database. She remembered what her instructor said in class, "Database administration is a big responsibility. You need to be proactive, informed, resourceful, and ready when the big waves of problems come. You should take advantage of any little feature available to help you better configure your database."

As you learned in previous chapters, Oracle9*i* introduced a new feature, Oracle Advice, to assist you in configuring major parts of the SGA. You learned about using the Oracle Advice feature for the Shared Pool Memory and the buffer cache. As you might have guessed, Oracle9*i* also provides an Advice feature for the PGA. This PGA Advice feature helps you determine if an adjustment to the PGA target is needed or not. When you set the PGA_AGGREGATE_TARGET parameter, you use the processes and steps outlined in a previous section. But, as you were advised, your initial setting might not be optimal, and you should therefore use the Advice feature to guide you. Oracle provides two ways of viewing the PGA Advice: one method is to use the dynamic performance views; another method is to use the Oracle Enterprise Manager. The following sections explore each method in detail.

Advice Using Dynamic Performance Views

Two views relate to the Advice feature for PGA: the V$PGA_TARGET_ADVICE view and the V$PGA_TARGET_ADVICE_HISTOGRAM view. This section examines the V$PGA_TARGET_ADVICE view. It is used to predict the impact on cache hits if you adjust the target from its current setting to a lower or higher value. Table 5-8 defines the columns in this view.

Table 5-8   V$PGA_TARGET_ADVICE view

Column	Description
PGA_TARGET_FOR_ESTIMATE	Predicted target value in bytes
PGA_TARGET_FACTOR	Target factor is the predicted target value compared to the current target
ADVICE_STATUS	ON indicates that Advice is enabled for the predicted target value; the other setting is OFF

Column	Description
BYTES_PROCESSED	Number of bytes processed for all operations used
ESTD_EXTRA_BYTES_RW	Estimated number of extra bytes which would be read or written for the predicted target value
ESTD_PGA_CACHE_HIT_PERCENTAGE	Estimated cache hit percentage: BYTES_PROCESSED / (BYTES_PROCESSED + ESTD_EXTRA_BYTES_RW)
ESTD_OVERALLOC_COUNT	Estimated number of memory overallocations for the predicated target value. A nonzero value indicates that the predicted target is not large enough.

To find out if the PGA target is properly set, issue the following query:

```
SQL> COLUMN PGA_TARGET_FOR_ESTIMATE HEADING "Estimated|Target"
SQL> COLUMN PGA_TARGET_FACTOR HEADING "Target|Factor"
SQL> COLUMN BYTES_PROCESSED HEADING "Bytes|Processed"
SQL> COLUMN ESTD_EXTRA_BYTES_RW HEADING "Est Extra|Bytes RW"
SQL> COLUMN ESTD_PGA_CACHE_HIT_PERCENTAGE HEADING "Est. Cache|Hit Pct"
SQL> COLUMN ESTD_OVERALLOC_COUNT HEADING "Est. Overalloc|Count"
SQL> SELECT PGA_TARGET_FOR_ESTIMATE,
  2          PGA_TARGET_FACTOR,
  3          BYTES_PROCESSED,
  4          ESTD_EXTRA_BYTES_RW,
  5          ESTD_PGA_CACHE_HIT_PERCENTAGE,
  6          ESTD_OVERALLOC_COUNT
  7     FROM V$PGA_TARGET_ADVICE
  8  /

Estimated    Target     Bytes   Est. Extra Est. Cache Est. Overalloc
   Target    Factor  Processed   Bytes RW    Hit Pct      Count
---------- ---------- ---------- ---------- ---------- ---------------
  10485760         1   10227712          0        100               1
  12582912       1.2   10227712          0        100               0
  14680064       1.4   10227712          0        100               0
  16777216       1.6   10227712          0        100               0
  18874368       1.8   10227712          0        100               0
  20971520         2   10227712          0        100               0
  31457280         3   10227712          0        100               0
  41943040         4   10227712          0        100               0
  62914560         6   10227712          0        100               0
  83886080         8   10227712          0        100               0
```

As you can see from the preceding results, the highlighted row with the Target Factor equal to 1 indicates that the PGA was configured by you—in other words, you set the PGA to the 10 MB value shown in the Estimated Target column. Also, a Target Factor of 2 means twice the value of current configuration of the PGA. You should also notice that the Est. Overalloc Count is a nonzero value, which indicates that the PGA target is not large enough. This implies that you would increase performance if you adjusted the target to a higher value, such as 12 MB.

You can use another dynamic performance advice view to get a detailed execution projection on a specific PGA target level. This is the V$PGA_TARGET_ADVICE_HISTOGRAM view. Table 5-9 defines the most commonly used columns of the V$PGA_TARGET_ADVICE_HISTOGRAM view.

Table 5-9   Most commonly used columns of V$PGA_TARGET_ADVICE_HISTOGRAM view

Column	Description
PGA_TARGET_FOR_ESTIMATE	Predicted target value in bytes
LOW_OPTIMAL_SIZE	Optimal lower boundary of workareas
HIGH_OPTIMAL_SIZE	Optimal upper boundary of workareas
ESTD_OPTIMAL_EXECUTIONS	Estimated number of executions within the workarea's lower and upper boundaries
ESTD_ONEPASS_EXECUTIONS	Estimated number of one-pass executions within the workarea's lower and upper boundaries
ESTD_MULTIPASSES_EXECUTIONS	Estimated number of multipass executions within the workarea's lower and upper boundaries
ESTD_TOTAL_EXECUTIONS	Estimated number of one-pass and multipass executions within the workarea's lower and upper boundaries

Before moving on to display the contents of this view, it is important to understand what is meant by **optimal**, **one-pass,** and **multipass** execution. The terms are defined as follows:

- Optimal execution: The workarea in PGA is large enough to allocate memory for the current operation.

- One-pass execution: The workarea in PGA is not large enough to allocate memory for the current operation and requires one extra step or pass to complete the operation.

- Multi-pass execution: The workarea in PGA is too small to allocate memory for the current operation and requires multiple extra steps and passes to complete the operation.

Figure 5-8 visually summarizes the execution threshold and response time for each of the three types of execution in the preceding list.

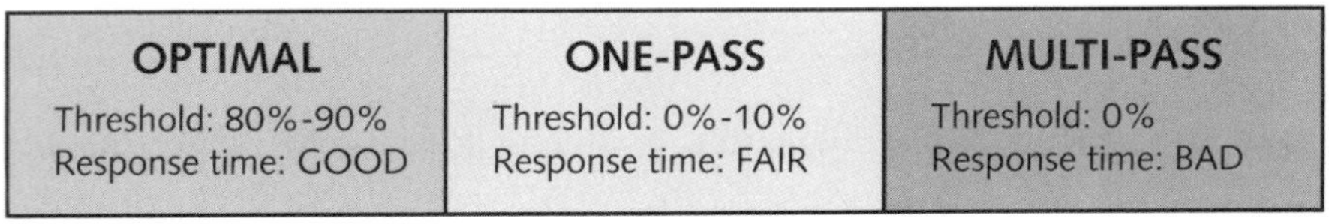

OPTIMAL	ONE-PASS	MULTI-PASS
Threshold: 80%-90%	Threshold: 0%-10%	Threshold: 0%
Response time: GOOD	Response time: FAIR	Response time: BAD

Figure 5-8   Execution threshold and response time

You can use the V$PGA_TARGET_ADVICE_HISTOGRAM dynamic performance view to determine optimal configuration of the PGA target. You can run the following query to get details on the PGA target of 10 MB:

```
SQL> SELECT LOW_OPTIMAL_SIZE/1024  LO_SIZE_KB,
  2         ROUND(HIGH_OPTIMAL_SIZE/1024) HI_SIZE_KB,
  3         ESTD_OPTIMAL_EXECUTIONS EST_OPTIMAL_EXEC,
  4         ESTD_ONEPASS_EXECUTIONS EST_ONEPASS_EXEC,
  5         ESTD_MULTIPASSES_EXECUTIONS EST_MULTIPASS_EXEC
  6    FROM V$PGA_TARGET_ADVICE_HISTOGRAM
  7   WHERE PGA_TARGET_FOR_ESTIMATE/1024/1024 = 10
  8   ORDER BY 1,2
  9  /
```

LO_SIZE_KB	HI_SIZE_KB	EST_OPTIMAL_EXEC	EST_ONEPASS_EXEC	EST_MULTIPASS_EXEC
0	1	0	0	0
1	2	0	0	0
2	4	0	0	0
4	8	0	0	0
8	16	2404	0	0
16	32	0	0	0
32	64	10	0	0
64	128	4	0	0
128	256	0	0	0
256	512	0	0	0
512	1024	0	0	0
1024	2048	0	0	0
2048	4096	0	0	0
4096	8192	0	0	0
8192	16384	0	0	0
16384	32768	0	0	0
32768	65536	0	0	0
65536	131072	0	0	0
131072	262144	0	0	0
262144	524288	0	0	0
524288	1048576	0	0	0
1048576	2097152	0	0	0
2097152	4194304	0	0	0
4194304	8388608	0	0	0
8388608	16777216	0	0	0
16777216	33554432	0	0	0
33554432	67108864	0	0	0
67108864	134217728	0	0	0
134217728	268435456	0	0	0
268435456	536870912	0	0	0
536870912	1073741824	0	0	0
1073741824	2147483648	0	0	0
2147483648	4294967295	0	0	0

The results of the preceding query show that EST_OPTIMAL_EXEC column value is optimal at a value of 0, which means that setting the PGA_AGGREGATE_TARGET parameter to a value between 128 KB and 256 KB is an adequate configuration. You should remember that multipass execution should be very close to 0; if not, consider increasing the PGA_AGGREGATE_TARGET value. Also, one-pass executions should be a very low number compared to optimal execution; if not, you should consider increasing the PGA_AGGREGATE_TARGET value

Advice Using Oracle Enterprise Manager

There is a new trend in database administration. Not so long ago—ten years—most DBA experts and professionals used the basic primitive command line SQL*Plus tool to perform most of their tasks. They were very familiar with all dynamic performance views and were resourceful with scripts and queries to perform their tasks. As with most software and IT fields, progress in software technology created a new generation of DBAs that use graphical user interface tools to replace old-fashioned scripts and queries. Drop-down menus, drop-down lists, charts, and all sorts of colorful database tools are being used to make the life of a DBA much easier. No need to remember what view to query or to write a script; you can accomplish your task with the click of a mouse. Many companies were created to develop tools to work with Oracle, and these companies developed all sorts of graphical user interface tools for DBAs, and Oracle jumped into the game by developing Oracle Enterprise Manager as an administration tool.

Oracle Enterprise Manager provides a graphical interface that you can use at any time to view PGA Advice. Part of this interface includes a Help feature that explains the contents of the screen. You can explore this feature by performing the following steps:

1. Open Oracle Enterprise Manager in either standalone or management server mode.

2. Click the **+** (plus) icon of Instance node.

3. Click the **Configuration** option as shown in Figure 5-9 and select the **Memory** tab.

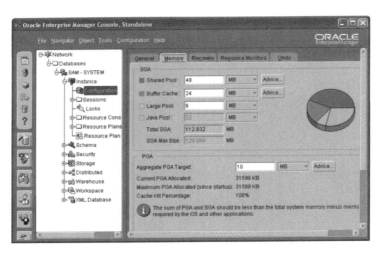

Figure 5-9   Oracle Enterprise Manager—Configuration

4. Click the **Advice** button in the PGA section. This causes a new screen to display the contents of the V$PGA_TARGET_ADVICE, as shown in Figure 5-10. As you can see, there are two check marks in the overflow column, 12 MB and 18 MB, indicating that the PGA target should be greater than 18 MB because the cache hit percentage is 100 percent. In other words, setting the PGA_AGGREGATE_TARGET parameter to 12 or 18 MB results in 46 to 60 percent of operations that would require more memory than allocated by the PGA_AGGREGATE_TARGET parameter, which forces Oracle to use temporary segments. This leads to performance degradation.

5

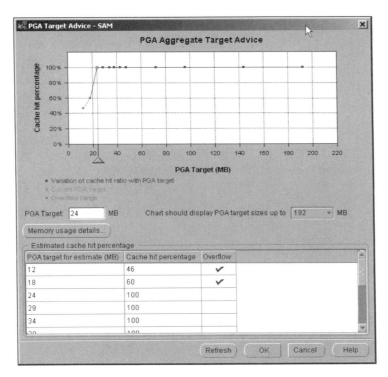

Figure 5-10   Oracle Enterprise Manager—PGA Target Advice

Figure 5-11 displays the number of optimal, one-pass, and multi-pass executions for any target value. In this screen you see the optimal size for operations of memory size 0 to 256 KB.

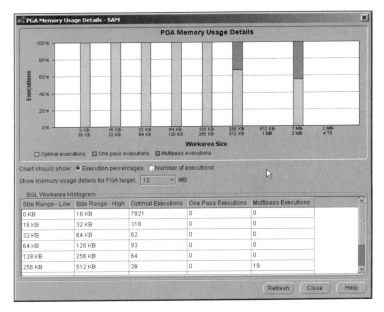

Figure 5-11   Oracle Enterprise Manager—PGA target histogram

Now that you know how to use the PGA Target Advice feature, you can tackle adjusting the PGA target.

Adjusting the PGA Target

While the database is up and running, the PGA_AGGREGATE_TARGET parameter can be adjusted dynamically. This parameter can be set to a value between 10 MB and 4 TB (terabytes). For instance, if you decide to adjust the parameter to 20 MB, you issue the following statement:

```
SQL> ALTER SYSTEM SET PGA_AGGREGATE_TARGET = 20M
  2  /

System altered.

SQL> SHOW PARAMETER PGA

NAME                                   TYPE        VALUE
-------------------------------------- ----------- ---------
pga_aggregate_target                   big integer 20971520
```

When using SQL*Plus and using OEM, if you set the PGA_AGGREGATE_TARGET parameter to an invalid value, you get the error displayed in Figure 5-12 and shown in the following code segment:

```
SQL> ALTER SYSTEM SET PGA_AGGREGATE_TARGET = 4M;
ALTER SYSTEM SET PGA_AGGREGATE_TARGET = 4M
*
ERROR at line 1:
ORA-02097: parameter cannot be modified because specified value is invalid
ORA-00093: pga_aggregate_target must be between 10M and 4096G-1
```

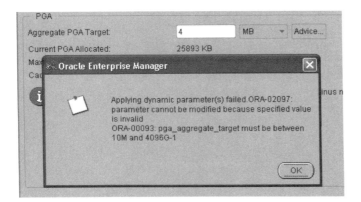

Figure 5-12   Oracle Enterprise Manager—error message

PGA DIAGNOSIS

Now that you understand the PGA use, components, and configuration, you need to delve into PGA diagnosis. Understanding diagnosis is, of course, a prerequisite for PGA tuning. The V$PROCESS view is useful for diagnosis because it contains information about active processes for all sessions. The structure of this view has been modified in Oracle9*i* to include PGA statistics for each process. These new PGA columns are listed in Table 5-10.

Table 5-10   V$PROCESS view

Column	Description
PGA_USED_MEM	Total number of bytes used by the process in PGA memory
PGA_ALLOC_MEM	Total number of bytes allocated to, used by, and free to the process in PGA memory
PGA_FREEABLE_MEM	Total number of bytes of allocated PGA memory that can be freed
PGA_MAX_MEM	Total number of bytes of PGA memory that were ever allocated by the process

You can issue the query that follows to get a listing of all current processes. From the results of the query, you can see which processes are using and allocating the most PGA memory. This query does not provide you with the get hit ratio, percentage threshold, or any performance indicators. It provides, instead, a current picture of PGA memory use and allocation by processes.

```
SQL> SELECT DECODE(BACKGROUND,
  2                    1, (SELECT NAME
  3                          FROM V$BGPROCESS
  4                         WHERE PADDR=P.ADDR),
  5                   'USER') PROCESS,
  6           PGA_USED_MEM,
  7           PGA_ALLOC_MEM,
  8           PGA_MAX_MEM
  9      FROM V$PROCESS P
 10     ORDER BY 1
 11  /

PROCESS      PGA_USED_MEM PGA_ALLOC_MEM PGA_MAX_MEM
----------   ------------ ------------- -----------
CKPT               164912       1128188     1128188
DBW0               136108       1180564     1180564
LGWR              4349880       5386656     5386656
PMON               132564        198892      198892
RECO               140876        207404      207404
SMON               186392        383956      383956
USER                    0             0           0
USER               141260        207404      207404
USER               934580       1064724     1064724
USER                56708        144936      144936
USER               442156        509800      509800
USER               309480      11133024    11133024
USER               153672        224496      224496
USER               156676        224496      224496
USER               156676        224496      224496
USER               156676        224496      224496
USER               156676        224496      224496
...
```

The results in the preceding code segment show that the maximum memory used by a user process is *934580* bytes, which is about 1 MB. Also, the most overallocated PGA memory for a user process is *11133024* bytes, which is about 10 MB, and 10 MB happens to be the maximum PGA memory ever allocated to all users. Of course, these numbers can be used to get a PGA memory allocation estimate for one user or all users, and to compare it to PGA_AGGREGATE_TARGET value.

Although the query yields no formal PGA configuration indicators, you can aggregate the memory used by background processes and user processes to get an idea of how much memory has been allocated and used by each category. To do so, use the following query. The results show that total memory used is within the target 10 MB.

```
SQL> SELECT DECODE(BACKGROUND,
  2                  1, 'BACKGROUND',
  3                  'USER') PROCESSES,
  4          COUNT(*) PROCESSES_COUNT,
  5          SUM(PGA_USED_MEM)/1024/1024 PGA_USED_MEM,
  6          SUM(PGA_ALLOC_MEM)/1024/1024 PGA_ALLOC_MEM,
  7          SUM(PGA_FREEABLE_MEM)/1024/1024 PGA_FREE_MEM,
  8          SUM(PGA_MAX_MEM)/1024/1024 PGA_MAX_MEM
  9    FROM V$PROCESS
 10    GROUP BY DECODE(BACKGROUND, 1, 'BACKGROUND', 'USER')
 11  /

PROCESSES   PROCESSES_COUNT PGA_USED_MEM PGA_ALLOC_MEM PGA_FREE_MEM PGA_MAX_MEM
---------- ---------------- ------------ ------------- ------------ -----------
BACKGROUND                6   4.87395096    8.10839462            0  8.10839462
USER                     59   10.3892059    24.5235252            0  24.8360252
```

It is useful to take this example a little further to see what percentage of allocated memory is used. You can infer that about 58 percent can be freed. This percentage is derived by subtracting 42 percent from 100 percent for user processes.

```
SQL> SELECT DECODE(BACKGROUND,
  2                  1, 'BACKGROUND',
  3                  'USER') PROCESSES,
  4          COUNT(*) PROCESSES_COUNT,
  5          round(SUM(PGA_USED_MEM)/
  6          SUM(PGA_ALLOC_MEM)*100) PGA_USED_ALLOC_PCT
  7    FROM V$PROCESS
  8    GROUP BY DECODE(BACKGROUND, 1, 'BACKGROUND', 'USER')
  9  /

PROCESSES   PROCESSES_COUNT PGA_USED_ALLOC_PCT
---------- ---------------- ------------------
BACKGROUND                6                 60
USER                     59                 42
```

Working With V$ WORKAREA Views

Unlike V$PROCESS, the V$SQL_WORKAREA view provides full PGA statistics for every statement submitted to the database. This view consists of many columns that provide statistical data. Table 5-11 lists some of the columns that are most frequently used.

Table 5-11   V$SQL_WORKAREA view

Column	Description
ADDRESS	Address in memory of the related statement
WORKAREA_ADDRESS	Address in PGA memory of the operation

Column	Description
OPERATION_TYPE	Type of operation applied to the statement, types are: BITMAP CREATE, BITMAP MERGE, BUFFERING, GROUP BY, HASH JOIN, or SORT (These operations are explained in more detail in Chapter 13.)
POLICY	Indicates whether PGA memory management for the related statement was allocated automatically or manually
ESTIMATED_OPTIMAL_SIZE	Memory needed to complete operation in memory (value expressed in kilobytes)
TOTAL_EXECUTIONS	Total number of executions for this operation
OPTIMAL_EXECUTIONS	Number of optimal executions
ONEPASS_EXECUTIONS	Number of one-pass executions
MULTIPASSES_EXECUTIONS	Number of multipass executions

To find out the number of executions and the memory used for each type of operation, use the query that follows. The results of the query can be plotted as a line chart to obtain a trend to determine if your application is excessive in submitting one or more operations of any type.

```
SQL> SELECT OPERATION_TYPE,
  2         COUNT(*),
  3         SUM(ESTIMATED_OPTIMAL_SIZE),
  4         SUM(TOTAL_EXECUTIONS)
  5    FROM V$SQL_WORKAREA
  6   GROUP BY OPERATION_TYPE
  7  /

OPERATION_TYPE           COUNT(*) SUM(ESTIMATED_OPTIMAL_SIZE) SUM(TOTAL_EXECUTIONS)
-------------------- ---------- --------------------------- ---------------------
BUFFER                        1                       10240                   155
CONNECT-BY (SORT)             1                       10240                   310
GROUP BY (SORT)              38                     1324032                   318
HASH-JOIN                     2                     1560576                     0
SORT                         94                     2807808                 17355
WINDOW (SORT)                 2                       20480                   262
```

Another use for this view is to identify the query that is consuming the most memory or the most executions of any operation type. Use the following query to get the top five queries using the most PGA memory, other than SYS or SYSTEM:

```
SQL> SELECT *
  2     FROM (
  3          SELECT U.USERNAME,
  4                 SUBSTR(S.SQL_TEXT,1,40) SQL,
  5                 SW.OPERATION_TYPE,
  6                 SUM(SW.ESTIMATED_OPTIMAL_SIZE) OPTIMAL_SIZE
  7            FROM V$SQL S, V$SQL_WORKAREA SW, DBA_USERS U
  8           WHERE S.ADDRESS = SW.ADDRESS
  9             AND U.USER_ID = S.PARSING_SCHEMA_ID
 10             AND USERNAME NOT IN ('SYS','SYSTEM')
 11          GROUP BY U.USERNAME,
 12                 SUBSTR(S.SQL_TEXT,1,40),
 13                 SW.OPERATION_TYPE
 14          ORDER BY OPTIMAL_SIZE DESC
 15          )
 16    WHERE ROWNUM < 6
 17  /

USERNAME   SQL                                       OPERATION_TYPE       OPTIMAL_SIZE
--------   ----------------------------------------  -------------------- ------------
TUNER      SELECT DISTINCT E.FIRST_NAME, E.LAST_NAM  SORT                       147456
TUNER      SELECT SHIPMENT_METHOD.SHIPMENT_DESCRIPT  GROUP BY (SORT)            147456
TUNER      SELECT SUPPLIER_NAME,         CONTACT_N   GROUP BY (SORT)            147456
TUNER      SELECT * FROM CUSTOMERS ORDER BY 2,3      SORT                        73728
TUNER      SELECT * FROM ALL_OBJECTS, TUNER.PRODUCT  SORT                        73728
```

Or submit the following queries to get the top 20 queries with the most executions of all users. The additional columns in the result from this query provide data on execution types.

```
SQL> SELECT *
  2      FROM (
  3          SELECT U.USERNAME,
  4                 SUBSTR(S.SQL_TEXT,1,30) SQL,
  5                 SW.OPERATION_TYPE,
  6                 SUM(SW.OPTIMAL_EXECUTIONS) OPT,
  7                 SUM(SW.ONEPASS_EXECUTIONS) ONE,
  8                 SUM(SW.MULTIPASSES_EXECUTIONS) MULTI
  9            FROM V$SQL S, V$SQL_WORKAREA SW, DBA_USERS U
 10           WHERE S.ADDRESS = SW.ADDRESS
 11             AND U.USER_ID = S.PARSING_SCHEMA_ID
 12           GROUP BY U.USERNAME,
 13                 SUBSTR(S.SQL_TEXT,1,30),
 14                 SW.OPERATION_TYPE
 15           ORDER BY OPT DESC
 16          )
 17      WHERE ROWNUM < 21
 18  /

USERNAME   SQL                             OPERATION_TYPE        OPT    ONE  MULTI
---------- ------------------------------- --------------------- ------ ---- -----
SYS        select job, nvl2(last_date, 1,  SORT                  17902     0     0
SYS        select q_name, state, delay, e  SORT                   2890     0     0
SYS        select i.obj#,i.ts#,i.file#,i.  SORT                    494     0     0
SYS        select name,intcol#,segcol#,ty  SORT                    324     0     0
SYS        select privilege#,level from s  CONNECT-BY (SORT)       310     0     0
SYSTEM     /* OracleOEM */ select case     WINDOW (SORT)           262     0     0
SYS        select i.obj#,i.ts#,i.file#,i.  GROUP BY (SORT)         238     0     0
SYS        select privilege#,level from s  BUFFER                  155     0     0
SYS        select grantee#,privilege#,nvl  GROUP BY (SORT)         148     0     0
SYS        select col#, grantee#, privile  GROUP BY (SORT)         142     0     0
SYSTEM     /* OracleOEM */ select case     SORT                    131     0     0
SYSTEM     SELECT U.USERNAME,        S.SQ  SORT                    130     0     0
SYS        select owner#,name,namespace,r  SORT                     86     0     0
SYSTEM     SELECT *     FROM (        SELE SORT                     77     0     0
SYS        select position#,sequence#,lev  SORT                     75     0     0
SYSTEM     /* OracleOEM */ SELECT round(p  SORT                     67     0     0
SYS        select col#,intcol#,charsetid,  SORT                     58     0     0
SYS        select col#,intcol#,ntab# from  SORT                     58     0     0
SYS        select col#,intcol#,toid,versi  SORT                     58     0     0
SYS        select l.col#, l.intcol#, l.lo  SORT                     58     0     0
```

V$SQL_WORKAREA_ACTIVE is another view that provides statistics for active statements submitted to the database. Table 5-12 provides a list of the most useful columns in this view.

Table 5-12   V$SQL_WORKAREA_ACTIVE view

Column	Description
OPERATION_TYPE	Type of operation such as SORT, HASH JOIN, GROUP BY, BUFFERING, BITMAP MERGE, or BITMAP CREATE
SID	Session identification number; this can be used to join this view with V$SESSION
EXPECTED_SIZE	Expected number of bytes for this operation expressed in kilobytes

Column	Description
ACTUAL_MEM_USED	Actual memory used by the operation expressed in kilobytes
MAX_MEM_USED	Maximum number of bytes used expressed in kilobytes
NUMBER_PASSES	Number of passes (0 for optimal, 1 for one pass, and >1 for multiple passes)
TEMPSEG_SIZE	Number of bytes in use from temporary tablespace
TABLESPACE	Tablespace name used for operations that needed temporary space on disk

5

Now that the columns in the V$SQL_WORKAREA_ACTIVE view have been explained, three typical uses for the view are described.

Use 1: You can use this view to identify sessions that are using temporary segments and how much space they are using. To display this information, issue the following query:

```
SQL> SELECT S.USERNAME,
  2         SW.OPERATION_TYPE,
  3         SW.TABLESPACE,
  4         SW.TEMPSEG_SIZE/1024/1024 SIZE_IN_MB
  5    FROM V$SQL_WORKAREA_ACTIVE SW,
  6         V$SESSION S
  7   WHERE S.SID = SW.SID
  8  /

USERNAME    OPERATION_TYPE       TABLESPACE                       SIZE_IN_MB
----------  -------------------  -------------------------------  ----------
DEMO        SORT                 TEMP                                   1197
```

The result of the query shows to what extent temporary disk segments were used because of either lack of PGA memory, or excessive use of operations that require more space than allocated or available. In this case, you need to examine the activities that this user is incurring.

Use 2: The following query lists all sessions and the amount of workarea space used by each session:

```
SQL> SELECT  S.USERNAME,
  2          SW.OPERATION_TYPE,
  3          SW.ACTUAL_MEM_USED/1024 USED_IN_KB
  4     FROM V$SQL_WORKAREA_ACTIVE SW,
  5          V$SESSION S
  6    WHERE SW.SID = S.SID
  7    ORDER BY SW.ACTUAL_MEM_USED DESC
  8   /

USERNAME    OPERATION_TYPE        USED_IN_KB
----------  --------------------  ----------
DEMO        SORT                         705
```

The results of the preceding query show that DEMO user has used about 705 KB of PGA memory, from which you can determine whether allocated PGA memory is adequate for most sessions that are incurring similar database activities.

Use 3: The following query lists all active queries and their memory allocation percentage to determine whether the workarea is sufficient to complete operations in memory:

```
SQL> SELECT  S.USERNAME,
  2          SUBSTR(Q.SQL_TEXT,1,30) SQL,
  3          SW.OPERATION_TYPE,
  4          ROUND((SW.EXPECTED_SIZE/
  5          SW.EXPECTED_SIZE+SW.ACTUAL_MEM_USED)*100)
  6           UNDER_ALLOC_PCT
  7     FROM V$SQL_WORKAREA_ACTIVE SW,
  8          V$SESSION S,
  9          V$SQL Q
 10    WHERE SW.SID = S.SID
 11      AND S.SQL_ADDRESS = Q.ADDRESS
 12    ORDER BY SW.ACTUAL_MEM_USED DESC
 13   /

USERNAME    SQL                              OPERATION_TYPE  UNDER_ALLOC_PCT
----------  -------------------------------  --------------  ---------------
DEMO        SELECT * FROM TMP A, TMP B ORD   SORT                         71
```

The result of the preceding query shows that the workarea is underallocated by 71 percent, by which you can infer that the PGA is not configured properly. If you want to see the memory area size in which execution is occurring most heavily, you can look at the workarea histogram provided by another dynamic performance view, named V$SQL_WORKAREA_HISTOGRAM. The following query shows that only areas between 8 KB and 256 KB are being used, which indicates that PGA configuration outside this region is not adequate.

```
SQL> SELECT LOW_OPTIMAL_SIZE/1024 LOWER_BOUND,
  2           ROUND(HIGH_OPTIMAL_SIZE/1024) UPPER_BOUND,
  3           OPTIMAL_EXECUTIONS OPTIMAL,
  4           ONEPASS_EXECUTIONS ONEPASS,
  5           MULTIPASSES_EXECUTIONS MULTIPASS,
  6           TOTAL_EXECUTIONS TOTAL_EXEC
  7      FROM V$SQL_WORKAREA_HISTOGRAM
  8   /

LOWER_BOUND UPPER_BOUND     OPTIMAL     ONEPASS   MULTIPASS  TOTAL_EXEC
----------- -----------  ----------  ----------  ----------  ----------
          0           1           0           0           0           0
          1           2           0           0           0           0
          2           4           0           0           0           0
          4           8           0           0           0           0
          8          16        4089           0           0        4089
         16          32         202           0           0         202
         32          64          34           0           0          34
         64         128         114           0           0         114
        128         256          36           0           0          36
        256         512           0           0           0           0
        512        1024           0           0           0           0
       1024        2048           0           0           0           0
       2048        4096           0           0           0           0
       4096        8192           0           0           0           0
       8192       16384           0           0           0           0
      16384       32768           0           0           0           0
      32768       65536           0           0           0           0
      65536      131072           0           0           0           0
     131072      262144           0           0           0           0
     262144      524288           0           0           0           0
     524288     1048576           0           0           0           0
    1048576     2097152           0           0           0           0
    2097152     4194304           0           0           0           0
    4194304     8388608           0           0           0           0
    8388608    16777216           0           0           0           0
   16777216    33554432           0           0           0           0
   33554432    67108864           0           0           0           0
   67108864   134217728           0           0           0           0
  134217728   268435456           0           0           0           0
  268435456   536870912           0           0           0           0
  536870912  1073741824          0           0           0           0
 1073741824  2147483648          0           0           0           0
 2147483648  4294967295          0           0           0           0
```

PGA Statistics

Like any other memory structure, PGA memory is an important database resource that you should configure optimally. Overallocation of memory wastes memory, and underallocation degrades performance. As mentioned earlier, Oracle provides performance statistics, which are copious and sometimes overwhelming. This section helps you understand how to use these statistics and how to disseminate statistical information.

In this section, you look at another dynamic view, named V$PGASTAT. As you can infer from the name, the V$PGASTAT view is exclusively for PGA memory. The structure of the view is simple and consists of three self-explanatory columns, NAME, VALUE, and UNIT. The following query displays the contents of this view. As you look at the query and examine the kind of information it supplies, take note that you have been presented with several dynamic performance views that enable you to investigate queries or operations that consume PGA memory. As you know, Oracle is also rich in database statistical data. Statistics are collected for all statements and operations in the database. Now, look at a view that contains statistics only on the PGA:

```
SQL> SELECT NAME, VALUE, UNIT
  2     FROM V$PGASTAT
  3  /

NAME                                           VALUE UNIT
----------------------------------------- ---------- -------
aggregate PGA target parameter              20971520 bytes
aggregate PGA auto target                    4194304 bytes
global memory bound                          1048576 bytes
total PGA inuse                             17004544 bytes
total PGA allocated                         43533312 bytes
maximum PGA allocated                       44996608 bytes
total freeable PGA memory                          0 bytes
PGA memory freed back to OS                        0 bytes
total PGA used for auto workareas                  0 bytes
maximum PGA used for auto workareas           959488 bytes
total PGA used for manual workareas                0 bytes
maximum PGA used for manual workareas              0 bytes
over allocation count                          15696
bytes processed                             65566720 bytes
extra bytes read/written                           0 bytes
cache hit percentage                             100 percent
```

The query displays information that contains a number of terms you may not recognize. These are defined in Table 5-13.

Table 5-13   Contents of V$PGASTAT dynamic performance view

PGA statistic name	Description
Aggregate PGA target parameter	PGA aggregate target value set by the PGA_AGGREGATE_TARGET parameter
Aggregate PGA auto target	Amount of allocated PGA memory when PGA_AGGREGATE_TARGET is set to AUTO.
Total PGA in use	Amount of PGA memory that is currently in use for all operations
Total PGA allocated	Amount of PGA memory allocated for the instance. This number should be less than the target; if not, you should increase the target.
Maximum PGA allocated	Maximum amount of PGA memory that was ever allocated for operations. Again, a consistently higher value than the PGA target indicates that the PGA is underallocated and you may consider increasing PGA memory.

PGA statistic name	Description
Total freeable PGA memory	Amount of PGA memory that can be freed for other uses. This is, therefore, the amount of PGA memory that has been overallocated.
PGA memory freed back to OS	Amount of PGA memory that was freed and was given back to operating system
Total PGA used for auto workareas	Amount of PGA memory used in workareas for operations running in AUTO mode
Maximum PGA used for auto workareas	Maximum amount of PGA memory ever used in workareas for operations that run in AUTO mode
Total PGA used for manual workareas	Amount of PGA memory used for operations running in manual mode
Maximum PGA used for manual workareas	Maximum amount of PGA memory that was ever allocated for operations running in MANUAL mode
Over allocation count	Number of times Oracle had to allocate memory over the PGA target value set by you. If this value is consistently increasing, it indicates that the PGA target is set too low.
Bytes processed	Number of bytes that were processed by all operations
Extra bytes read/written	Number of bytes that were processed by one or multiple pass operations because PGA was underallocated
Cache hit percentage	Percentage of optimal operations to one or multiple operations. Of course, a consistently high percentage indicates that PGA memory is underallocated. This value can be calculated using the following formula: `bytes processed/ ( bytes processed + extra bytes read/written)`

The results of the preceding query certainly indicate that the PGA memory is adequately set and no further adjustment or tuning is required. As you might expect, there are more statistics that you can use to diagnose the PGA. Next, you look at how to use V$SYSSTAT to diagnose PGA problems.

More PGA Statistics Using the V$SYSSTAT View

The V$SYSSTAT dynamic performance view contains statistics that cover the entire system from the startup of the Oracle instance. There are three relevant statistics that you can use to diagnose PGA memory allocation. These statistics are displayed by submitting the following query:

```
SQL> SELECT NAME, VALUE
  2    FROM V$SYSSTAT
  3    WHERE NAME LIKE 'workarea executions%'
  4  /

NAME                                          VALUE
----------------------------------------- ----------
workarea executions-optimal                    5098
workarea executions-onepass                     100
workarea executions-multipass                    12
```

NOTE In the code segment, `session pga memory` and `session pga memory max` are statistical values found in V$SYSSTAT, but are not used in a system context; they are only in a session context.

Listing these values is not very helpful, unless you interpret the numbers or derive some useful percentage to tell you the percentage of one-pass executions compared to optimal executions. The following query works through a number of extra steps to obtain the execution percentage for each type.

```
SQL> SELECT NAME WORKAREA_EXECUTION,
  2              ROUND(VALUE/
  3              ((SELECT SUM(VALUE)
  4                 FROM V$SYSSTAT
  5                 WHERE NAME LIKE '%workarea executions%'))
  6              *100) PCT
  7      FROM V$SYSSTAT
  8    WHERE NAME LIKE '%workarea executions%'
  9  /

WORKAREA_EXECUTION                            PCT
----------------------------------------- ----------
workarea executions-optimal                     98
workarea executions-onepass                      2
workarea executions-multipass                    0
```

The results indicate that 98 percent of the executions are optimal, two percent are one-pass, and there are no multipass executions. This means that the overall PGA allocation is in good shape as long as these number stay in the same range. You can refer to Figure 5-8 for threshold interpretation.

PGA and Oracle Enterprise Manager

Oracle Enterprise Manager provides a number of tools that are useful in diagnosing memory, and one of these is the Database Health Overview performance tool. However, this tool does not provide direct diagnostic capability for the PGA memory structure, but it provides diagnosis of the machine's RAM. In this section, you walk through steps to see these diagnostic data using the Database Health Overview performance tool.

1. Open the Performance Overview tool from the Diagnostics Pack toolbar.

2. The main screen displays two sections of interest. As shown in Figure 5-13, the first section is entitled Host Memory Use, which displays how much memory the database has used from the operating system and how much free space (Pagefile) remains. Note that at all times, 20 percent of the system memory should be left free.

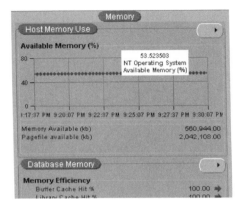

Figure 5-13   Oracle Enterprise Manager—Host Memory Use

3. You should also examine the second section of the main screen, which is entitled Top Consumers, as shown in Figure 5-14. It displays the sessions that are using the highest levels of system resources. As you can see from the figure, three tabs enable you to display information about the CPU sessions. Because the Sessions By Memory tab is activated, the screen displays the top five sessions for PGA consumption.

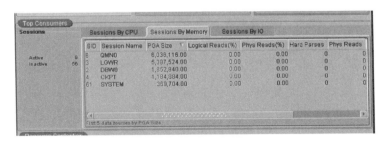

Figure 5-14   Oracle Enterprise Manager—Top Consumers

4. Double-click a session to see its full details. For this example, double-click the SYSTEM session to display Figure 5-15. You can then examine the session's CPU activity, memory use, and activities to diagnose problems.

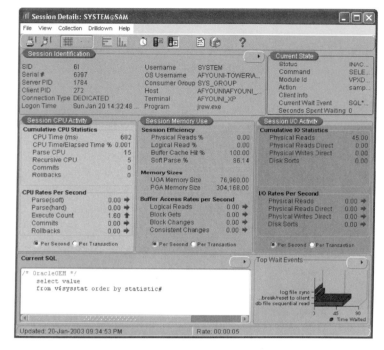

Figure 5-15   Oracle Enterprise Manager—Session Details

This concludes the first part of the chapter on diagnosing and tuning the PGA memory. The second part of this chapter explains the sort area of the PGA structure.

TUNING SORT OPERATIONS

Sort operations are expensive, especially if they are not performed in memory. In previous sections, you learned how to use PGA in automatic memory management to allocate memory to each session as needed. However, if you decide to control the different workarea sizes yourself, you ought to pay close attention to the SORT workarea because improper configuration of this area could hinder performance. In this part of the chapter, you learn why sort operations occur, how to prevent them, and finally, how to tune them.

Sort Operations

A database manager overheard one of his DBAs complaining about queries running in production by the application. The manager went to the DBA inquiring about his complaints. The DBA showed him three different queries that look similar to the query forms presented as follows:

```
SELECT DISTINCT ...    SELECT DISTINCT    SELECT ...       SELECT DISTINCT
FROM ...               FROM ...           FROM ...         FROM ...
WHERE ...              WHERE ...          WHERE ...        WHERE ...
GROUP BY ...           ORDER BY ...       GROUP BY ...     GROUP BY ...
ORDER BY ...                              ORDER BY ...
```

The database manager asked if developers were writing the queries and asked the DBA to meet with the developers.

The DBA held a quick meeting with the developers and presented the queries. Most of the developers agreed that the queries should be rewritten and confirmed the need for an ORDER BY clause when a GROUP BY clause (or) operation was present unless the results needed to be sorted in a different manner. The developers agreed that the same case applied to DISTINCT and ORDER BY or DISTINCT and GROUP BY. The developers decided to look into the issue and change code to remove unnecessary sorting operations.

A day later, one of the developers met with the DBA and told him they had corrected the problem. Being curious, the DBA asked who had written the queries, and the developer replied that a SQL generator tool that adds the ORDER BY clause by default had been used. The DBA and the developer agreed that the developers should conduct code reviews to catch this type of error.

Before you learn how to tune sort operations, you need to understand how they are caused. Ideally, your application should submit as few statements as possible that require sorting. Why should you minimize the number of sort operations? Simply because sort operations consume memory and CPU resources, and worse, if memory is not large enough, they can cause undesirable additional I/O by using disk space as temporary sorting space. In this section, you are shown all the causes of sorting operations. Table 5–14 presents these causes with an example for each.

NOTE

Oracle automatically allocates PGA memory to all dedicated sessions instead of using one SORT_AREA_SIZE for all sessions.

Table 5-14 Sort operations

Statement or operation	Example

SELECT UNIQUE	`SELECT UNIQUE FIRST_NAME,`
	`LAST_NAME`
	`FORM CUSTOMERS;`

SELECT DISTINCT	`SELECT DISTINCT JOB_ID` `FROM EMPLOYEES;`

SELECT ... ORDER BY	`SELECT FIRST_NAME,`
	`LAST_NAME`
	`FROM CUSTOMERS`
	`ORDER BY 1, 2;`

SELECT ... GROUP BY	`SELECT JOB_ID, SUM(SALARY)`
	`FROM EMPLOYEES`
	`GROUP BY JOB_ID;`

SELECT ... CONNECT BY	`SELECT lpad(' ',2*(level-1)) ||`
	`FIRST_NAME || ' ' ||`
	`LAST_NAME "Employee"`
	`FROM EMPLOYEES`
	`START WITH MANAGER_ID IS NULL`
	`CONNECT BY PRIOR`
	`EMPLOYEE_ID = MANAGER_ID`

CREATE INDEX	`CREATE INDEX IDX_EMP_ID` `ON EMPLOYEES(EMPLOYEE_ID);`

UNION set operations	`SELECT FIRST_NAME, LAST_NAME`
	`FROM CUSTOMERS`
	`UNION SELECT FIRST_NAME, LAST_NAME`
	`FROM EMPLOYEES;`

MINUS set operations	`SELECT FIRST_NAME, LAST_NAME`
	`FROM CUSTOMERS`
	`MINUS`
	`SELECT FIRST_NAME, LAST_NAME`
	`FROM EMPLOYEES;`

INTERSECT set operations	`SELECT FIRST_NAME, LAST_NAME`
	`FROM CUSTOMERS`
	`INTERSECT`
	`SELECT FIRST_NAME, LAST_NAME`
	`FROM EMPLOYEES;`

Un-indexed Table Joins	This is caused when two tables are being joined to columns that are not indexed.

Preventing Sort Operations

Now that you know the statements that trigger sorting and the impact of sorting on performance, you should learn, practice, and preach avoiding the submittal of statements that result in sort operations. Before you learn how to prevent sorting for each cause listed in Table 5-14, you should remember that the best place and time to prevent these operations is during the system development life cycle, specifically in the design and development phases. You should be asking yourself why and when sorting is needed. Most of the time, sorting is required to display the data in a specific order on a screen or in a report. In that case, the best thing to do is to sort the data at the client side or in the application server where the application resides rather than on the server side, especially if the amount of the sorted data is not large; otherwise, you may want to perform sorting on the database side.

If you actually follow this guideline, you will have few friends in the development field, simply because they prefer to get the data sorted without having to do it themselves. Another reason that developers do not follow this guideline is because some languages are not efficient at sorting. In any case, you should always question why any sort operations are being used. Table 5-15 shows you how to avoid sort operations.

Table 5-15 Sort operations preventive measures

Statement or operation	Preventive measure
SELECT UNIQUE	Remove duplicates using code on the application side
SELECT DISTINCT	Remove duplicates using code on the application side
SELECT ... ORDER BY	Sort data on the application side
SELECT ... CONNECT BY	Use application code
UNION set operations	Use UNION ALL and remove duplicates using application code
Un-indexed Table Joins	Create indexes on columns used in WHERE clause

Prevention of unnecessary sort operations can be critical to database performance whether the PGA is managed manually or automatically.

Sort Operation Diagnosis

Once you decided to manage PGA memory yourself by setting WORKAREA_SIZE_POLICY to MANUAL, you need to make sure that the SORT_AREA_SIZE parameter is always set properly. This parameter can be set dynamically on the session level or deferred for new sessions and can be monitored using V$SYSSTAT view or V$SESSTAT view for session statistics.

When you are setting the SORT_AREA_SIZE parameter systemwide in the deferred mode, issue the following statement:

```
SQL> ALTER SYSTEM SET SORT_AREA_SIZE = 1024 DEFERRED
/

System altered.
```

The DEFERRED option only impacts new sessions, not existing ones. Also, you can issue a different statement specifically for your own session. For example, if you are logged in as TUNER, you can issue the following statement (Note: This alternative statement only works for the user who submitted it):

```
SQL> ALTER SESSION SET SORT_AREA_SIZE = 1024
  /

Session altered.
```

Before exploring sort diagnosis, you walk through a sample scenario. Suppose your database has been configured for manual memory management and you have a CUSTOMERS table that has 4000 records used for reporting. The report that you need to generate is supposed to be ordered by customer name. Use the steps that follow to generate this report. Note that these steps include statements to set your database in manual memory management.

STEP 1: Log in as SYSTEM and show the setting of PGA memory management:

```
SQL> SHOW PARAMETER WORKAREA

NAME                                   TYPE          VALUE
------------------------------------   -----------   -----
workarea_size_policy                   string        AUTO
```

STEP 2: If memory management is set to MANUAL in your database, you can skip this step. Otherwise, you need to change the configuration dynamically by issuing this statement:

```
SQL> ALTER SYSTEM SET WORKAREA_SIZE_POLICY = MANUAL
  2  /

System altered.
```

STEP 3: Find out what SORT_AREA_SIZE is set to:

```
SQL> SHOW PARAMETER SORT_AREA_SIZE

NAME                                   TYPE          VALUE
------------------------------------   -----------   -----
sort_area_size                         integer       4096
```

STEP 4: Log in as TUNER and set your session to have the SORT_AREA_SIZE set to 1 KB. If the setting for your database is different from 4 KB/1 KB, issue the statement that follows:

```
SQL> ALTER SESSION SET SORT_AREA_SIZE = 1024
  2  /

Session altered.
```

5

> When setting SORT_AREA_SIZE, you cannot use KB or MB as part of the value.
> Use 1024 if you want a 1 KB setting.
>
> **TIP**

STEP 5: As SYSTEM user, get the session identification number for TUNER and record it:

```
SQL> SELECT USERNAME, PROGRAM, SID
  2    FROM V$SESSION
  3    WHERE USERNAME = 'TUNER'
  4   /

USERNAME            PROGRAM                                   SID
----------------    ----------------------------------       ----
TUNER               sqlplusw.exe                               62
```

STEP 6: As SYSTEM user, issue the following query to get sort statistics for TUNER:

```
SQL> SELECT NAME, VALUE
  2    FROM V$STATNAME N, V$SESSTAT S
  3    WHERE N.STATISTIC# = S.STATISTIC#
  4      AND NAME LIKE 'sort%'
  5      AND SID=62
  6   /

NAME                                                     VALUE
-----------------------------------------------------    ----------
sorts (memory)                                                3
sorts (disk)                                                  0
sorts (rows)                                                  6
```

STEP 7: As TUNER, issue the following statement to generate a customer report:

```
SQL> SELECT LAST_NAME, FIRST_NAME, PHONE
  2    FROM CUSTOMERS
  3    ORDER BY 1, 2
  4   /
```

> If you incur this error, "ORA-01114: IO error writing block to file %s (block #
> %s)," it is most likely that you have run out of space in the temporary file.
>
> **TIP**

STEP 8: Repeat Step 6, to get sort statistics for the TUNER session:

```
SQL> SELECT NAME, VALUE
  2    FROM V$STATNAME N, V$SESSTAT S
  3   WHERE N.STATISTIC# = S.STATISTIC#
  4     AND NAME LIKE 'sort%'
  5     AND SID=62
  6  /

NAME                                              VALUE
-------------------------------------------- ----------
sorts (memory)                                        3
sorts (disk)                                          1
sorts (rows)                                       4006
```

As you can see, sorting 4000 rows has caused one I/O because there was not enough space in memory for SORT_AREA_SIZE. This is not a significant performance problem by itself, but if this parameter is set improperly and many sessions are connected and retrieving large number of rows, it would be significant and users could notice some delays.

Now examine how to diagnose sort memory problems. You can do it at two levels: on the system level for the Oracle instance or on a session level specific for a session. The following query displays sort statistics for all connected users:

```
SQL> SELECT S.SID,
  2          S.USERNAME,
  3          S.OSUSER,
  4          S.PROGRAM,
  5          SN.NAME,
  6          SS.VALUE
  7    FROM V$SESSION S,
  8         V$SESSTAT SS,
  9         V$STATNAME SN
 10   WHERE SS.STATISTIC#=SN.STATISTIC#
 11     AND S.SID = SS.SID
 12     AND SN.NAME LIKE '%sort%'
 13     AND S.USERNAME NOT IN('SYS', 'SYSTEM')
 14     AND S.USERNAME IS NOT NULL
 15   ORDER BY S.USERNAME
 16  /

SID  USERNAME    OSUSER                      PROGRAM      NAME            VALUE
---- ----------  --------------------------- ------------ --------------- ----------
  11 TUNER       AFYOUNI-TOWER\Administrator vb6.exe      sorts (memory)        3
  11 TUNER       AFYOUNI-TOWER\Administrator vb6.exe      sorts (disk)          0
  11 TUNER       AFYOUNI-TOWER\Administrator vb6.exe      sorts (rows)          6
  12 TUNER       AFYOUNI-TOWER\Administrator vb6.exe      sorts (memory)        3
  12 TUNER       AFYOUNI-TOWER\Administrator vb6.exe      sorts (rows)          6
  12 TUNER       AFYOUNI-TOWER\Administrator vb6.exe      sorts (disk)          0
  13 TUNER       AFYOUNI-TOWER\Administrator vb6.exe      sorts (memory)        3
  62 TUNER       AFYOUNI-TOWER\Administrator sqlplusw.exe sorts (memory)        3
  62 TUNER       AFYOUNI-TOWER\Administrator sqlplusw.exe sorts (disk)          1
  62 TUNER       AFYOUNI-TOWER\Administrator sqlplusw.exe sorts (rows)       4006
```

It is useful to explore one more dynamic performance view called V$SORT_USAGE, which contains current sort operation usage statistics for every connect session. You can use this information to determine which session is using the most temporary space and to investigate why excessive temporary space is being used. See the query that follows for an example:

```
SQL> SELECT USERNAME,
  2          SESSION_ADDR,
  3          SESSION_NUM,
  4          TABLESPACE,
  5          CONTENTS,
  6          BLOCKS,
  7          SQLADDR
  8     FROM V$SORT_USAGE
  9  /

USERNAME    SESSION_  SESSION_NUM TABLESPACE        CONTENTS      BLOCKS SQLADDR
----------  --------  ----------- ----------------  ---------  ---------- --------
SYSTEM      682309E8        20079 TEMP              TEMPORARY        512 65B80FA4
```

System Level Diagnosis

Issue the following query to display a percentage of how many sorts were done on disk versus in memory for the whole system using the V$SYSSTAT view. Most Oracle experts agree that the threshold for disk sort ratios should be less than five percent (sort ratio is the percentage of sort operations that use temporary segments). Your goal is to have most, if not all, sort operations performed in memory and not resort to using temporary disk space. Achieving this goal reduces I/O trips which are detrimental to performance. If the sort ratio is higher than the threshold, you should increase the SORT_AREA_SIZE. Note that you could also use the following formula to determine sort ratio:

DISK.VALUE/(DISK.VALUE + MEM.VALUE)

```
SQL> SELECT DISK.VALUE DISK,
  2          MEM.VALUE MEMORY,
  3          ROUND(
  4              (DISK.VALUE/MEM.VALUE)*100, 2
  5              ) SORT_RATIO
  6     FROM V$SYSSTAT DISK, V$SYSSTAT MEM
  7    WHERE DISK.NAME = 'sorts (disk)'
  8      AND MEM.NAME  = 'sorts (memory)'
  9  /

      DISK      MEMORY SORT_RATIO
---------- ----------- ----------
        12       54868        .02
```

Session Level Diagnosis

For this type of diagnosis you need to use V$SESSTAT view. Submit the following statement to display the sort ratio for all sessions. Again, the threshold is five percent. If the sort ratio for the session is high, you may need to increase the value of the SORT_AREA_SIZE parameter for the session using the ALTER SESSION SET SORT_AREA_SIZE statement.

```
SQL> SELECT S.SID,
  2          S.USERNAME,
  3          S.PROGRAM,
  4          DISK.VALUE DISK,
  5          MEM.VALUE MEMORY,
  6          ROUND(
  7               (DISK.VALUE/MEM.VALUE)*100, 2
  8               ) SORT_RATIO
  9    FROM V$SESSTAT DISK,
 10          V$SESSTAT MEM,
 11          V$STATNAME N,
 12          V$SESSION S
 13   WHERE N.STATISTIC# = DISK.STATISTIC#
 14     AND N.STATISTIC# = MEM.STATISTIC#
 15     AND (N.NAME = 'sorts (disk)'
 16          OR N.NAME  = 'sorts (memory)')
 17     AND S.SID = DISK.SID
 18     AND S.SID = MEM.SID
 19     AND MEM.VALUE <> 0
 20   /
```

SID	USERNAME	PROGRAM	DISK	MEMORY	SORT_RATIO
5		ORACLE.EXE	53	53	100
6		ORACLE.EXE	4	4	100
7		ORACLE.EXE	31738	31738	100
8		ORACLE.EXE	5512	5512	100
9	SYS	sqlplusw.exe	221	221	100
11	TUNER	vb6.exe	3	3	100
12	TUNER	vb6.exe	3	3	100
13	TUNER	vb6.exe	3	3	100
14	TUNER	vb6.exe	3	3	100
15	TUNER	vb6.exe	3	3	100
16	TUNER	vb6.exe	3	3	100
17	TUNER	vb6.exe	3	3	100
18	TUNER	vb6.exe	3	3	100
19	TUNER	vb6.exe	3	3	100
20	TUNER	vb6.exe	3	3	100
21	TUNER	vb6.exe	3	3	100
58	TUNER	vb6.exe	3	3	100
59	TUNER	vb6.exe	3	3	100
60	TUNER	vb6.exe	3	3	100
61	SYSTEM	jrew.exe	14556	14556	100
62	TUNER	sqlplusw.exe	3	3	100
63	SYSTEM	dbSearch.exe	38	38	100
64	SYSTEM	jrew.exe	158	158	100
65	SYSTEM	jrew.exe	273	273	100
66	SYSTEM	jrew.exe	10	10	100
67	SYSTEM	sqlplusw.exe	68	66	103.03
62	TUNER	sqlplusw.exe	1	1	100
67	SYSTEM	sqlplusw.exe	24	22	109.09

5

SORT_AREA_RETAINED_SIZE Parameter

Suppose you set the SORT_AREA_SIZE to a large value because you are anticipating large sort operations. Oracle allocates this memory when it is needed and when the operation is completed, it releases the memory. Because you're expecting more sort operations of this nature, it would be appropriate and wise to retain some of this memory for these future operations. In this case, you can use SORT_AREA_RETAINED_SIZE. Like SORT_AREA_SIZE, this parameter can be set dynamically.

NOTE

Oracle does not recommend manual PGA memory management, which means that SORT_AREA_SIZE and SORT_AREA_RETAINED_SIZE parameters are not used when memory management is set to AUTO.

CREATING TEMPORARY TABLESPACES

It is important to understand the concept of PGA memory, especially if you are using applications that require sort operations, such as DSS and data warehouse. Sometimes, you may need to perform large sort operations and might not have enough space in memory to allocate to the PGA. In this case, these operations may resort to using a temporary space holder on disk, specifically on temporary segments within the Oracle database. This section shows you how to create temporary tablespaces.

First, you should know that most experts recommend having at least two temporary segments, one for use by SYS/SYSTEM and another for all other users. This is done to reduce contention. To create a temporary tablespace, you can use the following steps:

Step 1: Display a list of all tablespaces, datafiles, and their sizes to find out if any temporary tablespace was created in the conventional method using the CREATE TABLESPACE ... TEMPORARY.

```
SQL> SELECT T.TABLESPACE_NAME,
  2         D.FILE_NAME,
  3         D.BYTES/1024/1024 SIZE_MB,
  4         T.CONTENTS
  5    FROM DBA_TABLESPACES T, DBA_DATA_FILES D
  6   WHERE T.TABLESPACE_NAME = D.TABLESPACE_NAME
  7   ORDER BY T.TABLESPACE_NAME
  8  /

TABLESPACE FILE_NAME                                    SIZE_MB CONTENTS
---------- ------------------------------------------- ---------- ---------
CWMLITE    C:\ORACLE\ORADATA\SAM\CWMLITE01.DBF              20 PERMANENT
DRSYS      C:\ORACLE\ORADATA\SAM\DRSYS01.DBF                20 PERMANENT
EXAMPLE    C:\ORACLE\ORADATA\SAM\EXAMPLE01.DBF          148.75 PERMANENT
INDX       C:\ORACLE\ORADATA\SAM\INDX01.DBF                 25 PERMANENT
ODM        C:\ORACLE\ORADATA\SAM\ODM01.DBF                  20 PERMANENT
SYSTEM     C:\ORACLE\ORADATA\SAM\SYSTEM01.DBF              400 PERMANENT
TOOLS      C:\ORACLE\ORADATA\SAM\TOOLS01.DBF                10 PERMANENT
UNDOTBS1   C:\ORACLE\ORADATA\SAM\UNDOTBS01.DBF             330 UNDO
USERS      C:\ORACLE\ORADATA\SAM\USERS01.DBF             81.25 PERMANENT
XDB        C:\ORACLE\ORADATA\SAM\XDB01.DBF              38.125 PERMANENT
```

5

Step 2: Get a list of all temporary files:

```
SQL> SELECT TS.TABLESPACE_NAME,
  2         TF.FILE_NAME,
  3         TF.BYTES/1024/1024 SIZE_MB
  4    FROM DBA_TABLESPACES TS, DBA_TEMP_FILES TF
  5   WHERE TS.TABLESPACE_NAME = TF.TABLESPACE_NAME
  6   ORDER BY TS.TABLESPACE_NAME
  7  /

TABLESPACE FILE_NAME                                  SIZE_MB
---------- ------------------------------------------ ----------
TEMP       C:\ORACLE\ORADATA\SAM\TEMP01.DBF             10000
```

Step 3: Create another temporary tablespace, preferably residing on a different disk or mount point. Before creating the tablespace, you must make sure you have enough space where the new tablespace will reside. Use the operating system utilities to determine if you have enough space:

```
SQL> CREATE TEMPORARY TABLESPACE TEMP01
  2    TEMPFILE 'D:\ORACLE\ORADATA\SAM\TEMP01.DBF' SIZE 10M
  3  /

Tablespace created.
```

Step 4: As the DBA, you should verify every step you perform, no matter how simple the step is. Repeat Step 2 to verify that you created the new tablespace correctly:

```
SQL> SELECT TS.TABLESPACE_NAME,
  2          TF.FILE_NAME,
  3          TF.BYTES/1024/1024 SIZE_MB
  4     FROM DBA_TABLESPACES TS, DBA_TEMP_FILES TF
  5    WHERE TS.TABLESPACE_NAME = TF.TABLESPACE_NAME
  6    ORDER BY TS.TABLESPACE_NAME
  7    /

TABLESPACE FILE_NAME                                      SIZE_MB
---------- -------------------------------------------  ----------
TEMP        C:\ORACLE\ORADATA\SAM\TEMP01.DBF               10000
TEMP01      D:\ORACLE\ORADATA\SAM\TEMP01.DBF                  10
```

Suppose that you meant to create TEMP01 as 10 GB, not 10 MB, and by mistake you typed "10 MB", and you did not verify your result. You can imagine the result.

Step 5: Having created temporary tablespace is not enough. Now you should assign this temporary tablespace to users. Look at the temporary tablespace set for TUNER user:

```
SQL> SELECT USERNAME,
  2          DEFAULT_TABLESPACE,
  3          TEMPORARY_TABLESPACE
  4     FROM DBA_USERS
  5    WHERE USERNAME = 'TUNER'
  6    /

USERNAME    DEFAULT_TABLESPACE          TEMPORARY_TABLESPACE
----------  --------------------------  --------------------
TUNER       USERS                       TEMP
```

Step 6: Now assign the new temporary tablespace to TUNER:

```
SQL> ALTER USER TUNER TEMPORARY TABLESPACE TEMP01
  2    /

User altered.
```

Step 7: Verify Step 6 and issue the following statement, which is a repeat of Step 5.

```
SQL> SELECT USERNAME,
  2          DEFAULT_TABLESPACE,
  3          TEMPORARY_TABLESPACE
  4     FROM DBA_USERS
  5    WHERE USERNAME = 'TUNER'
  6  /

USERNAME     DEFAULT_TABLESPACE            TEMPORARY_TABLESPACE
----------   --------------------------    --------------------
TUNER        USERS                         TEMP01
```

 NOTE You can assign many users to the same temporary tablespace, but only one tablespace to a user.

If you are using Oracle Enterprise Manager, you could create this tablespace using the following steps:

Step 1: Double-click on the **Storage** node in the navigation panel to expand it, if necessary. Then click on the Tablespaces option as shown in Figure 5-16.

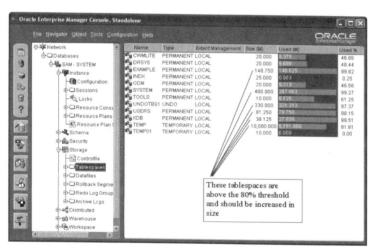

Figure 5-16   Oracle Enterprise Manager—Tablespaces option

In the right panel, there is a quick overview chart displaying all tablespaces, sizes of the tablespaces, and percent of usage. As you noticed, temporary tablespace TEMP is over the 80 percent threshold. Most DBAs use 80 percent, and DBAs who tolerate risks use a 90 percent threshold.

Step 2: Right-click on the **Tablespace** option, and click on the **Create** option, as in Figure 5-17.

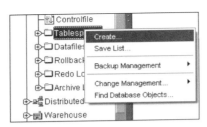

Figure 5-17   Oracle Enterprise Manager—Create menu option

A new screen is displayed in which you can fill in all data for the new temporary tablespace, as shown in Figure 5-18. When you have finished entering all the data, you can press the **Create** button.

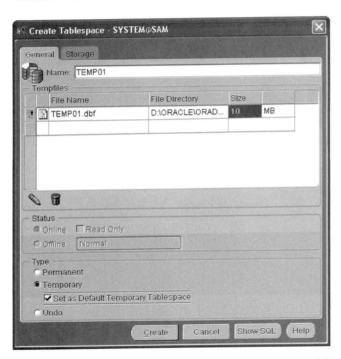

Figure 5-18   Oracle Enterprise Manager—Create Tablespace

If you have created a new temporary tablespace and you want it to be the default temporary tablespace for all users, issue the following statement:

NOTE

```
ALTER DATABASE DEFAULT TEMPORARY TABLESPACE
```

As mentioned earlier, the recommended threshold for all tablespaces usage should be 80 percent. You can check if the temporary tablespace has reached the threshold using Oracle Enterprise Manager or you can issue a query to get a quick report of tablespaces over the 80 percent threshold

NOTE Often a temporary tablespace is reported to be above the threshold, but it is not because the space has not yet been released. You need to find the activities that are using temporary space to take corrective action.

Another dynamic performance view that Oracle provides is V$SORT_SEGMENT which contains physical storage statistical data about every sort segment being used in temporary type tablespace.

CHAPTER SUMMARY

- The PGA is memory allocated from RAM (random access memory) on the host machine where Oracle resides.
- The PGA memory component is allocated when a user establishes a connection to the Oracle server.
- PGA memory is deallocated automatically when the user process is terminated gracefully.
- A dedicated Oracle database server processes requests for a single user process. The dedicated Oracle database server mode is the default mode.
- A shared Oracle database server handles requests for all user processes on a network.
- PGA memory management can be set to either manual mode or automatic mode.
- The PGA_AGGREGATE_TARGET parameter limits the total memory used for all user processes.
- Oracle and DBA experts recommend the use of automatic memory management for the PGA.
- The PGA Target Advice feature helps identify if an adjustment to the PGA target is needed.
- The V$PGA_TARGET_ADVICE view predicts the impact on cache hits of adjusting the target from its current setting to a lower or higher value.
- The V$SQL_WORKAREA view provides full PGA statistics for every statement submitted to the database.
- The V$SQL_WORKAREA_ACTIVE view also provides statistics for active statements submitted to the database.
- The V$PGASTAT view is a dynamic performance view specifically for the PGA.
- Sort operations are expensive, especially if they are not performed in memory.
- Initialization parameters presented in this chapter include the following:
  - BITMAP_MERGE_AREA_SIZE
  - CREATE_BITMAP_AREA_SIZE
  - HASH_AREA_SIZE
  - PGA_AGGREGATE_TARGET
  - SORT_AREA_RETAINED_SIZE

- SORT_AREA_SIZE
- WORKAREA_SIZE_POLICY

◻ Views used in this chapter include the following:

- DBA_USERS
- V$BGPROCESS
- V$PGA_TARGET_ADVICE
- V$PGA_TARGET_ADVICE_HISTOGRAM
- V$PGASTAT
- V$PROCESS
- V$SESSION
- V$SESSTAT
- V$SORT_SEGMENT
- V$SORT_USAGE
- V$SQL
- V$SQL_WORKAREA
- V$SQL_WORKAREA_ACTIVE
- V$SQL_WORKAREA_HISTOGRAM
- V$STATNAME
- V$SYSSTAT

REVIEW QUESTIONS

1. When running in dedicated server mode, PGA memory is part of the SGA. (True/False)

2. PGA memory management can be automatic or manual regardless of the server mode. (True/False)

3. The threshold for optimal executions is 90 percent. (True/False)

4. Bitmap operations are the most expensive operations for PGA memory. (True/False)

5. Use V$SYSSTAT to get session and system statistics. (True/False)

6. V$PGASTAT provides statistics specifically for PGA memory. (True/False)

7. The V$PROCESS view cannot be used for PGA diagnosis. (True/False)

8. The PGA Advice feature assists you in adjusting the PGA target. (True/False)

9. The V$SQL_WORKAREA view provides full statistics on every SQL statement submitted to the database. (True/False)

10. Use V$SESSTAT and V$PGASTAT to get PGA statistics on the session level and system level respectively. (True/False)

11. Write a query that displays the total number of sessions performing sort operations.

12. Describe the difference between automatic and manual memory management, and explain which mode you recommend.

13. Outline the steps to set up PGA advice and explain why you would use it.

14. How and why would you use the SORT_AREA_SIZE parameter?

15. Write a query that displays a list of temporary segments being used for sort operations.

16. Write a query that displays the total number of statements that performed sort operations.

17. Write a query that displays all the different PGA operations submitted to the database.

18. Write a statement that would produce the following Oracle error:
```
ORA-00093: pga_aggregate_target must be
        between 10M and 4096G-1
```

19. When would you use the SORT_AREA_RETAINED_SIZE parameter, and what size would you set it to?

20. How can you reduce sort operations?

EXAM REVIEW QUESTIONS: ORACLE9*i* PERFORMANCE TUNING (#1Z0-033)

1. When you set PGA to automatic memory management, which parameter is ignored?

   a. SORT_AREA_RETAINED_SIZE

   b. PGA_AGGREGATE_TARGET

   c. PGA_TARGET_ADVICE

   d. CREATE_BITMAP_WORKAREA_SIZE

2. What parameter would you set to enable manual memory management?

   a. SORT_AREA_SIZE

   b. PGA_WORK_POLICY

   c. PGA_WORKAREA_SIZE_POLICY

   d. PGA_WORK_SIZE_POLICY

   e. SORT_WORKAREA_SIZE

3. Which view would you use to get statistical data about the PGA Advice feature?

   a. V$PGA_CACHE_ADVICE

   b. V$SYSSTAT

   c. V$PGASTAT

   d. V$PGA_TARGET_ADVICE

   e. V$PGASTAT_ADVICE

4. If you use the V$SYSSTAT view, which value indicates that the PGA memory target is too low?

   a. 'workarea executions—disk'

   b. 'workarea executions—multipass'

   c. 'sorts (memory)'

   d. 'sorts (disk)'

   e. 'area executions—multiple'

   f. 'sorts (optimal)'

5. Which statement does not cause a sort operation?

   a. SELECT MAX(SAL) FROM EMPLOYEE ORDER BY SAL;

   b. SELECT DISTINCT SAL FROM EMPLOYEE;

   c. CREATE INDEX TDX_EMP_ID ON EMPLOYEE(EMP_ID);

   d. SELECT SUM(SAL) GROUP BY JOB_ID;

   e. None of the above

   f. All of the above

6. The modified V$PROCESS view contains new columns that are relevant to PGA statistics for every process in the database. Which column would you query to determine if the PGA target is being honored?

   a. PGA_USED_MEM

   b. PGA_ALLOC_MEM

   c. PGA_FREEABLE_MEM

   d. PGA_MAX_MEM

7. In what server mode is the automatic PGA memory management applicable?

    a. Dedicated

    b. Shared

    c. Dedicated and shared

    d. MTS

    e. MTS and shared

    f. MTS, shared, and dedicated

    g. None of the above

8. You set the parameter for the PGA target in automatic memory management to 10 GB. Which statement is true?

    a. You get an error because the PGA target exceeded the upper bound allowed.

    b. The setting causes no errors.

    c. You need to restart the instance for the setting to take effect.

    d. It is not possible to set the PGA target to 10 GB because it is set automatically by Oracle.

    e. It is set automatically, but only for new sessions.

9. Which view gives information about the number of temporary segment bytes that sort operations are consuming? (There are two correct answers.)

    a. V$SYSSTAT

    b. V$PGASTAT

    c. V$SQL_WORKAREA_ACTIVE

    d. V$SQL_WORKAREA

    e. V$SQLSTAT

10. What is the minimum value to which the PGA target can be set?

    a. 10 MB

    b. 1 MB

    c. 4 MB

    d. 100 MB

    e. No minimum limit

5

11. When you are working with the SORT_AREA_SIZE parameter, what must you be running in?

    a. Shared server mode

    b. Shared server mode, but in manual PGA memory management

    c. Dedicated server mode

    d. Dedicated server mode, but in manual PGA memory management

    e. A and C

    f. B and D

    g. A and D

    h. B and C

12. PGA memory consists of four working areas. Which of the four is a valid PGA working area?

    a. Sort area

    b. Join area

    c. Bitmap area

    d. Hash area

    e. Index area

13. Which of the following statistical values should be zero?

    a. 'workarea executions—optimal'

    b. 'workarea executions—multipass'

    c. 'workarea executions—onepass'

    d. 'workarea memory allocated'

14. Which two parameters can be changed dynamically?

    a. BITMAP_MERGE_AREA_SIZE

    b. CREATE_BITMAP_AREA_SIZE

    c. SORT_AREA_SIZE

    d. HASH_AREA_SIZE

15. Which of the following statements causes a sort operation?

 a. SELECT ... UNION ALL ... SELECT

 b. CREATE INDEX ...

 c. SELECT SUM(SALARY) ...

 d. SELECT ... CONNECT BY

HANDS-ON PROJECTS

5

Please complete the projects provided below.

1. Reread the Performance Problem presented at the start of the chapter, think through the problem in terms of the concepts you have learned in this chapter, and answer the questions posed by W. PROB.

 a. Should W. PROB use PGA_AGGREGATE_TARGET or SORT_AREA_SIZE? Why?

 b. What value do you recommend be set?

 c. Write the steps needed to implement your recommendations.

2. Your manager left you a voicemail message asking you to assist Bob who is a DBA working in a different department. After talking with Bob over the phone about the problem he is having, he e-mailed you the following query and its results:

```
SQL> SELECT *
  2    FROM V$SYSSTAT
  3    WHERE NAME LIKE 'sorts%'
  4  /

STATISTIC# NAME                                             CLASS      VALUE
---------- ----------------------------------------    ----------  ----------
       188 sorts (memory)                                    64    24263196
       189 sorts (disk)                                      64         363
       190 sorts (rows)                                      64  4535485856
```

He said that he performed a quick health check after a couple customers complained about the performance of the database, and he found nothing alarming. Bob told you that while researching Oracle Metalink, he stumbled into this query and he ran it, but did not know how to interpret the results. Answer the following questions:

a. What other information about the database should Bob provide?

b. Interpret the results of the query based on the information provided and assumptions made in the previous step.

c. Based on the results of the query, what do you recommend that Bob do?

d. Are there other tasks Bob should perform or queries he should issue?

e. If you think Bob should perform a query, do you think adding a query to calculate sort ratios to database health check queries would be beneficial? If not, write any other query you suggest should be included.

3. Your manager asked you to interview a new DBA to be hired to assist you in administering the 14 databases that you are currently managing.

4. You are having a consistent problem with TEMP tablespace. Users are getting temporary segments errors when executing certain queries. After you investigate the problem, you notice that the source of the problem is one specific query that is sorting a huge amount of data.

a. What query do you submit to find out which statement is causing the problem?

b. Should you increase the SORT_AREA_SIZE parameter and set the SORT_AREA_RETAINED_SIZE parameters?

c. What do you recommend to rectify the problem?

d. If you implement your recommendation, how you do you determine if the problem is fixed?

5. While you were browsing your favorite Oracle newsgroup, you came across the following question posted by a DBA who needs help. Help this DBA by giving him the correct answer to his question:

"Could someone help me determine how much PGA memory each background process is consuming?"

6. The other day, you read an article in a database technology magazine praising the automatic memory management feature. You got excited and decided to see if your database is taking advantage of this feature. Answer the following questions:

a. How do you determine if your database is using the automatic feature?

b. What query would you submit to monitor this feature?

c. What is the threshold at which you should take necessary action?

7. Explain the graph shown in Figure 5-19 that was obtained from the Oracle Enterprise Manager.

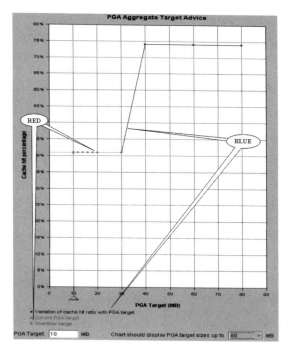

Figure 5-19   PGA Target Advice

8. Lately, your database has been running a bit sluggishly, but this morning the unexpected happened. You got an `Out of memory` error. You have about 300 users, and there are on average 50 to 60 concurrent sessions. The maximum sort operation requires 100 MB. You have 8 GB RAM, and your database SGA is sized 5 GB.

   a. Why did this problem occur?

   b. How do you fix it?

9. Your manager held a meeting with all the DBAs in your team. She asked if anyone would volunteer to collect statistical data about users and their memory consumption. So you volunteered to do the task, because this was a perfect opportunity for you to practice what you learned from the Oracle9*i* Performance Tuning book. Outline the steps you would take to perform this task.

10. Write a procedure that takes a session number and returns detailed information about the session, SQL statements submitted, and sort statistics. Your procedure should display one additional line to indicate if a session has reached the sort ratio threshold.

11. You took over a database that was monitored by a DBA consultant whose
contract ended. Then you received an e-mail from him with the following
code:

```
SQL> SELECT SN.STATISTIC#,
  2         SN.NAME, ST.VALUE
  3    FROM V$STATNAME SN, V$SYSSTAT ST
  4    WHERE SN.NAME LIKE '%pga memory%'
  5      AND SN.STATISTIC# = ST.STATISTIC#
  6  /

STATISTIC# NAME                                    VALUE
---------- ------------------------------     ----------
        20 session pga memory                  34570276
        21 session pga memory max              36601892


SQL> SELECT VALUE,
  2         N.NAME|| '('||S.STATISTIC#||')' NAME,
  3         S.SID,
  4         SS.USERNAME
  5    FROM V$SESSTAT S , V$STATNAME N, V$SESSION SS
  6    WHERE S.STATISTIC# = N.STATISTIC#
  7      AND S.SID = SS.SID
  8      AND N.NAME LIKE '%pga memory%'
  9      AND USERNAME IS NOT NULL
 10    ORDER BY VALUE
 11  /

     VALUE NAME                                    SID USERNAME
---------- ------------------------------     ---------- --------
    220460 session pga memory(20)                22 SYSTEM
    220460 session pga memory(20)                21 SYSTEM
    220460 session pga memory max(21)            21 SYSTEM
    220460 session pga memory max(21)            22 SYSTEM
    417068 session pga memory(20)                40 SYSTEM
    509824 session pga memory(20)                19 SYSTEM
    679212 session pga memory max(21)            40 SYSTEM
   2082688 session pga memory max(21)            19 SYSTEM
```

Explain how this report is used and what its benefits are.

12. Figure 5-20 shows Oracle Enterprise Manager. You have been monitoring a DSS application database all day, and its memory usage has been consistent.

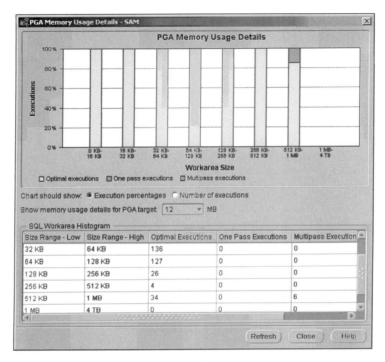

Figure 5-20   PGA target advice histogram

a. From what dynamic performance view is the contents of the screen derived?

b. Write a query that produces a report in a similar format. (*Note*: your numbers will differ from those in the figure.)

c. Are the results displayed in Figure 5-20 alarming? If yes, why, and what would you do?

CASE PROJECTS

1. Sorting Things Out

You have just met with the business manager of the ACME Order System about new requirements to generate a report for all orders that have been placed. The report is supposed to be sorted by annual quarters, order date, and total amount. A summary is also to be included at the end of the report showing, for each quarter, the number of orders and total amount. After you wrote the report, you determined that the report is running too slowly.

You decided to investigate the problem by running the report in automatic PGA memory management and manual memory management to obtain sort statistics for each mode and then to compare them. Set up an Oracle instance with the following settings:

- Automatic mode: PGA target is 10 MB

- Manual mode: Sort area size is 10 MB

    1. Try to optimize the sort operation by writing all necessary queries to generate a report.

    2. Run queries obtained in Step a in three different sessions.

    3. For each mode, record sort statistics for individual sessions and systems and compare them.

    4. Analyze the results and explain which mode has better performance throughput.

CASE PROJECTS

2. What Sort of Problem Is This?

A DBA on your team was at your office cube talking about the new database that recently went into production. Looking over your desk, he found the following report.

PGA TARGET FOR ESTIMATE	PGA TARGET FACTOR	ADV	BYTES PROCESSED	ESTD EXTRA BYTES RW	ESTD PGA CACHE HIT PERCENTAGE	ESTD OVERALLOC_COUNT
10485760	1	ON	11274240	17879040	39	2
12582912	1.2	ON	11274240	17879040	39	2
14680064	1.4	ON	11274240	17879040	39	2
16777216	1.6	ON	11274240	17879040	39	2
18874368	1.8	ON	11274240	17879040	39	2
20971520	2	ON	11274240	17879040	39	2
31457280	3	ON	11274240	17879040	39	2
41943040	4	ON	11274240	4469760	72	0
62914560	6	ON	11274240	4469760	72	0
83886080	8	ON	11274240	4469760	72	0

Being curious, he picked it up and started examining the output and asked you the following questions. Answer the following questions:

    1. How did you get this report?

    2. What do I have to do to get this type of information from my database?

    3. What does this report mean?

    4. Are the results alarming? Why?

    5. What would happen if you set your PGA target level to 10 MB?

After explaining the report outcome to your DBA colleague, he asked you to perform a demonstration for him. To perform the demonstration, complete the following tasks:

1. Run dbSessions using the dbSessions_chapter05.qry files and the logon information presented in Figure 5-21.

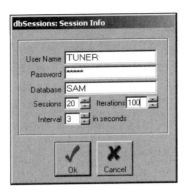

Figure 5-21   dbSessions logon information

2. Write the query that produces the same output as discussed in this case project.

3. Does your system have a PGA performance problem?

PART

III

Tuning Storage

CHAPTER

6

OPTIMIZING DATA STORAGE

In this chapter you will:

♦ Examine the relationship between the physical and logical architecture of Oracle data storage structures

♦ Learn to work with Oracle block structures

♦ Specify extent options when creating table segments and other segments

♦ Size and analyze segments and detect segment problems

♦ Analyze index problems and rebuild indexes

♦ Learn ten best practices for optimizing data storage

Chapter 6 is the first chapter in the Tuning Storage section of this textbook, which contains three chapters. This chapter emphasizes configuring storage efficiently to prevent performance degradation and to avoid storage waste. The chapter first presents the physical structure of Oracle architecture as illustrated in Figure 6-1, which shows the hierarchal structure of a logical data unit as well as a physical data unit. The chapter continues with an examination of the following three data units: Oracle blocks, extents, and segments. You learn what each data unit is, how to use it, how to configure it, and how it impacts performance.

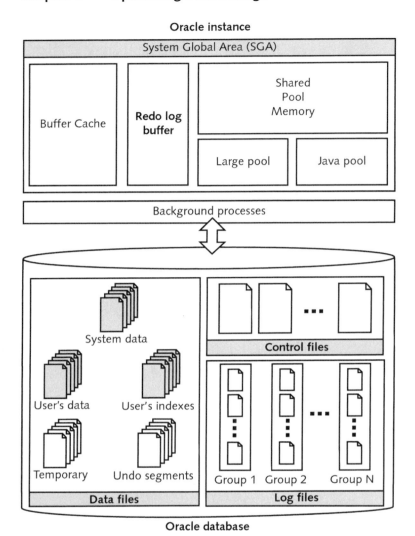

Figure 6-1 Oracle instance and database architecture highlighting data storage

Performance Problem

This section outlines an actual performance problem. As you look it over, imagine yourself as the DBA who reported it and keep it in mind as you proceed through the chapter. The chapter presents concepts relevant to the problem. In the first Hands-on Project at the end of the chapter, you are asked to use the concepts you have learned to provide a solution, or partial solution, to this performance problem.

From: Joe Store <mailto: joe_store@data.com >

Dates: 11-Jul-02 13:25

Subject: Row Chaining Problem

I have a database that has an Oracle block size of 8092. This database is used for an application that stores big images in large object columns. In the last few weeks, I have noticed that the database is showing a high ratio of row chaining. I have followed a procedure that I found at one of the DBA Web sites to eliminate row chaining, but it did not help at all. Why am I having this problem and what should I do?

J.

6

PHYSICAL ARCHITECTURE

Oracle provides a flexible storage structure to enable you to best configure storage for optimal data organization and retrieval. In this section you look at the physical and logical architecture of Oracle data storage structures and their relationships to each other, as shown in Figure 6-2.

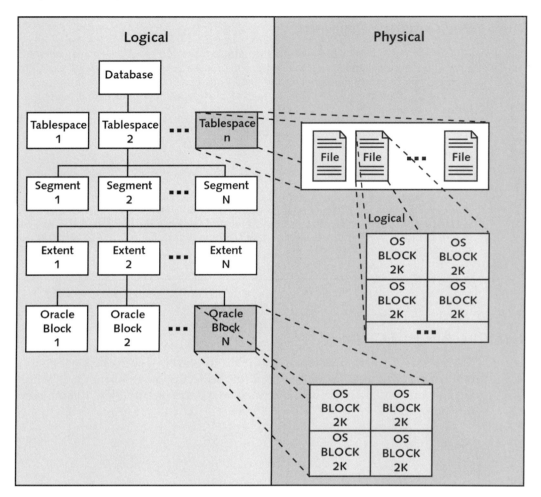

Figure 6-2   Oracle physical architecture illustrating logical and physical data units

Before you are presented with the explanation of Figure 6-2, you need to understand the definition of logical entities and physical entities within the context of Oracle data storage. A logical entity is a record stored in the database, whereas a physical entity is an entity that occupies blocks and sectors in disk storage. As you can see in Figure 6-2, a database may have one or many **tablespaces**, and each tablespace should be created for a specific purpose. A tablespace may have one or many files associated to it, and a file is a physical entity formatted by Oracle. Furthermore, each tablespace may have one or many segments, and a segment is a logical entity stored as a record in the system.

Each **segment** may consist of one or many **extents**, and each extent may be composed of many Oracle blocks. Each Oracle block is a multiple of operating system blocks, which can be 2 KB, 4 KB, 8 KB, 16 KB, or 32 KB. Also notice in Figure 6-2 that the physical architecture is composed of both logical entities (tablespaces, segments, extents, and Oracle blocks) and physical entities (files and operating system blocks). Finally, note that the smallest data storage entity is the Oracle block.

At this point, you may be asking, "Why has Oracle created this complex architecture?" The answer is simply to allow flexibility and optimization of data allocation. With this architecture, you can quickly access, pick and choose the size of Oracle blocks depending on the application type. You can also optimize the database by allocating segments in different tablespaces that reside on different files and disks.

In the next section, you explore Oracle blocks and segments in all aspects of storage optimization.

ORACLE BLOCK OVERVIEW

You already know that you need to create a table to store data for future use. You should also be aware that you, as a DBA, should act diligently when creating a table. It is not as simple as issuing a CREATE TABLE statement. In fact, creating a table involves a process of data and storage analysis. It is during the design phase of an application that you must first define the purpose of the data and identify how the data will be used. In this context, the term "use" includes the amount of data to be retrieved, the frequency of data update, and an evaluation of whether the data might be deleted. The answer to these questions must be part of the database storage design. Based on these factors, you determine the block specification for each table.

When creating a table, you should specify storage parameters and options as listed in Figure 6-3. These parameters are classified into block-related and extent-related parameters, and they are explained later in this section.

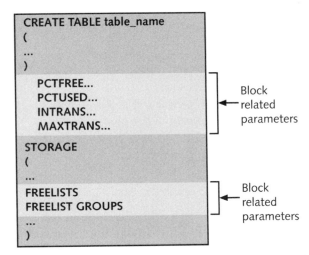

Figure 6-3   Syntax for creating a table showing block parameters

Before learning about block options, you can benefit from studying a quick overview of the **Oracle block structure**, which is the smallest data unit in the Oracle database, as shown in Figure 6-4.

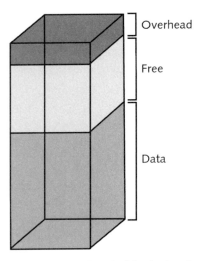

Overhead

Free

Data

Figure 6-4   Oracle block structure

As you can see from Figure 6-4, the block is divided into three major parts:

- **Overhead:** The first part of the Oracle block contains specific data about the block such as:
  - Block address: A physical address of the block within the file
  - ID of the block using the object: Block identification
  - Segment type: Type of segment (undo, table, index, and so on)
  - Table directory: Contains information about the table that has rows in current block
  - Row directory: Contains address of each row in current block

- **Free:** This part of the Oracle block is reserved as free space in the block for future updates of rows within the block or growth in the block overhead.

- **Data:** This part of the Oracle block stores rows for a specific segment.

Oracle Block Size

Jackie is a senior DBA who has been working at a banking institution for five years. For her performance and technical skills, she has been praised and complimented by everyone. Two months ago, Jackie got a new assignment to build the first new marketing data warehouse database. She was very excited about the fact she will be doing something new and different. So, she created the database from an existing create script template she used for all existing databases. The new data warehouse application went into production smoothly and reports were generated without a glitch. But, not so long, ago she started receiving requests to speed up the reports.

She started a full diagnosis of all queries used by the reports and could not find anything significant. So she went on diagnosing tablespaces and table allocation; again she found nothing. She went further, looking at memory and the database configuration and found minor issues that she fixed, but the fixes did not improve the speed of the reports. At that time, she told the business manager that the reports were as optimal as possible and there was nothing she could do to resolve the problem.

A few months later, she got another request to build a data warehouse database for customer activities. She assigned the project to a junior DBA named Hadi, who had been recently hired to assist her with daily routine tasks. When the time came to create the new database, Jackie gave him the create script template she had used for the last data warehouse application. While Jackie and Hadi were reviewing the scripts, Hadi asked why the DB_BLOCK_SIZE parameter was set to 4 KB. Jackie went white and murmured quietly to herself, "How could I have forgotten? That's it!"

Jackie created a new database changing the DB_BLOCK_SIZE parameter to 32 KB on the staging machine with the same configuration as production, loaded all the data, and ran the same reports. The reports were almost twice as fast as those running in production.

When creating a new database, you must first define the size of the Oracle block for the database. This is an important decision. The DB_BLOCK_SIZE initialization parameter specifies the block size. Although Oracle9i allows blocks of different sizes in one database, it is best to select one block size that will be used for most of the data stored in different segments. For special tables, you can create other segments with sizes different than the default block size. If you select the wrong size, there are two possible implications. First, the wrong size can negatively affect performance. Second, you may need to reorganize data in most segments and reconfigure the Buffer Cache. To select the optimal size, DBA experts consult guidelines, such as those shown in Figure 6-5.

NOTE
Some OLTP applications may require segments with larger block sizes than those outlined in the guidelines in Figure 6-5, or it may be necessary to have segments with different block sizes than the default size set by the DB_BLOCK_SIZE parameter. In either case, you should always try to optimally configure and implement databases to meet business requirements.

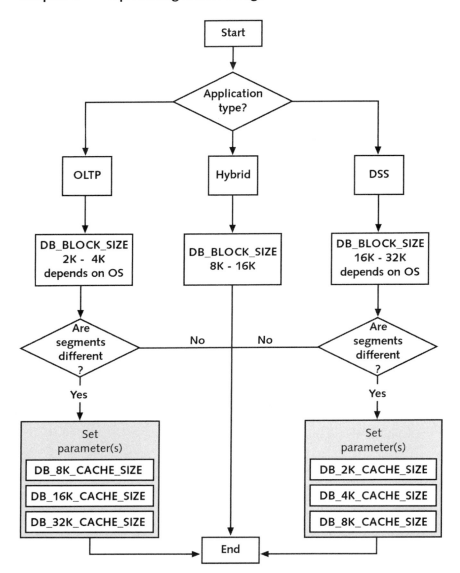

Figure 6-5   Flowchart of Oracle block size guidelines

Figure 6-5 shows that if the database is an OLTP, you should set a 2 KB to 4 KB block size depending on the operating system (OS) block. If the OS block is set to 4 KB by the system administrator, you should set the DB_BLOCK_SIZE to 4 KB.

Another way of approaching block size is using small block sizes for small rows and large block sizes for large rows.

NOTE

To better understand sizing blocks, consider the guidelines specifying small block size for OLTP and large block sizes for DSS applications, as shown in Table 6-1. As you study Table 6-1, remember that Oracle retrieves data in blocks, rather than rows.

Table 6-1 Guidelines for Oracle block sizes by application types

Application	Size	Justification
OLTP	Small	Because OLTP applications generate small transactions, it would be ideal to retrieve as few rows as possible for each transaction, such as updating, deleting, inserting, and retrieving. If the block size is too large, the block retrieves more rows than needed and eventually requires more Buffer Cache to fit all these blocks for different transactions. Or, the Buffer Cache flushes blocks to free up memory which in turn increases I/O.
Hybrid	Medium	Because hybrid applications are neither OLTP nor DSS, a medium-sized block may meet requirements for medium-sized transactions.
DSS	Large	DSS applications store and retrieve large amounts of data for reporting purposes. If an Oracle data block is set to a size that is too small, only a few rows can fit in one block. This means that an attempt to retrieve all rows will cause a high level of I/O. Note that DSS applications involve few updates, deletions, and inserts after being loaded.

Consider a time sheet Web application used for a large company. This application allows employees to enter their working hours each week. To decide on the block size, you need to determine whether the application type is OLTP, hybrid, or DSS. There will be many transactions entered throughout the weekdays with peak times on Fridays between 2:00 p.m. and 5:00 p.m., and on Mondays between 8:00 a.m. and 11:00 a.m. Normally these transactions shorten updating, inserting, or deleting a few rows. Knowing these facts, you can conclude that this application is an OLTP type. In this case, you can follow the guidelines listed in Table 6-1.

Oracle Block Options

Now that you understand how to determine block sizes, you can consider block options. Table 6-2 presents block options that are specified when you create a table segment or other segments.

Table 6-2 Block option descriptions

Block option	Description
PCTFREE	Percent free: This option specifies the percent of the block to be reserved as free for future row updates and block overhead growth. The default value is 10.
PCTUSED	Percent used: This option specifies how much of the block is used before the block is added back to the free list. Oracle maintains a structure called FREELISTS, which contains a list of all free blocks. The default value is 40.

Block option	Description
INITRANS	Initial transaction: This is the number of initial concurrent transactions for the block. The default value is 1 for table segments and 2 for index segments.
MAXTRANS	Maximum transaction: This is the maximum number of concurrent transactions for the block. The default value is 255.
FREELISTS	FREELISTS: This is the number of lists in a FREELIST GROUP, which contains a list of blocks that are free for new inserts. A block stays in the FREELIST to be used until the block hits the PCTFREE ceiling and goes back on the list until it hits the PCTUSED value. For applications with a high number of concurrent transactions, you may want to increase the default value of 1 to 8 or 16.
FREELIST GROUPS	Number: This is the number of FREELIST GROUPS in a segment. An application with a high number of transactions may require more than groups two or four.

The information in this table is derived from the online documentation that Oracle provides at the Oracle Technology Network site: *www.otn.oracle.com*.

Of all block parameters, PCTFREE is the most important option because improperly setting this option can lead to either performance degradation or space wastage. In the next section you learn how PCTFREE is used internally.

PCTFREE Overview

As outlined in Table 6-2, **PCTFREE** (percent free) is a block option that specifies the percent of the block to be reserved as free for future row updates and block overhead growth. The default value is 10. In this section, you see an illustration of Oracle's internal use of PCTFREE through three examples. The first example shows how an improper value of PCTFREE impacts performance through row chaining and row migration. The second example shows how an improper setting of PCTFREE results in wasted storage. The third example shows how the proper setting of PCTFREE improves performance and prevents storage waste.

The following glimpse into the life of a DBA demonstrates the use of PCTFREE in reality. Moe, a database expert, just joined a small local collection agency to lead a team of two junior DBAs. Moe spent the first two months becoming familiar with all the different projects and databases in production. He asked both DBAs to get him a full survey of all databases. A few days later, he summoned both DBAs to his office to review all the surveys they had prepared. Moe started the meeting by saying, "I was surprised that all the tables in all the different databases are configured with the same PCTFREE—40. How do you explain this?" The DBAs responded by saying that they had set the PCTFREE to 40 because it seemed like a reasonable number. They had not had time to analyze each table and compute PCTFREE, and the setting seemed to be working in a satisfactory manner. Their chaining row ratios were very low, so they assumed everything was fine. Moe listened with amazement to his two DBAs and replied, "Have you ever thought about disk space wastage? Just because disk space is cheap doesn't mean we can waste it." He said he would generate an analysis report showing for each table how much space was allocated and estimating how much space was consumed.

Is Moe asking for too much? No, he is not. Regardless of the cost of space, you as the DBA should treat storage as a valuable resource that should not be wasted. In addition, the junior DBAs took the easy way out and ignored guidelines that could have provided them with better settings for PCTFREE.

Row Migration

Row migration occurs when a row is updated, and the size of the updated row becomes too large for the block in which it resides. When this occurs, Oracle tries to find another block with enough space to migrate the entire row to the newly identified block. When a block is found, Oracle establishes a pointer to the new address and the original row header stays where it is.

Row Chaining

6

Row chaining occurs when a row is too big to fit in one block. In this case, Oracle keeps a portion of the row in the original block and the rest of the row is chained to another block.

Example 1 (Figure 6-6):   Figure 6-6 shows a block from an existing table that stores several rows. A small percentage of this block is set aside for future updates (PCTFREE is a very small value—0 percent to 10 percent). Of all the rows in the block, only five will be updated. The sequence of events is outlined as follows:

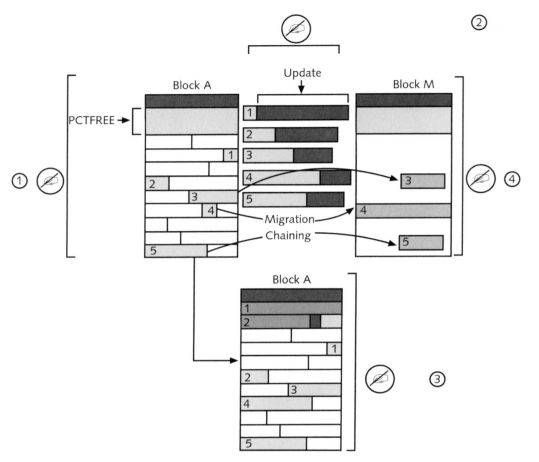

Figure 6-6 Example 1—Row chaining and migration resulting from an improper setting of PCTFREE

Event 1: Several rows are stored in block A.

Event 2: Five rows, marked 1 to 5, will be updated. Of course, any growth in these rows will go into the reserved free space.

Event 3: Row 1 and 2 have grown, and space for this growth was allocated from the free space specified by PCTFREE. However, there is no room for rows 3, 4, and 5 to grow in the reserved free space.

Event 4: Row 4 is too large to fit into block A, so Oracle searches for another block into which it can migrate the whole row. It finds block M, so the entire row 4 is stored in block M, and a pointer from block A is established to point to the row in block M. This process is called row migration.

For other rows, Oracle looks for another block in which to store data. Because block M has data that needs to be stored, it is chained to the row stored in block A. This is also row chaining. Row chaining negatively affects performance, because every time you retrieve Row 1, you must read block A and block M. Row chaining occurs because the reserved free space is not adequate.

TIP
Row migration is caused by updates. Row chaining is caused by both updates and the insertion of a row that is too big to fit in one block.

Example 2 (Figure 6-7): In this example, you see a table with a large amount of free space reserved for future updates. If the table is not updated, the reserved space is wasted storage.

6

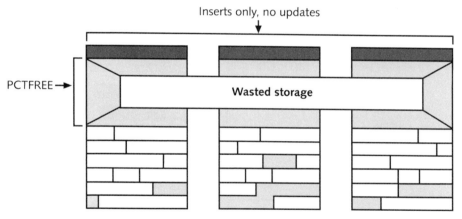

Inserts only, no updates

PCTFREE→

Wasted storage

Figure 6-7   Example 2—Wasted storage space resulting from improperly setting PCTFREE

Example 3 (Figure 6-8): In Example 3, you see several different scenarios in which the reserved free space is adequate for the transaction activities.

In the first scenario, which is labeled "1" in Figure 6-8, a table is created with a small PCTFREE because no updates are expected.

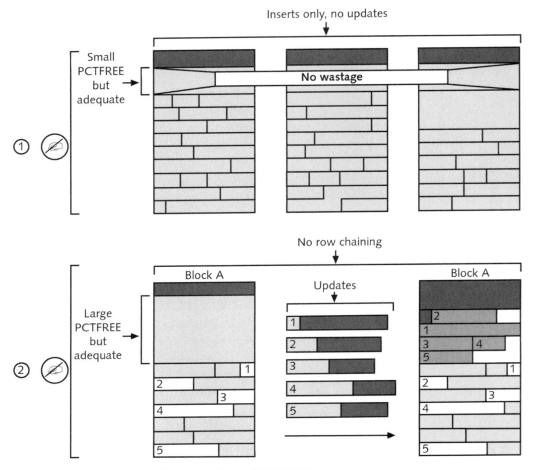

Figure 6-8   Example 3—Proper setting of PCTFREE

In the second scenario, which is labeled "2" in Figure 6-8, a table is created with a large PCTFREE because high levels of updating activity are expected.

PCTFREE Computation

In the previous sections, you learned how improperly setting PCTFREE can degrade performance or waste space. Your next step is to learn how to estimate the correct value for PCTFREE. To compute this value, you need to find the average growth of a row compared to its row size. This section presents two formulas for computing the PCTFREE.

TIP

If you alter a table to modify PCTFREE, existing blocks are not impacted and new allocated blocks take the new value of PCTFREE.

The PRODUCTS table structure in the TUNER schema is shown in the following code segment. You will be using this table to compute the PCTFREE value. Before starting, you should select the columns that are most likely to be updated and grow from their initial value. PRODUCT_ID, CATEGORY_ID, and STATUS will probably not be modified, and the likelihood of PRODUCT_NAME being updated is also slim. However, PRODUCT_DESC and especially COMMENTS will be updated frequently.

```
SQL> DESC PRODUCTS
 Name                        Null?    Type
 --------------------------- -------- --------------
 PRODUCT_ID                  NOT NULL NUMBER(4)
 CATEGORY_ID                          NUMBER(2)
 PRODUCT_NAME                         VARCHAR2(80)
 PRODUCT_DESC                         VARCHAR2(512)
 STATUS                               CHAR(1)
 COMMENTS                             VARCHAR2(1024)
```

For example, the PRODUCT_DESC column initial value could be "This is a cooking machine," but later be updated to "This is the best product for cooking gourmet snacks and fancy dinners."

"This is a cooking machine" is 25 characters.

"This is the best product for cooking gourmet snacks and fancy dinners" is 70 characters.

The growth in this column value is 45 characters, which is 45 bytes (each character is one byte). So you need to account for this growth and you must have enough space reserved for this growth for all rows residing in this table. Now you can follow the steps to compute PCTFREE value using these two methods:

Method 1: Estimation Without Data

As the title of this section suggests, in this method you compute this value without having sample data to compute the average initial row length.

Step 1: Compute the maximum row length of the PRODUCTS table by using the criteria listed in Table 6–3.

Table 6-3 Data type sizes

Data type	Number of bytes
VARCHAR2(n) or CHAR(n)	N bytes; each character is one byte
DATE	7 bytes
NUMBER(p, s)	Floor ((p+1)/2) + 1; add one extra byte for signed numbers
NUMBER	19 bytes

From the structure of the PRODUCTS table, the following results are obtained as listed in Table 6–4.

Table 6-4 PRODUCTS table data sizing (1)

Column	Data type	Bytes
PRODUCT_ID	NUMBER(4)	3
CATEGORY_ID	NUMBER(2)	2
PRODUCT_NAME	VARCHAR2(80)	80
PRODUCT_DESC	VARCHAR2(512)	512
STATUS	CHAR(1)	1
COMMENTS	VARCHAR2(1024)	1024
Total number of bytes		1622

As an alternative method, you could use the following query to calculate the maximum row length for each table in a specific schema. When running this query as SYSTEM, the query prompts you to enter a user name, and then it displays the results as shown in the following code segment:

```
SQL> SELECT TABLE_NAME "Table Name",
  2         SUM( DECODE( SUBSTR(DATA_TYPE,1,1),
  3               'N', TRUNC( ( NVL(DATA_PRECISION,38) + 1 )
  4                   / 2, 0 ) + 1 ,
  5               'D', 7, DATA_LENGTH ) ) "Max Length"
  6    FROM DBA_TAB_COLUMNS
  7   WHERE OWNER = UPPER('&Schema_Owner')
  8   GROUP BY TABLE_NAME
  9  HAVING SUM( DECODE( SUBSTR(DATA_TYPE,1,1),
 10               'N', TRUNC( ( NVL(DATA_PRECISION,38) + 1 )
 11                   / 2, 0 ) + 1 ,
 12               'D', 7, DATA_LENGTH ) ) > 0
 13   ORDER BY 2 DESC , 1
 14  /
Enter value for schema_owner: tuner

Table Name                      Max Length
------------------------------  ----------
PRODUCTS                              1622
SUPPLIERS                             1558
CUSTOMERS                             1367
ORDERS                                1056
PROMOTIONS                             102
PRODUCT_PRICES                          99
ORDER_LINES                             87
CATEGORIES                              82
JOBS                                    82
PAYMENT_METHOD                          82
SHIPMENT_METHOD                         82
EMPLOYEES                               77
PRODUCT_INVENTORY                       57
DEPARTMENTS                             54
EMPLOYEE_RANKS                          42
TRANS_DEMO                              40
SALES_COMMISSION                        23
PRODUCT_SUPPLIER                         6
```

Step 2: In this step, you estimate the initial average row length. So for each column, you estimate the number of bytes of its value, as shown in Table 6-5.

Table 6-5 PRODUCTS table data sizing (2)

Column	Data type	Bytes
PRODUCT_ID	NUMBER(4)	2
CATEGORY_ID	NUMBER(2)	2
PRODUCT_NAME	VARCHAR2(80)	50
PRODUCT_DESC	VARCHAR2(512)	80
STATUS	CHAR(1)	1
COMMENTS	VARCHAR2(1024)	20
	Total number of bytes	155

Step 3: You must now determine the average growth. Using the maximum row length and average row length, you estimate the growth caused by updates:

```
Est. Average Growth = (Max Row - Avg Row)/2
Where:
       Max Row = Maximum row length
       Avg Row = Average row length
       Est. Average Growth = (1622 - 155)/2 = 733.51467
```

Step 4: Compute PCTFREE using the following formula:

```
PCTFREE = (Est. Average Growth/Maximum Row Length) * 100
PCTFREE = 733.5/1622 * 100
PCTFREE = 45 percent
```

In this case, the PCTFREE value is 45 percent, which should be rounded up to 50 percent. Although you may think that this value is too high, in some cases, the value may be as high as 70 percent.

Method 2: Estimation Using Existing Data

In this method, you compute the PCTFREE value using a different formula and using existing data.

Step 1: Analyze the PRODUCTS table using the following command statement as SYSTEM:

```
SQL> ANALYZE TABLE TUNER.PRODUCTS
  2      ESTIMATE STATISTICS SAMPLE 30 PERCENT
  3  /

Table analyzed.
```

Step 2: Get table statistics using the following query:

```
SQL> SELECT TABLE_NAME, AVG_ROW_LEN
  2    FROM DBA_TABLES
  3   WHERE OWNER = 'TUNER'
  4     AND TABLE_NAME = 'PRODUCTS'
  5  /

TABLE_NAME                      AVG_ROW_LEN
------------------------------- -----------
PRODUCTS                                125
```

Step 3: Get the average growth for each column as shown in Table 6-6.

Table 6-6 PRODUCTS table data sizing (3)

Column	Data type	Bytes
PRODUCT_ID	NUMBER(4)	0
CATEGORY_ID	NUMBER(2)	0
PRODUCT_NAME	VARCHAR2(80)	40
PRODUCT_DESC	VARCHAR2(512)	256
STATUS	CHAR(1)	0
COMMENTS	VARCHAR2(1024)	512
	Total number of bytes	562

Step 4: Apply values obtained in Steps 2 and 3 to the following formula:

```
PCTFREE = (Average Growth - Average Row Length)*100/
          Maximum Row Length *100
PCTFREE = (808 - 125) * 100 / 1622
PCTFREE = 42 percent
```

In this case, the PCTFREE value is 42 percent, which should be rounded up to 45 percent or 50 percent.

PCTFREE and PCTUSED Computation Guidelines

The previous section showed you how to estimate the correct value for PCTFREE. But if you dislike arithmetic, you will like this section better than the last. When creating new tables, use the guidelines shown in Figure 6-9 to avoid the process of computing PCTFREE. As previously described, **PCTUSED** (percent used) is a block option that specifies how much of the block is used before the block is added back to the free list. Oracle maintains a structure called FREELISTS, which contains a list of all free blocks. The default value is 40.

6

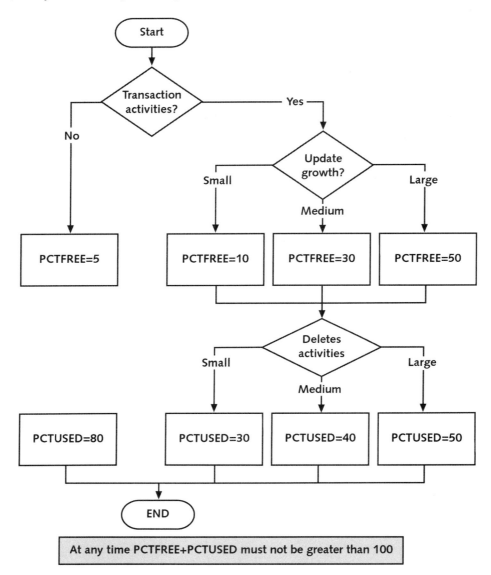

Figure 6-9   Flowchart of PCTFREE and PCTUSED guidelines

High-water Mark

When you are a DBA, your learning of new things about Oracle does not stop, and it will never end. Another piece of the storage puzzle is the HWM. Simply put, the **high-water mark (HWM)** is a marker of how much storage is allocated for a segment. Although the high-water mark is stored in the segment header, it is associated with empty blocks. When a new segment is created, the HWM is set at the beginning of the segment. As rows are inserted, the HWM advances forward five blocks at a time. When rows are deleted from the table, the HWM does not adjust backward. However, when the TRUNCATE statement truncates a table, the HWM is reset to the beginning of the segment. See Figure 6-10 and the steps that follow for an illustration.

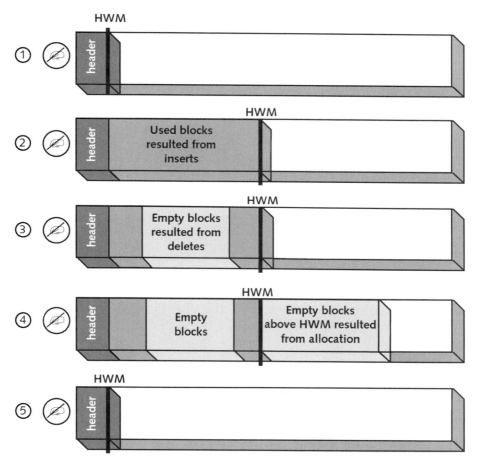

Figure 6-10   High-water mark illustration

Figure 6–10 illustrates the process of setting a HWM at the creation of a segment as follows:

1. The new segment is created. HWM is at the beginning of the segment.

2. As rows are inserted into the segments, the HWM advances forward.

3. Rows are deleted in a block below the HWM resulting in empty blocks. HWM does not go backward. To reclaim these empty blocks, you may need to reorganize the table by moving the segment to another segment in the same table or to a new tablespace using the following statement:

```
SQL> ALTER TABLE TUNER.CUSTOMERS MOVE
  2  /

Table altered.
```

4. New blocks were allocated as a result of the new extent allocation. The HWM still did not go backward. You can use the ALTER TABLE statement to deallocate these blocks:

```
SQL> ALTER TABLE TUNER.CUSTOMERS DEALLOCATE UNUSED
  2  /

Table altered.
```

5. The TRUNCATE TABLE statement resets the HWM.

EXTENT MANAGEMENT

So far, you have learned about the smallest data unit in Oracle, the block. It's time now to move to the next logical data unit, which is the extent. An **extent** is a group of Oracle blocks that is allocated for a segment when a segment is created. An important property of an extent is that the blocks it contains are physically contiguous. Extents are also allocated whenever space is needed for new data or updates. Extents are deallocated when space is freed by deletes or updates. The action of allocation and deallocation uses a significant amount of I/O. Also the allocation can degrade the performance of the database if its extents are being allocated and deallocated constantly while statements are being issued.

NOTE

Your prime objective is to avoid allocation of extents while statements are inserting or updating.

Extent options are specified when you create a table, index, or any other segment type. If not specified when the segment is created, an extent inherits extent specifications from the tablespace in which the segment resides. If a tablespace is created without specifying extents, the extents inherit default values from Oracle. The next section explains each extent option that can be specified when you create a table segment or other segments.

Extent Options

Figure 6-11 illustrates the syntax for creating a table segment. As you examine the syntax, pay special attention to the extent section, which specifies all options for storage parameters. Table 6-7 describes each option.

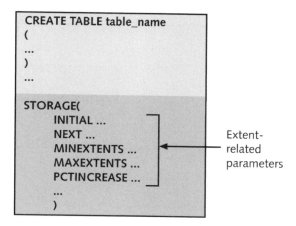

Figure 6-11   Syntax for creating a table highlighting extent options

Table 6-7   Description of extent options

Extent option	Description
INITIAL	Size of the first allocated extent
NEXT	Size of the next allocated extent
MINEXTENTS	Number of initial extents to be allocated when the segment is created
MAXEXTENTS	Maximum number of extents that can be allocated
PCTINCREASE	Percent increase: **PCTINCREASE** tells Oracle to increase the next extent with the percentage specified by this value. The default value is 50. This is used as a fudge factor to accommodate data growth.

The information in this table is derived from the online documentation that Oracle provides at the Oracle Technology Network site: *www.otn.oracle.com.*

The following examples illustrate the use of these extent parameters.

Example 4 (Figure 6-12):

```
INITIAL      1 MB
NEXT         2 MB
PCTINCREASE  0
MINEXTENTS   3
MAXEXTENTS   10
```

6

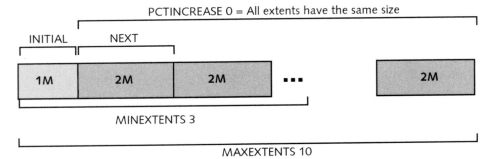

Figure 6-12   Example 4—Physical illustration of an extent

```
SQL> CREATE TABLE TBL
  2  (
  3    NUM NUMBER
  4  )
  5  STORAGE(
  6         INITIAL 1M
  7         NEXT    2M
  8         MINEXTENTS 3
  9         MAXEXTENTS 10
 10         PCTINCREASE 0
 11         )
 12    TABLESPACE DD_TS
 13  /

Table created.

SQL> SELECT SEGMENT_NAME, EXTENT_ID, BYTES
  2    FROM DBA_EXTENTS
  3    WHERE SEGMENT_NAME = 'TBL'
  4    ORDER BY 2
  5  /

SEGMENT_NAME                       EXTENT_ID     BYTES
-------------------------------- ---------- ----------
TBL                                       0    1064960
TBL                                       1    2109440
TBL                                       2    2109440
```

Example 5 (Figure 6-13):

```
INITIAL       500 KB
NEXT          1 MB
PCTINCREASE   20
MINEXTENTS    4
MAXEXTENTS    UNLIMITED
```

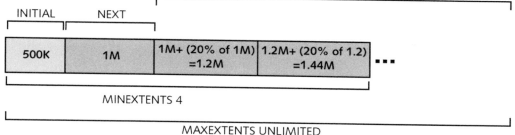

Figure 6-13   Example 5—Physical illustration of an extent

```
SQL> CREATE TABLE TBL
  2  (
  3    NUM NUMBER
  4  )
  5  STORAGE(
  6         INITIAL 500K
  7         NEXT    1M
  8         MINEXTENTS 4
  9         MAXEXTENTS UNLIMITED
 10         PCTINCREASE 20
 11         )
 12   TABLESPACE DD_TS
 13 /

Table created.

SQL> SELECT SEGMENT_NAME, EXTENT_ID, BYTES
  2    FROM DBA_EXTENTS
  3    WHERE SEGMENT_NAME = 'TBL'
  4    ORDER BY 2
  5  /

SEGMENT_NAME                    EXTENT_ID      BYTES
------------------------------- ----------- ----------
TBL                                      0     512000
TBL                                      1    1064960
TBL                                      2    1269760
TBL                                      3    1515520
```

Example 6 (Figure 6-14):

```
INITIAL       100 KB
NEXT          200 KB
PCTINCREASE   100
MINEXTENTS    4
MAXEXTENTS    UNLIMITED
```

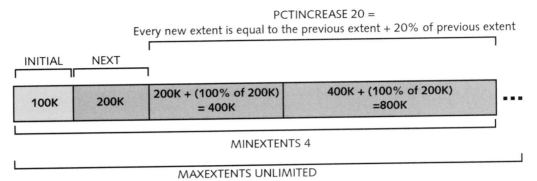

Figure 6-14   Example 6—Physical illustration of an extent

```
SQL> CREATE TABLE TBL
  2  (
  3    NUM NUMBER
  4  )
  5  STORAGE(
  6          INITIAL 100K
  7          NEXT    200K
  8          MINEXTENTS 4
  9          MAXEXTENTS UNLIMITED
 10          PCTINCREASE 100
 11          )
 12    TABLESPACE DD_TS
 13 /

Table created.

SQL> SELECT SEGMENT_NAME, EXTENT_ID, BYTES
  2     FROM DBA_EXTENTS
  3     WHERE SEGMENT_NAME = 'TBL'
  4     ORDER BY 2
  5  /

SEGMENT_NAME                          EXTENT_ID      BYTES
------------------------------------- ---------- ----------
TBL                                           0     102400
TBL                                           1     204800
TBL                                           2     409600
TBL                                           3     819200
```

You used the DBA_EXTENTS data dictionary view, which contains all extents allocated for a segment.

Oracle provides two methods of extent management, which you can employ when creating table segments. First is the traditional method, which is not recommended. This is the data dictionary management method. The second method is local management. The next section describes each method with examples for specifying extent management.

Data Dictionary Extent Management

As stated previously, before the release of Oracle 8*i*, you could manage extents only by using **data dictionary extent management**. When you use the data dictionary, Oracle uses system tables to determine which extents are free and which are used. Oracle uses two specific system tables: FET$ contains all free extents, and UET$ contains all used extents. To better understand the function of these two tables, log on as SYSTEM and follow the steps as follows.

NOTE

Only one method of extent management can be used if the SYSTEM tablespace is using local extent management.

6

Step 1: Determine the extent management method for SYSTEM tablespace:

```
SQL> SELECT  TABLESPACE_NAME,
  2             EXTENT_MANAGEMENT EXTENT_MGMT,
  3             ALLOCATION_TYPE,
  4             SEGMENT_SPACE_MANAGEMENT
  5      FROM DBA_TABLESPACES
  6  /

TABLESPACE_NAME  EXTENT_MGMT  ALLOCATION_TYPE  SEGMENT_SPACE_MANAGEMENT
---------------  -----------  ---------------  ------------------------
SYSTEM           DICTIONARY   USER             MANUAL
UNDOTBS          LOCAL        SYSTEM           MANUAL
TOOLS            LOCAL        SYSTEM           MANUAL
USERS            LOCAL        SYSTEM           AUTO
TEMP             LOCAL        UNIFORM          AUTO
TS_01            LOCAL        SYSTEM           AUTO
DD_TS            DICTIONARY   USER             AUTO
```

If SYSTEM tablespace extent management is LOCAL, you cannot proceed with these steps. Notice that the EXTENT_MANAGEMENT column has two values:

- **LOCAL:** Indicates that extent management is local

- **DICTIONARY:** Indicates that extent management is using the data dictionary

Step 2: Create a new tablespace with data dictionary extent management:

```
SQL> CREATE TABLESPACE DD_TS
  2      DATAFILE
  3      'C:\ORACLE\ORADATA\SAM\DD_TS01.DBF' SIZE 10M
  4      EXTENT MANAGEMENT DICTIONARY
  5  /

Tablespace created.
```

Step 3: Verify tablespace creation:

```
SQL> SELECT TABLESPACE_NAME,
  2         EXTENT_MANAGEMENT EXTENT_MGMT,
  3         ALLOCATION_TYPE,
  4         SEGMENT_SPACE_MANAGEMENT
  5    FROM DBA_TABLESPACES
  6  /

TABLESPACE_NAME EXTENT_MGMT  ALLOCATION_TYPE  SEGMENT_SPACE_MANAGEMENT
--------------- ------------ ---------------- ------------------------
SYSTEM          DICTIONARY   USER             MANUAL
UNDOTBS         LOCAL        SYSTEM           MANUAL
TOOLS           LOCAL        SYSTEM           MANUAL
USERS           LOCAL        SYSTEM           AUTO
TEMP            LOCAL        UNIFORM          AUTO
TS_01           LOCAL        SYSTEM           AUTO
DD_TS           DICTIONARY   USER             AUTO
```

Notice that the ALLOCATION_TYPE column has different values that indicate how extents will be allocated:

- **USER:** Allocated by you as the DBA

- **SYSTEM:** Allocated by Oracle

- **UNIFORM:** All extent allocation will be automatic and the same size

Step 4: Get the tablespace identification number:

```
SQL> SELECT TS#
  2    FROM V$TABLESPACE
  3   WHERE NAME = 'DD_TS'
  4  /

       TS#
----------
         7
```

Step 5: Create a new table residing on the new tablespace DD_TS:

```
SQL> CREATE TABLE TBL_DD
  2  (
  3    NUM    NUMBER
  4  )
  5  STORAGE
  6       (
  7            INITIAL 1M
  8            NEXT    1M
  9            MINEXTENTS 4
 10       )
 11  TABLESPACE DD_TS
 12  /

Table created.
```

Step 6: Retrieve all rows from UET$ to find all extents used in DD_TS:

```
SQL> SELECT *
  2    FROM UET$
  3    WHERE TS# = 7
  4  /
```

SEGFILE#	SEGBLOCK#	EXT#	TS#	FILE#	BLOCK#	LENGTH
6	2	2	7	6	522	385
6	2	0	7	6	2	260
6	2	1	7	6	262	260
6	2	3	7	6	907	580

Step 7: Select all rows in FET$ belonging to tablespace DD_TS:

```
SQL> SELECT *
  2    FROM FET$
  3    WHERE TS# = 7
  4  /
```

TS#	FILE#	BLOCK#	LENGTH
7	6	1487	1074

By examining the code, you can see how Oracle uses the results. Oracle consults and updates these two tables each time an extent is allocated or deallocated and could incur more I/O trips than required. Do not try to use the results in Steps 6 and 7 to derive any information regarding administering extents. Oracle uses the contents of UET$ and FET$.

Step 8: Obtain the size of the initial extent for table TBL_DD:

```
SQL> SELECT TABLE_NAME,
  2            INITIAL_EXTENT
  3     FROM DBA_TABLES
  4    WHERE TABLE_NAME = 'TBL_DD'
  5  /

TABLE_NAME    INITIAL_EXTENT
------------  --------------
TBL_DD               1048576
```

Notice that the initial extent is the same value (1 MB) as specified when the table was created.

Local Extent Management

Oracle improved on dictionary extent management by introducing **local extent management,** which is more efficient in retrieving information about extents allocation. It is called "local" because the information about extents is stored locally within the tablespace, where the extents reside. The extents list is represented as a map of bits for each extent indicating whether it is used or free, as illustrated in Figure 6-15.

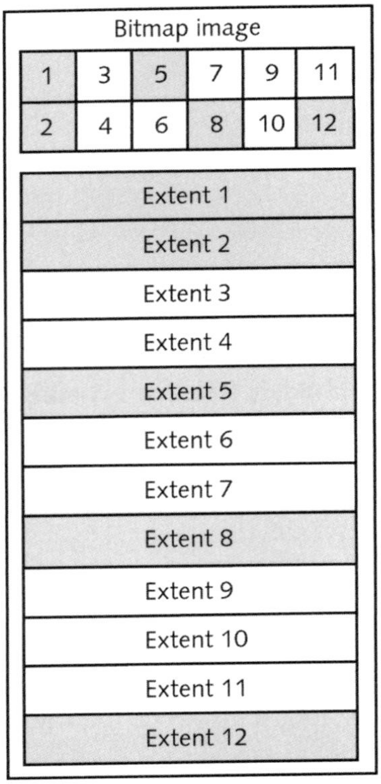

Figure 6-15   Local extent management—illustration of extents bit map image

As you can see in Figure 6-15, Oracle keeps a bit for each extent. The bit is turned on (highlighted) to indicate that the extent is in use, and turned off to indicate that the extent is available. The bitmap image consumes 64 KB of tablespace. When an extent is allocated or deallocated, the corresponding bit is turned on or off respectively without updating system tables.

TIP   LMT stands for "locally managed tablespace," which refers to local extent management. DMT stands for dictionary-managed tablespace, which refers to data dictionary extent management.

Log on as SYSTEM and use the following steps to create a table residing in a tablespace with local extent management.

Step 1: Verify SYSTEM tablespace is locally managed:

```
SQL> SELECT  TABLESPACE_NAME,
  2          EXTENT_MANAGEMENT EXTENT_MGMT,
  3          ALLOCATION_TYPE
  4     FROM DBA_TABLESPACES
  5  /

TABLESPACE_NAME                    EXTENT_MGMT ALLOCATION_TYPE
---------------------------------- ----------- ---------------
SYSTEM                             LOCAL       SYSTEM
TEMP                               LOCAL       UNIFORM
TOOLS                              LOCAL       SYSTEM
USERS                              LOCAL       SYSTEM
UNDO_TS01                          LOCAL       SYSTEM
```

Step 2: Create a new tablespace called LM_TS that is dictionary managed:

```
SQL> CREATE TABLESPACE LM_TS
  2     DATAFILE
  3     'C:\ORACLE\ORADATA\SAM\LM_TS01.DBF' SIZE 10M
  4     EXTENT MANAGEMENT DICTIONARY
  5  /

CREATE TABLESPACE LM_TS
*
ERROR at line 1:
ORA-12913: Cannot create dictionary managed tablespace
```

As the error shows, you cannot create a dictionary-managed tablespace if the SYSTEM tablespace is locally managed.

Step 3: Attempt to retrieve data from UET$ and FET$. No rows should be returned because these tables are not used for extent management:

```
SQL> SELECT * FROM UET$
  2  /

no rows selected

SQL> SELECT * FROM FET$
  2  /

no rows selected
```

Step 4: Create a LM_TS tablespace, this time using local extent management:

```
SQL> CREATE TABLESPACE LM_TS
  2    DATAFILE
  3    'C:\ORACLE\ORADATA\SAM\LM_TS01.DBF' SIZE 10M
  4    EXTENT MANAGEMENT LOCAL
  5  /

Tablespace created.
```

NOTE

Although large extents are good because space is preallocated and dynamic allocation is avoided while transactions are occurring, large extents can cause problems in importing tables because they require large amounts of space ahead of time.

Step 5: Create the new table TBL_L1 residing in LM_TS tablespace:

```
SQL> CREATE TABLE TBL_L1
  2  (
  3   NUM  NUMBER
  4  )
  5  STORAGE(
  6          INITIAL 4M
  7         )
  8  TABLESPACE LM_TS
  9  /

Table created.
```

Step 6: Create another table called TBL_L2 that also resides in LM_TS tablespace:

```
SQL> CREATE TABLE TBL_L2
  2  (
  3    NUM   NUMBER
  4  )
  5  TABLESPACE LM_TS
  6  /

Table created.
```

Step 7: Retrieve the initial extent value for both tables TBL_L1 and TBL_L2:

```
SQL> SELECT  TABLE_NAME,
  2          INITIAL_EXTENT
  3    FROM USER_TABLES
  4   WHERE TABLE_NAME LIKE 'TBL_L%'
  5  /

TABLE_NAME                       INITIAL_EXTENT
------------------------------   --------------
TBL_L1                                  4194304
TBL_L2                                    65536
```

At this point, it is important to understand the difference between the initial extents of TBL_L1 and TBL_L2. When TBL_L1 was created, you specified 4 MB as the initial extent. This specification overrides the initial extent value of the tablespace where the table resides. TBL_L2 table, on the other hand, inherited the initial extent value from the tablespace.

NOTE

You can use both methods of extent management if you create SYSTEM tablespace using data dictionary extent management.

Remember that Oracle and most DBA experts highly recommend local extent management. It enhances performance and does not generate any redo entries resulting from allocation and deallocation of extents.

NOTE

When you choose automatic segment allocation, PCTUSED and FREELIST are ignored.

Before you explore the next logical data unit, you should note one final point on this topic. Suppose your database employs tablespaces that are dictionary managed and you wanted to switch them to locally managed. What would you do? Oracle has supplied a DBMS package specifically for this purpose. Chapter 7 details this package and how to change extent management.

6

Extents Report

There are times when you need to find out how many extents are being used by a segment and whether a segment is nearing the maximum extents or not. In this case, you can use the following query, which displays a report showing extent usage for each tablespace:

```
SQL> SELECT T.TABLESPACE_NAME,
  2          T.MAX_EXTENTS MAX_EXTENTS,
  3          S.TOTAL_EXTENTS TOTAL_EXTENTS,
  4          CEIL(DF.TOTAL_SIZE/(1024*1024)) TOTAL_SIZE,
  5          CEIL(S.TOTAL_USED/(1024*1024)) TOTAL_USED,
  6          CEIL(T.NEXT_EXTENT/(1024*1024)) NEXT_EXTENT
  7    FROM DBA_TABLESPACES T,
  8         (SELECT TABLESPACE_NAME,
  9                 SUM(EXTENTS) TOTAL_EXTENTS,
 10                 SUM(BYTES) TOTAL_USED
 11           FROM DBA_SEGMENTS
 12          GROUP BY TABLESPACE_NAME) S,
 13         (SELECT TABLESPACE_NAME,
 14                 SUM(BYTES) TOTAL_SIZE
 15           FROM DBA_DATA_FILES
 16          GROUP BY TABLESPACE_NAME) DF
 17   WHERE T.TABLESPACE_NAME = S.TABLESPACE_NAME
 18     AND T.TABLESPACE_NAME = DF.TABLESPACE_NAME
 19   ORDER BY TABLESPACE_NAME
 20  /
```

TABLESPACE_NAME	MAX_EXTENTS	TOTAL_EXTENTS	TOTAL_SIZE	TOTAL_USED	NEXT_EXTENT
DD_TS	249	4	10	2	1
SYSTEM	249	1861	200	107	1
TS_01	2147483645	996	100	65	
UNDOTBS	2147483645	36	50	6	
USERS	2147483645	2648	1000	171	

This report shows, for example, that the DD_TS tablespace is configured to have a maximum of 248 extents and four extents are already used. This information is important if the total of extents used is 247. This indicates that this tablespace will run out of extent in the near future, which means you need to be proactive. One of the actions you could take is simply to raise the extent limit to a higher number.

SEGMENTS SIZING

In this section, you briefly explore the different types of segments available in Oracle. Then you concentrate on the most commonly used segments—the TABLE and INDEX segments. You learn how to size, analyze, and detect problems. Then you learn how to analyze INDEX segments and to reorganize indexes. A segment is a logical data unit that stores different database objects. Segments add a level of data organization to increase data access efficiency and reduce contention.

Segment Types

Different database objects contain many types of segments, and each segment serves a specific purpose. Table 6-8 lists all the segment types available in Oracle.

Table 6-8   Segment types available in Oracle

Segment type	Description
INDEX PARTITION	Used for a partitioned index
TABLE PARTITON	Used for partitioned tables—a partitioned table is a table that is physically divided into several independent parts that could reside on the same tablespace or different tablespaces.
TABLE	Most commonly used segment type; stores data in a normal table and in index-organized tables (IOTs)
CLUSTER	Special type of segment which clusters two tables based on a hierarchal relationship
INDEX	Stores column(s) values and row(s) for fast data retrieval
ROLLBACK	Used for undo data
DEFERRED ROLLBACK	Used for undo data residing in an undo segment with status pending offline
TEMPORARY	Used for storing data temporarily
CACHE	Used by Oracle only
LOBSEGMENT	Stands for large object segment and is used for columns with data type LOB, CLOB, NCLOB, and BLOB
LOBINDEX	Stands for large object index segment and is used for index columns with data types LOB, CLOB, NCLOB, and BLOB

The information in this table is derived from the online documentation that Oracle provides at the Oracle Technology Network site: *www.otn.oracle.com.*

You can use the DBA_SEGMENTS dictionary view to display data about all segments created in your database. For example, the following query displays all segments created by TUNER:

```
SQL> SELECT SEGMENT_NAME,
  2          SEGMENT_TYPE TYPE,
  3          TABLESPACE_NAME TABLESPACE,
  4          BLOCKS,
  5          EXTENTS
  6    FROM DBA_SEGMENTS
  7   WHERE OWNER = 'TUNER'
  8  /

SEGMENT_NAME        TYPE   TABLESPACE BLOCKS EXTENTS
------------------  -----  ---------- ------ -------
SUPPLIERS           TABLE  USERS          32       4
SHIPMENT_METHOD     TABLE  USERS           8       1
DEPARTMENTS         TABLE  USERS           8       1
JOBS                TABLE  USERS           8       1
EMPLOYEES           TABLE  USERS           8       1
SALES_COMMISSION    TABLE  USERS           8       1
PROMOTIONS          TABLE  USERS           8       1
CATEGORIES          TABLE  USERS           8       1
PRODUCTS            TABLE  USERS          96      12
PRODUCT_SUPPLIER    TABLE  USERS          16       2
PRODUCT_PRICES      TABLE  USERS          64       8
PRODUCT_INVENTORY   TABLE  USERS          32       4
PAYMENT_METHOD      TABLE  USERS           8       1
CUSTOMERS           TABLE  USERS         128      16
ORDERS              TABLE  USERS         256      17
ORDER_LINES         TABLE  USERS         512      19
EMPLOYEE_RANKS      TABLE  USERS           8       1
TRANS_DEMO          TABLE  USERS           8       1
CHN_TBL             TABLE  USERS         384      18
SYS_C003111         INDEX  USERS           8       1
SYS_C003113         INDEX  USERS           8       1
SYS_C003115         INDEX  USERS           8       1
SYS_C003117         INDEX  USERS           8       1
SYS_C003119         INDEX  USERS           8       1
SYS_C003121         INDEX  USERS           8       1
SYS_C003123         INDEX  USERS           8       1
SYS_C003125         INDEX  USERS           8       1
SYS_C003127         INDEX  USERS          24       3
SYS_C003130         INDEX  USERS          24       3
SYS_C003133         INDEX  USERS          40       5
SYS_C003135         INDEX  USERS          24       3
SYS_C003137         INDEX  USERS           8       1
SYS_C003139         INDEX  USERS          16       2
SYS_C003141         INDEX  USERS          32       4
SYS_C003144         INDEX  USERS         640      20
SYS_C003146         INDEX  USERS           8       1
```

Table Segment Sizing

No one can deny that the cost of disk storage has declined tremendously in the last decade. Over the same period, the advances in hardware technology have made storage technology increasingly faster and more efficient. Regardless of the cost and efficiency, it is still important to organize, allocate, and size your tables efficiently. This section presents two methods for sizing tables properly.

When you want to allocate storage for a new table, you need to answer the following questions. Usually, a business analyst should be able to assist you in getting these answers:

- How many rows will this table initially contain?

- What is the percentage of growth per time period (day, week, month, quarter, or year)?

- What type of activities will be conducted on this table (inserts, deletes, or updates)?

Consider the CUSTOMERS table in TUNER schema. It must initially store about one million customers, and it is predicted to grow about 10 percent per month. This table has a high number of INSERTS and UPDATES and a low number of DELETES. Knowing these facts, you can use any of the following methods to compute storage requirement.

NOTE Of the several types of table-sizing methods, some are complex and account for all the different structures, such as INITRANS and FREELIST. Some sizing methods account for column and block overhead. Most sizing methods yield very close results. Here are two methods for estimating table size.

Method 1: Using Maximum Row Length

In this method, you use the following formula to estimate a table size:

```
Estimated table size = MRL * (1 + PF/100) * NOR * FACTOR
Where:
        MRL = Maximum row length
        PF = PCTFREE
        NOR = Number of rows
        FACTOR = 20 percent or any desired percentage of
        number of rows as a fudge factor
```

Now, follow these steps to use this formula.

Step 1: Use the following query to compute the maximum row length:

```
SQL> SELECT TABLE_NAME "Table Name",
  2           SUM( DECODE( SUBSTR(DATA_TYPE,1,1),
  3                 'N', TRUNC( ( NVL(DATA_PRECISION,38) + 1 )
  4                     / 2, 0 ) + 1 ,
  5                 'D', 7, DATA_LENGTH ) ) "Max Length"
  6      FROM USER_TAB_COLUMNS
  7     WHERE TABLE_NAME = 'CUSTOMERS'
  8     GROUP BY TABLE_NAME
  9    HAVING SUM( DECODE( SUBSTR(DATA_TYPE,1,1),
 10                 'N', TRUNC( ( NVL(DATA_PRECISION,38) + 1 )
 11                     / 2, 0 ) + 1 ,
 12                 'D', 7, DATA_LENGTH ) ) > 0
 13     ORDER BY 2 DESC , 1
 14   /


Table Name                          Max Length
----------------------------------  ----------
CUSTOMERS                                 1367
```

This gives you an MRL equal to 1367 bytes.

Step 2: You need to determine PCTFREE. To do so, you can use the guidelines presented in Figure 6-9. Based on given activity levels for this table, you get PCTFREE 50 and PCTUSED 30. Therefore PF is 50.

Step 3: The number of initial rows is equal to one million. You can use this value for the initial storage requirements for this table or you can determine space requirements for one year. For a full year, the total number of rows is as follows:

```
1 million * 10% * 12 = 13200000 rows
```

Therefore, NOR is 13200000.

Step 4: Compute the FACTOR value, which is 20 percent of NOR. In this case, it is 2640000 rows.

Step 5: Combining all the values, you get:

```
Estimated table size = 1367 * (1 + 50/100) * (13200000 * 1.2)
Estimated table size = 10826640000 bytes
Estimated table size = 10826640000/(1024 * 1024 * 1024) = 10 GB
```

Therefore, you need 10 GB to store the estimated number of rows for one year. Now consider how to create this table by specifying block and extents options. Notice that only the INITIAL extent is specified, because you will be creating this on a tablespace with local extent management. Also, INITIAL is allocated as 100 MB because you will be inserting about one million rows initially, which will require large amounts of space. The proper INITIAL value is actually computed using this formula: 1 M rows $*$ 1367 $*$ 0.5 $=$ 651 MB, which is very large. Huge extents are not highly recommended because of space requirements. So the moderate value of 100 MB is selected.

```
SQL>   CREATE TABLE CUSTOMERS
          (
          ...
          )
       PCTFREE 50
          PCTUSED 30
          INITRANS 1
          MAXTRANS 255
          STORAGE(
                      INITIAL 100M
                  )
          TABLESPACE ...
       /
```

Method 2: Using Average Row Length

In this method, you use the following formula to estimate table size:

```
Number of blocks = (ROWS * SZ)/ (BLK * (1 - PF/100))
Where:
          ROWS = Estimated number of rows
          SZ = Average row size (assume it is 200)
          BLK = Block size
          PF = PCTFREE
```

Step 1: Obtain an estimated number of rows. This value was computed in Method 1, Step 3.

6

Step 2: Obtain a full description of the CUSTOMERS table structure. This yields COLS = 16:

```
SQL> DESC CUSTOMERS
 Name                          Null?     Type
 ----------------------------  --------  --------------
 SALES_REP_ID                            NUMBER(4)
 CUSTOMER_ID                   NOT NULL  NUMBER(8)
 CUSTOMER_SSN                            VARCHAR2(9)
 FIRST_NAME                              VARCHAR2(20)
 LAST_NAME                               VARCHAR2(20)
 ADDR_LINE                               VARCHAR2(80)
 CITY                                    VARCHAR2(30)
 STATE                                   VARCHAR2(30)
 ZIP_CODE                                VARCHAR2(9)
 PHONE                                   VARCHAR2(15)
 EMAIL                                   VARCHAR2(80)
 CC_NUMBER                               VARCHAR2(20)
 CREDIT_LIMIT                            NUMBER
 GENDER                                  CHAR(1)
 STATUS                                  CHAR(1)
 COMMENTS                                VARCHAR2(1024)

OR

SQL> SELECT COUNT(*)
  2    FROM USER_TAB_COLUMNS
  3   WHERE TABLE_NAME = 'CUSTOMERS'
  4  /

  COUNT(*)
----------
        16
```

Step 3: Obtain the block size used for your database:

```
SQL> SHOW PARAMETER DB_BLOCK_SIZE

NAME                                   TYPE         VALUE
------------------------------------   -----------  -----
db_block_size                          integer      8192
```

Step 4: Combining all the values you get:

```
Number of blocks = (ROWS * SZ)/(BLK * (1 - PF/100))
Number of blocks = (13200000 * 200)/(8192 * (1 - 50/100))
Number of blocks = 651691 blocks = 5 GB
```

As you probably noticed, this method gave different values than Method 1 because in Method 1 you used maximum row size rather than average row size. If you used average row size, your yield would be approximately 4.4 GB.

Analyzing Tables and Table Statistics

The Oracle Optimizer uses statistics to determine the fastest way to retrieve data from tables. If the tables are created and no statistics are generated for the Optimizer, it can't determine how best to retrieve data. To use Oracle Optimizer effectively, you need to analyze tables and other segments on a regular basis. Analyzing tables generates statistics that are stored in system tables to be available for viewing.

You can use the ANALYZE command or the DBMS_UTILITY supplied by Oracle in the DBMS package. When analyzing a table, you must specify whether you want Oracle to analyze every row in the table or only sample rows. To analyze every row in the table, you should specify the **COMPUTE STATISTICS** method. To sample the table, specify the **ESTIMATE STATISTICS** method. Statistics are populated in the base system tables that contain data about the users' data and can be seen using one of the following data dictionary views: DBA_TABLES, ALL_TABLES, or USER_TABLES. Also, when a table is analyzed, all of its columns are analyzed to generate its statistics. You can view statistics by using DBA_TAB_COLUMNS, ALL_TAB_COLUMNS, or USER_TAB_COLUMNS. Table 6-9 describes columns that are populated when the table is analyzed.

Table 6-9   Statistical columns

Column	Description
NUM_ROWS	Total number of rows in the table
BLOCKS	Number of blocks in the table that are below the high-water mark
EMPTY_BLOCKS	Number of empty blocks that are above the high-water mark
AVG_SPACE	Average free space in the used blocks that are below the high-water mark
CHAIN_CNT	Number of rows that are chained and migrated as a result of updates and lack of storage in the reserved free space
AVG_ROW_LEN	Average row length (size) in the table
LAST_ANALYZED	Last time and date the table was analyzed

The information in this table is derived from the online documentation that Oracle provides at the Oracle Technology Network site: *www.otn.oracle.com*.

Now follow these steps to learn how to analyze tables and see what statistics are generated.

Step 1: Log on as SYSTEM and list all tables owned by the TUNER schema using the following query:

```
SQL> SELECT TABLE_NAME,
  2          NUM_ROWS,
  3          BLOCKS,
  4          EMPTY_BLOCKS,
  5          AVG_SPACE,
  6          CHAIN_CNT,
  7          AVG_ROW_LEN,
  8          LAST_ANALYZED
  9     FROM DBA_TABLES
 10    WHERE OWNER = 'TUNER'
 11    /

TABLE_NAME        NUM_ROWS BLOCKS EMPTY_BLOCKS AVG_SPACE CHAIN_CNT AVG_ROW_LEN LAST_ANALYZED
----------------- -------- ------ ------------ --------- --------- ----------- -------------
CATEGORIES
CUSTOMERS
DEPARTMENTS
EMPLOYEES
EMPLOYEE_RANKS
JOBS
ORDERS
ORDER_LINES
PAYMENT_METHOD
PRODUCTS
PRODUCT_INVENTORY
PRODUCT_PRICES
PRODUCT_SUPPLIER
PROMOTIONS
SALES_COMMISSION
SHIPMENT_METHOD
SUPPLIERS
```

NOTE   If your tables are already analyzed (which means you have data in statistical columns), you may want to delete statistical data by executing the following command: EXEC*DBMS_STATS.DELETE_SCHEMA_STATS('TUNER').

Step 2: To analyze all tables, use the Oracle-supplied package called DBMS_UTILITY with the ESTIMATE STATISTICS option. This package employs many procedures for different purposes. The procedure you need from this package is ANALYZE_SCHEMA, as demonstrated in the following code segment.

TIP   When analyzing tables, it is recommended to use the ESTIMATE method with a 20 percent row sample, especially if the schema tables contain large amounts of data.

```
PROCEDURE ANALYZE_SCHEMA
Argument Name        Type                      In/Out  Default?
------------------   ----------------------    ------  --------
SCHEMA               VARCHAR2                   IN
METHOD               VARCHAR2                   IN
ESTIMATE_ROWS        NUMBER                     IN      DEFAULT
ESTIMATE_PERCENT     NUMBER                     IN      DEFAULT
METHOD_OPT           VARCHAR2                   IN      DEFAULT

Where:
   METHOD:              COMPUTE scan every single row in the table
                        ESTIMATE uses sample number of rows
                        DELETE removes all statistics.
   ESTIMATE_ROWS:    Number of estimated rows to be used for in the
                  analyze process. (used with ESTIMATE method)
   ESTIMATE_PERCENT: Percentage of total rows to be used in the analyze
                        process. (used with ESTIMATE method)
   METHOD_OPT:          Method options to indicate one of the following:
                        —  FOR TABLE
                        —  FOR ALL [INDEXED] COLUMNS [SIZE n]
                        —  FOR ALL INDEXES
```

6

If Step 1 produces any values for statistical columns, you can delete them by using DBMS_UTILITY.ANALYZE_SCHEMA with DELETE for the METHOD parameter, as shown in the code segment that follows. In addition to the Oracle-supplied PL/SQL package, there is another very useful package called DBMS_SPACE. The next section explains this package.

```
SQL> EXEC DBMS_UTILITY.ANALYZE_SCHEMA('TUNER', 'DELETE');

PL/SQL PROCEDURE SUCCESSFULLY COMPLETED.
```

Step 3: Using the DBMS_UTILITY and the ESTIMATE method, you must analyze the full schema of TUNER for 30 percent of the rows in each table as follows:

```
SQL> exec dbms_utility.analyze_schema('TUNER', 'ESTIMATE', NULL, 30)

PL/SQL procedure successfully completed.
```

Step 4: Now you can query DBA_TABLES to see all the statistics:

```
SQL> SELECT TABLE_NAME,
  2         NUM_ROWS,
  3         BLOCKS,
  4         EMPTY_BLOCKS,
  5         AVG_SPACE,
  6         CHAIN_CNT,
  7         AVG_ROW_LEN,
  8         LAST_ANALYZED
  9    FROM DBA_TABLES
 10   WHERE OWNER = 'TUNER'
 11  /
```

TABLE_NAME	NUM_ROWS	BLOCKS	EMPTY_BLOCKS	AVG_SPACE	CHAIN_CNT	AVG_ROW_LEN	LAST_ANALYZED
CATEGORIES	18	5	3	8002	0	17	23-FEB-02
CUSTOMERS	4357	122	6	966	0	197	23-FEB-02
DEPARTMENTS	99	5	3	7457	0	29	23-FEB-02
EMPLOYEES	294	5	3	5343	0	44	23-FEB-02
EMPLOYEE_RANKS	0	5	3	8069	0	0	23-FEB-02
JOBS	99	5	3	7608	0	21	23-FEB-02
ORDERS	9916	180	76	2695	0	96	23-FEB-02
ORDER_LINES	108038	496	16	1462	0	28	23-FEB-02
PAYMENT_METHOD	9	5	3	8044	0	14	23-FEB-02
PRODUCTS	5001	88	8	869	0	125	23-FEB-02
PRODUCT_INVENTORY	5001	28	4	2536	0	29	23-FEB-02
PRODUCT_PRICES	7739	58	6	1121	0	48	23-FEB-02
PRODUCT_SUPPLIER	5001	13	3	3112	0	11	23-FEB-02
PROMOTIONS	27	5	3	7874	0	34	23-FEB-02
SALES_COMMISSION	9	5	3	8052	0	10	23-FEB-02
SHIPMENT_METHOD	11	5	3	8041	0	13	23-FEB-02
SUPPLIERS	1000	28	4	2658	0	150	23-FEB-02
TRANS_DEMO	2	5	3	8066	0	13	23-FEB-02

You can use the physical statistics about each table to determine, for instance, if there is row chaining (row chaining is explained in detail in subsequent sections), the total number of rows, and the average row size. But most important, the Oracle Optimizer needs this information to make the proper decisions on data retrieval.

Not only table statistics are generated by the ANALYZE statement—statistics are generated for all columns in the table. The following query displays statistics for all columns in ORDERS table:

```
SQL> SELECT COLUMN_NAME,
  2           NUM_DISTINCT,
  3           LOW_VALUE,
  4           HIGH_VALUE,
  5           DENSITY,
  6           NUM_NULLS,
  7           NUM_BUCKETS,
  8           LAST_ANALYZED,
  9           SAMPLE_SIZE
 10      FROM USER_TAB_COLUMNS
 11     WHERE TABLE_NAME = 'ORDERS'
 12  /
```

COLUMN_NAME	NUM_DISTINCT	LOW_VALUE	HIGH_VALUE	DENSITY	NUM_NULLS	NUM_BUCKETS	LAST_ANALYZED	SAMPLE_SIZE
ORDER_ID	9916	C202	C3020110	.000100847	0	1	26-FEB-02	9916
ORDER_DATE	9452	77C50B140C3918	78660B110C3929	.000105798	0	1	26-FEB-02	9916
CUSTOMER_ID	3658	C30B0105	C35B2863	.000273373	0	1	26-FEB-02	9916
EMPLOYEE_ID	43	C20E5F	C26163	.023255814	0	1	26-FEB-02	9916
SHIP_DATE	359	78660B0C0C3901	78660B110C393C	.002785515	0	1	26-FEB-02	9916
SHIPMENT_METHOD_ID	10	C102	C10B	.1	0	1	26-FEB-02	9916
PAYMENT_METHOD_ID	8	C102	C109	.125	0	1	26-FEB-02	9916
PAID	2	4E	59	.5	0	1	26-FEB-02	9916
ORDER_STATUS	3	47	52	.333333333	1647	1	26-FEB-02	9916
COMMENTS	9916	2020687D3B30507D4D2B7E232	7E7E58523942444E4B4F3D795	.000100847	0	1	26-FEB	
		8284A59545D2760674D663C71	65F532D593C5661537A75356C					
		417836442C28	4C2E444D77524E					

You can also use the Oracle Enterprise Manager with the Schema option on the navigation panel to view all tables owned by the TUNER schema as well as general information about each table, as shown in Figure 6-16.

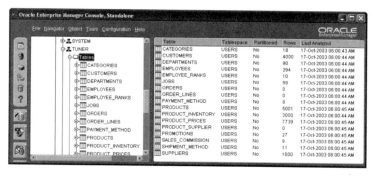

Figure 6-16   Oracle Enterprise Manager—Schema Manager, showing TUNER tables

Figure 6-17 displays statistics for the ORDER_LINES table. This screen is displayed when you double-click the ORDER_LINES table shown in Figure 6-16.

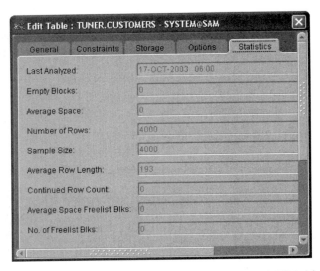

Figure 6-17   Schema Manager—ORDER_LINES table statistics

Another Oracle-supplied package that generates useful statistics is DBMS_STATS, which is discussed in more detail in Chapter 12.

If you use Oracle Enterprise Manager, you can follow these steps to analyze any schema or table. These steps analyze the TUNER.ORDERS table using the ESTIMATE method option for 20 percent of the rows.

Step 1: Log on to Oracle Enterprise Manager and click the **Analyze Wizard**, as shown in Figure 6-18.

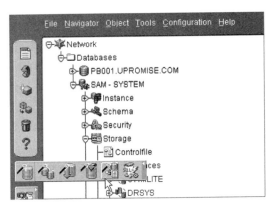

Figure 6-18   Oracle Enterprise Manager—launching the Analyze Wizard

Step 2: Clicking the Analyze Wizard displays actions that you can use to analyze. Select the **Estimate Statistics** radio button and change the Percent textbox from **10** to **20** because 20 percent of the rows will provide a better estimate sample than 10 percent. Then click **Next**, as in Figure 6-19.

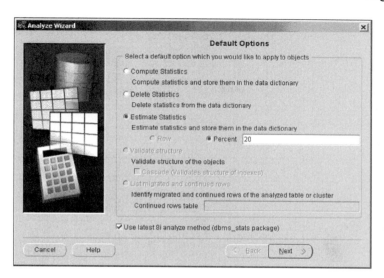

Figure 6-19 Oracle Enterprise Manager—Analyze Wizard main screen

Step 3: A screen is displayed showing in the left pane a tree of all objects with all associated schemas. Now select the **TUNER schema** and **ORDERS table**. Then click the **right arrow** button (>) and click **Next**, as shown in Figures 6-20 and 6-21.

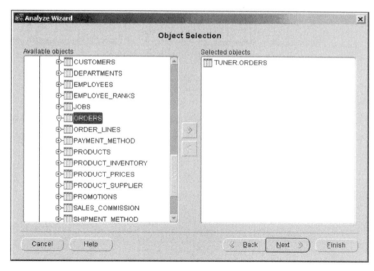

Figure 6-20 Using the Analyze Wizard to select an object

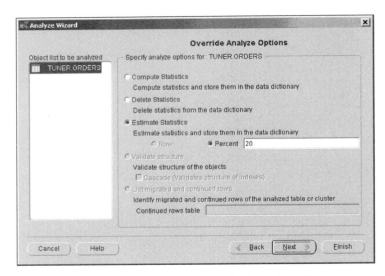

Figure 6-21   Clicking Next to override default options

Step 4: Clicking the **Next** button pictured in Figure 6-21 brings up a summary confirmation screen, as shown in Figure 6-22.

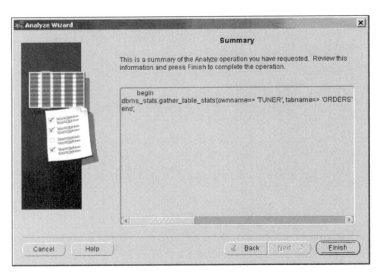

Figure 6-22   Summary of operations entered

Notice that you can highlight the text to get or see the command that will be executed to analyze the table. Click on the **Finish** button to display a progress window, followed by another screen indicating the completion of the analyze task, as shown in Figure 6-23.

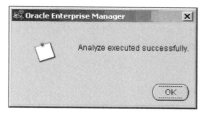

Figure 6-23 Analyze Wizard completion screen

DBMS_SPACE Package

This section delves further into the DBMS_SPACE, which is the Oracle-supplied PL/SQL package that provides three procedures for obtaining statistical data about physical segment storage. Table 6-10 describes the three DBMS_SPACE procedures.

6

Table 6-10 DBMS_SPACE package description

Procedure	Description of information provided

FREE_BLOCKS	Free blocks for any object:
	
	`Argument Name       Type        In/Out Default?`
	`----------------    ---------   ------ --------`
	`SEGMENT_OWNER       VARCHAR2    IN`
	`SEGMENT_NAME        VARCHAR2    IN`
	`SEGMENT_TYPE        VARCHAR2    IN`
	`FREELIST_GROUP_ID   NUMBER      IN`
	`FREE_BLKS           NUMBER      OUT`
	`SCAN_LIMIT          NUMBER      IN     DEFAULT`
	`PARTITION_NAME      VARCHAR2    IN     DEFAULT`

SPACE_USAGE	Block usage; procedure cannot be used if the tablespace is not using auto segment management.
	
	`Argument Name       Type       In/Out Default?`
	`----------------    --------   ------ --------`
	`SEGMENT_OWNER       VARCHAR2   IN`
	`SEGMENT_NAME        VARCHAR2   IN`
	`SEGMENT_TYPE        VARCHAR2   IN`
	`UNFORMATTED_BLOCKS  NUMBER     OUT`
	`UNFORMATTED_BYTES   NUMBER     OUT`
	`FS1_BLOCKS          NUMBER     OUT`
	`FS1_BYTES           NUMBER     OUT`
	`FS2_BLOCKS          NUMBER     OUT`
	`FS2_BYTES           NUMBER     OUT`
	`FS3_BLOCKS          NUMBER     OUT`
	`FS3_BYTES           NUMBER     OUT`
	`FS4_BLOCKS          NUMBER     OUT`
	`FS4_BYTES           NUMBER     OUT`
	`FULL_BLOCKS         NUMBER     OUT`
	`FULL_BYTES          NUMBER     OUT`
	`PARTITION_NAME      VARCHAR2   IN     DEFAULT`

Procedure	Description of information provided

UNUSED_SPACE	Unused space for a database object:
	
	`Argument Name                   Type      In/Out Default?`
	`------------------------ -------- ------ --------`
	`SEGMENT_OWNER                   VARCHAR2 IN`
	`SEGMENT_NAME                    VARCHAR2 IN`
	`SEGMENT_TYPE                    VARCHAR2 IN`
	`TOTAL_BLOCKS                    NUMBER   OUT`
	`TOTAL_BYTES                     NUMBER   OUT`
	`UNUSED_BLOCKS                   NUMBER   OUT`
	`UNUSED_BYTES                    NUMBER   OUT`
	`LAST_USED_EXTENT_FILE_ID        NUMBER   OUT`
	`LAST_USED_EXTENT_BLOCK_ID NUMBER   OUT`
	`LAST_USED_BLOCK                 NUMBER   OUT`
	`PARTITION_NAME                  VARCHAR2 IN      DEFAULT`

The information in this table is derived from the online documentation that Oracle provides at the Oracle Technology Network site: *www.otn.oracle.com*.

At this point it is useful to more fully examine the third procedure, UNUSED_SPACE. Suppose you wanted to get information about unused space for the ORDERS table. To do so, you could use the procedure outlined in the following code segment. You must create a PL/SQL block to capture all returned values from the procedure:

```
SQL> DECLARE
  2
  3     V_OWNER         VARCHAR2(30) := '&OBJECT_OWNER';
  4     V_NAME          VARCHAR2(30) := '&OBJECT_NAME';
  5     V_TYPE          VARCHAR2(30) := '&OBJECT_TYPE';
  6
  7     V_TOT_BLKS      NUMBER;
  8     V_TOT_BYTES     NUMBER;
  9     V_UNUSED_BLKS   NUMBER;
 10     V_UNUSED_BYTES  NUMBER;
 11     V_P1            NUMBER;
 12     V_P2            NUMBER;
 13     V_P3            NUMBER;
 14
 15  BEGIN
 16
 17     DBMS_SPACE.UNUSED_SPACE(
 18                            V_OWNER,
 19                            V_NAME,
 20                            V_TYPE,
 21                            V_TOT_BLKS,
 22                            V_TOT_BYTES,
 23                            V_UNUSED_BLKS,
 24                            V_UNUSED_BYTES,
 25                            V_P1,
 26                            V_P2,
 27                            V_P3
 28                            );
 29
 30     DBMS_OUTPUT.PUT_LINE('Object: '||V_OWNER||'.'||V_NAME||' - Type: '||V_TYPE);
 31     DBMS_OUTPUT.PUT_LINE('Total number of blocks    = ' || V_TOT_BLKS);
 32     DBMS_OUTPUT.PUT_LINE('Total number of bytes     = ' || V_TOT_BYTES);
 33     DBMS_OUTPUT.PUT_LINE('Total number unused blocks = ' || V_UNUSED_BLKS);
 34     DBMS_OUTPUT.PUT_LINE('Total number unused bytes  = ' || V_UNUSED_BYTES);
 35
 36  EXCEPTION WHEN OTHERS THEN
 37     DBMS_OUTPUT.PUT_LINE(SQLERRM);
 38  END;
 39  /
Enter value for object_owner: TUNER
Enter value for object_name: CUSTOMERS
Enter value for object_type: TABLE
Object: TUNER.CUSTOMERS - Type: TABLE
Total number of blocks    = 128
Total number of bytes     = 1048576
Total number unused blocks = 0
Total number unused bytes  = 0

PL/SQL procedure successfully completed.
```

As you can see, this procedure showed that 64 blocks are free, which amounts to 512 KB. You can use this number as an indicator of how many of the total blocks or bytes are free to obtain a growth trend of the table, which helps you to perform storage capacity planning.

The following PL/SQL block generates block usage for a specific table:

```
DECLARE

    V_UNF        NUMBER;
    V_UNFB       NUMBER;
    V_FS1        NUMBER;
    V_FS1B       NUMBER;
    V_FS2        NUMBER;
    V_FS2B       NUMBER;
    V_FS3        NUMBER;
    V_FS3B       NUMBER;
    V_FS4        NUMBER;
    V_FS4B       NUMBER;
    V_FULL       NUMBER;
    V_FULLB      NUMBER;


    V_OWNER     VARCHAR2(30)  := 'TUNER';
    V_SEGMENT   VARCHAR2(30)  := 'ORDERS';

BEGIN

    FOR b IN (SELECT TABLESPACE_NAME,
                     SEGMENT_NAME,
                     SEGMENT_TYPE,
                         PARTITION_NAME
                FROM DBA_SEGMENTS
               WHERE OWNER = UPPER(V_OWNER)
                 AND SEGMENT_NAME LIKE '%' || UPPER(V_SEGMENT) || '%') LOOP

       DBMS_SPACE.SPACE_USAGE(V_OWNER,
                              B.SEGMENT_NAME,
                              B.SEGMENT_TYPE,
                              V_UNF,
                              V_UNFB,
                              V_FS1,
                              V_FS1B,
                              V_FS2,
                              V_FS2B,
                              V_FS3,
                              V_FS3B,
                              V_FS4,
                              V_FS4B,
                              V_FULL,
                              V_FULLB,
                              B.PARTITION_NAME );

       DBMS_OUTPUT.PUT_LINE ('========================================');
       DBMS_OUTPUT.PUT_LINE (V_OWNER    || ' ' ||B.SEGMENT_TYPE
                                        || ' ' ||B.SEGMENT_NAME );
       DBMS_OUTPUT.PUT_LINE ('========================================');
```

```
       DBMS_OUTPUT.PUT_LINE('TABLESPACE                  : '|| B.TABLESPACE_NAME);
       DBMS_OUTPUT.PUT_LINE('TOTAL UNFORMATTED BYTES     : '|| V_UNF  || ' ('|| V_UNFB  ||')');
       DBMS_OUTPUT.PUT_LINE('TOTAL BLOCKS   0 - 25% FREE : '|| V_FS1  || ' ('|| V_FS1B  ||')');
       DBMS_OUTPUT.PUT_LINE('TOTAL BLOCKS  26 - 50% FREE : '|| V_FS2  || ' ('|| V_FS2B  ||')');
       DBMS_OUTPUT.PUT_LINE('TOTAL BLOCKS  51 - 75% FREE : '|| V_FS3  || ' ('|| V_FS3B  ||')');
       DBMS_OUTPUT.PUT_LINE('TOTAL BLOCKS  76 -100% FREE : '|| V_FS4  || ' ('|| V_FS4B  ||')');
       DBMS_OUTPUT.PUT_LINE('TOTAL FULL                  : '|| V_FULL || ' ('|| V_FULLB ||')');

    END LOOP;

END;
/


==========================================
TUNER TABLE ORDERS
==========================================
TABLESPACE                : USERS
TOTAL UNFORMATTED BYTES    : 0 (0)
TOTAL BLOCKS   0 - 25% FREE : 0 (0)
TOTAL BLOCKS  26 - 50% FREE : 0 (0)
TOTAL BLOCKS  51 - 75% FREE : 0 (0)
TOTAL BLOCKS  76 -100% FREE : 46 (376832)
TOTAL FULL                 : 134 (1097728)

PL/SQL procedure successfully completed.
```

Detecting and Resolving Chained Rows

A database manager for a large financial cooperation was reading the weekly system statistics report sent automatically by the Operations Department. This report contained memory, CPU, and I/O statistics for each system hosting one or more databases. He noticed some alarming numbers for one of the systems hosting a recent database commissioned into production and that was on the mission–critical list. So, he called the operation manager asking to confirm the report numbers. The operation manager confirmed the numbers, and furthermore, he pulled the daily reports to determine when these numbers started to climb. A few minutes later, he got a full chart of the numbers starting with the first day of production. He told the database manager that I/O activities had been climbing up since day one. The database manager called the DBA administering the database and asked her to investigate the problem.

The DBA did a full check on database configurations that could cause I/O problems such as file allocation, tablespace layout, disk configuration, sort activities, row chaining, and migration. After a full investigation that took about seven hours, the DBA went to her manager with her findings. She explained that the problem was arising in four central tables that had high ratios of row chaining and migration due to incorrect configuration of PCTFREE. She told her manager that the problem was rectified and that she would keep an eye on it.

Chaining is considered a big problem, especially when the table is highly active with transaction and data retrieval. Monitoring and detecting row chaining should be on the priority list of the DBA. In this section, you are presented with a step-by step procedure to detect and eliminate row chaining and row migration. In addition to the step-by step procedure, you are provided with a PL/SQL procedure that performs all these steps in one script. Finally, this section ends with a flowchart of how to detect and eliminate row chaining.

As you noticed in the previous section, one of the statistical values generated is the CHAIN_CNT column. This column is very important from a performance point of view. It indicates whether PCTFREE is set properly or not. You should be alarmed if the percentage of chained rows is one percent or higher.

For example, suppose you analyzed a medium-sized table of one million rows and the statistics showed that two percent of the rows were chained (20,000 rows). That is extremely high. This indicates a problem in the block specification, particularly PCTFREE. Ideally, this value should be much smaller and close to zero percent.

NOTE Tables that contain columns with raw data or large object (LOB) data types most often experience a high ratio of row chaining and row migration regardless of the size of the Oracle block being used.

What should you do with a table that has too many chained rows? Your first thought should be to eliminate the chaining, and your second thought should be to eliminate the cause of the chaining. The chaining is often caused by an underestimation of expected transaction activity levels. In any case, use the following steps to detect, eliminate, and then restructure the table with chained rows.

Step 1: Log on as TUNER and create a table called CHN_TBL as follows:

```
SQL> CREATE TABLE CHN_TBL
  2  (
  3    NUM     NUMBER(6),
  4    TEXT    VARCHAR2(255)
  5  )
  6  PCTFREE 10
  7  PCTUSED 60
  8  TABLESPACE USERS
  9  /

Table created.
```

Step 2: Verify table creation and PCTFREE setting:

```
SQL> SELECT TABLE_NAME,
  2          PCT_FREE,
  3          PCT_USED
  4    FROM USER_TABLES
  5   WHERE TABLE_NAME = 'CHN_TBL'
  6  /

TABLE_NAME                      PCT_FREE   PCT_USED
------------------------------ ---------- ----------
CHN_TBL                               10
```

Notice that PCTUSED is null even though you specified this value when you created the table. The null value is acceptable because PCTUSED is ignored when using local extent management. PCTFREE, however, *is* set to the value you indicated in the creation statement.

Step 3: Populate the table with 25,000 rows using the following PL/SQL block, making sure you have enough space on USERS tablespace where CHN_TBL resides:

```
SQL> BEGIN
  2      FOR I IN 1..25000 LOOP
  3          INSERT INTO CHN_TBL VALUES(
  4              I, 'this is a test text #'||I);
  5      END LOOP;
  6      COMMIT;
  7  END;
  8  /

PL/SQL procedure successfully completed.
```

Step 4: Verify row count.

```
SQL> SELECT COUNT(*)
  2      FROM CHN_TBL
  3  /
  COUNT(*)
----------
     25000
```

Step 5: Display statistics for CHN_TBL.

```
SQL> SELECT NUM_ROWS,
  2           BLOCKS,
  3           EMPTY_BLOCKS,
  4           AVG_SPACE,
  5           CHAIN_CNT,
  6           AVG_ROW_LEN,
  7           LAST_ANALYZED
  8      FROM USER_TABLES
  9     WHERE TABLE_NAME = 'CHN_TBL'
 10  /

NUM_ROWS BLOCKS EMPTY_BLOCKS AVG_SPACE CHAIN_CNT AVG_ROW_LEN LAST_ANALYZED
-------- ------ ------------ --------- --------- ----------- -------------
```

Step 6: Analyze CHN_TBL table, using the COMPUTE statistics method option only:

```
SQL> ANALYZE TABLE CHN_TBL COMPUTE STATISTICS;

Table analyzed.
```

Step 7: Display table statistics again, and notice that there are no chained rows (CHAIN_CNT=0):

```
SQL> SELECT NUM_ROWS,
  2          BLOCKS,
  3          EMPTY_BLOCKS,
  4          AVG_SPACE,
  5          CHAIN_CNT,
  6          AVG_ROW_LEN,
  7          LAST_ANALYZED
  8    FROM USER_TABLES
  9   WHERE TABLE_NAME = 'CHN_TBL'
 10   /

NUM_ROWS BLOCKS EMPTY_BLOCKS AVG_SPACE CHAIN_CNT AVG_ROW_LEN LAST_ANALYZED
-------- ------ ------------ --------- --------- ----------- -------------
   25000    180           76      2562         0          34 23-FEB-02
```

Step 8: To incur row chaining, you need to update some rows. The following PL/SQL block updates 1000 rows:

```
SQL> BEGIN
  2      FOR I IN 1..1000 LOOP
  3          UPDATE CHN_TBL SET
  4              TEXT = TEXT || TEXT || TEXT || TEXT || TEXT
  5              WHERE NUM = I;
  6      END LOOP;
  7      COMMIT;
  8  END;
  9  /

PL/SQL procedure successfully completed.
```

Step 9: You must analyze the table again to generate fresh statistics:

```
SQL> ANALYZE TABLE CHN_TBL COMPUTE STATISTICS;

Table analyzed.
```

Step 10: Display the table statistics again. Notice that there are 773 chained rows out of the 1000 that were updated. This value is detrimental to performance.

```
SQL> SELECT NUM_ROWS,
  2         BLOCKS,
  3         EMPTY_BLOCKS,
  4         AVG_SPACE,
  5         CHAIN_CNT,
  6         AVG_ROW_LEN,
  7         LAST_ANALYZED
  8    FROM USER_TABLES
  9   WHERE TABLE_NAME = 'CHN_TBL'
 10  /

NUM_ROWS BLOCKS EMPTY_BLOCKS AVG_SPACE CHAIN_CNT AVG_ROW_LEN LAST_ANALYZED
-------- ------ ------------ --------- --------- ----------- -------------
   25000    180           76      2344       773          38 23-FEB-02
```

Step 11: Now, you must create a table that will hold the rowids for all chained rows. The structure of this table is supplied by Oracle in the ORACLE_HOME\rdbms\admin folder. The script is called UTLCHN1.SQL. This script creates a table called CHAINED_ROWS:

```
SQL> @C:\ORACLE\ORA92\RDBMS\ADMIN\UTLCHN1.SQL

Table created.
```

Step 12: You must analyze the table to insert the rowid for every chained row by using the ANALYZE statement:

```
SQL> ANALYZE TABLE CHN_TBL
  2     LIST CHAINED ROWS
  3  /

Table analyzed.
```

Step 13: Verify that the number of chained rows inserted into the CHAINED_ROWS table matches the number obtained in Step 10 (773):

```
SQL> SELECT COUNT(*)
  2    FROM CHAINED_ROWS
  3  /

  COUNT(*)
----------
       773
```

Step 14: Create a temporary table called CHN_TMP to hold all chained rows, and verify the creation of the table:

```
SQL> CREATE TABLE CHN_TMP AS
  2      SELECT * FROM CHN_TBL
  3        WHERE ROWID IN (SELECT HEAD_ROWID
  4                               FROM CHAINED_ROWS
  5                        )
  6  /

Table created.

SQL> SELECT COUNT(*)
  2      FROM CHN_TMP
  3  /

  COUNT(*)
----------
       773
```

Step 15: Delete all chained rows in the original table CHN_TBL:

```
SQL> DELETE CHN_TBL
  2    WHERE ROWID IN (SELECT HEAD_ROWID
  3                           FROM CHAINED_ROWS
  4                    )
  5  /

773 rows deleted.

SQL> COMMIT;

Commit complete.
```

Step 16: Redefine PCTFREE to 50 percent and PCTUSED to 30 percent and reorganize the table. Increasing PCTFREE leaves more room in each block for increasing row size through updates. (PCTUSED is ignored.)

```
SQL> ALTER TABLE CHN_TBL
  2      PCTFREE 50--(was 10)
  3      PCTUSED 30--(was 60)
  4  /

Table altered.

SQL> ALTER TABLE CHN_TBL MOVE
  2  /

Table altered.
```

Step 17: Reinsert all rows in CHN_TMP table, and commit:

```
SQL> INSERT INTO CHN_TBL
  2     SELECT * FROM CHN_TMP
  3   /

773 rows created.

SQL> COMMIT;

Commit complete.
```

Step 18: Analyze the table to verify that all chained rows have been eliminated, and list its statistics:

```
SQL> ANALYZE TABLE CHN_TBL COMPUTE STATISTICS
  2   /

Table analyzed.

SQL> SELECT  NUM_ROWS,
  2            BLOCKS,
  3            EMPTY_BLOCKS,
  4            AVG_SPACE,
  5            CHAIN_CNT,
  6            AVG_ROW_LEN,
  7            LAST_ANALYZED
  8     FROM USER_TABLES
  9    WHERE TABLE_NAME = 'CHN_TBL'
 10   /

NUM_ROWS BLOCKS EMPTY_BLOCKS AVG_SPACE CHAIN_CNT AVG_ROW_LEN LAST_ANALYZED
-------- ------ ------------ --------- --------- ----------- -------------
   25000    318           66      4607         0          38 23-FEB-02
```

Step 19: Drop both tables, CHAINED_ROWS and CHN_TMP:

```
SQL> DROP TABLE CHAINED_ROWS
  2   /

Table dropped.

SQL> DROP TABLE CHN_TMP
  2   /

Table dropped.
```

Exporting and importing tables may eliminate row chaining and row migration.

NOTE

Now, you might be asking if chaining is really eliminated? The answer is "No, but the chaining has been reduced." Although you changed PCTFREE, existing rows that will be updated will still incur row chaining because they still reside on blocks with PCTFREE set to 10. Changing PCTFREE to 50 does not impact existing used blocks. Follow these steps to see this in action.

Step 1: Update another 1000 rows that were not previously updated:

```
SQL> BEGIN
  2      FOR I IN 1001..2000 LOOP
  3          UPDATE CHN_TBL SET
  4              TEXT = TEXT || TEXT || TEXT || TEXT || TEXT
  5              WHERE NUM = I;
  6      END LOOP;
  7      COMMIT;
  8  END;
  9  /

PL/SQL procedure successfully completed.
```

Step 2: Analyze the table again:

If the CHAINED_ROWS table does not exist, you can create it using the following command: @C:\oracle\ora92\rdbms\admin\utlchn1.sql.

NOTE

```
SQL> ANALYZE TABLE CHN_TBL
  2      LIST CHAINED ROWS
  3  /

Table analyzed.
```

Step 3: List the statistics:

```
SQL> ANALYZE TABLE CHN_TBL COMPUTE STATISTICS
  2  /

Table analyzed.

SQL> SELECT NUM_ROWS,
  2          BLOCKS,
  3          EMPTY_BLOCKS,
  4          AVG_SPACE,
  5          CHAIN_CNT,
  6          AVG_ROW_LEN,
  7          LAST_ANALYZED
  8    FROM USER_TABLES
  9   WHERE TABLE_NAME = 'CHN_TBL'
 10  /

NUM_ROWS BLOCKS EMPTY_BLOCKS AVG_SPACE CHAIN_CNT AVG_ROW_LEN LAST_ANALYZED
-------- ------ ------------ --------- --------- ----------- -------------
   25000    318           66      4399       463          42 23-FEB-02
```

As you can see, the number of chained rows decreased from 773 to 463. This is a 40 percent improvement in the number of chained rows.

The next question is this: how do you eliminate chaining totally? You need to rebuild the table by dropping and recreating, or you can monitor and fix it as you go.

The process of eliminating chained rows is a lengthy one. It would be very convenient if there were a script that eliminates the chained rows in one easy step. Fortunately, there is. The following script is of a single command that does exactly what you need. You should run this script as user SYSTEM:

```
EXECUTE IMMEDIATE 'ANALYZE TABLE ||
It should be
EXECUTE IMMEDIATE 'ANALYZE TABLE ' ||

DECLARE
    v_owner       VARCHAR2(30) := UPPER('&owner');
    v_table_name  VARCHAR2(30) := UPPER('&table_name');
    v_pctfree     NUMBER := &pct_free;
    v_pctused     NUMBER := &pct_used;
    v_chain_cnt   NUMBER := 0;
    v_count       NUMBER := 0;
BEGIN

    EXECUTE IMMEDIATE 'ANALYZE TABLE ' || v_owner || '.' || v_table_name ||
    ' ESTIMATE STATISTICS SAMPLE 10 PERCENT';

    SELECT CHAIN_CNT INTO v_chain_cnt
      FROM DBA_TABLES
     WHERE OWNER = v_owner
       AND TABLE_NAME = v_table_name;

    IF v_chain_cnt > 0 THEN

        SELECT COUNT(*)
          INTO v_count
          FROM USER_TABLES
         WHERE TABLE_NAME = 'CHOCHO_CHAINED_ROWS';

        IF v_count > 0 THEN
           EXECUTE IMMEDIATE 'DROP TABLE chocho_chained_rows';
        END IF;

        EXECUTE IMMEDIATE 'CREATE TABLE chocho_chained_rows ( ' ||
                          'owner_name VARCHAR2(30), ' ||
                          'table_name VARCHAR2(30), ' ||
                          'cluster_name VARCHAR2(30), ' ||
                          'partition_name VARCHAR2(30), ' ||
                          'subpartition_name VARCHAR2(30), ' ||
                          'head_rowid ROWID, ' ||
                          'analyze_timestamp DATE )';

        DBMS_OUTPUT.PUT_LINE('Number of chained rows for <'||v_owner||'.'||v_table_name||
                        '> = '|| TO_CHAR(v_chain_cnt));
        EXECUTE IMMEDIATE 'ANALYZE TABLE ' || v_owner || '.' || v_table_name ||
                        ' LIST CHAINED ROWS INTO chocho_chained_rows';
        EXECUTE IMMEDIATE 'CREATE TABLE chocho_chained_temp AS SELECT * FROM ' ||
                        v_owner || '.' || v_table_name || ' WHERE rowid IN '||
```

```
                              '(SELECT head_rowid FROM chocho_chained_rows)';
         EXECUTE IMMEDIATE 'DELETE FROM ' || v_owner || '.' || v_table_name ||
                              ' WHERE rowid IN ' ||
                              '(SELECT head_rowid FROM chocho_chained_rows)';
         EXECUTE IMMEDIATE 'ALTER TABLE '|| v_owner || '.' || v_table_name ||
                              ' PCTFREE ' || v_pctfree || ' PCTUSED ' || v_pctused;
         EXECUTE IMMEDIATE 'INSERT INTO ' || v_owner || '.' || v_table_name ||
                              ' SELECT * FROM chocho_chained_temp';
         EXECUTE IMMEDIATE 'DROP TABLE chocho_chained_rows';
         EXECUTE IMMEDIATE 'DROP TABLE chocho_chained_temp';
         DBMS_OUTPUT.PUT_LINE('Chained rows eliminated');
      ELSE
         DBMS_OUTPUT.PUT_LINE(
            'There are no chained rows for <'||v_owner||'.'||v_table_name||'>');
      END IF;
   EXCEPTION
      WHEN OTHERS THEN
         DBMS_OUTPUT.PUT_LINE('ERROR: '||SQLERRM);
   END;
   /
```

For a summary of the steps for detecting and eliminating row chaining, see Figure 6-24.

6

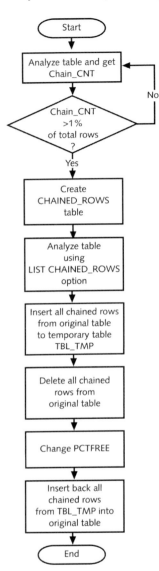

Figure 6-24   PL/SQL procedures for detecting and eliminating chained rows

INDEX SEGMENT

INDEX segments are used extensively to retrieve data quickly. In most cases, if an index never existed, or is missing on a column used in a WHERE clause, the query runs very slowly.

As a table grows or shrinks through the insertion of rows, deletion of rows, and updating of column values, any index associated with the table is updated along with the table and may become unbalanced. In this way, the associated index ultimately may become a performance liability. To prevent indexes from becoming unbalanced, a reorganization of the index is warranted. How will you know if an index needs rebuilding or not? You can analyze the index and then run a query to indicate if an index reorganization is required or not.

NOTE

The reason that an index may become a liability when it is unbalanced by deletions is that, as the rows are deleted, the index space is not automatically reclaimed. This is known as index browning.

Consider this example. An application user reported to you that lately every time she queries the ORDERS table, the query takes a long time to return information. You decide to investigate whether the index is unbalanced.

The following steps outline the process for analyzing, detecting, and resolving an unbalanced index (browned index):

Step 1: Get the index name of the suspected table:

```
SQL> SELECT INDEX_NAME, COLUMN_NAME
  2    FROM USER_IND_COLUMNS
  3   WHERE TABLE_NAME = 'ORDERS'
  4   ORDER BY COLUMN_POSITION
  5  /

INDEX_NAME                          COLUMN_NAME
-----------------------------       -----------
SYS_C003141                         ORDER_ID
```

Step 2: Analyze the index:

```
SQL> ANALYZE INDEX SYS_C003141 VALIDATE STRUCTURE
  2  /

Index analyzed.
```

Step 3: Issue the following query to determine if the index is unbalanced. The threshold for this ratio is 20 percent. If the unbalanced ratio is more than 20 percent, you should rebuild the index.

```
SQL> SELECT ROUND(DEL_LF_ROWS_LEN/
  2          LF_ROWS_LEN * 100) BALANCE_RATIO
  3    FROM INDEX_STATS
  4    WHERE NAME = 'SYS_C003141'
  5  /

BALANCE_RATIO
-------------
           23
```

Step 4: Since the ratio is higher than 20 percent, you need to rebuild the index:

```
SQL> ALTER INDEX SYS_C003141 REBUILD ONLINE
  2  /

Index altered.
```

TEN BEST PRACTICES

This list summarizes ten best practices for optimizing storage, which have been presented in this chapter. The list has no particular order:

1. Use large block sizes for large rows.

2. Use small block sizes for OLTP. Use large block sizes for DSS.

3. Use local extent management rather than dictionary extent management.

4. Use a low PCTFREE value for DSS applications.

5. Use a high PCTFREE value for OLTP applications.

6. Always specify storage parameters when creating tables and indexes.

7. Always perform segment-sizing analysis before creating a table or index.

8. Monitor, detect, and eliminate row chaining and row migration.

9. Analyze tables in an OLTP application on a periodic basis.

10. Monitor the usage of extents.

CHAPTER SUMMARY

- A database can have one or many tablespaces.
- Each tablespace can have one or many segments.
- Each segment can consist of one or many extents.
- An extent can be composed of many Oracle blocks.
- An Oracle block is a multiple of operating system blocks.
- A block is composed of overhead, which is reserved free space for future updates and space for row inserts.
- OLTP applications work most effectively with small Oracle blocks.
- DSS applications work most effectively with large Oracle blocks.
- PCTFREE specifies the percentage of the block to be reserved as free for future row updates and block overhead growth.
- The PCTFREE option specifies how much of the block is used before it is added back to the free list.
- The sum of PCTFREE and PCTUSED values should not exceed 100.
- A high-water mark is an indicator of the number of blocks allocated by inserts.
- Extents are either locally managed or data dictionary managed.
- Data dictionary extent management uses system tables to determine which extents are free and which are used.
- Local extent management uses a bitmap image residing in the tablespace to indicate which extent is free or used.
- The Oracle Optimizer uses statistics to determine the fastest way to retrieve data from tables.
- Statistics are populated in the base system tables that contain data about the user's data. Statistics can be seen by using any of the data dictionary views.
- The Oracle-supplied PL/SQL package called DBMS_SPACE is used to get physical statistical data about segment storage.
- CHAIN_CNT column is an indicator showing whether PCTFREE is set properly or not.
- The percentage of the chained rows in a table should not be one percent or higher.
- When an index is unbalanced due to deletes, it is a performance liability.
- An index becoming unbalanced is also known as index browning.
- Initialization parameters presented in this chapter include the following:

  - DB_BLOCK_SIZE

❑ Views used in this chapter include the following:

- DBA_DATA_FILES
- DBA_EXTENTS
- DBA_SEGMENTS
- DBA_TAB_COLUMNS
- DBA_TABLES
- DBA_TABLESPACES
- INDEX_STATS
- V$TABLESPACE

❑ Oracle-supplied PL/SQL packages used in this chapter include the following:

- DBMS_ADMIN_SPACE
- DBMS_SPACE
- DBMS_STATS
- DBMS_UTILITY

REVIEW QUESTIONS

1. You can create a tablespace with dictionary extent management if the SYSTEM tablespace is created with local extent management. (True/False)

2. Existing blocks are not impacted when you redefine PCTFREE for a table. (True/False)

3. You use the LIST CHAINED ROWS option to eliminate row chaining. (True/False)

4. A high-water mark is reset when you delete rows. (True/False)

5. PCTUSED is part of the STORAGE option of the CREATE TABLE or ALTER TABLE statement. (True/False)

6. PCTFREE is used for the future growth of data that results from inserts. (True/False)

7. Row chaining is a result of a small PCTUSED. (True/False)

8. You can use DBA_EXTENTS to view statistics about each table. (True/False)

9. Table and column statistics are generated when you analyze a table. (True/False)

10. Describe three ways of analyzing a table by scanning every row.

11. Write a query that displays extents information for each table owned by TUNER.

12. Write a query that displays the type of extent management for each tablespace.

13. Display the settings for all extent and block options for each table owned by the DEMO schema.

14. Display all row and column statistics for the CUSTOMERS table in the TUNER schema.

15. Provide two reasons for analyzing a table.

16. Explain the side effects of setting PCTFREE improperly.

17. Provide a SQL or PL/SQL script to generate a report that displays each table for a schema and the number of rows in the table.

18. Write a query that displays a table name and number of bytes used for a given schema.

19. Generate a report that displays each index with its corresponding balance ratio for a given schema.

20. Display all the different segment types created in your database.

EXAM REVIEW QUESTIONS: ORACLE9i PERFORMANCE TUNING (#1Z0-033)

1. If there are no update activities on a table, to what value would you set PCT-FREE?

   a. 0

   b. 5

   c. 10

   d. 20

   e. 50

2. Local extent management uses which of the following?

   a. FET$ and UET$ tables

   b. Data dictionary tables

   c. DBA views

   d. Extents bitmap image in the tablespace

3. Which view would you use to detect if an index is unbalanced (browned)?

   a. DBA_INDEXES

   b. DBA_INDEX_STATS

   c. INDEX_STATS

   d. DBA_IND_COLUMNS

   e. INDEX_STAT_COLUMNS

4. Which Oracle-supplied packages can you use to analyze database objects?

   a. DBMS_STATISTICS

   b. DBMS_UTILS

   c. DBMS_UTILITY

   d. DBMS_STATS

   e. DBMS_SPACE

   f. DBMS_SPACE_ADMIN

5. Which statement is true about Oracle blocks for a DSS application?

   a. Oracle blocks should be small.

   b. Oracle blocks should be large.

   c. Oracle blocks should be small and OS blocks should be small.

   d. Oracle blocks should be small and OS blocks should be large.

   e. Oracle blocks should be large and OS blocks should be small.

   f. Oracle blocks should be large and OS blocks should be large.

6. What are the two types of extent management available in Oracle?

   a. Local extent management

   b. UET$ and FET$ management

   c. Data dictionary management

   d. Local dictionary management

   e. Local data management

   f. Data image management

7. What causes row migration?

   a. Updates

   b. Updates and inserts

   c. Inserts

   d. Updates and deletes

   e. Inserts and deletes

8. How do you resolve row migration?

   a. Choose a large Oracle block.

   b. Analyze the table regularly.

   c. Set PCTFREE to a low value.

   d. Set PCTFREE to a high value.

9. Which statement is true about an OLTP application?

   a. PCTFREE should be small.

   b. PCTUSED should be set to the same value as PCTFREE.

   c. PCTINCREASE increases should be large.

   d. PCTFREE and PCTINCREASE should not exceed 100.

   e. PCTFREE should be large.

   f. PCTFREE and PCTUSED should not exceed 100.

10. Which statement do you use to reorganize an index?

    a. ALTER INDEX...REORGANIZE

    b. ANALYZE INDEX...VALIDATE

    c. ALTER INDEX... ORGANIZE

    d. ALTER INDEX... REBUILD

    e. ANALYZE INDEX... REBUILD

11. Which statement do you use to deallocate extents?

    a. ALTER TABLE... MOVE

    b. ALTER TABLE... DEALLOCATE

    c. ALTER TABLE... STORAGE(...)

    d. ALTER TABLE... REDEFINE

    e. ANALYZE TABLE...VALIDATE

6

12. What action should you take to achieve DBA objectives?

    a. Make sure that all extents are uniform.

    b. Ensure that dynamic allocation does not occur.

    c. Size the table properly to avoid data storage wastage.

    d. Allocate large extents.

    e. Ensure that extents are growing in proper speed.

13. What analyze method option is recommended when analyzing a large table?

    a. COMPUTE

    b. DELETE

    c. ANALYZE

    d. ESTIMATE

    e. DBMS_STATS

14. Which columns do you use to determine if there is index browning?

    a. DEL_LF_ROWS_LEN and LF_ROWS_LEN

    b. BR_ROWS_LEN and BR_DEL_LF_ROWS

    c. BR_ROWS_LEN and BR_ROWS

    d. LF_ROWS and DEL_LF_ROWS

    e. DEL_LF_ROWS_LEN and LF_ROWS

15. What are the two criteria for configuring an Oracle block?

    a. Type of application

    b. Type of database

    c. Type of transactions

    d. Type of operating system

    e. Type of segment

    f. Type of extent management

HANDS-ON PROJECTS

Please complete the projects provided below.

1. Reread the Performance Problem at the start of the chapter. Think of it in terms of the concepts you have learned in this chapter and answer Joe's question.

2. You were asked by your team leader to estimate the size of the CUSTOMERS table of TUNER schema. To meet the requirements of your team leader, create a PL/SQL script to generate the estimated size for any given table.

3. You were asked to do a lunch-hour seminar to explain row migration and chaining to developers.

   a. Outline how row migration and row chaining occur.

   b. Write steps to demonstrate row chaining to your audience

4. Consider the following table structure for an OLTP application that will have high update activities. Compute PCTFREE and PCTUSED values.

```
SQL> DESC PRODUCT_DESCRIPTIONS
 Name                              Null?     Type
 ---------------------------       --------  ---------------
 PRODUCT_ID                        NOT NULL  NUMBER(6)
 LANGUAGE_ID                       NOT NULL  VARCHAR2(3)
 TRANSLATED_NAME                   NOT NULL  NVARCHAR2(50)
 TRANSLATED_DESCRIPTION            NOT NULL  NVARCHAR2(2000)
```

5. You are asked to create a new database for a DSS application. The database is for read-only purposes, in other words, no transactions.

   a. What would you choose for a block size?

   b. What would you choose as a value for PCTFREE?

   c. What type of extent management would you select?

6. You read an article in *Oracle Magazine* about the benefits of local extent management, which triggered you to start employing this new feature.

   a. Outline the steps you would take to create a table using local extent management for a database that has a SYSTEM tablespace that is dictionary managed.

   b. Outline the steps you would take to create a table using local extent management for a database that has a SYSTEM tablespace that is locally managed.

6

7. A developer is writing a new form to display all information in the EMPLOY-EES table of the TUNER schema. Part of his code must allocate enough memory for one record. He asked if you can compute the maximum number of bytes for one row for the following table. How would you do it?

```
CREATE TABLE STUDENT (
        STUDENT_ID              NUMBER NOT NULL,
        STUDENT_FNAME           VARCHAR2(20) NULL,
        STUDENT_LNAME           VARCHAR2(20) NULL,
        STUDENT_ADDRESS         VARCHAR2(255) NULL,
        STUDENT_CITY            VARCHAR2(30) NULL,
        STUDENT_STATE           VARCHAR2(2) NULL,
        STUDENT_ZIPCODE         VARCHAR2(20) NULL,
        MAJOR                   VARCHAR2(10) NULL,
        PHONE                   VARCHAR2(15) NULL,
        REGISTERED              DATE NULL
);
```

8. Using the DBMS_SPACE package, compute the number of free blocks for the CUSTOMERS and EMPLOYEES segments.

9. Write a query that generates the following report:

TABLESPACE_NAME	TS_MAX_EXTENTS	TS_TOTAL_EXTENTS	SEGMENT_NAME	TYPE	TBL_EXTENTS
USERS	2147483645	2648	SUPPLIERS	TABLE	4

CASE PROJECTS

1. A Balancing Act

You are asked by your manager to demonstrate to the development team unbalanced indexes. Part of your demonstration is to perform the following:

1. Create a new table with the following structure:

```
CREATE TABLE COURSE (
        COURSE_ID               NUMBER NOT NULL,
        COURSE_TITLE            VARCHAR2(125) NOT NULL,
        CREDIT_HOURS            NUMBER NULL
);
```

2. Create an index on the COURSE_TITLE column.

3. Insert 10000 rows using a PL/SQL procedure.

4. Show whether the index is balanced or unbalanced.

5. Perform task(s) to make the index unbalanced.

6. How would you fix the unbalanced indexes?

2. Chaining Demonstration

A junior DBA asked you about row chaining and row migration. To explain to her how it happens and the impact of row chaining on performance, you perform the following tasks:

1. Create a new table called CH06CASE2 that has two columns: NUM as NUMBER and TEXT as VARCHAR2(80). Make sure you set the PCTFREE value for this table to 80 and PCTUSED to 10. This table will have a high level of update activity.

2. Populate the table with 50,000 rows using the following PL/SQL block.

3. Show table statistics.

4. Update the table using the following PL/SQL block.

5. Analyze statistics and explain the results.

6. Did the updates in Step 4 result in any chained or migrated rows?

7. Compare and explain results of Steps 3 and 5.

8. Drop the CH06CASE2 table and repeat Steps 1–7 using a PCTFREE value of 30.

9. Compare and explain storage usage when PCTFREE is 80 percent and when it is 30 percent.

6

7

OPTIMIZING TABLESPACES

In this chapter you will:

- ◆ Understand the impact of RAID configuration on performance
- ◆ Learn the concept of tablespaces and their use
- ◆ Learn to use the Oracle-managed Files feature
- ◆ Monitor data file I/O activities
- ◆ Detect and diagnose data file contention
- ◆ Learn about the use of external files
- ◆ Use the DBMS_SPACE_ADMIN package to upgrade tablespaces
- ◆ Perform capacity-planning functions
- ◆ Become familiar with best practices for optimizing tablespaces

Chapter 6 explained the three physical storage structures in Oracle, which are the Oracle block, extent, and segment. Chapter 8 moves on to higher structures, tablespaces, and data files. This chapter presents tablespaces from two perspectives: first, the role and use of optimally configured tablespaces; and second, storage issues such as sizing, allocation, and capacity planning.

By now you have seen Figure 7-1 so often that you can probably close your eyes and picture it. The highlighting of Figure 7-1 tips you off that the chapter focuses on the physical data file components, which are associated with tablespaces. First, you are introduced to RAID disk configuration used for Oracle databases, and then you learn details about different types of tablespaces, how to create them, and how to allocate them. Because data files are the essence of tablespaces, you learn about the different types of data files available in Oracle, how to detect file contention, and how to produce useful reports about tablespaces and data files.

Oracle instance

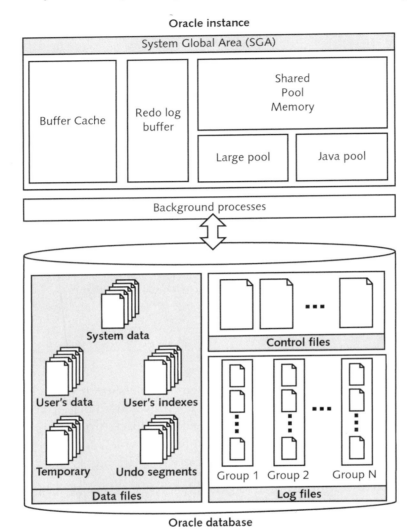

Figure 7-1   Oracle architecture showing physical components of the database

Performance Problem

This section outlines an actual performance problem. As you look it over, imagine yourself as the DBA who reported it and keep it in mind as you proceed through the chapter. The chapter presents concepts relevant to the problem. In the first Hands-on Project at the end of the chapter, you are asked to use the concepts you have learned to provide a solution, or partial solution, to this performance problem.

From: *Kari Space <mailto: kspace@tablespace.com>*

Date: *11-Aug-02 14:20*

Subject: *temp Segments*

Hello,

I am trying to execute a query which pulls information from four different tables. The query is supposed to retrieve a huge amount of data (approximately 100,000 rows). Unfortunately, this afternoon I received the following answer:

"ORA-01658: unable to create INITIAL extent for segment in tablespace DATA01"

This concerns me because it wasn't happening this morning. I have been testing some proC programs, and sometimes I have to kill these programs. Could the testing have polluted the temp file? Is there any way to clean the temp file or enlarge it?

I am an assistant DBA and our DBA is on vacation sun tanning...

All help is welcomed!

Kari

RAID CONFIGURATION

As you read through this chapter, you will encounter terms for RAID disk configuration and other related terminology. **RAID** is an acronym for Redundant Array of Inexpensive Disks, and is sometimes referred to as a Redundant Array of Independent Disks. Whatever the terminology, the sole purpose of the RAID is to protect data in case of disk media failure without any performance cost or compromise. When database files are configured properly, performance is enhanced by reducing I/O contention. RAID disks can be configured or arranged in four different levels to serve specific purposes. RAID levels 0+1, and 5 are most commonly used, and each RAID level has its trade-offs between strengths and weaknesses, as described in the sections that follow.

RAID Level 0 Characteristics

These are the characteristics of RAID level 0 (see Figure 7-2):

- Provides efficient storage using storage space stripes of equally sized operating system blocks. The blocks are taken from each disk.

- Has no fault tolerance. If one of the drives fails, the whole array fails.

- Allows simultaneous read/write operations on all disks

- Provides a performance advantage by reducing disk contention

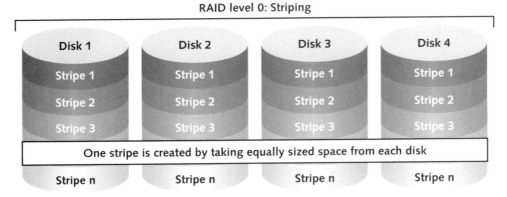

Figure 7-2   RAID level 0 with disk striping

RAID Level 1 Characteristics

These are the characteristics of RAID level 1 (see Figure 7-3):

- Mirrors each drive with another disk

- Provides the same data on each mirrored disk

- Presents the disk pair as one disk to the operating system

- Provides the backup feature that if one disk fails, data is still available from the other disk

- Ensures the best fault tolerance configuration against disk failure

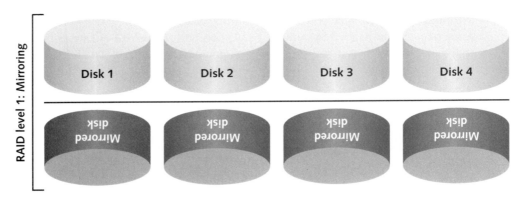

Figure 7-3   RAID level 1 with disk mirroring

RAID Level 0+1 Characteristics

These are the characteristics of RAID level 0+1 (see Figure 7-4):

- Provides the most efficient fault tolerance

- Is the most expensive solution (known as the rich man's solution)

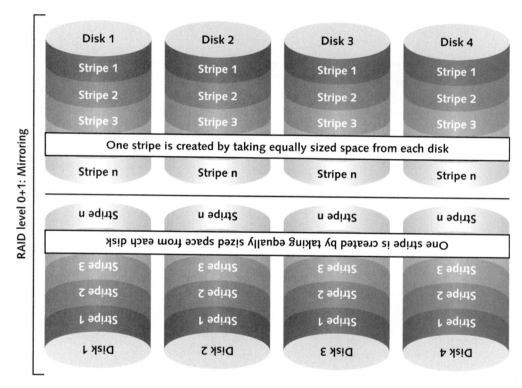

Figure 7-4   RAID level 0+1 showing how disks are arranged and striped for this configuration

RAID Level 5 Characteristics

These are the characteristics of RAID level 5 (see Figure 7-5):

- Provides striped disks

- Ensures fault tolerance if one disk fails

- Reserves one disk for parity checking

- Has the performance disadvantage that every write causes a parity update

- Is the least expensive solution (known as the poor man's solution)

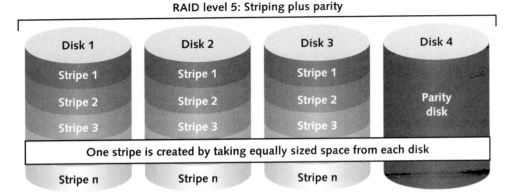

Figure 7-5   RAID level 5 showing how one disk is reserved (taken away) for parity

For Oracle databases, most DBAs use one of two configurations, either RAID level 0+1 or RAID level 5. The simple determinant factor for selecting a RAID level is your budget. Simply put, if money is no object, use RAID level 0+1; otherwise use RAID level 5.

How is RAID information put to use? As a system administrator, you use what you know about RAID as background information when you are building a new machine or reconfiguring disk storage.

Now that RAID is not a foreign term to you, it is time to start learning about the core chapter topic—the tablespace concept. The next section presents an overview of tablespaces and their use.

TABLESPACES

Most DBA experts consider the tablespace an important concept because it provides a methodology for efficiently organizing data. A **tablespace** is a logical entity that serves as a logical container for physical data files, as well as a logical container for logical segments. Chapter 6 introduced the hierarchical physical structure of tablespaces, in which a tablespace can have one or more segments and have one or more associated data files. This section delves more deeply into tablespace concepts.

Tablespace Overview

Before studying tablespaces in detail, you need to eliminate two common misconceptions:

- A table is not a file.
- A table is not a tablespace.

A tablespace is a logical entity for organizing data and file allocation. As you already know, data eventually resides in data files that are stored on disks. Oracle has created the concept of tablespace to group certain physical data files as one large, logical file for storing data. Also, you can allocate tables to different tablespaces based on the type of data used in the tablespace and its expected use.

To better understand, consider an analogy for the tablespace concept. Imagine a company that has different departments, and each department serves a specific function for the company. Each department is physically located on a different floor in the building. Table 7–1 outlines the analogy by showing building counterparts for each database entity.

Table 7-1 Tablespace analogy example

Company	Database entity	Database type
Building	Database	Physical
Department	Tablespace	Logical
Occupied space	Data file	Physical
Cube or office	Table	Physical
Furniture and other objects	Objects	Physical
Employee	Data	Physical

All the departments, employees, furniture, and other objects that belong to the company are housed in the building. Similarly all tablespaces, tables, database objects, and data are all housed in the database. A department is a concept, not a tangible object, and is used to organize employees who serve similar functions or serve the same purpose. In concept, a tablespace is similar to a department; a tablespace organizes tables that have similar functions.

For better communication, most companies locate employees of the same department in one area. In addition, departments that frequently work together are placed close together, as shown in Figure 7-6.

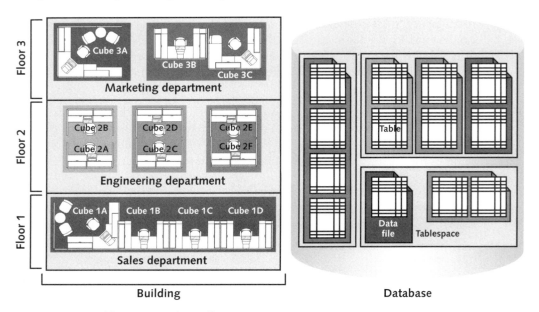

Figure 7-6 Tablespace analogy illustration

As mentioned earlier, a tablespace is a logical entity with no physical attributes. However, data files are associated with or belong to a tablespace, so the end result is that there is a specific space allocated to the tablespace that is called the tablespace size. And here is the $1 million question. Why do you need the notion of a tablespace? The answer is that a tablespace enables you to organize and manage database data based on data file types and functions. Also, having a tablespace allows you to allocate data files on different disks to reduce disk and file contention.

Figure 7-7 illustrates the relationship between a tablespace and data file. A database may have one or more tablespaces and a tablespace is associated to one or more data files.

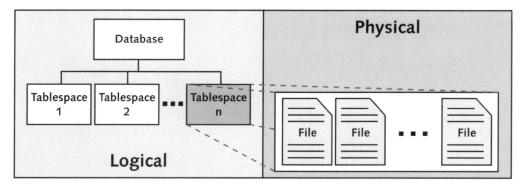

Figure 7-7 Database, tablespace, and data file relationships

The next section explores the different types or functions of tablespaces.

Types of Tablespaces

Tablespaces can be categorized by both type and function. Each type is used for a specific function. Figure 7-8 shows tablespace types and outlines functions for each type.

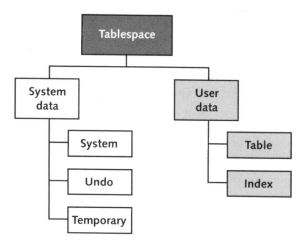

Figure 7-8   Tablespace types available in Oracle

A data file may contain objects from one tablespace only.

NOTE

Figure 7-8 shows five types of Oracle tablespaces. Each type of tablespace stores the following kinds of data:

- **System:** Stores system tables for the Oracle data dictionary

- **Undo:** For storing UNDO segments

- **Temporary:** Holds data temporarily. Temporary tablespaces are specifically used for sorting operations.

- **Table:** Stores user data

- **Index:** Stores indexes for user data

The use of different tablespace types is presented later in this chapter.

All tablespaces should be owned by SYS (owner of the database data dictionary) to avoid administration problems.

TIP

Tablespace Management

By now you must have observed a trend in Oracle9i database management, which is to automate maintenance and leave much of the work to Oracle. Tuning tablespace storage is a tricky business; you need to allocate the right size of data files and configure the default storage with the right extents. On top of that you need to make sure that database objects residing within the same tablespace do not increase contention.

When you are working as a DBA, you will probably appreciate help from any source to reduce some of this work. The new automatic features of Oracle9i are an excellent solution. However, if you are the type of person who likes the challenge of manually administering databases, specifically tablespaces, you can still do so, because this chapter will arm you with the appropriate background and tools. Be forewarned, however, that the pleasure of managing extents yourself does not justify the loss of time that could be spent on more useful projects. As illustrated in Figure 7-9, the two methods of managing free space in a tablespace are extent management and space management.

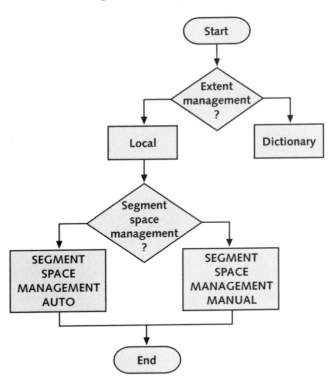

Figure 7-9 Flow chart for selecting extent and space management

Those new to database management often face extent management and space management problems. If you search the Internet for these types of problems, you are overwhelmed with the number of search hits returned. Here is a common problem listed by a junior DBA. His message says:

"Hello all DBAs,

I am new to DBA problems, so I have no idea how to resolve this one. I have been getting this error almost every day:

ORA-01658: UNABLE TO CREATE INITIAL EXTENT FOR SEGMENT IN TABLESPACE TSB.

Could you please tell me the cause of this problem and how to solve it? I am currently adding a data file to the tablespace. This is the temporary solution I put in place. Please provide a permanent solution. It's urgent!"

A DBA responded to this problem by listing the following possible reasons for receiving the error and their corresponding solutions:

- **Problem 1:** Not enough space on the tablespace for the new object to create its initial extent

- **Solution:** Add more space to existing tablespace, resize existing data, or add more files to tablespace.

- **Problem 2:** Storage clause used in the CREATE TABLESPACE, CREATE TABLE, or CREATE INDEX statement. To be more specific, extent setting might not be proper.

- **Solution:** Change initial extent setting to a smaller value.

- **Problem 3:** Tablespace fragmentation. Your tablespace might be highly fragmented and might therefore not have enough contiguous space for the initial extent.

- **Solution:** Find out if the tablespace is fragmented by issuing the following query:

```
SELECT FREE.TABLESPACE_NAME TABLESPACE,
       CEIL(TOT.TOTAL) TOTAL_SIZE,
       CEIL(FREE.FREE) FREE_SPACE,
       100 - CEIL( (FREE.FREE / TOT.TOTAL) * 100) USED_PCT,
       FRAG_PCT,
       DECODE ((CEIL(FRAG_PCT / 10)) ,
               0,'| .......... |',
               1,'| +......... |',
               2,'| ++........ |',
               3,'| +++....... |',
               4,'| ++++...... |',
               5,'| +++++..... |',
               6,'| ++++++.... |',
               7,'| +++++++... |',
               8,'| ++++++++.. |',
               9,'| +++++++++. |',
              10,'| ++DANGER++ |') FRAGMENTATION
  FROM (SELECT TABLESPACE_NAME,
               CEIL(SUM(BYTES)/1048576) TOTAL,
               COUNT(*) DATA_FILES
          FROM SYS.DBA_DATA_FILES
         GROUP BY TABLESPACE_NAME) TOT,
       (SELECT TABLESPACE_NAME TABLESPACE_NAME,
               CEIL(SUM(BYTES)/1048576) FREE,
               COUNT(*) FRAGMENTS,
               CEIL(100 - (MAX(BYTES) / SUM(BYTES)) * 100) FRAG_PCT
          FROM SYS.DBA_FREE_SPACE
         GROUP BY TABLESPACE_NAME) FREE
 WHERE FREE.TABLESPACE_NAME = TOT.TABLESPACE_NAME
 ORDER BY FRAG_PCT
 /
```

If you receive ORA-00379, you need to increase the number of buffers for block nK where n is 2, 4, 8, 16, or 32.

If you observe a high percentage of fragmentation, you can apply the following steps to reorganize the tablespace:

- **Step 1:** Back up the tablespace.

- **Step 2:** Export all objects residing in the tablespace.

- **Step 3:** Drop the tablespace and its contents.

- **Step 4:** Re-create the tablespace with a new definition.

- **Step 5:** Re-import all objects

The solutions provided to the problems are definitely valid. However, this problem can be at least partially prevented and fully controlled if the DBA adapts the Oracle features of extent management and space management. In the next section you are presented with the details of these features.

Extent Management

Within the category of extent management are the following two categories of tablespace management:

- **Dictionary-managed tablespace (DMT):** uses the system data dictionary to manage free space using the PCTUSED parameter and FREELIST structure. This method is not recommended, because your time is better spent elsewhere.

- **Locally managed tablespace (LMT):** uses a bitmap image of free extents within the tablespace.

Segment Space Management

Within the category of segment space management are the following two categories of tablespace administration:

- **Automatic space management (ASM):** eliminates the need for you to manage free space. Oracle ignores PCTUSED, FREELISTS, and FREELIST GROUPS storage parameters.

- **Manual space management (MSM):** makes you responsible for administering free space using PCTFREE and FREELIST structures. Again, this is not recommended.

Automatic Space Management

This section discusses the pluses and minuses of automatic space management. When considering the negative aspects of automatic space management, do not discard the possibility of using it. Even though it is a useful tool that can relieve you of much extraneous work, segment management has a number of shortcomings, which you should understand. As mentioned earlier, automatic segment management frees you from configuring the default storage that impacts free space. However, automatic space management involves at least one undesirable side effect that may show up and that you cannot control. The side effect is row chaining, which is a serious performance problem.

Some DBA experts warn against automatic space management by demonstrating the details of row chaining and your helplessness against it. However, row chaining can happen even if you do not use automatic space management, especially when DBAs set PCTFREE improperly, do not follow guidelines, or use no PCTFREE computation method. Row chaining is caused by improper configuration of PCTFREE. If any factors used in setting up the tablespace are guessed incorrectly, the whole estimation process is worthless.

So, now you know a negative side effect of this feature, and you know that it has the positive effect of freeing up your time. What are the other advantages? One important advantage is that ASM reduces contention for freelists. To understand this benefit, take a look at how freelist contention occurs. When a new row is inserted, it is added to the cache buffer. When these blocks are to be written to the data file, Oracle checks the freelists to determine which blocks are free. If there are no activities on the table other than the inserts, then there is no noticeable wait (this wait is called a "buffer busy wait"). However, when many activities occur simultaneously, some activities must wait for the freelists to become free, and in this case contention occurs.

NOTE

Automatically, the SMON background process shrinks automatically managed segments when extents for the segment are freed.

The fact that automatic space management works with local extent management means that automatic space management uses a bitmap image rather than freelists to determine which blocks are free. With this new method of maintaining free blocks and extents, Oracle has made it a point to allow many simultaneous activities without any waits.

It is best to use the automatic space management feature with an understanding that you still need to perform routine physical checkups. And actually, you should evaluate these space management features application-by-application, database-by-database, and finally table-by-table. In general, it is best to use ASM until you see the chaining side effect impact performance. You can turn on this feature by including the SEGMENT SPACE MANAGEMENT option in the CREATE TABLESPACE statement. Here are a few examples.

Example 1: This example illustrates creating a tablespace with automatic segment space management. This time, the tablespace is created successfully because the tablespace is using local extent management:

```
SQL> CREATE TABLESPACE TEST1
  2     DATAFILE 'C:\ORACLE\ORADATA\SAM\TEST01.DBF' SIZE 10M
  3     EXTENT MANAGEMENT LOCAL
  4     SEGMENT SPACE MANAGEMENT AUTO
  5   /

Tablespace created.
```

Example 2: The following query demonstrates the creation of a tablespace with manual segment space management:

```
SQL> CREATE TABLESPACE TEST2
  2     DATAFILE 'C:\ORACLE\ORADATA\SAM\TEST02.DBF' SIZE 10M
  3     EXTENT MANAGEMENT LOCAL
  4     SEGMENT SPACE MANAGEMENT MANUAL
  5   /

Tablespace created.
```

Example 3: The following query illustrates that the CREATE TABLESPACE statement fails if you try to create a tablespace with automatic segment space management *and* data dictionary extent management:

```
SQL> CREATE TABLESPACE TEST1
  2     DATAFILE 'C:\ORACLE\ORADATA\SAM\TEST01.DBF' SIZE 10M
  3     EXTENT MANAGEMENT DICTIONARY
  4     SEGMENT SPACE MANAGEMENT AUTO
  5  /
  SEGMENT SPACE MANAGEMENT AUTO
                              *
ERROR AT LINE 4:
ORA-30572: AUTO SEGMENT SPACE MANAGEMENT NOT VALID WITH DICTIONARY
EXTENT MANAGEMENT
```

Example 4: The following statement illustrates that the CREATE TABLESPACE command fails if you try to create a tablespace with DICTIONARY extent management if SYSTEM tablespace is the LOCAL extent management:

```
SQL> CREATE TABLESPACE TEST2
  2     DATAFILE 'C:\ORACLE\ORADATA\SAM\TEST2.DBF' SIZE 5M
  3     EXTENT MANAGEMENT DICTIONARY
  4  /
CREATE TABLESPACE TEST2
*
ERROR at line 1:
ORA-12913: Cannot create dictionary managed tablespace

SQL> SELECT TABLESPACE_NAME, EXTENT_MANAGEMENT
  2    FROM DBA_TABLESPACES
  3   WHERE TABLESPACE_NAME = 'SYSTEM'
  4  /

TABLESPACE_NAME                 EXTENT_MANAGEMENT
------------------------------- -----------------
SYSTEM                          LOCAL

1 row selected.
```

Tablespace Creation Options

It is very easy to create a tablespace. You can actually do this by simply issuing the one-line command, CREATE TABLESPACE TEST, provided you are using the Oracle-managed File (OMF) feature discussed later in this chapter. However, if you look at the full syntax of the CREATE TABLESPACE statement, you find many options that are available for various purposes, which you may want to employ as part of the tablespace attributes.

```
CREATE [TEMPORARY|UNDO] TABLESPACE tablespace
   [DATAFILE datafile_tempfile_specification]
   [MINIMUM EXTENT integer K|M]
   [BLOCKSIZE integer K]
   [LOGGING|NOLGGING]
   [FORCE LOGGING]
   [DEFAULT STORAGE [COMPRESS|NOCOMPRESS]
           default_storage_clause]
   [ONLINE|OFFLINE]
   [PERMENANT|TEMPORARY]
   [extent_management_clause]
   [segment_management_clause]
```

The code just cited is the complete syntax for creating a tablespace. The following sections examine each option that can be used with the CREATE TABLESPACE statement, so that you can understand its use and its effects on performance.

[TEMPORARY|UNDO] Option

This option indicates whether the tablespace created will be used for UNDO purposes or for TEMPORARY use. UNDO tablespace is used to store a "before" image of the data before it is modified. TEMPORARY tablespace is used for sorting. When there is a long sort operation that cannot be performed in memory, temporary space is required to split the operation into smaller pieces, as shown here:

```
CREATE UNDO TABLESPACE ...

Or

CREATE TEMPORARY TABLESPACE SAM_DATA
   TEMPFILE 'filename' ...
```

[DATAFILE datafile_tempfile_specification] Option

In this option, you are specifying the location, name, and size of the data file that will be associated with the tablespace. The complete syntax for this specification is as follows:

```
DATAFILE|TEMPFILE 'filename' SIZE K|M REUSE
   [AUTOEXTEND OFF|ON [NEXT integer K|M MAXSIZE UNLIMITED|integer K|M]]
```

The significant part of this file specification is the AUTOEXTEND clause, specifically when ON is selected. Turning this option on specifies that Oracle extends the size of the file when the file becomes full. You can put a cap limit on the file size or let it be unlimited. The advantage of this option is that if space is needed to perform transactions, the user does not get any errors, because Oracle allocates space automatically. Setting AUTOEXTEND with MAXSIZE UNLIMITED, you are basically indicating to Oracle that if the file needs to be extended, Oracle should increase the size of the file to the maximum space on the disk. Regardless, with the AUTOEXTEND turned on, you need to keep monitoring tablespace usage, be aware of any growth trends, and if you notice sudden growth, you must get a complete explanation of why it happened. You may be able to justify taking no action, but you still must have an explanation.

[MINIMUM EXTENT integer K|M] Option

This option cannot be used if tablespace is dictionary managed or if the tablespace is a temporary tablespace. This option is used to specify the minimum size of an extent that can be allocated in the tablespace.

[BLOCKSIZE integer K] Option

This option is used when you need to create a tablespace with a different Oracle block size than the standard size that the DB_BLOCK_SIZE initialization parameter specifies. This option is applicable to permanent tablespaces only.

[LOGGING|NOLOGGING] Option

This option specifies the default logging option for all objects residing within the tablespace. When LOGGING is turned on, Oracle generates redo entries for any creation or altering of a database object within the tablespace. NOLOGGING generates no redo entries, but impacts performance costs very little.

[FORCE LOGGING] Option

This option forces Oracle to generate redo entries for any object creation or modification residing within the tablespace regardless of the setting of the LOGGING or NOLOGGING option.

[COMPRESS|NOCOMPRESS] Option

COMPRESS notifies Oracle to compress data in a data segment. Data is compressed at the block level, so that rows within the block are compressed, thus eliminating repeating values for columns and therefore increasing memory per block. When data is retrieved, Oracle decompresses the data. This process has no impact on retrieving data but does impact updating and deleting data. For this reason, Oracle and DBA experts recommend using the COMPRESS option for DSS database applications, because DSS databases do not have a tremendous volume of update activities.

[DEFAULT STORAGE [COMPRESS|NOCOMPRESS] default_storage_clause] Option

This option is used to set the default storage parameter for database objects residing within the tablespace. Of course, objects can override these values, as shown in the previous chapter. The following code segment presents the complete syntax for the default storage clause, which is applicable for dictionary extent management.

```
DEFAULT STORAGE( INITIAL integer [ K | M ]
               | NEXT integer [ K | M ]
               | MINEXTENTS integer
               | MAXEXTENTS { integer | UNLIMITED }
               | PCTINCREASE integer
               | FREELISTS integer
               | FREELIST GROUPS integer
               | OPTIMAL [ integer [ K | M ] | NULL ]
               | BUFFER_POOL { KEEP | RECYCLE | DEFAULT }
               )
```

[ONLINE|OFFLINE] Option

When you use the ONLINE setting, this option makes the tablespace available immediately. OFFLINE makes it unavailable until altered.

[PERMANENT|TEMPORARY] Option

The PERMANENT option indicates that the database objects residing within the tablespace are to be held permanently; otherwise, the data objects are held temporarily.

[extent_management_clause] Option

This option notifies Oracle whether extent management is data dictionary managed or locally managed. The full syntax for this option is as follows:

```
EXTENT MANAGEMENT DICTIONARY|
            LOCAL [AUTOALLOCATE|UNIFORM
                                SIZE integer K|M]
```

When considering this option, remember from Chapter 6 that LOCAL is the preferred and recommended method of extent management. However, in the syntax for LOCAL, you indicate whether all extents are of UNIFORM size or are auto-allocated under Oracle discretion.

[segment_management_clause] Option

This option is applicable only for permanent and locally managed tablespaces. It tells Oracle whether the management of space within the tablespace is automatic or manual. If this option is set to AUTO, Oracle ignores settings of PCTUSED and FREELISTS.

```
SEGMENT SPACE MANAGEMENT AUTO|MANUAL
```

TIP

You cannot use a relative path when specifying a data file specification; instead, you must use an absolute path.

The following query lists all tablespaces, and some attributes, created in the database:

```
SQL> SELECT TABLESPACE_NAME,
  2         STATUS,
  3         CONTENTS,
  4         EXTENT_MANAGEMENT EXTENT_MGMT,
  5         ALLOCATION_TYPE ALLOCATION,
  6         SEGMENT_SPACE_MANAGEMENT SEGMENT_MGMT
  7    FROM DBA_TABLESPACES
  8  /

TABLESPACE_NAME  STATUS    CONTENTS   EXTENT_MGMT  ALLOCATION  SEGMENT_MGMT
---------------  -------   ---------  -----------  ---------   ------------
SYSTEM           ONLINE    PERMANENT  LOCAL        SYSTEM      MANUAL
TEMP             ONLINE    TEMPORARY  LOCAL        UNIFORM     MANUAL
CWMLITE          ONLINE    PERMANENT  LOCAL        SYSTEM      AUTO
DRSYS            ONLINE    PERMANENT  LOCAL        SYSTEM      AUTO
EXAMPLE          ONLINE    PERMANENT  LOCAL        SYSTEM      AUTO
INDX             ONLINE    PERMANENT  LOCAL        SYSTEM      AUTO
ODM              ONLINE    PERMANENT  LOCAL        SYSTEM      AUTO
TOOLS            ONLINE    PERMANENT  LOCAL        SYSTEM      AUTO
USERS            OFFLINE   PERMANENT  DICTIONARY   USER        MANUAL
XDB              ONLINE    PERMANENT  LOCAL        SYSTEM      AUTO
TEMP01           OFFLINE   TEMPORARY  LOCAL        UNIFORM     MANUAL
UNDO_TS01        ONLINE    UNDO       LOCAL        SYSTEM      MANUAL
LM_TS            ONLINE    PERMANENT  LOCAL        SYSTEM      MANUAL
```

As you can see, the CONTENTS column is the type of data stored within the tablespace. Now take a look at the following rows:

TEMP row: TEMP tablespace is accessible and used for storing temporary data mainly for sorting. Extent management is LOCAL with uniform extent size (meaning all extents have the same size) with extent allocation performed by the system. Segment space management is manual.

USERS row: USERS tablespace is not accessible because it is offline. It is used for storing data permanently. Extent management is LOCAL with extent allocation managed by the DBA. Segment space management is also manual.

The next section examines the type of tablespace management Oracle offers and how each management type influences performance.

Tablespace Examples

The following two examples of CREATE TABLESPACE demonstrate the use of different options and their purposes.

Example 1: This example creates a tablespace for a large table that is mainly used for reporting purposes in an OLTP application database. Before creating this tablespace, make sure that DB_32K_CACHE_SIZE is configured as shown in Figure 7-10.

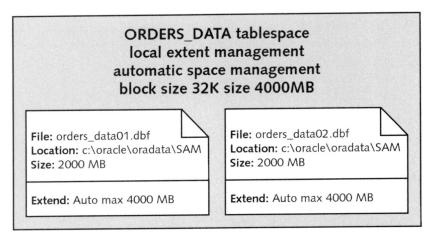

Figure 7-10 Example 1 showing a tablespace using local extent and automatic space management

```
SQL> CREATE TABLESPACE ORDERS_DATA
  2      DATAFILE 'C:\ORACLE\ORADATA\SAM\ORDERS_DATA01.DBF'
  3              SIZE 2000 M AUTOEXTEND ON MAXSIZE 2000 M ,
  4           'D:\ORACLE\ORADATA\SAM\ORDERS_DATA02.DBF' SIZE 2000M
  5              SIZE 2000 M AUTOEXTEND ON MAXSIZE 2000 M
  6      BLOCKSIZE 32K
  7      EXTENT MANAGEMENT LOCAL
  8      SEGMENT SPACE MANAGEMENT AUTO
  9  /

Tablespace created.
```

Example 2: This example creates a tablespace to contain a table with a high volume of transactions. The forecasted growth of the table residing within this tablespace is 1 GB for one year as shown in Figure 7-11.

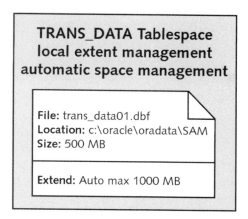

Figure 7-11   Example 2 showing a tablespace with AUTOEXTEND on

```
SQL> CREATE TABLESPACE TRANS_DATA
  2      DATAFILE 'C:\ORACLE\ORADATA\SAM\TRANS_DATA01.DBF'
  3             SIZE 500 M AUTOEXTEND ON MAXSIZE 10000 M
  7      EXTENT MANAGEMENT LOCAL
  8      SEGMENT SPACE MANAGEMENT AUTO
  9  /

Tablespace created.
```

Altering Tablespace Status

The status of a tablespace can be altered to fit its use. Most often, changing the tablespace status does not influence performance directly. However there are some performance implications for each status. Listed here is the ALTER TABLESPACE statement that changes the tablespace status:

```
ALTER TABLESPACE tablespace
    [ONLINE|OFFLINE NORMAL|TEMPORARY|IMMEDIATE]
    [BEGIN|END BACKUP]
    [READ ONLY|WRITE]
```

The following sections explain the meaning and implications of each status.

READ ONLY Status

This status indicates that tables residing within this tablespace can be read, but not updated. The performance benefit is that the tablespace is not backed up with every hot backup. A backup is needed only once after the tablespace is switched to READ-ONLY. When the ALTER statement is issued, Oracle commits all pending transactions for the tablespace; in other words, a checkpoint is set.

```
SQL> ALTER TABLESPACE TEST1 READ ONLY
  2  /

Tablespace altered.
```

READ WRITE Status

This status indicates that all tables residing within the tablespace will be updated. The performance implication is that more write activities on the tablespace will occur. Of course, for backups, this means that the database needs to back up this tablespace.

```
SQL> ALTER TABLESPACE TEST1 READ WRITE
  2  /

Tablespace altered.
```

OFFLINE Status

OFFLINE status indicates that the tablespace will be unavailable, and therefore, any database object residing within this tablespace will not be accessible. There is no performance implication when a tablespace is offline. Normally, when a tablespace is taken offline, a checkpoint is performed. All pending transactions will be written to the tablespace. This status has the following three options:

- **Normal:** A checkpoint must occur (default).

- **Immediate:** A checkpoint does not occur. This option is used most often for tablespace or data file recovery.

- **Temporary:** A checkpoint does not occur (similar to IMMEDIATE). This option is used for tablespace or data file recovery only.

```
SQL> ALTER TABLESPACE TEST1 OFFLINE
  2  /

Tablespace altered.
```

ONLINE Status

This status indicates that the tablespace is available, and all database objects residing within it are accessible. There is no performance implication.

```
SQL> ALTER TABLESPACE TEST1 ONLINE
  2  /

Tablespace altered.
```

BEGIN BACKUP Status

BEGIN BACKUP status is used for open database backup purposes. All tables within the tablespace are accessible. Although transactions on the tablespace are permitted, committed data are not written to the tablespace while in BEGIN BACKUP status. Instead, committed data are written to redo log files, deferring checkpoints on the tablespace until it is no longer in a backup mode. To end backup mode you need to use the ALTER TABLESPACE statement with the END BACKUP status. The performance implication is an increase in redo entries as well as the number of archived logs.

```
SQL> ALTER TABLESPACE TEST1 BEGIN BACKUP
  2  /

Tablespace altered.

...

SQL> ALTER TABLESPACE TEST1 END BACKUP
  2  /

Tablespace altered.
```

Tablespace Sizing

DBA students often ask how much space should be allocated to tablespaces. The answer is not clear-cut because the amount of space depends on what objects it will contain.

So far in this chapter, you have learned or reviewed most of the concepts about tablespaces. In this section, you learn how to size a tablespace. In other words, when you create a tablespace, how much space should you allocate to the files belonging to it: 1 GB, 2 GB, or some other value? The answer to this question depends on what tables or indexes will reside in the tablespace and the expected growth over a period of time. Chapter 6 presents a method to estimate the size of a table, and this section expands on that knowledge by showing how to size a tablespace as well as allocate tables to different tablespaces.

Tablespace sizing is the process of computing an approximate size of a tablespace based on objects allocated or assigned to it. The best way to understand how to size a tablespace is to examine examples. Suppose you have a new module that requires the creation of three medium-sized tables that are functionally related, and one other large table. Table 7-2 presents table sizes; note that these sizes are relative and some DBAs may not agree with these size classifications.

Table 7-2 Table volume

Table size	Number of rows
Small	0–100,000
Medium	100,001–1,000,000
Large	1,000,001–10,000,000
Huge	Over 10,000,000

First, since the three medium-sized tables are related—CUSTOMERS, BALANCES, and OPTIONS—you should place them in one tablespace, and the fourth large table, RECORD_CALLS, resides in another tablespace. Organization of tables is quite important from two points of view, administration and performance.

From an administration point of view, when you place related tables in a single tablespace, you are isolating dependencies among the modules of an application. For instance, if one module needs maintenance, you can change the status of the tablespace without impacting other modules. Here is another example: If a recovery is required because of data corruption, you can recover part of the application without impacting the whole database. From a performance point of view, transactions should be distributed among different tablespaces and files to reduce contention. Modules that are intertwined with respect to tablespaces cause contention, particularly when modules have similar levels of activity.

Now return to the example to complete analysis of this concept. Table 7-3 presents the maximum row length for this example.

```
Estimated Table Size = MRL * (1 + PF/100) * NOR * FACTOR
Where:
        MRL:            Maximum row length
        PF:             PCTFREE
        NOR:            Number of Rows
        FACTOR:         10% or any desired percentage of number of rows
                        as a fudge factor.
```

Applying the below formula from Chapter 6 produces the following results:

```
Estimated Table Size = MRL * (1 + PF/100) * NOR * FACTOR
```

Table 7-3 Scenario table volume

Table name	Maximum row length	Number of rows	Percent free	Total size
CUSTOMERS	1450 bytes	1,000,000	40	2.7 GB
BALANCES	200 bytes	1,000,000	10	0.3 GB
OPTIONS	551 bytes	1,000,000	10	0.7 GB
RECORD_CALLS	250 bytes	10,000,000	10	3.1 GB

By examining Table 7-3, you can see that you are creating two tablespaces to distribute data evenly, the first tablespace with a total of 3.7 GB to hold tables CUSTOMERS, BALANCES and OPTIONS, and another tablespace with 3.1 GB to hold RECORD_CALLS. These estimates can be used as initial sizes when you are creating these tablespaces. As you know, the number of rows is an estimate for the size of the table. Of course, if you know exactly the number of rows, use that instead of the estimate. Once you have created the tablespace, you need to monitor its usage to determine if you need more space.

The following query generates a tablespace size report, excluding temporary tablespaces:

```
SQL> SELECT  FREE.TABLESPACE_NAME TABLESPACE,
  2          TOT.TOTAL,
  3          (TOT.TOTAL - FREE.FREE_SPACE) USED_SPACE,
  4          FREE.FREE_SPACE FREE_SPACE,
  5          CEIL(((TOTAL - FREE.FREE_SPACE) /
  6                TOT.TOTAL) * 100) "% USED",
  7          CEIL((FREE.FREE_SPACE /
  8                TOT.TOTAL) * 100) "% FREE",
  9          DATA_FILES FILES
 10     FROM (SELECT TABLESPACE_NAME,
 11                  CEIL(SUM(BYTES) / 1024 / 1024) TOTAL ,
 12                  COUNT(*) DATA_FILES
 13             FROM SYS.DBA_DATA_FILES
 14            GROUP BY TABLESPACE_NAME) TOT,
 15          (SELECT TABLESPACE_NAME TABLESPACE_NAME,
 16                  CEIL(SUM(BYTES) / 1024 / 1024)
 17                  FREE_SPACE
 18             FROM SYS.DBA_FREE_SPACE
 19            GROUP BY TABLESPACE_NAME) FREE
 20    WHERE FREE.TABLESPACE_NAME = TOT.TABLESPACE_NAME
 21    ORDER BY USED_SPACE
 22  /

TABLESPACE   TOTAL USED_SPACE FREE_SPACE % USED % FREE FILES
----------- ----- ---------- ---------- ------ ------ -----
INDX            25          0         25      0    100     1
ORDER_DATA       2          0          2      0    100     2
UNDO_TS01       35          3         32      9     92     1
LM_TS           10          6          4     60     40     1
TOOLS           10          6          4     60     40     1
CWMLITE         20          9         11     45     55     1
ODM             20          9         11     45     55     1
DRSYS           20          9         11     45     55     1
XDB             39         38          1     98      3     1
USERS           97         93          4     96      5     1
EXAMPLE        149        148          1    100      1     1
SYSTEM         410        397         13     97      4     1
```

Having read up to this point gives you the equivalent of a Tablespace 101 course. The next section exposes you to advanced topics on tablespaces and data files. The next section also shows you how to use the Oracle Enterprise Manager to get a graphical report of all tablespaces. Figure 7-12 presents a snapshot of a tablespace summary obtained by clicking the **Tablespaces** option under **Storage** node in the navigation pane.

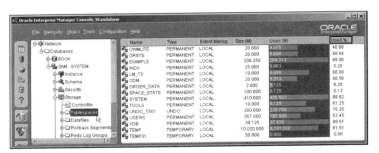

Figure 7-12   Oracle Enterprise Manager displaying a tablespace summary report

Tablespace Allocation

Over the years, proper data allocation has enhanced performance and noticeably reduced contention. In this context, data allocation means the allocation of tables as well as the allocation of data files. At this point, it is useful to delve into both table and data file allocation.

Table Allocation

Table allocation distributes tables among different application tablespaces. One of the Oracle Flexible Architecture (OFA) objectives is to separate the application data from system data by placing each type of data on separate disks. For example, system data dictionary should reside within a tablespace specifically for system data. Undo data should reside within a tablespace assigned for the purpose of undo operations, and temporary data should reside within a temporary tablespace. In addition, user data should be allocated among different tablespaces based on data function and transaction activity. Index data should reside on tablespaces dedicated for indexes, and table data should reside in tablespaces used for data only, and so on. The idea behind this practice is to reduce contention. When you submit a query or an update statement, it is most likely that all types of data (user data, indexes, temporary, and system data and undo data) residing in tablespaces will be accessed simultaneously. If all data resides on one or a few tablespaces, multiple processes compete to access data at the same moment. Figure 7-13 illustrates a typical data type separation that avoids contention.

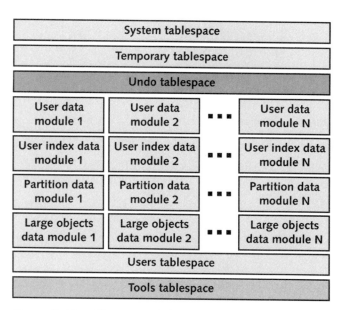

Figure 7-13   The optimal flexible architecture objective of data separation

Data File Allocation

Data file allocation places data files across all mount points (disks) in the system based on data type and function, as well as disk configuration. Some DBAs allocate all data files in one location in a RAID configuration, because all disks are striped. Placing files in different locations might not help, because the underlying mount point is taken from all disks. Although this is true, it does not mean that allocating files based on functionality and data does not add any value. In fact, it has been proven by many DBA experts that allocation of files enhances performance. In addition, OFA highly recommends the separation of files on different mount points.

Consider the following configuration for a new Oracle database that has been migrated from an existing Microsoft SQL Server.

- **System:**
  - 64 GB RAM
  - RAID configuration 0+1 for eight disks, each 60 GB
  - 4 CPUs

- **Application:**
  - Project-tracking system for a nationwide contracting company specializing in plowing, irrigation systems, plumbing, landscaping, and other types of work

- **Data Model:** See Figure 7-14.

- **Core Tables:**
  - COMPANY (small, three indexes) < 1 GB
  - CONTRACTOR (medium, five indexes) 2 GB
  - CLIENT (medium, four indexes) 10 GB
  - EXPENSE (huge, partitioned, two indexes) 50 GB
  - PROJECT (large, partitioned, 10 indexes) 32 GB
  - CLIENT_STAFF(large, three indexes) 21 GB
  - ITEM (huge, partitioned, three indexes) 52 GB
  - CATEGORY (small, one index) < 1 GB
  - TASK (huge, partitioned, four indexes) 72 GB

- **Other Tables:**
  - Reference tables and operation tables (medium) 1 GB

- **Data Space:**
  - 242 GB for tables
  - 48 GB for indexes
  - 290 GB for total space required

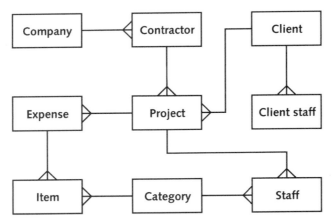

Figure 7-14   Data model of a nationwide general contracting company

Figure 7-15 illustrates tablespace allocation and table allocation for the contracting company example.

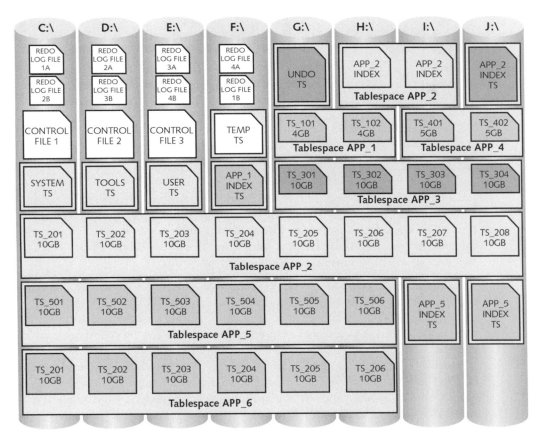

Figure 7-15 Map layout of tablespace and data file allocation

Note that C:\ represents a mount point, which is a logical drive. In this figure, you see an attempt to distribute all data across all mount points without overloading any specific mount point.

Table 7-4 lists the table allocation for each tablespace.

Table 7-4 Tablespace and table map

Tablespace	Table
APP_1	COMPANY
	CONTRACTOR
	CATEGORY
	OTHER TABLES
APP_2	TASK
APP_3	PROJECT
APP_4	CLIENT

Tablespace	Table
APP_5	EXPENSE
APP_6	ITEM
APP_7	CLIENT_STAFF

NOTE   Tablespace names should follow a convention that you should develop as part of the company standards. Usually tablespace names used for application data are named with the application acronym.

Looking at the contractor company example, you probably realize that coming up with an allocation map for a small application like this may take several hours. Is it really worth the time? The answer is: absolutely. Allocation mapping is a very good practice to adopt and the gain from using this practice is long term. Again, the benefit from balanced data load and I/O across all mount points is reduced contention.

Take for example tablespace APP_2, which will hold the TASK table. Because the TASK table is partitioned, each partition should reside on a different mount point. Of course, partitioning a table requires analysis and this example is simplified to make the point. In this example, you decide to have eight partitions only. Also, for tablespace APP_1, you see that data and indexes are on different mount points to reduce contention. This is how the allocation reduces contention. When a query is submitted to retrieve specific rows, index data will be accessed at the same time. If both data and index data reside on the same mount point, contention will cause a wait period. In this example, you have balanced data allocation and I/O load over all mount points.

Tablespace Map

The previous section described allocating tables and data files and showed that you had direct control over the whole process of tablespace allocation. In contrast, this section presents the tablespace map in which you do not have direct control over how space for a table is mapped. A **tablespace map** is a physical layout of extents for each segment residing in the tablespace. Tablespace maps provide a quick view to determine tablespace fragmentation. Why is a tablespace map so important? Because it tells you if extents for a table are fragmented. When you detect a fragmented table, you may need to reorganize the table to improve performance.

There are two ways to display a tablespace graphically: first, using Oracle Enterprise Manager (the preferred method); and second, using a query that displays a report.

Oracle Enterprise Manager Tablespace Map Tool

The Tablespace Map tool is a graphical user interface program that is part of the Oracle Enterprise Manager. It provides a display of the characteristics of each tablespace, tables residing within it, and its extents. It also provides an analysis feature to give a status report of the tablespace. To become familiar with the tool, follow these steps to display a map of the USERS tablespace.

Step 1: Log on to Oracle Enterprise Manager and select the tablespace for which you wish to display a map, and then click on the **Tablespace Map** utility icon from the Tuning Pack option, as shown in Figure 7-16. Select the tablespace that you want to display. A window displays a map of tablespace, as shown in Figure 7-17.

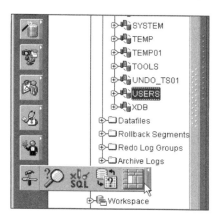

Figure 7-16   Oracle Enterprise Manager—Tablespace Map utility icon

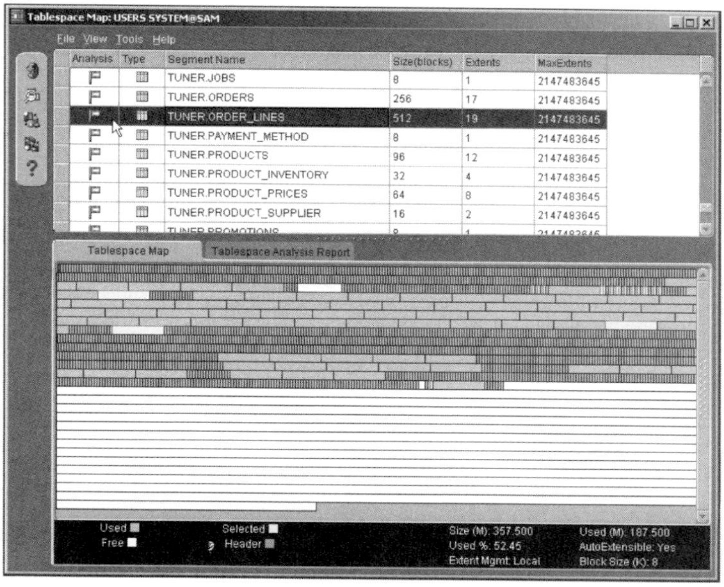

Figure 7-17   Tablespace Map utility window showing USERS tablespace map

As you can see in Figure 7-17, the table TUNER.ORDER_LINES is selected. The map highlights the blocks used by this table. In this case, it shows that space used by this table is not fully contiguous.

Step 2: To get a summary analysis report of the tablespace, click the **Tablespace Analysis** icon on the vertical toolbar on the left of the screen, as shown in Figure 7-18.

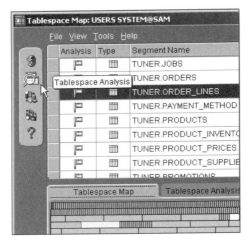

Figure 7-18   Tablespace Analysis icon

Step 3: When this icon is clicked, a Work In Progress dialog box is displayed, as shown in Figure 7-19.

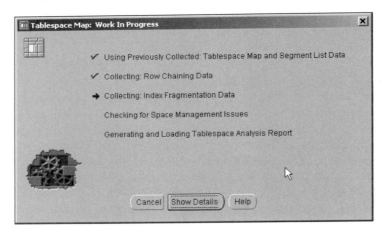

Figure 7-19   Tablespace Analysis Work In Progress dialog box

When the analysis is finished, a summary report is displayed, as shown in Figure 7-20.

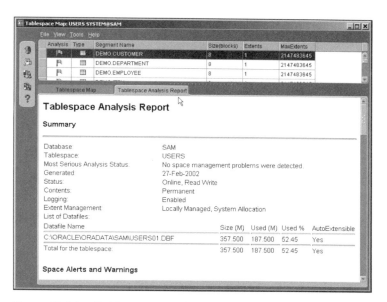

Figure 7-20   Tablespace Analysis summary results

The steps you have just finished demonstrate the first method for displaying a tablespace map using Oracle Enterprise Manager. The second method of obtaining this information is using a query statement, which is not as graphical as the previous method. The following query displays extents and blocks allocated for ORDER_LINES data segments using the DBA_EXTENTS view:

```
SQL> SELECT SEGMENT_NAME,
  2          EXTENT_ID,
  3          BLOCK_ID,
  4          BYTES,
  5          BLOCKS
  6    FROM DBA_EXTENTS
  7   WHERE TABLESPACE_NAME = 'USERS'
  8     AND SEGMENT_NAME = 'ORDER_LINES'
  9   ORDER BY 3
 10  /

SEGMENT_NAME   EXTENT_ID   BLOCK_ID      BYTES      BLOCKS
------------- ----------- ---------- ---------- ----------
ORDER_LINES            0       3873      65536           8
ORDER_LINES            1       4473      65536           8
ORDER_LINES            2       4617      65536           8
ORDER_LINES            3       4633      65536           8
ORDER_LINES            4       4649      65536           8
ORDER_LINES            5       4657      65536           8
ORDER_LINES            6       4681      65536           8
ORDER_LINES            7       4697      65536           8
ORDER_LINES            8       4705      65536           8
ORDER_LINES            9       4721      65536           8
ORDER_LINES           10       4745      65536           8
ORDER_LINES           11       4761      65536           8
ORDER_LINES           12       4777      65536           8
ORDER_LINES           13       4785      65536           8
ORDER_LINES           14       4809      65536           8
ORDER_LINES           15       4825      65536           8
ORDER_LINES           16       5001    1048576         128
ORDER_LINES           17       5257    1048576         128
ORDER_LINES           18       5513    1048576         128
```

The next query uses the DBA_SEGMENTS view to display all data segments of type
TABLE owned by TUNER and the space used by each segment in the USERS tablespace:

```
SQL> SELECT SEGMENT_NAME,
  2         TO_CHAR(SUM(BYTES)/1024/1024, '999.99') SIZE_MB
  3    FROM DBA_SEGMENTS
  4   WHERE TABLESPACE_NAME = 'USERS'
  5     AND OWNER = 'TUNER'
  6     AND SEGMENT_TYPE = 'TABLE'
  7   GROUP BY OWNER,SEGMENT_NAME
  8   ORDER BY 2 DESC
  9  /

SEGMENT_NAME                       SIZE_MB
------------------------------     -------
ORDER_LINES                           4.00
CHN_TBL                               3.00
ORDERS                                2.00
CUSTOMERS                             1.00
PRODUCTS                               .75
PRODUCT_PRICES                         .50
SUPPLIERS                              .25
PRODUCT_INVENTORY                      .25
PRODUCT_SUPPLIER                       .13
JOBS                                   .06
SHIPMENT_METHOD                        .06
SALES_COMMISSION                       .06
PAYMENT_METHOD                         .06
EMPLOYEE_RANKS                         .06
DEPARTMENTS                            .06
CATEGORIES                             .06
PROMOTIONS                             .06
TRANS_DEMO                             .06
EMPLOYEES                              .06
```

7

To put these concepts into practice, examine the following question that was posted on one of the DBA Web forums by a junior DBA. She writes:

"I am getting an error UNABLE TO EXTEND on one big index residing alone in a tablespace used by an application. I checked the tablespace usage and I found out that there is a plenty of space for the next extent. Can you explain why I am getting this error?"

In reply to this note, a DBA responded by instructing her to coalesce free space to eliminate fragmentation using the COALESCE option in the ALTER TABLESPACE statement. **Table coalescing** is a process of defragmenting tablespace by combining contiguous small extents together.

The Oracle statement ALTER TABLESPACE...COALESCE defragments some tablespaces. However, many DBAs doubt the effectiveness of this statement, because it does not defrag (defragment) the entire tablespace. This statement actually combines multiple smaller, adjacent free extents into a single large free extent. If two free extents are not next to each other, they are not combined and no physical movement of data takes place. Here is an example of the statement:

```
SQL> ALTER TABLESPACE USERS COALESCE
/

Tablespace altered.
```

NOTE

if PCTINCREASE is set to 0 or all extents are of the same size, you do not need to use the TABLESPACE...COALESCE statement.

Of course, you can also use DBMS_SPACE, as shown in Chapter 6, to display information on free blocks, space used, and unused space. One more report that is also helpful in displaying statistics about tablespace usage is shown here:

```
SQL> SELECT T.TABLESPACE_NAME,
  2          DF.BLOCKS,
  3          SUM(FS.BLOCKS) FREE,
  4          COUNT(*) "PIECES",
  5          MAX(FS.BLOCKS) LARGEST,
  6          MIN(FS.BLOCKS) SMALLEST,
  7          ROUND(AVG(FS.BLOCKS)) AVERAGE
  8    FROM DBA_FREE_SPACE FS,
  9         DBA_DATA_FILES DF,
 10         DBA_TABLESPACES T
 11   WHERE T.TABLESPACE_NAME=FS.TABLESPACE_NAME
 12     AND T.TABLESPACE_NAME = DF.TABLESPACE_NAME
 13   GROUP BY T.TABLESPACE_NAME,DF.BLOCKS
 14  /
```

TABLESPACE_NAME	BLOCKS	FREE	PIECES	LARGEST	SMALLEST	AVERAGE
ODM	2560	1368	1	1368	1368	1368
XDB	4880	24	1	24	24	24
INDX	3200	3192	1	3192	3192	3192
DRSYS	2560	1320	1	1320	1320	1320
LM_TS	1280	424	2	376	48	212
TOOLS	1280	496	1	496	496	496
USERS	12320	448	9	152	8	50
SYSTEM	52480	1640	1	1640	1640	1640
CWMLITE	2560	1360	2	1328	32	680
EXAMPLE	19040	16	1	16	16	16
UNDO_TS01	4480	4056	8	2016	8	507
ORDER_DATA	128	480	4	120	120	120

The next section demonstrates how to resize a tablespace by adding or removing space.

Tablespace Resizing

It is often necessary to add space to a tablespace. Circumstances requiring the addition of space include the following: 1) you issued a query to display a tablespace report showing that tablespace APP_DATA is above the threshold; 2) using Oracle Enterprise Manager, you find out that the APP_DATA tablespace is close to the threshold; or 3) you get a pager alert telling you that one of the tablespaces has reach the 90 percent threshold. In these circumstances, you can either resize existing data files by adding more space, or you can add new files.

The following statement illustrates how to resize an existing file for the USERS tablespace by adding an extra 1 GB to an existing space of 1 GB:

```
SQL> ALTER DATABASE
  2      DATAFILE 'C:\ORACLE\ORADATA\SAM\USERS01.DBF'
  3      RESIZE   2000 M
  4  /

Database altered.
```

NOTE   To reduce the size of the tablespace, you would substitute a smaller value, say 500 MB instead of 2000 MB. In this way, you reduce the size of the current tablespace. You can perform this operation, as long there is no data within the 500 MB space that you are removing.

NOTE   Once a data file is created, it cannot be removed until the tablespace is dropped.

Another method for increasing tablespace size is to add another file to the existing tablespace as shown in this statement:

```
SQL> ALTER TABLESPACE "USERS"
  2      ADD
  3      DATAFILE 'C:\ORACLE\ORADATA\SAM\USERS02.DBF'
  4      SIZE 1000M
  5  /

Tablespace altered
```

NOTE   You can also use ALTER TABLESPACE...RESIZE.

You must remember that every time you add a file or a tablespace, you must ensure that your backup script accounts for the new physical or logical files. In other words, your scripts should use the data dictionary to obtain current tablespace and/or data file information.

Moving and Renaming Data Files

As a DBA, you need to move data files around for a variety of reasons: for making space, for performing load balancing on disks, or for other reasons. In these situations, you can use the ALTER DATABASE or the ALTER TABLESPACE statement. The following steps demonstrate how you rename or move a file using the ALTER TABLESPACE statement:

Step 1: Determine the destination of the file to be moved and make sure there is enough space for the file.

Step 2: Inform your users that the data within the tablespace will not be available, and then bring the tablespace to an OFFLINE state.

```
SQL> ALTER TABLESPACE LM_TS OFFLINE
  2  /

Tablespace altered.
```

Step 3: Copy the file you want to move to the new destination using the Oracle command OCOPY or your operating system COPY command. Both options are shown in the following code segments:

```
SQL> HOST OCOPY C:\ORACLE\ORADATA\SAM\LM_TS01.DBF
D:\ORACLE\ORADATA\SAM\LM_TS01.DBF
```

Or

```
SQL> HOST COPY C:\ORACLE\ORADATA\SAM\LM_TS01.DBF D:\ORACLE\ORADATA\SAM\LM_TS01.DBF
```

Step 4: Verify that the file has been copied.

Step 5: Rename the moved data file(s) for the tablespace in the control file by issuing the following statements:

```
SQL> ALTER TABLESPACE LM_TS RENAME DATAFILE
  2    'C:\ORACLE\ORADATA\SAM\LM_TS01.DBF' TO
  3    'D:\ORACLE\ORADATA\SAM\LM_TS01.DBF'
  4  /

Tablespace altered.
```

Or

```
SQL> ALTER DATABASE LM_TS RENAME DATAFILE
  2     'C:\ORACLE\ORADATA\SAM\LM_TS01.DBF' TO
  3     'D:\ORACLE\ORADATA\SAM\LM_TS01.DBF'
  4  /

Tablespace altered.
```

The advantage of using the latter statement to rename the data file in the control file is that the ALTER TABELSPACE statement can be issued only when the database is open, whereas the ALTER DATABASE statement can be issued when the database is open and in a mount state.

Step 6: Verify that the name of the file has been changed in the control file:

```
SQL> SELECT NAME
  2     FROM V$DATAFILE
  3  /

NAME
----------------------------------------
C:\ORACLE\ORADATA\SAM\SYSTEM01.DBF
C:\ORACLE\ORADATA\SAM\UNDO_TS01.DBF
C:\ORACLE\ORADATA\SAM\CWMLITE01.DBF
C:\ORACLE\ORADATA\SAM\DRSYS01.DBF
C:\ORACLE\ORADATA\SAM\EXAMPLE01.DBF
C:\ORACLE\ORADATA\SAM\INDX01.DBF
C:\ORACLE\ORADATA\SAM\ODM01.DBF
C:\ORACLE\ORADATA\SAM\TOOLS01.DBF
C:\ORACLE\ORADATA\SAM\USERS01.DBF
C:\ORACLE\ORADATA\SAM\XDB01.DBF
D:\ORACLE\ORADATA\SAM\LM_TS01.DBF
C:\ORACLE\ORADATA\SAM\ORDERS_DATA01.DBF
C:\ORACLE\ORADATA\SAM\ORDERS_DATA02.DBF
```

Step 7: Put the tablespace back online:

```
SQL> ALTER TABLESPACE LM_TS ONLINE
  2  /

Tablespace altered.
```

Step 8: Verify that the status of the tablespace is online:

```
SQL> SELECT TABLESPACE_NAME, STATUS
  2     FROM DBA_TABLESPACES
  3  /

TABLESPACE_NAME                      STATUS
------------------------------       ---------
SYSTEM                               ONLINE
...
LM_TS                                ONLINE
ORDER_DATA                           ONLINE
```

Step 9: Use the operating system DELETE command to carefully remove the old file:

```
SQL> HOST DELETE C:\ORACLE\ORADATA\SAM\LM_TS01.DBF
```

Do not perform these types of operations during operation hours, because they make some of the data unavailable and may degrade performance, especially if the data file(s) are large. In addition, perform a backup before resizing the tablespace in case anything goes wrong. With these techniques, you can use the backup for recovery, and you can keep the business community informed when data is unavailable or has to be restored. In simple words, regardless of how small an operation is, take precautions to prevent any disaster, which may disrupt service. Should disruptions occur, ensure recovery by making backups.

Transportable Tablespaces

Refreshing databases and moving data from one database to another are routine tasks for DBAs. Certainly, Oracle EXP (export) and IMP (import) utilities are ideal for performing these routine tasks. Oracle EXP (export) and IMP (import) utilities work well for small to medium tables, but when it comes to large amounts of data, these utilities are not efficient and may require a considerable amount of time. Therefore, for a tablespace that contains large amounts of data, the transportable tablespace feature was created. Oracle provides **transportable tablespaces** to move and copy a tablespace from one database to another. Figure 7-21 illustrates the concept of transportable tablespaces.

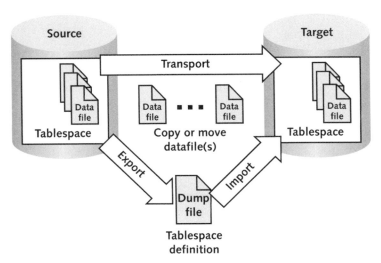

Figure 7-21 Overview of the architecture of transportable tablespace feature

You can follow these steps to transport a tablespace in one database to another. In this example you move the tablespace rather than copy it.

Step 1: Make sure that the following criteria are met:

- The OS platforms for source and target databases are compatible in version and block size. Consult with your system administrator to get the version and block size.

- The CHARACTERSET setting should be the same for both databases. Use the NLS_DATABASE_PARAMETERS dictionary view to verify this.

- The tablespace must be self-contained, and no referential integrity constraints can exist outside of the transported tablespace.

- The transported tablespace must not contain any function-based indexes.

- The target database must not have the same tablespace name.

- Owners of database objects residing within the transported tablespace in the source database must exist in the target tablespace.

Step 2: You can use the Oracle-supplied package called DBMS_TTS to check if any constraint violations exist. This package is owned by SYS. If for some reason this package does not exist, you can create it by using two Oracle-supplied scripts: dbmssql.sql and dbmsplts.sql, which are found in the ORACLE_HOME/rdbms/admin folder. In this step, you execute the procedure DBMS_TTS.TRANSPORT_SET_CHECK. The results of the procedure will be stored in the TRANSPORT_SET_VIOLATIONS table. In this case, the SOURCE database is SAM, and the TARGET database is BOOK. The transported tablespace is LM_TS.

```
SQL> EXEC DBMS_TTS.TRANSPORT_SET_CHECK('LM_TS',TRUE)

PL/SQL procedure successfully completed.

SQL> SELECT * FROM TRANSPORT_SET_VIOLATIONS
  2  /

VIOLATIONS
------------------------------------------------------------------------
Sys owned object  BLB in tablespace LM_TS not allowed in pluggable set
Sys owned object  TBL_L1 in tablespace LM_TS not allowed in pluggable set
Sys owned object  TBL_L2 in tablespace LM_TS not allowed in pluggable set
```

NOTE

You cannot transport any of the following tablespaces: SYSTEM, UNDO, or TEMPORARY.

As you can see, the table contains rows, which means that the transported tablespace has outside constraints and will require transport of the additional tablespace(s) that contain the constraints. Therefore, select another tablespace to transport, such as TRANSPORT_TS:

```
SQL> EXEC DBMS_TTS.TRANSPORT_SET_CHECK('TRANSPORT_TS', TRUE);

PL/SQL procedure successfully completed.

SQL> SELECT * FROM TRANSPORT_SET_VIOLATIONS
  2  /

no rows selected
```

As you can see in the result, there are no rows. This mean there is no violation and you can proceed to the next step.

Step 3: Get a listing of all data files belonging to the transported tablespace.

Step 4: You must set transported tablespace in the TARGET database to the READ ONLY state.

```
SQL> ALTER TABLESPACE TRANSPORT_TS READ ONLY
  2  /

Tablespace altered.
```

Step 5: Using the Oracle export utility EXP, export the definition of the transported tablespace from the target database. Create a parameter file called transport_exp.par with the following contents:

```
userid='sys/manager as sysdba'
TRANSPORT_TABLESPACE=y
TABLESPACES=TRANSPORT_TS
FILE=transport.dmp
```

Then issue the following command from the operating system prompt (see Figure 7-22):

```
C:\temp>exp parfile=transport_exp.par
```

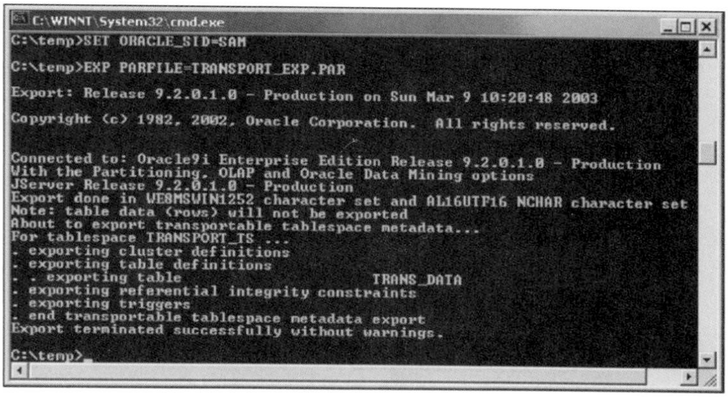

Figure 7-22 Exporting the transported tablespace definition from the source database

Step 6: Use the operating system MOVE command to copy the data files belonging to the tablespace:

```
C:\temp>copy c:\oracle\oradata\sam\transport_ts01.dbf
c:\oracle\oradata\book\transport_ts01.dbf
        1 file(s) copied.
```

Step 7: Use the Oracle import utility IMP to import the definition of the transported tablespace on the target database. Create a parameter file called transport_imp.par with the following text as its contents:

```
userid='system/manager as sysdba'
TRANSPORT_TABLESPACE=y
DATAFILES='c:\ORACLE\ORADATA\BOOK\TRANSPORT_TS01.DBF'
TABLESPACES=TRANSPORT_TS
FILE=c:\temp\transport.dmp
```

Next, issue the following commands, as shown in Figure 7-23:

```
C:\temp>SET ORACLE_SID=BOOK

C:\temp>imp parfile=transport_imp.par
```

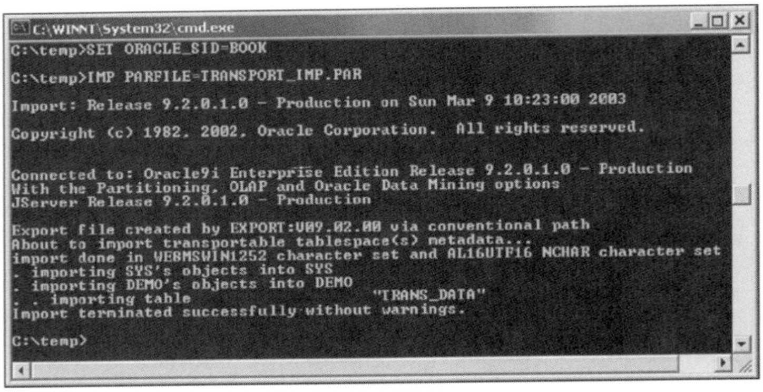

Figure 7-23 Importing the transported tablespace definition into a target database

Step 8: Change the transported tablespace on the target database to READ WRITE status:

```
SQL> ALTER TABLESPACE TRANSPORT_TS READ WRITE
  2  /

Tablespace altered.

SQL> SELECT COUNT(*) FROM DEMO.TRANS_DATA
  2  /

  COUNT(*)
----------
     50000
```

Step 9: Now clean up the transported tablespace from the source database by dropping tablespace TRANSPORT_TS and removing its data files:

```
SQL> DROP TABLESPACE TRANSPORT_TS INCLUDING CONTENTS
  2  /

Tablespace dropped.
```

Issue the following Windows command to remove the data file:

```
C:\temp>DEL C:\ORACLE\ORADATA\SAM\TRANSPORT_TS01.DBF
```

As you can see, this is quite a tedious process, so you would not want perform these steps on small tablespaces. It is meant for large tablespaces of 10 GB or more. The time spent performing these steps is the same time it takes to transfer the data file from one location to another. Using the EXP and IMP utilities on smaller files, the steps take less time.

At this point in the chapter, you have examined every aspect of creating and administering tablespaces. With this preparation, you are ready to study how to monitor tablespace space usage and fragmentation.

Tablespace Monitoring

As a DBA, one of your primary responsibilities is to ensure that you *never* run out of space on any tablespace in your database. How is this accomplished? You must monitor your tablespaces using all available tools. Tools for tablespace monitoring range from the most basic SQL statements, through the more advanced Oracle Enterprise Event Manager, to tools developed by various third-party software companies.

This section presents various queries that you can embed in shell scripts that can be executed periodically.

Tablespace Report (Usage)

The following query displays a graphic report on tablespace usage and can be modified to display tablespace fragmentation as illustrated earlier in this chapter:

```
SQL> SELECT FREE.TABLESPACE_NAME TABLESPACE,
  2          DATA_FILES FILE_CNT,
  3          CEIL(TOT.TOTAL) TOTAL_SIZE,
  4          CEIL(FREE.FREE) FREE_SPACE,
  5          CEIL(TOT.TOTAL - FREE.FREE) USED_SPACE,
  6          100 - CEIL( (FREE.FREE / TOT.TOTAL) * 100) USED_PCT,
  7          DECODE ((CEIL(10-(FREE.FREE / TOT.TOTAL) * 10)),
  8                   0,'| .......... |',
  9                   1,'| +......... |',
 10                   2,'| ++........ |',
 11                   3,'| +++....... |',
 12                   4,'| ++++...... |',
 13                   5,'| +++++..... |',
 14                   6,'| ++++++.... |',
 15                   7,'| +++++++... |',
 16                   8,'| ++++++++.. |',
 17                   9,'| +++++++++. |',
 18                  10,'| ++DANGER++ |') USAGE_CHARTED
 19    FROM (SELECT TABLESPACE_NAME,
 20                CEIL(SUM(BYTES)/1048576) TOTAL ,
 21                COUNT(*) DATA_FILES
 22           FROM SYS.DBA_DATA_FILES
 23          GROUP BY TABLESPACE_NAME) TOT,
 24         (SELECT TABLESPACE_NAME TABLESPACE_NAME,
 25                CEIL(SUM(BYTES)/1048576) FREE
 26           FROM SYS.DBA_FREE_SPACE
 27          GROUP BY TABLESPACE_NAME) FREE
 28   WHERE FREE.TABLESPACE_NAME = TOT.TABLESPACE_NAME
 29   ORDER BY USED_PCT
 30   /
```

TABLESPACE	FILE_CNT	TOTAL_SIZE	FREE_SPACE	USED_SPACE	USED_PCT	USAGE_CHART
LM_TS	1	10	4	6	60	| ++++++.... |
TOOLS	1	10	4	6	60	| ++++++.... |
USERS	1	358	170	188	52	| ++++++.... |
CWMLITE	1	20	11	9	45	| +++++..... |
ODM	1	20	11	9	45	| +++++..... |
DRSYS	1	20	11	9	45	| +++++..... |
EXAMPLE	1	207	2	205	99	| ++DANGER++ |
UNDO_TS01	1	300	29	271	90	| ++DANGER++ |
SYSTEM	1	410	5	405	98	| ++DANGER++ |
XDB	1	39	1	38	97	| ++DANGER++ |
TEST3	1	20	20	0	0	| .... |
SPACE_STATS	1	100	100	0	0	| .... |
OMF_TS	1	100	100	0	0	| .... |
ORDER_DATA	2	2	2	0	0	| .... |
INDX	1	25	25	0	0	| .... |

As you can see, three tablespaces are almost full. This report should prompt you to add more space to these tablespaces.

Next Extent Report

The following report displays data segments in which a tablespace has too little space for a segment to extend. Normally, it should return no rows. If rows are returned, you should add space to the tablespaces showing in the results of the report.

```
SQL> SELECT  S.OWNER,
  2          S.SEGMENT_TYPE,
  3          S.SEGMENT_NAME,
  4          S.TABLESPACE_NAME,
  5          S.NEXT_EXTENT/1024/1024 NEXT_EXTENT,
  6          TS.MAX_SPACE/1024/1024  MAX_SPACE
  7    FROM DBA_SEGMENTS S,
  8          (SELECT TABLESPACE_NAME,
  9                  MAX(BYTES) MAX_SPACE
 10            FROM DBA_FREE_SPACE
 11           GROUP BY TABLESPACE_NAME) TS
 12   WHERE S.TABLESPACE_NAME = TS.TABLESPACE_NAME
 13     AND SEGMENT_TYPE IN ('TABLE',
 14                          'INDEX',
 15                          'CLUSTER',
 16                          'TABLE PARTITION',
 17                          'INDEX PARTITION')
 18     AND NEXT_EXTENT > MAX_SPACE
 19   /

no rows selected    <- This is a good thing
```

Used and Free Extents Report

This report displays all used extents for a data segment within a tablespace and the free extents available on the same tablespace. You can use this report to view segments that proportionally have more extents allocated than other segments. This type of information helps determine if there is a need to move a segment from a current tablespace to another to reduce possible space contention.

```
SQL> SELECT DE.OWNER,
  2          DE.SEGMENT_NAME,
  3          DF.FILE_NAME,
  4          DE.BLOCK_ID,
  5          DE.BYTES/1024/1024 SIZE_MB
  6    FROM DBA_EXTENTS DE, DBA_DATA_FILES DF
  7   WHERE DE.TABLESPACE_NAME = 'USERS'
  8     AND DE.FILE_ID = DF.FILE_ID
  9  UNION ALL
 10  SELECT 'FREE',
 11          NULL,
 12          NULL,
 13          NULL,
 14          BYTES/1024/1024
 15    FROM DBA_FREE_SPACE
 16   WHERE TABLESPACE_NAME = 'USERS'
 17  /

OWNER SEGMENT_NAME                     FILE_NAME                           BLOCK_ID SIZE_MB
----- ---------------------------     ---------------------------------   -------- -------
DEMO  LOCATION                        C:\ORACLE\ORADATA\BOOK\USERS01.DBF         9   .0625
DEMO  DEPARTMENT                      C:\ORACLE\ORADATA\BOOK\USERS01.DBF        17   .0625
DEMO  JOB                             C:\ORACLE\ORADATA\BOOK\USERS01.DBF        25   .0625
DEMO  EMPLOYEE                        C:\ORACLE\ORADATA\BOOK\USERS01.DBF        33   .0625
DEMO  SALARY_GRADE                    C:\ORACLE\ORADATA\BOOK\USERS01.DBF        41   .0625
DEMO  PRODUCT                         C:\ORACLE\ORADATA\BOOK\USERS01.DBF        49   .0625
DEMO  PRICE                           C:\ORACLE\ORADATA\BOOK\USERS01.DBF        57   .0625
DEMO  CUSTOMER                        C:\ORACLE\ORADATA\BOOK\USERS01.DBF        65   .0625
DEMO  SALES_ORDER                     C:\ORACLE\ORADATA\BOOK\USERS01.DBF        73   .0625
DEMO  ITEM                            C:\ORACLE\ORADATA\BOOK\USERS01.DBF        81   .0625
DEMO  I_LOCATION$LOCATION_ID          C:\ORACLE\ORADATA\BOOK\USERS01.DBF        89   .0625
DEMO  I_DEPARTMENT$DEPARTMENT_ID C:\ORACLE\ORADATA\BOOK\USERS01.DBF        97   .0625
DEMO  I_JOB$JOB_ID                    C:\ORACLE\ORADATA\BOOK\USERS01.DBF       105   .0625
DEMO  I_EMPLOYEE$EMPLOYEE_ID          C:\ORACLE\ORADATA\BOOK\USERS01.DBF       113   .0625
DEMO  I_SALARY_GRADE$GRADE_ID         C:\ORACLE\ORADATA\BOOK\USERS01.DBF       121   .0625
DEMO  I_PRODUCT$PRODUCT_ID            C:\ORACLE\ORADATA\BOOK\USERS01.DBF       129   .0625
DEMO  I_PRICE                         C:\ORACLE\ORADATA\BOOK\USERS01.DBF       137   .0625
DEMO  I_CUSTOMER$CUSTOMER_ID          C:\ORACLE\ORADATA\BOOK\USERS01.DBF       145   .0625
DEMO  I_SALES_ORDER$ORDER_ID          C:\ORACLE\ORADATA\BOOK\USERS01.DBF       153   .0625
DEMO  I_ITEM                          C:\ORACLE\ORADATA\BOOK\USERS01.DBF       161   .0625
FREE                                                                            23.6875
```

Total Database Size

This report displays the total size of the database:

```
SQL> SELECT A.DF "Data Files Size in MB",
  2         B.TF "Temp Files Size in MB",
  3         C.LF "Log Files in MB",
  4         A.DF + B.TF + C.LF "Total Size"
  5     FROM (SELECT SUM(BYTES/(1024*1024)) DF
  6             FROM DBA_DATA_FILES) A,
  7          (SELECT SUM(BYTES/(1024*1024)) TF
  8             FROM DBA_TEMP_FILES) B,
  9          (SELECT SUM(BYTES/(1024*1024)) LF
 10             FROM V$LOG) C
 11  /

Data Files Size in MB Temp Files Size in MB Log Files in MB Total Size
-------------------- -------------------- --------------- ----------
             906.875                   40             300   1246.875
```

7

Oracle-Managed Files

There are many ways to learn to become a good, efficient DBA. You can be trained by a good instructor, you may pick up a good book on the subject of DBAs, you might have an opportunity to be mentored by a senior and experienced DBA, or you can learn the hard way by making mistakes—with luck, not on a production database. Jim, a junior DBA, is having problems and has posted a question to the one of the DBA Web sites. He asks:

"We have a policy at work to assign a tablespace for every user account created. The other day, I had to drop a user. So I dropped all the database objects the user owned and the tablespace assigned to him. Since I may get this request over and over, I created a script for this. When I tested my script, I kept getting the same message every time that I tried to build the tablespace. The error says that the data file already exists, but when I check the data file names I have in the database, it does not exist. Here is the error:

ORA-01119: error in creating database file 'games_data'

ORA-27038: skgfcre: file exit

OSD-04010: <create> option specified, file already exist

My question is this: can I use the REUSE option or is there other way to resolve this problem?"

First, you are probably hoping Jim is not playing or working with a production database. Using the REUSE option might be dangerous especially if the DBA enters a data file that is in use by other databases or other tablespace. The other part of the question is this: is there is any other way to resolve this problem? The answer is yes. Jim can use the Oracle-managed Files feature of Oracle9*i*. As you examine the example situations presented in this section, you will understand how Jim could have benefited from this feature and made his life much easier.

Now, how would you like to create a tablespace without having to specify any parameters? You can do so by issuing the following statement:

```
SQL> CREATE TABLESPACE TEST
  2  /

Tablespace created.
```

To configure your database to use Oracle Managed Files (OMF), you must set the `db-create_file_dest` initialization parameter to a valid data file directory.

The ease of creating a tablespace with the CREATE TABLESPACE TEST command is made possible by the new Oracle9*i* feature called **Oracle-managed files (OMF).** To better understand this feature, examine the following situations in which it is put to use.

Situation 1: A new DBA contractor is hired to help out the DBA group. One day he gets a call from the business team requesting that he add a new tablespace for a new module. He creates the tablespace with two data files on the same disk, one 2 GB and another 4 GB. Later he realizes that they are on the wrong disk, so he drops the new tablespace in preparation for recreating it somewhere else. He also wants to remove the data files that were created, but by mistake he removes the wrong data files. If he had been using the OMF feature, this would not have happened.

Situation 2: You are paged five minutes after midnight and notified that one of the tablespaces is 90 percent full. So you run to your computer at home and log in to find out that there is a process inserting a large number of rows. You need to quickly add more space to the tablespace by adding a new file. You cannot increase the size of the existing file, because it has already reached the operating system size limit. You add one file successfully. The next morning, you run a query to get a full listing of all the data files and see the new file. You are surprised to find that the new file name does not adhere to your company's naming conventions! You wish that your manager had listened to you when you requested the new OMF feature.

Situation 3: A DBA on your team is performing some tablespace maintenance, and he needs to drop many tablespaces, 15 of 10 GB each. After he moves database objects residing within the tablespaces to other tablespaces, he successfully drops all these tablespaces. Next he needs to delete all the corresponding data files, using the OS delete command. He deletes all except for two files, which he forgot because he was interrupted by a phone call about a database problem on another database. Two data files with a total size of 20 GB. Oops! He wishes he had used the OMF feature.

As these situations show, it is easy for a DBA to create new problems in the process of trying to correct existing problems. In each situation, the DBA made an error while performing database maintenance. OMF could have prevented all these problems. We all make mistakes, and therefore even the most experienced and cautious DBA can delete the wrong file by mistake. The OMF feature is a safeguard against such mistakes, because with OMF, Oracle manages all data files as well as other files, such as control files, and redo log files. Oracle creates a new file and name based on a naming convention, and when you want to delete the tablespace, Oracle removes the data file. The following steps illustrate how to configure your database to use OMF.

Step 1: Get the value for these parameters:

```
SQL> SHOW PARAMETER DB_CREATE

NAME                                TYPE          VALUE
----------------------------------- -----------   ------------
db_create_file_dest                 string
db_create_online_log_dest_1         string
db_create_online_log_dest_2         string
db_create_online_log_dest_3         string
db_create_online_log_dest_4         string
db_create_online_log_dest_5         string
```

As you see, these parameter values are not set; therefore, OMF is not active. Table 7-5 explains each parameter.

Table 7-5 Initialization parameters for Oracle-managed files

Parameter	Description
DB_CREATE_FILE_DEST	Data file destination where Oracle is able to create data files. You cannot include more than one destination. The destination can be modified dynamically.
DB_CREATE_ONLINE_LOG_DEST_N	Control file and log file destination where Oracle can create these files. N is 1–5.

The information in this table is derived from the online documentation that Oracle provides at the Oracle Technology Network site: *www.otn.oracle.com*.

NOTE

OMF and non-OMF data files can coexist within the same database and tablespace.

Step 2: Change the setting of DB_CREATE_FILE_DEST:

```
SQL> ALTER SYSTEM SET
  2      DB_CREATE_FILE_DEST='C:\ORACLE\ORADATA\SAM'
  3  /

System altered.
```

Step 3: Create a tablespace by simply issuing the following statement:

```
SQL> CREATE TABLESPACE OMF_TS;

Tablespace created.
```

Step 4: Verify the creation of the tablespace and the data file in database:

```
SQL> SELECT TABLESPACE_NAME, FILE_NAME
  2    FROM DBA_DATA_FILES
  3    ORDER BY 1
  4   /

TABLESPACE_NAME FILE_NAME
--------------- ------------------------------------------------
CWMLITE         C:\ORACLE\ORADATA\SAM\CWMLITE01.DBF
DRSYS           C:\ORACLE\ORADATA\SAM\DRSYS01.DBF
EXAMPLE         C:\ORACLE\ORADATA\SAM\EXAMPLE01.DBF
INDX            C:\ORACLE\ORADATA\SAM\INDX01.DBF
LM_TS           D:\ORACLE\ORADATA\SAM\LM_TS01.DBF
ODM             C:\ORACLE\ORADATA\SAM\ODM01.DBF
OMF_TS          C:\ORACLE\ORADATA\SAM\O1_MF_OMF_TS_Z6Q15500_.DBF
ORDER_DATA      C:\ORACLE\ORADATA\SAM\ORDERS_DATA01.DBF
ORDER_DATA      C:\ORACLE\ORADATA\SAM\ORDERS_DATA02.DBF
SYSTEM          C:\ORACLE\ORADATA\SAM\SYSTEM01.DBF
TOOLS           C:\ORACLE\ORADATA\SAM\TOOLS01.DBF
UNDO_TS01       C:\ORACLE\ORADATA\SAM\UNDO_TS01.DBF
USERS           C:\ORACLE\ORADATA\SAM\USERS01.DBF
XDB             C:\ORACLE\ORADATA\SAM\XDB01.DBF
USERS           C:\ORACLE\ORADATA\SAM\USERS01.DBF
XDB             C:\ORACLE\ORADATA\SAM\XDB01.DBF
```

NOTE   The default size of the Oracle-managed file is 100 MB.

As you can see, the file was created automatically. Observe that the file name convention is %T_MF_%TS_%U_.DBF

where:

%T is a thread number (instance number)

%TS is the tablespace name

%U is a unique name of eight alphanumeric characters

NOTE   You can always check the alert log to verify the creation of the Oracle-managed file. Figure 7-24 illustrates the contents of the alert log; as you can see from the shaded lines in the alert log, the tablespace was created successfully.

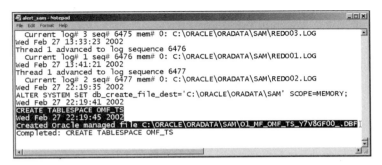

Figure 7-24   Contents of the Oracle alert log when an Oracle-managed file is created and an entry is recorded in the alert

Step 5: Verify the existence of the file at the operating system level, as shown in Figure 7-25.

7

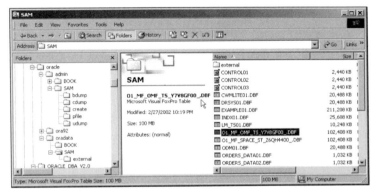

Figure 7-25   Windows Explorer showing the data file created by the Oracle-managed File feature

No redo entries are generated when an Oracle-managed file is deleted.

NOTE

Now, drop the newly created tablespace OMF_TS. Oracle removes the file automatically.

```
SQL> DROP TABLESPACE OMF_TS
  2      INCLUDING CONTENTS AND DATAFILES
  3  /

Tablespace dropped.
```

The example shows that the data file was removed automatically, so you have no more worries.

A disadvantage of the OMF feature should be noted here. With OMF, only one destination can be set at one time. You can overcome this limitation by creating each tablespace one at a time and change the destination each time. This process may sound cumbersome, but the benefits of having OMF outweigh the bother of changing this parameter each time.

NOTE

The Oracle-managed file process can also be applied to control files and log files.

MONITORING DATA FILE I/O ACTIVITIES

If you were to picture the computer hardware architecture or open your computer to look inside, you would see that the disk storage is connected to the motherboard through cables, whereas RAM memory is on the motherboard. This should tell you that any data traveling from disk to memory and from memory to disk takes time. These trips are referred to as Input/Output or **I/O activities**. Any unnecessary trips from RAM to disk and vice versa slow down the operation issued by the user.

In Oracle as well as other databases, unnecessary I/O activities cause application slowdown that can sometimes be detrimental to the database performance. Because of this, you should monitor I/O activities in your database to determine which file is more active than others. You should also monitor I/O activities from an operational perspective, which is discussed in Chapter 10. Figure 7-26 illustrates all I/O activities on different files by different processes for one transaction.

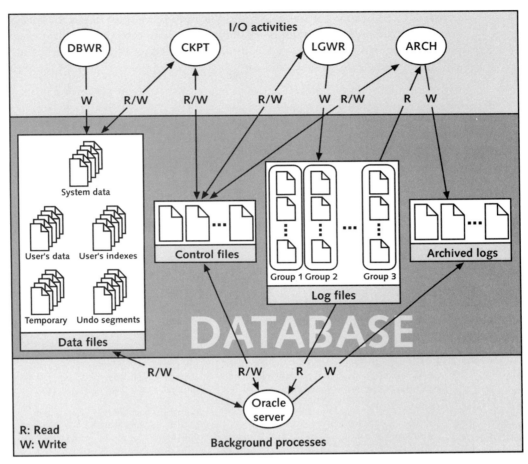

Figure 7-26 I/O activities of Oracle background processes on files

Note the following observations about the I/O activities:

- The volume of I/O activity for the Oracle server is high.

- Three processes access the data files. Therefore, contention problems could occur if all three processes access the files at the same time for many different transactions by different users.

- If all files reside on one disk and the database is highly active, contention would certainly increase.

DETECTING AND DIAGNOSING DATA FILE CONTENTION

So far in this chapter, you have taken an extensive tour of tablespaces from two perspectives, administrative and performance. Now you finish up this tour by learning about the data files types, data file I/O activities, and statistics that help you detect the overloading of I/O activities. There are two types of files, data files and temporary files. Obviously, **data files** contain permanent data and temporary files contain temporary data that is necessary for sort operations. As explained earlier, you should allocate data files on different mount points based on the files' functionality and use.

First, examine the four dynamic performance views that help get information and statistics about database files.

V$DATAFILE: This view contains information about files obtained from the control file. You can query this view when the database is in MOUNT and OPEN states (Refer to Appendix A for more details on MOUNT and OPEN states). This view does not include any temporary files.

```
SQL> SELECT FILE#,
  2         NAME,
  3         STATUS,
  4         ENABLED,
  5         BYTES,
  6         BLOCK_SIZE
  7    FROM V$DATAFILE
  8  /

FILE# NAME                                     STATUS  ENABLED          BYTES BLOCK_SIZE
----- ---------------------------------------- ------- ---------- ----------- ----------
    1 C:\ORACLE\ORADATA\SAM\SYSTEM01.DBF       SYSTEM  READ WRITE   429916160       8192
    2 C:\ORACLE\ORADATA\SAM\UNDO_TS01.DBF      ONLINE  READ WRITE    36700160       8192
    3 C:\ORACLE\ORADATA\SAM\CWMLITE01.DBF      ONLINE  READ WRITE    20971520       8192
    4 C:\ORACLE\ORADATA\SAM\DRSYS01.DBF        ONLINE  READ WRITE    20971520       8192
    5 C:\ORACLE\ORADATA\SAM\EXAMPLE01.DBF      ONLINE  READ WRITE   155975680       8192
    6 C:\ORACLE\ORADATA\SAM\INDX01.DBF         ONLINE  READ WRITE    26214400       8192
    7 C:\ORACLE\ORADATA\SAM\ODM01.DBF          ONLINE  READ WRITE    20971520       8192
    8 C:\ORACLE\ORADATA\SAM\TOOLS01.DBF        ONLINE  READ WRITE    10485760       8192
    9 C:\ORACLE\ORADATA\SAM\USERS01.DBF        ONLINE  READ WRITE   100925440       8192
   10 C:\ORACLE\ORADATA\SAM\XDB01.DBF          ONLINE  READ WRITE    39976960       8192
   11 D:\ORACLE\ORADATA\SAM\LM_TS01.DBF        ONLINE  READ WRITE    10485760       8192
   12 C:\ORACLE\ORADATA\SAM\ORDERS_DATA01.DBF  ONLINE  READ WRITE     1048576       8192
   13 C:\ORACLE\ORADATA\SAM\ORDERS_DATA02.DBF  ONLINE  READ WRITE     1048576       8192
```

V$TEMPFILE: This view contains information about all temporary files. You can query this view when the database is in MOUNT and OPEN states.

```
SQL> SELECT FILE#,
  2         NAME,
  3         STATUS,
  4         ENABLED,
  5         BYTES,
  6         BLOCK_SIZE
  7    FROM V$TEMPFILE
  8  /

FILE# NAME                              STATUS  ENABLED         BYTES BLOCK_SIZE
----- -------------------------------- ------- ---------- ---------- ----------
    1 C:\ORACLE\ORADATA\SAM\TEMP01.DBF ONLINE  READ WRITE 1.0486E+10       8192
    2 D:\ORACLE\ORADATA\SAM\TEMP01.DBF ONLINE  READ WRITE    5242880       8192
```

V$FILESTAT: This view contains read/write statistics on all data files. See Table 7-6 for a description of this view.

Table 7-6 V$FILESTAT dynamic performance view

Column	Description
FILE#	Data file identification number
PHYRDS	Total number of reads on the data file
PHYWRTS	Total number of writes on the data file
PHYBLKRD	Total number of blocks read from the data file
PHYBLKWRT	Total number of blocks written to the data file
The following columns will have a value of 0 when the TIMED_STATISTICS initialization parameter is turned off.	
READTIM	Total time spent in reads from the data file. This value is expressed in milliseconds.
WRITETIM	Total time spent in writes to this data file. This value is expressed in milliseconds.
AVGIOTIM	Average time spent in reads and writes. This value is expressed in milliseconds.
LSTIOTIM	Time spent for the last read/write on this data file. This value is expressed in milliseconds.
MINIOTIM	Minimum time spent on a read or write on the data file. This value is expressed in milliseconds.
MAXIOWTM	Maximum time spent on a write to the data file. This value is expressed in milliseconds.
MAXIORTM	Maximum time spent on a read from the data file. This value is expressed in milliseconds.

The information in this table is derived from the online documentation that Oracle provides at the Oracle Technology Network site: *www.otn.oracle.com.*

7

```
SQL> SELECT FILE#,
  2          PHYRDS,
  3          PHYWRTS
  4    FROM V$FILESTAT
  5  /

     FILE#      PHYRDS     PHYWRTS
---------- ---------- ----------
         1      11219         536
         2         94        8846
         3        306           4
         4        316           4
         5        796           4
         6          8           4
         7        223          17
         8        202           4
         9       1053           4
        10       1218           4
        11         13           4
        12          2           9
        13          2           9
```

V$TEMPSTAT: This view contains statistical values for temporary files:

```
SQL> SELECT FILE#,
  2          PHYRDS,
  3          PHYWRTS
  4    FROM V$TEMPSTAT
  5  /

     FILE#      PHYRDS     PHYWRTS
---------- ---------- ----------
         1          8           1
         2          5           0
```

In addition to the views described in the preceding paragraphs, there are two dictionary views that show information about files, DBA_DATA_FILES and DBA_TEMP_FILES. These views contain information about files, but the files can only be queried when the database is open.

The following query generates a data file usage report:

```
SQL> TITLE 'Datafile Usage Report|Values are expressed in MB'
SQL> column file_name format a50 set lines 120
SQL> set pages 9999
SQL> select file_name, total_size, used_size,
  2          total_size - used_size free_size
  3     from (select file_id, file_name, bytes/(1024*1024) total_size
  4             from dba_data_files) f,
  5          (select file_id,  sum(bytes)/(1024*1024) used_size
  6             from dba_free_space
  7             group by file_id) e
  8    where e.file_id=f.file_id
  9    /

Fri Mar 07                                                      page    1
                          Datafile Usage Report
                          Values are expressed in MB


FILE_NAME                                          TOTAL_SIZE  USED_SIZE  FREE_SIZE
-------------------------------------------------- ----------  ---------  ---------
C:\ORACLE\ORADATA\SAM\SYSTEM01.DBF                        500    63.6875   436.3125
C:\ORACLE\ORADATA\SAM\TS_TRY01.DBF                        100    41.5625    58.4375
C:\ORACLE\ORADATA\SAM\CWMLITE01.DBF                        20     10.625      9.375
C:\ORACLE\ORADATA\SAM\DRSYS01.DBF                          20    10.3125     9.6875
C:\ORACLE\ORADATA\SAM\EXAMPLE01.DBF                    148.75       .125    148.625
C:\ORACLE\ORADATA\SAM\INDX01.DBF                           25    24.9375      .0625
C:\ORACLE\ORADATA\SAM\ODM01.DBF                            20    10.6875     9.3125
C:\ORACLE\ORADATA\SAM\TOOLS01.DBF                          10      3.875      6.125
C:\ORACLE\ORADATA\SAM\USERS01.DBF                          65     1.0625    63.9375
C:\ORACLE\ORADATA\SAM\XDB01.DBF                        38.125      .1875    37.9375
C:\ORACLE\ORADATA\SAM\TS_3001.DBF                         100    42.4375    57.5625
C:\ORACLE\ORADATA\SAM\TS_SUPER01.DBF                      100      42.25      57.75
C:\ORACLE\ORADATA\SAM\UNODTB21.ORA                         55    49.6875     5.3125
C:\ORACLE\ORADATA\SAM\TEST01.DBF                          10     9.9375      .0625
C:\ORACLE\ORADATA\SAM\TEST02.DBF                          10     9.9375      .0625
C:\ORACLE\ORADATA\SAM\OEM_REPOSITORY.DBF           40.0078125          6 34.0078125
```

NOTE

Physical writes and physical block writes may be the same. All writes are single blocks.

Diagnosis of Data Files Contention

The following query can be used to get a ratio of how many files are READ overloaded. Most DBA experts agree on a threshold of 20 percent for READ or WRITE overloaded ratio. The remedy for overload is to move tables from one tablespace to another.

```
SQL> SELECT ROUND((SELECT COUNT(*)
  2            FROM V$FILESTAT
  3            WHERE PHYRDS >= (SELECT AVG(PHYRDS)
  4                                FROM V$FILESTAT)
  5         )
  6         /
  7         (SELECT COUNT(*) FROM V$DATAFILE) * 100)
  8         READS_RATIO
  9  FROM DUAL
 10  /

READS_RATIO
-----------
         15
```

The following query detects WRITE overloaded files:

```
SQL> SELECT ROUND((SELECT COUNT(*)
  2            FROM V$FILESTAT
  3            WHERE PHYWRTS >= (SELECT AVG(PHYWRTS)
  4                                FROM V$FILESTAT)
  5         )
  6         /
  7         (SELECT COUNT(*) FROM V$DATAFILE) * 100)
  8         WRITES_RATIO
  9  FROM DUAL
 10  /

WRITES_RATIO
------------
          8
```

The following query displays statistics for total reads and writes for each data file name, to see which file is being hit the hardest:

```
SQL> SELECT DF.NAME FILE_NAME,
  2         FS.PHYRDS READS,
  3         FS.PHYWRTS WRITES
  4     FROM V$DATAFILE DF, V$FILESTAT FS
  5    WHERE DF.FILE#=FS.FILE#
  6  /

FILE_NAME                                  READS  WRITES
---------------------------------------    -----  ------
C:\ORACLE\ORADATA\SAM\SYSTEM01.DBF         11219     539
C:\ORACLE\ORADATA\SAM\UNDO_TS01.DBF           94    8921
C:\ORACLE\ORADATA\SAM\CWMLITE01.DBF          306       4
C:\ORACLE\ORADATA\SAM\DRSYS01.DBF            316       4
C:\ORACLE\ORADATA\SAM\EXAMPLE01.DBF          796       4
C:\ORACLE\ORADATA\SAM\INDX01.DBF               8       4
C:\ORACLE\ORADATA\SAM\ODM01.DBF              223      17
C:\ORACLE\ORADATA\SAM\TOOLS01.DBF            202       4
C:\ORACLE\ORADATA\SAM\USERS01.DBF           1053       4
C:\ORACLE\ORADATA\SAM\XDB01.DBF             1218       4
D:\ORACLE\ORADATA\SAM\LM_TS01.DBF             13       4
C:\ORACLE\ORADATA\SAM\ORDERS_DATA01.DBF        2       9
C:\ORACLE\ORADATA\SAM\ORDERS_DATA02.DBF        2       9
```

NOTE

As important as knowing which file is experiencing the greatest amount of I/O activity, you also need to know the aggregate I/O per mount point.

As you see, the C:\ORACLE\ORADATA\SAM\XDB01.DBF file is being read the most often, excluding the SYSTEM data file (C:\ORACLE\ORADATA\SAM\SYSTEM01.DBF). You may want to investigate why. Is this a trend or is it just a one-time occurrence? Answers to these questions can help you allocate table and data files optimally.

EXTERNAL FILES

In many circumstances, you will want to load data from a Microsoft Excel spreadsheet or some other text file. You may need a text file for database lookups that may also be required for other modules outside the database. In this case, you can use the Oracle feature for external files. An **Oracle external file** is a non-Oracle file that can be in any format. This file is accessed by Oracle when an external table is associated to it and defined with the same structure of the file. Figure 7-27 illustrates the architecture of the external tables. This figure shows that the data is actually saved in an external operating system file.

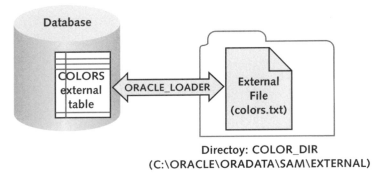

Directoy: COLOR_DIR
(C:\ORACLE\ORADATA\SAM\EXTERNAL)

Figure 7-27   Architectural overview of external tables

First, consider the process for creating a table with data residing in an external file. Then you will be shown the performance implications of this process. To work through the process, follow these steps:

Step 1: Create a text file with the following data and call it colors.txt. This file should reside within the ORADATA/SAM/EXTERNAL directory or another directory that is relevant to the application. For this practice, the file resides in the ORADATA/SAM/EXTERNAL directory.

```
100, white
200, blue
300, black
400, green
500, yellow
600, brown
700, cyan
800, grey
```

Step 2: You must create an alias for an Oracle directory where the document will reside.

```
SQL> CREATE DIRECTORY COLOR_DIR AS
  2      'C:\ORACLE\ORADATA\SAM\EXTERNAL'
  3  /

Directory created.
```

Step 3: Create a table called colors with two columns as shown here:

```
SQL> CREATE TABLE COLORS
  2  (
  3     CODE        NUMBER(3),
  4     DESCRIPTION VARCHAR2(20)
  5  )
  6  ORGANIZATION EXTERNAL
  7  (
  8     TYPE ORACLE_LOADER
  9     DEFAULT DIRECTORY COLOR_DIR
 10     ACCESS PARAMETERS
 11     (
 12        RECORDS DELIMITED BY NEWLINE
 13        FIELDS TERMINATED BY ','
 14     )
 15  LOCATION ('COLORS.TXT')
 16  )
 17  REJECT LIMIT 0
 18  /

Table created.
```

Step 4: Retrieve data from the table:

```
SQL> SELECT *
  2      FROM COLORS
  3  /

      CODE DESCRIPTION
---------- -------------
       100 white
       200 blue
       300 black
       400 green
       500 yellow
       600 brown
       700 cyan
       800 grey

8 rows selected.
```

This table is unusual, because it does not reside within a tablespace, and it has no data file associated to it. It is treated as a file that is managed by the operating system. To get information about the table, you need to query DBA_EXTERNAL_LOCATIONS and DBA_EXTERNAL_TABLES. The query that follows displays information about existing external tables:

```
SQL> SELECT OWNER,
  2          TABLE_NAME,
  3          LOCATION,
  4          DIRECTORY_NAME
  5    FROM DBA_EXTERNAL_LOCATIONS
  6  /

OWNER   TABLE_NAME                LOCATION      DIRECTORY_NAME
------  ------------------------  ------------  --------------
SH      SALES_TRANSACTIONS_EXT    sh_sales.dat  DATA_FILE_DIR
SYS     COLORS                    COLORS.TXT    COLOR_DIR
```

The benefits of external tables using external files are outlined in the following list:

- External read-only tables are useful when data needs to be accessed by both the database and modules outside of the database.

- External tables act as staging tables, so there is no need to create staging data when loading data to an Oracle database.

- The setup of external tables is quick and does not require the use of SQL*Loader or any third-party tool.

- Query response time is very fast for small tables.

The limitations of external tables and files are outlined in the following list:

- You can perform only one DML operation on external files and tables: SELECT.

- Query response time noticeably increases as the file size increases and is poor when a table is medium sized or larger.

The following query demonstrates that data manipulation on external tables is not allowed:

```
SQL> INSERT INTO COLORS (CODE, DESCRIPTION)
  2           VALUES (900, 'Magenta')
  3  /
INSERT INTO COLORS (CODE, DESCRIPTION)
            *
ERROR at line 1:
ORA-30657: operation not supported on external organized table
```

For more details on this topic, consult with the Oracle9*i* online documentation found at *www.otn.oracle.com.*

DBMS_SPACE_ADMIN Package

Most adventurous DBAs like to jump-start and use any new database feature that makes their lives easier, and one day you might be one of them. As you learned earlier in previous sections of this chapter, the automatic space management feature is only available in Oracle9*i*, not earlier versions of Oracle. So, what happens if an existing database is upgraded from Oracle8*i* to Oracle9*i* or it is created by a DBA who does not use the automatic features that Oracle9*i* offers? If this happens, you might ask yourself whether you need to re-create these tablespaces or just alter them. This section explains converting dictionary-managed tablespaces to locally managed tablespaces.

Oracle provides a PL/SQL supplied package called DBMS_SPACE_ADMIN that is created specifically for locally managed tablespaces. Table 7-7 lists all the functions and procedures found in this package:

Table 7-7 DBMS_SPACE_ADMIN function and procedure listing

Function and procedure name
FUNCTION SEGMENT_NUMBER_BLOCKS RETURNS NUMBER(126)
FUNCTION SEGMENT_NUMBER_EXTENTS RETURNS NUMBER(126)
PROCEDURE SEGMENT_CORRUPT
PROCEDURE SEGMENT_DROP_CORRUPT
PROCEDURE SEGMENT_DUMP
PROCEDURE SEGMENT_MOVEBLOCKS
PROCEDURE SEGMENT_VERIFY
PROCEDURE TABLESPACE_FIX_BITMAPS
PROCEDURE TABLESPACE_FIX_SEGMENT_STATES
PROCEDURE TABLESPACE_MIGRATE_FROM_LOCAL
PROCEDURE TABLESPACE_MIGRATE_TO_LOCAL
PROCEDURE TABLESPACE_REBUILD_BITMAPS
PROCEDURE TABLESPACE_REBUILD_QUOTAS
PROCEDURE TABLESPACE_RELOCATE_BITMAPS
PROCEDURE TABLESPACE_VERIFY

The information in this table is derived from the online documentation that Oracle provides at the Oracle Technology Network site: *www.otn.com*.

The following procedure converts dictionary-managed tablespaces to locally managed tablespaces: TABLESPACE_MIGRATE_TO_LOCAL. The following steps show you how to make the conversion.

Step 1: Get a listing of all tablespaces showing the extent management type:

```
TABLESPACE_NAME                      EXTENT_MANAGEMENT
------------------------------       -----------------
SYSTEM                               DICTIONARY
UNDOTBS                              LOCAL
TOOLS                                LOCAL
USERS                                LOCAL
TEMP                                 LOCAL
TS_BLA                               LOCAL
DD_TS                                DICTIONARY
TS_DATA                              LOCAL
```

Step 2: Execute the TABLESPACE_MIGRATE_TO_LOCAL procedure to convert the extent management. If the table is large, this may take some time:

```
SQL> EXEC DBMS_SPACE_ADMIN.TABLESPACE_MIGRATE_TO_LOCAL('DD_TS')

PL/SQL procedure successfully completed.
```

Step 3: Verify the conversion:

```
TABLESPACE_NAME                      EXTENT_MANAGEMENT
------------------------------       -----------------
SYSTEM                               DICTIONARY
UNDOTBS                              LOCAL
TOOLS                                LOCAL
USERS                                LOCAL
TEMP                                 LOCAL
TS_BLA                               LOCAL
DD_TS                                LOCAL
TS_DATA                              LOCAL
```

CAPACITY PLANNING

Capacity planning is probably not as complicated as you might expect, especially if your objective is to forecast how much space you need for a database for the coming years. At the same time, you should not underestimate the importance of capacity planning, because it involves planning for other resources such as memory, network, and other physical and logical resources.

Capacity planning is a way to plan and forecast how much storage will be needed for growth of all the databases in operation. Capacity planning involves all sorts of statistics to help forecast future needs as accurately as possible. Capacity planning is a routine task, one of the DBA's core responsibilities, which should be performed four times a year. When considering capacity planning, you should examine it from three perspectives:

- Nonproduction databases

- New production databases

- Production database growth

In this section, you are introduced to a method for planning storage capacity for production database growth only. The approach for each perspective is quite different from the others. The following sections treat each of these methods separately.

Capacity Planning for Nonproduction Databases

Nonproduction databases are used to support three teams: development, quality assurance, and integration. With nonproduction databases, you have more control of the amount of data you support. In most cases, running out of space in these databases is not catastrophic. You can always resolve such a situation by deleting unwanted data. So what do need to plan? You need to have a strategy for the new databases that you construct for new applications. A rule of thumb for the amount of space you will need is 20 percent of the initial size of the data set when it goes to production.

Capacity Planning for New Production Databases

For new production databases, you need to work with the business and system analysts to determine the initial number of rows for each table that will be created. When working with these colleagues, you can use these estimates in the table size formula. You should add a 20 percent fudge factor to the total number of rows obtained for all table sizes as well as the sizes of the redo log files and control files. Table 7-8 presents a template for computing initial database size.

Table 7-8   Template for capacity planning

Table/File	Quantity/Rows	Size	Total in MB
Redo log files	8	50 MB	400
Control files	3	35 MB	105
Table 1	1254782	127 bytes	152
Table 2			
		TOTAL	Xxxxx

Capacity Planning for Production Database Growth

Statistics are essential for capacity planning. On a daily or weekly basis, you should collect two sets of measurements: total space and used space (from these you derive available space), or total space and space available (from these you derive used space). You can collect these for the whole database or for each tablespace. It is recommended that you collect statistics at the tablespace level. To become familiar with the process, follow these steps to prepare and collect space measurements for the database.

Step 1: You need to create a table to serve as a repository for space measurements. The structure of this table is displayed in the following statement:

```
SQL> CREATE TABLESPACE SPACE_STATS
  2      EXTENT MANAGEMENT LOCAL
  3      SEGMENT SPACE MANAGEMENT AUTO
  4   /

Tablespace created.

SQL> CREATE TABLE SPACE_STATS_DATA
  2   (
  3       RUN_DTTM         DATE,
  4       TOTAL_SPACE      NUMBER,
  5       USED_SPACE       NUMBER,
  6       AVAIL_SPACE      NUMBER
  7   )
  8   TABLESPACE SPACE_STATS
  9   /

Table created.
```

Step 2: On a daily or weekly basis, issue the following query to collect these measurements and store them in the SPACE_STATS_DATA table:

```
SQL> INSERT INTO SPACE_STATS_DATA
  2      SELECT SYSDATE,
  3             TOT.TOTAL,
  4             (TOT.TOTAL - FREE.FREE_SPACE) USED_SPACE,
  5             FREE.FREE_SPACE FREE_SPACE
  6        FROM (SELECT CEIL(SUM(BYTES) / 1024 / 1024) TOTAL
  7                FROM SYS.DBA_DATA_FILES
  8             ) TOT,
  9             (SELECT CEIL(SUM(BYTES) / 1024 / 1024)
 10                    FREE_SPACE
 11               FROM SYS.DBA_FREE_SPACE
 12*            ) FREE
SQL> /

1 row created.

SQL> COMMIT
  2  /

Commit complete.

SQL> SELECT *
  2    FROM SPACE_STATS_DATA
  3  /

RUN_DTTM   TOTAL_SPACE USED_SPACE AVAIL_SPACE
---------  ----------- ---------- -----------
09-MAR-03          936        726         210
```

Step 3: Repeat Step 2 every day or every week, or on the periodic basis you have set.

Step 4: To illustrate an example, imagine that you run Step 2 on a weekly basis for one month. You could get a result that looks like the following:

```
SQL> SELECT *
  2    FROM SPACE_STATS_DATA
  3  /

RUN_DTTM   TOTAL_SPACE USED_SPACE AVAIL_SPACE
---------  ----------- ---------- -----------
09-MAR-03          936        726         210
16-MAR-03          936        755         181
23-MAR-03          936        823         113
30-MAR-03          936        845          91
```

Step 5: Analyze the results using a Microsoft Excel spreadsheet or any other tool, as shown in Figure 7-28.

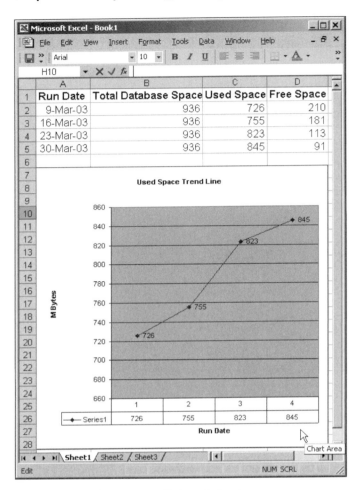

Figure 7-28   Space growth trend chart

Step 6: The chart in Figure 7–28 shows that the growth in one month is as follows:

$(845 - 726)/936 = 13\%$ of database size

To conclude, if the database were to grow the same amount again, this will lead to 845 + 119 = 964 MB which is 28 MB more than the current size. So 28 MB additional space is needed per the computed trend.

As you can see, this process is quite simple once the measurement data is collected. In addition, you should automate this process using a stored procedure and the DBMS_JOB scheduling mechanism provided by Oracle.

Best Practices

To help you become an effective DBA, this section summarizes the best practices for optimizing tablespaces that are recommended in this chapter.

1. Use locally managed tablespace.

2. Use automatic space management.

3. Use Oracle-managed files.

4. Place data on separate tablespaces and separate mount points even if your system is configured with RAID.

5. Use RAID level 0+1 if you can afford it; otherwise, use RAID level 5.

6. Monitor your tablespace on an hourly basis, especially for a high-transactional database with a threshold of 80 percent.

7. Monitor tablespaces to determine if there is enough space for the next extent.

8. Try to use the transportable tablespace feature when copying and moving a large amount of data from one database to another.

9. Gather space statistics to facilitate storage capacity planning for existing production databases.

10. When you create a new tablespace for an existing database, you must perform the necessary modifications to database backup scripts.

Chapter Summary

- The sole purpose of the RAID is to protect data from performance costs and compromise in case of disk media failure.

- RAID level 0+1 is striping and mirroring, whereas level 5 is striping and parity check.

- The ideal configuration is RAID level 0+1.

- The RAID level 5 configuration is not suitable for OLTP applications.

- A tablespace is a logical entity that serves as a logical container for physical data files as well as a logical container for logical segments.

- The three different types of tablespaces are system, undo, and temporary.

- A dictionary-managed tablespace uses the system data dictionary to manage free space with the PCTUSED parameter and FREELIST structure.

- A locally managed tablespace uses a bitmap image of free extents within the tablespace.

- Automatic space management eliminates DBA management of free space.

- In automatic space management, Oracle ignores the following storage parameters: PCTUSED, FREELISTS, and FREELIST GROUPS.

- Automatic space management reduces contention because it does not use freelists.

- Tables residing within tablespaces with READ ONLY status can be read, but not updated.

- Tables residing within tablespaces with READ WRITE status can be updated.

- The three tablespace status types are OFFLINE NORMAL, TEMPORARY, and IMMEDIATE.

- Tablespaces with a status of ONLINE are available, and all database objects residing within them are accessible.

- Tablespaces with a status of BEGIN BACKUP or END BACKUP are used for open database backup.

- One of the Oracle Flexible Architecture (OFA) objectives is to separate different types of data into separate tablespaces.

- Tablespace mapping indicates whether extents for a table are fragmented.

- The statements ALTER TABLESPACE...COALESCE are used to defragment tablespace extents.

- The ALTER TABLESPACE...RESIZE option and ALTER TABLESPACE...ADD DATAFILE option are used to increase or reduce the size of the tablespace.

- The ALTER DATABASE or ALTER TABLESPACE statements move or rename data files within a tablespace.

- A transportable tablespace can transfer a huge amount of data from one database to another.

- With the Oracle-managed Files (OMF) feature, Oracle manages all data files and other files, such as control files and redo log files.

- External files are used for external tables in which data resides in a formatted file outside the database.

- The DBMS_SPACE_ADMIN function is used for locally managed tablespaces, specifically for converting data dictionary-managed tablespaces to locally managed tablespaces.

- The objective of capacity planning is to forecast how much space you need for a database for the coming years.

- Initialization parameters presented in this chapter include the following:

  - DB_BLOCK_SIZE

  - TIMED_STATISTICS

  - DB_CREATE_FILE_DEST

  - DB_CREATE_ONLINE_LOG_DEST_1

  - DB_CREATE_ONLINE_LOG_DEST_2

  - DB_CREATE_ONLINE_LOG_DEST_3

  - DB_CREATE_ONLINE_LOG_DEST_4

  - DB_CREATE_ONLINE_LOG_DEST_5

- Views used in this chapter include the following:

  - DBA_DATA_FILES

- DBA_EXTENTS
- DBA_EXTERNAL_LOCATIONS
- DBA_EXTERNAL_TABLES
- DBA_FREE_SPACE
- DBA_SEGMENTS
- DBA_TABLESPACES
- DBA_TEMP_FILES
- NLS_DATABASE_PARAMETERS
- V$DATAFILE
- V$FILESTAT
- V$LOG
- V$TEMPFILE
- V$TEMPSTAT

◻ Oracle supplied PL/SQL packages used in this chapter include the following:

- DBMS_ADMIN_SPACE
- DBMS_JOB
- DBMS_SPACE
- DBMS_TTS

REVIEW QUESTIONS

1. A tablespace is a physical entity that creates data files. (True/False)

2. Oracle-managed files and files that are not Oracle managed cannot coexist in the same database. (True/False)

3. The best RAID configuration for an OLTP application is level 5. (True/False)

4. A database can have locally and dictionary-managed extent tablespaces. (True/False)

5. The FREELISTS setting is not ignored when the tablespace uses automatic segment space management. (True/False)

6. You can read and write to a tablespace when it is on ONLINE. (True/False)

7. You may see more redo activities when a tablespace is in BEGIN BACKUP mode. (True/False)

8. Optimal Flexible Architecture states that all data can reside on the same directory as long as a RAID level 0+1 configuration is used. (True/False)

9. Using the transportable tablespace feature does not enhance performance of the database. (True/False)

10. The sole benefit of tablespaces is to allow the DBA to administer space automatically. (True/False)

11. Write a report that displays free space for each tablespace.

12. Write a query that computes the total space consumed by all tablespaces.

13. Explain the differences between automatic and manual space management and how you would use each one.

14. Write a statement that moves the file(s) of a tablespace from one location to another.

15. Write a query that detects if a file(s) for a specific tablespace is (are) READ overloaded.

16. Why would you use external files? Provide an example.

17. Give an example of why you would use the transportable tablespace feature and explain the example.

18. List four methods to add space to a tablespace.

19. The other day while browsing the Internet, you came across a question posted on one of the database forums. Provide an answer to the following question:

    "Can someone explain how to determine if I've run out of space in one of my data files and tablespace?"

20. You are driving home during rush hour on a busy highway when you get a phone call on your work cellular phone. A DBA in your team tells you that one of the data files for a tablespace is corrupted. He asks you what he should do. Explain the impact of a corrupted file on performance.

EXAM REVIEW QUESTIONS: ORACLE9*i* PERFORMANCE TUNING (#1Z0-033)

1. What is the result of the following statement?

```
SQL> DROP TABLESPACE TEST INCLUDING CONTENTS;
```

   a. All objects within the tablespace are deleted.

   b. All objects within the tablespaces are dropped.

   c. The tablespace is removed, including the data file.

   d. The tablespace and objects are removed.

   e. The statement fails because of invalid syntax.

2. A tablespace is called a locally managed tablespace when:

   a. Oracle manages extents

   b. You manage extents

   c. Oracle manages segments

   d. You manage segments

   e. Oracle manages extents and segments

   f. You manage extents and segments

3. What initialization parameter would you need to use Oracle-managed files?

   a. EXTENT_MANAGEMENT

   b. ORACLE_FILE_MANAGEMENT

   c. DB_CREATE_FILE_DEST

   d. ORACLE_FILE_DEST

   e. FILE_EXTENT_MANGEMENT

   f. CREATE_FILE_DEST

4. Which storage parameter is ignored when using automatic segment space management?

   a. PCTFREE

   b. PCTINCREASE

   c. PCTUSED

   d. STORAGE clause

   e. INITIAL

5. You want to create a tablespace using an Oracle-managed file. Which statement is true?

   a. CREATE TABLESPACE TEST DATAFILE;

   b. CREATE TABLESPACE TEST;

   c. CREATE TABLESPACE TEST...FILE MANAGEMENT AUTO;

   d. CREATE TABLESPACE TEST 100M;

7

6. Which statement cannot be used with an external table?

    a. DROP TABLE TEST;

    b. DELETE TABLE TEST;

    c. SELECT * FROM TEST;

    d. ALTER TABLE TEST

    e. RENAME TABLE TEST TO TEST2;

7. What Oracle-supplied PL/SQL package do you use to convert a dictionary-managed tablespace to a locally managed tablespace?

    a. DBMS_SPACE

    b. DBMS_MIGRATE_TO_LOCAL

    c. DBMS_SPACE_ADMIN

    d. DBMS_ADMIN_SPACE

    e. DBMS_MIGRATE_ADMIN

8. Which clause do you use to manage free space automatically?

    a. SEGMENT SPACE MANAGEMENT AUTO

    b. SPACE MANAGEMENT AUTO

    c. SEGMENT MANAGEMENT AUTO

    d. SPACE SEGMENT MANAGEMENT AUTO

9. How do you determine if a file is an Oracle-managed file?

    a. Check the parameter setting of the Oracle-managed file.

    b. Check the alert log file.

    c. Check the size of the file.

    d. Check the FILE_NAME in DBA_DATA_FILES.

10. Which query do you use to determine if your database is employing different Oracle block sizes? Choose two.

    a. Query initialization parameter view V$PARAMETER.

    b. Query V$TABLESPACE dynamic view.

    c. Query DBA_TABLESPACE dictionary view.

    d. Query DBA_DATA_FILES dictionary view.

    e. Query V$DATAFILE dynamic view.

11. Which statement is true?

    a. When an external table is created, a new record is added to the DBA_DATA_FILES showing the new external file.

    b. Files controlled by OMF do not include log files or control files.

    c. Automatic segment space management cannot be used if extent data dictionary is managed.

    d. Space management is the best way to manage PCTFREE.

12. Which statement(s) do you use to find out how much free space is available in a tablespace?

    a. Query DBA_FREE_SPACE.

    b. Query DBA_DATA_FILES.

    c. Use the DBMS_SPACE package.

    d. Query DBA_EXTENTS.

    e. Use DBMS_FREE_SPACE package.

    f. Use DBMS_FREE package.

13. You want to create a new table that will contain a large amount of data (millions of rows). The table will also have an index. Which method is correct?

    a. Create the table and index within the same tablespace.

    b. Create the table and index within the same tablespace, but place the data files for the tablespace on different disks.

    c. Create the table and index within different tablespaces on different disks.

    d. Create the table and index within different tablespaces.

14. Where is free and used extent information stored for locally managed tablespaces?

    a. In dynamic performance views

    b. In data dictionary views

    c. Within the tablespace

    d. In memory

    e. In a system tablespace

    f. In a temporary tablespace

15. What is the benefit(s) of automatic space management?

    a. It eliminates the need to set PCTUSED and FREELISTS.

    b. There will be no buffer busy waits.

    c. It eliminates the need to use data dictionary extent management.

    d. A and C

    e. B and C

    f. A and C

    g. All of the above

HANDS-ON PROJECTS

HANDS-ON PROJECTS

Please complete the projects provided below.

1. Reread the Performance Problem at the start of the chapter. Think of it in terms of the concepts you have learned in this chapter and answer the following questions:

    a. Outline the problem being presented by Kari.

    b. Explain why Kari is having this problem.

    c. What should Kari do to prevent this problem from occurring again?

2. Interpret the following results of the query:

```
SQL> select name, phyrds, phywrts
  2    from v$datafile df, v$filestat fs
  3    where df.file# = fs.file#
  4  /
```

NAME	PHYRDS	PHYWRTS
C:\ORACLE\ORADATA\SAM\SYSTEM01.DBF	54832	1582
C:\ORACLE\ORADATA\SAM\TS_TRY01.DBF	1876	4
C:\ORACLE\ORADATA\SAM\CWMLITE01.DBF	306	4
C:\ORACLE\ORADATA\SAM\DRSYS01.DBF	316	4
C:\ORACLE\ORADATA\SAM\EXAMPLE01.DBF	796	4
C:\ORACLE\ORADATA\SAM\INDX01.DBF	8	4
C:\ORACLE\ORADATA\SAM\ODM01.DBF	198	4
C:\ORACLE\ORADATA\SAM\TOOLS01.DBF	202	4
C:\ORACLE\ORADATA\SAM\USERS01.DBF	884	703
C:\ORACLE\ORADATA\SAM\XDB01.DBF	1218	4
C:\ORACLE\ORADATA\SAM\TS_3001.DBF	4308	4
C:\ORACLE\ORADATA\SAM\TS_SUPER01.DBF	1854	4
C:\ORACLE\ORADATA\SAM\UNODTB21.ORA	35	13968
C:\ORACLE\ORADATA\SAM\TEST01.DBF	5	10
C:\ORACLE\ORADATA\SAM\TEST02.DBF	4	10
C:\ORACLE\ORADATA\SAM\OEM_REPOSITORY.DBF	1349	2143

3. Perform the following tasks to demonstrate the benefit of local extent management and automatic space management:

   a. Create a tablespace called CH7 using local extent management and automatic space management.

   b. Create a table with the following structure:
```
CREATE TABLE EX73
(
    NUM         NUMBER,
    TEXT        VARCHAR2(255)
)
TABLESPACE CH7
/
```

   c. Populate this table with 10000 rows.

   d. Analyze the table EX73 and record the CHAIN_CNT value: _____

   e. Update 2000 rows of EX73 setting the TEXT column to a text value that increases the size of the column considerably.

   f. Analyze the table EX73 again and record CHAIN_CNT value: _____

   g. What do you notice about row chaining and how would you fix it?

4. Create a table map for the ORDERS table in TUNER schema.

5. Write a statement that displays the total space used by the database.

6. While you were on vacation, you got a pager call asking you to call your manager. You went to the closest telephone, called him, and he told you this: "One of the databases is generating an error when users try to add rows. I tried to add more space to the existing tablespace, but it's no use and I'm still getting an error. What should I do?" Explain how you would handle this problem.

7. Your manager read an article about Oracle-managed files. The next day he asks you to explain it to him.

   a. How would you explain the implication(s) of using this feature?

   b. What effort is required when starting to use OMF?

   c. What would you do about existing data files that are not OMF?

8. You just had an interview for a DBA position. During the interview, the hiring manager pulled out a sheet of questions and asked you to illustrate how data should be allocated. Then he asked you what you would do if all the files for one of the databases you're going to manage reside on one mount point? Provide an explanation.

9. Use the OMF feature to create a 20 MB tablespace with a block size of 16 KB.

10. You've been working diligently to prevent your tablespace from running out of space. You have installed a sophisticated tool to alert you when 80 percent usage of the tablespace is reached. One day while you are shopping, your pager beeps showing that one of the tablespaces for the application is 83 percent used. You tell yourself that when you get home you will add more space. Unfortunately, the pager beeps again within five minutes to tell you that the tablespace is full. Describe four different actions that you could have taken to prevent this from happening.

11. You just get to work at 7:00 a.m., when your boss calls you to his office and says, "You've been doing a great job and you are a very valuable asset to our team." So you ask, "What's the problem?" He tells you that the DBA he hired last month has really done it this time; he deleted the wrong data file making nearly the entire database nonfunctional.

   a. How can losing one data file impact the database functioning so severely?

   b. What does it take to prevent this from happening again?

12. Write a report that generates a list of all segments in the database owned by the TUNER schema indicating the number of extents free and used and the percent of extent fragmentation.

CASE PROJECTS

Table and Tablespace Allocation

You were hired as a DBA consultant to help with the administration and tuning of the ACME Company database schema introduced in Chapter 2. Your hiring manager explained the importance of this application and gave you the following estimates of row count levels by the end of this year, as listed in Table 7-9.

Table 7-9   Estimates of table row counts

Table name	Row count
PRODUCTS	1812334
SUPPLIERS	345033
CUSTOMERS	12302321
ORDERS	32404324
PROMOTIONS	2345
CATEGORIES	122
JOBS	234
PAYMENT_METHOD	102
SHIPMENT_METHOD	12
EMPLOYEES	8005
DEPARTMENTS	232
PRODUCT_PRICES	632332
PRODUCT_INVENTORY	674432
ORDER_LINES	174322243
PRODUCT_SUPPLIER	31233232
SALES_COMMISSION	11
EMPLOYEE_RANKS	100

Your manager explained further that when the database was created, no one paid much attention to tables and tablespace allocation or capacity planning. She also stated that the machine on which the database is residing does not have the capacity to host the database in a year. In addition she said that the previous DBA did not use any of the automatic features. To resolve this problem, perform the following tasks that she requested:

1. Design an allocation map for all tables and tablespaces showing a diagram similar to Figure 7-15.

2. Recommend a disk configuration and provide the number of disks and size for each.

3. Determine the appropriate storage size needed to host the database.

4. Provide a CREATE statement for one of the tablespaces using automatic features.

# CHAPTER 8

TUNING UNDO SEGMENTS

In this chapter you will:

♦ Learn the rollback concept

♦ Learn about UNDO segments and their purposes

♦ Configure and size rollback segments

♦ Configure and size UNDO segments

♦ Diagnose rollback segments

♦ Diagnose UNDO segments

♦ Diagnose UNDO segments with Oracle Enterprise Manager

♦ Use the flashback query

♦ Solve common UNDO segment problems

♦ Learn best practices for optimizing transactions by decreasing undo data

Memory is a resource that requires your careful attention to ensure that it is not wasted, but rather used optimally to enhance, rather than degrade performance. In Chapters 2 through 5, you examined almost every important aspect of tuning the Oracle memory structures of the SGA. This chapter marks the end of examining the physical structure of the Oracle database, which is illustrated in Figure 8-1. As a DBA, you should know that Oracle users cannot perform any transactions without the UNDO segments shown in the data files sector of the figure.

Undo segments, also known as undo structure and rollback structure, are physical segments that reside on a tablespace. Undo is a new term introduced in Oracle9*i* to replace the term rollback. In this chapter, you come to understand the purpose of the undo structure and its importance to the Oracle instance. In addition, you learn how to configure and size this structure and finally how to diagnose it to proactively prevent problems. The chapter presents common problems that you may face as a DBA and supplies strategies for avoiding these problems. Finally, you learn how to optimize database transactions using DBA best practices.

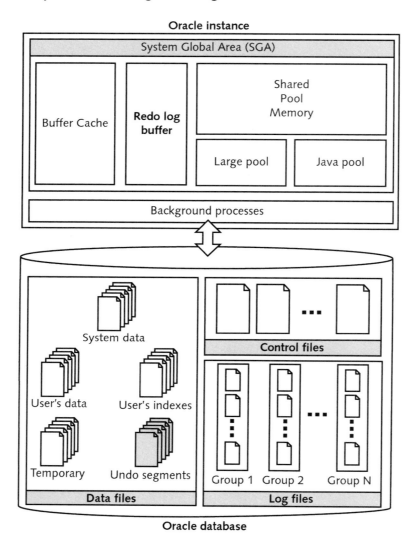

Figure 8-1   Oracle logical and physical architecture

Performance Problem

This section outlines an actual performance problem. As you look it over, imagine yourself as the DBA who reported it, and keep it in mind as you proceed through the chapter. The chapter presents concepts relevant to the problem. In the first Hands-on Project at the end of the chapter, you are asked to use the concepts you have learned to provide a solution, or partial solution, to this performance problem.

From: Howard Jones <mailto:HJones@undo.com>

Date: 23-Nov-02 09:23

Subject: ORA-00600: internal error code, arguments: [3668], [1], [2], [122], [122], [4],

Hello,

As I was trying to import a user schema, it failed with a warning. When I checked the errors produced by the IMP utility, I saw the following error: "insufficient temp spaceavailable." So I checked my disk space and found that the 50 GB disk space is entirely used up and there is 0 bytes of free space. I also checked the undo tablespace and found that undo segments tablespace undo_ts01 grew in size to 25GB. The following are my initialization parameter file settings:

```
undo_management = auto

undo_tablespace = undo_ts01
```

To release the space from the undo_ts01, I shut down and restarted the database. No progress. The undo_ts01 is still consuming 25GB using dba_rollback_segs view. Next I tried to take the undo segments offline like this:

```
SQL> ALTER ROLLBACK SEGMENT _sysys$ OFFLINE;
```

Everything resulted in errors, so I took the data file belonging to the undo_ts01 offline using DROP option:

```
SQL> alter database

  2   datafile 'D:\ORACLE\ORADATA\HISQ\UNDOTBS01.DBF'

  3   offline drop;
```

Then I shut down the database and deleted the previously listed data file and restarted the database by changing the initialization file using the following settings (pointing the undo tablespace to a different tablespace):

```
undo_management = auto

undo_tablespace = USERS
```

When I restarted the database, I ended up with following errors:

```
ORA-01157: cannot identify/lock data file 2 -

see DBWR trace file

ORA-01110: data file 2:

'D:\ORACLE\ORADATA\TEST\UNDO_TS01.DBF'
```

Then I tried undo_management=manual, and I got the same error again! I took a trace file of the control file and removed the data file mentioned previously. When I tried to open the database, I got the following error:

```
ORA-00600: internal error code, arguments: [3668], [1], [2], [122], [122], [4], [], []
```

Please help!!!

Howard

ROLLBACK CONCEPT

About 20 years ago, software technology was crude, unfriendly, and unforgiving. Because programmers wrote code on punch cards, one small program could consist of a deck of 100 cards, and if one card were misplaced, the program could not run. Technology advanced with the introduction of terminals connected to a mainframe; it still required patience and determination, however, to use these terminals to write and debug a program. The introduction of personal computers with the DOS operating system perpetuated the unforgiving process, because typing the wrong command introduced an error that was not easy to fix. Software applications did not offer capabilities to easily undo mistakes until recently. Today, the undo/redo feature is a standard with all new application software.

For example, even Notepad, which is a primitive application typically provided with the Microsoft Windows operating system, has the Undo feature, which allows you to undo the last operation you performed, as shown in Figure 8-2.

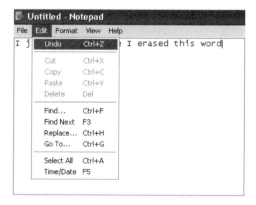

Figure 8-2   Notepad program showing the Undo menu option

Oracle provides a similar feature that allows the user to undo the last operation performed on the database. In an Oracle9i database, this operation is actually a transaction, which consists of either a single statement or a set of DML statements. Figure 8-3 shows examples of three transactions.

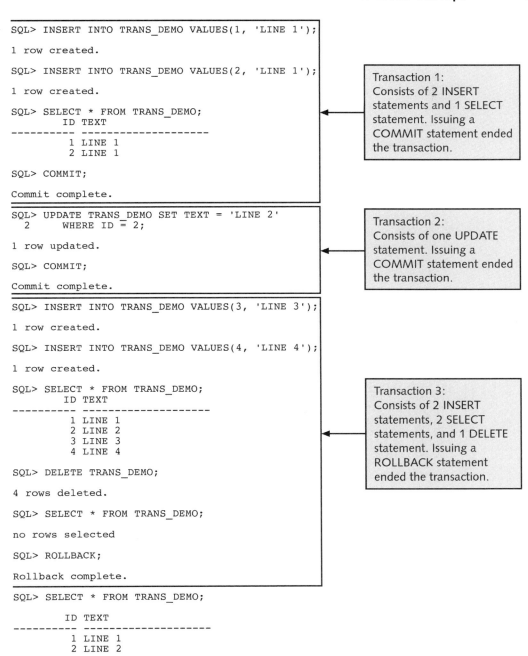

```
SQL> INSERT INTO TRANS_DEMO VALUES(1, 'LINE 1');

1 row created.

SQL> INSERT INTO TRANS_DEMO VALUES(2, 'LINE 1');

1 row created.

SQL> SELECT * FROM TRANS_DEMO;
        ID TEXT
---------- --------------------
         1 LINE 1
         2 LINE 1

SQL> COMMIT;

Commit complete.
```

Transaction 1:
Consists of 2 INSERT statements and 1 SELECT statement. Issuing a COMMIT statement ended the transaction.

```
SQL> UPDATE TRANS_DEMO SET TEXT = 'LINE 2'
  2      WHERE ID = 2;

1 row updated.

SQL> COMMIT;

Commit complete.
```

Transaction 2:
Consists of one UPDATE statement. Issuing a COMMIT statement ended the transaction.

```
SQL> INSERT INTO TRANS_DEMO VALUES(3, 'LINE 3');

1 row created.

SQL> INSERT INTO TRANS_DEMO VALUES(4, 'LINE 4');

1 row created.

SQL> SELECT * FROM TRANS_DEMO;
        ID TEXT
---------- --------------------
         1 LINE 1
         2 LINE 2
         3 LINE 3
         4 LINE 4

SQL> DELETE TRANS_DEMO;

4 rows deleted.

SQL> SELECT * FROM TRANS_DEMO;

no rows selected

SQL> ROLLBACK;

Rollback complete.
```

Transaction 3:
Consists of 2 INSERT statements, 2 SELECT statements, and 1 DELETE statement. Issuing a ROLLBACK statement ended the transaction.

```
SQL> SELECT * FROM TRANS_DEMO;

        ID TEXT
---------- --------------------
         1 LINE 1
         2 LINE 2
```

Figure 8-3   Examples of an Oracle undo transaction

UNDO segments are an essential part of the Oracle architecture. Without them, no transaction could be allowed to affect the database. Why are UNDO segments required? The answer is easy; UNDO segments are needed to store the image of the data before it is updated, as shown in Figure 8-4. As you can see, Step 1 saves the data in an UNDO segment before it is updated, so that it can be put back if the operator decides to undo the transaction by using the ROLLBACK statement. If the UNDO segment is not available, undo is not possible.

Rollback segments refer to Manual Undo Management and UNDO segments refer to Automatic Undo Management.

NOTE

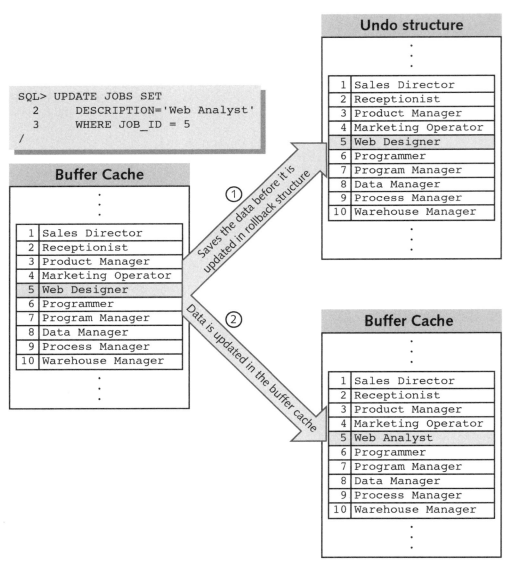

Figure 8-4 Detailed illustration of an UPDATE statement

Now that you understand the concept and importance of the UNDO segment, you next examine how UNDO segments are implemented in Oracle. Upcoming sections present an overview of rollback and UNDO segments and how Oracle uses these terms.

UNDO SEGMENTS OVERVIEW

As you learned in the previous section, the concept of UNDO segments is fairly simple. Whenever you make a change in the data, Oracle saves the old data and then allows you to change it back before the change is made permanent. The old data is saved in a data file within a tablespace, specifically within an UNDO segment. Before the release of Oracle9*i*, Oracle named this storage location the rollback segment, but with the release of Oracle9*i*, the name has changed to UNDO segment. To help you understand how the concept of a segment relates to other basic Oracle concepts, Figure 8-5 presents the logical and physical structure of tablespaces, data files, and segments, and shows the relationship among them.

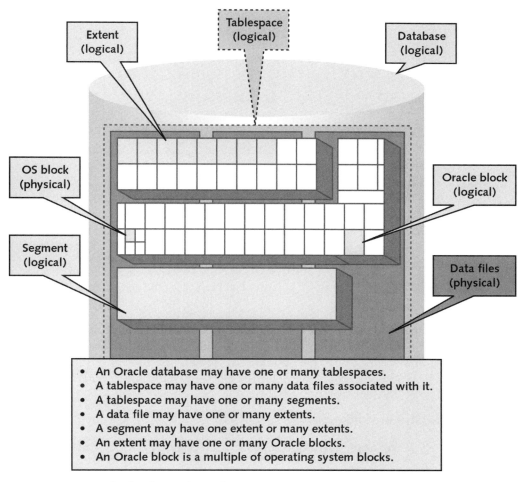

Figure 8-5   Oracle database physical structures

In the next section, you learn the difference between rollback and UNDO segments. You start by looking at rollback segments.

Rollback and Undo Segments

As you already know, there are several types of segments in an Oracle database, and each segment is used for a specific purpose. The following query lists all the different types of segments created in a database. For example, TABLE segments are used for storing tables and **ROLLBACK segments** are UNDO segments used for storing rollback data, which is also known as the **before image**.

```
SQL> SELECT DISTINCT SEGMENT_TYPE
  2      FROM DBA_SEGMENTS
  3  /

SEGMENT_TYPE
------------------
CACHE
CLUSTER
INDEX
INDEX PARTITION
LOBINDEX
LOBSEGMENT
NESTED TABLE
ROLLBACK
TABLE
TABLE PARTITION
```

Like other segments, rollback segments reside in tablespaces that are created for segment storage. One of the Optimal Flexible Architecture (OFA) guidelines is to separate different types of data to reduce contention. It is highly recommended to place indexes, tables, system tables, and UNDO segments on separate tablespaces as well as on different disks whenever possible. See Figure 8-6 for an illustration of tablespace allocation; the following list outlines each tablespace:

- **Table tablespace**: Contains data belonging to the database application or to users of the database

- **Index tablespace**: Contains index data for index objects owned by the application or users of the database

- **ROLLBACK (UNDO) segments tablespace**: Contains the before image used to rollback a transaction or to recover transactions in case of database failure

- **System tablespace**: Contains database metadata (system data dictionary)

- **Temporary tablespace**: Contains temporary data for sort operations

Notice in Figure 8-6 that different types of data are separated into different tablespaces to serve two basic purposes—data organization and reduction of I/O contention.

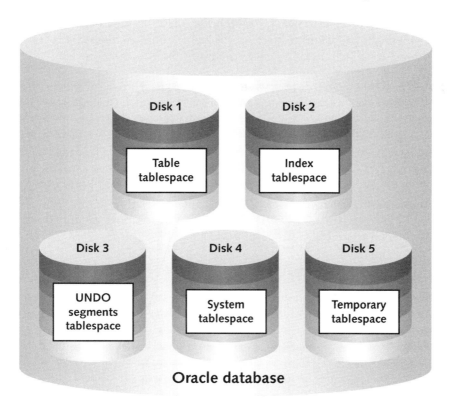

Figure 8-6   Tablespace layout that follows Optimal Flexible Architecture guidelines

This section examines the difference between rollback and UNDO segments. Rollback and UNDO segments serve the same purpose—they are both physical structures for storing the BEFORE image—but they are managed differently. Oracle9*i* introduced UNDO segments as a new method to manage rollback segments automatically, to reduce the burden on you, the DBA. Rollback segments always reuse and purge extents allocated for transactions to store the BEFORE image. Undo segments work differently; they retain the BEFORE image for the duration you specify before reusing these extents. An **extent** is a physical and logical grouping of Oracle blocks.

Before Oracle9*i*, the task of managing rollback segments required significant attention to proper sizing, configuration, monitoring, and tuning. There was no clear-cut formula that you could use to size them. Although you learn in upcoming sections how to configure and diagnose these segments to support the databases that use them or databases that have not been upgraded, most DBA experts are relieved that Oracle9*i* has introduced automatic UNDO segments management.

Guidelines for using rollback segments are not straightforward. Oracle sometimes deprecates a feature in one release and completely withdraws support for this feature in the next release. And so it is with UNDO segments. Oracle does not recommend using rollback segments in Oracle9*i*. So, if you want to manage UNDO segments in your database, you should use rollback segments. If you want to exert your valuable efforts on higher-level issues or other Oracle features, use the automatic management of UNDO segments.

NOTE

You may not use both rollback segments and UNDO segments in the same database unless you are migrating from an earlier version to Oracle9*i*.

To sum up this section, using rollback segments entails the manual management of UNDO segments, and if you are using the recommended UNDO segments, Oracle automatically manages UNDO segments. Now that you understand that the terms rollback segments and UNDO segments are the same in principal, you are ready to examine in more detail the purpose of UNDO segments. The next section details the purpose and functions of UNDO segments to help you understand their importance.

Purpose of Undo Segments

The rollback concept presented at the beginning of this chapter does not tell the whole story about UNDO segments. Undo segments have three functions, which are detailed in this section.

Transaction Rollback

The first function of UNDO segments to be examined is the **transaction rollback**. Suppose you submit a DML statement that changes data in a table, and then you decide against committing the change and want to undo it instead. When you issue a ROLLBACK statement, the uncommitted changes that you made are thereby undone. This is possible because of the UNDO segments mechanism. Oracle saves the BEFORE image in the UNDO segments until the transaction is committed or rolled back. When a ROLLBACK statement is issued, Oracle knows exactly where to get the data from the UNDO segments, because the part of the segments that is saving the BEFORE image stores the transaction number, block id, and other necessary data associated with the user transaction, as shown in Figure 8-7.

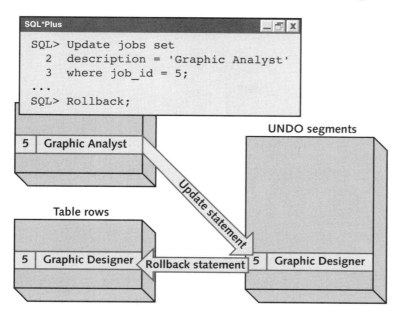

Figure 8-7   Rolling back a transaction

To better understand the rollback transaction concept, follow the steps in this example:

Step 1: Log on as TUNER and update one row in the EMPLOYEE table, but do not commit changes.

Step 2: View your changes by retrieving data for the row you updated.

Step 3: Undo your changes by issuing a ROLLBACK statement.

Step 4: Retrieve the row again to see that the original data is there.

Read Consistency

The second function of UNDO segments to be examined is **read consistency**. To understand this function, study the example presented in Figure 8-8. The figure shows that user 1 issues an UPDATE statement to change the value of the DESCRIPTION column in the JOBS table. User 1 then issues a SELECT statement to verify her changes but does not commit. Some time later, user 2 issues an UPDATE statement to change the DESCRIPTION column in the JOBS table, but his statement affects a different row than the user 1 update. User 2 decides to confirm his changes and issues a SELECT statement to see his changed information. User 2 does not see the changes of user 1 because user 1 did not commit her changes. So you see, Oracle preserves the old image until each transaction is committed and provides this data to ensure that for read consistency, users don't see each other's uncommitted changes.

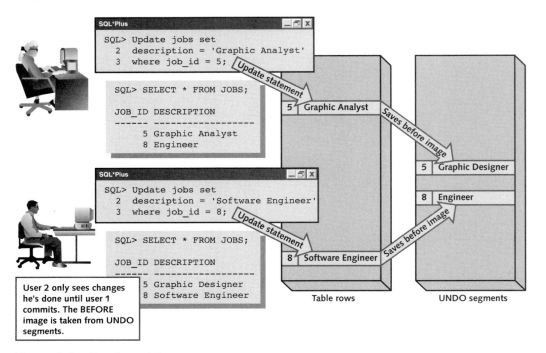

Figure 8-8   Read consistency

Figure 8-8 demonstrates the concept of read consistency, which is when you make data changes; other users do not see these changes until you commit your work. Figure 8-8 shows that user 2 cannot see changes made by user 1 until user 1 commits these changes. To better understand the sequence of events, follow the steps outlined in this example:

Step 1: Log on as TUNER and update a row in the CUSTOMER table, but do not commit the changes.

Step 2: Retrieve the row you updated to see your changes by issuing a SELECT statement.

Step 3: From a different session, log on as TUNER again and query the CUSTOMER table to retrieve the data you updated in Step 1. You should not see the changes you made in Step 1 because the changes were not committed.

When the Oracle system crashes, it is an implicit rollback, meaning that all pending transactions are rolled back.

NOTE

Transaction Recovery

The third function of UNDO segments to be examined is **transaction recovery**. To understand transaction recovery, consider the following example. Suppose that the database you are administering crashed during peak time in the middle of many uncommitted transactions. Of course, your priority is to recover the database as fast as possible without losing any transactions. Oracle attempts to recover the database automatically on its own. Any pending transactions that were occurring at the time of failure are rolled back. Oracle restores the BEFORE image data for these transactions from the UNDO segments.

Follow these steps to experience an example of the transaction recovery process.

Step 1: Log on as TUNER and update three rows in the JOBS table, but do not commit the changes.

Step 2: Issue a SELECT statement to see your changes.

Step 3: Shut off your computer while your database is running.

Step 4: Turn your computer on, and start your database if it has not already started.

Step 5: Log on again as TUNER.

Step 6: Retrieve the three rows you updated, and notice that the older values have been brought back from the UNDO segments.

In this example, you can see that when the computer was turned off with a transaction pending, Oracle restarted and rolled back this pending transaction.

8

MANAGEMENT OF UNDO SEGMENTS

As stated previously, there are two methods for managing UNDO segments: manual management and automatic management. Oracle and DBA experts recommend automatic management. In this section, you learn how to configure UNDO segment management using both methods.

Manual Management

DBAs choose to use manual management over the new automatic feature for a number of reasons:

- Many DBAs do not trust new features until they are tested, used, and proven by the industry.

- Some DBAs do not feel familiar and comfortable with new technicalities of the features, and so they stick to what they know.

- DBAs might not have enough time to test the new feature to ensure that it presents no major problems.

- To better understand the benefits of manually managing UNDO segments, consider the following scenario. Suppose you have been asked to build a new Oracle9*i* database for an existing database application. You have configured this database before and feel satisfied with its performance, so you have decided to use the rollback configuration in the new Oracle9*i* database. This is a classic example of an instance in which you would select manual management over automatic management of UNDO segments.

The necessary rollback segments configuration is composed of two tablespaces used for rollback segments, one sized at 1000 MB and another sized at 5000 MB. You have decided to have five segments on the small tablespace and one segment on the large tablespace (later in the chapter there are guidelines for optimally configuring rollback segments).

As you prepare to study the steps to configure the database for this example, you might ask: "What does it mean to have five segments on one tablespace?" As mentioned previously, the rollback segments are one type of segment residing on one tablespace. You can create one segment or many segments. If you create one segment for a database with a high level of transaction activities, there will be significant contention among the competing transactions, which will cause some transactions to wait until other transactions have completed, which in turn will degrade performance. To prevent this type of contention, you can create additional segments that can be used by all transactions.

Now, you are ready to configure your database with manual UNDO segments (also known as rollback segments). After the database has been created, you use the following steps to configure your database to manual management mode and create rollback segments.

Step 1: Shut down the database gracefully.

```
SQL> SHUTDOWN IMMEDIATE
Database closed.
Database dismounted.
ORACLE instance shut down.
```

Step 2: Modify your initialization parameter file by setting the following parameters:

UNDO_MANAGEMENT = MANUAL

Step 3: Start the database.

```
SQL> STARTUP PFILE=C:\ORACLE\ADMIN\SAM\PFILE\INIT.ORA
ORACLE instance started.

Total System Global Area   135338868 bytes
Fixed Size                    453492 bytes
Variable Size              109051904 bytes
Database Buffers            25165824 bytes
Redo Buffers                  667648 bytes
Database mounted.
Database opened.
```

Step 4: Verify the settings for UNDO segments management:

```
SQL> SHOW PARAMETER UNDO_MANAGEMENT

NAME                                 TYPE        VALUE
------------------------------------ ----------- ------
undo_management                      string      MANUAL
```

Step 5: Show the settings for the parameter ROLLBACK_SEGMENTS to determine if there are any segments online. As you can see, there are no segments online.

```
SQL> SHOW PARAMETER ROLLBACK_SEGMENTS

NAME                                 TYPE        VALUE
------------------------------------ ----------- -----
rollback_segments                    string
```

8

Step 6: Find out if previously created public segments exist.

NOTE

Rollback segments have two ownership classifications:

■ **PUBLIC:** Every user can access and use the segment.

■ **User name:** The segment belongs to a specified user and is accessed only by owner (this classification is usually referred to as a private rollback segment.)

```
SQL> SELECT OWNER, SEGMENT_NAME, STATUS
  2      FROM DBA_ROLLBACK_SEGS
  3  /

OWNER   SEGMENT_NAME                    STATUS
------  ------------------------------  --------
SYS     SYSTEM                          ONLINE
PUBLIC  _SYSSMU1$                       OFFLINE
PUBLIC  _SYSSMU2$                       OFFLINE
PUBLIC  _SYSSMU3$                       OFFLINE
PUBLIC  _SYSSMU4$                       OFFLINE
PUBLIC  _SYSSMU5$                       OFFLINE
PUBLIC  _SYSSMU6$                       OFFLINE
PUBLIC  _SYSSMU7$                       OFFLINE
PUBLIC  _SYSSMU8$                       OFFLINE
PUBLIC  _SYSSMU9$                       OFFLINE
PUBLIC  _SYSSMU10$                      OFFLINE
```

From these results, you can see that SYSTEM created public segments when the database was in Automatic Undo Management mode. The names of public segments starts with an underscore (_). In addition, SYS owns one segment that is for system use only.

Step 7: Create a tablespace for rollback segments. It is recommended to include the RBS in the name of the tablespace to indicate that it is used for manual rollback segments. In this case, name it RBS01

```
SQL> CREATE UNDO TABLESPACE RBS01
  2      DATAFILE
  3      'C:\ORACLE\ORADATA\SAM\RBS01.DBF' SIZE 1000M
  4  /

Tablespace created.
```

Step 8: Create five segments residing on tablespace RBS01 as shown in the following code segment:

```
SQL> CREATE PUBLIC ROLLBACK SEGMENT RBS01
  2      TABLESPACE RBS01 STORAGE ( INITIAL 10M NEXT 10M
  3      OPTIMAL 50M MINEXTENTS 2 MAXEXTENTS UNLIMITED)
  4  /

Rollback segment created.

SQL> CREATE PUBLIC ROLLBACK SEGMENT RBS02
  2      TABLESPACE RBS01 STORAGE ( INITIAL 10M NEXT 10M
  3      OPTIMAL 50M MINEXTENTS 2 MAXEXTENTS UNLIMITED)
  4  /

Rollback segment created.

SQL> CREATE PUBLIC ROLLBACK SEGMENT RBS03
  2      TABLESPACE RBS01 STORAGE ( INITIAL 10M NEXT 10M
  3      OPTIMAL 50M MINEXTENTS 2 MAXEXTENTS UNLIMITED)
  4  /

Rollback segment created.

SQL> CREATE PUBLIC ROLLBACK SEGMENT RBS04
  2      TABLESPACE RBS01 STORAGE ( INITIAL 10M NEXT 10M
  3      OPTIMAL 50M MINEXTENTS 2 MAXEXTENTS UNLIMITED)
  4  /

Rollback segment created.

SQL> CREATE PUBLIC ROLLBACK SEGMENT RBS05
  2      TABLESPACE RBS01 STORAGE ( INITIAL 10M NEXT 10M
  3      OPTIMAL 50M MINEXTENTS 2 MAXEXTENTS UNLIMITED)
  4  /

Rollback segment created.
```

Step 9: Use the same method to create another tablespace with one rollback segment residing on it:

```
SQL> CREATE UNDO TABLESPACE RBS02
  2      DATAFILE
  3      'C:\ORACLE\ORADATA\SAM\RBS02.DBF' SIZE 5000M
  4  /

Tablespace created.

SQL> CREATE PUBLIC ROLLBACK SEGMENT RS_BATCH
  2      TABLESPACE RBS02 STORAGE ( INITIAL 10M NEXT 10M
  3      OPTIMAL 50M MINEXTENTS 2 MAXEXTENTS UNLIMITED)
  4  /

Rollback segment created.
```

Step 10: Verify the creation of the rollback segments by using the following query:

```
SQL> SELECT OWNER, SEGMENT_NAME, STATUS
  2      FROM DBA_ROLLBACK_SEGS
  3  /

OWNER   SEGMENT_NAME                    STATUS
------  ------------------------------  -------
SYS     SYSTEM                          ONLINE
PUBLIC  RBS01                           OFFLINE
PUBLIC  RBS02                           OFFLINE
PUBLIC  RBS03                           OFFLINE
PUBLIC  RBS04                           OFFLINE
PUBLIC  RBS05                           OFFLINE
PUBLIC  RS_BATCH                        OFFLINE
```

NOTE

When you create a new rollback segment, it is offline, which means it cannot be used. You need to turn it online to make it usable.

Step 11: You can turn these segments online automatically by setting the ROLLBACK_SEG-MENTS parameter in the initialization parameter file and restarting the database:

```
SQL> show parameter rollback_segments

NAME                              TYPE          VALUE
-----------------  -----------  ----------------------------
rollback_segments        string rs01, rs02, rs03, rs04, rs05,
                                              rs_batch


OWNER   SEGMENT_NAME                      STATUS
------  ----------------------------  --------
SYS     SYSTEM                            ONLINE
PUBLIC RBS01                             ONLINE
PUBLIC RBS02                             ONLINE
PUBLIC RBS03                             ONLINE
PUBLIC RBS04                             ONLINE
PUBLIC RBS05                             ONLINE
PUBLIC RS_BATCH                          ONLINE
```

In setting the ROLLBACK_SEGMENTS parameters, you encountered the following new terms and statements:

1. The UNDO_MANAGEMENT parameter indicates the management mode for the database. This parameter can be set to one of two settings: AUTO or MANUAL.

2. The ROLLBACK_SEGMENTS parameter is set to any rollback segment that you want to turn online when an Oracle instance is started. No set value indicates that no segments will be turned online. This parameter cannot be turned on if the UNDO_MANAGEMENT parameter is set to AUTO.

3. The DBA_ROLLBACK_SEGS view contains information about all the public and private segments that were created for this database.

4. The CREATE_UNDO_TABLESPACE parameter specifies the storage to be used for UNDO segments.

5. The CREATE PUBLIC ROLLBACK SEGMENT statement creates public or private segments. (The next section explains storage parameters.)

It is worthwhile to examine one more query that produces a listing of all tablespaces. This is useful for determining which tablespace is used for UNDO segments.

```
SQL> SELECT TABLESPACE_NAME, CONTENTS, STATUS
  2    FROM DBA_TABLESPACES
  3    ORDER BY 2
  4    /

TABLESPACE_NAME                    CONTENTS   STATUS
--------------------------------   ---------  ------
SYSTEM                             PERMANENT  ONLINE
CWMLITE                            PERMANENT  ONLINE
DRSYS                              PERMANENT  ONLINE
EXAMPLE                            PERMANENT  ONLINE
ODM                                PERMANENT  ONLINE
USERS                              PERMANENT  ONLINE
XDB                                PERMANENT  ONLINE
TOOLS                              PERMANENT  ONLINE
INDX                               PERMANENT  ONLINE
TEMP                               TEMPORARY  ONLINE
TEMP01                             TEMPORARY  ONLINE
RBS01                              UNDO       ONLINE
RBS02                              UNDO       ONLINE
```

8

As you can see, you created the two online tablespaces: RBS01 and RBS02.

Automatic Management

Ruby just graduated from a DBA program offered by one of the local training schools in her town. She was hired as a junior DBA consultant for a nationwide consulting firm. On her first week of employment, she was placed at a client site assisting a team of DBAs performing routine tasks. On her first day at the client site, she was confronted with a problem and was not sure how to resolve it, so she sent an e-mail to her instructor asking for advice on how to tackle this problem. She wrote:

"My client has 14 rollback segments and 30 concurrent users logged in performing transactions. Users are facing unusually long waits on rollback segments especially when we have many of them online. What do you recommend I do?"

Do you want to face similar problems, or do you prefer to have a worry-free approach? This section presents details on how to configure your database to use automatic UNDO segments.

Manual management of UNDO segments is not recommended and requires significant management effort. As stated previously, Oracle9*i* introduced the automatic management of UNDO segments to free you for more important tasks. Of course, every DBA's objective is to have the optimal database performance with the least effort, and you should feel fortunate to be working with current databases. Fifteen years ago, many DBAs struggled with the tedious task of managing the rollback segments of Oracle 5 and could not imagine the ease of Automatic Undo Management.

The UNDO_MANAGEMENT initialization parameter cannot be changed dynamically.

NOTE

You will set four parameters to configure your database for Automatic Undo Management. The following SQL*Plus query displays the four parameters, and Table 8-1 describes them:

```
SQL> SHOW PARAMETER UNDO

NAME                                 TYPE        VALUE
------------------------------------ ----------- --------
undo_management                      string      MANUAL
undo_retention                       integer     10800
undo_suppress_errors                 boolean     FALSE
undo_tablespace                      string      UNDOTBS1
```

AUM stands for Automatic Undo Management, and SMU for System-Managed Undo.

TIP

Table 8-1 Automatic Undo Management initialization parameters

Parameter	Value
UNDO_MANAGEMENT	Possible values for this parameter include: AUTO for Automatic Undo Management and MANUAL for Manual Undo Management. The default value is AUTO.
UNDO_RETENTION	This parameter specifies in seconds how long the BEFORE image is to be stored in the UNDO segments. The default value is 900 seconds, which is 15 minutes.
UNDO_SUPRESS_ERRORS	This parameter instructs Oracle to suppress errors generated by issuing rollback segment operations when the database is configured in AUM. Possible values are TRUE or FALSE. The default value is FALSE, which means errors are not suppressed.
UNDO_TABLESPACE	This parameter specifies the undo tablespace assigned for UNDO segments in AUM.

The information in this table is derived from the online documentation that Oracle provides at the Oracle Technology Network site: *www.otn.oracle.com*.

Only one undo tablespace can be online.

NOTE

To strengthen your understanding of the four parameters outlined in Table 8-1, imagine yourself in another scenario. Suppose after running your Oracle9*i* database in Manual Undo Management mode for three months and researching your options, you decide to switch your database to AUM. Follow these steps to configure your database:

Step 1: Begin by dropping existing tablespaces created for rollback segments. Note that you could leave existing tablespaces to be used for AUM. You may need to turn all rollback segments offline before dropping tablespaces.

```
SQL> ALTER ROLLBACK SEGMENT RBS01 OFFLINE
  2  /

Rollback segment altered.

SQL> ALTER ROLLBACK SEGMENT RBS02 OFFLINE
  2  /

Rollback segment altered.

SQL> ALTER ROLLBACK SEGMENT RBS03 OFFLINE
  2  /

Rollback segment altered.

SQL> ALTER ROLLBACK SEGMENT RBS04 OFFLINE
  2  /

Rollback segment altered.

SQL> ALTER ROLLBACK SEGMENT RBS04 OFFLINE
  2  /

Rollback segment altered.

SQL> DROP TABLESPACE RBS01
  2  /

Tablespace dropped.
```

NOTE

The following statement demonstrates how to create an undo tablespace in the CREATE DATABASE statement:
```
SQL> CREATE DATABASE BLA
        . . .
     UNDO TABLESPACE UNDO_TS01
         DATAFILE 'C:\ORACLE\ORADATA\BLA\
UNDO_TS01.DBF' SIZE 100M
        . . .
```

Step 2: If you dropped all undo tablespaces because they were named RBS, you must create at least one UNDO segment. In this case you can call it UNDO_TS01:

```
SQL> CREATE UNDO TABLESPACE UNDO_TS01
  2      DATAFILE
  3      'c:\oracle\oradata\SAM\undo_ts01.dbf' size 1000M
  4  /
```

NOTE If a tablespace is either used by an active transaction or it is the only undo tablespace that exists, you cannot drop it.

Step 3: Shut down the database gracefully:

```
SQL> SHUTDOWN IMMEDIATE
Database closed.
Database dismounted.
ORACLE instance shut down.
```

NOTE Whenever Oracle creates an UNDO segment automatically, it records the event in the alert log file.

Step 4: Modify the initialization parameter file to set the following parameters:

```
UNDO_MANAGEMENT=AUTO
UNDO_RETENTION=900
UNDO_SUPPRESS_ERRORS=FALSE
UNDO_TABLESPACE=UNDO_TS01
```

NOTE If your database is set to Automatic Undo Management and you do not specify a tablespace, an alert is written to the alert log when you start the database, and Oracle does not allow any user transactions.

Step 5: Start the database:

```
SQL> STARTUP PFILE=C:\ORACLE\ADMIN\SAM\PFILE\INIT.ORA
ORACLE instance started.

Total System Global Area   135338868 bytes
Fixed Size                    453492 bytes
Variable Size              109051904 bytes
Database Buffers            25165824 bytes
Redo Buffers                  667648 bytes
Database mounted.
Database opened.
```

NOTE

You cannot drop an undo tablespace if the tablespace is being used by an active transaction or it is the only undo tablespace.

Step 6: Verify the settings:

8

```
SQL> SHOW PARAMETER UNDO

NAME                                 TYPE         VALUE
------------------------------------ ----------- ---------
undo_management                      string       AUTO
undo_retention                       integer      900
undo_suppress_errors                 boolean      FALSE
undo_tablespace                      string       undo_ts01
```

Step 7: Verify the undo tablespace:

```
SQL> SELECT TABLESPACE_NAME, CONTENTS, STATUS
  2      FROM DBA_TABLESPACES
  3   ORDER BY CONTENTS
  4  /

TABLESPACE_NAME                      CONTENTS   STATUS
------------------------------------ ---------- ------
SYSTEM                               PERMANENT  ONLINE
CWMLITE                              PERMANENT  ONLINE
DRSYS                                PERMANENT  ONLINE
INDX                                 PERMANENT  ONLINE
TOOLS                                PERMANENT  ONLINE
XDB                                  PERMANENT  ONLINE
USERS                                PERMANENT  ONLINE
ODM                                  PERMANENT  ONLINE
EXAMPLE                              PERMANENT  ONLINE
TEMP                                 TEMPORARY  ONLINE
TEMP01                               TEMPORARY  ONLINE
UNDO_TS01                            UNDO       ONLINE
```

Step 8: Verify the UNDO segments:

```
SQL> SELECT OWNER, SEGMENT_NAME, TABLESPACE_NAME, STATUS
  2     FROM DBA_ROLLBACK_SEGS
  3  /

OWNER    SEGMENT_NAME     TABLESPACE_NAME              STATUS
------   ---------------  ---------------------------  -------
SYS      SYSTEM           SYSTEM                       ONLINE
PUBLIC   _SYSSMU1$        UNDO_TS01                    ONLINE
PUBLIC   _SYSSMU2$        UNDO_TS01                    ONLINE
PUBLIC   _SYSSMU3$        UNDO_TS01                    ONLINE
PUBLIC   _SYSSMU4$        UNDO_TS01                    ONLINE
PUBLIC   _SYSSMU5$        UNDO_TS01                    ONLINE
PUBLIC   _SYSSMU6$        UNDO_TS01                    ONLINE
PUBLIC   _SYSSMU7$        UNDO_TS01                    ONLINE
PUBLIC   _SYSSMU8$        UNDO_TS01                    ONLINE
PUBLIC   _SYSSMU9$        UNDO_TS01                    ONLINE
PUBLIC   _SYSSMU10$       UNDO_TS01                    ONLINE
```

As you can see from the steps in the preceding practice, you need only create one undo tablespace for UNDO segments, set the AUM, and off you go. Oracle manages the number of segments to put online or offline and the settings of these segments.

At this point, you can distinguish between the two undo management modes and can set your database in each mode. You are therefore ready to learn the guidelines for sizing segments for each mode and the sizing procedures for UNDO segments.

SIZING GUIDELINES

Proper configuration of any parameter or any database component is the first step to achieving optimal performance. Some settings are based on previous or existing databases, some settings are based on experience, and others are based on guidelines that are set by either Oracle or DBA experts, or both. For UNDO segments, you will use guidelines as well as a process for initial sizing. You start by examining the rollback segments as manual UNDO segments and the UNDO segments as automatic UNDO segments.

Sizing Rollback Segments

Tuning rollback segments is a tricky task. As a DBA, you must pay attention to the type of transactions, longevity of transactions, and most importantly, the concurrency of these transactions. In addition, you must pay attention to these issues from the minute the database application is in the conception phase until at least three months after the database is in production.

You previously used the CREATE ROLLBACK SEGMENT statement without an explanation of the storage parameters. Table 8-2 outlines guidelines associated with each storage option.

Table 8-2 Guidelines for rollback segments storage parameters

Storage option	Description	Recommended value
INITIAL	Number of bytes allocated for the first extent	Should be set to the average transaction size multiplied by the number of concurrent transactions
NEXT	Number of bytes allocated for new extents. INITIAL & NEXT must be set the same size.	Should be the same size as INITIAL extents
OPTIMAL	Number of rollback segments bytes allocated at all times to avoid shrinking of the segment to a size less than the optimal setting. This value should not be below or equal to INITIAL+NEXT extent setting.	Should be set to the average size of the largest transactions multiplied by the number of concurrent transactions
MINEXTENTS	Number of extents to be allocated initially. This value cannot be less than two extents.	Two to twenty extents
MAXEXTENTS	Total number of extents that can be allocated for the rollback segment. This value could be defaulted to UNLIMITED.	UNLIMITED

The information in this table is derived from the online documentation that Oracle provides at the Oracle Technology Network site: *www.otn.oracle.com*.

Now that you understand the storage parameters of rollback segments more fully, you can learn how to calculate the average number of transactions and the number of concurrent transactions. To accomplish this, you use the dynamic performance view V$TRANSACTION. This view contains statistical data for each pending transaction in the database. Table 8–3 lists only the columns of the V$TRANSACTION view that are used in the query:

Table 8-3 Most frequently used columns of V$TRANSACTION view

Column	Description
ADDR	Transaction address in memory
XIDUSN	Rollback segment identification number, used to join with V$ROLLNAME to display rollback segment name
STATUS	Status of the transaction
USED_UBLK	Number of rollback segment blocks used for the transaction

The information in this table is derived from the online documentation that Oracle provides at the Oracle Technology Network site: *www.otn.oracle.com*.

You can obtain the average transaction size by following these steps:

Step 1: Determine the peak time for transaction activities.

Step 2: Issue the following query during peak activity:

```
SQL> SELECT ADDR, XIDUSN, STATUS, USED_UBLK
  2    FROM V$TRANSACTION
  3  /

ADDR          XIDUSN STATUS             USED_UBLK
-------- ---------- ---------------- ----------
79395D64          2 ACTIVE               16080
7939ABAC          1 ACTIVE                 137
7939F9F4          4 ACTIVE                3005
```

This query displays all active transactions with the number of blocks used by each rollback segment. You are examining the total number of concurrent transactions as well as the total number of blocks. From the results of this query, you can see that the total number of concurrent transactions is three and the total number of used blocks is 19222 (that is, Oracle blocks), which yields to 6407 blocks for the average transaction. Another way to get these results is by issuing the following query:

```
SQL> SELECT COUNT(*) CONCURRENT_TRANS,
  2          AVG(USED_UBLK) AVERAGE_TRANSACTION_SIZE
  3    FROM V$TRANSACTION
  4  /

CONCURRENT_TRANS AVERAGE_TRANSACTION_SIZE
---------------- ------------------------
               3              6407.33333
```

Step 3: You need to set INITIAL extent equal to 6408 (average transaction size) multiplied by eight concurrent transactions, which equals 51264 Oracle blocks. Set the NEXT extents to 51264 Oracle blocks, as well.

To compute the OPTIMAL storage, determine the average size of the large transactions. Suppose that large transactions are consuming between 10000 to 15000 blocks. This means that the median of large transaction is 12500 blocks; therefore, set OPTIMAL to 12500 blocks.

The V$ROLLSTAT dynamic performance view can also help you determine how to set rollback segments storage options. The content of this view is statistical data for every online rollback segment in the database. Table 8-4 describes the most frequently used columns of the V$ROLLSTAT view.

Table 8-4 Most frequently used columns of V$ROLLSTAT view

Column	Description
USN	Rollback segment identification number
EXTENTS	Number of extents allocated in the rollback segment
RSSIZE	Size of the rollback segment in bytes
WRITES	Number of bytes written to the rollback segment
XACTS	Number of active transactions in the rollback segment
GETS	Number of rollback segment header gets. Every time space in rollback segments is requested, a get is recorded.
WAITS	Number of times a request had to wait for a header get
SHRINKS	Number of times the rollback segments was shrunk
WRAPS	Number of times the rollback segments wrapped to the beginning of the segment, because it ran out of space
EXTENDS	Number of times the rollback segment extended
AVESHRINK	Average size of the rollback segment shrinkage
AVEACTIVE	Average size of active extents
STATUS	Rollback status (ONLINE, OFFLINE, PENDING OFFLINE, FULL)

The information in this table is derived from the online documentation that Oracle provides at the Oracle Technology Network site: *www.otn.oracle.com*.

Table 8-4 presents column descriptions of V$ROLLSTAT and includes three important columns: EXTENDS, SHRINKS, and WRAPS. You should understand the implications of these three columns on performance. Figure 8-9 illustrates these three terms as they are explained in this list:

1. The rollback segment structure contains a segment header (one data block) where it stores transaction tables and controls the writing of transactions to the segment. Each transaction frequently accesses the header. An extent is a physical allocation of space, and every segment must have at least two extents.

2. This is a rollback segment with two extents and no transactions.

3. Transaction 1 is stored within the allocated extents; no additional space is required.

4. Transaction 2 required an additional extent. This mean that the rollback segment extended one extent to fit this transaction, and this operation is referred to as an EXTENDS.

5. Because transaction 2 was committed, data in rollback segments is no longer needed, so the rollback shrinks back to OPTIMAL size. In this case the segment gives up one extent. This operation is referred to as SHRINKS. The SMON (System Monitor) background process is responsible for shrinking UNDO segments as required.

6. Transaction 1 is too large to fit into the segment and therefore it wraps around to write over from the beginning of the segment. This operation is known as a WRAPS.

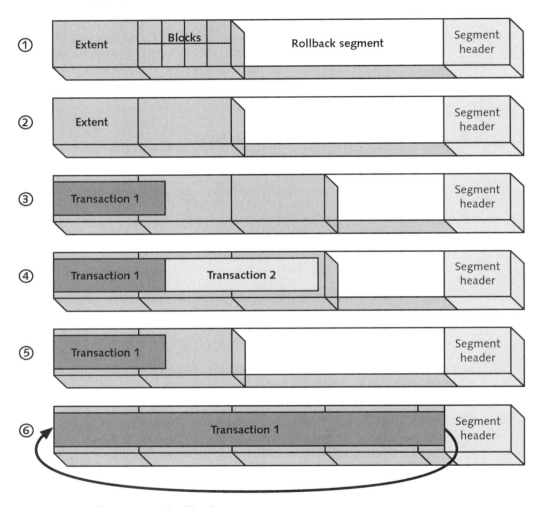

Figure 8-9   Illustration of rollback segments terms

Table 8-5 presents rollback segment guidelines to assist you in configuring the number of rollback segments and their size for different types of applications. When you examine Table 8-5, you should be able to answer the following question: "What does SMALL segment size and LARGE segment size mean?" The answer to this question is based on the type of application transaction. Normally, transactions for an OLTP application are considered to be small, because the processing involves only updating, inserting, or deleting a few rows. So the amount of space needed for an OLTP transaction is small.

Table 8-5   Rollback segment guidelines for different types of applications

Application Type	Number of segments	Size of segment	Extent size
OLTP	Many	Small	8 KB, 16 KB, 32 KB, 64 KB
DSS	Few	Large	128 KB, 256 KB, 512 KB, 1 MB
Hybrid	Many	Many Small Few Large	For OLTP transactions, follow OLTP guidelines. For DSS transactions, follow DSS guidelines.

In addition to rollback segment guidelines, you should know facts about the cost of DML statements with respect to rollback segment generation. The following list outlines the cost of different transaction types:

- **DELETE:** Is the most expensive transaction, because it must save the BEFORE image of the whole row.

- **UPDATE:** Is the next most expensive transaction. It stores the BEFORE image of only the columns that were modified.

- **INSERT:** Is the least expensive transaction, because it saves only the rowid of the row in the rollback. The BEFORE image is restored by merely removing the new row.

- **INDEX:** Is another expensive transaction, because it involves changes in the table as well as in the index as it saves the old index value, as well as the new index value in the rollback segment.

The TRUNCATE command purges all records in a table without the capability to undo the command. This command is more efficient than the DELETE statement if the rows to be purged do not need to be rolled back. The TRUNCATE command does not save the before image in the rollback segments.

For example, suppose a customer orders four items from the ACME Company. This transaction requires the addition of one row in the ORDERS table and four rows in the ORDER_LINES table. The rollback segment cost is the amount of space needed to store the rowid for five rows. With transactions for a DSS application, you usually insert a large number of rows; such an insertion requires a larger amount of space than for OLTP. Again, you need to quantify small and large amounts of space. This is done by measuring the transaction size as was outlined earlier in this section.

Transactions involving Large Object columns do not use rollback segments. They use, instead, segment space specified by the PCTVERSION clause.

It is useful for you to learn another method for calculating the volume of undo data for any rollback segment. Suppose the PRODUCT_PRICES table is refreshed nightly via a feed process and you want to know how much undo data is generated by this process in a development environment. There are at least two approaches to refresh this table.

Approach 1

To determine how much undo data is generated by the feed process, follow these steps:

1. Read a line from the feed file.

2. Find a product match in the PRODUCT_PRICES table for this line and update the price; if there is no match, perform Step 3. If a row exists in the table but does not exist in the feed file, perform Step 4.

3. Insert a new row with the new processed values.

4. Delete the existing row that does not have a match in the feed file.

In this approach, Steps 2, 3, and 4 generate undo data, whereas in Approach 2, only Step 2 generates undo data.

Approach 2

1. Delete all rows from the table.

2. Insert all rows into the table from a file.

Focusing again on undo data measurement, follow these steps to compute the volume of the undo data that Approach 2 produces:

Step 1: Log on as SYSTEM and get the current statistics for each rollback segment using the V$ROLLSTAT. Issue the following query:

```
SQL> SELECT USN,
  2          RSSIZE,
  3          WRITES,
  4          SHRINKS,
  5          EXTENDS
  6      FROM V$ROLLSTAT
  7  /

       USN      RSSIZE      WRITES    SHRINKS     EXTENDS
---------- ---------- ---------- ---------- ----------
         0      385024      296220          0           0
        21      122880    44405892          0           0
        22      122880    44343024          0           0
        23      122880    44327790          0           0
```

Step 2: Log on as TUNER, and create a temp table to hold all the data in the PRODUCT_PRICES table. Submit the following query:

```
SQL> CREATE TABLE PP_TEMP AS
  2      SELECT * FROM PRODUCT_PRICES
  3  /
```

Step 3: Delete the PRODUCT_PRICES table:

```
SQL> DELETE PRODUCT_PRICES
  2  /
```

Step 4: Insert all data back into PRODUCT_PRICES using the temporary table:

```
SQL> INSERT INTO PRODUCT_PRICES
  2      SELECT * FROM PP_TEMP
  3  /
```

Step 5: As SYSTEM, issue the following query to get the statistics of the rollback segments as in Step 1:

```
SQL> SELECT USN,
  2         RSSIZE,
  3         WRITES,
  4         SHRINKS,
  5         EXTENDS
  6    FROM V$ROLLSTAT
  7  /
```

USN	RSSIZE	WRITES	SHRINKS	EXTENDS
0	385024	296220	0	0
21	122880	44488212	0	0
22	122880	44422176	0	0
23	3137536	47049788	0	16

Step 6: Notice that the size and writes of rollback segment 23 have changed. In this step, you need to calculate the difference between the before and after transactions as shown in Table 8-6.

Table 8-6 Before and after transactions calculation

Rollback segment 23	RSSIZE value	WRITES value
Before	122880	44327790
After	3137536	47049788
Difference	3014656	2721998

As you can see, the undo data volume is 2721998 bytes which is about 2.6 MB.

Step 7: Drop the temp table PP_TEMP:

```
SQL> DROP TABLE PP_TEMP
  2  /
```

From the complexity of the steps you have performed, you can see why Oracle introduced the automatic UNDO segments. Now you are ready to learn how to size these UNDO segments.

Sizing Undo Segments

At this point, you can appreciate learning another way to manage UNDO segments without worrying so much about the size of transactions and number of segments. To size automatic UNDO segments, you must determine how much committed data you want to keep in the UNDO segments before it is overwritten. This is related to the UNDO_RETENTION parameter, which tells Oracle how long committed data should stay in the UNDO segments before it is overwritten.

To put this into perspective, suppose you decided to retain committed data in the UNDO segments for one hour. This means that to avoid errors caused by running out of space, you need enough space on the UNDO segments for all transactions submitted in that hour. If you know the number of generated undo blocks per second, the formula becomes obvious. The following formula for sizing automatic undo management specifies that the undo space required is equal to the undo retention time multiplied by the number of generated bytes per second.

```
Undo Size = undo retention * undo bytes
```

The terms used in the formula are defined as follows:

- **Undo retention:** duration in seconds required to retain undo data in UNDO segments

- **Undo bytes:** number of bytes generated for undo data by all transactions per second

You already know the value of undo retention from the UNDO_RETENTION parameter value that you set based on business requirements. The second part of the formula is undo bytes, which can be obtained from the V$UNDOSTAT dynamic performance view, which contains statistics about all UNDO segments that are online. Table 8-7 describes the column of this view.

NOTE

Each row in V$UNDOSTAT represents a ten minute interval.

Table 8-7   Column description of the V$UNDOSTAT view

Column	Description
BEGIN_TIME	Start of the time interval, each interval is ten minutes
END_TIME	End of time interval
UNDOTSN	Tablespace number that is active for this interval
UNDOBLKS	Number of undo blocks consumed for this interval
TXNCOUNT	Number of transactions during this interval
MAXQUERYLEN	The longest execution for a query in seconds during this interval
MAXCONCURRENCY	Maximum number of concurrent transactions during this interval
UNXPSSTEALCNT	Number of times Oracle attempted to steal unexpired extents from other transactions during this interval
UNXPBLKRELCNT	Number of unexpired blocks removed from an UNDO segment to be used by other transactions in this interval
UNXPBLKREUCNT	Number of unexpired blocks reused by transactions
EXPSTEALCNT	Number of times Oracle attempted to steal expired extents from other transactions during this interval
EXPBLKRELCNT	Number of expired blocks stolen from other segments for this interval
EXPBLKREUCNT	Number of expired blocks reused within the same segment in this interval
SSOLDERRCNT	Number of times the SNAPSHOT TOO OLD Oracle error, ORA-01555, occurred. This is caused by wrapping.
NOSPACEERRCNT	Number of times a request for space failed because there was no space available

The information in this table is derived from the online documentation that Oracle provides at the Oracle Technology Network site: *www.otn.oracle.com*.

NOTE

When configuring Automatic Undo Management for a Real Application Cluster, you must create an undo tablespace for each instance.

Using this view, you can get the number of undo blocks used for a certain period of time from the UNDOBLKS column value. You'll probably need to issue the following query during peak time when the database is busy with transactions:

```
SQL> SELECT SUM(UNDOBLKS)/
  2         SUM( (END_TIME - BEGIN_TIME)*24*60*60)
  3         BLOCKS_PER_SECOND
  4    FROM V$UNDOSTAT
  5  /

BLOCKS_PER_SECOND
-----------------
       1797.48061
```

Date difference results in days. 1 day is 24*60*60

Of course, you are looking for bytes per second, not blocks per second, so you need to multiply this number by the block size, which is set by the DB_BLOCK_SIZE parameter. In this case, it is 8192, which results in a value of 14724961.15712 bytes per second. Applying this value and the undo retention value (1 hour = 60*60) to the formula results in the following:

```
Undo Size = undo retention * bytes per second
Undo Size = (60*60) * 14724961.15712 = 53009860165.632
Undo Size = 53009860165.632/1024/1024/1024 = 49.34 GB
```

In addition to this value, you need to add space for the overhead that Oracle uses (one Oracle block) and add extra space for exceptional transactions that may take more space. A reasonable value is 1% to 5%. In this case, if a 1% buffer is used, 49.86 GB is required for the UNDO segments.

You could consider this value very large, but don't be surprised. If your application is generating this amount of undo data and your business requirement is to retain one hour of UNDO segments, this value becomes understandable. Also, you probably noticed that if the retention duration is much higher, it requires proportionally more space.

To pull all these concepts together and derive one query to compute the undo size value, examine this query:

```
SQL>  SELECT UNDO_RETENTION *
  2          ( BLOCKS_PER_SECOND * BLOCK_SIZE ) * 1.01
  3          UNDO_SIZE
  4    FROM (SELECT VALUE UNDO_RETENTION
  5             FROM V$PARAMETER
  6            WHERE NAME = 'undo_retention'
  7          ) RETENTION,
  8          (SELECT VALUE BLOCK_SIZE
  9             FROM V$PARAMETER
 10            WHERE NAME = 'db_block_size'
 11          ) BLOCK,
 12          (SELECT SUM(UNDOBLKS)/
 13                 SUM( (END_TIME - BEGIN_TIME)*24*60*60)
 14                 BLOCKS_PER_SECOND
 15             FROM V$UNDOSTAT
 16          ) UNDO_BLOCKS
 17  /

     UNDO_SIZE
--------------
52285115.98368
```

You can see that this query is handy for determining the UNDO segments needed for the undo retention feature. Another point needs to be emphasized at this time: This query provides a close estimate of the UNDO segment size for a database in production, meaning databases that are already created. What about new databases? The answer is to collect these measurements while an application in development is in the *testing* phase. To start, use the highest reading as a size for the UNDO segments.

NOTE
If you want to switch the undo tablespace from one to another undo tablespace, use the following statement:
```
SQL> ALTER SYSTEM SET UNDO_TABLESPACE=UNEWUNDO_TS;
```

When you issue this statement, all new transactions are to be stored in the new tablespace and pending transactions that are stored in an UNDO segment in the old tablespace will show the status of PENDING_OFFLINE when viewing V$ROLLSTAT.

Your result is used to create an undo tablespace or resize an existing tablespace to the proper size as shown in this query:

```
SQL> CREATE UNDO TABLESPACE UNDO_TS01
  2  DATAFILE
  3  'c:\oracle\oradata\SAM\undo_ts01.dbf' size 52285116
  4  /
```

After you establish rollback segments or UNDO segments for your database, your next step is to monitor these structures to ensure that you do not get errors during transactions. The cost of transaction failure is summarized by this list:

- Lost time for the user to re-enter the transaction

- Loss application credibility because of frequent errors

- User frustration when he needs to re-enter transactions

- Excessive DBA time spent on fixing this error impedes progress on more important issues

In the next section, you learn how to diagnose rollback segments to proactively prevent errors. You learn to diagnose UNDO segments in both Automatic Undo Management and Manual Undo Management modes.

Diagnosing Rollback Segments

No matter what magic or precision formula you use, you still need to monitor rollback or UNDO segments to detect problems before they occur. As mentioned previously, experiencing errors during transactions because of UNDO segment space issues should not happen. These must be eliminated. In this section, you explore different methods for diagnosing rollback or UNDO segments.

To understand these concepts in a real-world context, imagine that you have just configured the rollback segments to the best of your ability for a database that will be commissioned next week. You need a rest and you deserve it, but the real work on the rollback segments has not yet started. You will have to spend time monitoring this component of the database to prevent any transaction losses or contention, and you therefore need to put diagnostic tools in place that alert you on a regular basis.

In this situation, you should consider three types of contention diagnosis: header contention, segment contention, and buffer contention. The following sections describe each type of diagnosis in detail, stating the cause, the remedy, and a query to detect the problem. You should also consult two dynamic performance views to troubleshoot rollback segments: V$ROLLSTAT, which was presented earlier in this chapter, and V$WAITSTAT, which contains system wait statistics.

Rollback Segments Statistics

Proper setting of the OPTIMAL option and optimal setting of the rollback segment can prevent unnecessary I/O caused by extending and shrinking of extents. First examine how this prevention works. The following query reports statistics obtained from the V$ROLL-STAT and V$ROLLNAME views:

```
SQL> SELECT NAME SEGMENT_NAME,
  2          OPTSIZE OPTIMAL,
  3          SHRINKS,
  4          WRAPS,
  5          EXTENDS,
  6          AVESHRINK,
  7          AVEACTIVE
  8     FROM V$ROLLSTAT S, V$ROLLNAME R
  9    WHERE S.USN = R.USN
 10    /

SEGMENT_NAME     OPTIMAL SHRINKS   WRAPS EXTENDS AVESHRINK  AVEACTIVE
------------  ---------- ------- ------- ------- --------- ----------
RBS00           50331648       0       8       0         0    3294913
RBS01           50331648       0       6       0         0    2456597
RBS02           50331648       0       6       0         0    2456059
RBS03           50331648       0       7       0         0    2734789
RBS04           50331648       0       6       0         0    2455860
RBS05           50331648       0       5       0         0    2146347
RBS06           50331648       0       6       0         0    2455860
RBS07           50331648       0       6       0         0    2456597
RBS08           50331648       0       6       0         0    2456059
RBS09           50331648       0       6       0         0    2456113
RBS10           50331648       0      10       0         0    4421498
RBS11           50331648       0       5       0         0    2147011
RBS12           50331648       0       5       0         0    2147011
RBS13           50331648       0       8       0         0    2985253
RBS14           50331648       0      10       0         0    5796779
RBS15           50331648       0       6       0         0    2456597
RBS16           50331648       0       3       0         0    2840903
RBS17           50331648       0       6       0         0    2455860
```

Table 8-8 shows how to interpret these results:

Table 8-8   Column values interpretation of the V$ROLLSTAT view

Column	Interpretation
SHRINKS	**Low:** This value should be checked with EXTENDS. **High:** This value indicates that the setting of the OPTIMAL value is not high enough.
WRAPS	**Low:** A value very close to zero is good. **High:** A high value indicates that the rollback segment is too small.

Column	Interpretation
EXTENDS	This value along with SHRINKS indicates whether or not OPTIMAL is set properly.

SHRINKS	EXTENDS	OPTIMAL
LOW	LOW	GOOD
LOW	HIGH	TOO SMALL
HIGH	LOW	TOO LARGE
HIGH	HIGH	BAD

Column	Interpretation
AVESHRINK	A HIGH value indicates that OPTIMAL is too small; otherwise, check EXTENDS and SHRINKS.
AVEACTIVE	If average active is much smaller than the OPTIMAL value, it indicates that the setting for OPTIMAL is too high. If average active is much larger than OPTIMAL, it indicates that the setting for optimal is too small. If average active is close to OPTIMAL, it indicates that OPTIMAL is set properly.

The information in this table is derived from the online documentation that Oracle provides at the Oracle Technology Network site: *www.otn.oracle.com*.

Looking at results with the assistance of this table, you can determine that the OPTIMAL value for most rollback segments is not set properly. Why should you worry about the OPTIMAL value? Simply, because improper settings of this value causes I/O which in turn degrades performance. I/O occurs because each time the rollback segment extends a new extent, it must be physically allocated. The same is true for shrinking, which deallocates extents.

Rollback Segment Block Header Contention

This type of diagnosis determines if there are transactions contending to write to the header of the rollback segment. If the header is busy, transactions must wait. To remedy this symptom, create more rollback segments. You should consult the V$ROLLSTAT view to determine if there is contention. The following query displays the header contention ratio for each rollback segment. The threshold of this ratio should be less than one percent.

```
SQL> SELECT NAME RBS_NAME,
  2          GETS,
  3          WAITS,
  4          ROUND ( (WAITS/GETS)*100 ,2) HEADER_RATIO
  5     FROM V$ROLLNAME R, V$ROLLSTAT S
  6    WHERE S.USN = R.USN
  7    /

RBS_NAME         GETS       WAITS HEADER_RATIO
---------- ---------- ---------- ------------
SYSTEM          10351          0            0
RBS00           41457          1            0
RBS01           40700          1            0
RBS02           40608          1            0
RBS03           41061          2            0
RBS04           39962          0            0
RBS05           40225          4          .01
RBS06           38512          0            0
RBS07           40058          3          .01
RBS08           39568          2          .01
RBS09           39462          0            0
RBS10           39106          1            0
RBS11           39324          1            0
RBS12           40430          2            0
RBS13           39214          1            0
RBS14           39484          4          .01
RBS15           39184          2          .01
RBS16           39135          0          .01
RBS17           38779          2          .01
RBS18           38400          4          .01
RBS19           38303          1            0
RBS20           38095          1            0
RBS21           38290          2          .01
RBS22           37551          5          .01
BIGRB1          90539         79          .09
```

8

As you can see, the results of this query show no alarming values that indicate serious contention for rollback segment block headers.

After determining that there is no serious contention for rollback segment block headers, you should issue the following query to determine the header ratio for all rollback segments. The threshold for this ratio is five percent.

```
SQL> SELECT  SUM(GETS),
   2          SUM(WAITS),
   3          ROUND (SUM(WAITS)/SUM(GETS)*100 ,2) HEADER_RATIO
   4    FROM V$ROLLNAME R, V$ROLLSTAT S
   5   WHERE S.USN = R.USN
   6  /

 SUM(GETS) SUM(WAITS) HEADER_RATIO
---------- ---------- ------------
   1729057      18460         1.07
```

Again, the result does not indicate any contention in the rollback segment configuration. In other words, transactions are not waiting for a header to be free; it is available almost 99 percent of the time.

Segment Header Contention

Segment header contention results when transactions are contending for updates in the segment header. The following query uses V$SYSTEM_EVENT to determine if there is contention. If you increase the number of rollback segments, there will be no waits.

```
SELECT EVENT,
       TOTAL_WAITS,
       TIME_WAITED
  FROM V$SYSTEM_EVENT
 WHERE EVENT LIKE '%undo%'
/
```

Rollback Segment Buffers Contention

This type of diagnosis determines if there is any contention for free rollback segments. Suppose you created too few rollback segments for a highly active database. As a result, transactions contend for free space on these segments.

To remedy this situation, first, examine the V$WAITSTAT dynamic performance view, which contains wait statistics related to rollback segments. Table 8-9 describes the wait statistics.

Table 8-9   Description of wait statistics for rollback segments

Statistics name	Description
SYSTEM UNDO HEADER	Number of times a transaction waited for header blocks of SYSTEM rollback segment
SYSTEM UNDO BLOCK	Number of times waited for blocks of SYSTEM rollback segment
UNDO HEADER	Number of times waited for header blocks of PUBLIC rollback segments
UNDO BLOCKS	Number of times waited for blocks of PUBLIC rollback segment

The information in this table is derived from the online documentation that Oracle provides at the Oracle Technology Network site: *www.otn.oracle.com*.

NOTE

The TIMED_STATISTICS parameter must be turned on to collect V$WAITSTAT statistics.

The following query displays a ratio to determine if there is contention for buffers that contain rollback segments. In other words, you are trying to compare the number of times the system waited for data blocks in rollback segments to the number of blocks read. A ratio that is consistently more than one percent implies that you should increase the number of rollback segments. This query uses V$WAITSTAT and V$SYSSTAT view:

```
SQL> SELECT ((W1.COUNT+W2.COUNT+W3.COUNT+W4.COUNT)/
  2          (ST1.VALUE+ST2.VALUE))*100 RATIO
  3    FROM V$WAITSTAT W1,
  4          V$WAITSTAT W2,
  5          V$WAITSTAT W3,
  6          V$WAITSTAT W4,
  7          V$SYSSTAT ST1,
  8          V$SYSSTAT ST2
  9   WHERE W1.CLASS = 'system undo header'
 10     AND W2.CLASS = 'system undo block'
 11     AND W3.CLASS = 'undo header'
 12     AND W4.CLASS = 'undo block'
 13     AND ST1.NAME = 'db block gets'
 14     AND ST2.NAME = 'db block changes'
 15   /

     RATIO
----------
 2.14733915
```

The result of this query is alarming because it is higher than one percent. If running this query at regular intervals results in a consistently high calculation of this ratio, you should consider creating more rollback segments. You may want to start by adding one rollback segment and continue monitoring. Add rollback segments until contention is stabilized with a ratio less than one percent.

As you can see, if any of these diagnoses detect contention, the remedy is quite simple: just create more rollback segments to reduce the contention. Although the remedy is simple, you can do without the constant monitoring, which requires your decisions on when to add and when not to add rollback segments.

Rollback Segment Usage

Monitoring is a routine task for DBAs. You may have fancy tools that automatically alarm you when a certain threshold is reached or you may have the basic scripts that you run periodically to produce the reports to be analyzed to detect problems. In either case, you need to write the query to be used by the fancy tool or the script. The following query can be used to produce a rollback segment usage report, which displays all current transactions and rollback segments used by the transaction:

```
SQL> SELECT R.NAME SEGMENT_NAME,
  2           S.USERNAME,
  3           S.OSUSER,
  4           S.SID,
  5           S.SERIAL#,
  6           T.USED_UBLK TRANS_USED,
  7           RS.AVEACTIVE,
  8           RS.EXTENDS,
  9           RS.WAITS,
 10           RS.SHRINKS,
 11           RS.WRAPS
 12     FROM V$ROLLSTAT RS,
 13           V$ROLLNAME R,
 14           V$SESSION S,
 15           V$TRANSACTION T
 16    WHERE RS.USN (+) = R.USN
 17      AND T.ADDR = S.TADDR(+)
 18      AND T.XIDUSN(+) = R.USN
 19    ORDER BY S.USERNAME
 20   /
```

SEGMENT_NAME	USERNAME	OSUSER	SID	SERIAL#	TRANS_USED	AVEACTIVE	EXTENDS	WAITS	SHRINKS	WRAPS
BIGRB1	SAM	SAMA	242	59718	665	397582678	0	79	0	34
RBS34	TUNER	SAMA	115	109	1	3117431	0	5	0	7
SYSTEM						0	0	0	0	0
RBS00						3294913	0	10	0	8
RBS01						2456597	0	2	0	6
RBS02						2456059	0	1	0	6
RBS03						2734789	0	3	0	7
RBS04						2455860	0	2	0	6
RBS05						2146347	0	5	0	5
RBS06						2455860	0	0	0	6
RBS07						2456597	0	4	0	6
RBS08						2456059	0	5	0	6
RBS09						2456113	0	1	0	6
RBS10	TUNER	SAMA	12	2311	3	4421498	0	5	0	10

Transactions Using Rollback Segments

This report displays all active transactions, the rollback segments used, and some session information:

```
SQL> SELECT R.NAME SEGMENT,
  2         S.SID,
  3         S.SERIAL#,
  4         S.USERNAME,
  5         T.STATUS,
  6         T.CR_GET,
  7         T.PHY_IO,
  8         T.USED_UBLK,
  9         T.NOUNDO,
 10         SUBSTR(S.PROGRAM, 1, 60) "COMMAND"
 11   FROM  V$SESSION S,
 12         V$TRANSACTION T,
 13         V$ROLLNAME R
 14   WHERE T.ADDR = S.TADDR
 15     AND T.XIDUSN = R.USN
 16   ORDER BY T.CR_GET, T.PHY_IO
 17  /

SEGMENT SID SERIAL# USERNAME STATUS CR_GET PHY_IO USED_UBLK NOU COMMAND
------- --- ------- -------- ------ ------ ------ --------- --- ---------------
RBS30   224     231 TUNER    ACTIVE      8      2         1 NO  JDBC-1.0-Client
BIGRB1  242   59718 TUNER    ACTIVE  29947 116985      1299 NO  JDBC-1.0-Client
```

Rollback Segments and Process Information

This report displays all rollback segments and the related processes that are currently using them:

```
SQL> SELECT R.NAME SEGMENT,
  2         P.PID,
  3         P.SPID,
  4         NVL(P.USERNAME, 'NO TRANSACTION') USERNAME,
  5         P.TERMINAL
  6    FROM V$LOCK L,
  7         V$PROCESS P,
  8         V$ROLLNAME R
  9   WHERE L.SID = P.PID(+)
 10     AND TRUNC (L.ID1(+)/65536) = R.USN
 11     AND L.TYPE(+) = 'TX'
 12     AND L.LMODE(+) = 6
 13   ORDER BY 1
 14  /

SEGMENT            PID SPID      USERNAME         TERMINAL
-------     ---------- --------- ---------------- -----------
BIGRB1                           NO TRANSACTION
RBS00                            NO TRANSACTION
RBS01                            NO TRANSACTION
RBS02                            NO TRANSACTION
RBS03                            NO TRANSACTION
RBS04                            NO TRANSACTION
RBS05                            NO TRANSACTION
RBS06                            NO TRANSACTION
RBS07                            NO TRANSACTION
RBS08                            NO TRANSACTION
RBS09              140 27763     oracle           UNKNOWN
RBS10                            NO TRANSACTION
```

Rollback Segments Duration

This report displays how long each segment has been online:

```
SQL> SELECT R.NAME,
  2         ROUND(24*((SYSDATE-STARTUP_TIME) -
  3              TRUNC(SYSDATE-STARTUP_TIME)) /
  4              (S.WRITES/S.RSSIZE),1) HOURS
  5     FROM V$INSTANCE I,
  6          V$ROLLNAME R,
  7          V$ROLLSTAT S
  8    WHERE R.USN = S.USN
  9      AND S.STATUS = 'ONLINE'
 10    /

NAME                                  HOURS
------------------------------   ----------
SYSTEM                             1418.6
RBS00                                   3
RBS01                                 3.8
RBS02                                 3.8
RBS03                                 3.6
RBS04                                 3.9
RBS05                                 4.6
RBS06                                 3.8
RBS07                                 4.2
RBS08                                 3.9
RBS09                                 4.3
RBS10                                 2.4
```

8

Commits and Rollbacks

This report displays the number of commits and rollbacks made in the system since the last startup. The results of this report can be saved for use in trend analysis to view the behavior of the application in terms of number of times an application issued rollback and commit statements. Also, the sum of COMMITS and ROLLBACKS is the total number of transactions issued against the database.

```
SQL> SELECT A.VALUE COMMITS,
  2         B.VALUE ROLLBACKS,
  3         A.VALUE + B.VALUE TOTAL
  4     FROM V$SYSSTAT A,
  5          V$SYSSTAT B
  6    WHERE A.NAME = 'USER COMMITS'
  7      AND B.NAME = 'USER ROLLBACKS'
  8    /

   COMMITS  ROLLBACKS       TOTAL
---------- ---------- ----------
   1921473    3718305     5639778
```

DIAGNOSING UNDO SEGMENTS

By now, you probably agree that manually managed rollback segments are outmoded. To clarify this point, in this section, you compare diagnosing in Automatic Undo Management mode with diagnosing in Manual Undo Management mode.

Undo segments are monitored for either UNDO segment size or undo retention. You must monitor the size to ensure that you have enough space allocated to retain undo statements for the retention period specified by the UNDO_RETENTION parameter. You can use the *counterpart* (one word) of V$ROLLSTAT, which is the dynamic performance view V$UNDOSTAT. V$UNDOSTAT provides the indicators detailed in the sections that follow.

Space Request Indicator

The space request indicator tells you whether a request for space failed due to lack of allocated space in the UNDO segment. A consistently high value indicates that the UNDO segments are too small and that you should increase their size. A value close to zero indicates the size is adequate. The following query displays the value of this indicator. The result of this query indicates that there is no problem with the size configuration of the UNDO segment:

```
SQL> SELECT SUM(NOSPACEERRCNT) NOSPACE_CNT
  2      FROM V$UNDOSTAT
  3  /

NOSPACE_CNT
-----------
          0
```

The V$UNDOSTAT view can be used in Manual or Automatic Undo Management.

NOTE

Snapshot Indicator

The snapshot indicator is one of the detection mechanisms that tells you whether the UNDO segment is too small and whether the transaction is too long. When the value of the snapshot indicator is consistently above zero, the segment is too small or a transaction takes too long. The following query reports the value of this indicator. The result is alarming, because it shows a value of 12 within 60 minutes of transactions. In this case, you should use V$TRANSACTION to examine the transaction submitted, and look at all concurrent transactions as well. Use the following query to obtain the value of this indicator:

```
SQL> SELECT SUM(SSOLDERRCNT) SNAPSHOT_CNT
  2     FROM V$UNDOSTAT
  3  /

SNAPSHOT_CNT
------------
          12
```

Steal Indicator

A consistent value above zero indicates that some transactions are taking unexpired extents away from other transactions because of lack of space. Unexpired extents are extents that are being used but are not yet released because they are still needed for undo retention. The following query can be used to get the steal indicator value. As you can see, the result is 0, which means that there were no incidents of stealing unexpired extents. Of course, a consistent value above 0 is alarming and should prompt you to increase the size of the UNDO segments.

```
SQL> SELECT SUM(UNXPSTEALCNT)
  2     FROM V$UNDOSTAT
  3  /

SUM(UNXPSTEALCNT)
-----------------
                0
```

In general, if you use automatic segment allocation for all tablespaces in the database, you need not be concerned about size. Oracle is able to extend as needed.

Transactions Peak Time

The following query displays a statistical report showing UNDO segment usage during peak time:

```
SQL> SELECT TO_CHAR(BEGIN_TIME, 'DD-MON-YYYY HH24:MI:SS') BEGIN_TIME,
  2          TO_CHAR(END_TIME, 'DD-MON-YYYY HH24:MI:SS') END_TIME,
  3          UNDOBLKS,
  4          TXNCOUNT,
  5          MAXCONCURRENCY
  6    FROM V$UNDOSTAT
  7   WHERE ROWNUM < 20
  8   ORDER BY UNDOBLKS DESC
  9  /

BEGIN_TIME           END_TIME              UNDOBLKS   TXNCOUNT MAXCONCURRENCY
-------------------- -------------------- ---------- ---------- --------------
06-FEB-2003 11:30:18 06-FEB-2003 11:40:18      10426       5896              3
06-FEB-2003 12:20:18 06-FEB-2003 12:30:18       5231      10233              1
06-FEB-2003 12:30:18 06-FEB-2003 12:40:18       1567      11074              1
06-FEB-2003 11:40:18 06-FEB-2003 11:50:18         20       6782              1
06-FEB-2003 11:20:18 06-FEB-2003 11:30:18         20       5041              1
06-FEB-2003 13:40:18 06-FEB-2003 13:50:18         19      16967              1
06-FEB-2003 13:00:18 06-FEB-2003 13:10:18         19      13602              1
06-FEB-2003 11:00:18 06-FEB-2003 11:10:18         19       3336              1
06-FEB-2003 12:50:18 06-FEB-2003 13:00:18         19      12756              1
06-FEB-2003 13:30:18 06-FEB-2003 13:40:18         18      16092              1
06-FEB-2003 10:50:18 06-FEB-2003 11:00:18         18       2390              1
06-FEB-2003 12:10:18 06-FEB-2003 12:20:18         17       9292              1
06-FEB-2003 12:00:18 06-FEB-2003 12:10:18         17       8495              1
06-FEB-2003 13:20:18 06-FEB-2003 13:30:18         16      15306              1
06-FEB-2003 13:10:18 06-FEB-2003 13:20:18         16      14481              1
06-FEB-2003 11:50:18 06-FEB-2003 12:00:18         16       7629              1
06-FEB-2003 11:10:18 06-FEB-2003 11:20:18         13       4052              1
06-FEB-2003 12:40:18 06-FEB-2003 12:50:18         12      11819              1
06-FEB-2003 13:50:18 06-FEB-2003 13:57:25         11      17582              1
```

Longest Transaction

The following query reports when the longest transaction occurred and the amount of undo blocks it used:

```
SQL> SELECT TO_CHAR(BEGIN_TIME, 'DD-MON-YYYY HH24:MI:SS') BEGIN_TIME,
  2          TO_CHAR(END_TIME, 'DD-MON-YYYY HH24:MI:SS') END_TIME,
  3          UNDOBLKS,
  4          TXNCOUNT,
  5          MAXCONCURRENCY
  6    FROM V$UNDOSTAT
  7   WHERE UNDOBLKS = (SELECT MAX(UNDOBLKS) FROM V$UNDOSTAT)
  8  /

BEGIN_TIME           END_TIME              UNDOBLKS   TXNCOUNT MAXCONCURRENCY
-------------------- -------------------- ---------- ---------- --------------
06-FEB-2003 11:30:18 06-FEB-2003 11:40:18      10426       5896              3
```

DIAGNOSING UNDO SEGMENTS WITH ORACLE ENTERPRISE MANAGER

In this section, you learn how to use Oracle Enterprise Manager to diagnose UNDO segments. Try out an example diagnosis by following these steps:

Step 1: Start Oracle Enterprise Manager Console.

Step 2: Select your database and click the **Instance>Configuration** option. Then click the **Undo** tab as shown in Figure 8-10.

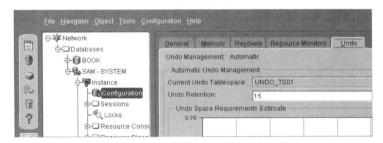

Figure 8-10   Oracle Enterprise Manager configuration option

Step 3: Display all undo parameters to see the current setting:

```
SQL> SHOW PARAMETER UNDO

NAME                                  TYPE         VALUE
------------------------------------- ------------ ---------
undo_management                       string       AUTO
undo_retention                        integer      60
undo_suppress_errors                  boolean      FALSE
undo_tablespace                       string       UNDO_TS01
```

Step 4: Get the current size of undo tablespace UNDO_TS01:

```
SQL> SELECT BYTES/1024/1024 SIZE_MB
  2    FROM DBA_DATA_FILES
  3   WHERE TABLESPACE_NAME = 'UNDO_TS01'
  4  /

   SIZE_MB
----------
        35
```

Step 5: Figure 8-11 displays the full content of the Undo tab.

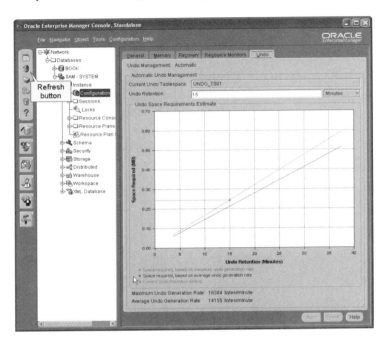

Figure 8-11   Oracle Enterprise Manager—before chart of the Undo segments tab

On the chart, you see two lines. The top line represents the space required to hold the maximum undo data generated by long transactions, and the bottom line represents the space required to hold the average undo data generated by transactions. Chart data is obtained from the undo statistics performance view called V$UNDOSTAT.

In the descriptions that follow, the chart shown in Figure 8-11 is referred to as the before chart.

Step 6: Log on as TUNER and delete the ORDER_LINES table:

```
SQL> DELETE ORDER_LINES
  2  /
```

Step 7: Refresh the Undo tab by clicking the **Refresh** button on the toolbar, as shown in Figure 8-12. In the descriptions that follow, this chart is referred to as after.

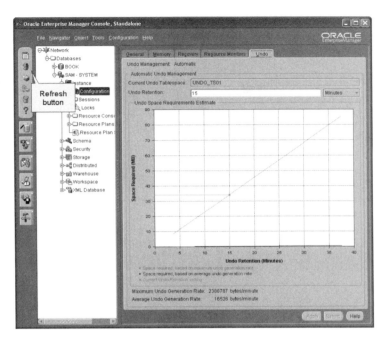

Figure 8-12 Oracle Enterprise Manager—after chart of the Undo segments tab

Step 8: Undo your changes by issuing this rollback statement:

```
SQL> ROLLBACK
  2  /
```

These steps show that from the before and after charts you can deduce whether the current size of the UNDO segments is adequate to fit the transaction. In addition, they show that the maximum undo data can be contained within the size of the tablespace for up to 540 seconds.

FLASHBACK QUERY

A DBA got a frantic call from one of the lead developers of an accounting database application. The developer was panicking because he updated the wrong 10 rows in production about three hours before. He asked the DBA if there was a way to revert the changes or display the rows before they were updated. He stressed to the DBA that backup recovery was not an option since the table to be recovered was required, and needed to be available and accessible at all times. The DBA responded, "Well, I'm unlucky and you're lucky. I am unlucky because I did not conduct an audit to discover that you have access to production. You are lucky because we just upgraded to Oracle9*i* and configured the database to use the new UNDO segments that support **flashback query.** Do you remember when you modified the table? I can flash back to the time when the changes were made and display those rows before you changed them."

The Oracle9i UNDO segments provide the capability of allowing users to go back in time and query the database as of that time. There are many scenarios similar to that just described in which there is a need to go back and query the database at a specific time in the past. Two main criteria are needed to enable this feature:

1. You must use automatic UNDO segments.

2. You must set the UNDO_RETENTION initialization parameter to a value specifying how long the before image can be retained in the UNDO segment before it is overwritten.

The following steps demonstrate how to perform a flashback query using the Oracle-supplied package, DBMS_FLASHBACK.

Step 1: Log on as tuner and create a table called FLASHBACK as follows:

```
SQL> CREATE TABLE FLASHBACK
  2  (
  3      NUM NUMBER
  4  )
  5  /

Table created.
```

Step 2: Insert one row into the newly created table and commit changes:

```
SQL> INSERT INTO FLASHBACK VALUES (100)
  2  /

1 row created.

SQL> COMMIT
  2  /
```

Step 3: Get the current time:

```
SQL> SELECT TO_CHAR(SYSDATE, 'HH24:MI:SS') TIME FROM DUAL
  2  /

TIME
--------------
10:03:07

1 row selected.
```

Step 4: Wait for five or 10 minutes and then update the FLASHBACK table and commit changes:

```
SQL> UPDATE FLASHBACK
  2     SET NUM = 9999
  3   WHERE NUM = 100
  4   /

1 row updated.

SQL> COMMIT
  2   /

Commit complete.
```

Step 5: Enable flashback using the DBMS_FLASHBACK.ENABLE_AT_TIME procedure. For more details on this package, consult the Oracle documentation, "Oracle9*i* Supplied PL/SQL Packages and Types Reference Release 2 (9.2)" found at *otn.oracle.com*.

```
SQL> EXEC DBMS_FLASHBACK.ENABLE_AT_TIME('11-SEP-2003 10:05:07')

PL/SQL procedure successfully completed.
```

Step 6: Display the contents of the FLASHBACK table. You should notice that the value of the NUM column value is set as it was after it was inserted.

```
SQL> SELECT *
  2     FROM FLASHBACK
  3   /

       NUM
----------
       100

1 row selected.
```

Step 7: When you are finished, disable the flashback query using the DBMS_FLASH-BACK.DISABLE procedure:

```
SQL> EXEC DBMS_FLASHBACK.DISABLE

PL/SQL procedure successfully completed.
```

That was not difficult at all. It is as simple as executing a procedure. Of course, this feature has some restrictions. For example, you are not allowed to perform DML statements while flashback is enabled. Other restrictions are related to the size of UNDO segments and the retention time specified by the UNDO_RETENTION initialization parameter.

Long Transactions

A senior developer is working on a process that updates a very large table. One of the business requirements of this process is to update all rows or none. In other words, if the process fails half way through, the process needs to revert all data changes. When the developer's code was ready, it was pushed to production. The first time it ran, it failed with this error: "ORA-01650 Error: Unable to extend rollback segment." The developer did not inform the DBA and persistently tried to solve this problem on his own, but no matter what he tried, he failed. Finally, he consulted the DBA on this issue. The DBA immediately asked him to use the SET TRANSACTION command, which is used to assign a specific rollback segment to one transaction to facilitate its completion and prevent rollback segment contention.

The SET TRANSACTION command is a statement issued at the start of a transaction to assign a large rollback segment specifically to the transaction without contending with other transactions. The assigned rollback segment is released automatically at the completion of the transaction by issuing a COMMIT or ROLLBACK statement. The following partial code segment provides an example:

```
SQL> SET TRANSACTION USE ROLLBACK SEGMENT RBS01
  2  /
...
SQL> INSERT INTO …
...
SQL> COMMIT
  2  /
```

You need to remember that the rollback segment you use for the transaction should be large enough to hold the whole transaction. Also, it is a good idea to keep this rollback segment offline until it is needed.

SOLVING COMMON UNDO SEGMENT PROBLEMS

Ideally, your database should run with no interruption, but of course, that is almost impossible. So you need to settle for running with minimal disruption. To achieve this objective, you should configure the UNDO segments optimally. Even though you try to proactively detect problems before they happen, interruptions occur. Setting the sizing of the rollback or UNDO segments improperly causes a set of recognizable problems. This section presents two common problems that many DBAs encounter.

ORA-01554 Error: Out of transaction slots in transaction tables

This error indicates one of three problems: there are too many concurrent transactions; there are more transactions than the TRANSACTIONS parameter has specified; or there are not enough rollback segments available. Although this error does not occur often, when it does, you need to shut down the database and change the TRANSACTIONS parameter value.

ORA-01555 Error: Snapshot too old

For ten days, a DBA was getting the ORA-01555 error message for one report that ran every night. It was working fine and suddenly it started to fail. The report did not change and the database configuration did not change. The DBA put his investigation helmet on to determine the cause of this problem. He researched and consulted with other colleagues on this matter, but to no use. Then he looked at all batch processes running at the time of the report, and bingo! Here it was—a process performing updates on the same table that the report was querying, and at about the same time the report ran. He had identified the cause of the error. The data requested by the report is a before image because the batch process was updating the data at the same time. The before image was overwritten by the batch process which caused the snapshot too old error. The DBA easily solved this problem by changing the schedule so that the batch process executed earlier than the report ran.

Some errors and failures can be tolerated, especially if the problem can be resolved easily. The occurrence of this type of error may not require any resolution. To understand when action is required, examine the circumstances that cause the error. The error occurs when:

- The before image that was requested by a query has been overwritten by another active transaction or by a current transaction.

- The System Change Number (SCN) being used by the transaction becomes out of date. Remember that the SCN number ensures that all data files are synchronized.

- The before image data in the rollback segment is overwritten after the transaction is committed.

- The slot in the segment head is reused.

When this error occurs, you should carefully examine the current transaction to determine if it is a recurring transaction or an isolated instance. If it is an isolated instance, no action is required. If it is a recurring instance, you should increase the size or number of the rollback segment or both.

ORA-01594 Error: Attempt to wrap into rollback segment

This error occurs when Oracle attempts to write to an extent that is too small. To solve the problem, increase the OPTIMAL value.

ORA-01650 Error: Unable to extend rollback segment

This error occurs when a large transaction requires a large amount of space in rollback segments, and the system is unable to allocate an extent in the rollback segment tablespace. To solve the problem, add space to the rollback segment tablespace.

This error can be prevented by monitoring the consumption of tablespaces and extents. Typically, you should be alerted when 80 percent of the tablespace is consumed and when 80 percent of the maximum extents is reached. If your MAXEXTENTS is unlimited, you should monitor tablespace to ensure that the amount of space allows rollback segments to extend. This error is more common in Manual Undo Management than in Automatic Undo Management.

BEST PRACTICES FOR DECREASING UNDO DATA

Many DBAs use checklists to reduce the risk of making mistakes due to oversights, or to avoid performance problems by practicing standard procedures and guidelines. In this section, you are presented with ten best practices (methods) for optimizing transactions by decreasing the generation of undo data.

1. Commit transactions frequently to reduce the amount of undo data that is generated.

2. When using long transactions, set the transaction to use a specific, large rollback segment. You can do this by following these steps:

   a. Create a large rollback segment for long transactions; keep this rollback segment offline. This step is done only once.

   b. Turn large rollback segments online.

   c. Assign rollback segments to long transactions using the SET TRANSACTION statement.

   d. Turn large rollback segments offline when the transaction is completed.

In Automatic Undo Management, SET TRANSACTION cannot be used.

TIP

3. Use locally managed extents because they do not generate undo data when allocating and deallocating extents.

To reduce undo data, some DBAs recommend setting the AUTOCOMMIT option to YES to automatically commit every DML statement issued by the user in a SQL*Plus session. This book does not recommend this practice, because it breaks transaction logic.

NOTE

4. When importing data using the Oracle IMP utility, set the COMMIT option to YES.

5. When exporting data using the Oracle EXP utility, set the CONSISTENT option to NO.

6. When loading data using the Oracle SQL*Loader, set the COMMIT option interval with the ROWS option.

7. Avoid extending and shrinking the rollback segment by setting OPTIMAL to accommodate most transactions.

8. Use the TRUNCATE command instead of the DELETE command if the deleted rows are not needed for recovery.

9. Use Automatic Undo Management.

10. Monitor undo activities to examine and analyze transaction behavior.

CHAPTER SUMMARY

8

- Oracle provides a feature that allows the user to undo the last DML operation performed on the database.
- Undo segments are an essential part of the Oracle architecture; no transaction is allowed without them.
- Oracle saves the data before it is changed in UNDO segments.
- Rollback or UNDO segments should reside in their own tablespaces to comply with OFA guidelines.
- Undo segments serve three purposes: transaction rollback, read consistency, and transaction recovery.
- Transaction rollback is the action of undoing the last transaction issued by a user.
- Read consistency states that data changes made by a user are not seen by other users until the user commits these changes.
- Transaction recovery is the action of restoring the before image data from UNDO segments when an Oracle instance crashes.
- There are two methods for managing UNDO segments: Manual Undo Management and Automatic Undo Management.
- Oracle and DBA experts recommend Automatic Undo Management.
- The UNDO_MANAGEMENT parameter indicates in which management mode the database is running.
- The ROLLBACK_SEGMENTS parameter is set to any rollback segment that you want to turn online when an Oracle instance is started.
- The DBA_ROLLBACK_SEGS view contains information about all the public and private segments that have been created for a database.

❏ Four parameters are set to configure a database for Automatic Undo Management: UNDO_MANAGEMENT, UNDO_RETENTION, UNDO_SUPPRESS_ERRORS, and UNDO_TABLESPACE.

❏ The optimal setting of the rollback segment prevents the unnecessary I/O caused by extending and shrinking of extents.

❏ Segment header contention results when transactions are contending for updates in the segment header.

❏ Oracle9*i* UNDO segments provide the capability of allowing a user to go back in time and query the database as of that time.

❏ The SET TRANSACTION command is a statement issued at the start of a transaction to assign a large rollback segment specifically to the transaction without contention from other transactions.

REVIEW QUESTIONS

1. You cannot create more than one undo tablespace in a database. (True/False)

2. Read consistency is defined as this circumstance: a user cannot see another user's changes before the changes are committed. (True/False)

3. If a database is in Automatic Undo Management, the V$TRANSACTION view cannot be used. (True/False)

4. The INSERT statement is the most expensive statement in regards to generated undo data. (True/False)

5. The UNDO_RETENTION parameter tells Oracle how long undo data should be retained in the UNDO segments. (True/False)

6. Oracle recommends the use of rollback segments for existing databases and UNDO segments for new databases. (True/False)

7. When an UNDO segment extent is deallocated manually, this is called SHRINK. (True/False)

8. A database cannot function without rollback segments. (True/False)

9. Write a query to display a list of all UNDO segments available online.

10. List all parameters that are related to Automatic Undo Management.

11. Suppose your database is running in Manual Undo Management. Write a query to display the statistics of all active segments.

12. List two ratios that alert you of rollback segment contention.

13. List all guidelines for rollback segment storage parameters.

14. Suppose your database is in Automatic Undo Management.

    a. Create a new undo tablespace called EXER14_UNDOTS with a size of 10 MB.

    b. Activate the EXER14_UNDOTS undo tablespace.

    c. Drop the EXER14_UNDOTS undo tablespace.

15. What is your objective when configuring Automatic Undo Management?

16. You are using the AUM feature of Oracle9i, which means that the database manages the rollback segments. Does this mean that you will not get any error related to ORA-01555 snapshot too old?

17. How does undo management work? When you set undo parameters in the initialization parameter file, does it mean that Oracle automatically manages UNDO segments and creates undo tablespace?

18. You issued a query that generated the following report:

```
TO_CHAR(END_TIME, TO_CHAR(BEGIN_TIM UNDOBLKS
----------------- ----------------- --------
31-JAN-2002 06:03 31-JAN-2002 05:59        1
31-JAN-2002 05:59 31-JAN-2002 05:49       21
31-JAN-2002 05:49 31-JAN-2002 05:29        0
31-JAN-2002 05:29 31-JAN-2002 05:19        1
31-JAN-2002 05:19 31-JAN-2002 05:09        3
31-JAN-2002 05:09 31-JAN-2002 04:39        0
31-JAN-2002 04:39 31-JAN-2002 04:29    21111
31-JAN-2002 04:29 31-JAN-2002 03:49        2
31-JAN-2002 03:49 31-JAN-2002 03:39       12
31-JAN-2002 03:39 31-JAN-2002 02:39        0
31-JAN-2002 02:39 31-JAN-2002 02:29        1
31-JAN-2002 02:29 31-JAN-2002 02:19        1
31-JAN-2002 02:19 31-JAN-2002 01:49        1
31-JAN-2002 01:49 31-JAN-2002 01:39        1
```

    a. What view did you use to generate this report?

    b. What does this report tell you?

19. Your Oracle9i database is running with UNDO_MANAGEMENT=AUTO. As you are browsing the alert log, you notice ORA-01594 errors. According to the error message, you should increase the optimal size of rollback segments. What should you do to eliminate these errors?

20. You are running an OLTP database application. You notice that the undo tablespace has grown to 5 GB. You perform a cold boot of your machine and restart the Oracle9*i* server. Then you log in to check if the space claimed by the undo tablespace is released, but to your surprise it is 99 percent used.

a. Why is Oracle using all this space?

b. How can you retrieve the space?

c. Should you be alarmed?

EXAM REVIEW QUESTIONS: ORACLE9*i* PERFORMANCE TUNING (#1Z0-033)

1. Which of the following statements does not generate undo data?

a. SET TRANSACTION USE ROLLBACK SEGMENT RBS01;

b. Using COMMIT=YES when using EXP utility

c. Using COMMIT=NO when using IMP utility

d. TRUNCATE TABLE EMP;

e. DELETE EMP;

2. Which two parameters must be set to configure your database to use Automatic Undo Management?

a. UNDO_TABLESPACES

b. ROLLBACK_SEGMENTS

c. UNDO_RETENTION

d. UNDO_MANAGEMENT

e. TRANSACTIONS_PER_ROLLBACK_SEGMENT

f. UNDO_SUPPRESS_ERRORS

3. Undo segments serve three purposes. Which of the following is irrelevant?

a. Read consistency

b. Transaction rollback

c. Automatic Undo Management

d. Transaction recovery

4. If you decide to set your database to use rollback segments rather than UNDO segments, which two statements would you use?

   a. UNDO_TABLESPACES

   b. ROLLBACK_SEGMENTS

   c. UNDO_RETENTION

   d. UNDO_MANAGEMENT

   e. TRANSACTIONS_PER_ROLLBACK_SEGMENT

   f. UNDO_SUPPRESS_ERRORS

5. Suppose you want to run a long transaction and assign a specific rollback segment for this transaction. Which statement is true?

   a. You need to use the SET TRANSACTION statement.

   b. Your database is set to Automatic Undo Management.

   c. Your database is set to Manual Undo Management.

   d. You need to set the ROLLBACK_SEGMENTS parameter to specify the segment to be used for the transaction.

6. What is the threshold for block header contention?

   a. 0 percent

   b. 1 percent

   c. 5 percent

   d. 90 percent

   e. 95 percent

   f. 100 percent

7. When you create a new OLTP database, which guideline would you use to create UNDO segments?

   a. Automatic Undo Management

   b. Many small rollback segments

   c. Few large rollback segments

   d. Extent size in the range of 8 KB to 64 KB

   e. Extent size above 64 KB

8

8. Your database is using rollback segments. Which view would you use to get rollback segment statistics?

   a. V$ROLLBACK_STAT

   b. V$ROLL_STATISTICS

   c. V$ROLLSTAT

   d. V$ROLL_STAT

   e. V$ROLLBACK_STATISTICS

9. Which view would you use to get the block header ratio?

   a. V$SYSSTAT

   b. V$SYSTEM_EVENT

   c. V$WAITSTAT

   d. V$UNDOSTAT

10. Which statement is true about Automatic Undo Management?

    a. Oracle manages all transactions automatically.

    b. Oracle manages undo space automatically.

    c. Oracle creates UNDO segments based on the number of tablespaces specified in the initialization parameter file.

    d. Oracle creates undo tablespace automatically.

11. Which statement would you use to switch the undo tablespace from UNDOTS1 to UNDOTS2?

    a. ALTER SYSTEM SET UNDO_TABLESPACE = UNDOTS2

    b. You must shutdown the database and set the UNDO_TABLESPACE parameter in the initialization parameter file. Then start up the database.

    c. ALTER UNDO TABLESPACE UNDOTS2 ONLINE;

    d. The following two statements:

       1. ALTER UNDO SEGMENT UNDOTS1 ONLINE;

       2. ALTER UNDO SEGMENT UNDOTS2 OFFLINE;

12. The V$UNDOSTAT view displays rows based on time intervals. What is the duration of this interval?

   a. one minute

   b. five minutes

   c. 10 minutes

   d. 15 minutes

   e. one hour

13. Which column in the V$UNDOSTAT view should always have a value of 0?

   a. TXNCOUNT

   b. SSOLDERRCNT

   c. UNDOTSN

   d. UNDOBLKS

   e. MAXCONCURRENCY

14. Which view would you use to compute the number of undo blocks used per second?

   a. V$UNDO_EXTENTS

   b. V$TRANSACTION

   c. V$SYSSTAT

   d. V$UNDOSTAT

15. Which parameter cannot be modified dynamically?

   a. UNDO_TABLESPACE

   b. UNDO_RETENTION

   c. UNDO_MANAGEMENT

   d. UNDO_SUPPRESS_ERRORS

8

HANDS-ON PROJECTS

Please complete the projects provided below.

1. Reread the Performance Problem presented at the start of this chapter. Think of it in terms of the concepts you have learned in this chapter, and answer the following questions:

   a. What caused Howard's problem to begin with?

   b. Why did this problem occur?

   c. Did Sheila's actions worsen the problem?

   d. After what action could Howard stop without escalating the problem?

   e. What do you recommend that Howard do?

2. Analyze the chart presented in Figure 8-13. If an action is necessary, make a recommendation.

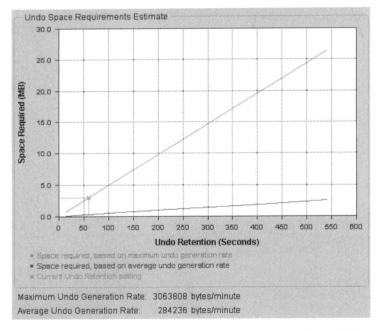

Figure 8-13   Oracle Enterprise Manager—chart of the UNDO segments tab

3. You received an e-mail requesting help from a friend who just started a new job as a junior DBA in a different company. Here is the e-mail:

```
From: Joe Doe [mailto:joe.doe@acme.com]
Sent: Thursday, February 06, 2003 4:05 PM
To: dba@oracle_tuning.com
Subject: Transactions
```

Hi there,

As you know I started my job yesterday and my manager has already assigned me a small project to investigate transactions for an existing database. So I ran this query several times and every time I ran it, the results were nearly the same. So I picked this:

```
SQL> SELECT ADDR, XIDUSN, UBABLK, STATUS, USED_UBLK, USED_UREC, SPACE
  2    FROM V$TRANSACTION
  3   ORDER BY 2
  4  /

ADDR         XIDUSN      UBABLK STATUS USED_UBLK  USED_UREC SPACE
--------- ---------- ----------- ------ --------- ---------- -----
F30974DC          1      469311 ACTIVE         1          6 NO
F30A1524          2      467034 ACTIVE         2         61 NO
F3094790          4      400247 ACTIVE         1          3 NO
F3099438          7      470818 ACTIVE         1         34 NO
F30974DC          9      463100 ACTIVE         1         24 NO
F3096370         14      108810 ACTIVE         1         41 NO
F3096370         15      470211 ACTIVE         1         20 NO
F30A2A0C         22      615214 ACTIVE         1          2 NO
F3096370         23      160607 ACTIVE         1         70 NO
F30974DC         24      280343 ACTIVE         2         21 NO
F3094790         27      315403 ACTIVE         1          7 NO
F30A2A0C         30      985429 ACTIVE         1          6 NO
F3099438         34      583765 ACTIVE         2         27 NO
F30A2A0C         36      445729 ACTIVE         1         16 NO
F3094790         40      332314 ACTIVE         3        116 NO
F30A2A0C         42     1035205 ACTIVE         1          3 NO
F30A2A0C         53      231696 ACTIVE         1         56 NO
```

Could you help me answer these questions?

When I asked my manager about the type of application this database is running, he didn't know. Can you tell what type of an application this is?

What is the query reporting?

How can I use the results of this query to help me determine if my database is configured optimally?

Your help is much appreciated.

Best regards,

Joe

4. You just upgraded your database from Oracle8i to Oracle9i, and you set it to use Automatic Undo Management. After a few days, you noticed that the UNDO segments were growing when large numbers of INSERTS operations were submitted, but they do not shrink afterwards. Answer the following:

   a. What would happen if you tried to modify the OPTIMAL value?

   b. What command would you issue to shrink the UNDO segments?

   c. Are the UNDO segments behaving normally?

5. Using Oracle 9i with Automatic Undo Management of UNDO segments, you got the following report. Analyze this report and explain the numbers for each column:

RBS No	Gets	Waits	Written	Wraps	Shrinks	Extends
0	512	0.00	25768	3	0	10
1	8306	0.00	2023668	19	5	11
2	8224	0.01	1898976	4	11	1
3	8292	0.00	2034636	43	5	19
4	8441	0.01	2414190	23	7	14
5	8316	0.03	1873476	46	12	29
6	8265	0.04	2040168	21	7	16
7	8270	0.03	1966492	19	14	21
8	8254	0.00	1954154	49	4	13
9	8294	0.00	2136208	19	5	22
10	8311	0.00	2085956	26	6	22
11	8461	0.04	2092652	69	27	27
12	8292	0.00	1937326	21	5	13

6. Users were experiencing several problems related to UNDO segments. After a lengthy investigation, you decided to call the Oracle consultant whom your company hired last year. After explaining the problem to her, she asked you the following questions:

   ■ How many concurrent transactions do you have?

   ■ How many concurrent sessions are active?

   ■ How frequent are the commits?

   ■ Do you have overnight batch jobs running?

   Write the queries that answer these questions.

7. Answer the following questions:

a. How can you use the query in the following code segment to diagnose UNDO segments problems?

b. Does the result of the query indicate any problems?

```
SQL> SELECT R.SEGMENT_NAME,
  2         S.EXTENTS,
  3         S.RSSIZE,
  4         S.WRITES,
  5    FROM V$ROLLSTAT S,
  6         DBA_ROLLBACK_SEGS R
  6    WHERE S.USN = R.SEGMENT_ID
  8  /

SEGMENT_NAME  EXTENTS     RSSIZE      WRITES
------------  -------  ----------  ----------
SYSTEM            228    18669568       28638
RBS18             111   581951488     5833798
RBS19              62   325050368     5106862
RBS20             447  2343559168     6747110
RBS21             132   692051968     5933376
RBS22             189   990896128     6718108
RBS23              62   325050368     6415450
RBS24             134   702537728    14012070
RBS25             124   650108928     5759408
RBS26              55   288350208    11457916
RBS27             313  1641013248     5669556
RBS28              43   225435648     5449484
RBS29              82   429907968     5979166
RBS30              62   325050368     4897766
RBS31              57   298835968     7300814
RBS32              44   230678528     5121834
RBS33             119   623894528     5856452
RBS34              51   267378688     5682046
RBS35              33   173006848    15159388
RBS36              98   513794048     6204726
RBS37             173   907010048     5001226
RBS38              88   461365248     5135002
RBS39             151   791666688     6638184
RBS40              50   262135808     4685504
RBLARGE1           33  1782571008   357641276
RBLARGE2            8   471851008     5776772
```

8

8. Calculate the undo bytes for your database for eight hours of undo retention.

9. For each session of the database referred to in Question 8, write a query to display the number of undo data used by the session.

10. You had an interview for a junior DBA position. During the interview, the perspective manager presented you with the following scenario about rollback segments:

Suppose your database is getting this error when an application process is trying to insert 5 million rows into a table using PL/SQL code.

```
ORA-01555: snapshot too old: rollback segment
number 6 with name "RBS01" too small
```

You are using an undo tablespace sized at 8 GB. There are 24 rollback segments in the undo tablespace with the following storage parameters:

```
Initial extent = 131072
Next Extent = <not given>
Min Extent = 2
Max Extents = 32765

Database configuration
----------------------
db_block_size=8192
undo_management=MANUAL
```

Answer the following:

a. Is this a good configuration? Why?

b. Do you need other information to better diagnose the problem?

c. What should you do to fix this problem?

11. As you already know, UNDO segments are used for three purposes:

a. Transaction rollback

b. Read consistency

c. Transaction recovery

Demonstrate each purpose of the UNDO segments.

12. You are working as a DBA consultant assisting a DBA team with routine tasks. Your client asked you to thoroughly assess one of the production databases. As you are taking health check readings, you discover that one ratio indicates that there is segment header contention as well as block header contention. Answer the following questions:

a. Explain the meanings of segment header and block header contention.

b. What two queries did you issue to get these ratios and what is the threshold for each one?

c. What action do you recommend to your client?

d. Explain whether this problem could have been prevented.

CASE PROJECTS

1. Rollback Segment Size

In this project, you learn to work with long-running transactions. Acme Order System gets a daily feed of new products from each supplier. The feed process takes all files for each supplier and merges them into one large file to be loaded into a staging table in the database and processed later. The crucial part of the process is the loading of a large file into a table. Identify all necessary steps that would show how improper sizing of rollback segments makes a significant difference in performance and error.

2. Flashback to the Past

In this project, you use the flashback? query feature of Oracle9i. A flashback query enables users to go back to a specific time and view their data at that time. The functionality of this powerful feature depends on configuring the database with Automatic Undo Management, because it uses the UNDO_RETENTION parameter to determine how far back you can query with this feature.

To use this feature, use the Oracle-supplied package, DBMS_FLASHBACK and follow these steps:

1. Log on as SYSTEM and ensure that the DBMS_FLASHBACK package is installed. If not, you can install it using DBMSTRAN.SQL, which is found under %ORACLE_HOME%\rdbms\admin.

2. Grant the EXECUTE privilege on DBMS_FLASHBACK package to TUNER.

3. Configure your database in Automatic Undo Management setting the UNDO_RETENTION parameter to one hour.

4. Get the SCN number using DBMS_FLASHBACK.GET_SYSTEM_ CHANGE_NUMBER and record it here: _____.

5. Log on as TUNER and retrieve all the rows in the EMPLOYEE_RANKS table.

6. Delete all rows in the EMPLOYEE_RANKS table and commit your changes. First you need to disable referential constraint in the ORDERS table.

7. Verify that the rows were deleted.

8. Perform three different transactions on different tables.

9. Suppose you just realized that the rows for that table were missing and you needed to see these rows before they were deleted. So you decided to flashback to the time when you deleted these rows. To do so, you issued the following statement as SYSTEM:

EXEC DBMS_FLASHBACK.ENABLE_AT_SYSTEM_ CHANGE_ NUMBER(scn_recorded)

If you get the following error, it means that the time given is not close to the time you deleted the rows. So you can change the time(?)record to a value more recent or less recent. Keep trying until the statement runs without an error:

ERROR at line 1:

ORA-08180: no snapshot found based on specified time

ORA-06512: at "SYS.DBMS_FLASHBACK", line 0

ORA-06512: at line 1

You must disable the flashback feature before you re-enable it.

NOTE

10. View the contents of the EMPLOYEE_RANKS table and save the output to a file. You will need the results to reinsert these rows again.

11. Disable the flashback query.

12. Edit the output to create insert statements.

13. Execute the edited file and re-enable the constraint that was disabled in Step 6.

8

IV

Advanced Tuning

9

DETECTING LOCK CONTENTION

In this chapter you will:

♦ Learn about locks and their uses

♦ Differentiate lock types

♦ Understand different lock modes

♦ Learn to distinguish between different locking levels

♦ Learn to use the LOCK statement

♦ Learn the impact of the SELECT...FOR UPDATE statement on transactions

♦ Work through some practical examples of locking

♦ Work with the DML_LOCKS initialization parameter

♦ Use the SET TRANSACTION statement in transactions

♦ Understand the workings of deadlocks

♦ Detect and resolve lock contention

♦ Learn the Best Practices for detecting lock contention

At this point in the book, you have gained a firm grasp on tuning the memory and storage areas. Gaining this knowledge is worth time and effort to ensure optimal performance. In this chapter, you switch gears to learn Oracle locking mechanisms, their behavior, and use. You learn how locks impact performance, as well as how to detect and resolve locking problems. This chapter not only explains the different types and levels of locks, it also demonstrates lock mode behavior through illustrations that you can follow and try on your own.

Performance Problem

This section outlines an actual performance problem. As you look it over, imagine yourself as the DBA who reported it and keep it in mind as you proceed through the chapter. The chapter presents concepts relevant to the problem. In the first Hands-on Project at the end of the chapter, you are asked to use the concepts you have learned to provide a solution, or partial solution, to this performance problem.

FROM: Tim Smith <mailto: tsmith@locks.com>
Date: 12-Dec-04 11:23
Subject: SELECT...FOR UPDATE

Hello DBAs,

A database application went into production three months ago at my office. At that time there were no complaints from users about performance. The DBAs monitoring reports and tools did not indicate any performance or configuration problems. Recently, users began complaining about sporadic performance degradation on different screens, especially when the user tries to commit data modifications.

The administering DBA performed a health check on the database at different times but could not detect anything, even though she tried to use the application to capture all queries and their progress. Can you please help me identify the problem and suggest a checklist to prevent and identify future occurrences.

Please help!!!

OVERVIEW OF LOCKS

Suppose you want to modify a value in a table, and you submit the usual UPDATE statement, but instead of getting the expected response informing you that the value is updated, you receive an error about an invalid column name. You parse the statement once, twice, then three times to make sure that the syntax is correct and resubmit the statement. This time you get an invalid data type error. What actually happened was that another user altered the structure at the same time you submitted your statements. What a coincidence!

Here is another common situation. Suppose you are on the phone with a customer who wants to change the address information for his account. You pull his record from the database and enter the new address information. When you click the Save button, instead of getting a successful completion message, you get the message: "Your request is being processed, please wait." You wait one, two, and three minutes and still get no response. Your customer is on the phone sighing and getting impatient! To kill time you start a conversation with the customer talking about everything except why he is waiting—an embarrassing situation.

These two situations could easily happen in a multiuser environment, in which applications and tables are concurrently shared, accessed, and updated by different users and processes. The likelihood that these incidents will occur is low, but because they can happen, they must be addressed.

The first situation can be prevented by locking the row or table momentarily while the update is being executed to prevent any other alteration of the table. The second situation can be prevented by using an application with an algorithm that detects if the updated table or row is busy and queues or aborts the request. This prevents the user from waiting to acquire the lock. Locking mechanisms can prevent both types of situations.

So, just what is a lock? A **lock** is a mechanism that protects a database object from being altered while it is being modified by other processes or users. Figure 9-1 is an illustration of a lock process. As you can see in the illustration, when a request for modification to the data or structure of an object is submitted, the Oracle server tries to acquire a lock on the object to secure it from being changed while the request is processed. If the Oracle server cannot acquire the lock, the Oracle server either waits or aborts with an error based on what type of lock and mode it encounters. If a lock is obtained, the object is locked and the request is processed. When the request for modification is completed, the lock is released automatically.

9

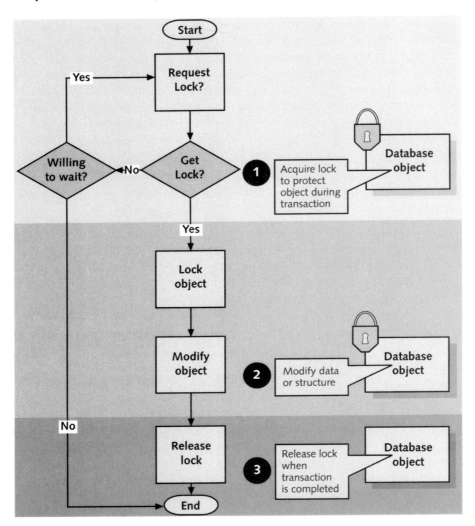

Figure 9-1   Oracle locking process

To protect objects from being modified by two different users at the same time, Oracle has created a complex data structure called locks for implementing a locking mechanism. This mechanism enforces locks in a serial manner using a queue structure known in Oracle as enqueue. An **enqueue** is a data structure for locks that notifies Oracle of the process waiting for a resource that is locked by another session. This mechanism works in a serialized manner on a first-come, first-served basis.

For instance, if two transactions to modify the same object are submitted at nearly the same time, the first transaction that is received locks the object for the duration of the transaction. When the transaction is completed (either committed or rolled back), that lock is released and a new lock is acquired for the next transaction. Locks are characterized as follows:

- They enforce consistency and integrity. Data and objects maintain their integrity and consistency for the duration of the transaction.

- They provide a queue structure that allows all sessions to join a queue for the object when the object is not available immediately.

- Oracle automatically handles lock mechanisms.

- The duration of the lock is equal to the length or processing time of the transaction submitted.

Although Oracle automatically manages locks, they are indirectly controlled by application logic in general and by transactions issued by the application specifically. Oracle's automatic hold and release of locks is determined by the start and completion of the transaction. The next section introduces you to the type of locks that are available in Oracle.

LOCK TYPES

Table 9-1 presents the three different types of locks that Oracle uses to protect objects during a transaction.

Table 9-1 Oracle lock types

Type	Description
DDL (Data Definition Language) locks	Protect schema objects during structure modification
DML (Data Manipulation Language) locks	Protect objects during a transaction
Internal locks	Managed by Oracle to protect internal database structures such as data files

The information in this table is derived from the online documentation that Oracle provides at the Oracle Technology Network site: *www.otn.oracle.com*.

The following sections describe DDL and DML locks as they are controlled directly or indirectly by the application. Internal locks are not discussed because they are managed efficiently by Oracle.

DDL Lock

When a CREATE, TRUNCATE, or ALTER statement is issued, Oracle automatically locks an object to ensure that no transactions are submitted against the object during the execution of the statement. If Oracle cannot lock the object because another transaction or user has locked it, the statement either waits or returns with an error. DDL locks are issued and released by Oracle automatically.

DML Lock

This lock is acquired at the start of a transaction and released at the completion of the transaction. As you already know, a transaction consists of one or many DML statements such as INSERT, UPDATE, and DELETE. A transaction is considered completed when a COMMIT or ROLLBACK statement is issued.

If a transaction is rolled back to a specific SAVEPOINT (a SAVEPOINT acts like a bookmark to control a transaction), all locks acquired before the savepoint are not released and locks acquired after the SAVEPOINT are released, as shown in Figure 9-2.

Two UPDATE statements were issued in this transaction with a SAVEPOINT statement between them. Each statement acquired a lock on the row being updated. When the rollback was issued to SAVEPOINT A, the second update statement undid the changes and the lock was released on the second row, but the first update statement was not rolled back. Therefore, the lock on the first row holds until the transaction is completed. This transaction ends when either a COMMIT or ROLLBACK statement is issued.

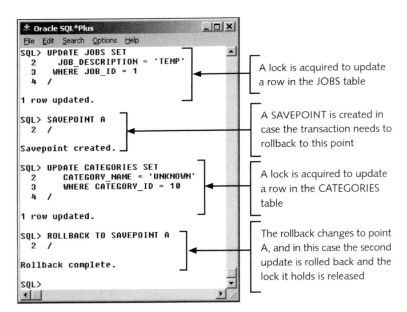

Figure 9-2   Lock process when rollback to a SAVEPOINT is issued

The next section presents the different types of lock modes to enhance your understanding of lock behaviors.

LOCK MODES

The previous section described the types of locks that Oracle uses; this section discusses lock modes. Oracle uses the acronyms listed in Table 9-2 to indicate lock modes, and it is a good idea to become familiar with them.

Table 9-2   Acronyms and descriptions of lock modes

Acronym	Mode	Description
RS (SS)	ROW SHARE (also known as SUBSHARE)	A transaction has locked rows in a table for updates, but allows other transactions to lock other rows in the table
RX	ROW EXCLUSIVE	A transaction has locked rows in a table for updates and does not allow other transactions to lock the table
S	SHARE	A transaction has locked a table in a mode that allows other transactions to lock the table in a SHARE mode but does not allow any updates on the table
SRX (SSX)	SHARE ROW EXCLUSIVE (also know as SHARE-SUBEXCLUSIVE)	Other transactions are not allowed to lock the table in SHARE MODE, and no DML statements are allowed
TM	N/A	Table-level lock
TX	N/A	Row-level lock
UUL	N/A	User-defined lock
X X	EXCLUSIVE	The table is locked and no other sessions are allowed to lock the table or submit DML statements to the table

9

The information in this table is derived from the online documentation that Oracle provides at the Oracle Technology Network site: *www.otn.oracle.com*.

Table 9-3 presents another summary of the different lock modes and summarizes when each mode is used automatically by Oracle. Note that Yes indicates that the operation is allowed and No indicates that the operation is not allowed.

NOTE

SHARE mode is the least restrictive locking mode, and EXCLUSIVE is the most restrictive.

Table 9-3   Lock modes and DML statements

Mode	Acquired	Query	Insert	Update	Delete	Lock
S	Used for referential integrity by Oracle	Yes	No	No	No	Yes in SHARE mode
RS	When SELECT...FOR UPDATE is issued	Yes	Yes	Yes	Yes on other rows	No
RX	When INSERT, UPDATE, or DELETE statements are issued	Yes	Yes	Yes on other rows	Yes on other rows	Yes on other rows
SRX	Used for referential integrity by Oracle	Yes	Yes	No	No	No in SHARE mode
X	Manually	No	No	No	No	No

Each time you issue an UPDATE statement, two locks are acquired: one lock on the table is ROW EXCLUSIVE, which secures the table from structure modifications during the transaction; the other lock is EXCLUSIVE, which locks the rows to be updated to prevent the selected rows from being updated by another process.

Figure 9-3 shows an instance of locks in use. In the session at the upper-left of the figure, three rows are being updated and the Oracle Enterprise Manager console displays the two locks acquired by this session.

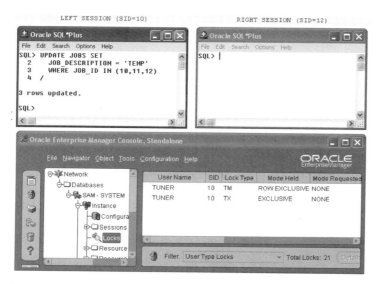

Figure 9-3   Locks being held when a row is updated

All the lock modes described to this point are for *DML* locks. *DDL* locks are also acquired and released automatically by Oracle, whenever a DDL statement is issued. Table 9-4 presents DDL statements and the lock mode held for each statement.

Table 9-4   DDL statements and lock modes

DDL Statement	Lock mode
AUDIT	SHARE
COMMENT	
CREATE FUNCTION	
CREATE PACKAGE	
CREATE PACKAGE BODY	
CREATE PROCEDURE	
CREATE TABLE	
CREATE TRIGGER	
CREATE SYNONYM	
CREATE VIEW	
ALTER ...	EXCLUSIVE

Locking Levels

Conceptually speaking, four levels of locks can be implemented in a database. Each level has a different purpose and a different implementation. The following sections outline the different levels.

Database Level

Database level locks the database to disallow any new sessions and transactions. One of the main purposes for locking a database is to perform maintenance without interference from user sessions. Usually, the DBA locks the database by setting it in a restrictive mode. In this mode only users with RESTRICTIVE SESSION privileges are allowed to log in. The other method is to place the database in READ ONLY mode, which disallows any transactions against the database, but allows sessions to run queries. READ ONLY mode is normally used for a STANDBY database or a database serving for reporting functions only.

The following statement can be used to put the database in a restrictive mode. As you can see, the system will not allow TUNER to log on because TUNER does not have the RESTRICTED SESSION privilege.

```
SQL> ALTER SYSTEM ENABLE RESTRICTED SESSION
  2  /

System altered.

SQL> CONN TUNER/TUNER@SAM
ERROR:
ORA-01035: ORACLE only available to users with RESTRICTED SESSION privilege
```

NOTE

Sessions that are already connected are not impacted by ALTER SYSTEM ENABLE RESTRICTED SESSION; only new sessions trying to connect are restricted.

You could also use ALTER SYSTEM QUIESCE RESTRICTED to lock the database from user's activities.

The following statement places the database in READ ONLY mode. As you can see by examining the code that follows, the system did not allow the transaction because the UNDO segment is offline because of the READ ONLY state of the database.

```
SQL> STARTUP MOUNT PFILE=C:\ORACLE\ADMIN\SAM\PFILE\INIT.ORA
ORACLE instance started.

Total System Global Area   135338868 bytes
Fixed Size                    453492 bytes
Variable Size              109051904 bytes
Database Buffers            25165824 bytes
Redo Buffers                  667648 bytes
Database mounted.
SQL> ALTER DATABASE OPEN READ ONLY
  2  /

Database altered.

SQL> CONNECT TUNER/TUNER@SAM
Connected.
SQL> UPDATE JOBS SET
  2     JOB_DESCRIPTION = 'TEMP'
  3     WHERE JOB_ID = 1
  4  /
UPDATE JOBS SET
       *
ERROR at line 1:
ORA-01552: cannot use system rollback segment for non-system tablespace
'USERS'
```

Table Level

Putting a table in table-level locks a whole table to prevent transactions on the table as well as any alteration of its structure. A table-level lock can be achieved by explicitly issuing a DML statement or by issuing a LOCK statement, which is discussed in further detail later in this chapter. Issuing any of the following statements locks the whole table. The lock on the table is maintained until the statement is committed or rolled back.

```
SQL> UPDATE EMPLOYEES SET
  2     SALARY = 30000
  3  /

294 rows updated.
```

```
SQL> DELETE EMPLOYEES
/

294 rows deleted.
```

```
SQL> SELECT *
  2     FROM JOBS
  3     FOR UPDATE
  4  /

    JOB_ID JOB_DESCRIPTION
---------- -------------------------------
         1 Sales Director
...
```

Row Level

This is the lowest level of locking that Oracle supports. A row-level lock prevents any other DML operations on that row to occur during an update. This is accomplished when a DML statement is issued to operate on one or more rows.

Column Level

Column level is not supported by Oracle. It is a lock that protects a column value in a row, but allows another transaction to change the value for another column on the same row. Figure 9-4 is an illustration of the lock level. If Oracle supported this type of lock, these two transactions shown in Figure 9-4 could run concurrently. But because Oracle does not support column-level locking, the result of these two transactions is that Transaction2 waits until Transaction1 is completed (committed or rolled back).

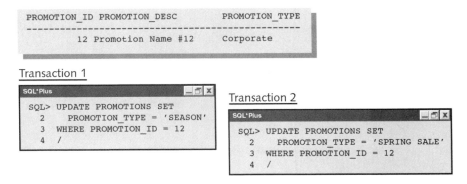

Figure 9-4   Column-lock level

LOCK STATEMENT

Oracle provides a statement that allows you to manually lock a table rather than having its lock be triggered automatically by a transaction. This statement is called LOCK. The following example presents the syntax of this statement followed by an illustration for each option.

```
SQL> LOCK TABLE table_name IN lock_mode MODE [NOWAIT];

Where lock_mode is:

      · SHARE
      · ROW SHARE
      · SHARE UPDATE is same as ROW SHARE
      · ROW EXCLUSIVE
      · SHARE ROW EXCLUSIVE
      · EXCLUSIVE

NOWAIT is specified when you do not want to wait to obtain a lock
because the object is already locked by another session or transaction.
When NOWAIT is specified, Oracle returns an error immediately indicating
that the object is currently locked and that the statement failed to
lock it.
```

Use the following steps to see a demonstration of each lock mode using the LOCK statement.

Step 1: Open the Oracle Enterprise Manager console and log on to your database.

Step 2: On the Navigation bar, click the **Instance** icon.

Step 3: Click the node for Locks that displays, as shown in Figure 9-5.

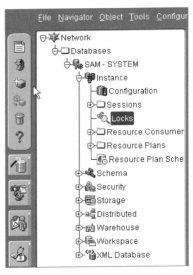

Figure 9-5   Option for Oracle Enterprise Manager Locks

Step 4: As shown in Figure 9-6, the right pane of the console window displays a list of locks held by all users. At the bottom of the screen, you can select from the drop-down list to view All Locks, BLOCKING/WAITING Locks, or User-type Locks. The default setting is User-type Locks.

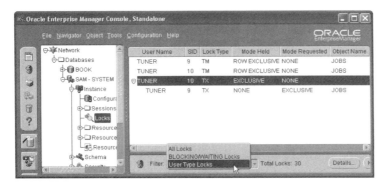

Figure 9-6   Lock type options within the locks main window

NOTE

A session that is holding a lock and blocking other sessions is known as a blocking lock.

Step 5: Select any row and double-click on it. A window opens, displaying details of the session, as shown in Figure 9-7.

9

Figure 9-7   Oracle Enterprise Manager showing session details of the holding lock

The following sections present illustrations of each lock mode. For each lock mode section there are at least two different demonstrations to show you the impact of the lock mode on other sessions.

SHARE (S) Lock Mode

Scenario 1: The session shown in the upper-left corner of Figure 9-8, locked the JOBS table in a SHARE mode, which disallows other sessions from locking the table in ROW EXCLUSIVE mode. ROW EXCLUSIVE mode is illustrated by the session shown in the upper-right corner, which issued an UPDATE statement. SHARE lock mode does not allow other sessions to perform any updates. The session shown in the upper-right corner of Figure 9-8 is waiting until the lock held by the session on the left is released.

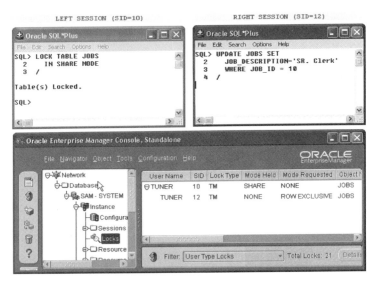

Figure 9-8   SHARE lock mode for Scenario 1

In the Oracle Enterprise Manager console, you see in the right pane that Session 12 is waiting for Session 10 to release the lock in order to perform its transaction.

Scenario 2: Figure 9-9 illustrates that a lock in SHARE mode allows another session to lock the table in a SHARE mode. The Oracle Enterprise Manager console shows that no session is waiting for another session.

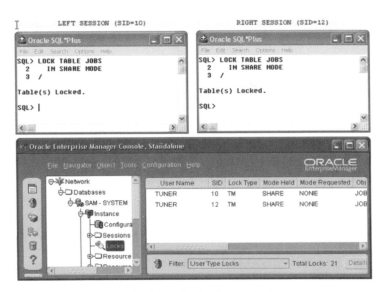

Figure 9-9   SHARE lock mode for Scenario 2

ROW SHARE (RS) Lock Mode

Scenario 1: Figure 9-10 shows that when the session in the upper-left corner locks the table in ROW SHARE mode, it allows other sessions to perform updates on the table. In the Oracle Enterprise Manager console, you can see that there are three locks held on the JOBS table: one SHARED table lock in session 10 and two locks by session 12, one EXCLUSIVE lock on the row and another ROW EXCLUSIVE lock on the table.

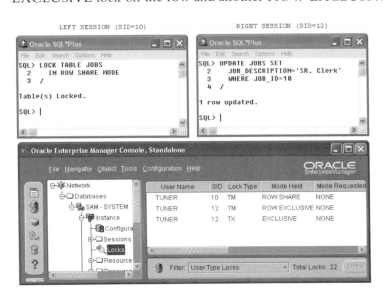

Figure 9-10   ROW SHARE lock mode for Scenario 1

Scenario 2: In this scenario, both sessions are holding ROW SHARE locks on the table jobs, as shown in Figure 9-11.

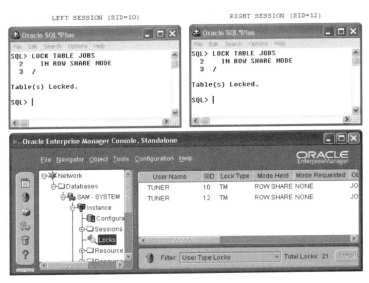

Figure 9-11   ROW SHARE lock mode for Scenario 2

ROW EXCLUSIVE (RX) Lock Mode

In Figure 9-12, the session shown in the upper-left corner has locked the table for updates but allows other sessions to lock the table for updates on different rows. Also, the same lock mode on the table (Figure 9-13) is allowed, but it does not allow other users to lock the table in SHARE mode (Figure 9-14).

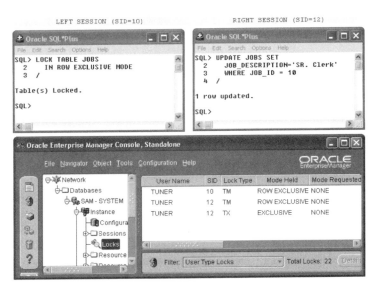

Figure 9-12   ROW EXCLUSIVE lock mode for Scenario 1

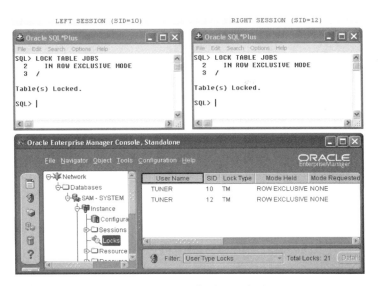

Figure 9-13   ROW EXCLUSIVE lock mode for Scenario 2

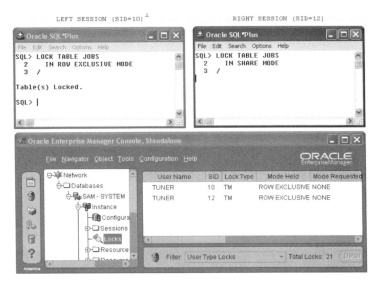

Figure 9-14 · ROW EXCLUSIVE lock mode for Scenario 3

SHARE ROW EXCLUSIVE (SRX) Lock Mode

In Figure 9-15 and 9-16, the session in the upper-left corner is holding a SHARE ROW EXCLUSIVE lock, which does not allow any updates (Figure 9-15) and does not allow other sessions to lock the table (Figure 9-16).

> SRX lock mode is equivalent to S and RX locks on the same table and at the same time.

TIP

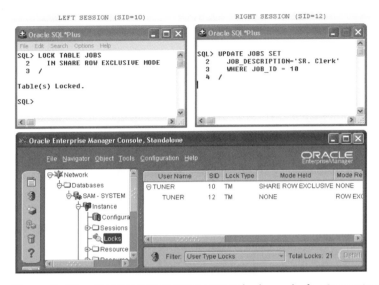

Figure 9-15   SHARE ROW EXCLUSIVE lock mode for Scenario 1

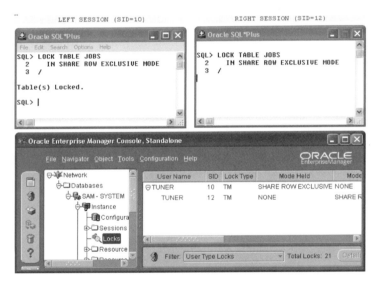

Figure 9-16   SHARE ROW EXCLUSIVE lock mode for Scenario 2

EXCLUSIVE (X) Lock Mode

The session shown in the upper-left corner of Figure 9-17 locks the table in EXCLUSIVE mode, which allows neither updates nor the unlocking of the table in any mode by other sessions.

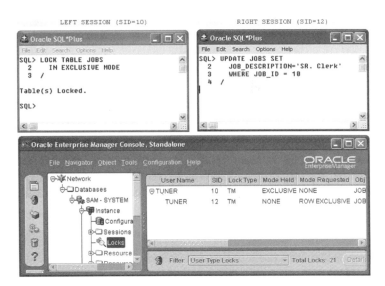

Figure 9-17   EXCLUSIVE lock mode

SELECT...FOR UPDATE STATEMENT

This section begins with a scenario designed to illustrate the practical implications of the SELECT...FOR UPDATE statement. In this scenario, when a new reporting module was deployed in the system of a small telecommunication company, users started to log many complaints about how slow the application had become. The Help desk was flooded with complaints and did not know how to resolve them. The Help desk manager finally held an urgent meeting with the database group to resolve the complaints. The database managers assigned the problems to one of the DBA contractors she had recently hired. The DBA was given little information about the problems; he was told that the users were experiencing long delays when they submitted their changes to be saved, and the response was varying from one minute to 15 minutes.

The DBA started his investigation by looking at the application code to analyze how transactions were managed and controlled. He also instructed the Help desk to inform him when anyone experienced delays. A whole day passed looking at all possibilities that he could imagine, but he could not come up with an answer until he overheard two Help desk employees discussing the fact that these problems started to occur when the new reporting module was installed. Nobody had mentioned this piece of information to him. The DBA immediately asked about the architecture of the new module and was told that the major component of this module was a new OLAP application used by business managers to generate analytical reports.

To determine if the reports were consuming all the CPU resources, he asked a developer to generate one of the reports. The report was very fast and the query generated by the OLAP application was reasonably efficient. This DBA was adamant about the fact that the cause of all these problems was the reporting module. Then he asked one of the managers to run a typical report. As the report was running, he examined the query executed by the report and voila—it was a FOR UPDATE clause in the SELECT statement. He looked at the application to see how the FOR UPDATE clause was used and noticed that one of the report options was checked. This option had a Help tip explaining its use, which read: "Check this to produce accurate and consistent reports." When this option was checked, the FOR UPDATE clause was added to the query.

The major purpose of the SELECT...FOR UPDATE clause is to safeguard the accuracy of reporting. This statement ensures that selected rows do not change while being read. The statement locks rows selected by the SELECT statement as well as all rows in the table that are in ROW SHARE mode and thus effectively disallows any updates to the table. Figure 9-18 shows that the session in the upper-right corner needs to acquire a lock on the row to be updated and needs to wait until the transaction in the upper-left session is completed. Once the session pictured on the upper-left corner issues a COMMIT or ROLL-BACK statement, the session on the upper-right can acquire the lock if it is next in line.

It should be clear that a SELECT...FOR UPDATE statement locks only the rows that are returned by the statement.

NOTE

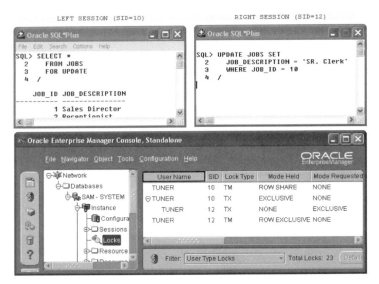

Figure 9-18 SELECT...FOR UPDATE statement

LOCKING EXAMPLES

You are now halfway through the chapter about detecting locks, and you have learned about the locks and how they work. You understand the different lock types and levels. You had a demonstration of each lock mode. So what is next? In this section, you are again presented with several locking examples to tie together and reinforce all the concepts presented earlier and to demonstrate two more practical examples of locking.

Example 1 (Figure 9-19) In this example notice that both sessions are able to secure a lock on the rows to be updated. Both sessions are holding ROW EXCLUSIVE locks. If the session shown in the upper-right corner of Figure 9-19 needs to be updated in the same manner as shown in the same row in the upper-left session, the session would not be able to secure the lock and therefore would wait until the session shown on the left completed its transaction.

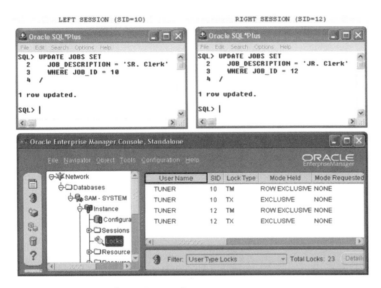

Figure 9-19 Locking Example 1

Example 2 (Figure 9-20) In this example, the following steps occurred:

1. The session on the left secured a ROW EXCLUSIVE lock on the row to be updated.

2. The session on the right issued a SELECT...FOR UPDATE on the same table.

3. Because the locked row in the session on the left is part of the rows that will be selected by the statement on the right, the session on the right cannot acquire a lock on the row updated by the session on the left.

4. The session on the right therefore has to wait until the session on the left completes its transaction.

Oracle always uses the least restrictive lock.

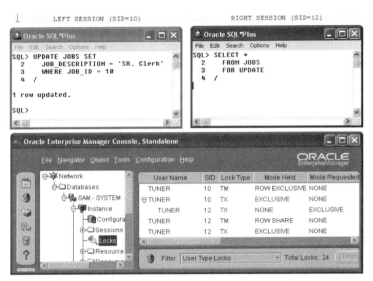

Figure 9-20   Locking Example 2

Example 3 (Figure 9-21) In this example, the session on the left is updating a row and has locked the table in ROW EXCLUSIVE mode and locked the row in EXCLUSIVE mode until a COMMIT or ROLLBACK is issued. The session on the right issued an ALTER statement, which required a lock on the table in EXCLUSIVE mode. Because the table is already locked, an error was returned saying the resource is busy.

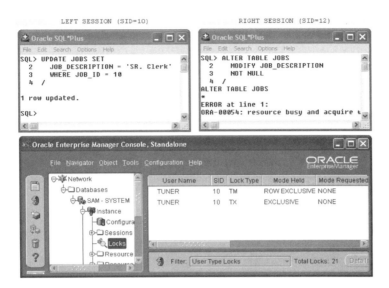

Figure 9-21   Locking Example 3

At this point in the chapter, you have seen various examples of locking and lock modes. Have you determined how locks impact performance? If not, review the examples in this section to see that lock contention impacts performance. Take Example 2 for instance. The session on the right needs to lock the table to protect data from being updated while the session is generating a summary report for management. It must do this because a lock is already placed on the row to be updated.

Examine another scenario for Example 2:

1. The session on the left does not end its transaction in a reasonable time.

2. Because of this, the session on the right starts to experience delays in processing the SELECT statement.

3. In addition, the SELECT...FOR UPDATE statement in the session on the right is locked.

4. The session on the left needs to update another row, but experiences delays in the update because the SELECT...FOR UPDATE statement in the session on the right is locked.

5. The data to be generated for the session on the right is based on a complex query and therefore takes a long time.

The most serious problems with lock contention are the delays that result in user dissatisfaction. To keep your users happy, you learn in the sections that follow the resources for detecting and resolving lock contention.

DML_LOCKS INITIALIZATION PARAMETER

This parameter informs Oracle of the maximum number of DML locks that can be used by an instance for UPDATE, INSERT, and DELETE statements. The default value of this parameter is derived and set to 4 multiplied by the value of the TRANSACTIONS parameter. This formula assumes that an average of four tables are touched in one transaction. As you can see 4 * 187 = 748.

```
SQL> SHOW PARAMETER DML_LOCKS

NAME                                     TYPE        VALUE
---------------------------------------- ----------- ------
dml_locks                                integer     748

SQL> SHOW PARAMETER TRANSACTIONS

NAME                                     TYPE        VALUE
---------------------------------------- ----------- ------
transactions                             integer     187
```

Suppose your application's average transaction impacts six tables and you have set the value of the transactions parameter to 100. In this case, DML_LOCKS should be set to 600.

The DML_LOCKS parameter allows values in the range of 20 to an unlimited value, inclusive. However, if DML_LOCKS is set to 0, it disables enqueue structures. To review, enqueue structures are used to serialize locking requests to database objects. Disabling enqueue structures might enhance performance, but you might not be able to issue statements to lock tables in exclusive mode. The ENQUEUE_RESOURCES parameter is derived from the SESSIONS parameter and informs Oracle of the maximum number of resources that can be locked at the same time.

The DML_LOCKS parameter cannot be set dynamically. You receive an error if you try to set it dynamically, as displayed in the following statement:

```
SQL> ALTER SYSTEM SET DML_LOCKS = 600
  2  /
ALTER SYSTEM SET DML_LOCKS = 600
                 *
ERROR at line 1:
ORA-02095: specified initialization parameter cannot be modified
```

To set DML_LOCKS, you must specify this parameter in the initialization parameter and then bounce the database:

```
DML_LOCKS=1000
```

SET TRANSACTION STATEMENT

You can enhance the performance of an application by specifying the behavior of a transaction. How is this done? This section explains the two settings you can use to enhance application performance. At the session level, you can set the transaction to behave in either a **SERIALIZABLE** or **READ COMMITTED** fashion:

- **SERIALIZABLE**: If a DML statement is attempting to update data in an object that has been updated and committed by another session, the DML statement fails.

- **READ COMMITTED:** If a DML statement is attempting to update data in an object that has been updated by another session and not committed at any time during the session, the DML statement waits until the other session completes its transaction. This is the default behavior as shown in all previous examples.

NOTE

The fundamental point of the SERIALIZABLE isolation level is to make sure that a transaction in this mode always sees the database as it was when the transaction began, regardless of what other transactions do (even if they insert, update, delete, and commit data). The fundamental point of the READ COMMITTED isolation level is that one transaction may see only database changes that have been committed by some other transaction.

Now that you have read how it works, you need to learn how to use the SET TRANSACTION statement. Follow these steps to demonstrate setting a transaction to be SERIALIZABLE:

TIP

To set SQL*Plus prompt to indicate which session you are working with, use:
```
SET SQLPROMPT "Session1 > "
```

Step 1: Open two different sessions using the TUNER account.

Step 2: In the second session, set the transaction isolation level to SERIALIZABLE:

```
SQL> SET TRANSACTION
  2    ISOLATION LEVEL SERIALIZABLE
  3  /

Transaction set.
```

Step 3: In the second session, select a row that will also be updated in the first session:

```
SQL> SELECT *
  2    FROM JOBS
  3   WHERE JOB_ID=99
  4  /

    JOB_ID JOB_DESCRIPTION
---------- ------------------------------
        99 Engineer
```

Step 4: In the first session, update the row selected in the second session and commit the changes:

```
SQL> UPDATE JOBS SET
  2    JOB_DESCRIPTION='SR. Clerk'
  3   WHERE JOB_ID=99
  4  /

1 row updated.

SQL> COMMIT;

Commit complete.
```

Step 5: In the second session, reselect the same row:

```
SQL> SELECT *
  2    FROM JOBS
  3   WHERE JOB_ID=99
  4  /

    JOB_ID JOB_DESCRIPTION
---------- ------------------------------
        99 Engineer
```

Step 6: In the second session, try to update the same row. An error is displayed:

```
SQL> UPDATE JOBS SET
  2    JOB_DESCRIPTION='ENGINEER'
  3   WHERE JOB_ID=99;
UPDATE JOBS SET
       *
ERROR at line 1:
ORA-08177: can't serialize access for this transaction
```

This example demonstrated that when session 2 sets the transaction isolation level to SERIALIZABLE, session 2 checks with session 1 to ensure that no changes are occurring during the transaction, and if session 1 makes changes to the same row and commits, the transaction for session 1 is void.

DEADLOCKS

A DBA received a call from her manager asking her what she did to resolve the latest deadlock incident. The DBA told her manager that she did not take any action. A day later the DBA received another call, but this time from a business manager of the application. He told her that he was concerned about the numerous deadlock incidents that the users were getting. He asked her if she could do something to prevent these annoyances. She explained that this is not a problem that could be fixed by changing the database configuration but is instead an application issue. The business manager was not convinced and escalated the issue to her manager.

So what is a **deadlock?** A deadlock occurs when two or more transactions are attempting and failing to process an object because it is locked. The transactions must wait until the locked objects are released.

A demonstration is provided here to help you understand how a deadlock can occur and how to resolve it. First, follow these steps to create a deadlock.

To begin, open two sessions using the TUNER account and align them side-by-side as illustrated in Figure 9-22.

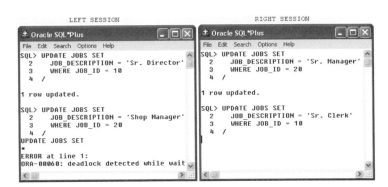

Figure 9-22   Sample deadlock

Step 1: For the session on the left, issue an update statement to update data in one row:

```
SQL> UPDATE JOBS SET
  2    JOB_DESCRIPTION = 'Sr. Director'
  3    WHERE JOB_ID = 10
  4  /
```

Step 2: For the session on the right, issue an update statement to change data for a different row in the same table:

```
SQL> UPDATE JOBS SET
  2    JOB_DESCRIPTION = 'Sr. Manager'
  3    WHERE JOB_ID = 20
  4  /
```

Step 3: For the session on the left, update the same row that was updated in Step 2. Notice that this session hangs (waits for the other session to release the lock on the row).

```
SQL> UPDATE JOBS SET
  2    JOB_DESCRIPTION = 'Shop Manager'
  3    WHERE JOB_ID = 20
  4  /
```

Step 4: For the session on the right, update the same row that was updated in Step 1. When this statement is issued, Oracle detects that a deadlock exists and an error is generated for the session on the left. The session on the right is still waiting for Step 1 to be completed, as illustrated in Figure 9-23.

```
SQL> UPDATE JOBS SET
  2    JOB_DESCRIPTION = 'Sr. Clerk'
  3    WHERE JOB_ID = 10
  4  /
```

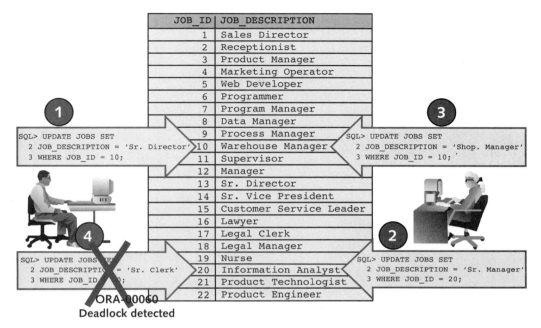

Figure 9-23   Illustration of the deadlock process

When Oracle detects a deadlock, an error is registered in the Alert log indicating the time it occurred as shown in the following code segment. In addition, a trace file is generated to the USER_DUMP_DEST folder that contains the rowid of the locking row.

Contents of the Alert log:

```
. . .
Sun Mar 23 16:51:21 2003
ORA-000060: Deadlock detected. More info in file
c:\oracle\admin\sam\udump\sam_ora_1840.trc.
```

9

Contents of the trace file sam_ora_1840.trc:

```
*** 2003-03-23 16:47:21.000
*** SESSION ID:(14.1006) 2003-03-23 16:47:21.000
DEADLOCK DETECTED
Current SQL statement for this session:
UPDATE JOBS SET
  JOB_DESCRIPTION = 'Shop Manager'
  WHERE JOB_ID = 20
The following deadlock is not an ORACLE error. It is a
deadlock due to user error in the design of an application
or from issuing incorrect ad-hoc SQL. The following
information may aid in determining the deadlock:
Deadlock graph:
                    ---------Blocker(s)--------  ---------Waiter(s)---------
Resource Name        process session holds waits  process session holds waits
TX-00010017-00004583      16      14    X              18      16          X
TX-00030003-0000457f      18      16    X              16      14          X
session 14: DID 0001-0010-00000002  session 16: DID 0001-0012-00000002
session 16: DID 0001-0012-00000002  session 14: DID 0001-0010-00000002
Rows waited on:
Session 16: obj - rowid = 00007731 - AAAHcxAAJAAAA5nAAJ
  (dictionary objn - 30513, file - 9, block - 3687, slot - 9)
Session 14: obj - rowid = 00007731 - AAAHcxAAJAAAA5nAAT
  (dictionary objn - 30513, file - 9, block - 3687, slot - 19)
Information on the OTHER waiting sessions:
Session 16:
  pid=18 serial=113 audsid=1199 user: 65/TUNER
  O/S info: user: AFYOUNI-TOWER\Administrator, term: AFYOUNI_XP, ospid: 196:3296, machine:
AFYOUNI\AFYOUNI_XP
            program: sqlplusw.exe
  application name: SQL*Plus, hash value=3669949024
  Current SQL Statement:
  UPDATE JOBS SET
  JOB_DESCRIPTION = 'Sr. Clerk'
  WHERE JOB_ID = 10
End of information on OTHER waiting sessions.
```

What should you do when this type of thing happens? Even though Oracle generated an error for the session on the left and rolled back the statement in Step 3, this session is still holding a lock on the first statement, and the session on the right is waiting for the lock to be released to complete its transaction. You can use two methods to resolve this problem, and both are fatal to the transaction in the session on the left:

- Issue a ROLLBACK statement to roll back the transaction in the session on the left. This might be possible especially if users are available to issue the ROLLBACK statement on that terminal.

- If you cannot issue a ROLLBACK statement, issue an ALTER SYSTEM KILL SESSION statement to terminate the session on the left. To do this, you need the SID (session id) and SERIAL# (serial number) values for the session, which you can obtain from the V$SESSION view.

```
SQL> SELECT USERNAME, SID, SERIAL#
  2    FROM V$SESSION
  3    WHERE USERNAME IS NOT NULL
  4  /

USERNAME                              SID     SERIAL#
------------------------------- ---------- ----------
SYS                                     9           5
TUNER                                  13        3009
SYSTEM                                 14        1071
SYSTEM                                 16         120
DEMO                                   17         287

SQL> ALTER SYSTEM KILL SESSION '13, 3009'
  2  /

System altered.
```

This section has walked you through a sample deadlock and showed you methods for resolution. If deadlocks occur frequently in an application, you have serious design problems, and the development team may be required to revisit the design and resolve issues at the application level.

DETECTING AND RESOLVING LOCK CONTENTION

At this point, you have looked at all aspects of locks except the tools for detecting them. This section presents the tools available from Oracle to detect lock contention and the steps necessary to resolve them. You start by looking at available views.

Lock Dynamic Performance Views

Oracle has a rich dictionary of views and performance views to assist you to optimally administer your Oracle databases. There are views for every topic or component of a database. Two main dynamic performance views provide helpful information about current lock activities: V$LOCK and V$LOCKED_OBJECT.

V$LOCK

The dynamic performance view V$LOCK contains information about all locks that are currently held by the system and by all connected sessions. Table 9-5 describes each column of this view.

Table 9-5 Dynamic performance view V$LOCK

Column	Description
ADDR	Address of the locked object in memory
KADDR	Address of the lock in memory
SID	Session identification number that is holding or acquiring the lock
TYPE	Type of lock, either system type or user type User type locks: • TX: Row Transaction lock • TM: DML lock • UL: User-defined locks System type locks are more specific to Oracle.
ID1	Lock identifier #1
ID2	Lock identifier #2
LMODE	0 = None 1 = Null 2 = Row Share (RS) or (SS) 3 = Row Exclusive (RX) or (SX) 4 = Share (S) 5 = Share Row Exclusive (SRX) or (SSX) 6 = Exclusive (X)
REQUEST	0 = None 1 = Null 2 = Row Share (RS) or (SS) 3 = Row Exclusive (RX) or (SX) 4 = Share (S) 5 = Share Row Exclusive (SRX) or (SSX) 6 = Exclusive (X)
CTIME	Elapsed time since lock was granted
BLOCK	Lock which is blocking another lock

The information in this table is derived from the online documentation that Oracle provides at the Oracle Technology Network site: *www.otn.oracle.com*.

The following query displays all locks held in the system:

```
SQL> SELECT *
  2     FROM V$LOCK
  3     ORDER BY SID
  4  /

ADDR      KADDR     SID TY    ID1    ID2 LMODE REQUEST CTIME BLOCK
--------  --------  --- --  ------ ----- ----- ------- ----- -----
682BE218  682BE228    2 MR    202      0     4       0 57337     0
682BE1CC  682BE1DC    2 MR    201      0     4       0 57337     0
682BE180  682BE190    2 MR     14      0     4       0 57337     0
682BE134  682BE144    2 MR     13      0     4       0 57337     0
682BE0E8  682BE0F8    2 MR     12      0     4       0 57337     0
682BE09C  682BE0AC    2 MR     11      0     4       0 57337     0
682BE050  682BE060    2 MR     10      0     4       0 57337     0
682BE004  682BE014    2 MR      9      0     4       0 57337     0
682BDFB8  682BDFC8    2 MR      8      0     4       0 57337     0
682BDF6C  682BDF7C    2 MR      7      0     4       0 57337     0
682BDF20  682BDF30    2 MR      6      0     4       0 57337     0
682BDED4  682BDEE4    2 MR      5      0     4       0 57337     0
682BDE88  682BDE98    2 MR      4      0     4       0 57337     0
682BDE3C  682BDE4C    2 MR      3      0     4       0 57337     0
682BDDF0  682BDE00    2 MR      2      0     4       0 57337     0
682BDDA4  682BDDB4    2 MR      1      0     4       0 57337     0
682BDCC0  682BDCD0    3 RT      1      0     6       0 57340     0
682BDB90  682BDBA0    4 XR      4      0     1       0 57341     0
682BDD0C  682BDD1C    5 TS      2      1     3       0 57335     0
67B9AEB0  67B9AFBC   14 TX 524328 17834     6       0   122     0
67B4E0C0  67B4E0D4   14 TM  30513     0     3       0   122     0
682BDC28  682BDC38   14 TX 589825 17773     0       6   105     0
67B91220  67B9132C   16 TX 589825 17773     6       0   108     1
67B4E144  67B4E158   16 TM  30513     0     3       0   108     0
```

As you can see, the results of this query are not obvious. To make this easier to read, it is a good idea to list only locks held by users, not locks held by Oracle. The shaded rows in the preceding code segment are locks held by users. Therefore, to get a more useful display of current lock activities, you must join this table with the V$SESSION view as in the query that follows. This query takes some time to execute, so be patient.

```
SQL> SELECT S.USERNAME,
  2         L.SID,
  3         L.TYPE,
  4         DECODE(L.LMODE   , 0, 'NONE'
  5                          , 1, 'NULL'
  6                          , 2, 'RS'
  7                          , 3, 'RX'
  8                          , 4, 'S'
  9                          , 5, 'SRX'
 10                          , 6, 'X'
 11                          , LMODE, LTRIM(TO_CHAR(LMODE,'990'))) LMODE,
 12         DECODE(L.REQUEST, 0, 'NONE'
 13                          , 1, 'NULL'
 14                          , 2, 'RS'
 15                          , 3, 'RX'
 16                          , 4, 'S'
 17                          , 5, 'SRX'
 18                          , 6, 'X'
 19                          , REQUEST, LTRIM(TO_CHAR(REQUEST,'990'))) REQUEST,
 20         L.ID1,
 21         L.ID2
 22    FROM V$SESSION S, V$LOCK L
 23   WHERE (S.SID = L.SID AND L.REQUEST != 0)
 24      OR (S.SID = L.SID
 25     AND L.REQUEST = 0
 26     AND LMODE != 4
 27     AND (ID1, ID2 ) IN (SELECT A.ID1, A.ID2
 28                           FROM V$LOCK A
 29                          WHERE REQUEST != 0
 30                            AND A.ID1 = L.ID1
 31                            AND A.ID2 = L.ID2 )
 32                        )
 33   ORDER BY ID1,ID2, L.REQUEST
 34   /
```

USERNAME	SID	TY	LMOD	REQU	ID1	ID2
TUNER	16	TX	X	NONE	589825	17773
TUNER	14	TX	NONE	X	589825	17773

V$SESSION view has important columns that identify the row, block, object, and file for which the session is waiting. The following is a structure description of this view highlighting the columns:

```
SQL> DESC V$SESSION
 Name                        Null?      Type
 --------------------------- --------   -------------
 SADDR                                  RAW(4)
 SID                                    NUMBER
 SERIAL#                                NUMBER
 AUDSID                                 NUMBER
 PADDR                                  RAW(4)
 USER#                                  NUMBER
 USERNAME                               VARCHAR2(30)
 COMMAND                                NUMBER
 OWNERID                                NUMBER
 TADDR                                  VARCHAR2(8)
 LOCKWAIT                               VARCHAR2(8)
 STATUS                                 VARCHAR2(8)
 SERVER                                 VARCHAR2(9)
 SCHEMA#                                NUMBER
 SCHEMANAME                             VARCHAR2(30)
 OSUSER                                 VARCHAR2(30)
 PROCESS                                VARCHAR2(12)
 MACHINE                                VARCHAR2(64)
 TERMINAL                               VARCHAR2(16)
 PROGRAM                                VARCHAR2(64)
 TYPE                                   VARCHAR2(10)
 SQL_ADDRESS                            RAW(4)
 SQL_HASH_VALUE                         NUMBER
 PREV_SQL_ADDR                          RAW(4)
 PREV_HASH_VALUE                        NUMBER
 MODULE                                 VARCHAR2(48)
 MODULE_HASH                            NUMBER
 ACTION                                 VARCHAR2(32)
 ACTION_HASH                            NUMBER
 CLIENT_INFO                            VARCHAR2(64)
 FIXED_TABLE_SEQUENCE                   NUMBER
 ROW_WAIT_OBJ#                          NUMBER
 ROW_WAIT_FILE#                         NUMBER
 ROW_WAIT_BLOCK#                        NUMBER
 ROW_WAIT_ROW#                          NUMBER
 LOGON_TIME                             DATE
 LAST_CALL_ET                           NUMBER
 PDML_ENABLED                           VARCHAR2(3)
 FAILOVER_TYPE                          VARCHAR2(13)
 FAILOVER_METHOD                        VARCHAR2(10)
 FAILED_OVER                            VARCHAR2(3)
 RESOURCE_CONSUMER_GROU                 VARCHAR2(32)
 PDML_STATUS                            VARCHAR2(8)
 PDDL_STATUS                            VARCHAR2(8)
 PQ_STATUS                              VARCHAR2(8)
 CURRENT_QUEUE_DURATION                 NUMBER
 CLIENT_IDENTIFIER                      VARCHAR2(64)
```

9

- ROW_WAIT_ROW#: Rowid of the row being locked

- ROW_WAIT_BLOCK#: Identification number of the block in which the blocked row resides

- ROW_WAIT_OBJ#: Identification number of the object in which the blocked row resides

- ROW_WAIT_FILE#: Identification number of the file in which the blocked row resides

DBA_BLOCKERS Dictionary View

This view has only one column, which is the session ID for the session(s) that are blocking other users:

```
SQL> DESC DBA_BLOCKERS
 NAME                      NULL?     TYPE
 --------------------- -------- ------
 HOLDING_SESSION                     NUMBER

SQL> SELECT *
  2    FROM DBA_BLOCKERS
  3  /

HOLDING_SESSION
---------------
             16
```

NOTE

If DBA_BLOCKERS and DBA_WAITERS do not exist, you can create them using CATBLOCK.SQL [found in the ORACLE_HOME/rdbms/admin folder).

DBA_WAITERS Dictionary View

This view displays the session IDs for sessions that are waiting for a lock to be released by the blocking session. The listing that follows describes the structure of the view and its contents:

```
SQL> DESC DBA_WAITERS
 Name                      Null?     Type
 ------------------------- --------  ------------
 WAITING_SESSION                     NUMBER
 HOLDING_SESSION                     NUMBER
 LOCK_TYPE                           VARCHAR2(26)
 MODE_HELD                           VARCHAR2(40)
 MODE_REQUESTED                      VARCHAR2(40)
 LOCK_ID1                            NUMBER
 LOCK_ID2                            NUMBER

SQL> SELECT WAITING_SESSION,
  2          HOLDING_SESSION,
  3          LOCK_TYPE,
  4          MODE_HELD
  5     FROM DBA_WAITERS
  6  /

WAITING_SESSION HOLDING_SESSION LOCK_TYPE   MODE_HELD
--------------- --------------- ----------- ---------
             14              16 Transaction Exclusive
```

9

V$LOCKED_OBJECT

Every now and then you may want to see what objects are locked and in what lock mode they are locked so that you can note which objects are in contention. In cases like this, you can use V$LOCKED_OBJECT view which contains all objects that are locked by different sessions. The following listing displays the structure of this view and the objects that are currently locked:

```
SQL> DESC V$LOCKED_OBJECT
 Name                 Null?     Type
 ----------------     --------  -----------
 XIDUSN                         NUMBER
 XIDSLOT                        NUMBER
 XIDSQN                         NUMBER
 OBJECT_ID                      NUMBER
 SESSION_ID                     NUMBER
 ORACLE_USERNAME                VARCHAR2(30)
 OS_USER_NAME                   VARCHAR2(30)
 PROCESS                        VARCHAR2(12)
 LOCKED_MODE                    NUMBER

SQL> SELECT  OBJECT_NAME,
  2          ORACLE_USERNAME,
  3          LOCKED_MODE
  4    FROM V$LOCKED_OBJECT L,
  5         DBA_OBJECTS O
  6   WHERE L.OBJECT_ID = O.OBJECT_ID
  7  /

OBJECT_NAME  ORACLE_USERNAME  LOCKED_MODE
-----------  ---------------  -----------
JOBS         TUNER                      3
JOBS         TUNER                      3
```

Blockers and Waiters

A junior DBA worked very hard to create a script to monitor any session that held a lock blocking other sessions. This script paged him every time a **blocking lock** occurred. He was excited that he could pinpoint the session causing delays. It did not take much time when his pager was flooded with alerts about blocking sessions. If that was not enough, every time he got a page and tried to log on and view the blocking session, the lock vanished. To relieve the frustration he called his professor and was surprised to hear that he should not be concerned about blocking sessions, but he should be concerned with sessions that hold locks blocking other sessions for lengthy periods such as five minutes and more. The professor said "What is important is to know why a session is holding a lock on an object for a long time while other sessions are waiting to acquire the lock in order to proceed with the transaction."

You will be asked many times to determine if a user is being blocked by another user. This usually occurs when a user experiences delays in DML statement response time. In cases like this, you can use any of the following two listed queries. In principal the two queries return similar results but use different dynamic performance views to display the results.

Query 1 (using DBA_WAITERS view):

```
SQL> SELECT 'Blocker('||BW.HOLDING_SESSION||':'||SB.USERNAME||') - SQL: '||BQ.SQL_TEXT BLOCKERS,
  2         'Waiter ('||BW.WAITING_SESSION||':'||SW.USERNAME||') - SQL: '||SQ.SQL_TEXT WAITERS
  3    FROM DBA_WAITERS BW,
  4         V$SESSION SB,
  5         V$SESSION SW,
  6         V$SQLAREA BQ,
  7         V$SQLAREA SQ
  8   WHERE BW.HOLDING_SESSION = SB.SID
  9     AND BW.WAITING_SESSION = SW.SID
 10     AND SB.PREV_SQL_ADDR   = BQ.ADDRESS
 11     AND SW.SQL_ADDRESS     = SQ.ADDRESS
 12     AND BW.mode_HELD <> 'None'
 13  /

BLOCKERS
------------------------------------------------------------------------------
WAITERS
------------------------------------------------------------------------------
Blocker(13:TUNER) - SQL: UPDATE JOBS SET   JOB_DESCRIPTION = 'Sr. Clerk'   WHERE JOB_ID = 10
Waiter (17:DEMO) - SQL: UPDATE TUNER.JOBS SET   JOB_DESCRIPTION = 'Sr. Clerk'   WHERE JOB_ID = 10

Blocker(13:TUNER) - SQL: UPDATE JOBS SET   JOB_DESCRIPTION = 'Sr. Clerk'   WHERE JOB_ID = 10
Waiter (14:SYSTEM) - SQL: UPDATE TUNER.JOBS SET   JOB_DESCRIPTION = 'Sr. Clerk'   WHERE JOB_ID = 10
```

Query 2 (using V$LOCK):

```
SQL> SELECT DISTINCT
  2         'Blocker('||LB.SID||':'||SB.USERNAME||') - SQL: '||QB.SQL_TEXT BLOCKERS,
  3         'Waiter ('||LW.SID||':'||SW.USERNAME||') - SQL: '||QW.SQL_TEXT WAITERS
  4    FROM V$LOCK LB, V$SESSION SB, V$LOCK LW, V$SESSION SW, V$SQL QB, V$SQL QW
  5   WHERE LB.SID = SB.SID
  6     AND LW.SID = SW.SID
  7     AND SB.PREV_SQL_ADDR = QB.ADDRESS
  8     AND SW.SQL_ADDRESS = QW.ADDRESS
  9     AND LB.ID1 = LW.ID1
 10     AND SW.LOCKWAIT IS NOT NULL
 11     AND SB.LOCKWAIT IS NULL
 12     AND LB.BLOCK = 1
 13  /

BLOCKERS
------------------------------------------------------------------------------
WAITERS
------------------------------------------------------------------------------
Blocker(13:TUNER) - SQL: UPDATE JOBS SET JOB_DESCRIPTION='Sr. Clerk' WHERE JOB_ID=10
Waiter (14:SYSTEM) - SQL: UPDATE JOBS SET JOB_DESCRIPTION='Sr. Clerk' WHERE JOB_ID=10

Blocker(13:TUNER) - SQL: UPDATE JOBS SET JOB_DESCRIPTION='Sr. Clerk' WHERE JOB_ID=10
Waiter (17:DEMO) - SQL: UPDATE JOBS SET JOB_DESCRIPTION='Sr. Clerk' WHERE JOB_ID = 10
```

UTLLOCKT.SQL Script

As previously stated, Oracle provides dynamic performance views that supply helpful information about current lock activities. In addition to the views, Oracle has created a script entitled UTLLOCKT.SQL that displays a treelike report listing all blocking and waiting sessions as displayed in the query that follows. This script resides under ORA-

CLE_HOME\rdbms\admin folder. When you run UTLLOCKT.SQL, it creates two temporary tables: DBA_LOCKS_TEMP and LOCK_HOLDERS. Note that all indented sessions (14 and 17) are waiting for session 13 to release its lock.

```
WAITING_SESSION LOCK_TYPE    MODE_REQUESTED MODE_HELD LOCK_ID1 LOCK_ID2
--------------- -----------  -------------- --------- -------- --------
13              None
   14           Transaction Exclusive       Exclusive 65559    18097
   17           Transaction Exclusive       Exclusive 65559    18097
```

DBMS_LOCK Package

Suppose you are building an application and want to manage on your own the locking mechanism that Oracle employs. Managing the mechanism on your own means that you issue the request for a lock for a specific mode, you name the lock, you change the lock type, and finally you release the lock. The DBMS_LOCK package is an Oracle-supplied PL/SQL stored package that enables you to create user-defined locks and manage them on your own. For more details on this package, consult the Oracle documentation, *Oracle9i Supplied PL/SQL Packages and Types Reference Release 2 (9.2)*.

Oracle Enterprise Manager

Oracle Enterprise Manager provides three different utilities for monitoring and detecting locks:

- Locks option of the Oracle Enterprise Manager console (introduced earlier in the chapter)

- Lock Manager (part of the Performance Pack)

- Locks option of Oracle Performance Manager, which employs many functions including the Lock Manager listed in Step 2

To become familiar with the Lock Manager, work through the steps that follow:

Step 1: Log on to the Oracle Enterprise Manager.

Step 2: On the tool bar on the left, click the **Diagnostics Pack** icon and then select the **Lock Manager**, as shown in Figure 9-24.

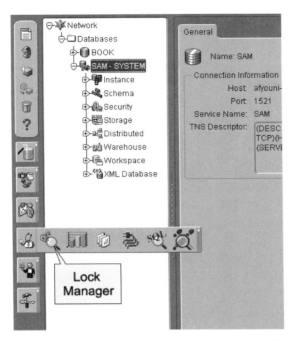

Figure 9-24   Oracle Enterprise Manager toolbar showing the Lock Manager icon

Step 3: The main window is displayed listing all locks in the system. This main window is refreshed every few seconds, according to the timing you set (see Figure 9-25).

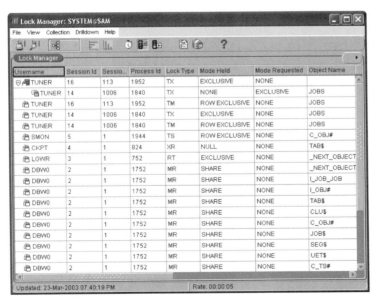

Figure 9-25   Lock Manager main window

Step 4: In the drill-down menu option, you can view only user lock types as shown in Figure 9-26.

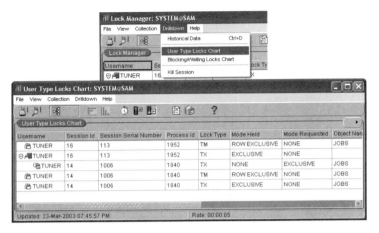

Figure 9-26   Lock Manager showing user lock types

Follow these steps to use the Locks option of Oracle Performance Manager, which assists DBAs in viewing the health of the database:

Step 1: In the Oracle Enterprise Manager, select the **Performance Manager** icon on the Diagnostic Pack toolbar, as illustrated in Figure 9-27.

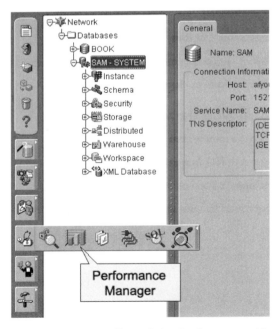

Figure 9-27   Toolbar of the Performance Manager Diagnostic Pack

Step 2: A double-paned Performance Manager screen is displayed (see the background screen of Figure 9-28). The left pane presents a tree structure of all performance options available in this tool, including the Locks option. The right pane shows details of each option. Figure 9-28 (foreground screen) displays details of Locks node and Lock Manager. For more details on how to use these tools, consult Oracle Enterprise Manager documentation.

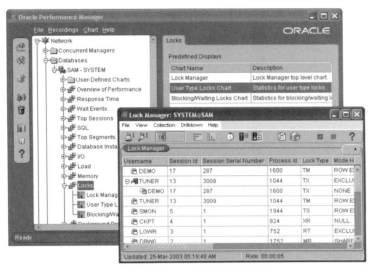

Figure 9-28   Performance Manager showing locks options

Resolving Lock Contention

Now that you've worked through the details of lock contention, it may help to examine a summary of the essence of resolving lock contention. Here is a recap of major points that were addressed in this chapter:

- Blocking locks can result in delays, especially when the blocking locks are held for a long time.

- Your database application should be designed to use short transactions to prevent blocking locks.

- You should monitor locks that are being held for more than one minute to determine the reason for the length of the lock hold.

When you detect a blocking lock, you should get the DML statement or the query that was issued, and based on that statement or query, respond as follows:

- Determine the session holding the statement, and if possible, contact the user and inquire how long he expects this statement to run and if it has run before.

- If the statement is a DML and is part of a transaction, you should consult the business manager to get an approval to terminate the session.

In summary, to resolve lock contention, you end the transaction if possible, or if not, you terminate the session by using ALTER SYSTEM KILL SESSION.

TEN BEST PRACTICES

This list summarizes ten best practices for detecting lock contention, which have been presented in this chapter. The list has no particular order:

1. Make sure that applications do not run long transactions.

2. Commit often to avoid locking row(s) for a long time.

3. Avoid using the LOCK command to lock tables.

4. Perform DDL operations during off-peak hours.

5. Perform long running queries and transactions during off-peak hours.

6. Ensure that developers use the least restrictive locking mode and carefully design transactions that prevent lock contention.

7. Monitor locks that are blocking others and investigate why these locks are being held.

8. Determine why blocking locks are being held for a long duration and try to prevent them.

9. Watch how frequently deadlocks are occurring and resolve them.

10. When a deadlock occurs, resolve it by rolling back the transaction or terminating the session.

CHAPTER SUMMARY

- A lock is a mechanism that protects a database object from being altered while it is being modified by other processes or users.

- An enqueue is a data structure for locks that informs Oracle of who is waiting for a resource that is locked by another session.

- Locks are held and released by Oracle automatically according to the start and completion of a transaction.

- Application logic indirectly controls locks.

- There are five different lock modes: SHARE, ROW SHARE, ROW EXCLUSIVE, SHARE ROW EXCLUSIVE, and EXCLUSIVE.

- The lock mode held by an ALTER statement is EXCLUSIVE.

- The lowest lock level Oracle provides is at the row level.

- DBAs use LOCK statements to manually lock a table in any desired lock mode.

- The FOR UPDATE clause of the SELECT statement is used for reporting accuracy. The row selected is locked in the ROW SHARE lock mode.

❐ The DML_LOCKS initialization parameter informs Oracle of the maximum number of locks an instance can have.

❐ Oracle supports two modes of transaction behavior, SERIALIZABLE and READ COMMITTED.

❐ The SET TRANSACTION statement defines the behavior of a transaction by using SERIALIZABLE or READ COMMITTED options.

❐ A deadlock occurs when two or more sessions are waiting for each other to release and acquire a necessary lock.

❐ When a transaction deadlock is detected, Oracle automatically rolls back the last statement.

❐ When a deadlock is detected, an entry is registered in the Alert log and the rowid of the locking row is entered in a trace file.

REVIEW QUESTIONS

1. DBAs manage locks. (True/False)

2. ROW SHARE is also known as SUBSHARE. (True/False)

3. EXCLUSIVE lock mode does not allow any other session to lock the object in any mode. (True/False)

4. SRX (also known as SSX) allows other transactions to lock the table in an (S) mode. (True/False)

5. You should never use the SELECT...FOR UPDATE statement because it locks a table from being updated. (True/False)

6. There are two rows displayed in V$LOCK for an update statement. (True/False)

7. RX lock mode results from an update statement. (True/False)

8. Deadlocks cannot be controlled by an application. (True/False)

9. When you issue a COMMENT statement on a table, the lock mode held by the statement is in SHARE. (True/False)

10. A NOWAIT clause informs Oracle that it should acquire the lock immediately without waiting for it to be released. (True/False)

11. Outline in detail the steps to produce a blocking lock.

12. Write a query that displays all objects and details about the objects that are locked.

13. Write a query that generates a report displaying the rowid and the object name for the locking row.

14. List all the different methods you can use to detect locks.

15. How do you resolve a blocking lock?

16. Write a query that shows the USERNAME, SID, SERIAL#, OSUSER, and QUERY for each lock held by users.

17. Simulate a deadlock with three different sessions.

9

18. Locate all errors, row, and lock information caused by the deadlock in Question 17.

EXAM REVIEW QUESTIONS: ORACLE9*i* PERFORMANCE TUNING (#1Z0-033)

1. Which statement is true about deadlocks?

    a. DBAs need do nothing because the transaction is rolled back.

    b. DML locks are acquired and managed by Oracle.

    c. ROW EXCLUSIVE is the least restrictive lock mode.

    d. Row-level locking is not supported by Oracle.

    e. DBAs must terminate the session that detected the deadlock.

2. Which statement is true when a lock is detected? You should:

    a. Terminate the session that is waiting for the lock.

    b. Terminate both the blocking session and the waiting session.

    c. Try to roll back the blocking transaction. If this is not possible, terminate the session.

    d. Do not terminate any sessions until a thorough investigation is completed.

    e. React only when someone complains.

3. How do you detect deadlock?

    a. By monitoring V$LOCK

    b. By monitoring ALERT.LOG

    c. From an application error ORA-00600

    d. By monitoring active sessions

4. Which situation could cause lock contention?

    a. Not enough locks

    b. Too many concurrent transactions

    c. Too many locks

    d. Long transactions

5. How long is a lock held?

   a. For the duration of the session

   b. For the duration of the statement that acquired the lock

   c. For as long as the object is being accessed

   d. For the duration of the transaction

6. When a deadlock occurs, what information is registered in the Alert log?

   a. Rowid of the locking row

   b. SID of the blocking row

   c. Name of the trace file that contains information about the deadlock

   d. Time, date, and ORA-00600

7. While working on a transaction, an end–user received an ORA-00600 error. What should he do and what should you do?

   a. The user should ask a DBA to immediately terminate the other session that caused the deadlock.

   b. The DBA should ask the user who caused the deadlock to roll back his transaction.

   c. The user should roll back his transaction.

   d. The user should ask a DBA to assist him in terminating his session.

   e. The user and DBA should wait for the other transaction to complete.

8. What view do you query to find locked objects?

   a. DBA_LOCKED_OBJECTS

   b. DBA_LOCK_OBJECTS

   c. DBA_LOCK_OBJECT

   d. V$LOCKED_OBJECTS

   e. V$LOCKED_OBJECT

   f. V$LOCK_OBJECT

9

9. What should be your objective when you are designing a database application?

   a. Make sure you explicitly lock the table at the start of the transaction and release the lock at the end of the transaction.

   b. Avoid manual table locks.

   c. Always detect locks before the start of a transaction.

   d. Perform frequent checks on currently held locks and their mode during transactions.

10. Which view do you query to locate a locking session?

    a. V$LOCK

    b. DBA_LOCKED_OBJECTS

    c. V$SESSION

    d. DBA_BLOCKERS

    e. V$SQL

11. Which script do you use to display a lock tree?

    a. UTLLOCKT.SQL

    b. UTLBLOCK.SQL

    c. CATBLOCK.SQL

    d. CATLOCK.SQL

    e. UTTLOCKL.SQL

12. What information do you need to know to terminate a session?

    a. Username and query submitted

    b. Username and SID

    c. Username and serial number

    d. SID and serial number

13. What statement locks a table and prevents others from locking it without waiting to acquire the lock?

    a. LOCK TABLE test IN EXCLUSIVE MODE NO WAIT

    b. LOCK TABLE test IN ROW EXCLUSIVE NO WAIT

    c. LOCK TABLE test IN EXCLUSIVE MODE NOWAIT

    d. LOCK TABLE test IN ROW EXCLUSIVE NOWAIT

14. Which statement locks objects in EXCLUSIVE mode?

    a. ALTER

    b. DDL

    c. DML

    d. DROP

15. What does SELECT...FOR UPDATE do?

    a. Locks all rows selected against updating

    b. Prevents other transactions from updating the table

    c. Prevents other sessions from reading the table

    d. Does not allow other sessions to perform SELECT...FOR UPDATE statements

---

HANDS-ON PROJECTS

HANDS-ON PROJECTS

9

Please complete the projects provided below.

1. Reread the Performance Problem at the start of the chapter. Think of it in terms of the concepts you have learned in this chapter and perform the tasks and answer the following questions:

    a. Provide one example that simulates the problem that the application is experiencing.

    b. Answer the questions posed by Tim Smith.

2. A new application went into production this morning. At lunch you decided to go shopping in the nearby mall. When you reached the mall, you started to receive one page per minute about an ORA-00600 error occurring in the database. Perform the tasks and answer the following questions:

    a. List all the possible causes that could have generated this error.

    b. How can you prevent this error?

    c. How would you resolve this error?

3. A customer service representative received a call from a client about an account issue that needed to be corrected. As the representative was about to press the Save button in the application to commit customer changes entered, the fire alarm sounded and he had to leave the building. When the fire alarm was over, he returned to his desk and noticed that the application that he was working on generated an error asking him to call the DBA, so he called you to report the problem.

   a. List the steps that you would take to investigate the problem.

   b. Suppose the error was ORA-000060. What action would you take?

4. A developer called you about a problem he was having with one of the forms he was working on. He stated, "The current form that I am writing works fine when no other instance of the form is running. But the moment I run another instance, it hangs." List all the possible causes of the problem and describe what you would advise him to do.

5. While your manager was on vacation, you got a voice mail from her asking you to study the lock behavior of the application by collecting lock statistics for one week. Outline all the steps necessary to accomplish this task.

6. Describe four different ways to lock a whole table.

7. Issue two statements that would result in a blocking and waiting situation. List all the Oracle Enterprise Manager tools for detecting or monitoring locks.

8. List all available lock modes available in Oracle and order them from least restrictive to most restrictive.

9. The CEO and the manager of the company you work for came to your cube. You were surprised to see them. Your manager said, "Bob I would like to introduce to you our CEO, Mr. Badry. Mr. Badry is having a problem with the database application you installed last week. Each time he wants to update information in the Executive form, it takes a long time to save. As you know Bob, Mr. Badry is a very busy man. Could you please help him?" Then Mr. Badry said, "Bob, I hear a lot of good things about you. Could you please take care of it right away? Oh, and by the way, I usually do this task every morning around 7:00 a.m."

Outline all the possible causes of Mr. Badry's performance problem.

CASE PROJECTS

Transactions and Deadlocks

A question was posted on one of the DBA Web sites asking for a demonstration of how deadlocks work and their impact on transaction performance. One of the experts replied with the following tasks. Using the TUNER schema, perform the following tasks. Make sure you only have two TUNER sessions open, one session opened by SYSTEM and the other session opened by the Oracle Enterprise Manager.

1. Create two sessions.

2. Make sure that the auto commit setting is off.

3. The company CEO issued a 10 percent raise. Issue an update statement to reflect the raise. Do not commit the changes.

4. In session 1, submit a query to list the first 10 rows of the EMPLOYEES table to see the changes.

5. Using the Oracle Enterprise Manager, view the status of the locks held and record the SID and lock mode for each lock.

6. In session 1, submit the same query as in Step 4, but this time add a FOR UPDATE clause.

7. Using the Oracle Enterprise Manager, view the status of the locks held. Are the same locks held as in Step 5? If not, what is different and why?

8. In session 2, change the LAST_NAME column from 20 characters to 30 characters. Explain what happens.

9. In session 2, try to lock the table manually in (S) mode. Explain what happens.

10. In session 2, update the first row in the EMPLOYEES table changing the first name to TOMMY. Explain what happens.

11. In session 2, select the last 10 rows in the table using SELECT...FOR UPDATE. Explain what happens.

12. Using the Oracle Enterprise Manager, view all held locks.

13. Using session 3 as SYSTEM, write a query or issue a statement that produces the same results as in Step 12.

14. In session 1, update the first row in the EMPLOYEES table. Set FIRST_NAME to TOM. Did a deadlock occur? If not, why?

15. If Step 4 did not produce a deadlock, using the existing session, write a statement for the proper session to produce a deadlock.

16. List all blocking locks and resolve them.

9

10

OTHER TUNING ISSUES

In this chapter you will:

- ◆ Understand the role of Oracle background processes
- ◆ Detect background process contention
- ◆ Understand the concept of latches
- ◆ Tune and monitor an operating system

This chapter presents information on Oracle background processes, latches, and operating system issues that you can apply to enhance database performance. The topics have little to do with each other, but are grouped here as miscellaneous topics that are important to learn as you understand more about your database and your system.

The first section of the chapter reviews how Oracle background processes work and shows you how to enhance their performance. The second section presents latches and how you can detect contention. And finally, the third section discusses operating system components to be examined when you have exhausted all your efforts to tune the application and database. In this chapter, you will also look at the various monitoring tools available in Windows and UNIX.

Performance Problem

This section outlines an actual performance problem. As you look it over, imagine yourself as the DBA who reported it and keep it in mind as you proceed through the chapter. The chapter presents concepts relevant to the problem. In the first Hands-on Project at the end of the chapter, you are asked to use the concepts you have learned to provide a solution, or partial solution, to this performance problem.

From: Jack Kellog <mailto: jkellog@str.com>

DATE: 13-Dec-02 12:20

SUBJECT: Heavy redo log activity and slow LGWR performance

Hello,

We are running Oracle9i (9.0.1) on Sun OS 5.8, and we have set the log_buffer to 1 MB, and the redo log file size to 500 MB (three redo log groups, two members each) for our batch jobs. We noticed the POOR performance of a simple sql insert statement: inserted into T2 (pkey) select pkey from T1 -- with 2.5 million rows it will take over seven minutes, which caused a bottleneck at redo log (LGWR), i.e., log write slow.

Here are the stats (V$sysstat):
redo synch writes 205
redo synch time 27916
redo entries 2519548
redo size 993708316
redo buffer allocation retries 5455
redo wastage 744276
redo writer latching time 0
redo writes 3310
redo blocks written 2003549
redo write time 407539
redo log space requests 13
redo log space wait time 1286
redo log switch interrupts 0
redo ordering marks 2

By comparison, it only took < 2 minute to do this by create table as select.

We would appreciate any insight into why we have such a bottleneck and how we can work around it.

Your help is much appreciated

Jack

TUNING BACKGROUND PROCESSES

As you already know, Oracle architecture consists of logical and physical components. The logical component comprises memory and background processes. Background processes are the core of the Oracle engine that makes Oracle one of the leading database management systems in the database arena. Oracle has invested significant amounts of man-hours and dollars to provide advanced features backed by efficient fundamental database functionality. Background processes are the backbone of Oracle, and for that reason they are written to operate very efficiently. However, Oracle provides flexibility that enables you to tune some of the background processes as discussed in this section.

NOTE A **process** is a program that performs a specific task. An Oracle process is a program that comprises several related programs that make up the database management system.

Figure 10-1 illustrates the architecture of the Oracle instance showing memory structure as well as the background processes. As you can see, these processes are an integral part of the Oracle instance, which acts as controller of the resources, as well as the interface to the physical component of the Oracle database. Appendix A provides an overview of Oracle architecture.

10

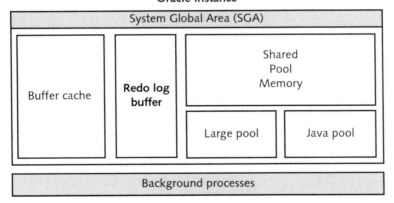

Figure 10-1   The instance architecture of Oracle showing memory and background processes as integral parts

Table 10-1 lists the main processes with a brief description of each. Notice that each background process is purposely restricted to a single specific task to reduce the amount of work for each process and increase its efficiency.

Table 10-1 Oracle's main background processes

Process	Name	Description
ARC*n*	Archiver	Reads the contents of the redo log file and writes it to a file called archived log. This process only runs if the database is in an ARCHIVELOG mode (n is 0-9).
CKPT	Checkpoint	Synchronizes all data files with System Change Numbers (SCNs)
DBW*n*	Database Writer or DB Writer	Writes the dirty block buffers to data files (n is 0-9)
LGWR	Log Writer	Writes all entries in the log buffer to redo log files
PMON	Process Monitor	Monitors status of other processes including user processes. When a process is defunct, PMON cleans up after it by releasing memory held by the defunct process.
SMON	System Monitor	Monitors and registers all events in the database to the alert file; performs automatic recovery

Oracle background processes do not require tuning to run efficiently because they are highly optimized. However, in some situations, Oracle provides you with flexibility to enhance performance. Figure 10-2 illustrates the I/O activities of an Oracle background process caused by one DML statement. Of all the main Oracle background processes, only the ARCH, CKPT, DBWR, and LGWR processes shown in Figure 10-2 can be enhanced.

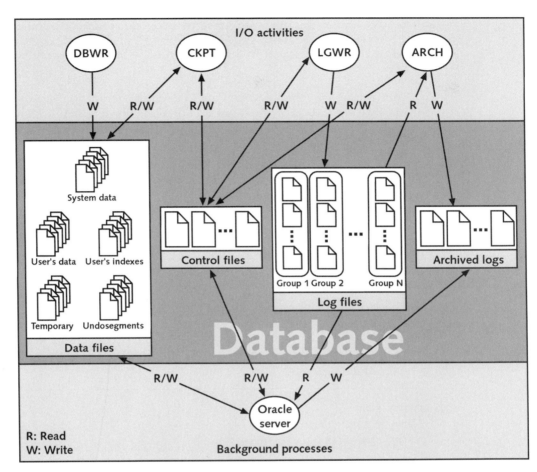

Figure 10-2   Background processes and I/O activities

ARCn Process

The **ARCn** process performs a single task: it archives the redo log file to a file called the archived log file. As you know, when you set a database in ARCHIVELOG mode, you are telling Oracle not to overwrite any redo log until the ARCn process has finished writing the redo log to an archived log. As illustrated in Figure 10-2, the number of reads for ARCn is 2 while the number of reads for LGWR is 1. This means that the ARCn process is working harder than the LGWR process and could lead to performance problems if ARCn does not keep pace with LGWR. For instance, suppose there are a huge number of transactions in the database that will fill up the redo log quickly. If the ARCn process fails for some reason or does not read and write the redo log quickly, users will notice performance degradation. The following list outlines reasons why an ARCn process could fail or fall behind the pace of LGWR:

- The ARCn process is not fast enough to write to the destination due to slow I/O channels, device speed, or contention on the device or destination.

- The ARC*n* process is not able to read redo logs due to LGWR contention.

- There is not enough space on the destination device to which archive logs are written.

- If your database is configured to write to a remote destination and is set to be mandatory, the ARC*n* process must wait until the file is written, which is a process that may be impacted by network traffic or bandwidth.

NOTE If the ARC*n* process cannot complete the writing of a redo log to an archived log file, the database literally halts operation and warnings are generated to the alert log.

To determine if the ARC*n* process is performing efficiently, monitor the frequency and duration of writes using any or all of the following methods.

System Events

Oracle keeps track of different wait events in the system. The V$SYSTEM_EVENT dynamic performance view contains information about events that caused a wait. It does not show an event that caused no wait. The V$EVENT_NAME view contains all events that may occur in the system. The events of interest related to the ARC*n* process are listed in the following results of the query:

```
SQL> SELECT NAME
  2    FROM V$EVENT_NAME
  3   WHERE NAME LIKE 'log file switch%'
  4  /

NAME
-------------------------------------------
log file switch (checkpoint incomplete)
log file switch (archiving needed)
log file switch (clearing log file)
log file switch completion

SQL> SELECT *
  2    FROM V$SYSTEM_EVENT
  3   WHERE EVENT LIKE 'log file switch (archiving%'
  4  /

no rows selected
```

Of the wait events listed, log file switch (archiving needed) is an event that indicates that the LGWR waited for the ARC*n* to archive the log to which it was trying to switch. A high value (above 0) indicates that the ARC*n* process is not fast enough. The column named VALUE holds this value.

V$ARCHIVED_LOG

This view contains control file information about archived logs and tells you how often an archived log is being generated and how long it takes to be written. The following query displays results for all archived logs generated in one day. The results show that the ARC*n* process is not highly active. The number of generated archived logs is low, and it is taking a long time to switch from one log file group to another. So, in this case, the results are not alarming.

```
SQL> SELECT NAME,
  2          BLOCKS,
  3          STATUS,
  4          TO_CHAR(FIRST_TIME,
  5                  'DD-MON-YYYY HH24:MI:SS') STARTED,
  6          TO_CHAR(COMPLETION_TIME,
  7                  'DD-MON-YYYY HH24:MI:SS') COMPLETE
  8     FROM V$ARCHIVED_LOG
  9    WHERE TRUNC(FIRST_TIME) = '11-MAR-2003'
 10    /

NAME           BLOCKS    S STARTED               COMPLETE
------------   --------- - -------------------   --------------------
arc_5607.arc   1023998 A 11-MAR-2003 00:23:00 11-MAR-2003 01:12:01
arc_5608.arc   1023998 A 11-MAR-2003 01:10:59 11-MAR-2003 03:07:32
arc_5609.arc   1023998 A 11-MAR-2003 03:06:29 11-MAR-2003 06:38:32
arc_5610.arc   1023998 A 11-MAR-2003 06:37:39 11-MAR-2003 08:48:34
arc_5611.arc   1023998 A 11-MAR-2003 08:47:39 11-MAR-2003 10:59:48
arc_5612.arc   1023998 A 11-MAR-2003 10:58:55 11-MAR-2003 13:24:50
arc_5613.arc   1023998 A 11-MAR-2003 13:23:47 11-MAR-2003 13:56:56
arc_5614.arc   1023998 A 11-MAR-2003 13:55:54 11-MAR-2003 14:50:35
arc_5615.arc   1023998 A 11-MAR-2003 14:49:27 11-MAR-2003 15:56:47
arc_5616.arc   1023998 A 11-MAR-2003 15:55:54 11-MAR-2003 17:16:29
arc_5617.arc   1023995 A 11-MAR-2003 17:15:34 11-MAR-2003 18:46:00
arc_5618.arc   1023998 A 11-MAR-2003 18:45:10 11-MAR-2003 20:16:39
arc_5619.arc   1023998 A 11-MAR-2003 20:15:45 11-MAR-2003 22:46:33
```

10

V$ARCHIVED_PROCESSES

This view shows the number of ARC*n* processes that are active and whether each process is busy or idle. The following query lists the contents of this view:

```
SQL> SELECT *
  2     FROM V$ARCHIVE_PROCESSES
  3  /

   PROCESS STATUS       LOG_SEQUENCE STAT
---------- ----------   ------------ ----
         0 ACTIVE                  0 IDLE
         1 ACTIVE                  0 IDLE
         2 STOPPED                 0 IDLE
         3 STOPPED                 0 IDLE
         4 STOPPED                 0 IDLE
         5 STOPPED                 0 IDLE
         6 STOPPED                 0 IDLE
         7 STOPPED                 0 IDLE
         8 STOPPED                 0 IDLE
         9 STOPPED                 0 IDLE
```

ARCn Configuration

To avoid performance problems generated by ARCn, Oracle provides a configuration to spawn more than one process of the ARCn. This distributes the load on more than one process and thus increases the chance that the ARCn process will be able to keep pace with the LGWR. The LOG_ARCHIVE_MAX parameter configures the maximum number of ARCn processes that Oracle can start. The default value is 2 and the maximum value is 10. The following statement shows the setting of this parameter:

```
SQL> SHOW PARAMETER LOG_ARCHIVE_MAX

NAME                                 TYPE        VALUE
------------------------------------ ----------- ------
log_archive_max_processes            integer     2
```

This parameter is set in the initialization parameter file and can be modified dynamically using the ALTER SYSTEM statement. The following statement changes the setting of this parameter from 2 to 5:

```
SQL> ALTER SYSTEM SET LOG_ARCHIVE_MAX_PROCESSES = 5
  2  /

system altered.
```

At any time, you can change this setting from 5 to 3 as follows:

```
ALTER SYSTEM SET LOG_ARCHIVE_MAX_PROCESSES = 3
  2  /

system altered.
```

CKPT Process

Have you ever wondered how Oracle knows which files need to be recovered and which are up to date? It is not a mystery. Oracle uses a mechanism called a **checkpoint**, which updates the control file at the heart of the database and other data files, with a System Change Number (SCN) to track which files are up to date.

Suppose a database has three data files and one control file as shown in Figure 10-3. The control file and File 1 have an SCN of 101, whereas Files 2 and 3 have numbers different than the current SCN. What does this mean? Files 2 and 3 are not up to date with the current SCN, and therefore if this instance fails, Oracle requires that these two files be recovered and synchronized with the current SCN. Having said that, the checkpoint mechanism serves two purposes: data consistency, in which all data files are kept synchronized, and data recovery, in which Oracle can determine based on the checkpoint stamp on each file whether it requires recovery or not.

10

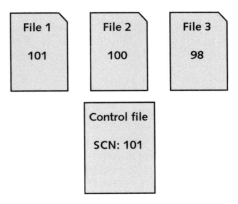

Figure 10-3   Illustration of file synchronization

By now you understand that the only task of a CKPT process is to update the headers of data files and the control file with timestamps and SCNs to make sure that all files are synchronized. What triggers a checkpoint? A CKPT process wakes up and makes an announcement when any of the following events occur:

- A log file switch occurs.

- A commit is issued.

- A checkpoint timeout occurs.

- A checkpoint interval occurs.

- A manual checkpoint is issued.

- A manual log file switch is issued.

- A database shutdown is issued.

- A tablespace is put in OFFLINE or BEGIN BACKUP status.

The CKPT process not only updates the headers of files, it signals the DBWn process to write the dirty block buffers to data files. There are two situations in which the CKPT process could impact the database: performance and recovery from database failure.

NOTE

By default, the CKPT process wakes up every three seconds.

A CKPT process that performs checkpoints frequently impacts performance because every time this process wakes up, it has to make I/O trips (writing). On the other hand, the more frequently a checkpoint occurs, the smaller the amount of data to be recovered. Infrequent checkpoints result in a greater amount of data that need to be recovered in case of database failure. It is desirable to balance the two factors, the number of checkpoints and the amount of data to be recovered in case of failure, and that is a difficult task.

Again, Oracle provides you with parameters to regulate the frequency of checkpoints. These parameters are examined in the next section.

Regulating Checkpoints

To regulate the frequency of checkpoints, Oracle supplies you with two main parameters listed here:

- **LOG_CHECKPOINT_INTERVAL**: This parameter tells Oracle the number of OS blocks that need to be written by LGWR to wake up the CKPT. For example, if this parameter was set to 10 KB and LGWR wrote 10 KB to log files since the last checkpoint, the CKPT process is triggered and a checkpoint is performed.

- **LOG_CHECKPOINT_TIMEOUT**: This parameter informs Oracle of the number of seconds the CKPT process has been idle. For example, if this parameter is set to eight seconds, the checkpoint is performed eight seconds after the last checkpoint. To disable this parameter, set it to zero.

Of course, setting these parameters regulates how frequently a checkpoint occurs. High LOG_CHECKPOINT_TIMEOUT and LOG_CHECKPOINT_INTERVAL values decrease the number of checkpoints and vice versa. To reach a well-balanced frequency of checkpoint occurrences, you most likely need to monitor how often a checkpoint is occurring. You can do so by setting the LOG_CHECKPOINT_TO_ALERT parameter in the initialization parameter file to true (the default value is false). This parameter tells

Oracle to record the timestamp to the alert log every time a checkpoint is performed. It is important to note that it is not recommended to set this parameter to true at all times, as it may slightly impact performance. When you know how frequently a check point is occurring during peak times, you get a feel for whether a checkpoint frequency requires adjustment or not. Ideally, as mentioned earlier, it is a balancing act. Less frequent means more data to be recovered in case of failure. Another factor to keep in mind is the size of the redo log file. The size contributes to how fast the file is filled and yields to a log switch.

Log File Switch (Checkpoint Incomplete) Event

As with the event presented in the previous section, there is an event that can be useful to determine if there is a problem with the performance of the CKPT process and the DBWn process. This event is called the log file switch (checkpoint incomplete). It is an indicator that LGWR has to wait until the checkpoint is completed before it starts writing to the redo log. The most likely cause of an incomplete checkpoint is that the Down process is not fast enough to write all dirty block buffers to the data files. Any consistent high value of this event requires you to either increase the number of processes of DBWn or balance the load on I/O or the number of checkpoints. In any of these cases, it does require diligent effort to monitor every little transaction to prevent this problem.

V$SYSSTAT View

Another indicator that Oracle provides through the V$SYSSTAT dynamic performance view are statistics about the number of checkpoints started and completed. These two statistics can be obtained by issuing the following query:

```
SQL> SELECT NAME, VALUE
  2    FROM V$SYSSTAT
  3   WHERE NAME LIKE 'background checkpoint%'
  4  /

NAME                                        VALUE
---------------------------------------- ----------
background checkpoints started               16
background checkpoints completed             15
```

If the value of `background checkpoints started` is greater than `background checkpoints completed` by more than one, it indicates that checkpoints are not being completed between log file switches which, in turn, indicates that the redo log file is not large enough. Therefore, you need to increase the size of the redo log file. Other available statistics are related to the DBWn process. These statistics are as follows:

- **DBWR checkpoint buffers written:** This statistic indicates the number of buffers written.

- **DBWR checkpoints:** This statistic indicates the number of times DBWn was signaled to scan the Buffer Cache for dirty blocks to write.

By examining the results of the query in conjunction with the frequency of checkpoints, you can determine an average number of blocks per checkpoint. In this case, the average blocks per checkpoint is about 3618 blocks.

```
SQL> SELECT NAME, VALUE
  2     FROM V$SYSSTAT
  3    WHERE NAME LIKE 'DBWR checkpoint%'
  4  /

NAME                                        VALUE
---------------------------------------- ---------
DBWR checkpoint buffers written             57893
DBWR checkpoints                               16
```

Oracle introduced two initialization parameters that contribute to regulating checkpoints, and they are listed here:

- **FAST_START_IO_TARGET:** This parameter specifies the target number of I/O operations to perform crash recovery. (This parameter is deprecated.)

- **FAST_START_MTTR_TARGET:** This parameter specifies the number of seconds Oracle should take to perform crash recovery, and the default value is 300 seconds. (MTTR stands for Mean Time To Recover.)

The LOG_CHECKPOINT_TIMEOUT, LOG_CHECKPOINT_INTERVAL, and FAST_START_IO_TARGET parameters are hard to set to achieve the right frequency of checkpoints. You should use the FAST_START_MTTR_TARGET parameter to regulate checkpoints because Oracle adjusts the frequency of checkpoints based on database activities to achieve this target.

```
SQL> SHOW PARAMETER FAST_START

NAME                                 TYPE         VALUE
------------------------------------ -----------  -----
fast_start_io_target                 integer      0
fast_start_mttr_target               integer      300
fast_start_parallel_rollback         string       LOW
```

NOTE

FAST_START_IO_TARGET and FAST_START_MTTR_TARGET can be set dynamically.

How do you determine the value (number of seconds) for FAST_START_MTTR_TARGET? This can be done using the following methodology:

- Assign an estimated value based on business requirements.

- Consult with the V$INSTANCE_RECOVERY dynamic performance view to get information about the actual, estimated, and target I/Os and redo blocks for recovery. The results of the view tell you how close you are to your target and whether your requirements are achievable or not.

The following example illustrates the use of the FAST_START_MTTR_TARGET parameter. For instance, if business requirements dictate that crash recovery should be targeted to three minutes, you can set this parameter using the ALTER SYSTEM statement as follows:

```
SQL> ALTER SYSTEM SET FAST_START_MTTR_TARGET = 180;

System altered.
```

After setting the parameter, you can view V$INSTANCE_RECOVERY to observe how close it is to the target. The following query displays the contents of this view:

```
SQL> SELECT *
  2     FROM V$INSTANCE_RECOVERY
  3  /

RECOVERY_ESTIMATED_IOS ACTUAL_REDO_BLKS TARGET_REDO_BLKS LOG_FILE_SIZE_REDO_BLKS
---------------------- ---------------- ---------------- -----------------------
LOG_CHKPT_TIMEOUT_REDO_BLKS LOG_CHKPT_INTERVAL_REDO_BLKS
--------------------------- ----------------------------
FAST_START_IO_TARGET_REDO_BLKS TARGET_MTTR ESTIMATED_MTTR CKPT_BLOCK_WRITES
------------------------------ ----------- -------------- -----------------
                    66             3431             3606                  184320
                  3606
                                   31             11              65023
```

To interpret the results, examine Table 10-2 for the description of each column in the view.

Table 10-2   V$INSTANCE_RECOVERY view

Column	Description
RECOVERY_ESTIMATED_IOS	Number of dirty block buffers
ACTUAL_REDO_BLKS	Actual number of redo blocks needed to recover
TARGET_REDO_BLKS	The target number of redo blocks needed to recover
LOG_FILE_SIZE_REDO_BLKS	Number of redo blocks required to prevent a log switch before a checkpoint is completed

Column	Description
LOG_CHKPT_TIMEOUT_REDO_BLKS	Number of redo blocks needed to comply with the LOG_CHECKPOINT_TIMEOUT parameter
LOG_CHKPT_INTERVAL_REDO_BLKS	Number of redo blocks needed to comply with the LOG_CHECKPOINT_INTERVAL parameter
FAST_START_IO_TARGET_REDO_BLKS	This number is obsolete and always NULL
TARGET_MTTR	MTTR target expressed in seconds
ESTIMATED_MTTR	MTTR time based on current operations
CKPT_BLOCK_WRITES	Number of blocks written by CKPT process

The information in this table is derived from the online documentation that Oracle provides at the Oracle Technology Network site: *www.otn.oracle.com*.

The results of the above query show that the estimated MTTR is 11 seconds, which is very good. This is much lower than the target of three minutes, which means that you have achieved your objective. Note that this view should be monitored to make sure that your objectives are attained most of the time.

DBWn Process

The **DBWn** (Database Writer) is another background process that can be tuned to enhance performance or reduce contention. The DBWn writes dirty block buffers to data files and ensures that there are always free buffers in the database Buffer Cache memory. What could happen to degrade the performance of this process? Here is a situation that could happen when a checkpoint is performed because of the occurrence of a log file switch. As mentioned in the previous section, a log file switch promptly signals DBWn to write dirty block buffers to data files. If another checkpoint happens while the DBWn is still writing, this causes contention and soon results in a performance problem. This means that the DBWn process must keep pace with checkpoints.

To prevent this problem from happening, you can configure the DBWn process with multiple processes to distribute the load of writing database block buffers or you can configure DBWn I/O slaves to assist it. An **I/O slave** is a process that works on behalf of the DBWn to distribute the load from one process to several processes. The following list details some of the reasons why DBWn may show performance degradation:

- Inadequate Buffer Cache configuration:
  - Buffer Cache is too small to find free buffers so it is required to clean some of the buffers to free them.
  - Buffer Cache is too big, so the current configuration of the DBWn processes is not sufficient to free buffers.

- I/O system is not adequate for fast performance.

To use this information, you need to know when to use multiple DBWn processes (the maximum possible processes is 10, numbered from 0 to 9). Next, you learn how to detect if there is a problem with DBWn contention. The following indicators help determine if tuning of the DBWn is necessary.

Free Buffer Waits Event

This indicator tells you that Oracle was not able to get a free block buffer as requested because the DBWn had not completed writing dirty database blocks to the data file to free up buffers. This wait event is obtained from the V$SYSTEM_EVENT dynamic performance view. The following query shows a high number of total waits for a free buffer. A consistently high value is an indication that the DBWn process is not doing the job efficiently, and this should prompt you to increase the number of DBWn processes or number of I/O slaves to decrease contention and distribute the workload.

```
SQL> SELECT EVENT, TOTAL_WAITS, TIME_WAITED
  2    FROM V$SYSTEM_EVENT
  3    WHERE EVENT LIKE 'free%'
  4  /

EVENT                TOTAL_WAITS TIME_WAITED
----------------     ----------- -----------
free buffer waits          33984     3184763
```

10

V$SYSSTAT View

You have seen before the dynamic view V$SYSSTAT, which contains system statistics. It is a useful view because it contains indicators that tell you if the Oracle instance and database components are performing optimally or not. In this case, you are interested in statistics about the DBWn process, which you can list by issuing the following query:

```
SQL> SELECT NAME, VALUE
  2    FROM V$SYSSTAT
  3   WHERE NAME LIKE '%DBW%'
  4   ORDER BY 1
  5  /

NAME                                        VALUE
------------------------------------- ---------
DBWR buffers scanned                    806393202
DBWR checkpoint buffers written          23355975
DBWR checkpoints                            11352
DBWR cross instance writes                      0
DBWR free buffers found                 728050573
DBWR fusion writes                              0
DBWR lru scans                            4437173
DBWR make free requests                   4437173
DBWR revisited being-written buffer         41389
DBWR summed scan depth                  806393202
DBWR transaction table writes              452361
DBWR undo block writes                    7398292
```

Of all of these listed statistics, you should focus on the following two that indicate if the DBWn is fast enough in responding to requests for free buffers:

- **DBWR free buffers found:** This indicates the number of buffers that were found free.

- **DBWR make free requests:** This statistic tells you the number of requests to make free buffers that the DBWn process received.

These two statistics indicate the average free (not dirty) buffers found per request to make a free buffer. A number close to 0 indicates that the DBWn process is working hard to make free buffers process, which signals a high level of contention. The following query shows that there is no contention and that the configuration of the DBWn process is all right:

```
SQL> SELECT ROUND(A.VALUE/B.VALUE) AVERAGE_FREE_PER_REQUEST
  2  FROM V$SYSSTAT A, V$SYSSTAT B
  3  WHERE A.NAME = 'DBWR free buffers found'
  4  AND B.NAME = 'DBWR make free requests'
  5  AND B.VALUE <> 0/

AVERAGE_FREE_PER_REQUEST
------------------------
164
```

Now that you have this information, what should you do if you determine that there is contention? Figure 10-4 guides you through configuring the DBWn process effectively. As you can see in this diagram, if the machine on which the database resides has more than one CPU, you can use the initialization parameter DB_WRITER_PROCESSES which indicates the number of DBWn processes that can be spawned (from 0 to 9). If the system has one CPU and your operating system supports asynchronous I/O, you can use DBWn I/O slaves by setting the initialization parameters DBWR_IO_SLAVES and DISK_ASYNCH_IO. When you use DBWR_IO_SLAVES, you have only one DBWR process.

NOTE
You may not use both options DB_WRITER_PROCESSES and DBWR_IO_SLAVES at the same time.

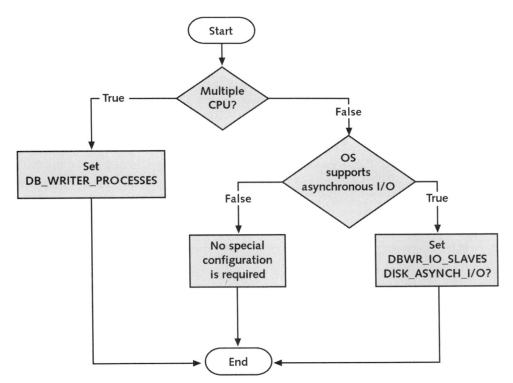

Figure 10-4   DBWR configuration flow chart

NOTE
DB_WRITER_PROCESSES, DBWR_IO_SLAVES, and DISK_ASYNCH_IO cannot be modified dynamically.

DETECTING BACKGROUND PROCESS CONTENTION

In Chapter 3, you studied the memory structure log buffer and learned that the LGWR is the background process that controls this structure and flushes redo entries to the redo log files. This section presents tuning issues connected with the LGWR and redo logs.

The LGWR process is highly efficient and usually does not contribute to performance problems by keeping other processes waiting. On the contrary, the LGWR process usually has to wait for other tasks to complete, so that it can continue performing its job. The configuration of the log buffer memory structure and the redo log files also impact LGWR performance.

Since the LGWR process does not require tuning, it is important to shed light on another factor that may impact the performance of the other background processes, such as ARC*n* and CKPT processes and the LGWR (although indirectly). This factor is the size of the redo log file. Before you start looking into how to tune the size of the redo logs, it is worthwhile to quickly review how the LGWR and redo log file work.

When users submit transactions to the database, every transaction is recorded in the log buffer. When the log buffer is one-third full, when a commit is issued, or when other events occur as discussed in Chapter 3, the LGWR flushes the log buffer and writes all these entries to the redo log file. If the database is in ARCHIVELOG mode, the ARC*n* process writes the contents of the redo log file before the LGWR overwrites it. The ARC*n* process also triggers the CKPT process to perform a checkpoint as indicated in the previous section in this chapter.

NOTE

The maximum size of the archived log is the size of the redo log file.

With this in mind, how does the size of the redo log file impact performance? If the size of the redo log file is too small, this leads to frequent log switches, which means more frequent checkpoints and more processes generated to the archive log. This in turn leads to increased I/O and therefore performance degradation. If the redo log file is too large, this means less frequent log switches and less I/O, but longer recovery time and possibly loss of transactions that occurred since the last archived log file. As a DBA, you need to give more consideration to the business requirements that dictate the acceptable amount of lost transactions than to the performance of the LGWR. This does not mean that performance is secondary.

How do you size redo logs? To answer this question, you should know that the number of redo log file groups and the size of the redo log file groups should be configured to accommodate 20 to 30 minutes of transactions. Many DBA experts agree on the following guidelines outlined in Table 10-3.

Table 10-3 Redo log size guidelines

Application type	Number of groups	Size of log file	Justification
OLTP	MANY (16–32)	SMALL (10 MB–100 MB)	Since transactions are normally small, not much space is required to hold this transaction in the redo log file. You need many redo logs to accommodate 20 to 30 minutes of transactions.
DSS	FEW (3–8)	LARGE (200 MB–500 MB)	Since transactions are normally large, the log file must be large enough to contain transactions without being quickly filled.
HYBRID	MEDIUM (8–16)	MEDIUM (100 MB–200 MB)	Requirements for HYBRID applications fall in the midpoint between OLTP and DSS applications.

Normally you define the size and number of redo log files at the time of database creation as shown in the following CREATE DATABASE statement:

```
CREATE DATABASE TEST
    LOGFILE 'd:\oracle\oradata\test\redoA1.log' size 10M,
            'd:\oracle\oradata\test\redoB1.log' size 10M
    MAXLOGFILES 32
    MAXLOGMEMBERS 3
    ...
  /
```

A LOGFILE clause tells Oracle to create a redo log file group in a specific location with a specific size. You must have at least two log file groups. The MAXLOGFILES clause defines the maximum number of logs that can be multiplexed for each group.

NOTE
When a redo log file is created, you cannot modify its size. You must create a new log file with the desired size and then drop the log file group with the wrong size.

If you determine that you need to add another log file group, you can issue the following command to add a group. For further information and details about administration of the redo logs, consult Oracle documentation.

```
ALTER DATABASE ADD LOGFILE GROUP n
    'd:\oracle\oradata\test\redoC1.log
```

You should make sure that all redo log file groups have the same size.

NOTE

As in the ARC*n* process section, you can monitor the frequency of log switches using V$LOG_HISTORY.

Finally, since redo log files are important, the loss or corruption of these files may result in a loss of transactions. Oracle allows you to multiplex these files on different locations. It is highly recommended that redo log files reside on separate mount points to avoid a single point of failure. In other words, if there are four disks (mount points) and you decide to create a redo log file with two members for each group, you should place them in such a way that if one disk is lost due to media failure, your database will still have all redo log groups as shown in Figure 10-5.

Figure 10-5   Configuration of a redo log multiplex

This figure shows that no matter which disk is lost, there will be a copy of the log file for each group on the other disks. This not only reduces the risk of losing redo log files, it is a configuration in which disk contention is balanced when accessing these files.

LATCHES

Chapter 9 introduced you to the concept of locks and how the Oracle locking mechanism protects data and database objects during a transaction. You also learned how to detect and resolve blocking locks that could frustrate the user who is waiting for locked data objects. Oracle has another mechanism that acts in a similar way on memory structures to protect them until a process completes its task. This mechanism is a structure called a latch. In this section, you examine a brief overview of latches and how to detect latch contention.

Because latches are efficient structures and are not tunable, it is not worth the time and effort to investigate them. Usually, when there is a serious or somewhat serious problem, you detect it by performing a routine health check on the major part of the memory structure.

NOTE

Oracle uses **latches** as sophisticated locking mechanisms to protect memory structure while a process is accessing the structure or working with it. Oracle controls and manages latches, so you don't need to tune them. However, improper configuration of SGA memory structures may result in latch contention.

As you learned in a previous chapter, the lock mechanism works like a queue—first come, first served. When a lock is requested and the lock cannot be acquired, the requester has to wait until the request is filled. Latches do not work like locks. Latch mechanisms are based on two types of requests:

- **Willing-to-wait request**: A request for a latch cannot be obtained immediately, so the process waits for it. Until the process obtains the latch, the function of waiting is referred to as **sleeping**. In the meantime, other requests for latches are served.

- **No-wait request**: A request is not willing to wait. Therefore, if it does not obtain the latch, it gives up on the request.

Many different latches are used for specific memory structures. You can get a list and statistics about these latches by querying the dynamic performance view V$LATCH. Table 10-4 describes the major columns of the V$LATCH view.

Table 10-4   V$LATCH view

Column	Description
NAME	Name of the latch
GETS	Number of times a willing-to-wait request for latch failed to acquire the latch the first time
MISSES	Number of times a willing-to-wait request for latch failed to acquire the latch the first time
SLEEPS	Number of times the process slept while waiting to acquire a latch
IMMEDIATE_GETS	Number of times a request for a no-wait latch was obtained immediately when it was requested
IMMEDIATE_MISSES	Number of times a no-wait request for a latch failed the first time
WAIT_TIME	Total wait time for the latch. You must turn on TIMED_STATISTICS to get a value for this column. If it is turned off, this column will have the value of 0.

The information in this table is derived from the online documentation that Oracle provides at the Oracle Technology Network site: *www.otn.oracle.com*.

The following query displays the contents of V$LATCH view:

```
SELECT NAME,
       GETS,
       MISSES,
       SLEEPS,
       IMMEDIATE_GETS,
       IMMEDIATE_MISSES
  FROM V$LATCH
 ORDER BY NAME
 /
```

If you issue the query as shown in the preceding code segment, you get a huge listing of all latches, which might overwhelm you. To avoid this, you can refine the query to get only the latches that had MISSES with a value higher than 0. The following query uses this criteria and displays a hit ratio of GETS and MISSES. Also, you can change GETS to IMMEDIATE_GETS and MISSES to IMMEDIATE_MISSES to display the hit ratio for latches in no-wait mode.

```
SQL> SELECT name,
  2          gets,
  3          misses,
  4          sleeps,
  5          round((gets-misses)/decode(gets,0,1,gets))
  6              *100 hit_ratio,
  7          round(sleeps/decode(misses,0,1,misses))
  8              *100 sleeps_misses
  9     from v$latch
 10    where gets != 0
 11      and misses>0
 12    order by name
 13  /
```

NAME	GETS	MISSES	SLEEPS	HIT_RATIO	SLEEPS_MISSES
checkpoint queue latch	29939245	1	1	100	100
dml lock allocation	10509293	1	1	100	100
enqueue hash chains	18166423	9	9	100	100
library cache	22581298	19	19	100	100
messages	7425118	60	115	100	200
mostly latch-free SCN	1081330	2	2	100	100
redo allocation	9076233	1031	1968	100	200

The results in the preceding code segment do not list any alarming numbers that would prompt you to take action. Assume one of these rows returned a consistent low hit ratio (a value less than one percent is considered a low ratio). If that happened, you would need to investigate for what resource this latch is used. For instance, if it is a redo copy latch, you need to investigate the Redo Log Buffer configuration. For more information on these latches, consult Oracle documentation.

Here is a list of some of the useful latches to watch for:

- redo allocation (Redo Log Buffer)

- redo copy (Redo Log Buffer)

- cache buffers LRU chain (Buffer Cache)

- enqueues (enqueues structures)

- row cache objects (data dictionary cache)

- library cache (library cache)

- shared pool (Shared Pool Memory)

- shared java pool (Shared Java Pool Memory)

The following is a list of dynamic performance views related to latches.

- **V$LATCH:** Contains statistics on all latches

- **V$LATCH_CHILDREN:** Contains statistics on child latches

- **V$LATCH_MISSES:** Contains statistics on latches that were not able to obtain a latch

- **V$LATCH_PARENT:** Contains statistics about parent latches. This view has a one-to-many relationship with V$LATCH_CHILDREN.

- **V$LATCHHOLDER:** Contains information about the sessions, including who is holding current latches

- **V$LATCHNAME:** Contains the latch number and latch name; used for looking up latch name using latch number

Not every DBA expert would agree with the following statement: latches are valuable internal mechanisms that Oracle uses efficiently. It is useful to run queries, but other than that, analyzing latches is a waste of time.

TUNING AND MONITORING AN OPERATING SYSTEM

Consider the following true story. A DBA contractor was hired to migrate an existing application that had been developed using Oracle Forms and data residing on an Oracle8*i* database system running on a UNIX computer. The application and the database had been running efficiently for three years before the migration. There had not been even one complaint related to performance. Users were happy, DBAs were working diligently and effortlessly to maintain the status quo, and the manager was satisfied and even bragged about his effectiveness in managing these talented DBAs. The contractor DBA was told when he was hired to migrate not only the database, but also the operating system and new hardware.

The contractor pulled off a marvelous job, completing all his assigned tasks on time and on budget. Everyone was excited to get the migrated application and database going. One hour of operation passed with no problem. After two hours of operation, things were getting better, but by the third hour performance degradation was noticeable and happy days were over. An emergency meeting was called to discuss what had happened and to take action to resolve the problem. The meeting included everyone: developers, DBAs, users, business managers, project managers, system administers, and VPs. It was a critical problem that had never occurred before.

In the meeting, after an intensive two–hour review of documentation and auditing results, it was determined that the problem was neither in the application nor in the database. The focus turned to the operating system level. The DBA contractor was on the hot seat, and when asked who installed and configured the operating system, the DBA replied that he did. In response, many eyebrows were raised and people looked at each other aghast.

After system administrators investigated the system for an hour, they determined that the problem was processes bound and related to semaphore configuration. (Semaphores are variables whose values denote the status of a resource that is shared by a number of processes.) Oracle9i release notes indicated that a certain number of semaphores must be set, but the DBA did not want to change the current configuration, so he decided to keep it as it was. This decision crippled the application when the system was loaded with requests.

Chapter 1 emphasized one major point: that little effort should be spent on tuning the operating system because the performance bottlenecks are usually tied to the application or the database. In this section, the discussion of the operating system is focused on two topics:

- Operating system tuning guidelines

- Operating system monitoring tools

No doubt, tuning the operating system is not the appropriate role of a DBA, especially if you are not very familiar with the operating system. However, you should be aware that tuning problems could arise if the performance degradation is not caused by the application or database configuration. When performance issues related to the operating system arise, you should turn to the system administrator to work on the system configuration to repair and eliminate the problem. Notice the terms *repair* and *eliminate*. If the performance is bound to the operating system, the database will definitely not perform well no matter how optimally it is configured. Therefore, operating system performance problems must be eliminated.

Before delving into operating system tuning issues, it is important to mention that the Oracle Corporation is one of the pioneers in supporting multiple operating systems. Oracle can be run on almost all major operating systems with the same architecture and with almost the same efficiency. However, it should be noted that major corporations run Oracle on UNIX. Now, look at the operating system tuning issues.

Operating System Tuning Issues

If you are tuning the operating system, two things are obvious: you are facing a serious performance problem with the current configuration of the operating system; and you have exhausted all tuning measures on the application and database. Figure 10-6 depicts the effort that system administrators should exert on tuning each component of the operating system and the time they should spend tuning these components. The chart is a compilation of several surveys and interviews of system administrators.

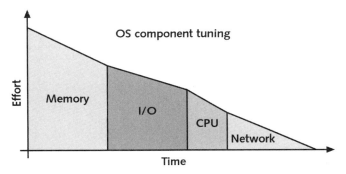

Figure 10-6   Tuning effort and time chart for an operating system

The chart shows that most system administrators spend their time on tuning memory and designing I/O-related factors but spend less effort and time on tuning the CPU. Tuning the network requires the least effort, but designing a good performance network backbone ranks second in time spent. The four factors that should be considered for tuning are as follows:

- Memory

- Input

- Output

- CPU

Memory

Oracle documentation emphasizes that the memory resource is expensive and important to the performance of the database. The DBA should plan on allocating an adequate amount of memory for the database and leave a portion of this memory to the operating system. Usually 50 percent of memory should be left for the operating system and for other applications residing and running on the computer. Actually, some DBA experts disagree with this guideline and recommend 80 percent for Oracle databases and 20 percent for the operating system. You can always take the middle of the road. The point is that there should be adequate memory left for the operating system to perform different tasks.

What are the consequences of inadequate memory for Oracle or the operating system? Simply, paging or swapping. Paging is for Windows operating systems and swapping for UNIX. Conceptually, the terms are synonymous and mean that the operating system offloads memory by moving the least used application to a disk, to what is called virtual memory. The term **disk thrashing** refers to a high level of I/O activity. Virtual memory affects the operating system in two ways: it requires more I/O and disk space.

Of course, you must have thought about the Oracle SGA memory. Will it ever be swapped or paged? Swapping and paging are possible and sometimes harmless, especially if the system is not constantly used. However, in some operating systems, the DBA can actually lock the SGA from being swapped or paged by setting the initialization parameter LOCK_SGA to true. This is a good idea if the database is not sharing memory with other databases or applications on the system.

Here's another true story to illustrate these points. A DBA consultant was hired to install Oracle on a new computer that would host a newly developed application. This DBA worked with the system administrator to make sure that all operating system setup processes required by Oracle were completed, and then he installed Oracle. Because of his expertise, his contract was extended to ensure that the performance of the application would be at a satisfactory level. He worked with developers and designers to configure the database optimally. Everything was working fine on the QA computer, and all tests were passed. Then, the day before the application was scheduled to be put into production, the consultant decided to do one more smoke test on the application on the production computer. It was a disaster.

Everyone started to worry, and wondered what happened. The code was the same, the database configuration was the same, the operating system configuration was the same, and finally, the hardware was the same. So what could be wrong? After ten straight hours of investigation and troubleshooting, the system administrator noticed that there was a hardware malfunction. Specifically, there were four disk controllers, one for every two disks. However, they were mistakenly configured by the hardware distributor as one controller for every four disks, which meant that two of the controllers were not configured. These two controllers were installed to distribute and balance the load of I/O to all controllers.

Input/Output (I/O)

There are numerous horror stories about inadequate configurations of disks and improper allocations of Oracle data files, which lead to high disk, I/O, and file contention. DBAs are always concerned, and rightfully so, when it comes to I/O because it can greatly impact the performance of the database. For this specific reason, system administrators and DBAs spend a great deal of time discussing, planning, and designing disk configurations and I/O balancing.

Oracle has a capability—called management of raw devices—for enhancing I/O performance, but that capability is not used very often because system administrators cannot control it. A **raw device** is a disk that is neither formatted nor managed by the operating system. It appears as a disk to the operating system. Oracle can manage these raw devices by creating data files on them and thereby bypassing the operating system. Because the amount of I/O seriously affects the performance of database applications, many third-party utilities and software packages were developed to enhance operating system I/O to provide better performance.

On the topic of I/O, some operating systems offer two types of I/O:

- **Synchronous (blocking) I/O:** When Oracle requests a read or write from or to a file, Oracle has to wait until the read or write operation is completed.

- **Asynchronous I/O:** When Oracle requests a read or write from or to a file, Oracle can continue without waiting for the read or write operation to complete. This feature provides an opportunity for Oracle to perform other tasks rather than waiting for the I/O operation to be completed. This feature is supported by most UNIX operating systems.

One more true story. A database specialist was hired to expedite the User Acceptance Test process for a database application running on Oracle8*i*. The project was initiated two years before user acceptance. Top-of-the-line hardware was purchased for the system and top software engineers worked on the development of the application.

For one of the application functions, the client requested a maximum five-minute response time, because the application involved extensive mathematical computations and the processing of millions of records. When the database specialist was hired, he was told that the response time for this specific function was 20 minutes, and he was asked to resolve this complicated problem. The specialist was given all the hardware specifications and application design documents, and all other documentation needed to review the application.

The project manager of the system indicated to the specialist that the project was already way over budget, and they were continuing with the project to maintain good public relations with the client, because the client had awarded them other projects and consultation assignments.

The database specialist started reviewing and optimizing the application by looking at every query submitted by the application. Then he looked at every possible configuration of the database and made sure everything was optimal. Next he examined the operating system and made sure that everything worked as it should. Because everything seemed fine, he decided to do a quick user acceptance test to see if there was any improvement. Response time did go down from 20 minutes to 18 minutes, but this was not a significant drop.

So, the specialist decided to deliver the bad news to the project manager and the VP of the department. He firmly stated that everything was running optimally but that the hardware was incapable of handling the load to produce the required response time. In summary he said: "The hardware has been fully upgraded and still does not have the needed capacity, so new hardware should be purchased. Current hardware has a limitation of four CPUs and you need at least four times the number of CPUs you have currently to run effectively and efficiently."

This story brings you to the next topic, which is the CPU.

CPU

On rare occasions, the CPU becomes a bottleneck to performance. Having said that, you must remember that you should not expect a one-horse carriage carrying eight people to move as fast as a four-horse carriage carrying the same number of people. The CPU should not be sitting idle all the time and should not be busy 100 percent of the time. Most experts agree that the CPU should be busy 80 to 90 percent of the time it is running; that is, it should have a busy rate of 80 to 90 percent. Of the 80 to 90 busy rate percentage, Oracle use should be no more than 50 percent. In other words, the CPU busy rate used by Oracle should be 40 percent to 45 percent. An operating system with more than one CPU has a big advantage. The multiple CPUs give the system a significant power advantage.

By this point in the chapter, you've had a quick tour of operating system tuning issues and you have some guidelines for each component of the operating system. What you need now is to be exposed to the various monitoring tools available to you in the operating systems, mainly Windows and UNIX. The next section does exactly that.

Operating System Monitoring Tools

This section introduces you to monitoring tools available in both the Windows and UNIX operating systems. These tools are used to monitor the three operating system components: memory, I/O, and CPU. You will look at Windows and then at UNIX, and this should be an interesting little tour.

Windows Monitoring Tools

Needless to say, the efficiency of the Microsoft Windows operating system is improving, but it is still not considered the operating system of professionals. If you are Windows savvy and familiar with this operating system's tools, you can use many GUI tools for various aspects of the operating system.

First, look at the oldest Windows performance tool, the Task Manager. This tool is used by pressing the Ctrl+Alt+Delete buttons, and it shows all the programs and processes that are currently running. Figure 10-7 shows the main screen of the Task Manager.

Figure 10-7   Windows Task Manager showing all programs running

As you can see, this screen displays all running programs. If you suspect some performance degradation, you can click on the Performance tab to view the CPU and memory performance, as illustrated in Figure 10-8.

10

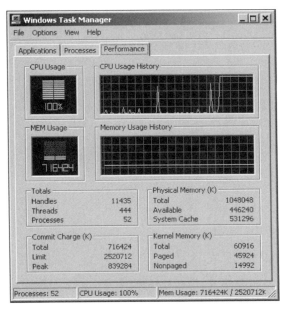

Figure 10-8   Task Manager Performance tab showing CPU and memory usage

You can see in this screen that CPU usage was at an acceptable level until some process started to consume most of the CPU. The memory usage looks stable and reasonable.

Windows has another tool called the Performance tool that you can access from Control Panel>Administrative Tools. This tool allows you to monitor several aspects of the operating system. Figure 10-9 displays the Performance main window.

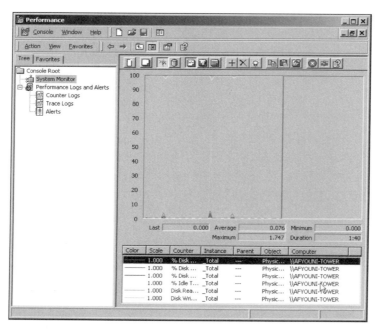

Figure 10-9   Windows Performance tool showing read and write activities

This window displays disk activities showing percentages of reads and writes. You can actually monitor any component of the system. To remove the current setting, click the Delete (X) button in the vertical toolbar; to add any setting, click the Add (+) button. Clicking the Add (+) button displays the screen shown in Figure 10-10.

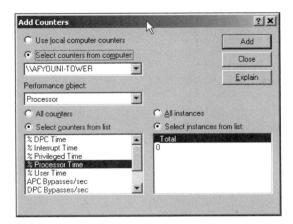

Figure 10-10   Performance configuration dialog box

This screen allows you to select any object to monitor its performance. This is available under the Performance object drop-down list. Other tools are available and can be used to monitor performance of the operating system. For more details, consult Windows documentation or your system administrator.

The next section introduces you to UNIX tools.

10

UNIX Monitoring Tools

UNIX provides a suite of tools that can be run from the command line, although they are not as pretty as the Windows tools. However, most DBAs are looking for a quick and easy tool to display the usage and performance of the operating system. The following is a list of these tools accompanied by screen snapshots. Consult the UNIX documentation for more information about these utilities.

This section explores monitoring tools of Unix operating system that are not available in Windows operating system.

NOTE

ps Command: This command displays all processes running on the system. The following is the result of a search for all DBWn database writers currently running:

```
SAM> ps -ef | grep -i dbw
   oracle 13001 12850   0 03:12:45 pts/1     0:00 grep -i dbw
   oracle 25654     1   0  Mar 04 ?          0:22 ora_dbw0_SA01
   oracle  4530     1   0  Feb 10 ?          2:31 ora_dbw0_SA02
   oracle 11996     1   0  Mar 11 ?          0:06 ora_dbw0_SAM
   oracle 21760     1   0  Mar 03 ?          1:01 ora_dbw0_SD01
   oracle 15876     1   0  Mar 12 ?          1:53 ora_dbw0_SQ01
```

mpstat Utility: This utility displays a statistics report on each processor in the system. The argument passed in the following example notifies the utility to pool statistics every one second.

The report displayed by the mpstat utility shows that there are four CPUs, numbered 0 to 3. Table 10-5 provides a description of each column.

```
SAM> mpstat 1
CPU minf mjf xcal  intr ithr  csw icsw migr smtx  srw syscl  usr sys  wt idl
  0    2   0   20   100   99   94    0    1    0    0   109    1   1    7  91
  1    2   0    1    80  226   43    0    1    0    0   110    1   0    6  93
  2    1   0   19   114  113   78    0    1    0    0   100    1   1    5  93
  3    2   0   24   119  119   82    0    1    0    0   112    1   1    6  92
CPU minf mjf xcal  intr ithr  csw icsw migr smtx  srw syscl  usr sys  wt idl
  0    5   0    0   100  100   10    0    1    0    0    33    0   0    0 100
  1    0   0  330   420  220  205    0    2    0    0   113    0   1   99   0
  2    0   0   12   106  106   55    0    9    0    0    84    0   0    4  96
  3    0   0   18   100  100  203    0    3    2    0   112    0   0    8  92
CPU minf mjf xcal  intr ithr  csw icsw migr smtx  srw syscl  usr sys  wt idl
  0    0   0   12   100  100  245    0    3    0    0   151    0   0    9  91
  1    0   0  324   422  222   34    0    1    0    0   135    0   0  100   0
  2    0   0   12   105  105   36    0    4    0    0    62    0   0    4  96
  3    0   0   12   104  104  132    0    1    0    0    74    0   0    9  91
```

You can see from the results that all CPUs are over 90 percent idle, which means that there are no activities on the system. Ideally, you want to see activities, which in turn bring CPU idle time down to a comfortable level of 10 percent to 20 percent.

Table 10-5 Description of mpstat utility columns

Column	Description
CPU	Processor ID
Minf	Minor faults
mjf	Major faults
xcal	Interprocessor cross-calls
intr	Interrupts
ithr	Interrupts as threads (not counting clock interrupts)
csw	Context switches
icsw	Involuntary context switches
migr	Thread migrations (to another processor)
smtx	Spins on mutexes (lock not acquired on first try)
srw	Spins on readers/writer locks (lock not acquired on first try)
syscl	System calls

Column	Description
usr	Percent user time
sys	Percent system time
wt	Percent wait time
idl	Percent idle time

iostat Utility: This utility displays an I/O statistics report similar to `mpstat`. You can pass an argument to poll statistics every desired number of seconds. The example that follows illustrates the use of this command. As you can see, the report shows that there are four devices (disks). The statistics do not show any alarming numbers that would prompt you to take action. In case there are consistently alarming numbers, such as a high percentage of service, you would need to investigate what files are being accessed on the device.

```
SAM> iostat -xnp
r/s w/s kr/s kw/s wait actv wsvc_t asvc_t %w %b  device
  0.0 0.0  0.0  0.0  0.0  0.0    0.0    0.0  0  0  server:/export/home/sam
  0.0 0.2  0.2  1.1  0.0  0.0   13.4   17.1  0  0  c0t0d0
  0.0 0.0  0.1  0.2  0.0  0.0   22.3   27.2  0  0  c0t0d0s2
  0.0 0.0  0.0  0.0  0.0  0.0    2.4   27.9  0  0  c0t0d0s6
```

Table 10-6 displays the description of each column.

Table 10-6   Description of iostat utility columns

Column	Description
disk	Name of the disk
r/s	Reads per second
w/s	Writes per second
Kr/s	Kilobytes read per second
Kw/s	Kilobytes written per second
wait	Average number of transactions waiting for service (queue length)
actv	Average number of transactions actively being serviced (removed from the queue, but not yet completed)
svc_t	Average service time, in milliseconds
%w	Percent of time there are transactions waiting for service (queue nonempty)
%b	Percent of time the disk is busy (transactions in progress)

vmstat Utility: Again like `mpstat` and `iostat`, this utility monitors virtual memory swapping and other system resources. The following is an example of this tool's display of statistics about usage of virtual memory and I/O and CPU usage. The report does not show alarming numbers on any aspect of the operating system.

10

```
SAM> vmstat 1
  procs        memory              page                    disk           faults        cpu
  r b w     swap   free   re  mf pi po fr de sr f0 s0 s1 s6   in   sy   cs us sy id
  0 0 0      824    648    7  62 100 165 180 0 2 0  0  2  0  406  644 2244  8  5 87
  0 2 0 2929176 64208    3   5   0 24 24  0 0 0  0  0  0  622  357  471  0  0 100
  0 1 0 2929176 64216    6   0   0 48 48  0 0 0  0  6  0  654  433  493  0  0 100
  0 1 0 2929176 64216    6   0   0 48 48  0 0 0  0  0  0  641  384  486  0  0 100
  0 1 0 2929176 64216    3   0   0 24 24  0 0 0  0  0  0  631  364  473  2  0 98
  0 1 0 2929176 64216    6   0   0 48 48  0 0 0  0  6  0  647  386  467  0  2 98
```

Table 10-7 describes each column.

Table 10-7   Description of vmstat utility columns

Column		Description
procs	r	Run queue length
	w	Number of processes blocked while waiting for I/O
	b	Idle processes which have been swapped
memory	swap	Free swap space in KB
	free	Free memory in KB
page	re	Pages reclaimed from the free list
	mf	Minor faults (page in memory, but not mapped)
	fr	Paged in from swap (KB/sec)
	pi	Paged out to swap (KB/sec)
	de	Freed or destroyed (KB/sec)
	po	Freed after writes (KB/sec)
	sr	Scan rate (pages)
disk		For each available disk, I/O disk activities per second
faults	in	Interrupts (per second)
	sy	System calls (per second)
	cs	Context switches (per second)
cpu	us	User CPU time (%)
	sy	Kernel CPU time (%)
	id	Idle and I/O wait CPU time (%)

sar Utility: The `sar` utility is a tool that generates statistical reports on most of the operating system components. To run this tool, you should pass an argument to notify it of what type of report you need to generate. The following list in Table 10-8 gives the arguments for some useful reports generated by `sar`.

Table 10-8   Reports generated by the sar utility

Argument	Report Description
a	Report use of file access system routines: iget/s, namei/s, dirblk/s
b	Report buffer activity
d	Report activity for each device (for example, disk or tape drive)
m	Report message and semaphore activities
p	Report paging activities
r	Report unused memory pages and disk blocks
v	Report status of process, i-node, and file tables
u	Report CPU utilization (the default)
w	Report system swapping and switching activity

The following is an example of output from the sar utility:

```
SAM> sar -p 1 5

SunOS sam 5.7 Generic_106541-23 sun4u     04/13/03

02:56:36  atch/s  pgin/s ppgin/s  pflt/s  vflt/s slock/s
02:56:37   5.88    0.00    0.00    3.92    6.86    0.00
02:56:38   0.00    0.00    0.00    0.00    2.00    0.00
02:56:39   8.91    0.00    0.00    0.00    0.00    0.00
02:56:40   7.92    0.00    0.00    0.00    0.00    0.00
02:56:42   2.00    0.00    0.00    0.00    0.00    0.00

Average    4.96    0.00    0.00    0.79    1.79    0.00




SAM> sar -u 1 5

SunOS sam 5.7 Generic_106541-23 sun4u     04/13/03

02:58:04   %usr    %sys    %wio   %idle
02:58:05    0       0       25      75
02:58:06    0       3       34      63
02:58:07    0       0       29      71
02:58:08    0       1       25      75
02:58:09    0       0       33      67

Average     0       1       29      70
```

10

To wrap up this section, note that you should always work with the system administrator who can provide you with reports similar to that reproduced here as output of the `sar` utility. Most of the time, system administrators monitor the system and are alerted when serious problems arise. For example, they may get an alert via e-mail or pager every time CPU utilization is over 95 percent. You should remember that your primary responsibility is to administer the databases that have been assigned to you.

CHAPTER SUMMARY

- Background processes are the core of the Oracle engine, which makes Oracle one of the leading database management systems in the database arena.

- Background processes have been written to be highly efficient because they are the backbone of Oracle systems.

- Oracle instance architecture consists of memory and background processes as one integral part.

- Of the Oracle background processes, only the performance of ARCH, CKPT, DBWR, and LGWR can be enhanced.

- When a database is in an ARCHIVELOG mode, you are notifying Oracle not to overwrite any redo log until the ARC*n* process has finished writing the log to an archived log.

- Log file switch (archiving needed) is an event that indicates that the LGWR waited for the ARC*n* to archive the log to which it was trying to switch.

- The V$ARCHIVED_LOG view contains control file information about archived logs including how often an archived log is being generated and how long it takes to write it.

- The V$ARCHIVED_PROCESSES shows the number of ARC*n* processes that are active and whether each process is busy or idle.

- The LOG_ARCHIVE_MAX parameter configures the maximum number of ARC*n* processes that Oracle can start.

- Oracle uses System Change Numbers (SCNs) to mark all data files and control files every time a checkpoint occurs.

- The checkpoint mechanism serves two purposes: data consistency, whereby all data files are kept synchronized; and data recovery, whereby Oracle determines whether it requires recovery or not based on the checkpoint stamp on each file.

- The LOG_CHECKPOINT_INTERVAL parameter informs Oracle of the number of OS blocks that LGWR must write to wake up the CKPT.

- The LOG_CHECKPOINT_TIMEOUT parameter informs Oracle of the number of seconds a CKPT process is idle.

- The log file switch (checkpoint incomplete) is an indicator that LGWR has to wait until the checkpoint is completed before it starts writing to the redo log.

- The FAST_START_MTTR_TARGET parameter specifies the number of seconds that should be required for a crash recovery.

- The DBWn process has the single function of writing dirty block buffers to data files.

- `Free buffer waits` is an event that determines if there is DBWn contention.

- DB_WRITER_PROCESSES indicates the number of DBWn processes that can be spawned (from 0 to 9).
- If the size of the redo log file is too small, frequent log switches occur.
- If the size of the redo log file is too large, longer recovery times occur.
- Latches are sophisticated locking mechanisms that Oracle uses to protect memory structure while processes are accessing it.
- A willing-to-wait request works this way: when a request for a latch cannot be obtained immediately, the process is willing to wait for it.
- A no-wait request works this way: when a request for a latch cannot be obtained immediately, the process gives up the request.
- System administrators spend most of their time and effort tuning and designing I/O related factors and less on tuning the CPU.
- In most cases, 50 percent of memory should be reserved for the operating system and other applications residing and running on the machine.
- Inadequate configurations of disks and improper allocations of Oracle data files lead to high levels of disk I/O, and file contention.
- Most experts agree that the average CPU busy rate should be 80 to 90 percent.

REVIEW QUESTIONS

1. CKPT wakes up every eight seconds. (True/False)
2. The size of the redo log file cannot be modified. (True/False)
3. DBWn is responsible for writing dirty logs to data files. (True/False)
4. You can configure Oracle to enhance the performance of all background processes. (True/False)
5. You should make sure that at least 70 percent of memory is free for the operating system. (True/False)
6. You can spawn more than one checkpoint process using the CKPT_PROCESSES parameter. (True/False)
7. The ARCHIVE_MAX_PROCESSES parameter notifies Oracle of the maximum number of processes that can be spawned. (True/False)
8. You must shut down the database to increase the number of DBWn processes. (True/False)
9. When monitoring CPU usage, the aim should be that the CPU be 90 percent idle all the time. (True/False)
10. Thrashing is the result of improper configuration of virtual memory. (True/False)
11. You should put more effort into tuning the operating system than the database. (True/False)

12. The LOG_CHECKPOINT_INTERVAL notifies Oracle of the number of seconds the CKPT process has been idle. (True/False)

13. You can spawn more than one DBWn process or I/O slave to clean dirty block buffers. (True/False)

14. Explain the purpose of the CKPT process and its impact on performance.

15. What statement would you use to increase or decrease the number of redo log files?

16. What is the purpose of redo log multiplexing and what is its impact on performance?

17. Write three queries to detect DBWn contention.

18. Outline the symptoms of frequent log file switches.

19. Write all the statements that cause log switches.

20. List all the tools you can use to detect all background process contention.

EXAM REVIEW QUESTIONS: ORACLE9i PERFORMANCE TUNING (#1Z0-033)

1. As you were routinely checking your database, you discovered that the allocation latch ratio is very high. What would you do?

    a. Increase the number of latches.

    b. Do nothing.

    c. Decrease the number of latches.

    d. Increase the size of the log buffer.

    e. Increase the size of the redo log buffer.

2. Which statement is not true about checkpoints?

    a. Checkpoints occur every time a commit is issued.

    b. Checkpoints signal DBWn to write dirty blocks.

    c. Checkpoints cannot be regulated.

    d. The main function of checkpoints is to synchronize all Oracle files.

3. Which statement about latches is true?

   a. Latches are not tunable.

   b. Latch contention is caused by the improper configuration of the number of latches.

   c. When latch contention is observed, you need to investigate the cause of the contention and then properly configure the number of latches.

   d. Latches are memory structures that protect data.

4. Which event would you use to find that the LGWR waited for the ARC*n* process?

   a. log file switch (archiving needed)

   b. log file switch (archiving waited)

   c. log file switch (archiving completed)

   d. log file switch (archiving required)

5. What is the threshold for the latch miss ratio?

   a. 0 percent

   b. 1 percent

   c. 10 percent

   d. 50 percent

   e. 90 percent

   f. 99 percent

   g. 100 percent

6. Which view would you use to determine the frequency of log switches?

   a. V$LOG

   b. V$LOGFILE

   c. V$LOG_HISTORY

   d. V$ARCHIVED_LOG

7. Which parameter would you set to determine the frequency of checkpoints?

   a. LOG_CHECKPOINT_INTERVAL

   b. LOG_CHECKPOINT_TIMEOUT

   c. LOG_CHECKPOINT_TO_ALERT

   d. LOG_CHECKPOINT_ALERT

10

8. Which statement about the ARC*n* process is true?

   a. Oracle dynamically increases and decreases the number of ARC*n* processes whenever it is necessary.

   b. The ARC*n* triggers LGWR to perform a log switch.

   c. The ARC*n* writes the dirty blocks in redo logs to archived files.

   d. If the ARC*n* cannot complete its job, the database continues operations and another ARC*n* process is spawned to catch up with the work.

   e. The ARC*n* works harder than the LGWR.

9. Which event can you use to find out if there was DBW*n* contention?

   a. `free buffer waits`

   b. `buffer waits`

   c. `busy waits`

   d. `buffer free waits`

10. Which condition must exist in order to use DBWR_IO_SLAVES?

    a. The operating system must support synchronous I/O.

    b. You must have only one DBWn process.

    c. You must have multiple DBWn processes.

    d. You must set an ASYNCHRONOUS_IO parameter.

11. Which statement about the LGWR is not true?

    a. The LGWR manages the log buffer.

    b. The LGWR wakes up when a checkpoint occurs.

    c. The LGWR flushes the buffer when it is one-third full.

    d. Contention is usually attributed to the ARC*n*, because the ARC*n* process cannot keep pace with other LGWR.

12. Which parameter would you set to spawn more than one DBWn process?

    a. DB_WRITER_PROCESS

    b. DBWR_PROCESS

    c. DB_WRITER_PROCESSES

    d. DATABASE_WRITER_PROCESSES

13. Which new parameter did Oracle introduce to control checkpoints?

    a. ARCHIVE_LAG_TARGET

    b. FAST_START_IO_TARGET

    c. LOG_CHECKPOINT_INTERVAL

    d. LOG_CHECKPOINT_TIMEOUT

14. For an OLTP application, what should be the size of the redo log?

    a. SMALL

    b. MEDIUM

    c. LARGE

15. What is true about FAST_START_MTTR_TARGET?

    a. It controls the frequency of checkpoints.

    b. It ensures that the frequency of log switches is met.

    c. It ensures that the number of redo blocks corresponds to the checkpoint target.

    d. It controls the CKPT.

10

HANDS-ON PROJECTS

HANDS-ON PROJECTS

Please complete the projects provided below.

1. Reread the Performance Problem at the start of the chapter. Think of it in terms of the concepts you have learned in this chapter and answer the following questions:

    a. What type of a database application is Jack supporting?

    b. Define and analyze Jack's problem.

    c. What recommendation would you offer to Jack?

2. Perform the following tasks:

    a. Enable checkpoint stamping to the alert log.

    b. Write all statements that will cause a checkpoint and verify the event in the alert log.

3. Write a query (script) that computes the frequency of log switches.

4. The other day you attended a database seminar about contention that emphasized the role of the DBA in preventing LGWR contention. Write a scenario for database configuration that would result in LGWR contention.

5. Your friend sent you an e-mail asking you to help him interpret the results of this query. What would you tell him?

```
SQL> SELECT LATCH#,
  2         NAME,
  3         GETS,
  4         MISSES,
  5         SLEEPS,
  6         WAITS_HOLDING_LATCH,
  7         SPIN_GETS
  8    FROM V$LATCH
  9   WHERE LATCH# IN (66,67);


LATCH# NAME                    GETS        MISSES      SLEEPS      WAITS_HOLDING SPIN
GETS
------ -------------------- ---------- ---------- ---------- ------------- -------
66        cache buffers chains 2.5564E+11   421669488    89537613        2831266
349986831
67        cache buffer handles 4182220471 4195183179   486726709      4195183179
3752176073
```

6. Configure your database and write statements to produce DBWn contention.

7. Write a report that displays all events related to LGWR.

8. Suppose your DSS database is set up with three small redo log file groups. Explain the performance implications of this configuration, if there are any.

CASE PROJECTS

Learning Process Project

Your instructor just explained the function of each Oracle background process. He or she asked you to perform the following tasks to reinforce what you just learned.

1. Log on as SYSTEM in two separate sessions and perform the following tasks.

2. Make sure your database is in ARCHIVELOG mode but not in AUTOMATIC mode.

3. Issue a simple transaction, switch the log file three times, and explain what happens.

4. Enable automatic archiving.

5. Set the FAST_START_MTTR_TARGET parameter to two minutes.

6. Display a list of all archive processes with their statuses and record the total number of archive processes. If zero, explain why.

7. Activate an archive that spawns three processes.

8. Increase the number of archive processes to five.

9. Perform the following transaction as a SYSTEM user. Observe the number of ARC*n* processes in another session.

```
CREATE TABLE EX10H1 (NUM NUMBER);

BEGIN
   FOR I IN 1..1000000 LOOP
      INSERT INTO EX10H1 VALUES(I);
      COMMIT;
      EXECUTE IMMEDIATE 'ALTER SYSTEM SWITCH LOGFILE';
   END LOOP;
END;
/
```

10. Determine if there is redo log contention or any other contention.

11. Using an operating system tool, observe if there are any performance problems (MEMORY, CPU, or I/O).

12. Observe if the MTTR target has been achieved.

13. What do you observe about this task and what do you conclude?

10

CHAPTER
11

ADVANCED TUNING TOPICS

In this chapter you will:

♦ Learn how to configure and monitor shared servers

♦ Understand distributed transactions

♦ Set up replications and use materialized views

♦ Understand the concept of Oracle Real Application Clusters

Suppose you have done your best to ensure that an Oracle instance is configured optimally and the database is running at peak performance—everything is working well. Do you stop there, or do you work on enhancing the performance of your application by employing Oracle features? As a competent DBA, you should most definitely continue to explore Oracle's available features.

Similar to Chapter 10 in title and content, this chapter discusses advanced features of Oracle and provides an overview of their use and function. Four topics are discussed in this chapter: shared servers, distributed transactions, replication, and Real Application Clusters. Each topic contains an overview, implementation details, and some performance issues with one exception. No implementation information is presented for the Real Application Cluster, because it is the most complicated of the four topics and discussion of its implementation is beyond the scope of this book.

Performance Problem

This section outlines an actual performance problem. As you look it over, imagine yourself as the DBA who reported it and keep it in mind as you proceed through the chapter. This chapter presents concepts relevant to the problem. In the first Hands-on Project at the end of the chapter, you are asked to use the concepts you have learned to provide a solution, or partial solution, to this performance problem.

FROM: Joanna Chair <mailto: joanna.chair@replication.com>
Date: 11-Jan-03 23:45
Subject: Dedicated or Shared
Rdbms Version: Oracle9i

I need help!!!

I am creating a new database using Oracle Database Configuration Assistant. I am now wondering if I should install the DB in dedicated or shared server mode.

The DB will be serving a WebLogic J2EE Application Server, which is talking to the DB via JDBC. This will be the only client that will be issuing queries to the DB.

So in this case, in which mode should I install the DB? If I install shared mode, what parameters do I need to use and what values should be used with it?

Regards, Joanna

SHARED SERVER CONFIGURATION AND MONITORING

In this section, you learn about the architecture of the two server configurations (dedicated and shared) that are available in Oracle. Later, you are shown how to configure and monitor shared servers followed by a summary outlining the advantages and disadvantages of shared servers.

To gain insight into the workings of shared servers, take a look at a typical situation often faced by DBAs. An application had been running in production for six months when a new database architect was hired to work on the new application features. She was given a set of functional specifications and a design document of the existing application.

NOTE

Client/server architecture is based on two logical program units. The program that submits a request is called a "client" and the program that receives and processes the request is called a "server."

She learned that the application was a financial application based on a two-tier client/server architecture. The front-end (client) was developed in Visual Basic and the back-end was an Oracle database server. There were approximately 1300 concurrent users. She was shocked when she found out that the database was running in dedicated server mode. Right away, she wrote a memo to the database manager explaining that the database would perform faster and have more resources available if the database were running in shared server mode. Her recommendations were accepted and the application performance improved immediately.

NOTE   Each layer in a client/server architecture is a logical program unit called a tier. So, a two-tier architecture comprises two separate logical program units. Three-tier comprises three, and so forth.

In the introductory story of this section, the database architect alerted the database manager that the application was using dedicated server mode when it should have been using shared server mode and that a shared server configuration would provide significant, noticeable advantages and enhancements which would benefit the application. The next section looks at each configuration and examines how each one works.

Dedicated Server Mode

Dedicated server is the most widely used mode and is the default Oracle configuration. It is a server process dedicated to serving requests for one specific user connection and session. Figure 11-1 illustrates that each client connected to the Oracle instance is being served by a dedicated server that serves a specific client. This dedicated server processes, executes, and returns the results of all SQL requests submitted by the client.

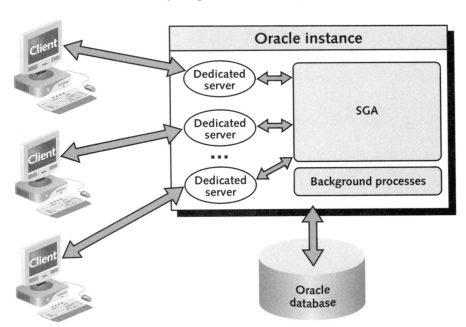

Figure 11-1   Dedicated server architecture overview

Figure 11-2 explains how a dedicated server is created and how it works.

1. Client initiates a request to connect to the database. Listener process picks up the request.

2. Listener process creates a dedicated server for the client.

3. Listener process tells the client the memory address of the dedicated server assigned to it.

4. Client connects to the dedicated server and submits requests to the database through the dedicated server. The dedicated server responds to the user's requests.

5. Dedicated server forwards the request to the SGA, which works on the request until it is complete.

6. Dedicated server returns results to client.

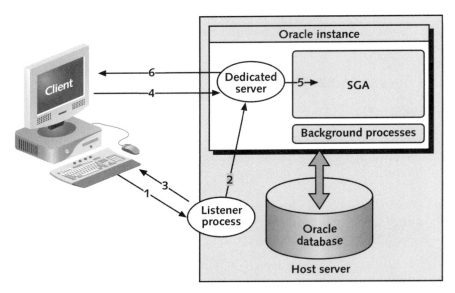

Figure 11-2   Dedicated server process

As an analogy, suppose you take your car to a neighborhood service station for repairs. You are greeted by the station owner who asks how he may help you. You tell him that your car needs repairs, so he directs you to Fred, the mechanic in his shop. The mechanic takes the details of your repair request and works on your car. When he finishes, he informs you that the job is completed. Figure 11-3 depicts this scenario.

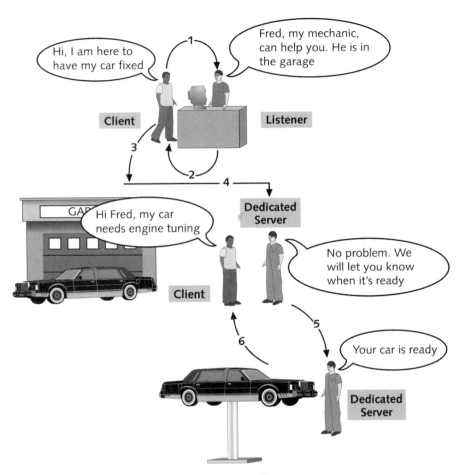

Figure 11-3   Dedicated server process analogy

The default server mode configuration of Oracle is a dedicated server, which requires no specific setup.

Shared Server Mode

A dedicated server process services a specific user connection, whereas a **shared server** process is shared among all user connections connecting in this mode. A shared server process receives and responds to all requests submitted by the users.

Before Oracle9*i* was released, the shared server was known as "Multithreaded Server (MTS)."

Figure 11-4 shows a shared server (process) that is concurrently serving all clients connected to an Oracle instance. Similar to a dedicated server, a shared server receives and responds to all SQL submitted by all clients.

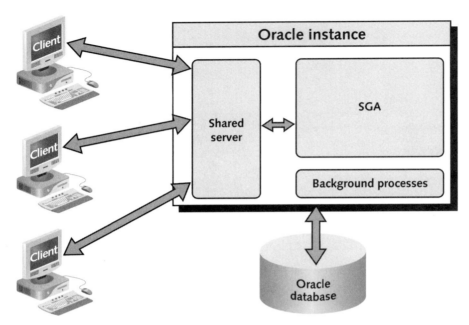

Figure 11-4   Shared server architecture

An Oracle shared server has a specific architecture of its own as depicted in Figure 11-5. As you see, the shared server is composed of three layers that interact with each other.

1. **Dispatcher layer:** Comprises one or many **dispatcher processes** acting as an interface between the user and Oracle. Each dispatcher process also controls server processes and assigns to them requests submitted by users.

2. **Server layer:** Comprises many **server processes**. Each server process handles the user requests assigned by the dispatcher.

3. **Queue layer:** A data structure that keeps a queue of requests and responses.

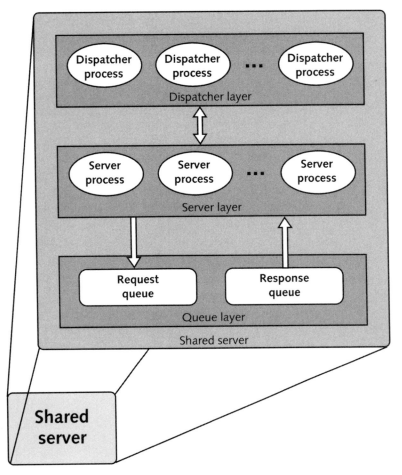

Figure 11-5   Shared server internal structure

You must have noticed that shared server architecture is more sophisticated and complex than dedicated server architecture; there's a good reason for that. The shared server must serve requests from many users with high efficiency. Figure 11-6 shows how a shared server works.

1. Client initiates a request to connect to the database. Listener process picks up the request.

2. Listener process tells the client the memory address of the shared server.

3. Client connects to the dispatcher.

4. Client submits a request to the database via the dispatcher process.

5. Dispatcher process places the request in a queue for server process handling.

6. Server process picks up the request from the queue for processing.

7. Server process works on the request until it is completed.

8. Server process places the results of the request in a response queue.

9. Dispatcher picks up the result of the request from the response queue.

10. Dispatcher sends the results of the request to the client.

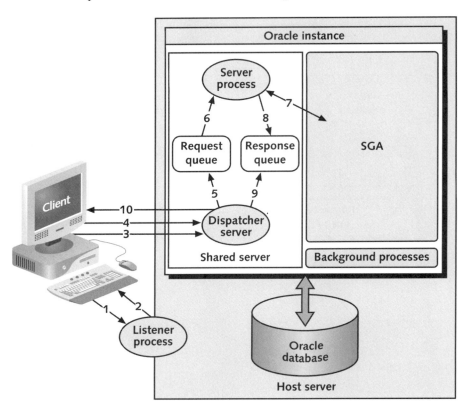

Figure 11-6   Shared server process

Look at an analogy of this process using another auto repair scenario. This time you take your car to a major car dealership. You enter the dealership where a receptionist greets you and asks what you need. You tell the receptionist that your car needs repairs, and he directs you to a repair consultant named Fred in the Service Department. Fred notes the details of your request and puts a job order in the job orders queue for any one of several mechanics available. A mechanic takes the job order, does the work, and when the job is completed, he returns the job order to Fred. Fred then informs you that the car is repaired. Figure 11-7 depicts this scenario.

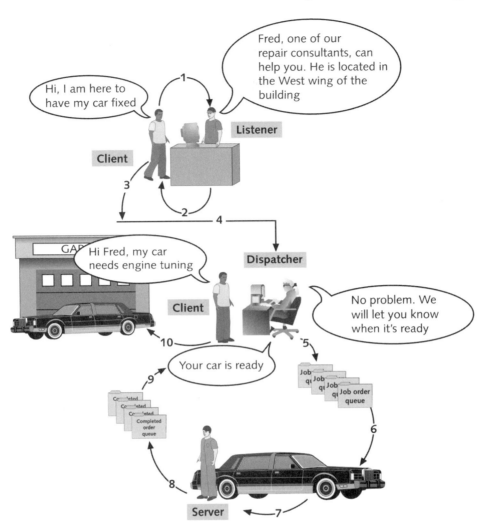

Figure 11-7   Shared server process analogy

Now that you understand how shared servers work, you are ready to learn how to configure the database of a server that is in shared server mode.

Configuring a Shared Server

Although the architecture of a shared server looks complicated, configuration is not as difficult as it appears. The process of configuring the database in shared server mode requires setting parameters in the Init.ora (initialization parameter) file on the database side and the service name in the Tnsnames.ora file on the client side (user), as shown in Figure 11-8. You must set up the database to start the required processes (dispatcher and server), and you must set up the client by telling it how to connect to the database in server mode.

NOTE

The local naming method of the Oracle Net Services uses the TNSNAME service to locate services. The TNSNAME service is usually stored in the Tnsnames.ora file.

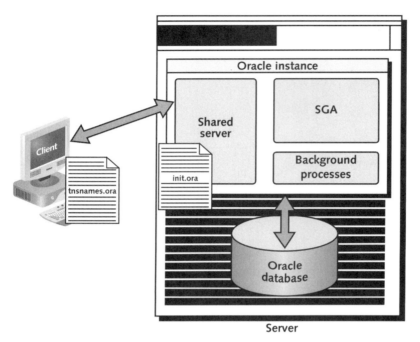

Figure 11-8   Names and locations of shared server and required files

Server Side Setup

As mentioned previously, initialization parameters must be configured. The following is a list of all required parameters for shared server mode configuration.

- **DISPATCHERS:** Sets the number of dispatcher processes to be initiated for the database (formerly known as MTS_DISPATCHERS)

- **MAX_DISPATCHERS**: Tells Oracle the maximum number of dispatcher processes that can be run concurrently (formerly known as MTS_MAX_DISPATCHERS)

- **SHARED_SERVERS:** Sets the number of server processes to be initiated (formerly known as MTS_SERVERS)

- **MAX_SHARED_SERVERS:** Tells Oracle the maximum number of servers that can be run concurrently (formerly known as MTS_MAX_SERVERS)

- **CIRCUITS:** Indicates the total number of virtual circuits for inbound and outbound network connections (formerly known as MTS_CIRCUITS); each connection is a circuit.

- **SHARED_SERVER_SESSIONS:** Indicates the total number of sessions allowed using shared servers (formerly known as MTS_SERVERS)

It looks confusing until you see the recommended guidelines, which assist in setting these parameters. Table 11-1 presents a recommended initial value for each of these parameters. Of course, after these values are configured and the database is operating, you need to monitor the performance of the shared server. If a problem arises, you go back and adjust these parameters.

Table 11-1   Shared server initialization parameters

Parameter	Recommended value	Dynamic or Static
DISPATCHERS (mandatory)	1 dispatcher per 1000 connections	Dynamic
MAX_DISPATCHERS (optional)	Default value of 5	Static
SHARED_SERVERS (optional)	1 server per 10 connections (0 value terminates all current shared servers)	Dynamic
MAX_SHARED_SERVERS (optional)	Default value of 20; should be based on the number of concurrent connections	Static
CIRCUITS (optional)	Default value of 170; change based on the number of concurrent connections	Static
SHARED_SERVER_SESSIONS (optional)	Default value of 165; set to limit the number of sessions using shared server	Static

The information in this table is derived from the online documentation that Oracle provides at the Oracle Technology Network site: *www.otn.oracle.com.*

NOTE
The DISPATCHERS parameter tells Oracle to initiate the specified number of dispatcher processes, but it may initiate more depending on the number of connections.

There is one more important item to learn: the setting of the DISPATCHERS initialization parameter. This is a complex structure, which is composed of many attributes. The most common attributes are listed below and the full structure of this parameter is outlined in Table 11-2.

- **PROTOCOL:** Tells Oracle the network protocol to be used; TCP is the protocol used in most cases.

- **ADDRESS:** Tells Oracle the address (HOST and PORT) in which the dispatcher resides

- **DESCRIPTION:** Describes each dispatcher

Table 11-2 Dispatcher initialization parameter value syntax

Value syntax
| ```
DISPATCHERS=(PROTOCOL = protocol) |
            (ADDRESS = address) |
            (DESCRIPTION = description ) |
            (DISPATCHERS = integer |
             SESSIONS = integer |
             CONNECTIONS = integer |
             TICKS = seconds |
             POOL = {1 | ON | YES | TRUE | BOTH |
             {IN | OUT} = ticks) | 0 | OFF | NO | FALSE | ticks} |
             MULTIPLEX = {1 | ON | YES | TRUE | 0 | OFF | NO |
             FALSE | BOTH | IN | OUT} | LISTENER = tnsname |
             SERVICE = service | INDEX = integer)
``` |

Consider the scenario presented at the beginning of the section, in which the database architect noticed that the number of concurrent sessions was 1300. Follow the outlined steps to configure the database (server) to use shared server mode.

Step 1: Shut down the database (you should connect as SYS to be able to perform this task):

```
SQL> SHUTDOWN IMMEDIATE
Database closed.
Database dismounted.
ORACLE instance shut down.
```

NOTE

Oracle shared server uses memory from the program global area memory (PGA).

Step 2: Set the appropriate parameters in the initialization parameter file. In this case, the number chosen is two to a maximum of three. Because the number of concurrent users is approximately 1300 and the guidelines recommend one dispatcher per 1000 connections, one dispatcher can handle all concurrent connections, and if Oracle decides that it requires more, it initiates them. However, in this case it is decided to specify two dispatchers for two reasons. First, the system can handle the resources consumed by two dispatchers. Second, having two dispatchers ensures that users do not encounter any performance issues. You should note that increasing the number of dispatchers requires more memory and CPU resources, which may impact the database if the system cannot spare these resources.
```

```
###########################################
# Shared Server Configuration
###########################################

dispatchers="(PROTOCOL=TCP) (PORT=5000)"
dispatchers="(PROTOCOL=TCP) (PORT=5001)"
max_dispatchers= 3
shared_servers= 100
max_shared_servers= 150
```

Step 3: Start up the database:

```
SQL> STARTUP PFILE=C:\ORACLE\ADMIN\SAM\PFILE\INIT.ORA
ORACLE instance started.

Total System Global Area  135338868 bytes
Fixed Size                   453492 bytes
Variable Size             109051904 bytes
Database Buffers           25165824 bytes
Redo Buffers                 667648 bytes
Database mounted.
Database opened.

SQL> SHOW PARAMETER DISPATCHER

NAME                             TYPE        VALUE
-------------------------------- ----------- ------------------------------
dispatchers                      string      (protocol=tcp) (PORT=5000),
                                             (protocol=tcp) (PORT=5001)
max_dispatchers                  integer     3
mts_dispatchers                  string      (protocol=tcp) (PORT=5000),
                                             (protocol=tcp) (PORT=5001)
mts_max_dispatchers              integer     3

SQL> SHOW PARAMETER SHARED_SERV

NAME                             TYPE        VALUE
-------------------------------- ----------- ------------------------------
max_shared_servers               integer     150
shared_server_sessions           integer     165
shared_servers                   integer     100
SQL> SHOW PARAMETER CIRCUITS

NAME                             TYPE        VALUE
-------------------------------- ----------- ------------------------------
circuits                         integer     170
mts_circuits                     integer     170
```

11

Step 4: Verify the creation of dispatchers:

```
SQL> SELECT NAME, NETWORK
  2     FROM V$DISPATCHER
  3  /

NAME        NETWORK
----------  --------------------------------------------------------
D000        (ADDRESS=(PROTOCOL=tcp)(HOST=afyouni-tower)(PORT=2546))
D001        (ADDRESS=(PROTOCOL=tcp)(HOST=afyouni-tower)(PORT=2547))
```

As you can see, Oracle picked a different port address than specified because the specified port was either not valid or not available. Notice that Oracle automatically assigns the names of the dispatchers, D000 and D001.

It's simple and easy to set up the shared server. The next task is to set up the client side.

Client-side Setup

You probably know that Oracle Network can connect to an Oracle database via different methods over different types of network protocols. No matter what method is used to connect, you always need to provide information about the connection. This information is referred to as a **connect string**, which tells Oracle the name to be resolved based on the resolution method. Oracle provides four different methods to connect to the database and each method has specific advantages. The most frequently used naming (resolution) method is local naming (also known as service naming) which uses Tnsnames.ora to store detailed information about all databases to which you want to connect. This file resides at the %oracle_home%\network\admin folder in Windows and at the `$ORACLE_HOME/net-work/admin` directory on UNIX. The content of the file resembles the following listing:

```
# TNSNAMES.ORA Network Configuration File:
C:\oracle\ora92\network\admin\tnsnames.ora
# Generated by Oracle configuration tools.

SAM =
  (DESCRIPTION =
    (ADDRESS_LIST =
      (ADDRESS = (PROTOCOL = TCP)
                 (HOST = afyouni-tower)
                 (PORT = 1521)
       )
    )
    (CONNECT_DATA =
      (SERVICE_NAME = SAM)
      (SERVER = DEDICATED)
    )
  )

BOOK =
  (DESCRIPTION =
    (ADDRESS_LIST =
      (ADDRESS = (PROTOCOL = TCP)
                 (HOST = afyouni-tower)
                 (PORT = 1521)
       )
    )
    (CONNECT_DATA =
      (SERVICE_NAME = BOOK)
      (SERVER = DEDICATED)
    )
  )
```

11

Each entry in the listing, SAM and BOOK, is a service name or a local name to connect to a database. In the listing, the two local names specify DEDICATED for the SERVER option. If you want to configure this entry to shared server mode, you must modify Tnsnames.ora and specify the value, SHARED, for the SERVER option.

NOTE

The Oracle shared server is best suited for OLTP because most of the requests are small, and this mode can scale up or down as needed.

You can query the SERVER column in V$SESSION to determine whether a session is connected using dedicated or shared server as displayed in this query:

```
SQL> SELECT USERNAME, STATUS, SERVER
  2     FROM V$SESSION
  3  /

USERNAME                              STATUS    SERVER
-----------------------------------   --------  ----------
                                      ACTIVE    DEDICATED
                                      ACTIVE    DEDICATED
                                      ACTIVE    DEDICATED
                                      ACTIVE    DEDICATED
                                      ACTIVE    DEDICATED
                                      ACTIVE    DEDICATED
                                      ACTIVE    DEDICATED
                                      ACTIVE    DEDICATED
SYS                                   ACTIVE    DEDICATED
DEMO                                  INACTIVE  NONE
```

NOTE   ACTIVE status indicates that the session is currently executing a statement, whereas INACTIVE means that the session is not currently performing any statements.

Notice that DEMO session has NONE as a value for the SERVER column, which indicates it is not DEDICATED. Although it does not say SHARED, it is a connection using a shared server.

Monitoring and Detecting a Shared Server Contention

As with any other Oracle component or functionality, Oracle provides performance views that you can use to administer and monitor the performance of the database. Shared server functionality has several views as listed in Table 11–3.

Table 11-3   Shared server performance views

View	Description of contents
V$CIRCUIT	Information about each connection to the dispatchers
V$DISPATCHER	Information about each dispatcher process
V$DISPATCHER_RATE	Rate statistics for each dispatcher process
V$QUEUE	Information about message queues in the shared queue structure
V$SHARED_SERVER	Information about the server process
V$SHARED_SERVER_MONITOR	Information about monitoring data for tuning a shared server

The information in this table is derived from the online documentation that Oracle provides at the Oracle Technology Network site: *www.otn.oracle.com*.

Using V$CIRCUIT

Most of the time, this view is joined with V$SESSION on the SADDR column (SADDR stands for "session address") to identify and investigate specific connected sessions. The following query shows that the user connection to the dispatcher process is TUNER. Table 11-4 lists some of the most commonly used columns.

```
SQL> SELECT V$SESSION.USERNAME,
  2         V$SESSION.STATUS SESSION_STATUS,
  3         V$SESSION.SERVER,
  4         V$CIRCUIT.STATUS CIRCUIT_STATUS
  5    FROM V$SESSION, V$CIRCUIT
  6   WHERE V$SESSION.SADDR=V$CIRCUIT.SADDR
  7  /

USERNAME SESSION_STATUS SERVER CRCUIT_STATUS
-------- -------------- ------ -------------
TUNER    INACTIVE       NONE   NORMAL
```

Table 11-4   Most frequently used columns of the V$CIRCUIT view

Column	Description
CIRCUIT	Circuit memory address
DISPATCHER	Memory address of dispatcher process
SERVER	Memory address of server process
WAITER	Memory address of the waiting server process
SADDR	Memory address of the session related to current connection
STATUS	Status of circuit: ■ BREAK—Currently interrupted ■ EOF—About to be removed ■ OUTBOUND—An outward link to a remote database ■ NORMAL—Normal circuit into the local database
QUEUE	Queue the circuit is currently on: ■ COMMON—On the common queue, waiting to be picked up by a server process ■ DISPATCHER—Waiting for the dispatcher ■ SERVER—Currently being serviced ■ NONE—Idle circuit
BYTES	Number of bytes that passed through this circuit (connection)
BREAKS	Number of interruptions for current circuit

The information in this table is derived from the online documentation that Oracle provides at the Oracle Technology Network site: *www.otn.oracle.com*.

This view does not serve much purpose in detecting contention; its main purpose is to identify all connections to dispatchers and servers.

NOTE If Oracle cannot start up a shared server, you should check the settings of PROCESSES and MAX_SHARED_SERVERS parameters.

Using V$DISPATCHER

Table 11-5 presents the most commonly used columns of this view.

Table 11-5 V$DISPATCHER view most commonly used columns

Column	Description
NAME	Name of the dispatcher process
NETWORK	Network address of the dispatcher
PADDR	Dispatcher process address
STATUS	Status of the dispatcher: ■ WAIT—Idle ■ SEND—Sending a message ■ RECEIVE—Receiving a message ■ CONNECT—Establishing a connection ■ DISCONNECT—Handling a disconnect request ■ BREAK—Handling a break ■ TERMINATE—In the process of terminating ■ ACCEPT—Accepting connections (no further information available) ■ REFUSE—Rejecting connections
ACCEPT	Indicates if this dispatcher is accepting new connections or not (YES: accepting, NO: not accepting)
MESSAGES	Number of messages processed by this dispatcher
BYTES	Number of bytes processed for all messages processed by this dispatcher
BREAKS	Number of interruptions using this dispatcher
OWNED	Number of circuits owned by this dispatcher
CREATED	Number of circuits created by this dispatcher
IDLE	Total idle time in hundredths of a second
BUSY	Total busy time in hundredths of a second

The information in this table is derived from the online documentation that Oracle provides at the Oracle Technology Network site: *www.otn.oracle.com*.

This view not only shows information about dispatcher processes but also contains statistical data that you could use to detect dispatcher contention. If there is contention, you must increase the number of dispatcher processes. One useful indicator from this view is the busy rate ratio. It can be obtained by using the BUSY and IDLE columns of V$DISPATCHER. The threshold is 50 percent. If this ratio is consistently higher than the threshold, you should consider adding more dispatchers. The following query displays the busy rate ratio:

```
SQL> SELECT NETWORK,
  2         ROUND(SUM(BUSY)/SUM(BUSY+IDLE)*100) BUSY_RATE
  3    FROM V$DISPATCHER
  4   GROUP BY NETWORK
  5   /

NETWORK                                                    BUSY_RATE
---------------------------------------------------------- ----------
(ADDRESS=(PROTOCOL=tcp)(HOST=afyouni-tower)(PORT=2546))          60
(ADDRESS=(PROTOCOL=tcp)(HOST=afyouni-tower)(PORT=2547))          10
```

Or you can use this query:

```
SQL> SELECT ROUND(SUM(BUSY)/SUM(BUSY+IDLE)*100) BUSY_RATE
  2    FROM V$DISPATCHER
  3   /

 BUSY_RATE
----------
        70
```

In this case, you have a busy rate ratio higher than 50 percent, which indicates that you should add another dispatcher. You can do so by issuing the following ALTER SYSTEM statement:

```
SQL> ALTER SYSTEM SET DISPATCHERS = '(PROTOCOL=TCP)(DISPATCHERS=3)'
  2   /

SQL> SELECT NAME, NETWORK FROM V$DISPATCHER
  2   /

NAME NETWORK
---- --------------------------------------------------------
D000 (ADDRESS=(PROTOCOL=tcp)(HOST=afyouni-tower)(PORT=2546))
D001 (ADDRESS=(PROTOCOL=tcp)(HOST=afyouni-tower)(PORT=2547))
D002 (ADDRESS=(PROTOCOL=tcp)(HOST=afyouni-tower)(PORT=2281))
```

NOTE

When a new dispatcher process is added, it is not available for existing and current connections, only for new connections.

If the busy rate is consistently low (less than 10 percent), you may want to reduce the number of dispatcher processes as follows:

```
SQL> ALTER SYSTEM SET DISPATCHERS = '(PROTOCOL=TCP)(DISPATCHERS=1)'
  2  /

System altered.

SQL> SELECT NAME, NETWORK FROM V$DISPATCHER
  2  /

NAME NETWORK
---- --------------------------------------------------------
D000 (ADDRESS=(PROTOCOL=tcp)(HOST=afyouni-tower)(PORT=2546))
D001 (ADDRESS=(PROTOCOL=tcp)(HOST=afyouni-tower)(PORT=2547))
D002 (ADDRESS=(PROTOCOL=tcp)(HOST=afyouni-tower)(PORT=2281))

Some time later

SQL> SELECT NAME, NETWORK FROM V$DISPATCHER
  2  /

NAME NETWORK
---- --------------------------------------------------------
D000 (ADDRESS=(PROTOCOL=tcp)(HOST=afyouni-tower)(PORT=2546))
D001 (ADDRESS=(PROTOCOL=tcp)(HOST=afyouni-tower)(PORT=2547))
```

Or you can issue the following statement to shut down a specific dispatcher process if it is idle or when it becomes idle:

```
SQL> ALTER SYSTEM SHUTDOWN 'D001'
  2  /

System altered.

SQL> SELECT NAME, NETWORK FROM V$DISPATCHER
  2  /

NAME NETWORK
---- --------------------------------------------------------
D000 (ADDRESS=(PROTOCOL=tcp)(HOST=afyouni-tower)(PORT=2546))
```

The results do not show that the number of dispatcher processes is down. The number of processes is reduced when the existing connections are terminated. You should bear in mind that Oracle fully controls the number of processes created based on the connection load.

Using V$DISPATCHER_RATE

This view was introduced in Oracle9i, and it contains a host of statistical data about dispatcher performance. The 66 columns of this view are classified into the four categories listed as follows:

- **CUR_** : Current statistics column

- **MAX_** : Maximum statistics value that is ever reached for this column

- **AVG_** : Historical average value for this column

- **TTL_** : Time To Live; this is a statistic value for the most recent time interval

- **SCALE_** : Scale values for the TTL_ columns

You cannot get a specific indicator from this view. However, you should note that if the current values in CUR_ columns are very close to the maximum values in MAX_ columns, it indicates that more dispatcher processes are needed.

Using V$QUEUE

Table 11-6 contains descriptions of all columns belonging to this view. This view provides yet another indicator of the average wait time in the queue.

Table 11-6   Columns in the V$QUEUE view

Column	Dispatcher
PADDR	Memory address of the process that owns this queue
TYPE	Type of queue:
	■ COMMON (server process) ■ DISPATCHER
QUEUED	Number of items in the queue
WAIT	Total time all items in the queue have waited; value expressed in hundredths of a second
TOTALQ	Total number of items that have ever been in the queue

The information in this table is derived from the online documentation that Oracle provides at the Oracle Technology Network site: *www.otn.oracle.com*.

The following query shows the average wait time in the queue for the dispatcher processes. The result shows that the average wait time for a dispatcher is less than one second. A number that is consistently higher than one second should prompt you to increase the number of dispatchers. Remember that the result is expressed in hundredths of a second.

```
SQL> SELECT SUM(WAIT)/SUM(TOTALQ) AVERAGE_WAIT
  2    FROM V$QUEUE
  3    WHERE TYPE = 'DISPATCHER'
  4  /

AVERAGE_WAIT
------------
  .006060606
```

The following code segment shows the average wait in the queue for server processes. Again, the result shows that there is no need to do anything because the average wait time is less than one second. As stated previously, if the average wait time is consistently greater than one second, you need to increase the number of server processes.

NOTE
If a session hangs one of the shared servers, you should query V$CIRCUIT and V$SESSION views to determine which session is causing this problem and kill it. You know that a session is hanging if the session does not respond for a long time.

```
SQL> SELECT SUM(WAIT)/SUM(TOTALQ) AVERAGE_WAIT
  2    FROM V$QUEUE
  3    WHERE TYPE = 'COMMON'
  4  /

AVERAGE_WAIT
------------
  .002777778
```

Using V$SHARED_SERVER

Table 11-7 presents column definitions for this view. Similar to V$DISPATCHER view, this view provides a busy rate indicator that tells you if the number of server processes is adequate. This indicator has a threshold of 50 percent; so if the busy rate indicator is consistently higher than 50 percent, you should consider increasing the number of server processes.

Table 11-7 Columns in the V$SHARED_SERVER view

Column	Description
NAME	Name of this server (S000, S001, S00N)
PADDR	Memory address of this server process
STATUS	Server status: ■ EXEC—Executing SQL ■ WAIT (ENQ)—Waiting for a lock ■ WAIT (SEND)—Waiting to send data to user ■ WAIT (COMMON)—Idle; waiting for a user request ■ WAIT (RESET)—Waiting for a circuit to reset after a break ■ QUIT—Terminating
MESSAGES	Total number of messages processed by this server process
BYTES	Total number of bytes processed for all messages by this server process
BREAKS	Total number of interrupts
CIRCUIT	Memory address of current circuit and connection being serviced by this server process
IDLE	Total idle time for this server process; value expressed in hundredths of a second
BUSY	Total busy time for this server process; value expressed in hundredths of a second
REQUESTS	Total number of requests serviced from the queue

The information in this table is derived from the online documentation that Oracle provides at the Oracle Technology Network site: *www.otn.oracle.com*.

The following query displays the busy rate for all server processes. The query does not show any alarming results.

```
SQL> SELECT ROUND(SUM(BUSY)/
  2             SUM(BUSY+IDLE)*100) BUSY_RATE
  3    FROM V$SHARED_SERVER
  4    WHERE STATUS != 'QUIT'
  5  /

 BUSY_RATE
----------
        10
```

Using V$SHARED_SERVER_MONITOR

This view is used to tell you if the MAX_SHARED_SERVERS parameter is set properly. This view has only five columns, as listed in Table 11-8.

Table 11-8   V$SHARED_SERVER_MONITOR view columns

Column	Description
MAXIMUM_CONNECTIONS	Highest number of circuits ever in use at any time since instance startup
MAXIMUM_SESSIONS	Highest number of shared server sessions ever in use at any time since instance startup
SERVERS_STARTED	Total number of shared servers initiated since instance startup
SERVERS_TERMINATED	Total number of shared servers stopped by Oracle since instance startup
SERVERS_HIGHWATER	Highest number of servers running at the same time since instance startup

The information in this table is derived from the online documentation that Oracle provides at the Oracle Technology Network site: *www.otn.oracle.com*.

If the SERVER_HIGHWATER column value is close to the value of the parameter, MAX_SHARED_SERVERS, you may need to raise the value of the parameter.

Now that you have learned how to monitor the performance of a shared server, you are ready to move on to the next section to learn about the pros and cons of shared server mode and the differences between dedicated servers and shared servers.

Advantages and Disadvantages of Shared Servers

Here is a list of advantages of the shared servers:

- They work well with a large pool of connections to the database.

- Resources used by shared servers are well balanced. This means that there is no waste of resources if some user connections are inactive, because resources that would have been used by those connections are used instead by the active connections.

- They scale down or up depending on the connection's load.

- They enable you to use both dedicated server mode and shared server mode.

- They are well suited for Web applications in which there are high percentages of connections and disconnections. Shared servers have less time overhead than dedicated servers.

- Connections are not rejected because resources are lacking. Shared servers can be configured to set a limit on the number of allowed connections.

- They work well with Oracle Connection Manager for connection pooling.

- They allow users to share dispatcher and server processes.

- They use less memory than dedicated servers, especially if user connections are not active.

NOTE   Even when the database is configured for shared server mode, you can still connect to the database using a dedicated server. In fact, DBA sessions should connect using dedicated servers to avoid contention with users.

Here is a list of disadvantages:

- Unlike dedicated servers, shared servers require DBA setup and configuration time and effort.

- DBAs are required to monitor the performance of the shared servers.

- Shared servers may not perform for all types of applications and sessions.

- DBAs must connect to shared servers using dedicated server mode.

- Tracing sessions using SQL Trace is not possible (discussed in Chapter 12).

- They are not suitable if you are already using middleware to handle user connections.

DISTRIBUTED TRANSACTIONS

You must have encountered database experts throwing around the term, "distributed transaction" in conversations, white papers, or technical articles, and you may have said to yourself, "I'd like to learn to set up an application that employs this concept!" If you have made this comment to yourself or you are unfamiliar with the term, this section will be especially useful. It presents distributed databases and distributed transactions, along with a comprehensive overview of distributed transactions. Instructions for creating DATABASE LINKS follow. The section concludes with some of the performance issues of which you should be aware.

Distributed Transactions Overview

Before jumping into a scenario that illustrates the implementation of a distributed transaction, it's important you understand the definition of the term. A **distributed transaction** comprises one or more DML statements executed on more than one database as a single transaction. A distributed transaction is established via the use of a database object called a DATABASE LINK.

Now here's the scenario. An insurance company has several applications that serve different business departments and functions. The chief information officer (CIO) has decided to share functionality and data across different applications and business units, when appropriate. One of the applications that is shared across all applications is the security application, which registers and authenticates all users. Since this application is a critical mission (the company's operations depend on it), it resides on highly available architecture where the host machine and the application are redundant, and it uses the advanced feature of Oracle Data Guard. If a user logs on to the financial application and uses this application, the user is authenticated and registered with the security application. Each time the user moves from one module to another, the application updates the security database. This means that the financial application requires the capability to issue transactions against the security database. Therefore, the financial application uses distributed transactions because it needs to read and write to two or more databases as a single transaction.

As you can see in Figure 11-9, if a user needs to update financial records for a customer, the transaction entails modifying a row in the financial application database as well as recording auditing information in the security database as one single transaction. If security information cannot be registered, the whole transaction is rolled back.

11

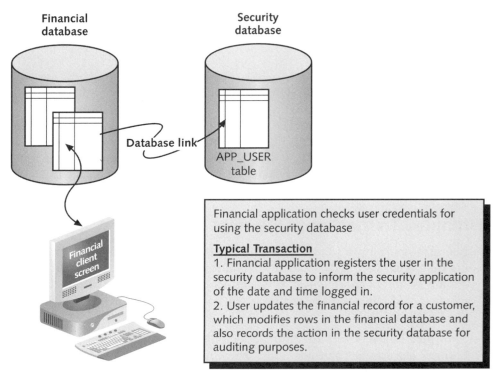

Figure 11-9 Architecture of the distributed transaction scenario

The illustration also shows that the link between the two databases allows the application to access data and issue DML statements to the security database as if it were issuing them to the financial database. This is transparent to the user and the application. The application does not need to do anything special; the database administrator sets it all up. This setup is established by creating a database object called a DATABASE LINK. This database object enables you to issue any DML statement from your local database to be executed in another database.

Oracle supports this sophisticated and complicated feature via a mechanism called Two-phase commit. This mechanism ensures that data changes by distributed transactions are committed in all databases. The two-phase commit has the following phases:

- **Preparation phase:** In this phase, the main database (local) informs all databases to prepare for a commit. This includes recording information about the transaction in the redo log and locking modified data.

- **Commit phase:** In this phase, the main database tells all involved databases to commit the changes. After the databases commit the changes, they notify the main database whether the commit failed or succeeded. Once all the databases have notified the main database that the commit is completed, changes in the main database are committed.

This was a brief overview. If you are interested in more details about this topic, you should consult Oracle9*i* documentation.

Because the foundation of a distributed transaction is a DATABASE LINK object, you should learn how to create it and issue transactions using this object. This is covered in the next section.

Creating and Using DATABASE LINKS

As indicated previously, you cannot implement distributed transactions without creating a DATABASE LINK object. The complete syntax to create a DATABASE LINK follows (refer to Figure 11-10):

```
CREATE [SHARED] [PUBLIC] DATABASE LINK dblink_name
   [ CONNECT TO { CURRENT_USER |
                  user IDENTIFIED BY password [AUTHENTICATED BY user
                                                IDENTIFIED BY password]
               } |
               AUTHENTICATED BY user IDENTIFIED BY password
   ]
[USING 'connect_string'];
```

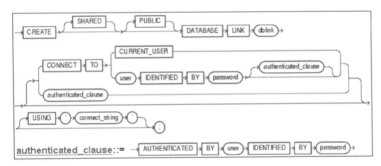

Figure 11-10   Create DATABASE LINK syntax

- **SHARED option**: Tells Oracle to create a DATABASE LINK that can be shared among multiple users

- **PUBLIC option**: Tells Oracle to allow all users to use the DATABASE LINK

- **CONNECT TO CURRENT_USER** (Authentication Method 1, known as CURRENT-USER): Tells Oracle to use the current user for authentication to the database to which you are trying to link

- **CONNECT TO** *user* **IDENTIFIED BY** *password* (Authentication Method 2, known as FIXED-USER):Tells Oracle to use the user and password provided in this clause for authentication to the database to which you are trying to link

- **AUTHENTICATE BY** (Authentication Method 3, known as CONNECTED-USER): Tells Oracle to use the credentials of the connected user who has an existing account in the database to which you are trying to link

- **USING connect_string**: This option tells Oracle the TNSNAME (service name) to use to connect to the database to which you are trying to link. The **connect_string** is a set of usernames, passwords, and services that usually has the following format: *username/password@service*.

Before you jump into the creation of the DATABASE LINK, you need to know about the initialization parameter DB_DOMAIN. This parameter tells Oracle the logical location of the database. A typical domain name is the name of a company, such as ACME.COM. Oracle uses this parameter by appending its value to the name of the database.

DB_DOMAIN cannot be modified dynamically.

NOTE

The following steps create a DATABASE LINK using the three authentication methods and using the CREATE DATABASE LINK statement to establish a link from the BOOK database to the SAM database, as shown in Figure 11-11.

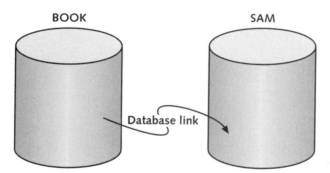

Figure 11-11   DATABASE LINK example

To use the DATABASE LINK, you must have a user account on the remote database.

NOTE

Step 1: You need to make sure that there is a TNSNAME (service name) for SAM in the Tnsnames.ora file because you are trying to connect to the SAM database from the BOOK database. Tnsnames.ora contains a TNSNAME entry as specified here:

Tnsnames.ora file usually resides at $ORACLE_HOME/network/admin.

NOTE

```
SAM =
  (DESCRIPTION =
    (ADDRESS_LIST =
      (ADDRESS = (PROTOCOL = TCP)(HOST = afyouni-tower)(PORT = 1521))
    )
    (CONNECT_DATA =
      (SERVER = DEDICATED)
      (SERVICE_NAME = SAM)
    )
  )
```

Step 2: Log on to the BOOK database as user SYSTEM and create a DATABASE LINK called TO_SAM_Mx where M stands for method and x stands for 1, 2, or 3. Using the rules for naming database objects, you can give the DATABASE LINK any valid name. Here are three statements for creating a DATABASE LINK:

Authentication Method 1 (CURRENT USER)

```
SQL> CONNECT SYSTEM@BOOK
Enter password: ******
Connected.

SQL> CREATE PUBLIC DATABASE LINK TO_SAM_M1
  2      CONNECT TO CURRENT_USER
  3      USING 'SAM'
  4  /

Database link created.
```

11

Authentication Method 2 (FIXED USER)

```
SQL> CREATE PUBLIC DATABASE LINK TO_SAM_M2
  2      CONNECT TO TUNER IDENTIFIED BY TUNER
  3       USING 'SAM'
  4  /

Database link created.
```

Authentication Method 3 (CONNECTED USER)

```
SQL> CREATE PUBLIC DATABASE LINK TO_SAM_M3
  2      USING 'SAM'
  3  /

Database link created.
```

Step 3: Verify each DATABASE LINK created in Step 2 by issuing the following statements:

```
SQL> SHOW PARAMETER DB_DOMAIN

NAME                          TYPE        VALUE
----------------------------- ----------- -------------------------
db_domain                     string      AFYOUNI.NET

SQL> SELECT 'METHOD #1: ' || GLOBAL_NAME METHOD
  2      FROM GLOBAL_NAME@TO_SAM_M1
  3  /

METHOD
--------------------------------------------------
METHOD #1: SAM.AFYOUNI.NET

SQL> SELECT 'METHOD #2: ' || GLOBAL_NAME METHOD
  2      FROM GLOBAL_NAME@TO_SAM_M2
  3  /

METHOD
--------------------------------------------------
METHOD #2: SAM.AFYOUNI.NET

SQL> SELECT 'METHOD #3: ' || GLOBAL_NAME METHOD
  2      FROM GLOBAL_NAME@TO_SAM_M3
  3  /

METHOD
--------------------------------------------------
METHOD #3: SAM.AFYOUNI.NET
```

You must have noticed the at symbol (@) in the FROM clause of the previous SQL statements. This symbol tells Oracle to execute the current statement at the database specified in the DATABASE LINK whose name follows the symbol (for example, issue the second SQL statement at DATABASE LINK TO_SAM_M2).

Step 4: You can view all DATABASE LINKS created in a database using DBA_DB_LINKS, as shown in this query:

```
SQL> SELECT * FROM DBA_DB_LINKS
/

OWNER  DB_LINK                    USERNAME     HOST   CREATED
------ -------------------------- ------------ ------ ---------
PUBLIC TO_SAM_M1.US.ORACLE.COM    CURRENT_USER SAM    27-APR-03
PUBLIC TO_SAM_M2.US.ORACLE.COM    TUNER        SAM    27-APR-03
PUBLIC TO_SAM_M3.US.ORACLE.COM                 SAM    27-APR-03
```

The following statements demonstrate distributed transactions:

Step 1: Log on to the BOOK database as user DEMO:

```
SQL> CONNECT DEMO@BOOK
Enter password: ****
Connected.
```

Step 2: Issue the following transaction that comprises the following:

- SELECT statement on remote database (SAM)

- SELECT statement on local database (BOOK)

- INSERT statement on local database (BOOK)

- INSERT statement on remote database (SAM) using DATABASE LINKTO_SAM_M2

- UPDATE statement on remote database (SAM)

```
SQL> SELECT * FROM CATEGORIES@TO_SAM_M2
  2  /

CATEGORY_ID CATEGORY_NAME
----------- ------------------------
          1 Hardware
          2 Software
          3 Appliances
          4 Apparel
          5 Grocery
          6 Medical Equipment
          7 Equipment
          8 Home Design
          9 Games
         10 Electrical
         11 Materials
         12 Carpentry
         13 Accessories
         14 Shoes
         15 Entertainment
         16 Electronics
         17 Books
         18 Office Supplies
```

11

```
SQL> SELECT * FROM LOCATION
  2  /

LOCATION_ID REGIONAL_GROUP
----------- ---------------
        122 NEW YORK
        124 DALLAS
        123 CHICAGO
        167 BOSTON

SQL> INSERT INTO LOCATION VALUES(999, 'OTTAWA')
  2  /

1 row created.

SQL> INSERT INTO CATEGORIES@TO_SAM_M2 VALUES
  2     (19, 'Misc. via db link')
  3  /

1 row created.

SQL> UPDATE CATEGORIES@TO_SAM_M2
  2     SET CATEGORY_NAME = 'Books, via db link'
  3     WHERE CATEGORY_ID = 17
  4  /

1 row updated.

SQL> SELECT * FROM CATEGORIES@TO_SAM_M2
  2  /

CATEGORY_ID CATEGORY_NAME
----------- --------------------------
          1 Hardware
          2 Software
          3 Appliances
          4 Apparel
          5 Grocery
          6 Medical Equipment
          7 Equipment
          8 Home Design
          9 Games
         10 Electrical
         11 Materials
         12 Carpentry
         13 Accessories
         14 Shoes
         15 Entertainment
         16 Electronics
         17 Books, via db link
         18 Office Supplies
         19 Misc. via db link
```

Step 3: Issue a commit.

Step 4: Log on as TUNER to SAM and verify that the data was committed.

Of course, if you issue a distributed transaction and you then issue a ROLLBACK statement, all changes made will be rolled back in each impacted database.

Oracle provides a useful dynamic performance view called V$DBLINK, which shows all pending transactions using a DATABASE LINK. The query shows a row after an update statement using a DATABASE LINK. All rows of V$DBLINK are removed the moment you disconnect from the current session.

```
SQL> UPDATE CATEGORIES@TO_SAM_M2
  2    SET CATEGORY_NAME = 'Books, via db link'
  3    WHERE CATEGORY_ID = 17
  4  /

1 row updated.

SQL> SELECT * FROM V$DBLINK
  2  /

DB_LINK                   OWNER_ID LOG HET PROTOC OPEN_CURSORS IN_ UPD COMMIT_POINT_STRENGTH
------------------------- -------- --- --- ------ ------------ --- --- ---------------------
TO_SAM_M2.US.ORACLE.COM          5 YES YES UNKN              0 YES YES                     1
```

You must have SELECT privilege on V$DBLINK to query this view.

NOTE

As stated previously, you can implement distributed transactions, which will be transparent to the application. You can establish this by using a synonym (a synonym is an alias name for a database object). Examine the following example. Suppose you want to access the CATEGORIES table residing on the SAM database from the BOOK database. As you learned previously, you would issue the following statement, which must specify the DATABASE LINK. That means you need to hard code it in your application.

```
SQL> SELECT * FROM CATEGORIES@TO_SAM_M2
  2  /
```

To avoid hard coding the DATABASE LINK in your application and to make it transparent, you will create a synonym as follows:

```
SQL> CREATE SYNONYM CATEGORIES FOR CATEGORIES@TO_SAM_M2
  2  /

Synonym created.
```

11

Now that you have established this synonym, you can issue the following query to display the contents of the CATEGORIES table residing in the SAM database without specifying a DATABASE LINK.

```
SQL> SELECT * FROM CATEGORIES
  2  /

CATEGORY_ID CATEGORY_NAME
----------- -----------------------------
          1 Hardware
          2 Software
          3 Appliances
          4 Apparel
          5 Grocery
          6 Medical Equipment
          7 Equipment
          8 Home Design
          9 Games
         10 Electrical
         11 Materials
         12 Carpentry
         13 Accessories
         14 Shoes
         15 Entertainment
         16 Electronics
         17 Books, via db link
         18 Office Supplies
         19 Misc. via db link

19 rows selected.
```

DATABASE LINK Performance Issues

Oracle provides initialization parameters to configure DATABASE LINKS for distributed transactions. However, these parameters do not have much influence on the performance of the distributed transactions or DATABASE LINKS. The following is a list of these parameters:

- **DBLINK_ENCRYPT_LOGIN:** Tells Oracle whether to use encryption when connecting to other databases

- **DISTRIBUTED_LOCK_TIMEOUT:** The amount of time in seconds to wait to obtain a lock on a desired resource

- **OPEN_LINKS:** Total number of open links per session

- **OPEN_LINKS_PER_INSTANCE:** Total number of open links per session

Now you're aware that you cannot do much to improve the performance of distributed transactions, but how can you ensure that performance is not degraded by distributed transactions? The solution is simple! The backbone (hardware and network) of distributed transactions is stable, fast, and capable of supporting fast distributed traffic between databases that are not residing on the same machine. If this backbone does not exist, you will be operating at a high risk of performance degradation.

REPLICATION

A development team for a medium-sized financial company encountered a small database challenge while reviewing the design of a new application. The review committee consisted of the chief architect, project manager, project leader, database administrator, and senior developers.

The new application under review required data from one specific table that already existed in production and belonged to a mission-critical application. This table was huge and still growing. The new application was also mission critical but did not have the same high availability requirements. In addition, the two applications would neither reside on the same database nor on the same machine. The data required by the new application could be out of date after five to ten minutes.

So the chief architect laid out two solutions to provide the data from the existing database to the new database:

- **Data feed:** Every ten minutes, the data from the table is extracted to a text file and then transferred to the new application host machine where the text file is loaded to the truncated table. Figure 11-12 depicts this process.

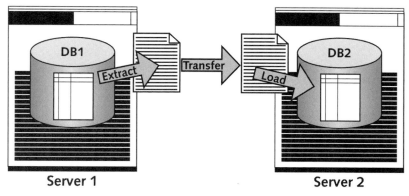

Figure 11-12   Data feed architecture

- **DATABASE LINK:** In this approach, a link is established from the new application to the existing application from which data will be accessed on demand, and data will not reside in the new application, as shown in Figure 11-13.

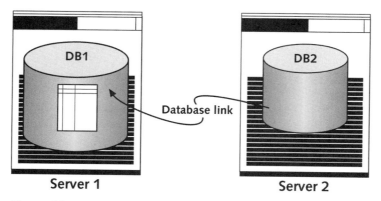

Figure 11-13 DATABASE LINK architecture

The chief architect outlined the major advantages and disadvantages of these two approaches in Table 11–9.

Table 11-9 Data feed versus DATABASE LINK

Function	Approach 1: Data feed	Approach 2: DATABASE LINK
High availability	Data is available even if SERVER1/DB1 (existing application) is down	If SERVER1/DB1 is down, data is not available
Development effort	Requires development effort and testing	Does not require any development effort
Database setup and administration	Requires minimal database setup and administration	Requires the effort of database setup, but it is not a complicated task. No administration required
Data status	At best, data might be ten minutes out of date	Data is up to date at all times
Synchronization effort	Requires an effort to synchronize the data if the table goes out of sync	No synchronization effort required
Performance	Heavy on performance (processing time) because it is performing three tasks, extract, transfer and load, and the table is huge. There is a risk that the process of updating the table may not be able to complete within a given window	Performance is not as good as when retrieving data from a table residing in the same database; also, performance depends on the number of rows being retrieved and the network connection between the bandwidth of the two linked machines

As the chief architect was explaining Table 11–9, he was interrupted with a question from the database administrator. "Did you consider a replication option?" The chief architect said, "Yes, I read about it and it seemed too complicated for what we need." The database administrator expanded the chief architect's table outline by adding a column for replication as in Table 11–10.

Table 11-10   Replication functionality

Function	Approach 3: Replication
High availability	Data will be available even if SERVER1/DB1 (existing application) is down
Development effort	No development effort is required
Database setup and administration	Requires database setup and minimal administration
Data status	At best, data might be one minute (not ten) out of date, or in the worst case, for the period the SERVER1/DB1 is down
Synchronization effort	Oracle takes care of synchronization
Performance	Performance is not affected when retrieving data. Only updated rows are refreshed. Performance of refreshing data depends on network connection

And then the database administrator explained the process to the audience. When he was finished, everyone applauded and agreed to go with the replication approach.

A happy ending, wasn't it? Of course! Replication delivered exactly what the development team was looking for without jeopardizing performance or data accessibility and integrity. So, what is replication? To answer this question, the following sections take you on a tour by presenting the concept of replication, types of replication, and the diagnosis of replication problems. Of course, this section is not meant to provide detailed information about replication but only to whet your appetite for the topic.

Replication Architecture Overview

Replication is an advanced feature of a database system that enables data objects to be replicated from one primary database to a secondary database. In other words, replication is the process of copying and maintaining changes to data objects. As the changes occur on the primary database, they are applied to the secondary database. For example, suppose you decide to replicate a database object (TABLE) as in Figure 11-14. If a new row is added to the table in the primary database, this row is replicated to the secondary database.

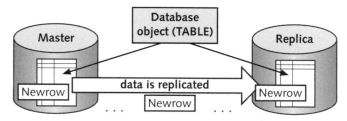

Figure 11-14   Replication architecture

Not only that, every time data is deleted, inserted, or updated in the primary database, these changes are applied automatically to the secondary database. The process of applying changes is called DATA REFRESH.

NOTE

The primary database is usually referred to as the master database or the master site, and the secondary database has many names: materialized view site, replica site, slave database, and slave site.

Of course, a TABLE object is not the only database object that can be replicated. Oracle supports the replication of the following objects:

- **Indexes:** Enables fast access to data stored in tables

- **Indextypes:** Enables the creation of new indexing schemes

- **Packages and package bodies:** Enables developers to package procedures, functions, and data variables within one object

- **Procedures and functions:** Enables users to write code in modules to perform a specific task or function

- **Synonyms:** Enables database object aliasing

- **Tables:** Represents the most common and the main database objects used to store data

- **Triggers:** Enables users to write code to be used when an event occurs

- **User-defined operators:** Enable developers and administrators to define their own operators to perform a specific operation

- **User-defined types and type bodies:** Allows developers to create their own user-defined data types and data objects

- **Views and object views**: Simplifies complicated queries and limits the scope of what data users can see

In the true story related in the beginning of this section, the DBA recommended the use of replication because it offered the benefits the development team was looking for which included data availability, performance, and minimal development effort. This DBA was aware of the benefits that replication offers and had worked on different types of applications that used replication. The benefits and the applications affected are outlined in the following lists:

- **Data availability**: Replication offers another layer of ensuring data availability and access in case of failure in the master site. Data can still be accessible through the replica sites.

- **Data synchronization**: Oracle replication provides a reliable means of ensuring that data is synchronized between replicated databases.

- **Development effort**: Replication is a function of Oracle that has been proven to be a robust feature. Developers or database administrators need not develop any code to replicate data.

- **Performance**: Oracle has invested resources to ensure that the process of replication is fast and reliable, provided the network connection between databases is reliable and has a high bandwidth and that the replicated databases are geographically adjacent to each other.

Here is a list of applications in which replication was used:

- Example 1: A master database site supporting the main Web site for a prominent financial company is replicated to three replica sites at different locations for high availability and fast access, as illustrated in Figure 11-15. Users can access the Web site that is geographically closest to them. A user on the West Coast can access the Web site residing in Replica 1. Context changes of the Web site are updated on the master site and replicated on a periodical basis to the replica sites.

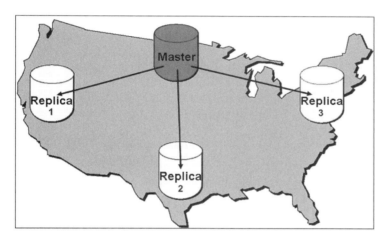

Figure 11-15 Example 1 of replication architecture

- Example 2: Consultants for one of the big consulting companies are equipped with notebook computers that have many software applications that they use. One of the applications is a time-keeping program, which maintains the hours worked by the consultant. This application has a small replica of the corporate headquarters' time-keeping database and, in fact, only records belonging to the consultant are kept locally on the database. The data is synchronized between headquarters and the notebook PC on demand, as shown in Figure 11-16. In this case, the application is used as a distributed database application to increase database performance and data synchronization. So in this case, the local database will have only records pertaining to the consultant where he or she can access his or her data anytime without the need to connect to headquarters. The local database is refreshed or synchronized when managers approve time cards and when a consultant updates his or her time card.

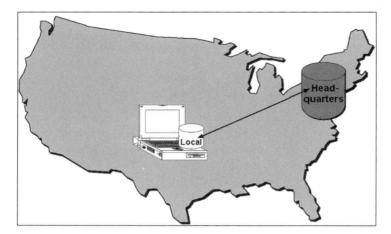

Figure 11-16 Headquarters of replication architecture

■ Example 3: A bank with several branches in the New England region uses replication for distributed transactions. This reduces the load on the master database at headquarters. Actually, every branch has a master database where transactions are replicated to all databases and then synchronized with headquarters daily.

When performance or maintenance of up-to-date data might be compromised, replication can be implemented in two ways, asynchronous and synchronous.

The **asynchronous replication** is also known as store-and-forward replication. With asynchronous replication, data changes on the master site are stored in the database first, and then periodically at a set time, the changes are forwarded to all replica sites. This method compromises the up-to-date factor because all replicas are behind the master site by a time equal to the duration of forwarding the changes. As the periods of time between replications increases, the data becomes less up-to-date and the number of changes forwarded increases. Performance is not impacted by any factor except by the longevity of refreshing periods.

Synchronous replication is also known as real-time-replication. Synchronous replication acts like a single transaction: any data changes on the master site are not stored until changes are stored on all replica sites. This method compromises performance. If one replica site takes longer to store changes, all sites must wait. However this method ensures that sites have consistent data.

Figure 11-17 presents a flowchart for each type of replication to demonstrate the behavior of each replication type. The main difference between the two types is the timing of data replication. Synchronous replication is performed immediately, whereas with asynchronous replication, the flowchart shows that the data changes are stored locally for later forwarding.

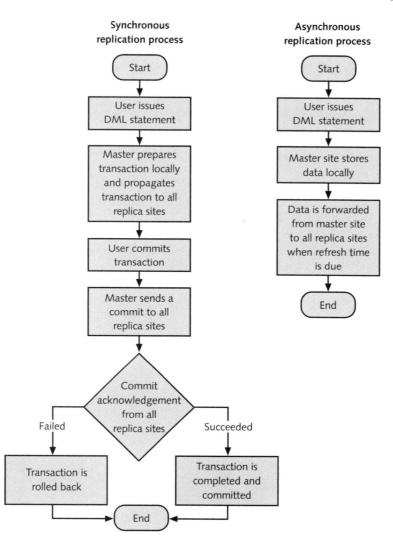

Figure 11-17   Asynchronous and synchronous process flowcharts

After learning about asynchronous and synchronous replications, you must be curious about the other types of replications available in Oracle. You might have guessed some of them. The next section presents an overview of the three types of replication applications supported by Oracle—each type can be synchronous or asynchronous.

Types of Replications

As indicated in the last section, there are three types of replication, and they vary in complexity and purpose.

Multimaster Replication

Consider the example of a law firm with offices in several major U.S. cities. An application was developed for all offices to share all accounting records, which are always kept synchronized and up to the minute. The type of replication used in this case is called multimaster replication.

NOTE

Multimaster replication is also known as peer-to-peer or *n*-way replication.

Multimaster replication occurs when all sites in the replication environment act as master and replica at the same time. This means that changes on any of the replicated objects, known as the replicated group, are applied to other master sites, and any changes on the replicated objects in another master site are applied to the master site. In this case, the master site is acting as master and replica (this is known as *n*-way replication). Figure 11-18 represents the architecture of a multimaster replication. As you can see, all master sites are replicating to the other master sites at the same time data is being replicated to it.

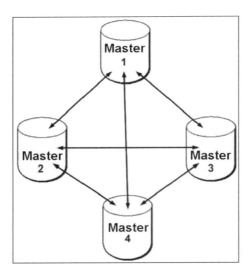

Figure 11-18   *Multimaster replication architecture*

As you might have guessed, this type of replication is advanced and requires a well-planned and thorough implementation. This implementation is usually used for two main purposes. The first purpose is to keep the application available at all times, called "high availability." If one master site is down, the application fails over to other master sites without any downtime. Multimaster replication is also used for load balancing, so that users access the master site that is geographically closest to them rather than all users accessing one central database.

Single-master Replication

This method is commonly used and is much less complicated than multimaster replication. In a **single-master replication** environment, you have one master site replicating to one or more replica sites, as shown in Figure 11-19.

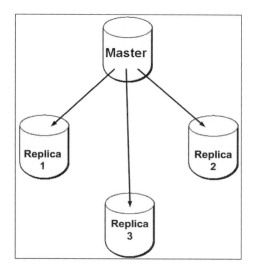

Figure 11-19   Single-master replication architecture

Materialized-view Replication

Materialized-view replication uses a materialized view to replicate full or partial data of one or more tables. A **materialized view** is a database object that stores the query and its results to provide indirect access to table data. A materialized view is created based on a query and a refresh schedule. The refresh schedule is used to rerun the base query to get up-to-date results. Materialized views provide better query performance than rerunning the query repeatedly. Materialized views are often used in data warehouse applications and in replication.

NOTE

Materialized views have an advantage over normal views in that the query for the materialized view does not need to be run to retrieve results because the results of the query have already been stored in the materialized view.

There are two types of materialized view replications:

- **Read-only materialized-view replication:** In this type, data is replicated through the use of a materialized view, which is in read-only mode. Data cannot be updated through the materialized view, only through the table in the master site, as shown in Figure 11-20.

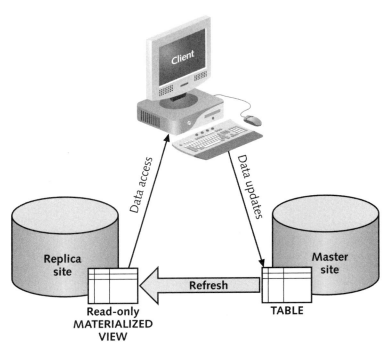

Figure 11-20   Architecture of a read-only materialized-view replication

NOTE

One disadvantage of materialized views compared to normal views is that the data in materialized views becomes outdated over time.

- **Updateable materialized–view replication:** With this type of replication, data is replicated from the master site using a materialized view. Any changes on the replica site are synchronized and refreshed with the master site. Users can update data directly to the master or replica site. See Figure 11–21.

NOTE

As you do with a table, you can specify storage parameters and tablespace to reside in a materialized view.

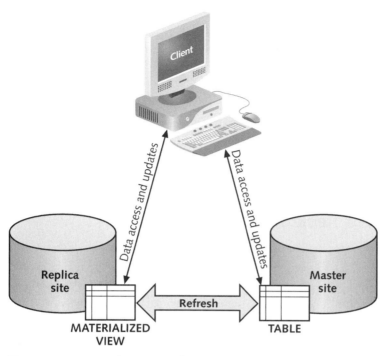

Figure 11-21   Architecture of an updateable materialized-view replication

Hybrid Replication

Hybrid replication combines multimaster replication and materialized-view replication, as illustrated in Figure 11-22.

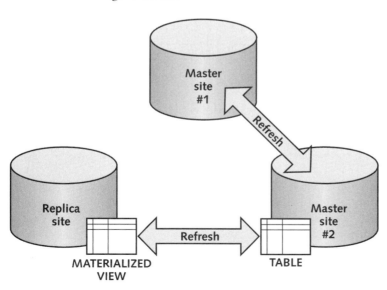

Figure 11-22   Hybrid replication architecture

Here is an example of a real application using hybrid replication. A company sells different products to several companies, and all product data resides on two master databases for high availability and load balancing. Users and administrators can use the two master sites to retrieve and update product data such as prices, inventory, and so on. A replica Web site is established for customers to access product data and other data pertaining to the customer. Customers are not allowed to access the master site for security reasons.

At this point you are ready to see how materialized-view replication works, and as a DBA you may find it interesting to learn how data is replicated from one database to another. In the next section, you learn how to set up this type of replication step by step. Of course, it would be more interesting to witness how multimaster replication works, but that is beyond the scope of this book.

Materialized-View Replication Setup

This brief portion of the replication section is dedicated to getting a feel for what's involved in setting up the simplest type of replication and using materialized views.

Although you can create materialized views to demonstrate replication using one database, in the steps outlined, you assume that you have two databases. In this case, the database for the master site is called SAM, and the database for the replica site is called BOOK. The data object replicated is the CUSTOMER table residing in the TUNER schema in both databases, (see Figure 11-23).

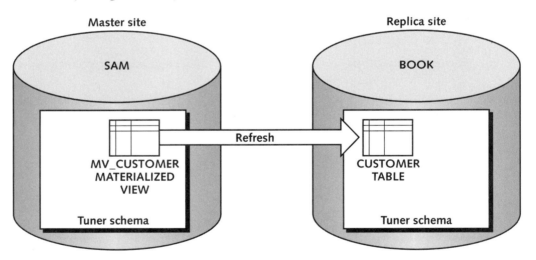

Figure 11-23   Replication scenario architecture

Step 1: Create a DATABASE LINK to allow the TUNER user in the BOOK database to access the TUNER object in the SAM database. Refer to the previous section for instructions on how to create a DATABASE LINK.

```
SQL> CONNECT TUNER@BOOK
Enter password: *****
Connected.

SQL> CREATE DATABASE LINK TO_SAM
  2    CONNECT TO TUNER IDENTIFIED BY TUNER
  3    USING 'SAM'
  4  /

Database link created.
```

Step 2: Verify DATABASE LINK:

```
SQL> SELECT * FROM GLOBAL_NAME@TO_SAM
  2  /

GLOBAL_NAME
----------------------------------------
SAM.AFYOUNI.NET
```

11

Step 3: Using the TUNER schema on the BOOK database, create a materialized view called MV_CUSTOMERS. See the statement that follows which creates a materialized view that will be refreshed every 10 minutes. Details of the CREATE statement are explained later.

```
SQL> CREATE MATERIALIZED VIEW "TUNER"."MV_CUSTOMERS"
  2    PARALLEL ( DEGREE DEFAULT ) CACHE
  3    TABLESPACE "USERS"
  4    BUILD IMMEDIATE
  5    USING INDEX
  6    TABLESPACE "USERS"
  7    REFRESH COMPLETE
  8    START WITH to_date('27-Apr-2003 10:04:17 AM','dd-Mon-yyyy HH:MI:SS AM')
  9    NEXT sysdate + 10/1440
 10    AS
 11    SELECT CUSTOMER_ID, FIRST_NAME, LAST_NAME, EMAIL, PHONE
 12      FROM CUSTOMERS@TO_SAM
 13  /

Materialized view created.
```

NOTE

Your MV_CUSTOMERS view may contain data different than that shown in Steps 4, 5, and 6.

Step 4: Verify that data is in MV_CUSTOMERS. Because the table has many rows, you display only the first five rows.

```
SQL> SELECT * FROM MV_CUSTOMERS
  2    WHERE ROWNUM < 6
  3  /

CUSTOMER_ID FIRST_NAME LAST_NAME EMAIL                          PHONE
----------- ---------- --------- ------------------------------ ----------
     802701 Emely      Ulmer     EUlmer@vieuykktxbsdgyc.ad      1432872794
     402724 Heriberto  Teixeira  HTeixeira@bnywenkmnsouqyi.gov  7933962285
     102008 Helga      Barr      HBarr@ccgsgzmxkeutrjy.gov      4155187511
     401989 Alfonso    Branch    ABranch@eyvmxphmrtqvxja.com    7667045227
     402022 Bud        Chew      BChew@hgfggptewvgosrx.net      4155081512
```

Step 5: Log on to TUNER on the SAM database and modify the EMAIL column value to 'emely.ulmer@acme.com' and commit your changes:

```
SQL> CONNECT TUNER@SAM
Enter password: *****
Connected.
SQL> UPDATE CUSTOMERS
  2      SET EMAIL = 'emely.ulmer@acme.com'
  3    WHERE CUSTOMER_ID = 802701
  4  /

1 row updated.

SQL> COMMIT
  2  /

Commit complete.
```

Step 6: Wait for a few minutes (a maximum of 10), because the materialized view is refreshed every 10 minutes. As TUNER on BOOK, display the row for CUSTOMER_ID 802701 in MV_CUSTOMERS. You should notice that the e-mail for the first row has changed (this means that the materialized view was refreshed).

NOTE

Materialized views are often used in data-warehousing applications because they improve the performance of the underlying query.

```
SQL> CONNECT TUNER@BOOK
Enter Password:*****
Connected.
SQL> SELECT * FROM MV_CUSTOMERS
  2   WHERE CUSTOMER_ID = 802701
  3  /


CUSTOMER_ID FIRST_NAME LAST_NAME EMAIL                PHONE
----------- ---------- --------- -------------------- ----------
     802701 Emely      Ulmer     emely.ulmer@acme.com 1432872794
```

Next, you examine the CREATE statement in the following code segment. It is quite complicated. Focus on the main options for refreshing the materialized view. You should consult Oracle9i documentation for more details on this CREATE statement.

```
CREATE MATERIALIZED VIEW [schema.]materialized_view
  [OF [schema.]object_type]
  [(scoped_table_ref_constraint)]
  ON PREBUILT TABLE [{WITH | WITHOUT} REDUCED PRECISION]
  | physical_properties materialized_view_props
  [USING INDEX
    [physical_attributes_clause | TABLESPACE tablespace]
      [physical_attributes_clause | TABLESPACE tablespace]...
  ]
  | USING NO INDEX
  [create_mv_refresh]

  [FOR UPDATE] [{DISABLE | ENABLE} QUERY REWRITE] AS subquery;
```

11

```
Where create_mv_refresh is

{ REFRESH
  { { FAST | COMPLETE | FORCE }
  | ON { DEMAND | COMMIT }
  | { START WITH | NEXT } date
  | WITH { PRIMARY KEY | ROWID } }
  | USING
    { DEFAULT [ MASTER | LOCAL ] ROLLBACK SEGMENT
    | [ MASTER | LOCAL ] ROLLBACK SEGMENT rollback_segment
    }
    [ DEFAULT [ MASTER | LOCAL ] ROLLBACK SEGMENT
    | [ MASTER | LOCAL ] ROLLBACK SEGMENT rollback_segment
    ]...
  }
  [ { FAST | COMPLETE | FORCE }
  | ON { DEMAND | COMMIT }
  | { START WITH | NEXT } date
  | WITH { PRIMARY KEY | ROWID } }
  | USING
    { DEFAULT [ MASTER | LOCAL ] ROLLBACK SEGMENT
    | [ MASTER | LOCAL ] ROLLBACK SEGMENT rollback_segment
    }
    [ DEFAULT [ MASTER | LOCAL ] ROLLBACK SEGMENT
    | [ MASTER | LOCAL ] ROLLBACK SEGMENT rollback_segment
    ]...
  ]...
| NEVER REFRESH
}
```

Here are some pointers on the preceding code segment:

- **BUILD IMMEDIATE:** Tells Oracle to build the view immediately

- **REFRESH option:** Tells Oracle to use the refresh mode for this materialized view. Available refresh modes are:

  - **FAST:** For incremental refresh. Only changes will be refreshed rather than all rows (this is good for performance, especially if the table is large and the refresh schedule is frequent).

  - **COMPLETE:** Refreshes all rows. This can take a toll on performance, especially for a large number of rows.

  - **FORCE:** Indicates that a refresh should do a FAST refresh if possible, otherwise a COMPLETE refresh.

  - **NEVER REFRESH:** Use this option if you do not intend to refresh the materialized view. This option does not allow you to refresh rows using any refresh mechanism such as the Oracle-supplied package DBMS_MVIEW.

  - **ON COMMIT:** Tells Oracle that a refresh must occur every time a transaction is committed on the master site

- **ON DEMAND:** Tells Oracle that a refresh will be done on demand using package DBMS_MVIEW

- **START WITH:** Specifies the first time to automatically refresh the materialized view

To help you pull together all this information, Figure 11-24 summarizes the options in a flowchart.

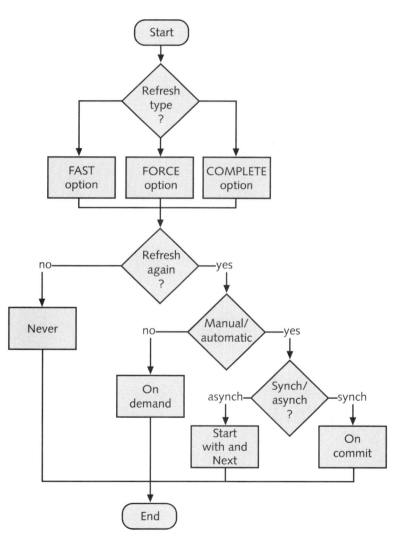

Figure 11-24 Flowchart guide for creating materialized views

Oracle provides a PL/SQL package, DBMS_MVIEW, to administer materialized views. To refresh a materialized view using this package, follow these steps:

Step 1: Log on as TUNER on the BOOK database and create the new materialized view, TUNER.MV_CATEGORIES, on the SAM database:

```
SQL> CONNECT TUNER@BOOK
Enter password: *****
Connected.

SQL> CREATE MATERIALIZED VIEW MV_CATEGORIES
  2      TABLESPACE USERS
  3      BUILD IMMEDIATE
  4      USING INDEX TABLESPACE USERS
  5      REFRESH FORCE ON DEMAND
  6      AS
  7      SELECT * FROM CATEGORIES@TO_SAM
  2  /

Materialized view created.

SQL> SELECT * FROM MV_CATEGORIES
  2  /

CATEGORY_ID CATEGORY_NAME
----------- --------------------
          1 Hardware
          2 Software
          3 Appliances
          4 Apparel
          5 Grocery
          6 Medical Equipment
          7 Equipment
          8 Home Design
          9 Games
         10 Electrical
         11 Materials
         12 Carpentry
         13 Accessories
         14 Shoes
         15 Entertainment
         16 Electronics
         17 Books, via db link
         18 Office Supplies
         19 Misc. via db link
```

Step 2: Log on as TUNER on SAM, delete CATEGORY_ID 19, and commit the changes:

```
SQL> CONNECT TUNER@SAM
Enter password: *****
Connected.
SQL> DELETE CATEGORIES
  2   WHERE CATEGORY_ID = 19
  3  /

1 row deleted.

SQL> COMMIT
  2  /

Commit complete.
```

Step 3: As TUNER on BOOK, display category information for the CATEGORY_ID 19:

```
SQL> CONNECT TUNER@BOOK
Enter password:*****
Connected.
SQL> SELECT * FROM MV_CATEGORIES
  2   WHERE CATEGORY_ID = 19
  3  /

CATEGORY_ID CATEGORY_NAME
----------- --------------------
         19 Misc. via db link
```

11

Step 4: As TUNER on BOOK, refresh the materialized view using the DBMS_MVIEW PL/SQL package and the REFRESH procedure as follows:

```
PROCEDURE REFRESH
 Argument Name              Type                    In/Out Default?
 --------------------       ----------------------  ------ --------
 TAB                        TABLE OF VARCHAR2(227)  IN/OUT
 METHOD                     VARCHAR2                IN     DEFAULT
 ROLLBACK_SEG               VARCHAR2                IN     DEFAULT
 PUSH_DEFERRED_RPC          BOOLEAN                 IN     DEFAULT
 REFRESH_AFTER_ERRORS       BOOLEAN                 IN     DEFAULT
 PURGE_OPTION               BINARY_INTEGER          IN     DEFAULT
 PARALLELISM                BINARY_INTEGER          IN     DEFAULT
 HEAP_SIZE                  BINARY_INTEGER          IN     DEFAULT
 ATOMIC_REFRESH             BOOLEAN                 IN     DEFAULT
```

Where
METHOD: C for COMPLETE, F for FAST or ? (question mark) for FORCE
REFRESH_AFTER_ERRORS: TRUE to continue if an error occurs while refreshing or FALSE to stop if an error occurs.
ATOMIC_REFRESH: TRUE to do refresh as one single transaction otherwise FALSE

```
Other functions and procedures
·  FUNCTION I_AM_A_REFRESH RETURNS BOOLEAN
·  FUNCTION PMARKER RETURNS NUMBER
·  PROCEDURE BEGIN_TABLE_REORGANIZATION
·  PROCEDURE DROP_SNAPSHOT
·  PROCEDURE END_TABLE_REORGANIZATION
·  PROCEDURE EXPLAIN_MVIEW
·  PROCEDURE EXPLAIN_REWRITE
·  PROCEDURE GET_LOG_AGE
·  PROCEDURE GET_MV_DEPENDENCIES
·  PROCEDURE PURGE_DIRECT_LOAD_LOG
·  PROCEDURE PURGE_LOG
·  PROCEDURE PURGE_MVIEW_FROM_LOG
·  PROCEDURE PURGE_SNAPSHOT_FROM_LOG
·  PROCEDURE REFRESH
·  PROCEDURE REFRESH_ALL
·  PROCEDURE REFRESH_ALL_MVIEWS
·  PROCEDURE REFRESH_DEPENDENT
·  PROCEDURE REFRESH_MV
·  PROCEDURE REGISTER_MVIEW
·  PROCEDURE REGISTER_SNAPSHOT
·  PROCEDURE SET_I_AM_A_REFRESH
·  PROCEDURE SET_UP
·  PROCEDURE TESTING
·  PROCEDURE UNREGISTER_MVIEW
·  PROCEDURE UNREGISTER_SNAPSHOT
·  PROCEDURE WRAP_UP

You can display the full package description by issuing:
SQL> DESC DBMS_MVIEW
```

```
SQL> EXEC DBMS_MVIEW.REFRESH('MV_CATEGORIES','C',NULL,TRUE,FALSE,0,0,0,TRUE)

PL/SQL procedure successfully completed.
```

Step 5: As TUNER on BOOK, perform Step 3 again. When the refresh was completed, it had refreshed all rows because the METHOD used is C for COMPLETE.

```
SQL> CONNECT TUNER@BOOK
Enter password:*****
Connected.
SQL> SELECT * FROM MV_CATEGORIES
  2   WHERE CATEGORY_ID = 19
  3  /

no rows selected
```

If you want to use a FAST refresh, you must create a **materialized–view log** to keep track of changes. This can be done by issuing CREATE MATERIALIZED VIEW LOG. For more details, consult Oracle9*i* documentation. Figure 11-25 shows the architecture for materialized–view logs.

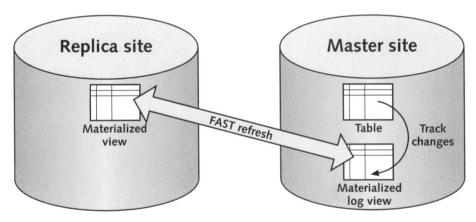

Figure 11-25   FAST refresh replication architecture

To set up the materialized–view log and use the FAST refresh method, follow these steps:

Step 1: As TUNER on BOOK, drop the existing materialized view, MV_CATEGORIES:

```
SQL> CONNECT TUNER@BOOK
Enter password:*****
Connected.
SQL> DROP MATERIALIZED VIEW MV_CATEGORIES
  2  /

Materialized view dropped.
```

Step 2: On the master site SAM as TUNER, create a materialized-view log:

```
SQL> CREATE MATERIALIZED VIEW LOG ON CATEGORIES
  2      TABLESPACE USERS
  3  /

Materialized view log created.
```

Step 3: On BOOK as TUNER, create the materialized view:

```
SQL> CREATE MATERIALIZED VIEW MV_CATEGORIES
  2      TABLESPACE USERS
  3      BUILD IMMEDIATE
  4      USING INDEX TABLESPACE USERS
  5      REFRESH FORCE ON DEMAND
  6      AS
  7      SELECT * FROM CATEGORIES@TO_SAM
  8  /

Materialized view created.
```

Step 4: Now add a row to categories in the SAM master site:

```
SQL> INSERT INTO CATEGORIES VALUES(21, 'Misc. via repl.')
  2  /

1 row created.

SQL> COMMIT
  2  /

Commit complete.
```

Step 5: As TUNER on BOOK, refresh MV_CATEGORIES using the DBMS_MVIEW package, this time using the FAST method:

```
SQL> EXEC DBMS_MVIEW.REFRESH('MV_CATEGORIES','F',NULL,TRUE,FALSE,0,0,0,TRUE)

PL/SQL procedure successfully completed.
```

Step 6: Verify that the data changes for the CATEGORIES table on the master site SAM are replicated to the slave site BOOK:

```
SQL> SELECT * FROM MV_CATEGORIES
  2  /

CATEGORY_ID CATEGORY_NAME
----------- --------------------
          1 Hardware
...
         21 Misc. via repl.

20 rows selected.
```

Why did you need to drop the materialized view? The answer is simple. The materialized-view log must be created before the materialized view in order to track all replication changes.

You just witnessed replication using SQL statements, which require you to know the syntax of CREATE MATERIALIZED VIEW. Oracle Enterprise Manager makes this job a little bit easier by providing a GUI interface. This option is available under the DISTRIBUTED node in the main navigation panel, as shown in Figure 11-26.

11

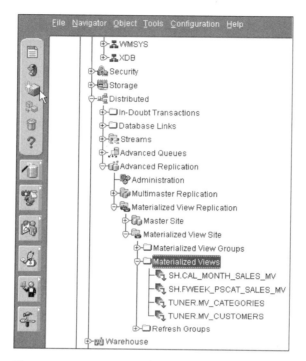

Figure 11-26   Oracle Enterprise Manager—Materialized Views node

To create a new materialized view, you can click on the Create button on the tool bar. Then select Materialized View in the Create dialog box, and click Create. A dialog box opens in which you can enter all necessary information about the materialized view, as shown in Figure 11-27.

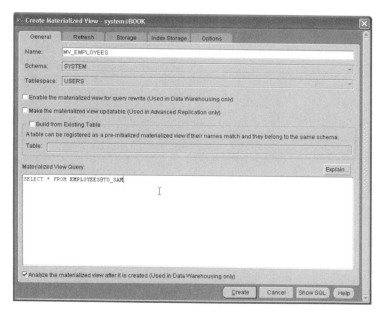

Figure 11-27   Oracle Enterprise Manager—Create Materialized View dialog box

NOTE

Use DBA_MVIEWS and DBA_MVIEW_LOGS to view all materialized views and materialized-view logs created in the database.

11

One set of options in CREATE MATERIALIZED VIEW is ENABLE or DISABLE QUERY REWRITE. So what is QUERY REWRITE? It tells the Oracle optimizer to rewrite the query using the materialized view instead of using the underlying base tables. This improves performance of the query. Oracle provides two initialization parameters that are related to Query Rewrite:

- **QUERY_REWRITE_ENABLED:** Enables query rewrites whenever Oracle Optimizer determines it will improve performance of the query; allowed values are FALSE or TRUE.

NOTE

Mode must be set in Oracle Optimizer to CHOOSE mode.

- **QUERY_REWRITE_INTEGRITY:** Tells Oracle how the integrity of the results should be enforced; allowed values are:

  - **ENFORCED:** Enables query rewrites only if the optimizer can ensure that the result will be consistent

- **TRUSTED:** Enables query rewrites using relationships that have been declared, but that are not enforced by Oracle

- **STALE_TOLERATED:** Enables query rewrites using unenforced relationships

NOTE

Initialization parameters for QUERY_REWRITE_ENABLED and QUERY_REWRITE_INTEGRITY can be set dynamically on the session and instance level.

This concludes your introduction to the exciting topic of replication. As stated previously, replication is more involved than what is presented in this chapter and requires careful and proper design, configuration, and implementation.

Diagnosing Replication Problems

Oracle Enterprise Manager offers a handy Advanced Replication feature, which allows you to create and configure sites for all of the replication types. In addition, this feature enables administering and monitoring replication. You can use this feature by clicking on Distributed>Advanced Replication>Administration on the navigation panel, as illustrated in Figure 11-28.

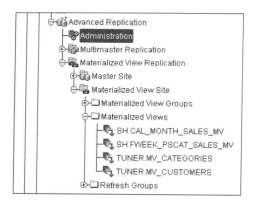

Figure 11-28   Oracle Enterprise Manager—Administration node

Once you click on Administration node, the topology of existing replication is displayed, as illustrated in Figure 11-29.

NOTE

The Legend can be displayed by pressing the Legend button located on the lower-right of the window. The Legend provides an explanation of existing topology.

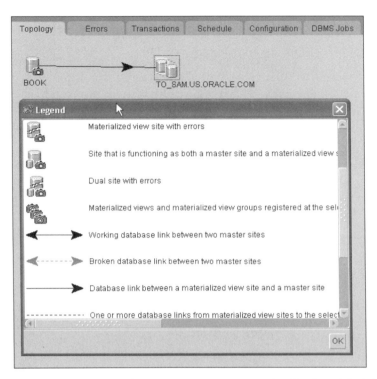

Figure 11-29   Oracle Enterprise Manager—Replication Administration window

As you can see, there are several tabs that contain more details about existing replication objects. For more information on this feature, consult Oracle9*i* Enterprise Manager documentation.

The following list outlines pointers and tips to diagnose replication problems. When you diagnose replication problems, make sure that:

- The underlying DATABASE LINK is working (you should be able to connect to the remote database from the local database as presented in the previous section).

- The scheduled interval value provided for the START WITH clause in the CREATE statement is valid.

- The scheduled interval for refreshing is longer than the execution time to refresh the data.

- The network connection between the two databases is stable.

- The maximum number of open links has not been reached for the replica site.

- You have enough storage for both the MATERIALIZED VIEW and MATERIALIZED VIEW LOG.

Real Application Clusters

With the release of version 9*i*, Oracle revamped many earlier features to ensure that their functionality is efficient and robust. The **Real Application Cluster**, formerly known as Oracle Parallel Server (OPS) and commonly referred to as RAC, is the new star feature of Oracle9*i*. Oracle9*i* RAC is a groundbreaking feature of database system, which distinguishes Oracle databases from the competition.

If you have been exposed to OPS, then you probably have an idea what RAC is about. If you are not familiar with OPS or RAC, you can benefit from this section, which presents a brief overview of RAC and its architecture, concluding with the purposes and benefits of RAC.

RAC Overview

Three years ago, a startup dot-com company was created with the idea of providing an information service. The founders of the company were three computer science graduates who had gone to school together. They had no idea what the future held! Due to a lack of investment money, the founders selected a shareware operating system and a shareware database system with a shareware Web server. In the first year the company picked up a reasonable number of clients, and the business started to make money, which was invested in marketing efforts without changing the architecture or the tools used.

The business was doing so well, with clients and money growing, that little attention was paid to the system architecture until the day the whole system was crippled because it could not handle the heavy load of transactions. That day was the beginning of the fall of the empire! The company faced not only performance problems, but they faced even more serious problems because the system would sporadically lose transactions and become unavailable.

Customer service personnel were overwhelmed with complaints and cancellations of service. Reports and articles in technical and business magazines and newspapers were knocking the company's service. The market lost confidence in the company. Of course, the founders realized that they needed to completely replace the software architecture by employing UNIX as operating system software, Oracle as the database system, and Apache for a Web server, coupled with strong middleware. Basically, the company invested a considerable amount of money, but it was too late, and the company went bankrupt six months later!

So what is the moral of this true story? Putting aside management and other business factors, the moral of the story is that the architectural layer used for the company was not scalable to the increased workload as the business grew.

Many companies invest huge amounts of money employing sophisticated and complex architecture to ensure two main requirements: *scalability* and *high availability*. Oracle9*i* RAC satisfies these two requirements and also provides increased performance and decreased possibilities of loss of transactions and data.

In the simplest terms, the Oracle Real Application Cluster is an architecture in which multiple Oracle instances access and work on one shared Oracle database. Figure 11-30 provides an illustration of this architecture.

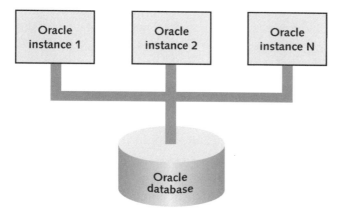

Figure 11-30   Basic architecture of Oracle Real Application Cluster

Oracle9*i* RAC provides the following benefits:

- **High availability:** Database downtime is decreased.

- **Scalability:** Oracle instance(s) and database can scale up or scale down, depending on business growth.

- **Increased performance and throughput:** RAC takes advantage of hardware resources to improve performance and efficiency.

- **Failover mechanism:** RAC supports the Oracle Data Guard feature that facilitates the failover to another instance and database in case of failure.

- **Manageability:** Once it is configured and implemented, there is little need for tuning.

Oracle9*i* RAC disadvantages include the following:

- **Hardware:** RAC requires more hardware resources than the normal setup of Oracle instance, specifically CPUs and memory resources.

- **Expertise:** Configuring and implementing RAC requires expertise.

CHAPTER SUMMARY

- ❏ Dedicated servers are more widely used than shared servers and are the default Oracle configuration.
- ❏ A client connected to an Oracle instance using dedicated server mode is served by a dedicated process.

- A shared server is a process shared among all users connecting in this mode.
- A shared server is composed of three layers that interact with each other: dispatcher, server, and queue structure.
- Configuring the database in shared server mode requires setting parameters in the Init.ora file on the database side and the service name in the Tnsnames.ora file on the client side.
- One useful indicator from V$DISPATCHER view is a ratio which is called the busy rate ratio. The threshold of this ratio is 50 percent.
- The average wait time in the queue for dispatcher processes should be less than one second.
- A distributed transaction comprises one or more DML statements executed on more than one database as one single transaction.
- Oracle supports distributed transactions via a mechanism called Two-phase commit.
- The foundation of a distributed transaction is a DATABASE LINK object.
- The at (@) symbol in the FROM clause tells Oracle to execute the current statement at the database specified in the DATABASE LINK whose name follows the symbol.
- Replication enables data objects to be replicated from one primary database to a secondary database.
- The process of applying changes that occur in a master site to a replica site is called DATA REFRESH.
- Types of replication include the following: multimaster replication, single-master replication, materialized-view replication, and hybrid replication.
- Multimaster replication occurs when all sites in the replication environment act as master and replica at the same time.
- Single-master site replication occurs when one master site replicates to one or more replica sites.
- A materialized-view replication uses a materialized view to replicate full or partial data of one or more tables.
- A materialized view is a database object that stores the query and its results to provide indirect access to table data.
- Hybrid replication is a combination of multimaster replication and materialized-view replication.
- An Oracle Real Application Cluster is an architecture in which multiple Oracle instances access and work on a shared Oracle database.
- Initialization parameters presented in this chapter include the following:
  - DISPATCHERS
  - MAX_DISPATCHERS
  - SHARED_SERVERS
  - MAX_SHARED_SERVERS
  - CIRCUITS
  - SHARED_SERVER_SESSIONS

- QUERY_REWRITE_ENABLED
- QUERY_REWRITE_INTEGRITY
- DBLINK_ENCRYPT_LOGIN
- DISTRIBUTED_LOCK_TIMEOUT
- OPEN_LINKS_PER_INSTANCE
- OPEN_LINKS
- DB_DOMAIN
- DBLINK_ENCRYPT_LOGIN

❏ Views used in this chapter include the following:

- DBA_DB_LINKS
- DBA_MVIEWS
- DBA_MVIEW_LOGS
- V$SESSION
- V$CIRCUIT
- V$DISPATCHER
- V$DISPATCHER_RATE
- V$QUEUE
- V$SHARED_SERVER
- V$SHARED_SERVER_MONITOR
- V$DBLINK

❏ PL/SQL Packages used in this chapter include the following:

- DBMS_MVIEW

REVIEW QUESTIONS

1. Dedicated server mode serves more than one user connection when the original connected user is idle. (True/False)

2. Shared server mode requires more resources than dedicated server mode. (True/False)

3. You use the tnsnames.ora file to instruct Oracle to connect in shared mode. (True/False)

4. You cannot connect using dedicated server mode when the database is configured in shared server mode. (True/False)

5. You do not need to configure the database to use a dedicated server. (True/False)

11

6. The MAX_DISPATCHERS initialization parameter sets the number of dispatcher processes to be initiated for the database. (True/False)

7. The MAX_SHARED_SERVERS initialization parameter is mandatory. (True/False)

8. The USING 'connect_string' option in the CREATE DATABASE LINK tells Oracle the TNSNAME for connecting. (True/False)

9. You use the @ symbol as a suffix to the DATABASE LINK name. (True/False)

10. A materialized-view replication is also known as an *n*-way replication. (True/False)

11. A materialized-view replication is simple to set up. (True/False)

12. Replication requires DATABASE LINK objects. (True/False)

13. You need to create a materialized-view log on the replica site to perform a FAST refresh. (True/False)

14. FORCE refresh forces a refresh no matter what errors or warnings occur while refreshing the materialized view. (True/False)

15. The query Rewrite tells the Oracle Optimizer to rewrite a query using the materialized view instead of the underlying base tables to improve performance of the query. (True/False)

16. Synchronous refresh may impact performance. (True/False)

17. Write a query that displays all materialized views that exist in your database.

18. If you have two databases, create a DATABASE LINK from one to another and verify that the link is working.

19. Display all DATABASE LINKS in your database.

20. List the three ways you can create a database, and provide an example of how and why you would use each method.

21. Write a query that displays information about all dispatcher processes.

EXAM REVIEW QUESTIONS: ORACLE9*i* PERFORMANCE TUNING (#1Z0-033)

1. What is the threshold of the dispatcher busy rate?

   a. 1 percent

   b. 5 percent

   c. 10 percent

   d. 50 percent

   e. 90 percent

2. Why would you use V$CIRCUIT?

   a. To display all dispatcher processes

   b. To display all server dispatcher processes

   c. To display all connected users

   d. To display all network connections

3. What would you do if you notice dispatcher contention?

   a. Increase the number of shared server processes.

   b. Increase the number of dispatcher processes.

   c. Increase both the number of dispatcher and server processes.

   d. Increase the number of queues.

4. Why would you query V$QUEUE?

   a. To determine the average wait time in the queue

   b. To determine the busy wait time in the queue

   c. To determine the rate of the queue

   d. To determine the size of the queue

5. Why would you query V$SHARED_SERVER_MONITOR?

   a. To display the high-water mark of servers

   b. To determine if the MAX_SHARED_SERVERS parameter is set properly

   c. To determine if the number of dispatchers and servers is set properly

   d. To display the maximum rate ratio of the shared server

6. What parameter would you use to limit the number of connections for a shared server?

   a. CIRCUITS

   b. PROCESS

   c. SESSIONS

   d. SHARED_SERVER_SESSIONS

7. Which initialization parameter is mandatory to set up an Oracle shared server?

    a. SHARED_SERVERS

    b. MAX_SHARED_SERVERS

    c. SHARED_SERVER_SESSIONS

    d. DISPATCHERS

    e. MAX_DISPATCHERS

    f. CIRCUITS

8. What two files do you need to configure for an Oracle shared server?

    a. INIT.ORA

    b. LISTENER.ORA

    c. TNS.ORA

    d. TNSNAMES.ORA

    e. SERVICE.ORA

9. Which application is an Oracle shared server is suited for?

    a. OLTP

    b. Web

    c. DSS

    d. All applications

    e. None of the above

10. What would you use to administer a materialized-view replication?

    a. DBMS_VIEW

    b. DBMS_MVIEW

    c. DBMS_MATVIEW

    d. DBMS_MATERIALIZED_VIEW

11. Which initialization parameter would you set to enable a query rewrite for the whole Oracle instance?

    a. QUERY_REWRITE_ENABLED

    b. QUERY_REWRITE

    c. GLOBAL_QUERY_REWRITE

    d. GLOBAL_ QUERY_REWRITE_ENABLED

12. Which option(s) would you include in the CREATE MATERIALIZED VIEW to establish synchronous refresh? (Select one.)

    a. START WITH and NEXT

    b. ON DEMAND

    c. ON COMMIT

    d. FORCE

13. Which option(s) would you include in the CREATE MATERIALIZED VIEW to establish an asynchronous refresh? (Select one.)

    a. START WITH and NEXT

    b. ON DEMAND

    c. ON COMMIT

    d. FORCE

14. Which statement is not true?

    a. A materialized view is like a table.

    b. You can specify storage parameters for a materialized view in the same way you can for a table.

    c. A materialized view can be created as read-only and updateable.

    d. A materialized view can be refreshed at any time.

15. What option is not valid for refreshing a materialized view?

    a. NEVER REFRESH

    b. ENFORCE

    c. FAST

    d. COMPLETE

11

HANDS-ON PROJECTS

HANDS-ON
PROJECTS

Please complete the projects provided below.

1. Reread the Performance Problem at the start of the chapter. Think of it in terms of the concepts you have learned in this chapter and answer the following questions:

    a. What do you recommend for Joanna to do?

    b. What values for the initialization parameters would you recommend?

2. List three ways you would use a materialized view. Provide an example for each.

3. Your manager has asked you to assist a developer in establishing a DATABASE LINK from a production database to a development database. Outline the reasons why you would not comply with this request.

4. Read a technical paper about the uses of Oracle shared servers. Outline all the uses of shared servers.

5. List all situations in which you would need to use a DATABASE LINK.

6. Your customer (an application user) called you complaining about the performance of the database you are administering. Your customer is using a database designated as a replica site. List two possible reasons for your customer's problem.

7. You and your colleague are interested in determining which consumes more resources, a dedicated or shared server. So you perform the following steps:

   a. Log on as TUNER and create a table called TAB_COMPARE with two columns: NUM as NUMBER and TEXT as VARCHAR2(80).

   b. Populate this table with 100,000 rows.

   c. Establish ten different dedicated server connections, and for each connection issue the procedure listed in the code segment that follows.

   d. Monitor resource usage (CPU and MEMORY) from the operating system and from the database, and record the outcome.

   e. Close all dedicated connections, establish 10 shared server connections, and issue for each connection the procedure listed in the code segment that follows.

   f. Repeat Step d.

   g. What did you notice?

```
DECLARE
   V_NUM NUMBER
BEGIN
   FOR I IN 1..100000 LOOP
      SELECT NUM
        INTO V_NUM
        FROM TAB_SHARED
       WHERE NUM = I;
      FOR J IN 1..10000 LOOP
         NULL;
      END LOOP;
   END LOOP;
END;
/
```

CASE PROJECTS

1. Switching from Dedicated to Shared Server Mode

Set up your database to accept connections in shared server mode and then perform the following tasks:

1. Establish one connection as dedicated server mode.

2. Establish another connection as shared server mode.

3. Determine how you can distinguish which session is dedicated and which is shared server mode.

4. Create a table called TAB_SHARED with one column NUM as NUMBER.

5. Establish another shared server mode connection and issue the following procedure. Then monitor the dispatcher and the shared server processes as the procedure is running.

```
DECLARE
    V_NUM NUMBER
BEGIN
    FOR I IN 1..100000 LOOP
        INSERT INTO TAB_SHARED VALUES(I);
        FOR J IN 1..100000 LOOP
            NULL;
                END LOOP;
                SELECT NUM
                    INTO V_NUM
                    FROM TAB_SHARED
                  WHERE NUM = I;
        END LOOP;
    END;
    /
```

11

6. What did you notice from Step 5?

7. Why would you switch from dedicated server mode to shared server mode?

2. Links and Transactions

If you have one database, create another database called BOOK. If you have two databases, proceed with the following tasks. Perform the following tasks:

1. On the PRIMARY database, log on as SYSTEM and create a table called TAB_LINK1 with one column NUM as NUMBER.

2. On the BOOK database, log on also as SYSTEM and create a table called TAB_LINK2 with one column NUM as NUMBER.

3. Create a database that allows SYSTEM to see TAB_LINK2 from the PRIMARY database. Verify that the link is working before you proceed with the next task.

4. Insert a new row into TAB_LINK1 and a new row into TAB_LINK2, but do not commit.

5. Display all pending transactions in both databases.

6. What did you notice? Can you tell which one is using a DATABASE LINK?

7. Roll back your transaction and then query both tables.

8. Explain what happened.

3. Will FAST Work?

CASE PROJECTS

Using the TUNER schema, perform the following tasks:

1. Create a materialized view that contains the total amount of sales for each customer. This materialized view should be refreshed only when necessary.

2. Update the order table by updating the amount in three rows.

3. Perform a COMPLETE refresh.

4. Do you see changes to the materialized view?

5. Add a new order for a customer.

6. Perform a FAST refresh. What happened?

7. Perform the necessary actions for a fast refresh.

If you do not have privileges to create a materialized view, connect as SYSTEM and issue the following statement: GRANT CREATE MATERIALIZED VIEW TO username;

NOTE

PART

V

Tools

CHAPTER
12

TUNING TOOLS

In this chapter you will:

♦ Understand and use the four basic diagnostic tools supplied with Oracle9*i*

♦ Use statistical tools to diagnose and tune a database

♦ Understand and use SQL tools

♦ Use data block corruption tools

♦ Use the resource management tools to regulate and distribute resource usage based on priorities

---

After reading this chapter, you will appreciate the tools that can assist you in diagnosing and tuning the database. Your job as a DBA is quite narrowly defined: you need to keep your customers (users) happy, and keep yourself happy by making sure your database is available and optimized. There is no canned formula or set of magic tricks that you can use to make your database perform optimally. How do you it? You can employ Oracle-provided tuning tools that facilitate the process of database optimization. These tools can be classified into the following functional categories:

- **Diagnostics:** Diagnose problems and performance issues.

- **Statistics:** Collect statistical data to determine the health of the database and perform trend analysis.

- **SQL:** Identify problematic queries.

- **Data block corruption:** Detect data block corruption in data files as well as database objects.

- **Analysis:** Gather object storage statistics.

- **Resource management:** Distribute CPU allocation to database users based on planned priorities.

This chapter presents an overview of each of these tools and shows you how to use them. Be forewarned that the focus of this chapter is on tool use, not on the analysis or interpretation of the results produced by the tool. The previous chapter, as well as the next chapter, deal with the analysis and interpretation of the results.

Performance Problem

This section outlines an actual performance problem. As you look it over, imagine yourself as the DBA who reported it and keep it in mind as you proceed through the chapter. The chapter presents concepts relevant to the problem. In the first Hands-on Project at the end of the chapter, you are asked to use the concepts you have learned to provide a solution, or partial solution, to this performance problem.

From: George Dunn <mailto: gdunn@tools.com>
Date: 21-Dec-03 11:23
Subject: SQL Tuning Tool

I am seeking advice on the Oracle database SQL tuning tools.

I would like to hear your recommendations on and experiences with various SQL tuning tools and find out which one is best for getting an Explain Plan for a query. Are you aware of similar competitive products? And how would you rank them?

We are planning to pick a product and we would greatly appreciate your feedback.

Best regards,

George Dunn

gdunn@tools.com

DIAGNOSTIC TOOLS

You've probably heard the saying, "Every little bit counts!" This is especially true for you as a DBA. Every tool, whether simple or sophisticated, can help you troubleshoot or diagnose problems. This section presents four basic tools, which are included in Oracle 9*i* at no additional cost, which can help you diagnose problems. You'll examine each one starting with the Alert log file, followed by V$ views, and finally, the two Oracle Enterprise Manager diagnostic tools.

Alert Log

The Alert log file is the heartbeat of the system, registering errors, events, and database activities. This file is updated by the SMON background process as illustrated in Figure 12-1.

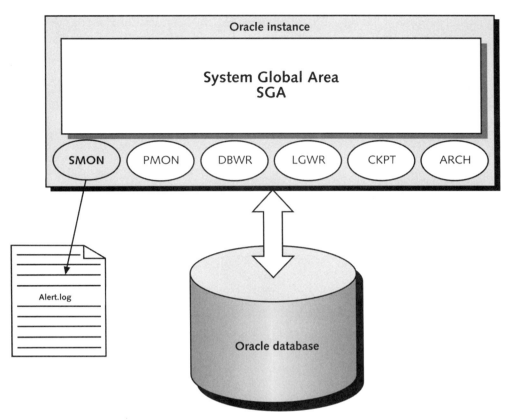

Figure 12-1   Oracle architecture showing the relationship between the SMON background process and the Alert log

The following sections describe the types of entries that the Alert log records.

Errors

The occurrence of any error that is related to an instance or physical structure is recorded in the Alert log. For example, an error is recorded when a background process fails. An error is recorded when a tablespace runs out of space or a deadlock occurs. And of course, there are many other possible errors that can occur. Because these types of errors have a system-wide (instance and database) effect, you need to monitor Alert log on a periodic basis, every five minutes, or 10 minutes maximum, through a UNIX or Windows script. Or you can employ a third-party tool to monitor the file. Some errors are not registered in the file, for example, a SQL statement that fails because of a syntactical error. Figure 12–2 demonstrates an error entry. The format of the entry is a date and time line followed by the trace file name and location, when applicable, and the ORA error with an error description.

Trace file has two meanings. First, a trace file can be a memory dump of a failed Oracle background process or user process. Database administrators and Oracle technical support specialists use the contents of such a trace file to determine the cause of a failure. Second, the term trace file can be used to mean the SQL activity of a session that is being traced. The contents of this trace file are used by database administrators to identify problematic queries.

```
alert_sam - Notepad                                              _ □ X
File  Edit  Format  Help
Thread 1 advanced to log sequence 25
  Current log# 3 seq# 25 mem# 0: C:\ORACLE\ORADATA\SAM\REDO03.LOG
Sat Jan 04 23:04:49 2003
Thread 1 advanced to log sequence 26
  Current log# 1 seq# 26 mem# 0: C:\ORACLE\ORADATA\SAM\REDO01.LOG
Sun Jan 05 08:39:42 2003
ALTER SYSTEM SET java_pool_size='0' SCOPE=SPFILE;
Sun Jan 05 08:41:37 2003
Shutting down instance: further logons disabled
Shutting down instance (immediate)
License high water mark = 7
Waiting for dispatcher 'D000' to shutdown          I
Sun Jan 05 08:41:37 2003
Errors in file c:\oracle\admin\sam\udump\sam_ora_1640.trc:
ORA-02097: parameter cannot be modified because specified value is invalid
ORA-01089: immediate shutdown in progress - no operations are permitted

All dispatchers and shared servers shutdown
Sun Jan 05 08:41:39 2003
ALTER DATABASE CLOSE NORMAL
Sun Jan 05 08:41:39 2003
SMON: disabling tx recovery
SMON: disabling cache recovery
```

Figure 12-2   Sample contents of the Alert log file

NOTE

The location of the Alert log is set by configuring BACKGROUND_DUMP_DEST. The name of the alert is alert_ORACLE_SID.log, where ORACLE_SID is the instance name for example: alert_SAM.log.

Startup and Shutdown

The Alert log records each time the database is signaled to shut down or start with the data and time of the occurrence.

Modified Initialization Parameters

Every time a database is started, Oracle records all modified initialization parameters in the Alert log.

Checkpoints

You can configure Oracle to record checkpoint time in the Alert log by setting the initialization parameter as follows: LOG_CHECKPOINT_TO_ALERT = TRUE. You can also determine when a checkpoint and incomplete checkpoints are completed.

Archiving

You can view the timing for all redo log sequences as well as archiving times (when an archive log is started and completed).

Physical Database Changes

As stated previously, any change to the physical structure of the database (not objects) is recorded in the Alert log. For example, the following actions are registered in the Alert log: creating a new tablespace, dropping a tablespace, resizing a data file, and adding a redo log file. Figure 12-3 shows entries for a tablespace that was dropped.

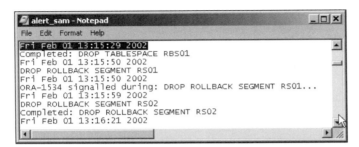

Figure 12-3   Alert log example showing an entry for tablespace changes

You must monitor the Alert log errors, specifically ORA-00600, which indicates an internal error and is usually a serious problem. When an error ORA-00600 occurs, you should work with Oracle Technical Support to investigate the trace file generated for this error.

Background Processes Trace

Each time a background process fails, an error is generated to the Alert log and a **trace file** is generated. Since these trace files are usually difficult to interpret, you should work with the Oracle Technical Support team to identify the type of problem, its cause, and action necessary to resolve the problem or prevent it from occurring again.

V$ Views

To introduce you to using V$ views as a diagnostic tool, first take a look at a true story about a person called Ali. Ali took an extensive DBA program at a prominent training school to become a database administrator. The instructor preached on a daily basis that the DBA should be familiar with most of the views that Oracle provides. In addition, the instructor constantly reminded the students to use these views with a command–line tool rather than a GUI tool, which degrades the learning process for students. Ali graduated from the program and got a job immediately. One day his manager came to his desk and asked him to generate a space-consumption report for an application. The manager needed to present the report to his VP immediately. Clearly, the manager wanted to know how much space was being used by all the objects of an application.

So, Ali went straight to his favorite GUI tool and started to look for an option that would give him this report. Unfortunately, he could not find such a feature. His manager sighed impatiently and then asked, "Can you issue a query to do this?" Of course Ali said, "Yes, but I need to look up the views that I need to query; just give me five minutes." The manager walked away saying, "I'm in the middle of a meeting, and I need it right away. Never mind!"

Fortunately for Ali, the manager's request was not a critical task. If it had been, Ali would not have had the luxury of research time. The moral of the story is that, in spite of all the colorful and good-looking screens that GUI tools provide, you still need to know intimately the views that Oracle provides. There are many instances in which a GUI tool cannot work because of the platform or environment. For instance, if you need to administer a tool remotely by using a Telnet session, you cannot use a GUI tool. This section presents a quick overview of the views available to you for diagnosing performance problems.

Oracle is rich with views that can provide you with information about your database and indicators on how the database is performing. Examine Figure 12-4 to understand the categorization of these views. In the figure, the dynamic performance views on the left are V$ views. The data in these views is flushed every time a database is shut down. The three types of views for the data dictionary, as shown on the right of the figure, include the following:

- DBA views: Display all objects that exist in the database.

- ALL views: Display all objects that are owned by the current user and the objects granted to the current user.

- USER views: Display all objects owned by the current user.

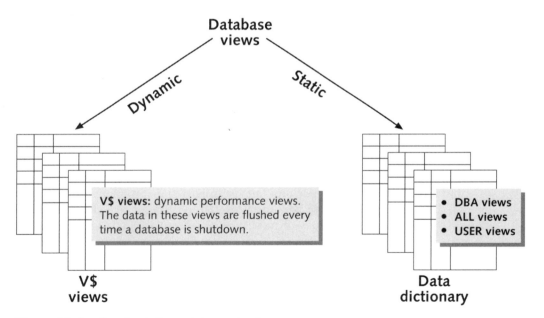

Figure 12-4   Oracle static and dynamic views

V$ views are synonyms for GV_ views that are populated from Oracle X$ base tables. Oracle provides a V$ view to display the definition of any view. This view is called V$FIXED_VIEW_DEFINITION. For example, if your inquiring mind wanted to get the definition of V$SESSION, you could issue the following query to get it. You need to log in as SYSTEM or SYS or as a user who has been granted the SELECT_CATALOG_ROLE role. As you can see, the result shows the V$SESSION view base query:

```
SQL> SELECT VIEW_DEFINITION
  2    FROM V$FIXED_VIEW_DEFINITION
  3   WHERE VIEW_NAME = 'V$SESSION'
  4  /

VIEW_DEFINITION
--------------------------------------------------------------------
select  SADDR , SID , SERIAL# , AUDSID , PADDR , USER# , USERNAME , CO
MMAND , OWNERID, TADDR , LOCKWAIT , STATUS , SERVER , SCHEMA# , SCHEMA
NAME ,OSUSER , PROCESS , MACHINE , TERMINAL , PROGRAM , TYPE , SQL_ADD
RESS , SQL_HASH_VALUE , PREV_SQL_ADDR , PREV_HASH_VALUE , MODULE , MOD
ULE_HASH , ACTION , ACTION_HASH , CLIENT_INFO , FIXED_TABLE_SEQUENCE ,
 ROW_WAIT_OBJ# , ROW_WAIT_FILE# , ROW_WAIT_BLOCK# , ROW_WAIT_ROW# , LO
GON_TIME , LAST_CALL_ET , PDML_ENABLED , FAILOVER_TYPE , FAILOVER_METH
OD , FAILED_OVER, RESOURCE_CONSUMER_GROUP, PDML_STATUS, PDDL_STATUS, P
Q_STATUS, CURRENT_QUEUE_DURATION, CLIENT_IDENTIFIER from GV$SESSION wh
ere inst_id = USERENV('Instance')
```

Performance views can be classified into several categories, which facilitates your search in case you have forgotten what view includes the information you are looking for. Figures 12-5 and 12-6 list the views in categories.

12

ARCHIVE
V$ARCHIVE
V$ARCHIVED_LOG
V$ARCHIVE_DEST
V$ARCHIVE_DEST_STATUS
V$ARCHIVE_PROCESSES
V$DELETED_OBJECT
V$PROXY_ARCHIVEDLOG
V$STANDBY_LOG

BACKUP
V$BACKUP
V$BACKUP_ASYNC_IO
V$BACKUP_CORRUPTION
V$BACKUP_DATAFILE
V$BACKUP_DEVICE
V$BACKUP_PIECE
V$BACKUP_REDOLOG
V$BACKUP_SET
V$BACKUP_SPFILE
V$BACKUP_SYNC_IO
V$RMAN_CONFIGURATION

CONTROLFILE
V$CONTROLFILE
V$CONTROLFILE_RECORD_SECTION

DATAFILES
V$COPY_CORRUPTION
V$DATAFILE
V$DATAFILE_COPY
V$DATAFILE_HEADER
V$FILESTAT
V$FILE_CACHE_TRANSFER
V$OFFLINE_RANGE
V$PROXY_DATAFILE

DATA GUARD
V$DATAGUARD_STATUS
V$MANAGED_STANDBY

DATABASE
V$COMPATSEG
V$DATABASE
V$DATABASE_BLOCK_CORRUPTION
V$DATABASE_INCARNATION
V$DBFILE
V$DBLINK
V$PWFILE_USERS
V$TABLESPACE
V$TYPE_SIZE

DIRECT PATH
V$LOADISTAT
V$LOADPSTAT

ENQUEUES
V$ENQUEUE_LOCK
V$ENQUEUE_STAT
V$HVMASTER_INFO

EVENTS
V$EVENT_NAME
V$SESSION_EVENT
V$SYSTEM_EVENT

FIXED VIEWS
V$FIXED_TABLE
V$FIXED_VIEW_DEFINITION
V$INDEXED_FIXED_COLUMN

GENERAL
V$COMPATIBILITY
V$LICENSE
V$OPTION
V$RESERVED_WORDS
V$VERSION

INSTANCE
V$ACTIVE_INSTANCES
V$AQ
V$BGPROCESS
V$CR_BLOCK_SERVER
V$DB_PIPES
V$ENABLEDPRIVS
V$FAST_START_TRANSACTIONS
V$GLOBAL_BLOCKED_LOCKS
V$GLOBAL_TRANSACTION
V$HS_AGENT
V$HS_PARAMETER
V$HS_SESSION
V$INSTANCE
V$INSTANCE_RECOVERY
V$MTTR_TARGET_ADVICE
V$PROCESS
V$RESOURCE
V$RESOURCE_LIMIT
V$STREAMS_APPLY_COORDINATOR
V$STREAMS_APPLY_READER
V$STREAMS_APPLY_SERVER
V$STREAMS_CAPTURE
V$THREAD
V$TIMER
V$TIMEZONE_NAMES
V$TRANSACTION
V$VPD_POLICY

LATCHES
V$LATCH
V$LATCHHOLDER
V$LATCHNAME
V$LATCH_CHILDREN
V$LATCH_MISSES
V$LATCH_PARENT

LOCKS
V$LOCK
V$LOCKED_OBJECT
V$LOCK_ELEMENT
V$TRANSACTION_ENQUEUE

LOGMINER
V$LOGMNR_CALLBACK
V$LOGMNR_CONTENTS
V$LOGMNR_DICTIONARY
V$LOGMNR_LOGS
V$LOGMNR_PARAMETERS
V$LOGSTDBY
V$LOGSTDBY_STATS

MAPPING
V$MAP_COMP_LIST
V$MAP_ELEMENT
V$MAP_EXT_ELEMENT
V$MAP_FILE
V$MAP_FILE_EXTENT
V$MAP_FILE_IO_STACK
V$MAP_LIBRARY
V$MAP_SUBELEMENT

MEMORY
V$BUFFER_POOL
V$BUFFER_POOL_STATISTICS
V$DB_CACHE_ADVICE
V$DB_OBJECT_CACHE
V$LIBRARYCACHE
V$LIBRARY_CACHE_MEMORY
V$PGASTAT
V$PGA_TARGET_ADVICE
V$PGA_TARGET_ADVICE_HISTOGRAM
V$ROWCACHE
V$ROWCACHE_PARENT
V$ROWCACHE_SUBORDINATE
V$SHARED_POOL_ADVICE
V$SHARED_POOL_RESERVED
V$SUBCACHE

Figure 12-5   V$ views classification, part 1

PARALLEL

V$EXECUTION
V$PARALLEL_DEGREE_LIMIT_MTH
V$PQ_SESSTAT
V$PQ_SLAVE
V$PQ_SYSSTAT
V$PQ_TQSTAT
V$PX_PROCESS
V$PX_PROCESS_SYSSTAT
V$PX_SESSION
V$PX_SESSTAT

PARAMETERS

V$NLS_PARAMETERS
V$NLS_VALID_VALUES
V$OBSOLETE_PARAMETER
V$PARAMETER
V$PARAMETER2
V$SPPARAMETER
V$SYSTEM_PARAMETER
V$SYSTEM_PARAMETER2

REAL APPLICATION CLUSTER

V$BH
V$CACHE
V$CACHE_LOCK
V$CACHE_TRANSFER
V$CLASS_CACHE_TRANSFER
V$FALSE_PING
V$GCSHVMASTER_INFO
V$GCSPFMASTER_INFO
V$GC_ELEMENT
V$GC_ELEMENTS_WITH_COLLISIONS
V$GES_BLOCKING_ENQUEUE
V$GES_CONVERT_LOCAL
V$GES_CONVERT_REMOTE
V$GES_ENQUEUE
V$GES_LATCH
V$GES_RESOURCE
V$GES_STATISTICS

RECOVERY

V$RECOVERY_FILE_STATUS
V$RECOVERY_LOG
V$RECOVERY_PROGRESS
V$RECOVERY_STATUS
V$RECOVER_FILE

REDO LOGS

V$LOG
V$LOGFILE
V$LOGHIST
V$LOG_HISTORY

RESOURCE MANAGER

V$RSRC_CONSUMER_GROUP
V$RSRC_CONSUMER_GROUP_CPU_MTH
V$RSRC_PLAN
V$RSRC_PLAN_CPU_MTH

SEGMENTS

V$SEGMENT_STATISTICS
V$SEGSTAT
V$SEGSTAT_NAME

SESSION

V$ACCESS
V$ACTIVE_SESS_POOL_MTH
V$CONTEXT
V$SESSION
V$SESSION_CONNECT_INFO
V$SESSION_CURSOR_CACHE
V$SESSION_LONGOPS
V$SESSION_OBJECT_CACHE
V$SESSION_WAIT
V$SESSTAT
V$SESS_IO

SGA

V$SGA
V$SGASTAT
V$SGA_CURRENT_RESIZE_OPS
V$SGA_DYNAMIC_COMPONENTS
V$SGA_DYNAMIC_FREE_MEMORY
V$SGA_RESIZE_OPS

SHARED SERVER (MTS)

V$CIRCUIT
V$DISPATCHER
V$DISPATCHER_RATE
V$QUEUE
V$QUEUEING_MTH
V$REQDIST
V$SHARED_SERVER
V$SHARED_SERVER_MONITOR

SQL

V$OBJECT_DEPENDENCY
V$OBJECT_USAGE
V$OPEN_CURSOR
V$SQL
V$SQLAREA
V$SQLTEXT
V$SQLTEXT_WITH_NEWLINES
V$SQL_BIND_DATA
V$SQL_BIND_METADATA
V$SQL_CURSOR
V$SQL_PLAN
V$SQL_PLAN_STATISTICS
V$SQL_PLAN_STATISTICS_ALL
V$SQL_REDIRECTION
V$SQL_SHARED_CURSOR
V$SQL_SHARED_MEMORY
V$SQL_WORKAREA
V$SQL_WORKAREA_ACTIVE
V$SQL_WORKAREA_HISTOGRAM
V$SYSTEM_CURSOR_CACHE

STATISTICS

V$MYSTAT
V$STATISTICS_LEVEL
V$STATNAME
V$SYSSTAT
V$WAITSTAT

TEMPORARY SEGMENTS

V$SORT_SEGMENT
V$TEMPFILE
V$TEMPORARY_LOBS
V$TEMPSEG_USAGE
V$TEMPSTAT
V$TEMP_CACHE_TRANSFER
V$TEMP_EXTENT_MAP
V$TEMP_EXTENT_POOL
V$TEMP_PING
V$TEMP_SPACE_HEADER

UNDO SEGMENTS

V$ROLLNAME
V$ROLLSTAT
V$UNDOSTAT

12

Figure 12-6 V$ views classification, part 2

NOTE

For a view description, consult Oracle9*i* documentation. For a structure description, use the DESC command from SQL*Plus.

You need to use the data dictionary DBA views to obtain information related to storage space. The following list identifies some useful views:

- DBA_FREE_SPACE

- DBA_EXTENTS

- DBA_SEGMENTS

- DBA_TABLESPACES

- DBA_DATA_FILES

- DBA_TABLES

- DBA_INDEXES

Initialization Parameters

The following sections describe initialization parameters that are used to configure the level of statistics collection.

STATISTICS_LEVEL Initialization Parameter

This parameter sets the level of statistics collection and can be dynamically set. Allowed values are:

- TYPICAL (this is the default setting for this parameter)

- BASIC

- ALL

Table 12-1 provides more details on these settings.

Table 12-1   STATISTICS_LEVEL initialization parameter

Level	BASIC	TYPICAL	ALL
Buffer Cache Advice	Not available	Available	Available
MTTR Advice	Not available	Available	Available
Timed Statistics	Available	Available	Available
Timed OS Statistics	Not available	Not available	Available
Segment Level Statistics	Not available	Available	Available
PGA Advice	Not available	Available	Available
Plan Execution Statistics	Not available	Not available	Available
Shared Pool Advice	Not available	Available	Available

The information in this table is derived from the online documentation that Oracle provides at the Oracle Technology Network site: *www.otn.oracle.com.*

You can view more information about the statistics level using the dynamic performance view, V$STATISTICS_LEVEL. Actually, Table 12-1 is populated from this view. The following query displays a list of statistics names and descriptions:

```
SQL> SELECT STATISTICS_NAME,
  2          DESCRIPTION
  3    FROM V$STATISTICS_LEVEL
  4  /

STATISTICS_NAME              DESCRIPTION
--------------------------   -------------------------------------------
Buffer Cache Advice          Predicts the impact of different cache sizes
                             on number of physical reads

MTTR Advice                  Predicts the impact of different MTTR settings
                             on number of physical I/Os

Timed Statistics             Enables gathering of timed statistics

Timed OS Statistics          Enables gathering of timed operating system
                             statistics

Segment Level Statistics     Enables gathering of segment access statistics

PGA Advice                   Predicts the impact of different values
                             of pga_aggregate_target on the performance
                             of memory intensive SQL operators

Plan Execution Statistics    Enables collection of plan execution statistics

Shared Pool Advice           Predicts the impact of different values
                             of shared_pool_size on elapsed parse time saved
```

TIMED_OS_STATISTICS Initialization Parameter

This parameter tells Oracle to collect operating system statistics for every client call to the database. It is recommended that this parameter be set to ON only when needed. This is only available when the STATISTICS_LEVEL is set to ALL.

TIMED_STATISTICS Initialization Parameter

This parameter tells Oracle whether to collect timed statistics for each call. Allowed values are TRUE or FALSE.

DB_CACHE_ADVICE Initialization Parameter

This parameter tells Oracle whether to collect advisory data for database caches.

Oracle Enterprise Manager

Although it is highly recommended that you use SQL queries to perform most of your DBA tasks, this does not mean that you should not use GUI tools. As a junior DBA, you should take every opportunity to perform your tasks using SQL to familiarize yourself with all available views, the data dictionary, and most the common queries. The use of a GUI is efficient and most of the time it displays output in a graphical or formatted manner. This section outlines the useful utilities that come with Oracle Enterprise Manager console. Oracle Enterprise Manager is structured into four different parts as illustrated in Figure 12-7:

1. Menu bar

2. Toolbar

3. Left panel (navigation)

4. Right panel (detail screen)

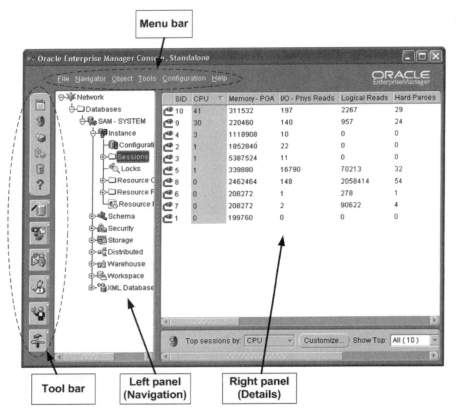

Figure 12-7   Oracle Enterprise Manager console window structure

Menu bar: Like any regular Windows application with a menu of options, Oracle Enterprise Manager provides menu options in a menu bar. The significant feature of this menu bar is that all options available in the toolbar are also available in the menu bar. Figure 12-8 highlights all available tools within the Oracle Enterprise Manager console.

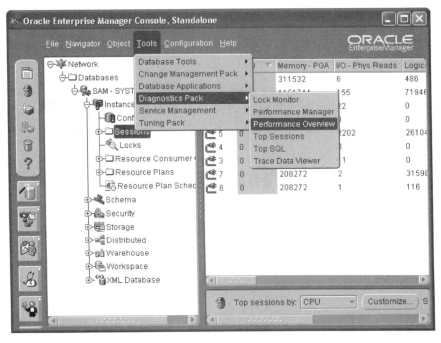

Figure 12-8   Oracle Enterprise Manager console showing the menu bar

Toolbar: For fast access, all tools are also available in this toolbar. Figure 12-9 shows all the options for each icon.

12

Figure 12-9 Oracle Enterprise Manager console showing toolbars

Left panel (navigation): As you can see in Figure 12-10, the navigation bar lists all the databases you have registered with the Oracle Enterprise Manager. For each database node there is a set of tools that assists you in administering and diagnosing your database.

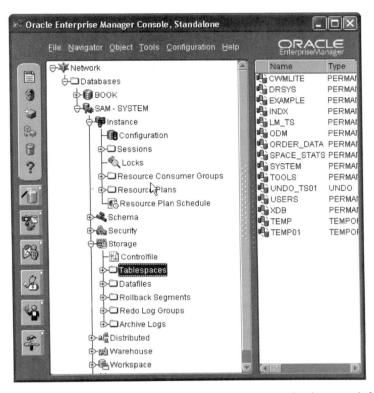

Figure 12-10 Oracle Enterprise Manager console showing left panel

12

Right panel (detail screen): This panel displays the details of any node or tool that is selected in the left panel. Since in Figure 12-11 the Sessions option is selected, the right panel shows details of sessions connected to the database, and you can drill down to get even more details for each session.

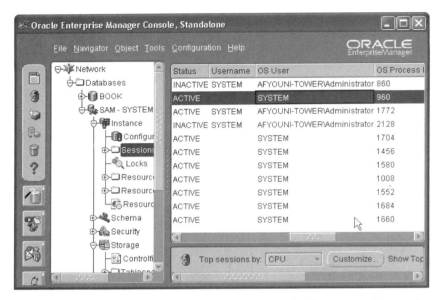

Figure 12-11   Oracle Enterprise Manager console showing right panel

As mentioned in many chapters, you should consult Oracle Enterprise Manager documentation for more details on its features, and do not get discouraged when exploring these features on your own. Most of these features are very intuitive.

STATISTICAL TOOLS

To begin thinking about how statistical tools can assist you in diagnosing and tuning a database, imagine yourself as a DBA who has been employed in a new job for only a few months. You were invited to your first weekly progress meeting organized by your immediate database manager. You thought this meeting would be like any other meeting in which projects were discussed to track progress. As expected, your manager started by asking each DBA in the team about current projects and when the first round was completed, he started another round demanding the status of each database administered by each DBA.

Every DBA was prepared except you. Each DBA provided a brief status on problems, performance issues, and capacity usage (memory, CPU, and disk storage). When it was your turn, you basically explained to your manager that you were not prepared at this time and you promised that at the next weekly meeting you would provide such information. Your manager thanked you for being frank and went on to other issues.

What would you do in this case? How would you provide such information? As a DBA, you are not just running scripts, which is the primary job of database operators (DBOs). You are also administering, troubleshooting, and tuning databases. In addition, you are constantly planning for resources capacity such as memory, CPU, and disk storage. Your manager relies on you to determine if current resources are capable of handling current database loads and activities.

Another question is this: How can you prevent performance problems? The answer to this question and the previous question is simple. You need to gather performance statistics on a periodic basis to gain a good overview of database activities and performance. You also need this statistical data to perform trend analysis, which can guide you in advanced planning for resources.

As you can see from the scenario, the need for statistical tools is apparent and important. In the past, Oracle provided a simple tool called UTLBSTAT/UTLESTAT, which was used until the introduction of another tool called STATSPACK.

This section describes both these tools and outlines their architecture and usage.

You should be warned that these tools provide reports that contain overwhelming amounts of statistical data.

UTLBSTAT/UTLESTAT

Not so long ago, UTLBSTAT/UTLESTAT was the tool that DBAs used to quickly collect the statistical performance data of a database. Although the tool is no longer supported with the advent of Oracle9*i*, it is still available and you can still use it as a means of diagnosing problems quickly without much setup or preparation.

UTLBSTAT is actually the name of a script called `UTLBSTAT.SQL` residing in ORA-CLE_HOME/rdbms/admin, the name of the script stands for:

- **UTL:** Utility

- **B:** Begin

- **STAT:** Statistics

When you run this script, it creates tables to store the results of queries issued against V$ dynamic performance views and thereby creates a snapshot of the database performance. UTLESTAT is the name of another script called `UTLESTAT.SQL` residing in the same location as its partner, `UTLESTAT.SQL`. The name of the script stands for:

- **UTL:** Utility

- **E:** End

- **STAT:** Statistics

When you run this script, it takes a final reading of database statistics, performs averages, creates a report, and then drops all tables created by UTLBSTAT. Figure 12-12 illustrates the architecture and process of UTLBSTAT/UTLESTAT.

12

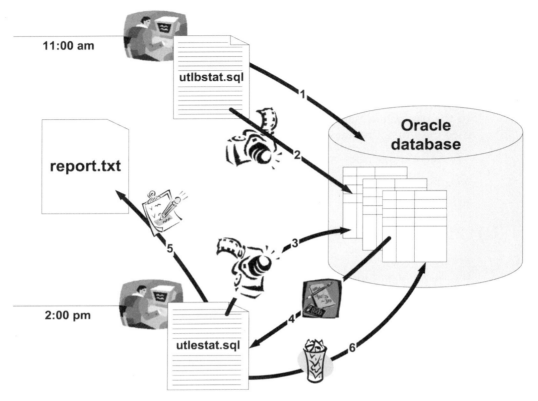

Figure 12-12   UTLBSTAT/UTLESTAT tool architecture and process

The illustration presents the following scenario. Suppose your customers have been noticing some performance degradation between 11:00 a.m. and 2:00 p.m. So you have decided to use UTLBSTAT/UTLESTAT as a quick way to collect database statistics during this period and you perform the following steps:

- At 11:00 a.m., you run the UTLBSTAT script, which performs the following tasks:

  1. Builds tables to store database statistics generated by UTLBSTAT.SQL. The names of these tables are prefixed with STATS$BEGIN_ .

  2. Runs statistical queries against the V$ dynamic performance views (initial reading)

- At 2:00 p.m., you run the UTLESTAT script, which performs the following tasks:

  1. Runs statistical queries against the V$ dynamic performance view (final reading)

  2. Computes statistical averages of initial and final readings

3. Writes a report to a report.txt file

4. Drops all tables created by UTLBSTAT

Now that you understand how this tool works, follow this step-by-step example to see what commands you must issue and how to retrieve and view the report results. Again, you should use this tool for a limited period when you suspect performance problems. Also, you should turn on the parameter TIMED_STATISTICS for more accurate CPU readings. Assuming that you suspect some performance contention between 9:00 a.m. and 10:00 a.m., you execute the following steps:

Step 1: At 9:00 a.m., log on as SYSTEM or SYS and turn on the TIMED_STATISTICS initialization parameter (this step is optional).

```
SQL> ALTER SYSTEM SET TIMED_STATISTICS=TRUE
  2  /

System altered.
```

Step 2: Run the UTLBSTAT script. Don't be concerned if you see errors during execution of this script. These errors result from dropping a UTLBSTAT table, which might not exist.

```
SQL> @C:\ORACLE\ORA92\RDBMS\ADMIN\UTLBSTAT
SQL> connect / as sysdba;
Connected.
SQL>
SQL> Rem ******************************************************
SQL> Rem                 First create all the tables
SQL> Rem ******************************************************
SQL>
...
SQL> Rem ******************************************************
SQL> Rem                 Gather start statistics
SQL> Rem ******************************************************
SQL>
...
SQL> commit;

Commit complete.
```

12

Step 3: Verify the creation of the STATS$BEGIN tables.

```
SQL> SELECT TABLE_NAME
  2    FROM USER_TABLES
  3   WHERE TABLE_NAME LIKE 'STATS$BEGIN%'
  4  /

TABLE_NAME
------------------------------
STATS$BEGIN_BCK_EVENT
STATS$BEGIN_DC
STATS$BEGIN_EVENT
STATS$BEGIN_FILE
STATS$BEGIN_LATCH
STATS$BEGIN_LIB
STATS$BEGIN_ROLL
STATS$BEGIN_STATS
STATS$BEGIN_WAITSTAT

9 rows selected.
```

Step 4: At 10:00 a.m., run the UTLESTAT script.

NOTE

Although it is not recommended to set the whole system in TRACE mode, you can allow users to turn on tracing for their own sessions by issuing ALTER SESSION SET SQL_TRACE=TRUE.

```
SQL> @C:\ORACLE\ORA92\RDBMS\ADMIN\UTLESTAT
...
SQL>
SQL> Rem *****************************************************
SQL> Rem              Gather Ending Statistics
SQL> Rem *****************************************************
SQL>
...
SQL>
SQL> Rem *****************************************************
SQL> Rem              Create Summary Tables
SQL> Rem *****************************************************
SQL>
...
SQL>
SQL> Rem *****************************************************
SQL> Rem              Output statistics
SQL> Rem *****************************************************
SQL>
...
SQL>
SQL> Rem *****************************************************
SQL> Rem              Drop Temporary Tables
SQL> Rem *****************************************************
...
```

Step 5: Retrieve Report.txt file. This report is usually located in C:\ or the location from which SQL*PLUS was started. You can use any text editor to open this file. You should be warned that the report contains an overwhelming amount of data. To get the relevant statistical data from it, you should know exactly what you are looking for. The following listing is a partial display of this report:

```
SQL>
SQL> column library        format a12 trunc;
SQL> column pinhitratio    heading 'PINHITRATI';
SQL> column gethitratio    heading 'GETHITRATI';
SQL> column invalidations heading 'INVALIDATI';
SQL> set numwidth 10;
SQL> Rem Select Library cache statistics.  The pin hit rate should be high.
SQL> select namespace library,
  2          gets,
  3          round(decode(gethits,0,1,gethits)/decode(gets,0,1,gets),3)
  4            gethitratio,
  5          pins,
  6          round(decode(pinhits,0,1,pinhits)/decode(pins,0,1,pins),3)
  7            pinhitratio,
  8          reloads, invalidations
  9      from stats$lib;

LIBRARY           GETS GETHITRATI       PINS PINHITRATI    RELOADS INVALIDATI
------------ ---------- ---------- ---------- ---------- ---------- ----------
BODY                  0          1          0          1          0          0
CLUSTER              10          1         10          1          0          0
INDEX               245          1        245          1          0          0
JAVA DATA             0          1          0          1          0          0
JAVA RESOURC          0          1          0          1          0          0
JAVA SOURCE           0          1          0          1          0          0
OBJECT                0          1          0          1          0          0
PIPE                  0          1          0          1          0          0
SQL AREA            748       .988       2318       .992          0          0
TABLE/PROCED        820       .998        839       .993          0          0
TRIGGER               2          1          2          1          0          0

11 rows selected.
...
SQL>
SQL> select n1.name "Statistic",
  2          n1.change "Total",
  3          round(n1.change/trans.change,2) "Per Transaction",
  4          round(n1.change/((start_users + end_users)/2),2)  "Per Logon",
  5          round(n1.change/((to_number(to_char(end_time,   'J'))*60*60*24 -
  6                      to_number(to_char(start_time, 'J'))*60*60*24 +
  7                      to_number(to_char(end_time,   'SSSSS')) -
  8                      to_number(to_char(start_time, 'SSSSS')))
  9              , 2) "Per Second"
 10      from
 11              stats$stats n1,
 12              stats$stats trans,
 13              stats$dates
 14      where
 15          trans.name='user commits'
 16       and  n1.change != 0
 17      order by n1.name;
```

12

```
Statistic                    Total Per Transact   Per Logon   Per Second
----------------------------  ------------ ------------ ------------ ------------
CPU used by this session          8            8          .89          .01
CPU used when call started        8            8          .89          .01
...
```

Step 6: Turn off the TIMED_STATISTICS initialization parameter:

```
SQL> ALTER SYSTEM SET TIMED_STATISTICS=FALSE
  2  /

System altered
```

This report contains statistical data about all aspects of the database. The report includes statistical readings in this specific order:

- Library cache

- Sessions and users

- System statistics

- System events

- Wait events

- Latch statistics

- Rollback segments statistics

- Modified initialization parameters

- Data dictionary

- Tablespace statistics

- Data files statistics

Of course, running and using this tool is only half of the job; you must also interpret the results of the report. Assume you are interested in memory statistics to determine the hit ratio of the library cache and data dictionary cache. Figure 12-13 shows the portion of the report related to the library cache. As you can see, the hit ratio for all different library spaces is above 90 percent, which means there is no contention in library cache and therefore the setting of the shared pool memory is proper.

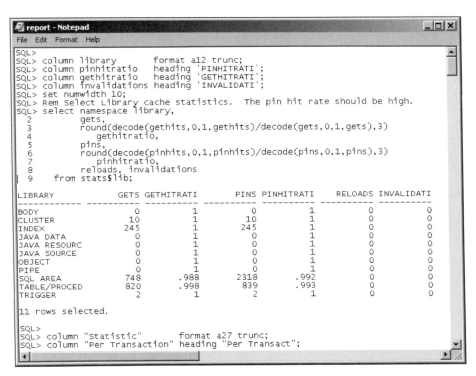

Figure 12-13   UTLBSTAT/UTLESTAT report.txt—library cache results

Figure 12-14 shows the portion of the report.txt file that is related to the data dictionary cache ratios. In this case, the number of get-misses for all parts of the data dictionary is less than 10 percent, which indicates that the setting of the shared pool is proper.

12

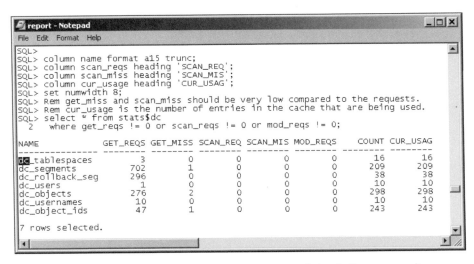

Figure 12-14   UTLBSTAT/UTLESTAT report.txt—data dictionary results

STATSPACK

To provide a more enhanced tool to collect statistics that help diagnose and troubleshoot the database performance, Oracle not so long ago introduced a new tool called STATSPACK to replace **UTLBSTAT/UTLESTAT**. Most DBAs have adopted this tool as the primary utility to gather statistics because it provides the following benefits:

- **Ease of use:** Is simple to use to gather statistics

- **Cost:** Is free with Oracle9*i* (requires no additional licensing fees)

- **Historical snapshots:** Captures and stores every reading in its repository for future comparisons and trend analysis

- **Reports:** Provides reports that are well organized and formatted

- **Procedure and scripts:** Provides several procedures for administering the repository of this tool

- **Multiple databases:** Supports more than one database

In this section, you learn the architecture of this tool followed by instructions on installing it, taking statistical readings, and finally, generating reports.

STATSPACK Architecture

STATSPACK is much more sophisticated than its predecessor UTLBSTAT/UTLESTAT in many aspects, such as the capability of collecting statistics and storing them in the repository for a time. It can also register all possible instance and database statistics that are available. Figure 12-15 depicts the architecture of STATSPACK, which consists of four main components as follows:

1. **Scripts:** Includes all scripts necessary for creating and maintaining the repository
2. **Repository:** Composed of tables, indexes, and sequences. The repository stores the collected data.
3. **PL/SQL stored package:** The engine of the STATSPACK tool that collects statistics
4. **Report:** A generated report resulting from analyzing snapshots of statistics taken at two different times

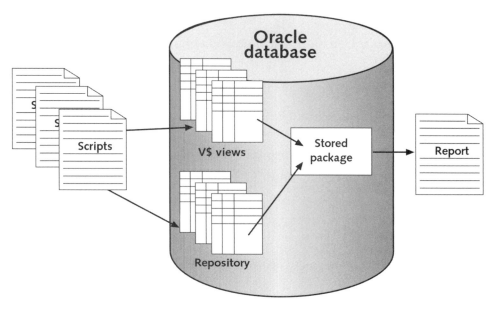

Figure 12-15   STATSPACK tool architecture

You can see that this tool reads V$ dynamic performance views, which contain statistical data since the startup of the instance. You should know that when the database is shut down, all statistical data in these views are flushed and they are populated again when the instance is started. Next is a quick overview for each component of STATSPACK.

STATSPACK Scripts

The STATSPACK tool comprises 18 files. To get a listing of all these files (as shown in Figure 12-16), issue the dir sp* command from the command prompt.

```
 Select Command Prompt                                             _ □ X
C:\oracle\ora92\rdbms\admin>dir sp*
 Volume in drive C is Local Disk
 Volume Serial Number is 7C45-6B8C

 Directory of C:\oracle\ora92\rdbms\admin

03/09/2002  08:19p             1,838 spauto.sql
04/17/2002  08:09p           103,896 spcpkg.sql
04/17/2002  08:09p               895 spcreate.sql
04/17/2002  08:09p            48,859 spctab.sql
04/17/2002  08:09p             9,344 spcusr.sql
04/17/2002  08:09p            86,176 spdoc.txt
03/09/2002  08:19p               794 spdrop.sql
03/09/2002  08:19p             5,030 spdtab.sql
03/09/2002  08:19p             1,423 spdusr.sql
04/01/2002  12:22p             8,722 sppurge.sql
04/17/2002  08:09p           137,070 sprepins.sql
03/09/2002  08:19p             1,330 spreport.sql
04/17/2002  08:09p            27,197 sprepsql.sql
03/09/2002  08:19p             2,955 sptrunc.sql
03/09/2002  08:19p               609 spuexp.par
04/18/2002  01:37p            31,700 spup816.sql
04/18/2002  01:37p            23,329 spup817.sql
04/18/2002  01:37p            19,129 spup90.sql
              18 File(s)        510,296 bytes
               0 Dir(s)  15,121,946,624 bytes free

C:\oracle\ora92\rdbms\admin>_
```

Figure 12-16   STATSPACK files and scripts

Each file is used for a specific task. The following list gives a brief description of each file.

- **spauto.sql:** Automates statistics gathering by taking a statistics snapshot every one hour

- **spcpkg.sql:** Creates the PL/SQL stored package STATSPACK

- **spcreate.sql:** Creates PERFSTAT user, a **repository**, and the stored package. Calls the following scripts:
  - spcusr.sql (stands for sp:STATSPACK c:CREATE usr:USER)
  - spctab.sql (stands for sp: STATSPACK c:CREATE tab:TABLES)
  - spcpkg.sql (stands for sp: STATSPACK c:CREATE pkg:PACKAGE)

- **spctab.sql:** Creates all tables and other objects for the STATSPACK repository

- **spcusr.sql:** Creates a user called PERFSTAT and grants this user all necessary privileges

- **spdoc.txt:** A useful text file that guides users on installing and maintaining STATSPACK

- **spdrop.sql:** Drops the STATSPACK repository and calls the following scripts:
  - spdtab.sql: (stands for sp:STATSPACK d:DROP tab:TABLES)
  - spdusr.sql: (stands for sp:STATSPACK d:DROP usr:USER)

- **spdtab.sql:** Removes all objects from the STATSPACK repository

- **spdusr.sql:** Removes the PERFSTAT user

- **sppurge.sql:** Deletes existing snapshots from the repository

- **sprepins.sql:** Generates a STATSPACK report named spreport.sql

- **spreport.sql:** Generates an analysis report of two existing snapshots and calls another script named sprepins.sql

- **sprepsql.sql:** Used by the SPREPORT.SQL script

- **sptrunc.sql:** Truncates all tables in the STATSPACK repository

- **spuexp.par:** An export parameter file used with the EXP utility to export all data in the STATSPACK repository

- **spup816.sql:** Upgrades the STATSPACK repository from earlier versions of Oracle to 8.1.6 (read STATSPACK documentation for upgrade procedures)

- **spup817.sql:** Upgrades the STATSPACK repository from Oracle 8.1.6 to 8.1.7 (read STATSPACK documentation for upgrade procedures)

- **spup90.sql:** Upgrades the STATSPACK repository from Oracle 8.1.7 to 9.x (read STATSPACK documentation for upgrade procedures)

STATSPACK Repositories

The following list briefly describes the contents of all tables within the STATSPACK repository:

- **STATS$BG_EVENT_SUMMARY:** Background events and background processes waits for the database

- **STATS$BUFFER_POOL_STATISTICS:** Statistical information about each buffer pool

- **STATS$DATABASE_INSTANCE:** Generic information about the database for which you are collecting statistics

- **STATS$DB_CACHE_ADVICE:** Buffer cache advisory statistics

- **STATS$DLM_MISC:** Miscellaneous statistical information

- **STATS$ENQUEUE_STAT:** Statistical data about enqueue structures to identify contention

- **STATS$FILESTATXS:** I/O statistics on data files

- **STATS$IDLE_EVENT:** One column storing idle events

- **STATS$INSTANCE_RECOVERY:** Statistical data about the instance mean time to recover (MTTR)

- **STATS$LATCH:** Data about latch contention statistics

- **STATS$LATCH_CHILDREN:** Additional statistical detail on latches. This table is populated when the statistical level of STATSPACK is set to 10.

- **STATS$LATCH_MISSES_SUMMARY:** Statistical data about latch misses

- **STATS$LATCH_PARENT:** Latch information

- **STATS$LEVEL_DESCRIPTION:** Description of each level of statistics snapshot collection

- **STATS$LIBRARYCACHE:** Statistical data about the library cache space of the shared pool memory

- **STATS$PARAMETER:** Initialization parameters that were modified

- **STATS$PGASTAT:** Statistical data about the PGA memory structure

- **STATS$PGA_TARGET_ADVICE:** Statistical advisory data for PGA memory configuration

- **STATS$RESOURCE_LIMIT:** Statistics on resource limits

- **STATS$ROLLSTAT:** Rollback segment statistics

- **STATS$ROWCACHE_SUMMARY:** Statistical data about the data dictionary memory cache

- **STATS$SEG_STAT:** I/O statistics for each collect segment

- **STATS$SESSION_EVENT:** Session events statistics

- **STATS$SESSTAT:** Table contents are identical to the V$SESSTAT view.

- **STATS$SGA:** The SGA memory configuration

- **STATS$SGASTAT:** Statistical data on the SGA

- **STATS$SHARED_POOL_ADVICE:** Statistical data on the shared pool advisory

- **STATS$SNAPSHOT:** Table is the storage heart of the STATSPACK repository. Every row in this table represents a snapshot of collected statistical data.

- **STATS$SQL_PLAN:** Used to view execution plan of recent SQL statements

- **STATS$SQL_PLAN_USAGE:** More information on execution plans of SQL statement

- **STATS$SQL_PLAN_WORKAREA_HISTOGRAM:** Statistics information about PGA workarea

- **STATS$SQLTEXT:** All the text of all top queries at the time of snapshot collection

- **STATS$SQL_STATISTICS:** Statistics for each top SQL query

- **STATS$SQL_SUMMARY:** Summary statistics for each collected SQL query

- **STATS$STAT_OBJ:** Information about database objects

- **STATS$STATSPACK_PARAMETER:** Default values for hit ratios and statistical thresholds

- **STATS$SYSSTAT:** Table contents are identical to V$SYSSTAT.

- **STATS$SYSTEM_EVENT:** System events statistics

- **STATS$TEMPSTATXS:** Statistics on temporary segments

- **STATS$UNDOSTAT:** Statistical data about undo segments

- **STATS$WAITSTAT:** All wait statistics that identify contention

Figure 12-17 presents the data model of the STATSPACK repository showing only the entities (each box represents an entity). As you can see, the model is centered on the STATS$SNAPSHOT entity.

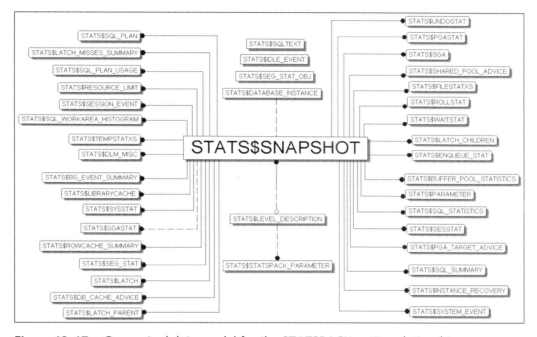

Figure 12-17   Conceptual data model for the STATSPACK entity relationship

STATSPACK PL/SQL Stored Package

STATSPACK package is the engine of this tool. This package contains the following five methods:

- **PROCEDURE MODIFY_STATSPACK_PARAMETER:** Modifies the thresholds of parameters (reconfigures STATSPACK hit ratios and other parameters' thresholds)

- **PROCEDURE QAM_STATSPACK_PARAMETER:** Provides the parameter default values from the STATS$STATSPACK_PARAMETER table

- **PROCEDURE SNAP:** Collects a statistics snapshot of the database. The collected statistics are stored in the repository and associated with a snapshot identification number.

- **FUNCTION SNAP RETURNS NUMBER(38):** Collects a statistics snapshot of the database. The collected statistics are stored in the repository and associated with a snapshot identification number, which is returned to the calling environment.

- **PROCEDURE STAT_CHANGES:** Used by the SPREPORT.SQL script to return differences between two statistics snapshots.

NOTE

To get the prototype of each procedure, you can use the DESC SQL*Plus command as shown in the code segment on SQL>DESC STATSPACK that follows.

STATSPACK Installation

Before using STATSPACK to collect statistics, you must install it. Here are step-by-step instructions.

Step 1: Log on as SYS (no other user can install STATSPACK):

```
SQL> CONNECT SYS/ORACLE@SAM AS SYSDBA
Connected.
```

Step 2: Create a tablespace called TS_PERF specifically for the use of PERFSTAT. The tablespace size depends on the number of historical snapshots you want to maintain in the repository. You should monitor the growth of this table and allocate more space as necessary or purge and delete data as soon as it is no longer needed.

```
SQL> CREATE TABLESPACE TS_PERF
  2      DATAFILE 'C:\ORACLE\ORADATA\SAM\TS_PERF_01.DBF'
  3      SIZE 200 M
  4      EXTENT MANAGEMENT LOCAL
  5  /

Tablespace created.
```

Step 3: Run SPCREATE.SQL to create the STATSPACK repository. Again, this script resides in the ORACLE_HOME/rdbms/admin directory. If this script fails, you should run SPDROP.SQL to drop all objects created, identify and solve the problem, and then repeat this step.

```
SQL> @c:\oracle\ora92\rdbms\admin\spcreate

...

Specify PERFSTAT password
Enter value for perfstat_password: perfstat

...

Specify PERFSTAT user's default   tablespace
Enter value for default_tablespace: ts_perf

...

Specify PERFSTAT user's temporary tablespace.
Enter value for temporary_tablespace: temp

...

NOTE:
SPCPKG complete. Please check spcpkg.lis for any errors.
```

NOTE

The CREATE script aborts if you choose SYSTEM as the tablespace for the repository.

12

Step 4: Check for errors in spcpkg.lis file, which is usually found in the location from which SQL*Plus was run. If you cannot locate it, use the Search utility. The contents of this file should contain no errors as shown in the following listing:

```
Creating Package STATSPACK...

Package created.

No errors.
Creating Package Body STATSPACK...

Package body created.

No errors.

NOTE:
SPCPKG complete. Please check spcpkg.lis for any errors.
```

Step 5: Connect as PERFSTAT and verify that all tables have been created. There should be one sequence, 41 tables, one package, and 42 indexes.

```
SQL> CONNECT PERFSTAT/PERFSTAT@SAM
Connected.

SQL> SELECT TABLE_NAME
  2    FROM USER_TABLES
  3    ORDER BY 1
  4  /

TABLE_NAME
------------------------------
STATS$BG_EVENT_SUMMARY
STATS$BUFFER_POOL_STATISTICS
STATS$DATABASE_INSTANCE
STATS$DB_CACHE_ADVICE
STATS$DLM_MISC
STATS$ENQUEUE_STAT
STATS$FILESTATXS
STATS$IDLE_EVENT
STATS$INSTANCE_RECOVERY
STATS$LATCH
STATS$LATCH_CHILDREN
STATS$LATCH_MISSES_SUMMARY
STATS$LATCH_PARENT
STATS$LEVEL_DESCRIPTION
STATS$LIBRARYCACHE
STATS$PARAMETER
STATS$PGASTAT
STATS$PGA_TARGET_ADVICE
STATS$RESOURCE_LIMIT
STATS$ROLLSTAT
STATS$ROWCACHE_SUMMARY
STATS$SEG_STAT
STATS$SEG_STAT_OBJ
STATS$SESSION_EVENT
STATS$SESSTAT
STATS$SGA
STATS$SGASTAT
STATS$SHARED_POOL_ADVICE
STATS$SNAPSHOT
STATS$SQLTEXT
STATS$SQL_PLAN
STATS$SQL_PLAN_USAGE
STATS$SQL_STATISTICS
STATS$SQL_SUMMARY
STATS$SQL_WORKAREA_HISTOGRAM
STATS$STATSPACK_PARAMETER
STATS$SYSSTAT
STATS$SYSTEM_EVENT
STATS$TEMPSTATXS
STATS$UNDOSTAT
STATS$WAITSTAT

41 rows selected.
```

```
SQL> SELECT OBJECT_TYPE, OBJECT_NAME, STATUS
  2    FROM USER_OBJECTS
  3    WHERE OBJECT_TYPE LIKE 'PACK%'
  4  /

OBJECT_TYPE          OBJECT_NAME  STATUS
-------------------  ------------ ------
PACKAGE              STATSPACK    VALID
PACKAGE BODY         STATSPACK    VALID
```

You just completed the installation of STATSPACK and are ready to gather statistics after you review statistics levels.

Statistic Levels

STATSPACK supports several levels of statistics collection. The levels are listed here with a description of the information each captures:

- **Level 0:** General statistics, including rollback segment, row cache, SGA, system events, background events, session events, system statistics, wait statistics, lock statistics, and latch information

- **Level 5:** High-resource usage SQL statements, along with all data captured by lower levels

- **Level 6:** SQL plan and SQL plan usage information for high-resource usage SQL statements, along with all data captured by lower levels

- **Level 7:** Segment-level statistics, including logical and physical reads, row lock, and buffer busy waits, along with all data captured by lower levels

- **Level 10:** Child latch statistics, along with all data captured by lower levels

NOTE

Statistics level 10 is only used when Oracle technical support asks you to set it.

You can get this list at any time from the database. Log on as PERFSTAT and issue the following query:

```
SQL> SELECT *
  2     FROM STATS$LEVEL_DESCRIPTION
  3  /

SNAP_LEVEL DESCRIPTION
---------- ----------------------------------------------------------------
         0 This level captures general statistics, including rollback segmen
           t, row cache, SGA, system events, background events, session even
           ts, system statistics, wait statistics, lock statistics, and Latc
           h information

         5 This level includes capturing high resource usage SQL Statements,
           along with all data captured by lower levels

         6 This level includes capturing SQL plan and SQL plan usage informa
           tion for high resource usage SQL Statements, along with all data
           captured by lower levels

         7 This level captures segment level statistics, including logical a
           nd physical reads, row lock, itl and buffer busy waits, along wit
           h all data captured by lower levels

        10 This level includes capturing Child Latch statistics, along with
           all data captured by lower levels
```

Gathering Statistics

Now that you are ready to gather statistics, you can use two methods provided by the STATSPACK stored package as outlined here.

Method 1: This method is simple. Just execute the SNAP procedure. This method does not give you the value of the snapshot identification number; you can get it by issuing the following query:

```
SQL> EXEC STATSPACK.SNAP

PL/SQL procedure successfully completed.

SQL> SELECT SNAP_ID, SNAP_TIME
  2     FROM STATS$SNAPSHOT
  3  /

   SNAP_ID SNAP_TIME
---------- ---------
         1 07-FEB-03
```

Method 2: In this method, you use the SNAP function, which returns the snapshot identification number. The following PL/SQL block executes and displays the snapshot identification number:

```
SQL> SET SERVEROUTPUT ON
SQL> DECLARE
  2      V_SNAPID     NUMBER;
  3  BEGIN
  4      V_SNAPID := STATSPACK.SNAP;
  5      DBMS_OUTPUT.PUT_LINE('SNAP ID = ' || V_SNAPID);
  6  END;
  7  /
  SNAP ID = 2

PL/SQL procedure successfully completed.

SQL> SELECT SNAP_ID, SNAP_TIME
  2    FROM STATS$SNAPSHOT
  3  /

   SNAP_ID SNAP_TIME
---------- ---------
         1 07-FEB-03
         2 07-FEB-03
```

NOTE

You may want to monitor space for the STATSPACK to make sure you do not run out of space while gathering statistics.

12

Automating Statistics Collection

You can automate the gathering of statistics by using the provided script named SPAUTO.SQL, which uses the Oracle-supplied package DBMS_JOB. The script provided by Oracle named SPAUTO.SQL schedules a job to take a snapshot every hour. If you decide to change the schedule, you should copy this script and modify the new script specifying a different timing schedule. To copy and modify the new script, you must know how to use DBMS_JOB.

The following listing is an example of how to run the SPAUTO.SQL script. The listing shows a partial output of the script.

```
SQL> @C:\ORACLE\ORA92\RDBMS\ADMIN\SPAUTO.SQL
SQL> Rem
SQL> Rem $Header: spauto.sql 16-feb-00.16:49:37 cdialeri Exp $
SQL> Rem
SQL> Rem spauto.sql

...

SQL> spool spauto.lis
SQL>
SQL> --
SQL> --   Schedule a snapshot to be run on this instance every hour, on the hour
SQL>
SQL> variable jobno number;
SQL> variable instno number;
SQL> begin
  2    select instance_number into :instno from v$instance;
  3    dbms_job.submit(:jobno, 'statspack.snap;', trunc(sysdate+1/24,'HH'), 'trunc(SYSDATE+1/24,''H
  4    commit;
  5  end;
  6  /

PL/SQL procedure successfully completed.

SQL>
SQL>
SQL> prompt

SQL> prompt       Job number for automated statistics collection for this instance
Job number for automated statistics collection for this instance
SQL> prompt       ------------------------------------------------------------------
------------------------------------------------------------------
SQL> prompt       Note that this job number is needed when modifying or removing
Note that this job number is needed when modifying or removing
SQL> prompt       the job:
the job:
SQL> print jobno

     JOBNO
----------
         1

...
SQL> prompt       -------------------
-------------------
SQL> prompt       The next scheduled run for this job is:
The next scheduled run for this job is:
SQL> select job, next_date, next_sec
  2    from user_jobs
  3    where job = :jobno;

       JOB NEXT_DATE NEXT_SEC
---------- --------- --------
         1 07-FEB-03 03:00:00

1 row selected.

SQL>
SQL> spool off;
```

Generating Reports

You went through all the trouble of collecting statistical data to analyze it. To perform statistical analysis, you can use the SPREPORT.SQL script, which produces a report that you can view using any text editor. The following listing demonstrates how to use this script. When you run the SPREPORT.SQL script, it prompts you for two values of snapshot IDs, low and high. In this case, you display a listing of all snapshots taken and then you run the script. Because the report is lengthy, the listing that follows shows only partial output of the report. The output of the report is spooled to a file named SAM_PERFOR-MANCE.LST that was entered when the prompt was displayed:

```
Enter value for report_name: SAM_PERFORMANCE
```

The location of the spooled file is in C:\ or the location from which you ran SQL*Plus. Note that the default statistic level is 5.

```
SQL> SELECT SNAP_ID, SNAP_TIME
  2    FROM STATS$SNAPSHOT
  3  /

   SNAP_ID SNAP_TIME
---------- ---------
         4 07-FEB-03
         5 07-FEB-03

SQL> @C:\ORACLE\ORA92\RDBMS\ADMIN\SPREPORT.SQL
SQL> Rem
SQL> Rem $Header: spreport.sql 22-apr-2001.15:44:01 cdialeri Exp $
SQL> Rem
SQL> Rem spreport.sql
SQL> Rem

. . .

Specify the Begin and End Snapshot Ids
~~~~~~~~~~~~~~~~~~~~~~~~~~~~~~~~~~~~~~~~
Enter value for begin_snap: 4
Begin Snapshot Id specified: 4

Enter value for end_snap: 5
End   Snapshot Id specified: 5


Specify the Report Name
~~~~~~~~~~~~~~~~~~~~~~~~~
The default report file name is sp_4_5.  To use this name,
press <return> to continue, otherwise enter an alternative.
Enter value for report_name: SAM_PERFORMANCE

Using the report name SAM_PERFORMANCE

. . .

STATSPACK report for

DB Name        DB Id       Instance    Inst Num Release     Cluster Host
-----------    ----------- ----------- -------- ----------- ------- --------------
SAM            2456380547 sam                 1 9.2.0.1.0   NO      AFYOUNI-TOWER
. . .
```

12

Report Structure

The report generated by SPREPORT.SQL contains overwhelming detail. It contains pages of statistical numbers and information. To help you to read this report, this section shows the structure of a report with statistical level 5. The report can be partitioned into 15 logical sections:

Section 1: Database and Instance Configuration Information

This section of the report displays information about the database and instance for which the report was generated:

```
STATSPACK report for

DB Name         DB Id       Instance      Inst Num Release      Cluster Host
-----------  -----------  ------------  -------- -----------  ------- -------------
SAM           2456380547 sam                  1 9.2.0.1.0    NO      AFYOUNI-TOWER

                Snap Id     Snap Time       Sessions Curs/Sess Comment
                -------  -----------------  -------- --------- -------------------
Begin Snap:        4 07-Feb-03 02:36:19       10       8.7
  End Snap:        5 07-Feb-03 02:36:23       10      10.3
  Elapsed:                 0.07 (mins)

Cache Sizes (end)
~~~~~~~~~~~~~~~~~
              Buffer Cache:        24M    Std Block Size:          8K
          Shared Pool Size:        48M       Log Buffer:        512K
```

Section 2: Database Load Information

This section displays database load statistics. For example, it gives you an average number of parses per second and other related statistics. This gives you an idea of the activity level of the database.

```
Load Profile
~~~~~~~~~~~~                        Per Second       Per Transaction
                                ---------------      ---------------
                Redo size:          112,060.00           448,240.00
            Logical reads:              233.50               934.00
            Block changes:              173.25               693.00
            Physical reads:               0.50                 2.00
           Physical writes:               0.00                 0.00
                User calls:               0.50                 2.00
                   Parses:                8.50                34.00
              Hard parses:                3.00                12.00
                    Sorts:               13.50                54.00
                   Logons:                0.00                 0.00
                 Executes:               13.00                52.00
             Transactions:                0.25

  % Blocks changed per Read:   74.20    Recursive Call %:     98.87
  Rollback per transaction %:   0.00      Rows per Sort:     183.28
```

Section 3: Hit Ratios

This section is useful in that it displays hit ratios of the instance memory structures and thereby supplies a quick overview of whether memory is configured optimally:

```
Instance Efficiency Percentages (Target 100%)
~~~~~~~~~~~~~~~~~~~~~~~~~~~~~~~~~~~~~~~~~~~~~~~
            Buffer Nowait %:  100.00      Redo NoWait %:  100.00
            Buffer  Hit  %:   99.79   In-memory Sort %:  100.00
            Library Hit  %:   96.36        Soft Parse %:   64.71
         Execute to Parse %:  34.62        Latch Hit %:   100.00
Parse CPU to Parse Elapsd %: 100.00      % Non-Parse CPU:  90.91


  Shared Pool Statistics      Begin   End
                              ------  ------
             Memory Usage %:  49.26   50.02
    % SQL with executions>1:  76.21   79.37
    % Memory for SQL w/exec>1: 65.74   76.08
```

Section 4: Top 5 Events

This section displays the top five events that consumed the most time:

```
Top 5 Timed Events
~~~~~~~~~~~~~~~~~~~                                         % Total
Event                                   Waits   Time (s) Ela Time
--------------------------------------- ------- -------- --------
CPU time                                              1    62.72
control file sequential read               54         0    31.77
log file parallel write                     3         0     2.57
db file sequential read                     2         0     2.54
control file parallel write                 2         0      .24
                     -------------------------------------------
Wait Events for DB: SAM  Instance: sam  Snaps: 4 -5
-> s  - second
-> cs - centisecond -      100th of a second
-> ms - millisecond -     1000th of a second
-> us - microsecond - 1000000th of a second
-> ordered by wait time desc, waits desc (idle events last)
```

12

Section 5: Top SQL

This section displays the SQL queries that were top consumers of resources and is therefore helpful for identifying problematic queries. The following is a partial listing of this section:

```
SQL ordered by Executions for DB: SAM   Instance: sam   Snaps: 4 -5
-> End Executions Threshold:      100

                                               CPU per    Elap per
   Executions   Rows Processed   Rows per Exec   Exec (s)   Exec (s)  Hash Value
  ------------ --------------- --------------- ----------- ---------- ----------
            4               4             1.0      0.00        0.00 1705880752
  select file# from file$ where ts#=:1

            1               1             1.0      0.00        0.00  189272129
  select o.owner#,o.name,o.namespace,o.remoteowner,o.linkname,o.su
  bname,o.dataobj#,o.flags from obj$ o where o.obj#=:1
  ...
```

Section 6: System Statistics

This section provides full system statistics. The following is a partial listing of this section:

```
Instance Activity Stats for DB: SAM   Instance: sam   Snaps: 4 -5

Statistic                                Total     per Second     per Trans
--------------------------------- ------------------- -------------- ------------
CPU used by this session                     55           13.8          55.0
CPU used when call started                   55           13.8          55.0
CR blocks created                             0            0.0           0.0
DBWR checkpoint buffers written               0            0.0           0.0
DBWR checkpoints                              0            0.0           0.0
DBWR transaction table writes                 0            0.0           0.0
DBWR undo block writes                        0            0.0           0.0
PX local messages recv'd                      0            0.0           0.0
```

Section 7: Tablespace Statistics

This section displays statistical information about tablespaces that have been hit most often, meaning those with many read/write activities:

```
Tablespace IO Stats for DB: SAM   Instance: sam   Snaps: 4 -5
->ordered by IOs (Reads + Writes) desc

Tablespace
------------------------------
               Av      Av     Av                     Av       Buffer Av Buf
        Reads Reads/s Rd(ms) Blks/Rd    Writes Writes/s    Waits Wt(ms)
-------------- ------- ------ ------- ------------ -------- ---------- ------
TS_PERF
            2       1   15.0     1.0         0         0          0    0.0
```

Section 8: File Statistics

Similar to Section 7, this section provides statistical information about data files that have the highest level of I/O activities (read/write):

```
File IO Stats for DB: SAM  Instance: sam  Snaps: 4 -5
->ordered by Tablespace, File

Tablespace              Filename
----------------------  --------------------------------------------------
             Av    Av    Av                        Av        Buffer Av Buf
        Reads Reads/s Rd(ms) Blks/Rd     Writes Writes/s    Waits Wt(ms)
-------------- ------- ------ ------- ------------ -------- ---------- ------
TS_PERF                 C:\ORACLE\ORADATA\SAM\TS_PERF_01.DBF
            2       1   15.0    1.0          0        0          0
```

Section 9: Buffer Pool Statistics

This section displays buffer pool statistics:

```
Buffer Pool Statistics for DB: SAM  Instance: sam  Snaps: 4 -5
-> Standard block size Pools  D: default,  K: keep,  R: recycle
-> Default Pools for other block sizes: 2k, 4k, 8k, 16k, 32k

                                               Free    Write  Buffer
     Number of Cache    Buffer  Physical  Physical  Buffer Complete    Busy
  P   Buffers Hit %      Gets     Reads    Writes   Waits    Waits   Waits
  --- --------- -----  --------- --------- --------- ------- -------- ------
  D     3,000  99.8      1,163         2         0       0        0       0
```

Section 10: Instance Recovery Statistics

This section displays statistical information about the mean time to recover (MTTR):

```
Instance Recovery Stats for DB: SAM  Instance: sam  Snaps: 4 -5
-> B: Begin snapshot,  E: End snapshot

  Targt Estd                              Log File  Log Ckpt  Log Ckpt
  MTTR  MTTR   Recovery   Actual   Target   Size    Timeout   Interval
  (s)   (s)    Estd IOs Redo Blks Redo Blks Redo Blks Redo Blks Redo Blks
  - ----- -----  --------- --------- --------- --------- --------- ---------
  B  65    46        455      7560      7159    184320      7159
  E  65    47        514      8566      8026    184320      8026
```

Section 11: Buffer Pool Advisory Statistics

The following is a listing of the buffer pool advisory statistics to guide you in properly configuring the size of the buffer cache:

```
Buffer Pool Advisory for DB: SAM   Instance: sam   End Snap: 5
-> Only rows with estimated physical reads >0 are displayed
-> ordered by Block Size, Buffers For Estimate


        Size for   Size     Buffers for   Est Physical      Estimated
P    Estimate (M) Factr       Estimate    Read Factor     Physical Reads
---  ------------ -----    ------------- -------------   ------------------
D             4    .2             500         19.85             389,210
D             8    .3           1,000          2.91              57,153
```

Section 12: PGA Aggregation Advisory Statistics

The following partial listing displays advisory statistics to identify whether the PGA is configured optimally or not:

```
PGA Aggr Target Stats for DB: SAM   Instance: sam   Snaps: 4 -5
 -> B: Begin snap    E: End snap (rows dentified with B or E contain data
    which is absolute i.e. not diffed over the interval)
 -> PGA cache hit % - percentage of W/A (WorkArea) data processed only in-memory
 -> Auto PGA Target - actual workarea memory target
 -> W/A PGA Used    - amount of memory used for all Workareas (manual + auto)
 -> %PGA W/A Mem    - percentage of PGA memory allocated to workareas
 -> %Auto W/A Mem   - percentage of workarea memory controlled by Auto Mem Mgmt
 -> %Man W/A Mem    - percentage of workarea memory under manual control

PGA Cache Hit % W/A MB Processed Extra W/A MB Read/Written
--------------- ---------------- ------------------------
          100.0                2                        0


                                          %PGA   %Auto  %Man
    PGA Aggr  Auto PGA  PGA Mem   W/A PGA   W/A    W/A    W/A   Global Mem
    Target(M) Target(M) Alloc(M)  Used(M)   Mem    Mem    Mem   Bound(K)
-   --------- --------- --------- --------- ------ ------ ----- ----------
B        24         8      32.5      0.0     .0     .0    .0     1,228
E        24         8      32.4      0.0     .0     .0    .0     1,228
         -------------------------------------------------------------------

PGA Aggr Target Histogram for DB: SAM   Instance: sam   Snaps: 4 -5
-> Optimal Executions are purely in-memory operations

    Low     High
 Optimal Optimal   Total Execs Optimal Execs 1-Pass Execs M-Pass Execs
 ------- -------   ----------- ------------- ------------ ------------
      8K     16K           64            64            0            0
     16K     32K            7             7            0            0
     32K     64K            3             3            0            0
     64K    128K            1             1            0            0
    256K    512K            2             2            0            0
         -------------------------------------------------------------------
```

```
PGA Memory Advisory for DB: SAM  Instance: sam  End Snap: 5
-> When using Auto Memory Mgmt, minimally choose a pga_aggregate_target value
   where Estd PGA Overalloc Count is 0

                                     Estd Extra    Estd PGA   Estd PGA
 PGA Target     Size      W/A MB   W/A MB Read/      Cache    Overalloc
 Est (MB)      Factr    Processed Written to Disk    Hit %      Count
 ----------    ------   --------- ---------------   --------  ----------
         12     0.5        27.0             0.0      100.0          1
         18     0.8        27.0             0.0      100.0          0
         24     1.0        27.0             0.0      100.0          0
         29     1.2        27.0             0.0      100.0          0
         34     1.4        27.0             0.0      100.0          0
         38     1.6        27.0             0.0      100.0          0
         43     1.8        27.0             0.0      100.0          0
         48     2.0        27.0             0.0      100.0          0
         72     3.0        27.0             0.0      100.0          0
         96     4.0        27.0             0.0      100.0          0
        144     6.0        27.0             0.0      100.0          0
        192     8.0        27.0             0.0      100.0          0
```

Section 13: Rollback Segments Statistics

The following is a partial listing of the rollback (undo) segments statistics:

```
Rollback Segment Stats for DB: SAM  Instance: sam  Snaps: 4 -5
->A high value for "Pct Waits" suggests more rollback segments may be required
->RBS stats may not be accurate between begin and end snaps when using Auto Undo
  managment, as RBS may be dynamically created and dropped as needed

          Trans Table    Pct   Undo Bytes
 RBS No      Gets       Waits    Written      Wraps  Shrinks  Extends
 ------  -------------- ------- --------------- -------- -------- --------
      0          1.0    0.00             0        0        0        0
      1          1.0    0.00             0        0        0        0
 ...
Rollback Segment Storage for DB: SAM  Instance: sam  Snaps: 4 -5
->Optimal Size should be larger than Avg Active

 RBS No   Segment Size     Avg Active    Optimal Size    Maximum Size
 ------  --------------- --------------- --------------- ---------------
      0        385,024               0                        385,024
      1        253,952          77,855                        385,024
 ...
```

Section 14: Latch Activity Statistics

This section displays latch activities that you can use to identify contention. The following is a partial listing of this section:

```
Latch Activity for DB: SAM  Instance: sam  Snaps: 4 -5
->"Get Requests", "Pct Get Miss" and "Avg Slps/Miss" are statistics for
   willing-to-wait latch get requests
->"NoWait Requests", "Pct NoWait Miss" are for no-wait latch get requests
->"Pct Misses" for both should be very close to 0.0

                                   Pct    Avg   Wait                    Pct
                          Get      Get    Slps  Time    NoWait NoWait
Latch                     Requests Miss   /Miss (s)     Requests  Miss
------------------------- -------- ------ ----- ------ ------------ ------
Consistent RBA                   4  0.0                0            0
SQL memory manager latch         1  0.0                0            2    0.0
```

Section 15: Memory Statistics

This section is composed of five parts:

- Data dictionary cache statistics

- Library cache statistics

- Shared pool statistics

- SGA allocation

- SGA breakdown statistics

The following listing displays the output of this section:

```
Dictionary Cache Stats for DB: SAM  Instance: sam  Snaps: 4 -5
->"Pct Misses"  should be very low (< 2% in most cases)
->"Cache Usage" is the number of cache entries being used
->"Pct SGA"     is the ratio of usage to allocated size for that cache


                           Get    Pct   Scan  Pct     Mod      Final
Cache                   Requests  Miss  Reqs  Miss    Reqs     Usage
-----------------------  --------  ----  ----  -----  --------  -------
dc_object_ids                 39   2.6     0              0       507
dc_objects                    77   0.0     0              0       834
dc_segments                   59   0.0     0              0       314
dc_tablespaces                 9   0.0     0              0        22
dc_usernames                  19   0.0     0              0        16
dc_users                      17   0.0     0              0        16
                        -------------------------------------------------


Library Cache Activity for DB: SAM  Instance: sam  Snaps: 4 -5
->"Pct Misses"  should be very low

                       Get  Pct       Pin     Pct             Invali-
Namespace          Requests Miss   Requests   Miss   Reloads  dations
----------------   -------- ----   --------   ----   -------  -------
SQL AREA                 27  0.0        190   11.1        21        0
TABLE/PROCEDURE         244  0.0        387    0.0         0        0
                   -------------------------------------------------------

Shared Pool Advisory for DB: SAM  Instance: sam  End Snap: 5
-> Note there is often a 1:Many correlation between a single logical object
   in the Library Cache, and the physical number of memory objects associated
   with it.  Therefore comparing the number of Lib Cache objects (e.g. in
   v$librarycache), with the number of Lib Cache Memory Objects is invalid

                                               Estd
Shared Pool   SP      Estd       Estd      Estd Lib LC Time
  Size for  Size  Lib Cache  Lib Cache   Cache Time   Saved   Estd Lib Cache
Estim (M) Factr  Size (M)   Mem Obj    Saved (s)    Factr   Mem Obj Hits
---------- ----- ---------  ---------  -----------  ------- ----------------
       24   .5        12       3,725       11,077     1.0        653,555
       32   .7        12       3,725       11,077     1.0        653,555
       40   .8        12       3,725       11,077     1.0        653,555
       48  1.0        12       3,725       11,077     1.0        653,555
       56  1.2        12       3,725       11,077     1.0        653,555
       64  1.3        12       3,725       11,077     1.0        653,555
       72  1.5        12       3,725       11,077     1.0        653,555
       80  1.7        12       3,725       11,077     1.0        653,555
       88  1.8        12       3,725       11,077     1.0        653,555
       96  2.0        12       3,725       11,077     1.0        653,555
           --------------------------------------------------------------

SGA Memory Summary for DB: SAM  Instance: sam  Snaps: 4 -5

SGA regions                   Size in Bytes
--------------------------   ----------------
Database Buffers                  25,165,824
Fixed Size                           453,492
Redo Buffers                         667,648
Variable Size                    109,051,904
                             ----------------
sum                              135,338,868
           --------------------------------------------------------------
```

12

```
SGA breakdown difference for DB: SAM   Instance: sam   Snaps: 4 -5

Pool    Name                          Begin value       End value    % Diff
------  ----------------------------  ----------------  ----------------  -------
java    free memory                     33,554,432        33,554,432    0.00
large   free memory                      8,179,380         8,179,380    0.00
large   session heap                       209,228           209,228    0.00
shared  1M buffer                        2,098,176         2,098,176    0.00
shared  Checkpoint queue                   282,304           282,304    0.00
shared  FileIdentificatonBlock             323,292           323,292    0.00
shared  FileOpenBlock                      695,504           695,504    0.00
shared  KGK heap                             3,756             3,756    0.00
shared  KGLS heap                        2,152,596         2,152,596    0.00
shared  KQR M PO                           734,740           734,740    0.00
shared  KQR S PO                           173,568           173,568    0.00
shared  KQR S SO                             1,280             1,280    0.00
shared  KSXR large reply queue             166,104           166,104    0.00
shared  KSXR pending messages que          841,036           841,036    0.00
shared  KSXR receive buffers             1,033,000         1,033,000    0.00
shared  MTTR advisory                        8,352             8,352    0.00
shared  PL/SQL DIANA                     3,191,200         3,191,200    0.00
shared  PL/SQL MPCODE                      398,752           398,752    0.00
shared  PLS non-lib hp                       2,068             2,068    0.00
shared  PX subheap                           2,600             2,600    0.00
shared  VIRTUAL CIRCUITS                   264,624           264,624    0.00
shared  character set object               274,508           274,508    0.00
shared  dictionary cache                 1,610,880         1,610,880    0.00
shared  enqueue                            171,860           171,860    0.00
shared  errors                                 580               580    0.00
shared  event statistics per sess        1,718,360         1,718,360    0.00
shared  fixed allocation callback              180               180    0.00
shared  free memory                     34,050,736        33,538,672   -1.50
shared  joxs heap init                       4,220             4,220    0.00
shared  kgl simulator                      678,916           678,916    0.00
shared  library cache                    4,317,556         4,343,784    0.61
shared  message pool freequeue             834,752           834,752    0.00
shared  miscellaneous                    6,408,336         6,412,536    0.07
shared  parameters                          17,096            17,096    0.00
shared  sessions                           410,720           410,720    0.00
shared  sim memory hea                      21,164            21,164    0.00
shared  sql area                         4,206,144         4,687,780   11.45
shared  table definiti                       2,408             2,408    0.00
shared  trigger defini                       3,372             3,372    0.00
shared  trigger inform                       1,076             1,076    0.00
shared  trigger source                       3,048             3,048    0.00
        buffer_cache                    25,165,824        25,165,824    0.00
        fixed_sga                          453,492           453,492    0.00
        log_buffer                         656,384           656,384    0.00
        ----------------------------------------------------------------
```

Section 16: Modified Initialization Parameter

This section lists all initialization parameters that were modified from their default values. The following is a partial listing of this section:

```
init.ora Parameters for DB: SAM  Instance: sam  Snaps: 4 -5

                                                          End value
Parameter Name              Begin value                (if different)
--------------------------- --------------------------------- --------------
aq_tm_processes             1
background_dump_dest        C:\oracle\admin\SAM\bdump
```

Deleting Snapshots

Suppose you decide to delete a snapshot that is not needed any longer. You can use a script called SPPURGE.SQL, which prompts you for two values: the LOW value of a snapshot ID and the HIGH value of a snapshot ID. Then the script inclusively deletes all snapshots within the given range. In this case, you are deleting snapshot ID 2, so the values for LOW and HIGH are both 2.

```
SQL> @C:\ORACLE\ORA92\RDBMS\ADMIN\SPPURGE
SQL> Rem
SQL> Rem $Header: sppurge.sql 20-mar-2002.18:02:43 vbarrier Exp $
...
SQL> prompt Specify the Lo Snap Id and Hi Snap Id range to purge
Specify the Lo Snap Id and Hi Snap Id range to purge
SQL> prompt ~~~~~~~~~~~~~~~~~~~~~~~~~~~~~~~~~~~~~~~~~~~~~~~~~~~~~~~~
~~~~~~~~~~~~~~~~~~~~~~~~~~~~~~~~~~~~~~~~~~~~~~~~~~~~~~~~
SQL> prompt Using &&LoSnapId for lower bound.
Enter value for losnapid: 2
Using 2 for lower bound.
SQL> prompt

SQL> prompt Using &&HiSnapId for upper bound.
Enter value for hisnapid: 2
Using 2 for upper bound.
SQL>
SQL>
...
SQL>
SQL> spool off
SQL> set feedback on termout on
SQL> whenever sqlerror continue
SQL> SELECT SNAP_ID, SNAP_TIME
  2    FROM STATS$SNAPSHOT
  3  /

  Snap Id SNAP_TIME
-------- ---------
        1 07-FEB-03

1 row selected.
```

12

Purging the Repository

If you decide to remove all snapshots collected in the repository, you can use the SPTRUNC.SQL script; you should, however, be cautious when executing this script. Data will be deleted and you will not be able to roll back. The following listing shows a snapshot being taken followed by a statement that truncates tables in the repository:

```
SQL> EXEC STATSPACK.SNAP

PL/SQL procedure successfully completed.

SQL> SELECT SNAP_ID, SNAP_TIME
  2    FROM STATS$SNAPSHOT
  3  /

 Snap Id SNAP_TIME
-------- ---------
       1 07-FEB-03
       3 07-FEB-03

2 rows selected.

SQL> @C:\ORACLE\ORA92\RDBMS\ADMIN\SPTRUNC.SQL
SQL> Rem
SQL> Rem $Header: sptrunc.sql 19-feb-2002.11:36:28 vbarrier Exp $
SQL> Rem
SQL> Rem sptrunc.sql
SQL> Rem
SQL> Rem Copyright (c) 2000, 2002, Oracle Corporation.  All rights reserved.
SQL> Rem
SQL> Rem    NAME
SQL> Rem        sptrunc.sql - STATSPACK - Truncate tables
SQL> Rem
SQL> Rem    DESCRIPTION
SQL> Rem        Truncates data in Statspack tables
SQL> Rem
SQL> Rem    NOTES
SQL> Rem        Should be run as STATSPACK user, PERFSTAT.
SQL> Rem
SQL> Rem        The following tables should NOT be truncated
SQL> Rem        STATS$LEVEL_DESCRIPTION
SQL> Rem        STATS$IDLE_EVENT
SQL> Rem        STATS$STATSPACK_PARAMETER
```

```
SQL> Rem
SQL> Rem     MODIFIED   (MM/DD/YY)
SQL> Rem     vbarrier   03/05/02 - Segment Statistics
SQL> Rem     cdialeri   04/13/01 - 9.0
SQL> Rem     cdialeri   09/12/00 - sp_1404195
SQL> Rem     cdialeri   04/11/00 - 1261813
SQL> Rem     cdialeri   03/15/00 - Created
SQL> Rem
SQL>
SQL> undefine anystring
SQL> set showmode off echo off;

Warning
~~~~~~~
Running sptrunc.sql removes ALL data from Statspack tables.  You may
wish to export the data before continuing.


About to Truncate Statspack Tables
~~~~~~~~~~~~~~~~~~~~~~~~~~~~~~~~~~~~
If you would like to continue, press <return>


Enter value for return:
Entered - starting truncate operation

Truncate operation complete

SQL> SELECT SNAP_ID, SNAP_TIME
  2    FROM STATS$SNAPSHOT
  3  /

no rows selected
```

12

Removing the Repository

Removing the repository is the easiest task of all, but can be dangerous, especially if you do it by mistake. Think twice before you remove a repository. To remove this repository, you must run the SPDROP.SQL script. The following steps outline the tasks you need to perform to remove repository:

Step 1: Log on as PERFSTAT and drop the repository:

```
SQL> @C:\ORACLE\ORA92\RDBMS\ADMIN\SPDROP.SQL
Dropping old versions (if any)
...
```

Step 2: Log on as SYSYEM and drop the tablespace created specifically for PERFSTAT (this step is optional). Make sure no other objects owned by other schemas are residing in this tablespace.

```
SQL> CONNECT SYSTEM@SAM
Enter password: ******
Connected.
SQL> SELECT SEGMENT_NAME
  2     FROM DBA_SEGMENTS
  3    WHERE TABLESPACE_NAME = 'TS_PERF'
  4   /

no rows selected

SQL> DROP TABLESPACE TS_PERF
  2   /

Tablespace dropped.
```

Step 3: Drop user PERFSTAT. This step is optional:

```
SQL> DROP USER PERFSTAT
  2   /

User dropped.
```

NOTE

If you are dropping the repository before recreating it, you should not drop the tablespace or the user.

SQL Tools

You probably know that most tuning problems arise from bad SQL queries submitted to the database. As a DBA, it is your right to audit every query to make sure it is optimally written and that it will not jeopardize the performance of the database. Here is a true story about a consultant's review of DBA queries.

An expert database administrator, charging $200.00 per hour, had a contract with a small company to convert an application written in Delphi and Crystal Reports, as the front-end and report writer respectively, to Oracle Forms and Reports. The consultant was given one month to complete his assignment. As the project deadline approached, the DBA of the company requested a meeting to discuss the optimization and tuning of all queries written by the consultant.

When the consultant and the DBA met, they discussed the importance of diagnosing problematic queries. The DBA confessed to the consultant that he was not an expert in SQL tuning and would appreciate her help in tuning the queries. The consultant was pleased with the DBA's initiative despite his lack of expertise in tuning queries. So the consultant asked the DBA to capture any queries submitted to the database and prepare an execution plan for each one. Then they would meet again to review all the queries, thus killing two birds with one stone: first, identifying bad queries, and second, training the DBA how to do it. The consultant was stunned to learn that the DBA did not know how to generate execution plans!

As a DBA, you need to know the ABCs of database administration, and knowing how to generate an execution plan equates to the first letter of this requirement. Interpreting and reading the execution plan is the next step in SQL tuning. In this section, you focus on learning the tools for generating the execution plan of a query. You will learn four Oracle-supplied tools that assist you in generating an execution plan.

Before you start learning each tool, you need to understand the term **execution plan**. The Oracle program named Oracle Optimizer has one task—to determine the best plan to retrieve data for the query. This plan is called the execution plan and sometimes is referred to as the **Explain Plan**.

In this chapter, you learn how to use available tools to generate execution plans, and in the next chapter, you learn how to identify and fix problematic queries.

EXPLAIN PLAN Command

To learn about the **EXPLAIN PLAN** command, imagine you are working in a progressive company as a database administrator. A developer pages you while you are in a meeting. The page says, "Please call me ASAP x1212, production problem—Doug." You are confused because you haven't received any alert from the system to indicate that there is a production problem. You excuse yourself and go to the nearest phone to call Doug and inquire what is going on. Doug answers the phone and explains, "As you know, we have a batch process that runs around 3:00 p.m. every day to do transaction verification. I have noticed that the process has been taking a long time lately, and today it took double the time it normally takes, and it is still running. We need your help to identify the problem!" So you say, "Okay, let me head to my desk, and I will look at the query and determine what's going on."

What would you do to find out if the query requires optimization? The answer is not as simple as you might think. Before you try to determine if the query is optimized, you need to see how Oracle is executing the query. To do that, you can use the EXPLAIN PLAN command.

How to Generate an Execution Plan

Execution plans are generated in two phases:

1. Preparation phase: performed once

2. Execution phase: performed every time you need to get the execution plan for a query

Preparation Phase—The following steps outline the tasks you need to perform to complete the preparation phase.

Step 1: Log on as SYSTEM to create a PLAN_TABLE owned by SYSTEM with read/write permission on this table granted to public. Or create a PLAN_TABLE for a specific user who needs to generate an execution plan for his queries. If PLAN_TABLE is created under

SYSTEM, there is a possibility that two users could delete each other's plans by mistake. If each user creates his own table, it will be used only for that specific user. To create PLAN_TABLE, you must execute an Oracle-supplied script residing in ORA-CLE_HOME/rdbms/admin/utlxplan.sql. This script only creates a table called PLAN_TABLE and does not grant privileges or create a synonym. In these steps you create PLAN_TABLE under SYSTEM:

```
SQL> CONNECT SYSTEM/MANAGER@SAM
Connected.

SQL> @C:\ORACLE\ORA92\RDBMS\ADMIN\UTLXPLAN

Table created.
```

Step 2: Verify the creation of this table:

```
SQL> DESC PLAN_TABLE
 Name                    Null?      Type
 ------------------      --------   --------------
 STATEMENT_ID                       VARCHAR2(30)
 TIMESTAMP                          DATE
 REMARKS                            VARCHAR2(80)
 OPERATION                          VARCHAR2(30)
 OPTIONS                            VARCHAR2(255)
 OBJECT_NODE                        VARCHAR2(128)
 OBJECT_OWNER                       VARCHAR2(30)
 OBJECT_NAME                        VARCHAR2(30)
 OBJECT_INSTANCE                    NUMBER(38)
 OBJECT_TYPE                        VARCHAR2(30)
 OPTIMIZER                          VARCHAR2(255)
 SEARCH_COLUMNS                     NUMBER
 ID                                 NUMBER(38)
 PARENT_ID                          NUMBER(38)
 POSITION                           NUMBER(38)
 COST                               NUMBER(38)
 CARDINALITY                        NUMBER(38)
 BYTES                              NUMBER(38)
 OTHER_TAG                          VARCHAR2(255)
 PARTITION_START                    VARCHAR2(255)
 PARTITION_STOP                     VARCHAR2(255)
 PARTITION_ID                       NUMBER(38)
 OTHER                              LONG
 DISTRIBUTION                       VARCHAR2(30)
 CPU_COST                           NUMBER(38)
 10_COST                            NUMBER(38)
 TEMP_SPACE                         NUMBER(38)
 ACCESS_PREDICATES                  VARCHAR2(4000)
 FILTER_PREDICATES                  VARCHAR2(4000)
```

Table 12-2 describes the most important columns in the **PLAN_TABLE** that retrieve the explain/execution plan. Each row generated in the execution plan is a step that is executed by Oracle.

Table 12-2 Commonly used columns of the PLAN_TABLE

Column	Description
STATEMENT_ID	An identifier of the plan for the submitted query
OPERATION	Name of the operation performed in this step
OPTIONS	Options used for the operation
OBJECT_NAME	Name of the object used in this step
OBJECT_TYPE	Type of object
OPTIMIZER	Optimizer mode
ID	Identification number of the step
PARENT_ID	Identification of the next step
COST	Estimated cost of the operation for the Cost-based Optimizer

The information in this table is derived from the online documentation that Oracle provides at the Oracle Technology Network site: *www.otn.oracle.com*.

Step 3: Create a public synonym to avoid the need to qualify the table name with the owner of the table, SYSTEM. This is needed for Oracle Enterprise Manager.

```
SQL> CREATE PUBLIC SYNONYM PLAN_TABLE FOR SYSTEM.PLAN_TABLE
  2  /

Synonym created.
```

Step 4: Grant read/write access on the table to any user who needs to determine a query execution plan. In this case, you provide access to TUNER schema.

```
SQL> GRANT SELECT, UPDATE, INSERT, DELETE ON PLAN_TABLE TO TUNER
  2  /

Grant succeeded.
```

You have just completed the preparation phase, which is performed only once. Now you are ready to move on to the execution phase.

Execution Phase—The following steps outline the tasks required to generate each new execution plan of a query.

Step 1: Log on as TUNER. In this step you need the query for which you want to generate an execution plan and you need to use an EXPLAIN PLAN statement. The syntax for this command is:

```
EXPLAIN PLAN [SET STATEMENT_ID = 'text']
   [INTO [schema .] table [@ dblink]] FOR statement;
Where:
```

12

■ **STATEMENT_ID**: This is an identifier for the query, which allows you to identify all the rows that belong to the execution plan of the query submitted. Although this clause is optional, it is a good idea to use it, especially if many users share the PLAN_TABLE.

■ **INTO [schema .] table[@ dblink]]**: This optional clause is used if you want the generated rows for the execution plan to be stored in a different table than the default table PLAN_TABLE. If you use a table other than the default, it must have the same data structure.

```
SQL> EXPLAIN PLAN
  2      SET STATEMENT_ID = 'QUERY1'
  3      FOR
  4   SELECT P.PRODUCT_NAME, SUM(OL.QUANTITY)
  5     FROM CUSTOMERS C, ORDERS O, ORDER_LINES OL, PRODUCTS P
  6    WHERE (C.FIRST_NAME = 'Omer' AND C.LAST_NAME = 'Plumley')
  7      AND C.CUSTOMER_ID = O.CUSTOMER_ID
  8      AND O.ORDER_ID = OL.ORDER_ID
  9      AND OL.PRODUCT_ID = P.PRODUCT_ID
 10    GROUP BY P.PRODUCT_NAME
 11   /

Explained.
```

Step 2: You must retrieve the execution plan from the PLAN_TABLE. There are many ways of writing a query to retrieve it. Notice that in the previous step you used a STATEMENT_ID = 'QUERY1' as an identifier for this query, but you can call it anything you like.

```
SQL> SELECT decode(id, 0, '',
  2     lpad(' ',2*(level- 1))||level||'.'||position)||' '||
  3     operation||' '||options||' '||object_name||' '||object_type||' '||
  4     decode(id,0,'Cost = '||position) "Execution Plan"
  5        FROM PLAN_TABLE
  6        CONNECT BY PRIOR ID = PARENT_ID
  7           AND UPPER(STATEMENT_ID) = 'QUERY1'
  8           START WITH ID = 0 AND UPPER(STATEMENT_ID) = 'QUERY1'
  9  /

Execution Plan
-------------------------------------------------------------------------
 SELECT STATEMENT     Cost = 21
   2.1 SORT GROUP BY
     3.1 NESTED LOOPS
       4.1 NESTED LOOPS
         5.1 NESTED LOOPS
           6.1 TABLE ACCESS FULL CUSTOMERS
           6.2 TABLE ACCESS BY INDEX ROWID ORDERS
             7.1 INDEX RANGE SCAN XIF15ORDERS NON-UNIQUE
         5.2 TABLE ACCESS BY INDEX ROWID ORDER_LINES
           6.1 INDEX RANGE SCAN PK_OL_ORDER_ID_PRODUCT_ID UNIQUE
       4.2 TABLE ACCESS BY INDEX ROWID PRODUCTS
         5.1 INDEX UNIQUE SCAN PK_PRO_PRODUCT_ID UNIQUE

12 rows selected.
```

As you can see in the query above, you used 'QUERY1' to identify all rows for the execution plan of the query you submitted.

NOTE The query you need to submit to retrieve the execution plan must include the CONNECT BY PRIOR ... START WITH clause, which displays the results in a treelike view.

At this point, you may be asking yourself, "Well, what does this output mean?" To understand the answer to this question, you'll have to wait for Chapter 13.

Of course, the query that retrieves the execution plan from the PLAN_TABLE is not trivial, especially if you write one from scratch. Because of its complexity, Oracle recognized the need of developing a PL/SQL package called DBMS_XPLAN to retrieve the execution plan from the plan table and format the output in a readable manner. This package contains only one function, which is named DISPLAY. The following listing is a description of this package:

```
SQL> DESC DBMS_XPLAN
FUNCTION DISPLAY RETURNS DBMS_XPLAN_TYPE_TABLE
 Argument Name            Type            In/Out Default?
 ----------------------   -------------   ------ --------
   TABLE_NAME             VARCHAR2        IN     DEFAULT
   STATEMENT_ID           VARCHAR2        IN     DEFAULT
   FORMAT                 VARCHAR2        IN     DEFAULT
```

12

As you can see, the DISPLAY function takes three parameters:

- **TABLE_NAME:** Name of the plan table. The default value is PLAN_TABLE.

- **STATEMENT_ID**: Specifies the statement ID of the execution plan to be retrieved.

- **FORMAT:** Specifies the level of details of the execution plan. Acceptable values are:

  - BASIC: Provides minimum details of the execution plan

  - TYPICAL: Provides most details of the execution plan. This is the default level of display format.

  - ALL: Provides maximum level of details of execution plan. Use this level of format for a parallel query.

  - SERIAL: Similar to TYPICAL, but does not display any details about parallel query

Referencing the execution plan for the previous query, the following steps demonstrate how to retrieve and display the execution plan.

Step 1: Log on as TUNER and execute the following EXPLAIN PLAN statement:

```
SQL> EXPLAIN PLAN
  2     SET STATEMENT_ID = 'QUERY1'
  3     FOR
  4  SELECT P.PRODUCT_NAME, SUM(OL.QUANTITY)
  5    FROM CUSTOMERS C, ORDERS O, ORDER_LINES OL, PRODUCTS P
  6   WHERE (C.FIRST_NAME = 'Omer' AND C.LAST_NAME = 'Plumley')
  7     AND C.CUSTOMER_ID = O.CUSTOMER_ID
  8     AND O.ORDER_ID = OL.ORDER_ID
  9     AND OL.PRODUCT_ID = P.PRODUCT_ID
 10   GROUP BY P.PRODUCT_NAME
 11  /

Explained.
```

Step 2: Retrieve the execution plan using DBMS_XPLAN:

```
SQL> SELECT * FROM table(DBMS_XPLAN.DISPLAY);

PLAN_TABLE_OUTPUT
-------------------------------------------------------------------------------

-------------------------------------------------------------------------------
| Id  | Operation                     | Name                      | Rows  | Bytes | Cost  |
-------------------------------------------------------------------------------
|   0 | SELECT STATEMENT              |                           |     1 |    57 |    21 |
|   1 |  SORT GROUP BY                |                           |     1 |    57 |    21 |
|   2 |   NESTED LOOPS                |                           |     1 |    57 |    19 |
|   3 |    NESTED LOOPS               |                           |     1 |    32 |    18 |
|   4 |     NESTED LOOPS             |                           |     1 |    24 |    16 |
|*  5 |      TABLE ACCESS FULL       | CUSTOMERS                 |     1 |    13 |    13 |
|   6 |      TABLE ACCESS BY INDEX ROWID| ORDERS                  |  9916 | 69412 |     3 |
|*  7 |       INDEX RANGE SCAN       | XIF15ORDERS               |     3 |       |     1 |
|   8 |     TABLE ACCESS BY INDEX ROWID | ORDER_LINES            |    11 |    88 |     2 |
|*  9 |      INDEX RANGE SCAN        | PK_OL_ORDER_ID_PRODUCT_ID |    11 |       |     1 |
|  10 |    TABLE ACCESS BY INDEX ROWID | PRODUCTS               |  5001 |  122K |     1 |
|* 11 |     INDEX UNIQUE SCAN        | PK_PRO_PRODUCT_ID         |     1 |       |       |
-------------------------------------------------------------------------------

Predicate Information (identified by operation id):
-----------------------------------------------------

   5 - filter("C"."FIRST_NAME"='Omer' AND "C"."LAST_NAME"='Plumley')
   7 - access("C"."CUSTOMER_ID"="O"."CUSTOMER_ID")
   9 - access("O"."ORDER_ID"="OL"."ORDER_ID")
  11 - access("OL"."PRODUCT_ID"="P"."PRODUCT_ID")

Note: cpu costing is off

27 rows selected.
```

As you can see, this package results in a remarkably better format and provides a greater level of detail with more information without the need to write a complex query to retrieve the execution plan. The following statement is an alternative way to retrieve the same results, but this time you are providing values for each parameter of the DISPLAY function.

```
SQL> SELECT * FROM table(DBMS_XPLAN.DISPLAY('PLAN_TABLE', 'QUERY1', 'TYPICAL'));
```

SQL*Plus Autotrace

To learn about SQL*Plus Autotrace, imagine that one of your company's SQL developers sent you an e-mail requesting that you generate the execution plan for a query she wants to implement in the application she is building. So you created it for her using the EXPLAIN PLAN command and sent it back to her with instructions on how to generate an execution plan on her own. A few hours later, she sent another e-mail asking you to do another query explaining that she was confused by your instructions and was not able to generate the execution plan.

What can you do to make this situation easier for both of you? You can use SQL*Plus **AUTOTRACE** which provides a simple way to generate an execution plan as well as query statistics without writing any query to retrieve the execution plan. The following steps demonstrate how you can use this simple tool.

Preparation Phase—As with the EXPLAIN PLAN command, you need to perform the following steps only once to use this tool.

Step 1: Log on as SYSTEM or SYS and verify that the PLUSTRACE role exists:

```
SQL> SELECT ROLE
  2    FROM DBA_ROLES
  3   WHERE ROLE LIKE 'PLUS%'
  4  /

no rows selected
```

Step 2: If the PLUSTRACE role does not exist, you must create it using an Oracle-supplied script named PLUSTRCE.SQL residing in the ORACLE_HOME/ORA92/SQLPLUS/ADMIN directory:

```
SQL> @C:\ORACLE\ORA92\SQLPLUS\ADMIN\PLUSTRCE.SQL
SQL>
SQL> drop role plustrace;
drop role plustrace
          *
ERROR at line 1:
ORA-01919: role 'PLUSTRACE' does not exist


SQL> create role plustrace;

Role created.

SQL>
SQL> grant select on v_$sesstat to plustrace;
grant select on v_$sesstat to plustrace
                *
ERROR at line 1:
ORA-00942: table or view does not exist


SQL> grant select on v_$statname to plustrace;
grant select on v_$statname to plustrace
                *
ERROR at line 1:
ORA-00942: table or view does not exist


SQL> grant select on v_$session to plustrace;
grant select on v_$session to plustrace
                *
ERROR at line 1:
ORA-00942: table or view does not exist


SQL> grant plustrace to dba with admin option;

Grant succeeded.
```

Step 3: Then you must create a PLAN_TABLE as shown in the previous section.

1. Execute the ULTXPLAN.SQL script.

2. Create PUBLIC synonym for PLAN_TABLE.

3. Grant SELECT, UPDATE, DELETE, INSERT privileges to the user.

Step 4: Grant the PLUSTRACE role to any user you want to allow to use the AUTO-TRACE tool:

```
SQL> GRANT PLUSTRACE TO TUNER
  2  /

Grant succeeded.
```

Execution Phase—To use this tool, issue the following SET command from SQL*Plus:

```
SET AUTOT[RACE] [OFF|ON|TRACE[ONLY]] [EXP[LAIN]] [STAT[ISTICS]]
```

Where:

- OFF: Turns off tracing

- ON: Turns tracing on in a mode that returns the results of the query following execution

- TRACEONLY: Turns tracing on in a mode that does not return the results of the query

- EXPLAIN: Generates and displays the Explain Plan for the query

- STATISTICS: Displays the query statistics described in Table 12-3

Table 12-3 Autotrace statistics description

Name	Description
recursive calls	Number of recursive calls generated at both the user and system level
db block gets	Number of times a CURRENT block was requested
consistent gets	Number of times a consistent read was requested for a block
physical reads	Total number of data blocks read from disk
redo size	Total number of bytes generated by redos
bytes sent via SQL*Net to client	Total number of bytes sent to the client
bytes received via SQL*Net from client	Total number of bytes received from the client
SQL*Net roundtrips to/from client	Total number of Oracle Net messages sent to and received from the client

Name	Description
sorts (memory)	Number of sort operations performed completely in memory
sorts (disk)	Number of sort operations that required at least one disk write
rows processed	Number of rows processed

Suppose you want to generate an execution plan for a query using this tool. The following steps demonstrate this process.

Step 1: Log on as TUNER and Set AUTOTRACE to ON:

```
SQL> SET AUTOTRACE TRACEONLY EXPLAIN STATISTICS
```

In this case, you are setting the trace to TRACEONLY, which means the results of the query are suppressed, but the AUTOTRACE option automatically generates both the execution plan and query statistics every time you submit a query.

Step 2: Although this step is optional, it is useful. You can set timing to ON to display how long a query takes to execute.

```
SQL> SET TIMING ON
```

Step 3: Submit the query for which you want to generate the execution plan:

```
SQL> SELECT P.PRODUCT_NAME, SUM(OL.QUANTITY)
  2    FROM CUSTOMERS C, ORDERS O, ORDER_LINES OL, PRODUCTS P
  3    WHERE (C.FIRST_NAME = 'Omer' AND C.LAST_NAME = 'Plumley')
  4      AND C.CUSTOMER_ID = O.CUSTOMER_ID
  5      AND O.ORDER_ID = OL.ORDER_ID
  6      AND OL.PRODUCT_ID = P.PRODUCT_ID
  7    GROUP BY P.PRODUCT_NAME
  8   /

Elapsed: 00:00:00.04

Execution Plan
-------------------------------------------------------------
   0        SELECT STATEMENT Optimizer=CHOOSE (Cost=21 Card=1 Bytes=57)
   1    0    SORT (GROUP BY) (Cost=21 Card=1 Bytes=57)
   2    1     NESTED LOOPS (Cost=19 Card=1 Bytes=57)
   3    2      NESTED LOOPS (Cost=18 Card=1 Bytes=32)
   4    3       NESTED LOOPS (Cost=16 Card=1 Bytes=24)
   5    4        TABLE ACCESS (FULL) OF 'CUSTOMERS' (Cost=13 Card=1
          Bytes=17)

   6    4          TABLE ACCESS (BY INDEX ROWID) OF 'ORDERS' (Cost=3
          Card=9916 Bytes=69412)

   7    6            INDEX (RANGE SCAN) OF 'XIF15ORDERS' (NON-UNIQUE)
          (Cost=1 Card=3)

   8    3          TABLE ACCESS (BY INDEX ROWID) OF 'ORDER_LINES' (Cost
          =2 Card=11 Bytes=88)

   9    8            INDEX (RANGE SCAN) OF 'PK_OL_ORDER_ID_PRODUCT_ID'
          (UNIQUE) (Cost=1 Card=11)

  10    2        TABLE ACCESS (BY INDEX ROWID) OF 'PRODUCTS' (Cost=1 Ca
          rd=5001 Bytes=125025)

  11   10          INDEX (UNIQUE SCAN) OF 'PK_PRO_PRODUCT_ID' (UNIQUE)
```

12

```
Statistics
-------------------------------------------------------------
         0  recursive calls
         0  db block gets
       183  consistent gets
        12  physical reads
         0  redo size
      1310  bytes sent via SQL*Net to client
       510  bytes received via SQL*Net from client
         3  SQL*Net roundtrips to/from client
         1  sorts (memory)
         0  sorts (disk)
```

Very simple! When you have finished generating the execution plan, you can turn off AUTOTRACE by issuing the following statement:

```
SQL> SET AUTOTRACE OFF
```

Going back to the scenario presented at the beginning of this section, you complete the preparation phase and then send the following instructions to the developer:

1. SET AUTOTRACE ON EXPLAIN STATISTICS (use TRACEONLY instead of ON if you do not want to display the results of the query)

2. SUBMIT QUERY

3. SET AUTOTRACE OFF when completely finished

SQL Trace and TKPROF

To become familiar with this topic, put yourself in this situation. A Web application has been running without any performance problems for several months. One of your routine tasks is to do a query audit to ensure that all queries submitted by the application are written optimally. So you want to conduct this audit on the application user during peak time.

What do you do? You could use V$ views to extract queries for all active sessions, and you could use V$SQL to capture all queries submitted to the database, and so on. After capturing the queries, you would need to generate an execution plan for each query to see the execution plan of the query. In addition to Oracle Enterprise Manager, there are many third-party tools that provide a means to extract these queries and their execution plans. But it is still necessary to distinguish which queries were submitted by the application. To accomplish this task, you can use SQL Trace and TKPROF. Figure 12-18 represents the process of using these two tools.

1. User logs on and establishes a connection to the database.

2. DBA retrieves session information for the user (session ID and serial number).

3. DBA turns on the tracing of the user's session.

4. User starts submitting queries normally.

5. As the queries are being executed by the database system, the database system generates a trace file for the session.

6. After a specific period, the DBA turns off tracing for the user session.

7. Because the generated trace file for the user is not readable, the DBA needs to run TKPROF to format the trace file.

8. The TKPROF tool reads the trace file.

9. TKPROF formats the trace file to a readable text file.

10. DBA reads the formatted text file using Notepad to analyze all submitted queries.

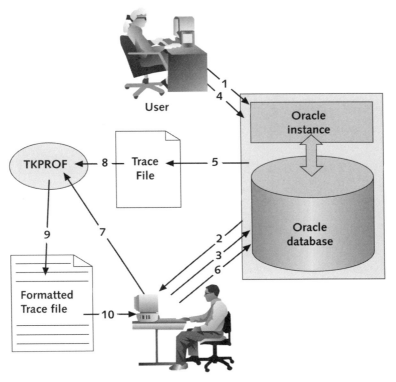

Figure 12-18   SQL trace architecture and process

Quite a lengthy process, isn't it? But, this process is not difficult. Getting the formatted trace file is half the battle; the other half is analyzing it, as described in Chapter 13.

The following step-by-step tasks outline how to trace a session to look at statistics and the execution plans for all queries submitted by the session.

Step 1: Using SQL*Plus, open a session as TUNER:

```
SQL> CONNECT TUNER/TUNER@SAM
Connected.
```

12

Step 2: Open another SQL∗Plus session as SYS:

NOTE You can set SQL TRACE for the whole Oracle instance by issuing the ALTER SYSTEM SET SQL_TRACE=TRUE command, but you should never use it, as it degrades the performance of the instance significantly.

```
SQL> CONNECT SYS@SAM AS SYSDBA
Enter password: ******
Connected.
```

Step 3: As SYS, retrieve session information for TUNER. You need the Session ID and serial number. Record this information on a piece of paper (11 and 6312).

```
SQL> SELECT USERNAME, SID, SERIAL#, STATUS
  2      FROM V$SESSION
  3  /

USERNAME          SID     SERIAL# STATUS
---------- ---------- ---------- --------
                    1           1 ACTIVE
                    2           1 ACTIVE
                    3           1 ACTIVE
                    4           1 ACTIVE
                    5           1 ACTIVE
                    6           1 ACTIVE
                    7           1 ACTIVE
                    8           1 ACTIVE
PERFSTAT            9          61 INACTIVE
TUNER              11        6312 INACTIVE
SYS                12        4189 ACTIVE
SYSTEM             13         429 INACTIVE
```

You also need the system process ID for the TUNER session, so you can submit the following enhanced query to supply more information about the session.

```
SQL> select s.username,
  2         s.sid,
  3         s.serial#,
  4         s.sid||','||s.serial# kill,
  5         p.spid system_pid,
  6         p.pid
  7    from v$session s, v$process p
  8   where s.username = 'TUNER'
  9     and s.paddr = p.addr
 10  /

USERNAME          SID    SERIAL# KILL       SYSTEM_PID        PID
---------- ---------- ---------- ---------- ------------ ----------
TUNER              11       6312 11,6312    2264                113
```

Step 4: As SYS, turn on SQL tracing for the TUNER session. For this, you need to use a PL/SQL-supplied package from Oracle named DBMS_SYSTEM. The procedure you will be using from this package is listed here.

```
PROCEDURE SET_SQL_TRACE_IN_SESSION
  Argument Name                        Type                     In/Out Default?
  ----------------------------------   ----------------------   ------ --------
  SID                                  NUMBER                   IN
  SERIAL#                              NUMBER                   IN
  SQL_TRACE                            BOOLEAN                  IN
```

As you can see, two of the parameters of this procedure are SID (session ID) and serial number. The last parameter, SQL_TRACE, accepts the values TRUE to turn on trace and FALSE to turn it OFF.

```
SQL> EXEC DBMS_SYSTEM.SET_SQL_TRACE_IN_SESSION( 11, 6312, TRUE)

PL/SQL procedure successfully completed.
```

Now, you can instruct the TUNER user to submit queries.

Step 5: As TUNER, submit the following queries:

```
SQL> SELECT * FROM CUSTOMERS
  2    WHERE CUSTOMER_ID = 1001
  3  /

...

SQL> SELECT * FROM EMPLOYEES
  2    WHERE EMPLOYEE_ID = 1001
  3  /

...

SQL> SELECT P.PRODUCT_NAME, SUM(OL.QUANTITY)
  2    FROM CUSTOMERS C, ORDERS O, ORDER_LINES OL, PRODUCTS P
  3    WHERE (C.FIRST_NAME = 'Omer' AND C.LAST_NAME = 'Plumley')
  4      AND C.CUSTOMER_ID = O.CUSTOMER_ID
  5      AND O.ORDER_ID = OL.ORDER_ID
  6      AND OL.PRODUCT_ID = P.PRODUCT_ID
  7    GROUP BY P.PRODUCT_NAME
  8  /
...
```

12

Step 6: As SYS, turn off SQL tracing for TUNER:

```
SQL> EXEC DBMS_SYSTEM.SET_SQL_TRACE_IN_SESSION(11, 6312, FALSE)

PL/SQL procedure successfully completed.
```

The TUNER user is free to disconnect or go on to other things. Starting with the next step, the participation of TUNER is not required.

Step 7: You need to retrieve the trace file. The trace file goes in the location specified by the initialization parameter USER_DUMP_DEST.

```
SQL> SHOW PARAMETER USER_DUMP_DEST

NAME                        TYPE         VALUE
------------------------    -----------  -------------------------
user_dump_dest              string       C:\oracle\admin\SAM\udump
```

The file is usually named SID_ORA_SPID.TRC where

- SID: Oracle System Identification (ORACLE_SID)

- SPID: Operating System Process Identification

For the TUNER session, the file name with the full path is:

```
C:\oracle\admin\sam\udump\SAM_ORA_2264.TRC
```

As mentioned previously, the file is not readable, and this means that you cannot use it for analysis until the coded text has been formatted. The following is a partial listing of this file:

```
Dump file c:\oracle\admin\sam\udump\sam_ora_2264.trc
Fri Feb 07 21:44:36 2003
ORACLE V9.2.0.1.0 - Production vsnsta=0
vsnsql=12 vsnxtr=3
Windows 2000 Version 5.0 Service Pack 3, CPU type 586
Oracle9i Enterprise Edition Release 9.2.0.1.0 - Production
With the Partitioning, OLAP and Oracle Data Mining options
JServer Release 9.2.0.1.0 - Production
Windows 2000 Version 5.0 Service Pack 3, CPU type 586
Instance name: sam

Redo thread mounted by this instance: 1

Oracle process number: 113

Windows thread id: 2264, image: ORACLE.EXE


*** 2003-02-07 21:44:36.000
*** SESSION ID:(11.6312) 2003-02-07 21:44:36.000
APPNAME mod='SQL*Plus' mh=3669949024 act='' ah=4029777240
====================
PARSING IN CURSOR #1 len=51 dep=0 uid=65 oct=3 lid=65 tim=383091544505 hv=653834925 ad='653ed0bc'
SELECT * FROM CUSTOMERS
   WHERE CUSTOMER_ID = 1001
END OF STMT
PARSE #1:c=0,e=2347,p=0,cr=0,cu=0,mis=1,r=0,dep=0,og=4,tim=383091540905
```

A common mistake is to forget to turn off tracing for the session. Forgetting could generate a large file that might consume all space on disk.

NOTE

Step 8: Now you can format the trace file using the command utility TKPROF. This utility has several options. To view all options, you can issue a command as displayed in Figure 12-19.

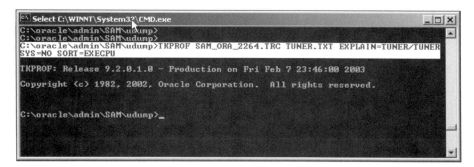

Figure 12-19   Help information for the Oracle TKPROF tool

To format the trace file, you must issue the following command as illustrated in Figure 12-20:

Figure 12-20   TKPROF command to format trace file generated by SQL trace

Here is an explanation of the command:

- TKPROF: The name of the tool
- SAM_ORA_2264.TRC: The trace file for the TUNER session
- TUNER.TXT: The formatted output file
- EXPLAIN: If you want the execution plan to be displayed, you must provide the username and password of the user. The PLAN_TABLE must already exist.
- SYS: If you want to show all commands executed by SYS on behalf of TUNER user, you specify YES; otherwise, NO.
- SORT: This tells TKPROF to sort queries issued during the tracing of an EXECPU (CPU execution). The query that spent the most CPU execution time is displayed first.

Step 9: Open the formatted text file. Figure 12-21 displays the content of this file.

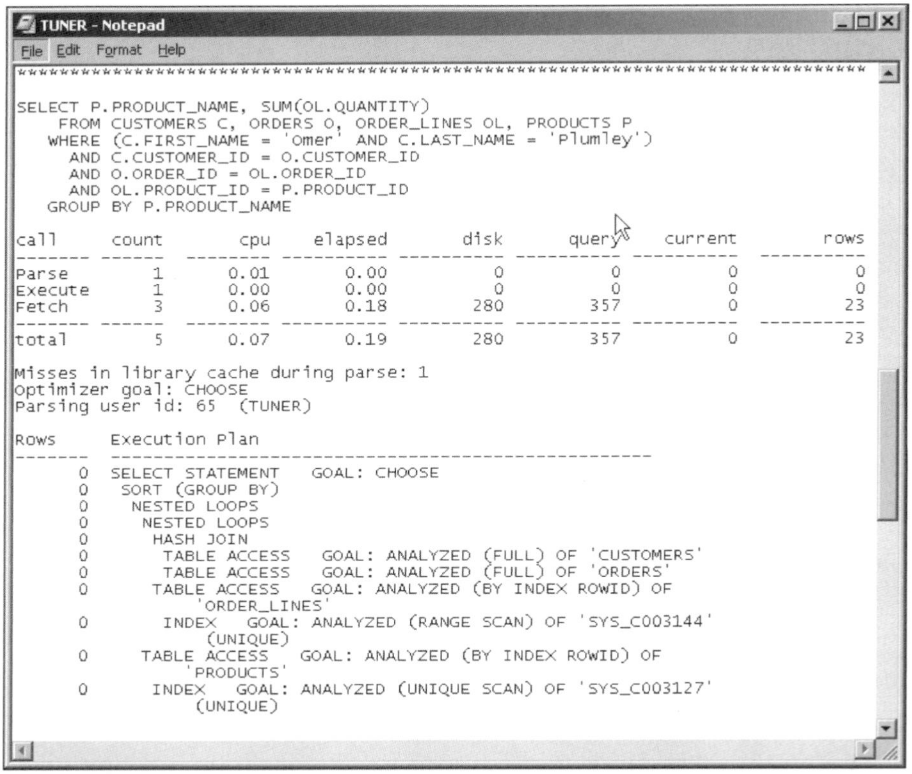


```
********************************************************************************

SELECT P.PRODUCT_NAME, SUM(OL.QUANTITY)
    FROM CUSTOMERS C, ORDERS O, ORDER_LINES OL, PRODUCTS P
   WHERE (C.FIRST_NAME = 'Omer' AND C.LAST_NAME = 'Plumley')
     AND C.CUSTOMER_ID = O.CUSTOMER_ID
     AND O.ORDER_ID = OL.ORDER_ID
     AND OL.PRODUCT_ID = P.PRODUCT_ID
   GROUP BY P.PRODUCT_NAME

call     count       cpu    elapsed       disk      query    current        rows
------- ------  -------- ---------- ---------- ---------- ----------  ----------
Parse        1      0.01       0.00          0          0          0           0
Execute      1      0.00       0.00          0          0          0           0
Fetch        3      0.06       0.18        280        357          0          23
------- ------  -------- ---------- ---------- ---------- ----------  ----------
total        5      0.07       0.19        280        357          0          23

Misses in library cache during parse: 1
Optimizer goal: CHOOSE
Parsing user id: 65  (TUNER)

Rows     Execution Plan
-------  ---------------------------------------------------
      0  SELECT STATEMENT   GOAL: CHOOSE
      0   SORT (GROUP BY)
      0    NESTED LOOPS
      0     NESTED LOOPS
      0      HASH JOIN
      0       TABLE ACCESS   GOAL: ANALYZED (FULL) OF 'CUSTOMERS'
      0       TABLE ACCESS   GOAL: ANALYZED (FULL) OF 'ORDERS'
      0      TABLE ACCESS   GOAL: ANALYZED (BY INDEX ROWID) OF
                 'ORDER_LINES'
      0       INDEX   GOAL: ANALYZED (RANGE SCAN) OF 'SYS_C003144'
                  (UNIQUE)
      0     TABLE ACCESS   GOAL: ANALYZED (BY INDEX ROWID) OF
                'PRODUCTS'
      0      INDEX   GOAL: ANALYZED (UNIQUE SCAN) OF 'SYS_C003127'
                 (UNIQUE)
```

Figure 12-21 Contents of the formatted SQL trace file by TKPROF

That's it. Now you are able to perform SQL tracing for any session.

NOTE

It is a common practice to audit SQL queries by randomly tracing application sessions using SQL Trace/TKPROF tools to identify problematic queries.

Oracle Enterprise Manager

A picture paints a thousands words. Oracle Enterprise Manager comes with a standard Sessions option, which presents a neatly formatted display of all connected sessions, as shown in Figure 12-22. As you can see, the selected session is TUNER user, and you can double-click on the selected session or right-click on it to view the details of the session.

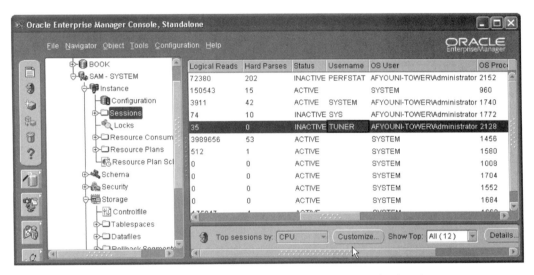

Figure 12-22   Oracle Enterprise Manager showing sessions node details

Figure 12-23 shows the details of the TUNER session with a graphical view of the execution plan of the query that was submitted by TUNER.

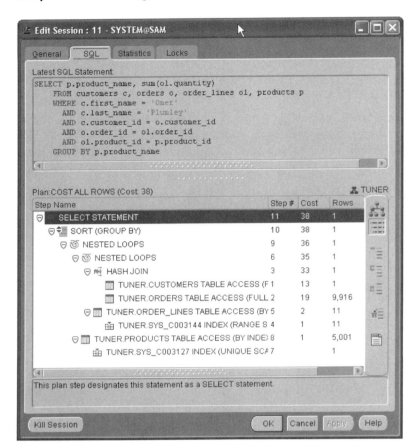

Figure 12-23   Oracle Enterprise Manager showing SQL submitted by the TUNER user

Top SQL tool is another tool you can use to display query information. This tool is accessed by clicking the Top SQL button on the Diagnostics Pack toolbar. This useful tool displays all queries sorted in the order you specify. You can right-click on any query and view the execution plan as shown in Figure 12-24. Once you select an Explain Plan option, a window displays the plan graphically, as in Figure 12-25, showing how the data is accessed and retrieved for the query. You can use options in this window to step through the execution plan with an explanation of each step at the bottom of the window.

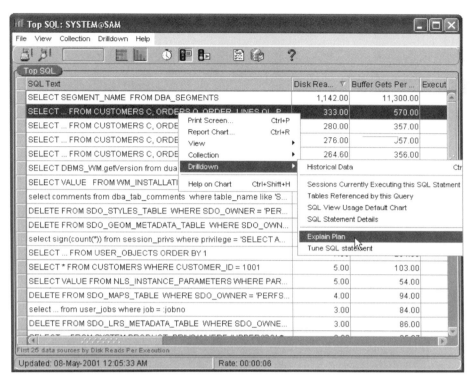

Figure 12-24   Oracle Enterprise Manager showing menu options for the Top SQL utility

12

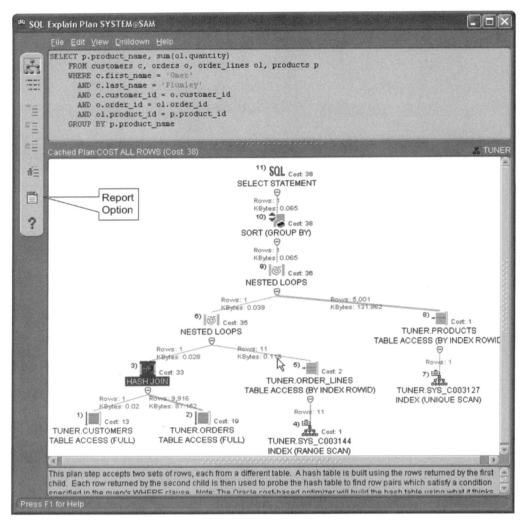

Figure 12-25 Top SQL utility of the Oracle Enterprise Manager showing the graphical Explain Plan option

This tool's best feature is the Report option, which displays a fully detailed report that you can save or print. Figure 12-26 shows a partial display of this report.

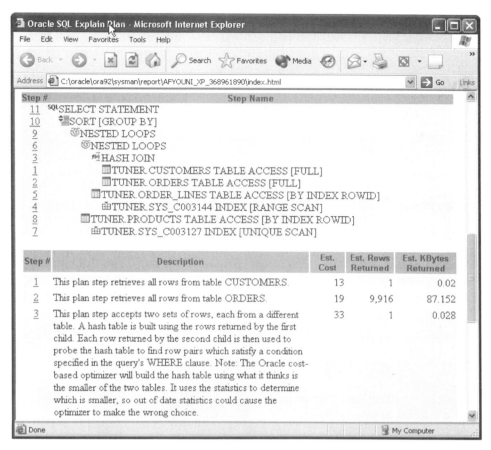

Figure 12-26   HTML report of the Oracle Enterprise Manager Explain Plan

DATA BLOCK CORRUPTION TOOLS

It was 3:00 a.m. when the phone rang at the DBA's house. "Hello, is this Joe?" asked the person on the other end of the line. "This is Linda from Acme Data Center. Sorry to bother you at this hour, but one of the database applications you are on-call for got an ORA-00600 alert error! Could you please look at the error and tell me what I should do? I have sent the application error log...thanks and sorry about the call."

Joe, the DBA, was now fully awake and ran to his home computer. He logged onto the company's virtual private network and read the Error log. Joe located the ORA-00600 error, which occurred after a query was submitted. Joe examined the query and didn't find anything odd, so he decided to submit the query himself from SQL*Plus. He got exactly the same error.

Joe examined the Alert log closely but could determine only that the trace file was created. He looked at the trace file, but could not make much out of it. Then Joe remembered what his instructor said about the 600 internal error: "When you get this error, you should report the problem to Oracle and send the trace file to them. Then investigate the problem." Joe looked at other queries that were submitted to the database and could not find any indicators of any major problems. Then he decided to detect for data block corruptions.

Detecting data block corruption is a task you will be doing every now and then. Oracle provides two tools to perform this task:

- DBVERIFY

- DBMS_REPAIR

You next explore how to use each tool to detect data block corruption.

DBVERIFY

This tool performs data file verification for corruption. It can scan an entire or partial data file whether it is online or offline. **DBVERIFY** takes as input the data file name, block size, and other parameters as listed in Figure 12-27. You can get this information by issuing the following command:

```
C:\DBV HELP=YES
```

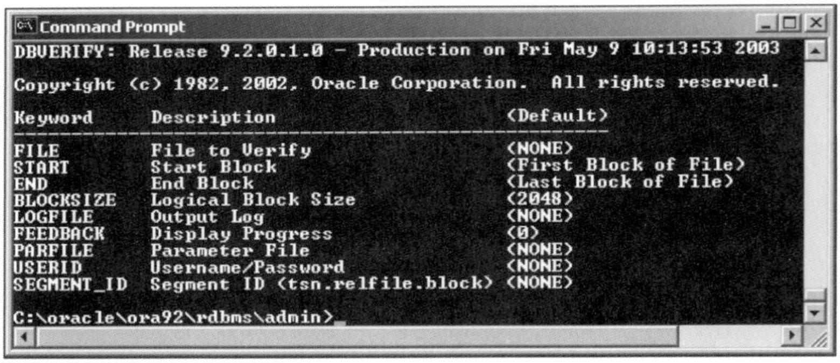

Figure 12-27   Help information for the DBVERIFY tool

You do not need to provide all these parameters. The following steps demonstrate how this tool is commonly used.

Step 1: Identify the file you want to verify, along with the tablespace, and block size. You must provide block size for the tool to verify data blocks within the data file.

```
SQL> SELECT T.NAME TABLESPACE,
  2          D.NAME DATAFILE,
  3          D.BLOCK_SIZE
  4    FROM V$TABLESPACE T, V$DATAFILE D
  5    WHERE T.TS# = D.TS#
  6    ORDER BY 1, 2
  7  /

TABLESPACE        DATAFILE                                  BLOCK_SIZE
---------------   ---------------------------------------   ----------
CWMLITE           C:\ORACLE\ORADATA\SAM\CWMLITE01.DBF             8192
DRSYS             C:\ORACLE\ORADATA\SAM\DRSYS01.DBF               8192
EXAMPLE           C:\ORACLE\ORADATA\SAM\EXAMPLE01.DBF             8192
INDX              C:\ORACLE\ORADATA\SAM\INDX01.DBF                8192
ODM               C:\ORACLE\ORADATA\SAM\ODM01.DBF                 8192
OEM_REPOSITORY    C:\ORACLE\ORADATA\SAM\OEM_REPOSITORY.DBF        8192
SYSTEM            C:\ORACLE\ORADATA\SAM\SYSTEM01.DBF              8192
TEST1             C:\ORACLE\ORADATA\SAM\TEST01.DBF                8192
TEST2             C:\ORACLE\ORADATA\SAM\TEST02.DBF                8192
TOOLS             C:\ORACLE\ORADATA\SAM\TOOLS01.DBF               8192
TS_PERF           C:\ORACLE\ORADATA\SAM\TS_PERF_01.DBF            8192
TS_TRY            C:\ORACLE\ORADATA\SAM\TS_TRY01.DBF              8192
UNODTB2           C:\ORACLE\ORADATA\SAM\UNODTB21.ORA              8192
USERS             C:\ORACLE\ORADATA\SAM\USERS01.DBF               8192
XDB               C:\ORACLE\ORADATA\SAM\XDB01.DBF                 8192
```

Step 2: From a Windows command line, you can issue the commands listed in Figure 12–28. The result of the verification indicates that there is no corruption. Note that data file verification may take some time, depending on the size of the data file.

Figure 12-28　DBVERIFY command and results

DBVERIFY checks the data file for block corruption, but it does not repair or fix corruption.

NOTE

DBMS_REPAIR

Although the name of this Oracle-supplied PL/SQL package implies that it repairs data **block corruption**, it really does not. So what does it do? Simply put, its primary use is to detect data block corruption of database objects such as tables and indexes. It also has other uses such as marking corrupted blocks to be skipped during data fetching. The following steps show how to detect data block corruption for a table.

Step 1: Log on as SYS and check to see if the REPAIR_TABLE exists. If not, you must create it because it is used by this package.

```
SQL> DESC REPAIR_TABLE
ERROR:
ORA-04043: object REPAIR_TABLE does not exist

SQL> BEGIN
  2      DBMS_REPAIR.ADMIN_TABLES (
  3          TABLE_NAME => 'REPAIR_TABLE',
  4          TABLE_TYPE => DBMS_REPAIR.REPAIR_TABLE,
  5          ACTION     => DBMS_REPAIR.CREATE_ACTION,
  6          TABLESPACE => 'SYSTEM');
  7  END;
  8  /

PL/SQL procedure successfully completed.
```

Step #2: You can use the CHECK_OBJECT procedure within the DBMS_REPAIR package:

```
SQL> DECLARE
  2      V_NUM NUMBER := 0;
  3  BEGIN
  4
  5      DBMS_REPAIR.CHECK_OBJECT (
  6          SCHEMA_NAME => 'TUNER',
  7          OBJECT_NAME => 'CUSTOMERS',
  8          REPAIR_TABLE_NAME => 'REPAIR_TABLE',
  9          CORRUPT_COUNT => V_NUM);
 10
 11      DBMS_OUTPUT.PUT_LINE('CORRUPTED BLOCKS: ' || V_NUM);
 12  END;
 13  /
CORRUPTED BLOCKS: 0

PL/SQL procedure successfully completed.
```

If you get the following error, it means that you skipped Step 1:

```
ERROR at line 1:
ORA-24130: table REPAIR_TABLE does not exist
ORA-06512: at "SYS.DBMS_REPAIR", line 284
ORA-06512: at line 5
```

The following is the modified PL/SQL block from Step 2 that is used to detect corruption for a whole schema:

```
SQL> DECLARE
  2      V_SCHEMA VARCHAR2(30) := 'DEMO';
  3      V_NUM NUMBER :=0;
  4      V_MAX NUMBER :=0;
  5  BEGIN
  6      SELECT MAX(LENGTH(TABLE_NAME))
  7        INTO V_MAX
  8        FROM DBA_TABLES
  9       WHERE OWNER = V_SCHEMA;
 10      FOR T IN (SELECT TABLE_NAME
 11                  FROM DBA_TABLES
 12                 WHERE OWNER=V_SCHEMA) LOOP
 13          V_NUM := 0;
 14          DBMS_REPAIR.CHECK_OBJECT (
 15              SCHEMA_NAME => V_SCHEMA,
 16              OBJECT_NAME => T.TABLE_NAME,
 17              REPAIR_TABLE_NAME => 'REPAIR_TABLE',
 18              CORRUPT_COUNT =>  V_NUM);
 19          DBMS_OUTPUT.PUT_LINE('TABLE_NAME: ' ||
 20                      RPAD(T.TABLE_NAME, V_MAX) ||
 21                      ' - CORRUPTED BLOCKS: ' || V_NUM);
 22      END LOOP;
 23  END;
 24  /
TABLE_NAME: CUSTOMER      - CORRUPTED BLOCKS: 0
TABLE_NAME: DEPARTMENT    - CORRUPTED BLOCKS: 0
TABLE_NAME: EMPLOYEE      - CORRUPTED BLOCKS: 0
TABLE_NAME: ITEM          - CORRUPTED BLOCKS: 0
TABLE_NAME: JOB           - CORRUPTED BLOCKS: 0
TABLE_NAME: LOCATION      - CORRUPTED BLOCKS: 0
TABLE_NAME: PRICE         - CORRUPTED BLOCKS: 0
TABLE_NAME: PRODUCT       - CORRUPTED BLOCKS: 0
TABLE_NAME: SALARY_GRADE  - CORRUPTED BLOCKS: 0
TABLE_NAME: SALES_ORDER   - CORRUPTED BLOCKS: 0
TABLE_NAME: TMP           - CORRUPTED BLOCKS: 0

PL/SQL procedure successfully completed.
```

Similarly, you can detect block corruption for indexes for a schema:

```
SQL> DECLARE
  2
  3        V_SCHEMA VARCHAR2(30) := 'DEMO';
  4        V_NUM NUMBER :=0;
  5        V_MAX NUMBER :=0;
  6
  7  BEGIN
  8
  9        SELECT MAX(LENGTH(INDEX_NAME))
 10          INTO V_MAX
 11          FROM DBA_INDEXES
 12         WHERE OWNER = V_SCHEMA;
 13
 14        FOR I IN (SELECT INDEX_NAME
 15                     FROM DBA_INDEXES
 16                    WHERE OWNER=V_SCHEMA) LOOP
 17          V_NUM := 0;
 18          DBMS_REPAIR.CHECK_OBJECT (
 19              SCHEMA_NAME => V_SCHEMA,
 20              OBJECT_NAME => I.INDEX_NAME,
 21              OBJECT_TYPE => DBMS_REPAIR.INDEX_OBJECT,
 22              REPAIR_TABLE_NAME => 'REPAIR_TABLE',
 23              CORRUPT_COUNT =>  V_NUM);
 24
 25          IF V_NUM > 0 THEN
 26              DBMS_OUTPUT.PUT_LINE('TABLE_NAME: ' ||
 27                        RPAD(I.INDEX_NAME, V_MAX) ||
 28                        ' - CORRUPTED BLOCKS: ' || V_NUM);
 29          END IF;
 30
 31      END LOOP;
 32  END;
 33  /

PL/SQL procedure successfully completed.
```

NOTE

If you discover that there is block corruption, you must recover that corrupted object from a backup.

Analyze Tools

Here is a real-world scenario to illustrate the use of the Analyze tools. Jim, the primary DBA of a production database that houses a data warehouse application, went on vacation for one month. The database manager handed over the administration to the secondary DBA, Tim, who was less familiar with the application. In the middle of each month, this data warehouse was completely refreshed. A day after the data was refreshed, Tim got a call from the business manager of the application. The tone of the manager was uneasy when she said, "What's going on? All our reports are running extremely slowly. We need to hand over these reports to executive management by the end of the day. What did you do?" Tim politely said, "Let me investigate this matter, and I will give you an update in one hour."

Tim was puzzled by this incident. As far as he could recall, he had completed all the tasks that Jim instructed him to do. What could be wrong? Tim remembered that he did not analyze the tables that would produce the statistics that Oracle Optimizer needs to make good decisions in determining the most efficient way to retrieve data. Not having this data influences the Optimizer to make the wrong decision. Tim analyzed all tables for the application and called the manager to tell her that the reports should run normally once again.

How did Tim analyze all tables? What tool did he use and how did he do it? The next section answers these questions. You can use four tools to analyze database objects to gather statistics and validate structure. This section looks at the three manual tools using SQL commands and PL/SQL stored procedure. The fourth tool uses the Oracle Enterprise Manager Analyze Wizard.

ANALYZE COMMAND

The ANALYZE command has been available for a long time and is commonly used. It can perform two simple tasks: gather storage statistics for the object and validate the structure of the object. As explained in the previous chapter, the ANALYZE command can perform analysis in two modes, COMPUTE or ESTIMATE. The following query generates ANALYZE statements to analyze all tables for a schema:

```
SQL> SELECT 'ANALYZE TABLE ' || TABLE_NAME
  2          || ' ESTIMATE STATISTICS SAMPLE 10 PERCENT;'
  3     FROM USER_TABLES
  4  /
...
```

The following query generates statements to analyze all tables and indexes for the current schema validating the structure of the table:

```
SQL> SELECT 'ANALYZE TABLE ' || TABLE_NAME ||
  2          ' VALIDATE    STRUCTURE;'
  3  FROM USER_TABLES
  4  UNION
  5  SELECT 'ANALYZE INDEX ' || INDEX_NAME ||
  6          ' VALIDATE    STRUCTURE;'
  7     FROM USER_INDEXES
  /
...
```

DBMS_UTILITY

This Oracle-supplied PL/SQL package contains several procedures that perform different tasks. One of these tasks is analyzing objects as the ANALYZE command does. The following listing displays two procedures that perform object analysis: ANALYZE_DATABASE to analyze all database objects and ANALYZE_SCHEMA to analyze all objects in a schema.

12

```
PROCEDURE ANALYZE_DATABASE
 Argument Name                              Type                          In/Out Default?
 ------------------------------            ----------------------        ------ --------
 METHOD                                     VARCHAR2                      IN
 ESTIMATE_ROWS                              NUMBER                        IN     DEFAULT
 ESTIMATE_PERCENT                           NUMBER                        IN     DEFAULT
 METHOD_OPT                                 VARCHAR2                      IN     DEFAULT

PROCEDURE ANALYZE_SCHEMA
 Argument Name                              Type                          In/Out Default?
 ------------------------------            ----------------------        ------ --------
 SCHEMA                                     VARCHAR2                      IN
 METHOD                                     VARCHAR2                      IN
 ESTIMATE_ROWS                              NUMBER                        IN     DEFAULT
 ESTIMATE_PERCENT                           NUMBER                        IN     DEFAULT
 METHOD_OPT                                 VARCHAR2                      IN     DEFAULT
```

```
SQL> EXEC DBMS_UTILITY.ANALYZE_SCHEMA('TUNER', 'ESTIMATE')

PL/SQL procedure successfully completed.
```

The following procedure provided by this package is worth mentioning. The COM-
PILE_SCHEMA procedure can compile all objects (triggers, procedures, functions, packages,
and views) for a schema:

```
PROCEDURE COMPILE_SCHEMA
 Argument Name                              Type                          In/Out Default?
 ------------------------------            ----------------------        ------ --------
 SCHEMA                                     VARCHAR2                      IN
 COMPILE_ALL                                BOOLEAN                       IN     DEFAULT
```

DBMS_STATS

Oracle recommends another tool for your use: DBMS_STATS. This package is sophisticated
and provides the following functions:

- Gathers storage statistics of database objects

- Sets storage statistics to database objects

- Transfers storage statistics from and to STAT$ and USER tables

- Gathers optimizer statistics

This package is actually used by the Oracle Enterprise Manager Analyze utility, which was
discussed in previous chapters. The following is an example of how to analyze all objects
in a schema using the GATHER_SCHEMA_STATS procedure. For more details on this
package, consult Oracle9i documentation.

```
SQL> EXEC DBMS_STATS.GATHER_SCHEMA_STATS('TUNER')

PL/SQL procedure successfully completed.
```

DBMS_DDL

In case you don't have enough tools to analyze objects, here is another—a procedure called ANALYZE_OBJECT that comes with DBMS_DDL. The following is an illustration of its use:

```
SQL> EXEC DBMS_DDL.ANALYZE_OBJECT('TABLE', 'TUNER', 'EMPLOYEES', 'COMPUTE')

PL/SQL procedure successfully completed.
```

RESOURCE MANAGEMENT TOOL

The Acme Company database is shared by the inventory and financial applications. The database is residing on hardware that is adequate depending on the time of the month. For instance, at the end of each month the financial application must generate all statements within a given time frame. In the past, the financial application was able to accomplish this, but recently it has been a struggle to get these statements out on time. The reason for this is the increase in and unpredictable nature of the number of inventory application reports.

You might be asking yourself why these two applications run on the same hardware. Two simple reasons: the increase in the load of the inventory application is sporadic, and the resources to house the applications on different machines are limited.

What is the solution for this problem? Oracle 9*i* provides a feature named the Database Resource Manager that was unavailable in 8*i*. This feature enables the DBA to manage hardware resources at the database level. Oracle introduced this feature to allow a DBA to regulate and distribute resource usage based on priorities that can be assigned to users.

The Database Resource Manager empowers the DBA to categorize users and application proxy users who are using the database into different categories. These categories are referred to as **resource consumer groups** and are used to allocate a percentage of CPU usage based on user priorities which are called the **resource plan**.

Database Resource Manager enables a DBA to guarantee a certain minimum percentage of the CPU resources to certain groups and to ensure that certain group users do not exceed a certain percentage of the CPU usage. Database Resource Manager provides the following benefits:

- Transfers the control of CPU resources from the operating system to the database and thus to the DBA

- Distributes CPU resources among users based on need and priority

12

- Allocates degree of parallelism to different groups based on need

- Prevents certain users from sporadically impacting applications that need CPU resources

- Allows DBAs to switch priority of CPU usage for users at any time

- Gives the DBA control of the amount of undo space for each consumer group

The next section presents the components and architecture of the Database Resource Manager.

Database Resource Manager Components

Oracle9*i* supplies the Database Resource Manager (DRM) so that DBAs can control user CPU usage and other resources usage. Figure 12-29 illustrates five components of the DRM. The DRM treats every user as a consumer who belongs to a **resource consumer group**.

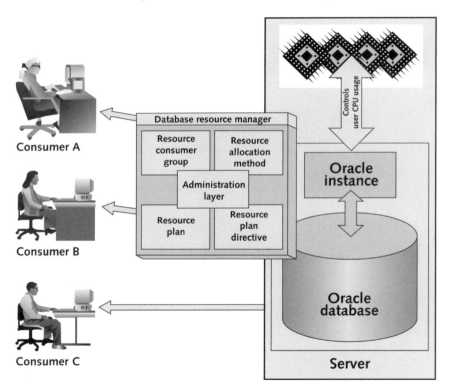

Figure 12-29   Architecture of the Oracle Database Resource Manager

Before you delve into how to use DRM, you need to know the definition of each component and its purpose.

Resource Consumer Group—A group of users or sessions grouped together because they have the same resource need and priority. The resource consumer group tells the DRM how resources are to be allocated for each consumer belonging to the group.

Resource Allocation Method—Tells the DRM the policy to be used when allocating resources to resource consumer groups. Table 12-4 presents the different methods available.

Table 12-4 Database Resource Manager allocation method

Method	Description
Round-Robin	Tells DRM to distribute CPU resources to each resource consumer group in a round-robin fashion
Emphasis	There are eight levels of priority from 1 to 8, in which level 1 is the highest priority. This method tells DRM to distribute CPU resources based on priority level using the following CPU allocation rules: ■ A consumer in a group with nonzero percentage has a higher priority to run. ■ At any priority level, the sum of percentages for a resource consumer group must not exceed 100 percent. ■ Any level that does not have any percentage explicitly specified is defaulted to 0% for all groups belonging to that level. ■ At any priority level the CPU resources are distributed based on percentages allocated to the consumer. ■ If CPU resources are not fully consumed, then consumer groups are allowed access to these resources starting from level 1.
Absolute	This method tells DRM the maximum number of processes that can be assigned to an operation for a consumer group. This limits the degree of parallelism.

The information in this table is derived from the online documentation that Oracle provides at the Oracle Technology Network site: *www.otn.oracle.com.*

Resource Plan—Tells the DRM how CPU resources are distributed to different consumer groups. Figure 12-30 illustrates how CPU resources are allocated for a plan for the Acme Company presented at the beginning of this section. As you can see, the Inventory Department has its own resource plan, and this plan allows the Inventory Department to get, at most, 20 percent of the CPU resources. For each group within the department, CPU resources are distributed among the three groups with 40 percent for the sales group, 40 percent for the marketing group, and 20 percent for the reporting group.

12

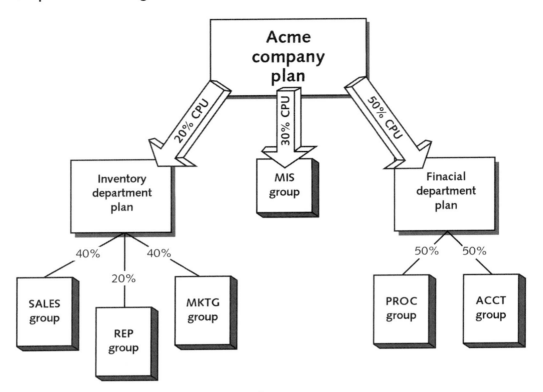

Figure 12-30   Acme Company resource plan

Figure 12-30 illustrates a multilevel resource plan, in which the Acme Company plan has one group and two subplans. In this case, the Inventory Department plan is considered a subplan for the Acme Company plan.

Resource Plan Directive—Specified by a DBA to associate a resource plan and resources with a resource consumer group

Administration Layer—Enables the DBA to administer DRM using DBMS_ RESOURCE_ MANAGER, an Oracle-supplied PL/SQL package

NOTE

To administer DRM, you must assign the ADMINISTER_RESOURCE_MANAGER system privilege to the user.

DEFAULT PLAN and CONSUMER GROUPS

Database Resource Manager comes with default resource consumer groups and a default plan named SYSTEM_PLAN.

The plan named SYSTEM_PLAN has three default groups (see Figure 12-31):

- **SYS_GROUP:** This group has priority level 1 with 100% CPU.

- **LOW_GROUP:** This group has priority level 2 with 100% CPU.

- **OTHER_GROUPS:** This group has priority level 3 with 100% CPU.

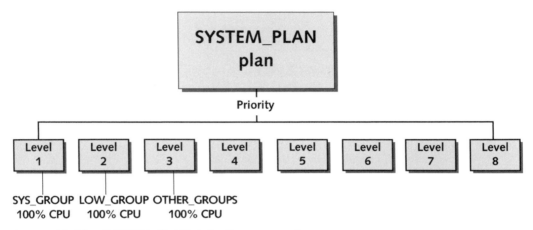

Figure 12-31   SYSTEM_PLAN default resource plan

There is one more default consumer group, DEFAULT_CONSUMER_GROUP, which is assigned automatically to each user.

Using the Database Resource Manager

To practice using the DRM, look back at the Acme Company scenario presented in Figure 12-30. You would need to create three plans and consumer groups, allocate resources to each plan, assign users to consumer groups, and finally associate the plan to the Oracle instance. Figure 12-32 illustrates the sequence of events for configuring resource management as follows:

1. First create a pending area, which is used as a staging area to construct resource plans, groups, and directives. You cannot configure resource management without creating this area.

2. Create all resource plans to be implemented. If a plan contains subplans, create the subplans first.

3. Create all the resource consumer groups to which database users will be assigned.

4. Create resource plan directives to associate resource plans to consumer groups.

5. Validate the configuration of the pending area.

6. Submit the validated plan to the database.

7. Assign existing database users to applicable consumer groups.

8. Associate the resource plan to the Oracle instance as the plan to be used to allocate CPU resources to users and sessions.

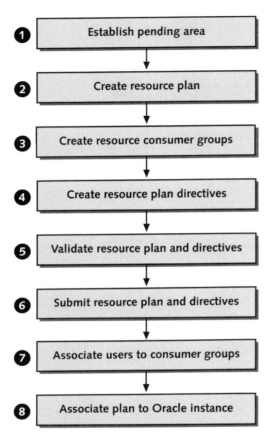

Figure 12-32   Sequence of events for configuring the Database Resource Manager

As mentioned previously, to configure resource management, you use the DBMS_RESOURCE_MANAGEMENT package. Table 12-5 lists the procedures contained in this package.

Table 12-5   Procedures of the DBMS_RESOURCE_MANAGER package

Category	Subprogram	Description
Pending area	CLEAR_PENDING_AREA	Clears all changes that were applied to the pending area
	CREATE_PENDING_AREA	Creates a staging area for configuring resource management. You must initiate this procedure before you proceed with any work.
	SUBMIT_PENDING_AREA	Submits changes that were applied to the pending area
	VALIDATE_PENDING_AREA	Validates changes that were applied to the pending area
Resource plan	CREATE_PLAN	Creates a resource plan
	CREATE_SIMPLE_PLAN	Creates a simple single-level resource plan consisting of eight different consumer groups
	DELETE_PLAN	Deletes an existing plan and the directive associated with it
	DELETE_PLAN_CASCADE	Deletes an existing plan and all the subplans belonging to it
	SWITCH_PLAN	Switches resource plan for a connected session
	UPDATE_PLAN	Updates information for an existing resource plan
Resource consumer group	CREATE_CONSUMER_GROUP	Creates a resource consumer group
	DELETE_CONSUMER_GROUP	Deletes an existing resource consumer group
	SET_INITIAL_CONSUMER_GROUP	Sets the initial resource consumer group for a user
	SWITCH_CONSUMER_GROUP_FOR_SESS	Switches a resource consumer group for a connected session
	SWITCH_CONSUMER_GROUP_FOR_USER	Switches a resource consumer group for an existing database user
	UPDATE_CONSUMER_GROUP	Updates information for an existing resource consumer group
Directive plan	CREATE_PLAN_DIRECTIVE	Creates a plan directive to associate resources and resource plans to consumer groups
	DELETE_PLAN_DIRECTIVE	Deletes an existing plan directive
	UPDATE_PLAN_DIRECTIVE	Updates information for an existing plan directive

12

The information in this table is derived from the online documentation that Oracle provides at the Oracle Technology Network site: *www.otn.oracle.com*.

The following steps demonstrate the process that establishes a configuration for the Acme Company, one phase at a time.

Step 1: To establish the pending area, log on as SYS and issue the following statement:

```
SQL> EXEC DBMS_RESOURCE_MANAGER.CREATE_PENDING_AREA;

PL/SQL procedure successfully completed.
```

Step 2: Create three resource plans: INV_PLAN, FIN_PLAN, and ACME_PLAN:

```
SQL> EXEC DBMS_RESOURCE_MANAGER.CREATE_PLAN('INV_PLAN', 'Inventory Department resource plan')

PL/SQL procedure successfully completed.

SQL> EXEC DBMS_RESOURCE_MANAGER.CREATE_PLAN('FIN_PLAN', 'Financial Department resource plan')

PL/SQL procedure successfully completed.

SQL> EXEC DBMS_RESOURCE_MANAGER.CREATE_PLAN('ACME_PLAN', 'Acme Company resource plan')

PL/SQL procedure successfully completed.
```

Step 3: Create six resource consumer groups:

```
SQL> EXEC DBMS_RESOURCE_MANAGER.CREATE_CONSUMER_GROUP('MIS_GROUP', 'MIS consumer group')

PL/SQL procedure successfully completed.

SQL> EXEC DBMS_RESOURCE_MANAGER.CREATE_CONSUMER_GROUP('SALES_GROUP', 'Sales consumer group')

PL/SQL procedure successfully completed.

SQL> EXEC DBMS_RESOURCE_MANAGER.CREATE_CONSUMER_GROUP('REP_GROUP', 'Report consumer group')

PL/SQL procedure successfully completed.

SQL> EXEC DBMS_RESOURCE_MANAGER.CREATE_CONSUMER_GROUP('MKTG_GROUP', 'Marketing consumer group')

PL/SQL procedure successfully completed.

SQL> EXEC DBMS_RESOURCE_MANAGER.CREATE_CONSUMER_GROUP('PROC_GROUP', 'Process consumer group')

PL/SQL procedure successfully completed.

SQL> EXEC DBMS_RESOURCE_MANAGER.CREATE_CONSUMER_GROUP('ACCT_GROUP', 'Accounting consumer group')

PL/SQL procedure successfully completed.
```

Step 4: Create a resource plan directive by using the procedure CREATE_PLAN_DIREC-TIVE. Table 12-6 describes every parameter in this procedure.

Table 12-6 Parameter descriptions of the CREATE_PLAN_DIRECTIVE procedure

Parameter	Description
PLAN	Name of resource plan
GROUP_OR_SUBPLAN	Name of resource consumer group or subplan
COMMENT	Remarks about the directive

Parameter	Description
CPU_P1	Specification of CPU usage percentage for priority level 1; default is NULL
CPU_P2	Specification of CPU usage percentage for priority level 2; default is NULL
CPU_P3	Specification of CPU usage percentage for priority level 3; default is NULL
CPU_P4	Specification of CPU usage percentage for priority level 4; default is NULL
CPU_P5	Specification of CPU usage percentage for priority level 5; default is NULL
CPU_P6	Specification of CPU usage percentage for priority level 6; default is NULL
CPU_P7	Specification of CPU usage percentage for priority level 7; default is NULL
CPU_P8	Specification of CPU usage percentage for priority level 8; default is NULL
ACTIVE_SESS_POOL_P1	Specification of the maximum number of concurrent active sessions for a resource consumer group; default is unlimited
QUEUEING_P1	Specification of time-out in seconds for a job waiting to be executed; default is unlimited
PARALLEL_DEGREE_LIMIT_P1	Specification of degree of parallelism for any operation, default is unlimited
SWITCH_GROUP	Specification of the consumer group to switch to after the job has waited for execution and a time-out has occurred
SWITCH_TIME	Specification of amount of time in seconds to wait for execution before the procedure is switched to another consumer group
SWITCH_ESTIMATE	Indication that Oracle will use an execution time estimate to switch to a different execution time. Accepted values are True or False.
MAX_EST_EXEC_TIME	Specification of maximum execution time allowed for a session; default is unlimited
UNDO_POOL	Specification of the maximum number of kilobytes on the total amount of undo generated by a consumer group; default is unlimited.

12

The information in this table is derived from the online documentation that Oracle provides at the Oracle Technology Network site: *www.otn.orcle.com*.

Note that every plan must have the resource consumer group OTHER_GROUPS assigned even if it is 0 percent CPU usage.

```
--ACME_PLAN
SQL> BEGIN
  2       DBMS_RESOURCE_MANAGER.CREATE_PLAN_DIRECTIVE(PLAN=>'ACME_PLAN',
  3                              GROUP_OR_SUBPLAN=>'INV_PLAN',
  4                                  COMMENT=>'Inventory Department Plan',
  5                                    CPU_P1=>20);
  6  END;
  7  /

PL/SQL procedure successfully completed.

SQL> BEGIN
  2       DBMS_RESOURCE_MANAGER.CREATE_PLAN_DIRECTIVE(PLAN=>'ACME_PLAN',
  3                              GROUP_OR_SUBPLAN=>'MIS_GROUP',
  4                                  COMMENT=>'MIS consumer group',
  5                                    CPU_P1=>30);
  6  END;
  7  /

PL/SQL procedure successfully completed.

SQL> BEGIN
  2       DBMS_RESOURCE_MANAGER.CREATE_PLAN_DIRECTIVE(PLAN=>'ACME_PLAN',
  3                              GROUP_OR_SUBPLAN=>'FIN_PLAN',
  4                                  COMMENT=>'Financial Team Plan',
  5                                    CPU_P1=>50);
  6  END;
  7  /

PL/SQL procedure successfully completed.

SQL> BEGIN
  2       DBMS_RESOURCE_MANAGER.CREATE_PLAN_DIRECTIVE(PLAN=>'ACME_PLAN',
  3                              GROUP_OR_SUBPLAN=>'OTHER_GROUPS',
  4                                  COMMENT=>'Other Groups',
  5                                    CPU_P1=>0);
  6* END;
SQL> /

PL/SQL procedure successfully completed.

--INV_PLAN
SQL> BEGIN
  2       DBMS_RESOURCE_MANAGER.CREATE_PLAN_DIRECTIVE(PLAN=>'INV_PLAN',
  3                              GROUP_OR_SUBPLAN=>'SALES_GROUP',
  4                                  COMMENT=>'Sales Group',
  5                                    CPU_P1=>40);
  6  END;
  7  /

PL/SQL procedure successfully completed.
```

```
SQL> BEGIN
  2       DBMS_RESOURCE_MANAGER.CREATE_PLAN_DIRECTIVE(PLAN=>'INV_PLAN',
  3                                      GROUP_OR_SUBPLAN=>'REP_GROUP',
  4                                               COMMENT=>'Reporting Group',
  5                                               CPU_P1=>20);
  6  END;
  7  /

PL/SQL procedure successfully completed.

SQL> BEGIN
  2       DBMS_RESOURCE_MANAGER.CREATE_PLAN_DIRECTIVE(PLAN=>'INV_PLAN',
  3                                      GROUP_OR_SUBPLAN=>'MKTG_GROUP',
  4                                               COMMENT=>'Marketing Group',
  5                                               CPU_P1=>40);
  6  END;
  7  /

PL/SQL procedure successfully completed.

SQL> BEGIN
  2       DBMS_RESOURCE_MANAGER.CREATE_PLAN_DIRECTIVE(PLAN=>'INV_PLAN',
  3                                      GROUP_OR_SUBPLAN=>'OTHER_GROUPS',
  4                                               COMMENT=>'Other Groups',
  5                                               CPU_P1=>0);
  6  END;
  7  /

PL/SQL procedure successfully completed.

--FIN_PLAN
SQL> BEGIN
  2       DBMS_RESOURCE_MANAGER.CREATE_PLAN_DIRECTIVE(PLAN=>'FIN_PLAN',
  3                                      GROUP_OR_SUBPLAN=>'PROC_GROUP',
  4                                               COMMENT=>'Process Group',
  5                                               CPU_P1=>50);
  6  END;
  7  /

PL/SQL procedure successfully completed.

SQL> BEGIN
  2       DBMS_RESOURCE_MANAGER.CREATE_PLAN_DIRECTIVE(PLAN=>'FIN_PLAN',
  3                                      GROUP_OR_SUBPLAN=>'ACCT_GROUP',
  4                                               COMMENT=>'Accounting Group',
  5                                               CPU_P1=>50);
  6  END;
  7  /

PL/SQL procedure successfully completed.
```

12

```
SQL> BEGIN
  2       DBMS_RESOURCE_MANAGER.CREATE_PLAN_DIRECTIVE(PLAN=>'FIN_PLAN',
  3                                    GROUP_OR_SUBPLAN=>'OTHER_GROUPS',
  4                                             COMMENT=>'Other Groups',
  5                                             CPU_P1=>0);
  6  END;
  7  /

PL/SQL procedure successfully completed.
```

Step 5: Validate the resource plan and directives.

```
SQL> EXEC DBMS_RESOURCE_MANAGER.VALIDATE_PENDING_AREA

PL/SQL procedure successfully completed.
```

Step 6: Submit the resource plan and directives.

```
SQL> EXEC DBMS_RESOURCE_MANAGER.SUBMIT_PENDING_AREA

PL/SQL procedure successfully completed.
```

Step 7: Associate users with consumer groups. In this step, you assign users to consumer groups as follows:

TUNER	➜	SALES_GROUP
DEMO	➜	MKTG_GROUP
SCOTT	➜	ACCT_GROUP
PERFSTAT	➜	MIS_GROUP
HR	➜	REP_GROUP

NOTE If any of the users previously listed do not exist, you can substitute for the missing user another user in your database; SYS and SYSTEM, however, cannot be substituted for a missing user.

To perform this task, you need to use another Oracle PL/SQL package called DBMS_RESOURCE_MANAGER_PRIVS. Table 12-7 lists all procedures and their descriptions.

Table 12-7 DBMS_RESOURCE_MANAGER_PRIVS procedures

Procedure	Description
GRANT_SWITCH_CONSUMER_GROUP	Grants permission to a user, role, or PUBLIC to switch to a consumer group
GRANT_SYSTEM_PRIVILEGE	Grants ADMINISTER_RESOURCE_MANAGER system privilege to a user or role
REVOKE_SWITCH_CONSUMER_GROUP	Revokes ADMINISTER_RESOURCE_MANAGER system privilege from a group
REVOKE_SYSTEM_PRIVILEGE	Revokes ADMINISTER_RESOURCE_MANAGER system privilege from a user or role

The information in this table is derived from the online documentation that Oracle provides at the Oracle Technology Network site: *www.otn.oracle.com.*

NOTE

For a user to switch from one consumer group to another, you must grant him permission to do so.

12

```
SQL> -- TUNER => SALES_GROUP
SQL> BEGIN
  2     DBMS_RESOURCE_MANAGER_PRIVS.GRANT_SWITCH_CONSUMER_GROUP('TUNER',
  3                                           'SALES_GROUP',
  4                                                   FALSE);
  5  END;
  6  /

PL/SQL procedure successfully completed.

SQL> -- DEMO => MKTG_GROUP
SQL> BEGIN
  2     DBMS_RESOURCE_MANAGER_PRIVS.GRANT_SWITCH_CONSUMER_GROUP('DEMO',
  3                                           'MKTG_GROUP',
  4                                                   FALSE);
  5  END;
  6  /

PL/SQL procedure successfully completed.

SQL> -- SCOTT => ACCT_GROUP
SQL> BEGIN
  2     DBMS_RESOURCE_MANAGER_PRIVS.GRANT_SWITCH_CONSUMER_GROUP('SCOTT',
  3                                           'ACCT_GROUP',
  4                                                   FALSE);
  5  END;
  6  /

PL/SQL procedure successfully completed.
```

```
SQL> -- PERFSTAT => MIS_GROUP
SQL> BEGIN
  2      DBMS_RESOURCE_MANAGER_PRIVS.GRANT_SWITCH_CONSUMER_GROUP('PERFSTAT',
  3                                                              'MIS_GROUP',
  4                                                                  FALSE);
  5  END;
  6  /

PL/SQL procedure successfully completed.

SQL> -- HR => REP_GROUP
SQL> BEGIN
  2      DBMS_RESOURCE_MANAGER_PRIVS.GRANT_SWITCH_CONSUMER_GROUP('HR',
  3                                                              'REP_GROUP',
  4                                                                  FALSE);
  5  END;
  6  /

PL/SQL procedure successfully completed.
```

Step 8: Associate the plan to an Oracle instance. In this task, you need to set the initialization parameter RESOURCE_MANAGER_PLAN to the ACME_PLAN. This parameter can be dynamically set.

```
SQL> ALTER SYSTEM SET RESOURCE_MANAGER_PLAN = ACME_PLAN
  2  /

System altered.

SQL> SHOW PARAMETER RESOURCE_MANAGER_PLAN

NAME                                 TYPE        VALUE
------------------------------------ ----------- ----------
resource_manager_plan                string      ACME_PLAN
```

Congratulations—you're finished!

Viewing Resource Manager Data

Table 12-8 lists DBA data dictionary views that contain data about the Database Resource Manager.

Table 12-8   Database Resource Manager DBA views

View	Description
DBA_RSRC_CONSUMER_GROUPS	Contains information about existing resource consumer groups
DBA_RSRC_CONSUMER_GROUP_PRIVS	Contains information about consumer group privileges assigned to users, roles, or PUBLIC

View	Description
DBA_RSRC_MANAGER_SYSTEM_PRIVS	Contains information about system privileges for the resource manager
DBA_RSRC_PLANS	Contains information about all existing resource plans
DBA_RSRC_PLAN_DIRECTIVES	Contains information about all resources and resource plans associated with consumer groups

The information in this table is derived from the online documentation that Oracle provides at the Oracle Technology Network site: *www.otn.oracle.com.*

The following code segment displays a list of all consumer groups created in this database:

```
SQL> SELECT CONSUMER_GROUP, CPU_METHOD
  2     FROM DBA_RSRC_CONSUMER_GROUPS
  3  /

CONSUMER_GROUP                  CPU_METHOD
------------------------------  -----------
OTHER_GROUPS                    ROUND-ROBIN
DEFAULT_CONSUMER_GROUP          ROUND-ROBIN
SYS_GROUP                       ROUND-ROBIN
LOW_GROUP                       ROUND-ROBIN
MIS_GROUP                       ROUND-ROBIN
SALES_GROUP                     ROUND-ROBIN
REP_GROUP                       ROUND-ROBIN
MKTG_GROUP                      ROUND-ROBIN
PROC_GROUP                      ROUND-ROBIN
ACCT_GROUP                      ROUND-ROBIN
```

12

Table 12-9 lists all V$ dynamic performance views used to monitor the Resource Manager configuration.

Table 12-9   Resource Manager V$ views

View	Description
V$RSRC_CONSUMER_GROUP	Current activities for all resource consumer groups
V$RSRC_CONSUMER_GROUP_CPU_MTH	All active resource consumer groups' methods
V$RSRC_PLAN	All active resource plans
V$RSRC_PLAN_CPU_MTH	All active resource plans' methods

The information in this table is derived from the online documentation that Oracle provides at the Oracle Technology Network site: *www.otn.oracle.com.*

The following query lists all active resource plans:

```
SQL> SELECT *
  2    FROM V$RSRC_PLAN
  3  /

NAME
----------------------
ACME_PLAN
INV_PLAN
FIN_PLAN
```

CHAPTER SUMMARY

❑ The Alert log file is the heartbeat of the system, registering errors, events, and database activities.

❑ Each time a background process fails, an error is generated to the Alert log and a trace file is generated.

❑ V$ views are synonyms for GV_ views that are populated from Oracle base tables.

❑ DBA data dictionary views obtain information related to storage space.

❑ The following parameters configure the level of statistics collection:

  ▪ STATISTICS_LEVEL

  ▪ TIMED_OS_STATISTICS

  ▪ TIMED_STATISTICS

  ▪ DB_CACHE_ADVICE

❑ UTLBSTAT/UTLESTAT is a simple tool for collecting performance statistics and generating reports.

❑ STATSPACK was developed to replace UTLBSTAT/UTLESTAT.

❑ STATSPACK is an enhanced tool for collecting statistics that help you diagnose and troubleshoot database performance.

❑ STATSPACK collects statistics and stores them in the repository for a period of time.

❑ The name of the STATSPACK tool is prefixed with STAT$.

❑ The gathering of statistics can be automated by using the provided script named SPAUTO.SQL.

❑ The SPREPORT.SQL script produces a report that can be viewed using any text editor.

❑ The SPPURGE.SQL script deletes a snapshot.

❑ The SPTRUNC.SQL script removes all snapshots collected in the repository.

❑ The EXPLAIN PLAN command generates an execution plan for a query.

❑ The DBMS_XPLAN package retrieves the execution plan from the plan table and formats the output to be readable.

❑ AUTOTRACE provides a simple way to generate an execution plan as well as query statistics without the need to write any query to retrieve the execution plan.

❑ SQL Trace and TKPROF work together to trace a session and generate an execution plan and statistics for a session.

❑ DBVERIFY and DBMS_REPAIR are tools that detect data block corruption.

❑ The following commands analyze database objects: ANALYZE, DBMS_STATS, DBMS_UTILITY, and DBMS_DDL.

❑ The Database Resource Manager distributes CPU and other resources to users based on priorities set by the DBA.

❑ No initialization parameters are presented in this chapter.

❑ Views used in this chapter include the following:

- DBA_SEGMENTS
- DBA_ROLES
- DBA_TABLES
- DBA_INDEXES
- DBA_RSRC_CONSUMER_GROUPS
- DBA_RSRC_CONSUMER_GROUP_PRIVS
- DBA_RSRC_MANAGER_SYSTEM_PRIVS
- DBA_RSRC_PLANS
- DBA_RSRC_PLAN_DIRECTIVES
- DBA_EXTENTS
- DBA_SEGMENTS
- DBA_TABLESPACES
- DBA_DATA_FILES
- DBA_TABLES
- DBA_INDEXES
- V$DATAFILE
- V$FIXED_VIEW_DEFINITION
- V$PROCESS
- V$RSRC_CONSUMER_GROUP
- V$RSRC_CONSUMER_GROUP_CPU_MTH
- V$RSRC_PLAN
- V$RSRC_PLAN_CPU_MTH
- V$SESSION

12

- V$SESSTAT
- V$STATISTICS_LEVEL
- V$TABLESPACE

◻ PL/SQL packages used in this chapter include the following:
  - DBMS_DDL
  - DBMS_JOB
  - DBMS_OUTPUT
  - DBMS_STATS
  - DBMS_SYSTEM
  - DBMS_REPAIR
  - DBMS_RESOURCE_MANAGER
  - DBMS_RESOURCE_MANAGER_PRIVS
  - DBMS_UTILITY
  - DBMS_XPLAN

REVIEW QUESTIONS

1. The BACKGROUND_DUMP_DESTINATION initialization parameter configures the location of the Alert log. (True/False)

2. You can view the date and time when an archive log is generated in the Alert log. (True/False)

3. When a trace file is generated, file information is recorded in the Alert log about the generated trace file. (True/False)

4. V$ views are flushed when an Oracle instance is started. (True/False)

5. You can use the V$FIXED_VIEW_DEFINITION to view the purpose of V$ views. (True/False)

6. ALL values for TIMED_STATISICS indicate that all types of statistics are enabled and collected. (True/False)

7. UTLBSTAT/UTLESTAT is still supported even though it was replaced by the STATSPACK tool. (True/False)

8. In concept, STATSPACK works similarly to UTLBSTAT/UTLESTAT. (True/False)

9. Use SPCUSR.SQL, SPCTAB.SQL, and SPCPKG to create all the components of STATSPACK. (True/False)

10. Use statistic level 10 for STATPACK when you need detailed statistics to analyze performance. (True/False)

11. You use SPPURGE.SQL when you want to purge all snapshots in the STATSPACK repository. (True/False)

12. You should run the ORACLE_HOME/rdbms/admin/utlxplan.sql script each time you need to use EXPLAIN PLAN command. (True/False)

13. The AUTOTRACE tool from SQL*Plus allows you to automatically generate query statistics. (True/False)

14. The TKPROF tool generates an execution plan for any session. (True/False)

15. You need system process identification numbers to identify the name of the trace file generated by the SQL Trace tool. (True/False)

16. If you want to detect whether a data file is corrupted or not, you can use DBV, but the data file must be offline. (True/False)

17. Oracle recommends the use of DBMS_STATS because it provides much functionality for analyzing database objects. (True/False)

18. You use the SET_INITIAL_CONSUMER_GROUP procedure to assign a database user to a resource consumer group. (True/False)

19. Your manager sent you an e-mail asking you to assist a developer who is trying to tune queries. Outline the steps you would take to assist the developer to tune his queries.

20. List the reasons why you would not use STATSPACK.

21. List reasons why you would not use the EXPAIN PLAN command to get the execution of a query.

22. List three disadvantages to using UTLBSTAT/UTLESTAT.

23. Outline steps to record checkpoint date and time to the Alert log.

24. List three reasons for using the Database Resource Manager and three reasons for not using it.

25. An Oracle expert once said that tuning a database is just like tuning a piano. What did this expert mean?

26. Generate a listing of all static and dynamic views.

12

Exam Review Questions: Oracle9i Performance Tuning (#1Z0-033)

1. A user called you the other day and asked you how he could generate the execution plan for his query. What tool would you recommend?

    a. The EXPLAIN PLAN command

    b. DBMS_XPLAN

    c. SQL Trace

    d. Oracle Enterprise Manager

2. What tool would you use to update and gather statistics for tuning analysis?

    a. DBMS_STATS

    b. DBMS_STATSPACK

    c. DBMS_UTILITY

    d. DBMS_DDL

    e. ANALYZE command

3. What parameter would you set to collect MTTR advisory statistics?

    a. MTTR_ADVICE

    b. STATISTICS_LEVEL

    c. TIMED_STATISTICS

    d. MTTR_STATISTICS

4. What should you do if you get an ORA-00600 error alert?

    a. Resolve the problem right away.

    b. Shut down the database and investigate the problem.

    c. Call Oracle technical support and investigate the problem further.

    d. Call Oracle technical support if the problem is persistent.

5. Which information is not registered in the Alert log file?

    a. Database startup and shutdown times

    b. Physical database changes

    c. Trace file information and content generated by a background process failure

    d. ORA-*xxxx* errors

6. What initialization parameter must you set to record checkpoint time in Alert log?

   a. No need to set any initialization parameters because this checkpoint cannot be recorded in the Alert log.

   b. Checkpoint time can be turned on using LOG_CHECK-POINT_TO_ALERT.

   c. LOG_CHECKPOINT

   d. CHECKPOINT_ALERT

7. What is the name of the file generated by UTLBSTAT/UTLESTAT?

   a. STAT.TXT

   b. REPORT.TXT

   c. UTLSTAT.TXT

   d. UTLBSTAT.TXT

   e. UTLESTAT.TXT

8. What is the username for the owner of the STATSPACK repository?

   a. STATS

   b. STATSPACK

   c. PERF

   d. PERFSTAT

   e. PERFPACK

   f. PERFSTATS

   g. PERFSTATSPACK

9. Which component of STATSPACK is not created or part of this tool?

   a. STATSPACK repository

   b. STATSPACK stored package

   c. STATSPACK scripts

   d. STATSPACK tablespace

12

10. Which STATSPACK script would you run to generate a report?

    a. sperepsql.sql

    b. spreport.sql

    c. sprep.sql

    d. sprepins.sql

    e. spstatrep.sql

11. Which STATSPACK view would you use to list time statistics collected by the STATSPACK package?

    a. STATS$DATABASE

    b. STATS$INSTANCE

    c. STATS$SNAPSHOT

    d. STATS$SYSSTAT

    e. STATS$STATSPACK_TIME

12. Which of the following is not a stored procedure of the STATSPACK tool?

    a. MODIFY_STATSPACK_PARAMETER

    b. QAM_STATSPACK_PARAMETER

    c. SNAP

    d. STAT_CHANGES

    e. STATSHOT

13. Which username would you use to log on before you install STATSPACK?

    a. SYSTEM

    b. DBA

    c. STATSPACK

    d. All of the above

    e. None of the above

14. Which statement is not a valid list of statistic levels for STATSPACK?

    a. 0, 1, 2, 3, 4, 5

    b. 0, 5, 6, 7, 8, 9

    c. 0, 5, 6, 7, 10

    d. 0, 6, 7, 8, 10

    e. 0, 6, 7, 8, 10

    f. 0, 6, 7, 9, 10

15. What STATSPACK facility would you use to automate collecting statistics?

    a. AUTOSTAT procedure

    b. DBMS_JOB package

    c. DBMS_STATSPACK package

    d. SPAUTO.SQL script

    e. SPASTAT.SQL script

16. Which tool does not generate an execution plan?

    a. EXPLAIN PLAN command

    b. Oracle Enterprise Manager

    c. DBMS_SQL_PLAN

    d. SQL Trace

17. What is required to generate an execution plan?

    a. PLAN table

    b. PLAN_TABLE table

    c. EXPLAIN PLAN command privilege

    d. access to the plan table

18. Which tool would you use to generate an execution plan when you issue a query?

    a. EXPLAIN PLAN command

    b. SQL Trace

    c. SQL*Plus AUTOTRACE facility

    d. TKPROF

12

19. What role does a user need to be able to use PLUSTRACE?

    a. AUTOTRACE

    b. TRACEPLUS

    c. SQLPLUSTRACE

    d. PLUSTRACE

20. To perform SQL tracing on a session, you need all the pieces of information listed below except one—which one?

    a. session ID

    b. SQL statement

    c. serial number

    d. process ID

    e. username

21. What database package would you use to initiate and terminate SQL tracing?

    a. DBMS_UTILITY

    b. DBMS_STATS

    c. DBMS_SQL_TRACE

    d. DBMS_SYSTEM

22. Which tool can detect data block corruption?

    a. DBV

    b. DBVERIFY

    c. DBMS_BLOCK_REPAIR

    d. DVERIFY

23. What is required to detect block corruption when you are using the DBMS_REPAIR package?

    a. Create REPAIR table.

    b. Create REPAIR_TABLE table.

    c. Privilege to repair table.

    d. Nothing is required.

24. Which resource is not controlled by the Database Resource Manager?

   a. CPU

   b. memory

   c. undo segments

   d. degree of parallelism

25. Rearrange the following actions in the correct order to configure the Database Resource Manager.

   a. Create pending area.

   b. Create resource plan.

   c. Create consumer groups.

   d. Create plan directives.

   e. Validate and submit changes.

   f. Assign users to consumer groups.

   g. Assign Resource Manager to the Oracle instance.

26. Which statement is not related to the Database Resource Manager?

   a. DBMS_RESOURCE_MANAGER

   b. DBMS_RESOURCE_MANAGER_PRIVS

   c. RESOURCE_MANAGER_PLAN

   d. RESOURCE_PLAN

12

HANDS-ON PROJECTS

Please complete the projects provided below.

1. Reread the Performance Problem set out at the start of the chapter. Think of it in terms of the concepts you have learned in this chapter and answer the following questions:

   a. What tool would you recommend and why?

   b. Answer the questions posed by George: "Are you aware of similar rival products? And how would you rank them?"

   c. Is there a need for other tools to generate an execution plan for a query? If so, indicate what is missing in the tools provided by Oracle.

2. One of the users from the Business Department sent you an e-mail complaining about the performance of the database when they run their daily reports. He explained that the reports are taking a long time, and this is hindering the department operations. He asked if you could prevent people from using the database while reports are running. Outline the steps that you would take to resolve this problem and the tools that you would use.

3. You work in a large organization in which contract personnel perform certain actions on an Oracle database. You need to be able to track all SQL statements to identify all problematic queries. You do not want to use SQL Trace because you do not have access to the trace files where they are generated. List three different tools that you can use and the steps for using each tool.

4. Using SQL*Plus, create two different sessions connecting as TUNER. Place one session to the left and the second to the right. Suppose you want to trace the session on the left; list preparation steps to perform this task.

5. As you were enjoying your lunch, you got a call from the vice president asking you to drop everything and come to her office. At her office you were surprised to see your manager there looking concerned. Your manager said that all users were noticing high performance problems and this had been going on for a while. List three tasks you missed that produced this problem. For each task, specify the tool you would use.

6. Suppose you have installed STATSPACK, and you want to perform trend analysis on the configuration of the shared pool. Outline the steps you would take to use STATSPACK to perform this task.

7. Write a script to automatically read the last query you submitted and generate the execution plan for the query without using the AUTOTRACE tool or EXPLAIN PLAN command.

8. Suppose you were hired as a manager for a database group of four DBAs managing several databases. On your first week at work you took an inventory of tools used by your DBAs and found that only one third-party tool was being used. Should you be concerned?

9. For each available method or tool, generate an execution plan for the following query using the TUNER schema.

   ■ SELECT * FROM CUSTOMERS, EMPLOYEES

CASE PROJECTS

1. Manage Resources

You were hired to manage a database for the Acme Company. After you assessed the current hardware and application loaded, you designed the resource plan illustrated in Figure 12-33. After you reviewed this plan with your manager, he asked you to implement this plan. Implement the plan.

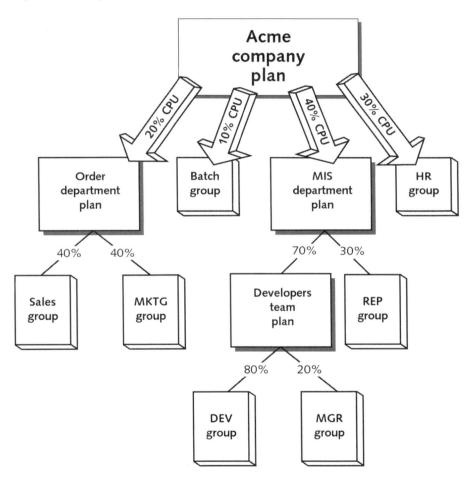

Figure 12-33   Acme Company resource plan

12

2. Where is the Corruption?

As a DBA for the Acme Company, you were given a script to execute, which performs the following tasks:

1. Connects as TUNER schema

2. As SYSTEM, create a tablespace called DBC with a size of 1 M

3. Creates a table called CODE_TBL that has two columns: CODE as Number and DESC as VARCHAR2(20) residing in DBC tablespace

4. Populates the table with 100 rows and commits changes

5. Makes tablespace DBC read-only

Now that you have executed the script, perform the following tasks:

1. Open the datafile of DBC tablespace with Notepad. (Do not use any other program.)

2. Select a chunk of the file and delete and save, overwriting the existing file.

3. Bounce the database.

4. Log in as TUNER and query CODE_TBL. What happened?

5. Detect if there is block corruption using DBVERIFY and DBMS_REPAIR.

Can you fix this corruption with these tools?

PART
VI

Application Tuning

SQL TUNING

In this chapter you will:

◆ Understand the difference between optimizer modes and goals

◆ Interpret execution queries

◆ Understand and use optimizer hints

◆ Use optimizer-related parameters

◆ Identify SQL queries that consume the highest amount of resources

◆ Understand the need for SQL standards

◆ Prevent slow SQL execution

◆ Work through SQL analysis examples

◆ Learn to use outlines

If you have worked in a company that uses information technology (needless to say, most of them do), you must have heard people around the office talking about a report taking too long to generate, a runaway query (a query that is running so slowly that it seems never to finish), or database applications taking ages to respond. Believe it or not, most of the time these types of problems are caused by badly written queries.

In Chapter 12, you learned how to use tools to perform various tuning tasks to detect and identify tuning performance problems, specifically problematic queries that degrade and consume system resources, which in turn degrade database performance. Knowing how to use these tools, however, is not sufficient; you need to be able to analyze the results generated by these tools in order to take the proper action.

In this chapter, you focus on one of the most common tuning performance problems in SQL statements. You learn how a statement is executed and the implications of this execution. You also learn the Oracle Optimizer modes, Rule-based and Cost-based, which determine how SQL statements execute. Next you delve into a list of initialization parameters that influence the optimizer. Then you shift gears to learn how to interpret execution plans produced by the optimizer. Once you understand how to analyze queries, you are shown how to use Oracle hints to influence the behavior of the optimizer. Then you will be presented with the dos and don'ts of writing queries and enhancing query performance. Finally, you learn how to use an Oracle feature called Outlines and Outline Manager.

Be warned, this chapter has plenty of query examples. Start SQL*Plus and put on your thinking cap—you are about to explore the world of query optimization.

Performance Problem

This section outlines an actual performance problem. As you look it over, imagine yourself as the DBA who reported it and keep it in mind as you proceed through the chapter. The chapter presents concepts relevant to the problem. In the first Hands-on Project at the end of the chapter, you are asked to use the concepts you have learned to provide a solution, or partial solution, to this performance problem.

From: Conny Kerry <mailto: conny.kerry@query.com>
Date: 23-Jan-03 03:15
Subject: Explain this!!!

Explain this for me please because I am stumped!

I have a query that is issued against a large table. Here is what the query looks like:

```
SELECT C1, C2, C3, C4
  FROM T1
 WHERE C1 = :1
   AND C4 BETWEEN :2 AND :3
```

Please note that an index exists on C1 and C4. Now here is the problem: when I use bind variables with BETWEEN in a WHERE clause, the query takes forever to return. But if I replace the bind variables :2 and :3 with their literal values, the query returns very quickly.

Confused,

Conny!!!

ORACLE OPTIMIZER

Li, a salesperson for a big, well known company, was traveling to Chicago for a conference and picked up an IT magazine at the airport. As she was browsing the magazine, she came across an article entitled "The Collapse of an Application: Bad Queries." She was interested in the topic because she markets and sells a database application. After reading every word of the article, she could not wait to talk to Ruby, the chief architect of the development team, to tell her what she had read, so she e-mailed Ruby as follows: "Hello, Ruby, I read an article about how bad queries can cause performance problems, and the author discussed Oracle's two optimizer modes and how each works. I am very concerned that the response time problem we are having in our application may be stemming from bad queries." Ruby replied, "Li, you are right to be concerned, and I'm glad that you mentioned it, because that is exactly the problem. I just put in a requisition to hire an application DBA consultant to tackle this problem! I assure you that we will get a handle on this."

Surprised? Don't be! It's a fact that bad queries exist in small and big companies. Before you start learning how to analyze queries and identify problematic queries, you need to look at how the Oracle optimizer generates an execution plan. By now, you already have some idea about Oracle optimizer, especially if you have read Chapter 12. So, what is it? The best way to answer this question is to offer an analogy.

Suppose you live in the city of Framingham in the Greater Boston area, as shown in Figure 13-1, which is about 20 miles from your job in Boston. As the figure shows, you can take several routes from Framingham to get to Boston. The question is, which route would you take? Route 90, 93, 95, 495, back roads, or a combination thereof? What are the criteria that would influence your selection of a particular route?

- Previous experience taking the route (statistics)
- Familiarity with route
- Distance to job
- Traffic congestion
- Weather reports

13

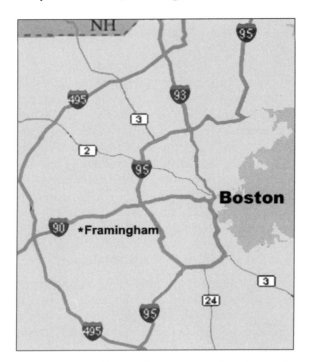

Figure 13-1   Greater Boston area showing major routes to Boston

So every morning you read and watch the weather and traffic reports. After a while you determine the best route to take every morning, if there are no unusual problems such as construction work or heavy traffic.

Now think of this analogy in the context of Oracle optimizer. Imagine that you are the optimizer and the action of going to work to Boston (target) is the action of accessing data from a data file (target). The Oracle optimizer can decide how to get to the data based on available statistics such as:

- Tables have been analyzed and statistics made available (previous experience of taking the route)

- Length of rows and tables (distance to the job)

- Amount of data to be retrieved (traffic congestion)

- Index availability (weather report)

- Syntax and statement ranking (familiarity with route)

As you can see, Oracle optimizer is an integral module of the Oracle engine, which can influence performance. **Oracle optimizer** is an algorithm that tries to determine the most efficient way to execute a SQL statement and retrieve data. Oracle optimizer performs the following functions when evaluating a SQL statement:

- Evaluates the expressions and conditions contained in the SQL statement

- Transforms complex queries into an equivalent join query

- Chooses an optimization goal, either the Cost-based Optimizer (CBO) or the Rule-based Optimizer (RBO)

- Determines how to access each table to retrieve data

- Determines the order of table joins for statements involving more than two tables

- Chooses the type of join to be performed for each pair

 The optimizer chooses the best and most efficient plan, which means the plan uses minimal resources and executes as fast as possible.

NOTE

Oracle optimizer is largely influenced by the mode in which it is set. The next section presents the different types of modes that can be configured.

Optimizer Modes

Oracle optimizer plays an important role in how SQL statements are executed and data is retrieved. As a result, SQL tuning is a major and primary task for the developer, and identifying problematic SQL statements has the highest priority for the DBA. For these specific reasons, Oracle has worked hard to provide different levels of optimization. These levels can be configured at the system (instance), session, or statement level.

Although Oracle optimizer is very efficient, it doesn't always pick the most efficient way of executing and retrieving data. For that reason, you need to generate an Explain Plan for the SQL statement (as shown in Chapter 12) to determine if the optimizer has picked the best method and if any enhancement is required. Before you get into interpreting Explain Plans, you need an overview of the different optimization modes to help understand how they differ and when each is used.

Different parameters are used to configure the **optimizer mode** for either all sessions or for individual sessions. To configure the optimizer for the whole system so that every session created uses this setting, use the initialization parameter, OPTIMIZER_MODE. On the other hand, if you want to use the optimizer only at the session level, use the OPTI-MIZER_GOAL parameter. Only the OPTIMIZER_GOAL parameter can be set dynamically. Figure 13-2 illustrates that OPTIMIZER_MODE is set in the initialization parameter file, whereas OPTIMIZER_GOAL is set by issuing the ALTER SESSION statement, which impacts the current session only.

13

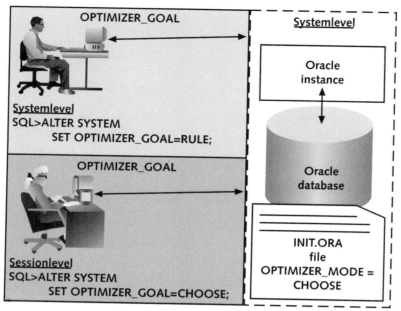

Figure 13-2   Optimizer mode and optimizer goal settings

Figure 13-3 illustrates the two modes, the Rule-based Optimizer (RBO), which is founded on SQL syntax and uses predetermined rules to execute a query, and the Cost-based Optimizer (CBO), which is based on statistics, which it uses to determine the execution plan. Note that the terms execution plan and Explain Plan are synonymous.

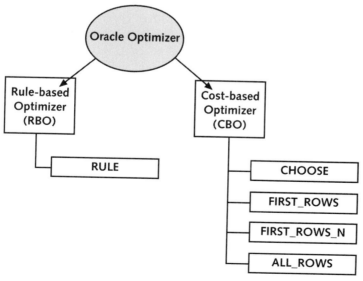

Figure 13-3   Optimizer mode settings

Rule-based Optimizer (RBO)

The **Rule-based Optimizer** determines the most efficient way to execute the SQL statement using a set of rules and a ranking system. This Optimizer evaluates the query using different execution paths to select the one that produces the lowest rank value.

Table 13-1 lists the ranks for all possible paths in the RBO—the lower the rank, the faster the path. As you can see, Rank 15 is a full table scan, which implies it is the slowest path to retrieve data. In contrast, Rank 1 accesses data by ROWID, which is the fastest way. A full table scan is a data access method used by the Oracle optimizer. With this method, the optimizer scans every row in a table to retrieve data.

Table 13-1   Rule-based Optimizer ranks

Rank	Path
1	Single row by ROWID
2	Single row by cluster join
3	Single row by hash cluster key with unique or primary key
4	Single row using primary or unique key
5	Cluster join
6	Hash cluster key
7	Indexed cluster key
8	Composite index
9	Single-column indexes
10	Bounded range search on indexed columns
11	Unbounded range search on indexed columns
12	Sort merge join
13	MAX or MIN on indexed column
14	ORDER BY indexed column
15	Full table scan

13

The information in this table is derived from the online documentation that Oracle provides at the Oracle Technology Network site: *www.otn.oracle.com*.

The following is an explanation of each rank with an example showing the Explain Plan. To get a feeling for this process, step through the examples that follow. Before trying these examples, first, log on as TUNER and set the OPTIMIZER_GOAL to RULE:

```
SQL> CONNECT TUNER/TUNER@SAM
Connected.

SQL> ALTER SESSION SET OPTIMIZER_GOAL=RULE
  2  /

Session altered.

SQL> SET AUTOTRACE TRACEONLY EXPLAIN
```

 NOTE   RBO does not need statistics to evaluate an execution path. Therefore the ANALYZE statement is not needed if the SYSYEM or statement being used is set to RBO.

Rank 1: This path is available when a SQL statement contains a WHERE clause identifying rows by ROWID:

```
SQL> SELECT EMPLOYEE_ID
  2     FROM EMPLOYEES
  3  WHERE ROWID = 'AAAHczAAJAAAA54AAR'
  4  /

Execution Plan
----------------------------------------------------------
  0        SELECT STATEMENT Optimizer=RULE
  1    0    TABLE ACCESS (BY USER ROWID) OF 'EMPLOYEES'
```

Rank 2: This path is available when two tables are clustered together. An example of a cluster is ACTIVITY and STATUS_CODE. These two tables will be clustered by CODE_ID:

```
SQL> CREATE CLUSTER CODES
  2  (CODE_ID NUMBER)
  3  /

Cluster created.

SQL> CREATE TABLE ACTIVITY
  2  (ACTIVITY_ID     NUMBER,
  3   DESCRIPTION     VARCHAR2(80),
  4   ACTIVITY_DATE   DATE,
  5   CODE_ID         NUMBER
  6  )
  7  CLUSTER CODES(CODE_ID)
  8  /

Table created.

SQL> CREATE TABLE STATUS_CODE
  2  (CODE_ID      NUMBER,
  3   DESCRIPTION VARCHAR2(20)
  4  )
  5  CLUSTER CODES(CODE_ID)
  6  /

Table created.

SQL> CREATE INDEX IDX_CODES ON CLUSTER CODES
  2  /

Index created.

SQL> INSERT INTO STATUS_CODE VALUES(1, 'ACTIVE');

1 row created.

SQL> INSERT INTO ACTIVITY VALUES(100, 'CALL DOCTOR', SYSDATE, 1);

1 row created.

SQL> SELECT *
  2    FROM ACTIVITY, STATUS_CODE
  3   WHERE ACTIVITY.CODE_ID = STATUS_CODE.CODE_ID
  4     AND STATUS_CODE.CODE_ID = 1
  5  /

Execution Plan
----------------------------------------------------------
   0      SELECT STATEMENT Optimizer=RULE
   1    0   NESTED LOOPS
   2    1     TABLE ACCESS (CLUSTER) OF 'STATUS_CODE'
   3    2       INDEX (UNIQUE SCAN) OF 'IDX_CODES' (NON-UNIQUE)
   4    1     TABLE ACCESS (CLUSTER) OF 'ACTIVITY'
```

13

Rank 3: This path is available only for hash cluster tables when the WHERE clause contains all columns of the cluster hash key, and the statement returns only one row:

```
SQL> CREATE CLUSTER GRADES_CLUSTER
  2  ( GRADE_ID    NUMBER)
  3  HASHKEYS 5
  4  /

Cluster created.

SQL> CREATE TABLE GRADES
  2  ( GRADE_ID    NUMBER,
  3    DESCRIPTION VARCHAR2(30)
  4  )
  5  CLUSTER GRADES_CLUSTER(GRADE_ID)
  6  /

Table created.

SQL> INSERT INTO GRADES VALUES(1, 'FINAL EXAM')
  2  /

SQL> COMMIT;

SQL> SELECT *
  2    FROM GRADES
  3   WHERE GRADE_ID = 1
  4  /

Execution Plan
-------------------------------------------------
   0      SELECT STATEMENT Optimizer=RULE
   1    0   TABLE ACCESS (HASH) OF 'GRADES'
```

Rank 4: This path is used when a column in the WHERE clause is the primary key or unique key. Oracle uses the index associated with the column to get to the row:

```
SQL> SELECT *
  2    FROM CUSTOMERS
  3   WHERE CUSTOMER_ID = 100
  4  /

Execution Plan
-----------------------------------------------------------
   0      SELECT STATEMENT Optimizer=RULE
   1    0   TABLE ACCESS (BY INDEX ROWID) OF 'CUSTOMERS'
   2    1     INDEX (UNIQUE SCAN) OF 'SYS_C003139' (UNIQUE)
```

Rank 5: This path is available if the two tables being joined reside in the same cluster:

```
SQL> SELECT *
  2    FROM ACTIVITY, STATUS_CODE
  3   WHERE ACTIVITY.CODE_ID = STATUS_CODE.CODE_ID
  4   /

Execution Plan
----------------------------------------------------
   0      SELECT STATEMENT Optimizer=RULE
   1    0   NESTED LOOPS
   2    1     TABLE ACCESS (FULL) OF 'STATUS_CODE'
   3    1     TABLE ACCESS (CLUSTER) OF 'ACTIVITY'
```

Rank 6: This path is available when all columns in the WHERE clause are part of the hash key cluster:

```
SQL> SELECT * FROM GRADES
  2   WHERE GRADE_ID = 1
  3   /

Execution Plan
-------------------------------------------
   0      SELECT STATEMENT Optimizer=RULE
   1    0   TABLE ACCESS (HASH) OF 'GRADES'
```

Rank 7: This path is available when all columns in the WHERE clause are part of the cluster index:

```
SQL> SELECT *
  2    FROM ACTIVITY
  3   WHERE CODE_ID = 1
  4   /

Execution Plan
----------------------------------------------------------
   0      SELECT STATEMENT Optimizer=RULE
   1    0   TABLE ACCESS (CLUSTER) OF 'ACTIVITY'
   2    1     INDEX (UNIQUE SCAN) OF 'IDX_CODES' (NON-UNIQUE)
```

13

Rank 8: This path is available when all columns in the WHERE clause are part of a composite index:

```
SQL> CREATE INDEX IDX_CUS_FIRST_LAST
  2      ON CUSTOMERS(FIRST_NAME, LAST_NAME)
  3  /

Index created.

SQL> SELECT CUSTOMER_ID, PHONE
  2      FROM CUSTOMERS
  3   WHERE FIRST_NAME = 'Codi'
  4       AND LAST_NAME  = 'Hatton'
  5  /

Execution Plan
----------------------------------------------------------
   0        SELECT STATEMENT Optimizer=RULE
   1    0     TABLE ACCESS (BY INDEX ROWID) OF 'CUSTOMERS'
   2    1       INDEX (RANGE SCAN) OF 'IDX_CUS_FIRST_LAST' (NON-UNIQUE)
```

Rank 9: This path is available when column(s) in the WHERE clause are individually indexed (index on each column):

```
SQL> CREATE INDEX IDX_CUS_PHONE
  2      ON CUSTOMERS(PHONE)
  3  /

Index created.

SQL> CREATE INDEX IDX_ZIP_CODE
  2      ON CUSTOMERS(ZIP_CODE)
  3  /

Index created.

SQL> SELECT CUSTOMER_ID, FIRST_NAME, LAST_NAME
  2      FROM CUSTOMERS
  3   WHERE PHONE = '9477997077'
  4       OR ZIP_CODE = '02112'
  5  /

Execution Plan
----------------------------------------------------------
   0        SELECT STATEMENT Optimizer=RULE
   1    0     CONCATENATION
   2    1       TABLE ACCESS (BY INDEX ROWID) OF 'CUSTOMERS'
   3    2         INDEX (RANGE SCAN) OF 'IDX_ZIP_CODE' (NON-UNIQUE)
   4    1       TABLE ACCESS (BY INDEX ROWID) OF 'CUSTOMERS'
   5    4         INDEX (RANGE SCAN) OF 'IDX_CUS_PHONE' (NON-UNIQUE)
```

Rank 10: This path is available when the WHERE clause contains a bounded expression such as BETWEEN or (> and <) or LIKE:

```
SQL> SELECT *
  2     FROM CUSTOMERS
  3   WHERE FIRST_NAME LIKE 'A%'
  4   /

Execution Plan
------------------------------------------------------------
   0        SELECT STATEMENT Optimizer=RULE
   1    0     TABLE ACCESS (BY INDEX ROWID) OF 'CUSTOMERS'
   2    1       INDEX (RANGE SCAN) OF 'IDX_CUS_FIRST_LAST' (NON-UNIQUE)
```

Rank 11: This path is available when the WHERE clause contains an unbounded expression such > or <:

```
SQL> CREATE INDEX IDX_CREDIT_LIMIT
  2     ON CUSTOMERS(CREDIT_LIMIT)
  3   /

Index created.

SQL> SELECT CUSTOMER_ID, PHONE
  2     FROM CUSTOMERS
  3   WHERE CREDIT_LIMIT > 2000
  4   /

Execution Plan
------------------------------------------------------------
   0        SELECT STATEMENT Optimizer=RULE
   1    0     TABLE ACCESS (BY INDEX ROWID) OF 'CUSTOMERS'
   2    1       INDEX (RANGE SCAN) OF 'IDX_CREDIT_LIMIT' (NON-UNIQUE)
```

13

NOTE

In a **range scan**, Oracle scans the rows of an object based on a range of values.

Rank 12: This path is available when joining two tables that do not reside in the same cluster. Oracle uses SORT-MERGE or NESTED LOOP to execute the statement:

```
SQL> CREATE INDEX IDX_PROD_CATEGORY_ID
  2     ON PRODUCTS(CATEGORY_ID)
  3  /

Index created.

SQL> SELECT *
  2     FROM CATEGORIES C, PRODUCTS P
  3    WHERE C.CATEGORY_ID = P.CATEGORY_ID
  4  /

Execution Plan
----------------------------------------------------------
   0          SELECT STATEMENT Optimizer=RULE
   1     0    NESTED LOOPS
   2     1      TABLE ACCESS (FULL) OF 'PRODUCTS'
   3     1      TABLE ACCESS (BY INDEX ROWID) OF 'CATEGORIES'
   4     3        INDEX (UNIQUE SCAN) OF 'SYS_C003125' (UNIQUE)
```

Rank 13: This path is available when a query contains a MAX or MIN:

```
SQL> SELECT MAX(CREDIT_LIMIT)
  2     FROM CUSTOMERS
  3  /

Execution Plan
----------------------------------------------------------
   0          SELECT STATEMENT Optimizer=RULE
   1     0    SORT (AGGREGATE)
   2     1      INDEX (FULL SCAN (MIN/MAX)) OF 'IDX_CREDIT_LIMIT' (NON-UNIQUE)
```

Rank 14: This path is available when an ORDER BY clause is included in the SQL statement and contains a primary key column:

```
SQL> SELECT *
  2     FROM CUSTOMERS
  3    ORDER BY CUSTOMER_ID
  4  /

Execution Plan
----------------------------------------------------------
   0          SELECT STATEMENT Optimizer=RULE
   1     0    TABLE ACCESS (BY INDEX ROWID) OF 'CUSTOMERS'
   2     1      INDEX (FULL SCAN) OF 'SYS_C003139' (UNIQUE)
```

Rank 15: This path is available when none of the previously described paths is used. In other words, no index was used and therefore this is a full table scan:

```
SQL> SELECT *
  2    FROM CUSTOMERS
  3    WHERE CITY = 'BOSTON'
  4  /

Execution Plan
------------------------------------------------
   0        SELECT STATEMENT Optimizer=RULE
   1    0     TABLE ACCESS (FULL) OF 'CUSTOMERS'
```

Cost-based Optimizer

When Oracle introduced the Rule-based Optimizer long ago, it was the only optimizer mode available. Oracle later introduced the Cost-based Optimizer as a better and recommended option. CBO is much more efficient than RBO because when evaluating an SQL statement, it considers consumption of all resources: the number of rows retrieved, table size, row size, block size, and other factors. CBO can be set to one of the following four settings:

- **CHOOSE:** Oracle chooses the best and most efficient path to execute and retrieve data. Optimizer can select a cost-access method when statistics are available or a rule-based access method if it is faster. This setting is the most common mode used.

- **ALL_ROWS:** Oracle uses cost-based access methods regardless of statistics availability. This optimizer priority is to retrieve all rows with the minimum amount of resource consumption. This option is often used in Web applications.

- **FIRST_ROWS:** Oracle uses a mix of cost-based access methods and heuristics to retrieve the first few rows quickly. This option is often used in FORMS client/server applications.

- **FIRST_ROWS_N:** (Where N is 1, 10, 100, or 1000.) Uses the cost-based access method to retrieve rows the most efficient way.

NOTE

So that CBO can determine how best to retrieve data, you should analyze tables in order. If statistics are not available, use RBO.

So how does CBO work? After the SQL statement is parsed, CBO considers all available storage statistics, generates all possible execution plans for the SQL statement, and selects the least expensive plan, as shown in Figure 13-4.

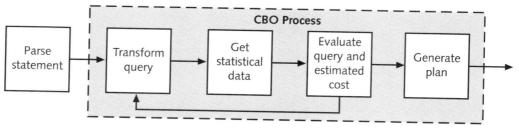

Figure 13-4   Cost-based Optimizer process

A plan with a cost of 1 (or near to 1) is faster than a plan with a cost of 200. A plan with a cost of 200 is better than 1000, and so forth. Again, the closer to 1, the better. Just in case you are wondering about a cost 0, you should know that no query costs 0.

The cost of the query is an indicator that tells you whether a query is efficient or not. For example, look at the following query and its Explain Plan. The total cost for this plan is 19 (looking at line 0). The CBO opted to execute this query using a full table scan because of three possibilities: no index on CUSTOMER_ID in the ORDERS table, or no statistical data to assist CBO, or a combination of both.

```
SQL> SELECT ORDER_ID, ORDER_DATE, PAID
  2     FROM ORDERS
  3     WHERE CUSTOMER_ID = 2022
  4   /

Execution Plan
--------------------------------------------------------------
   0         SELECT STATEMENT Optimizer=CHOOSE (Cost=19 Card=3 Bytes=57)
   1    0    TABLE ACCESS (FULL) OF 'ORDERS' (Cost=19 Card=3 Bytes=57)
```

The next step determines if the table has been analyzed before executing this query. In this case, you see that the table has been analyzed and that CBO chose to perform a full table scan. But is a full table scan bad or good? The answer is, it is bad when the table is large (has many rows) and good if the table is small.

```
SQL> SELECT LAST_ANALYZED
  2     FROM USER_TABLES
  3     WHERE TABLE_NAME = 'ORDERS'
  4   /

LAST_ANALYZED
-------------
11-FEB-03
```

Now, add an index to this table and run the same query again. This time you see that the cost has been lowered to 13, but CBO is still choosing a full table scan.

```
SQL> CREATE INDEX IDX_ORD_CUSTOMER
  2     ON ORDERS(CUSTOMER_ID)
  3  /

SQL> SELECT *
  2    FROM CUSTOMERS
  3   WHERE CITY = 'BOSTON'
  4  /

Execution Plan
-----------------------------------------------------------------------------
   0        SELECT STATEMENT Optimizer=CHOOSE (Cost=13 Card=12 Bytes=2316)
   1    0     TABLE ACCESS (FULL) OF 'CUSTOMERS' (Cost=13 Card=12 Bytes=2316)
```

NOTE

CBO uses a full table scan if the number of rows retrieved exceeds 20 percent of the total number of rows in the table.

You may be puzzled as to why CBO did not use the index that was created specifically to expedite row access. There are two possible reasons. The index was created but not analyzed, so CBO does not have sufficient information. The other reason could be that CBO decided a full table scan was faster, even though the index was analyzed. In this case, it is most likely that you did not analyze the index. Therefore, you should analyze the index and rerun the query to see if the cost is lower. Now look at the results. The cost has been lowered to 4, which is much better than what you started with (19). The index is now being used, and producing excellent results.

NOTE

Every time you analyze a table, all indexes belonging to it are analyzed. However, you can analyze an index in the same way you analyze a table. You use the ANALYZE command or one of the DBMS Oracle-supplied stored packages. In addition, you can display the time when the index was analyzed by viewing LAST_ANALYZED column in USER_INDEXES, ALL_INDEXES, or USER_INDEXES data dictionary views.

13

```
SQL> ANALYZE INDEX IDX_ORD_CUSTOMER ESTIMATE STATISTICS SAMPLE 20 PERCENT
  2  /

Index analyzed.

SQL> SELECT ORDER_ID, ORDER_DATE, PAID
  2    FROM ORDERS
  3   WHERE CUSTOMER_ID = 2022
  4  /

Execution Plan
----------------------------------------------------------------
   0        SELECT STATEMENT Optimizer=CHOOSE (Cost=4 Card=3 Bytes=57)
   1    0     TABLE ACCESS (BY INDEX ROWID) OF 'ORDERS' (Cost=4 Card=3 Bytes=57)
   2    1       INDEX (RANGE SCAN) OF 'IDX_ORD_CUSTOMER' (NON-UNIQUE) (Cost=1 Card=3)
```

As mentioned previously, you should not assume that using an index is always good, especially when the table is small. Also, you should not think that a cost of 1 is good. Yes, it is good that you can lower the cost to less than 19 and closer to 1, but you also need to look at the statistics of the query, the number of I/O trips, CPU consumption, memory consumption, and other factors. These factors together tell you how optimized the query is. You can feel comfortable about this query if you see that it is efficient.

 If the data in a table is constantly changing (extremely transactional), it is highly recommended to analyze the table on a periodical basis in order for the CBO to make a proper decision.

Table 13-2 presents the CBO access method with a description of each path. This table can be used to interpret the results of the execution plan of a query.

Table 13-2   Cost-based Optimizer access paths

Access path	Explanation
Bitmap joins	Oracle joins two tables using bitmap indexes. Available when the column in the WHERE clause is part of bitmap index. Used with bitmap indexes.
Cartesian joins	Oracle joins two or more tables without a WHERE clause to join them. Used when a WHERE clause condition to join two tables is missing.
Cluster scans	Oracle scans the cluster index to retrieve rows. Used when rows to be retrieved reside in a table that is part of a cluster index.
Fast full index scans	Oracle uses the index to perform a full table scan. Used when one of the columns in the query has a not null constraint and is indexed.
Full outer joins	Oracle joins the two tables by doing a combination of left and right outer joins.
Full scans	Full table or index scan
Full table scans	Oracle scans all blocks that are under the high-water mark to determine whether each row satisfies these conditions or not: ■ Used when a high degree of parallelism is being used for the SQL statement ■ Used when an index is not found ■ Used when many rows are being retrieved ■ Used when statistics are not up to date ■ Used when a table is small
Hash-join outer joins	Same as hash joins but with an outer join

Access path	Explanation
Hash joins	Oracle joins two tables by building a hash table of the smaller table in memory: ■ Used when one of the tables is large and the other table is small ■ Used when a large percentage of data must be joined with another table
Hash scans	Used to retrieve rows using a hash key in a cluster
Index joins	An index join of indexes that make up the columns selected in a query
Index-range scans	Used when a range of rows is selected using bounded or unbounded operators
Index-range scans descending	The same as index range scans except results are returned in descending order
Index scans	Uses columns that are part of an index to retrieve rows
Index-unique scans	Used when the statement contains a unique or primary key
Nested-loop joins	Two sets of data are joined using one data set as the outer loop, called the driving table, and another set as the inner loop, the driven table. It is important for the driving table to be smaller than the driven table.
Nested-loop outer joins	A nested loop joined with an outer join
ROWID scans	Oracle accesses the row by scanning the index for the ROWID. This is used when all columns in the WHERE clause are part of the index.
Sample table scans	Oracle scans each block by scanning a random number of rows from each as a sample. This is used when a SELECT statement is issued with a SAMPLE BLOCK clause.
Sort-merge joins	Oracle joins rows from two different tables.
Sort-merge outer joins	A sort-merge join with an outer join

13

The information in this table is derived from the online documentation that Oracle provides at the Oracle Technology Network site: *www.otn.oracle.com.*

INTERPRETING SQL EXECUTION PLANS AND STATISTICS

In Chapter 12 you were introduced to all sorts of different tools for generating execution plans for a SQL statement. Now, you are ready to read and interpret results. In this section you learn how to do that by looking at five different queries using a different tool for each query with RBO and CBO Optimizers.

Query Example 1

You are working at Acme Company as a DBA. You get a business request to generate a report of all orders and products for customers residing in Dallas, Texas, so you write the following query to generate the report. But being a diligent DBA, you want to make sure that the query is optimal. You decide to create an Explain Plan using RBO and CBO generated by the Oracle Enterprise Manager, as displayed in Figure 13-5.

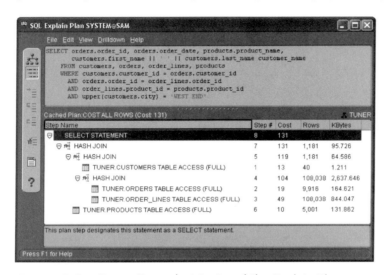

Figure 13-5   Query Example 1 text and the Explain Plan generated by Oracle Enterprise Manager

Explain Plan results always show the Optimizer mode used to execute the query.

NOTE

The Explain Plan of this query is read as follows:

1. All rows in the CUSTOMERS table are retrieved.

2. All rows in the ORDERS table are retrieved.

3. All rows in the ORDER_LINES table are retrieved.

4. A hash join is performed on the two data sets ORDERS and ORDER_LINES, having ORDERS as the driving table because it is smaller than ORDER_LINES.

5. A HASH JOIN is performed on two data sets: the resultant set of the HASH JOIN in Step 4 and the data set from the CUSTOMERS table. The driving table is CUSTOMERS because it is the smaller of the two.

6. All rows from the PRODUCTS table are retrieved.

7. A hash join is performed on two data sets: the resultant set of the hash join in Step 5 and the data set from the PRODUCTS table.

You can see that this Explain Plan resulted in the high cost of 131 and most of the cost is incurred in Step 4, which is a join with every row in the CUSTOMERS table. Reducing the number of rows retrieved from the CUSTOMERS table to only those needed enhances the performance. That means that using an index to select only those customers living in an area known as the West End of Dallas has a positive impact on the Explain plan.

So, add an index on the CITY column, and change the condition in the WHERE clause

From: `upper(customers.city) = 'WEST END'`

To: **`customers.city = 'West End'`**

```
SQL> CREATE INDEX IDX_CUS_CITY
  2      ON CUSTOMERS(CITY)
  3  /

Index created.

SQL> SELECT orders.order_id, orders.order_date, products.product_name,
  2          customers.first_name || ' ' || customers.last_name customer_name
  3     FROM customers, orders, order_lines, products
  4    WHERE customers.customer_id = orders.customer_id
  5      AND orders.order_id = order_lines.order_id
  6      AND order_lines.product_id = products.product_id
  7      AND customers.city = 'West End'
  8  /
...
```

You need to modify the condition because the index cannot be used if the column is part of an expression, as in UPPER(CITY). There are two ways to resolve this problem. You can remove the UPPER function, or you can create a function-based index that is based on that expression.

Figure 13-6 illustrates the Explain Plan for the modified query. As you can see, the cost was reduced by almost half, from 113 to 68, and therefore the query will perform better. What about the Rows column in Figures 13-5 and 13-6? Do you notice a difference in these numbers? This column indicates the total number of rows retrieved for each step.

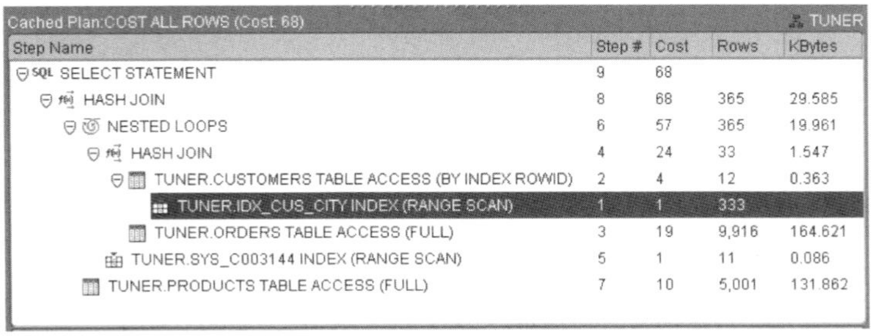

Step Name	Step #	Cost	Rows	KBytes
Cached Plan:COST ALL ROWS (Cost: 68)				TUNER
SELECT STATEMENT	9	68		
HASH JOIN	8	68	365	29.585
NESTED LOOPS	6	57	365	19.961
HASH JOIN	4	24	33	1.547
TUNER.CUSTOMERS TABLE ACCESS (BY INDEX ROWID)	2	4	12	0.363
TUNER.IDX_CUS_CITY INDEX (RANGE SCAN)	1	1	333	
TUNER.ORDERS TABLE ACCESS (FULL)	3	19	9,916	164.621
TUNER.SYS_C003144 INDEX (RANGE SCAN)	5	1	11	0.086
TUNER.PRODUCTS TABLE ACCESS (FULL)	7	10	5,001	131.862

Figure 13-6   Explain Plan for a modified query

Is this it? Not really. You can still modify the performance of this query by trying to eliminate full table scans, especially on the ORDERS table, because it is a large table. You can do so by checking if the CUSTOMER_ID column in the ORDERS table is indexed. If there is no index, then you should create one. Compare the result of an RBO for the same query with the same indexes in the Explain Plan as shown in Figure 13-7.

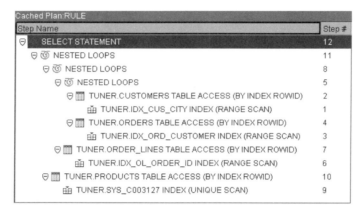

Figure 13-7   Execution plan for query Example 1 using the Rule-based Optimizer

As you can see, there is a huge difference between CBO and RBO Explain Plans. Notice that none of the tables are being accessed with full table scans. This would be very good if all tables were large. So how do you decide which one to use? You do that by looking at execution statistics for both as well as the response time.

Query Example 2

Suppose a developer sends you a query and asks you to check whether it is fully optimized. In response, you use the AUTOTRACE facility to generate an Explain Plan and statistics:

```
SQL> SET AUTOTRACE TRACEONLY EXPLAIN STATISTICS
SQL> SELECT P.PRODUCT_NAME, PI.QTY_ON_HAND
  2    FROM PRODUCTS P, PRODUCT_INVENTORY PI,
  3         PRODUCT_SUPPLIER PS, SUPPLIERS S
  4   WHERE P.PRODUCT_ID = PI.PRODUCT_ID
  5     AND P.PRODUCT_ID = PS.PRODUCT_ID
  6     AND PS.SUPPLIER_ID = S.SUPPLIER_ID
  7     AND S.SUPPLIER_NAME = 'Lyon Inc.'
  8     AND P.PRODUCT_ID NOT IN (SELECT PRODUCT_ID
  9                                FROM ORDER_LINES OL, ORDERS O
 10                               WHERE OL.ORDER_ID = O.ORDER_ID
 11                                 AND O.ORDER_DATE BETWEEN '12-JUN-00' AND '12-JUN-02')
 12  /

Elapsed: 00:00:01.03

Execution Plan
----------------------------------------------------------
   0      SELECT STATEMENT Optimizer=CHOOSE (Cost=96 Card=2 Bytes=142)
   1    0   NESTED LOOPS (Cost=96 Card=2 Bytes=142)
   2    1     HASH JOIN (ANTI) (Cost=94 Card=2 Bytes=128)
   3    2       NESTED LOOPS (Cost=16 Card=8 Bytes=408)
   4    3         HASH JOIN (Cost=8 Card=8 Bytes=192)
   5    4           TABLE ACCESS (FULL) OF 'SUPPLIERS' (Cost=4 Card=2 Bytes=34)
   6    4           INDEX (FAST FULL SCAN) OF 'SYS_C003130' (UNIQUE)
                      (Cost=3 Card=5001 Bytes=35007)
   7    3         TABLE ACCESS (BY INDEX ROWID) OF 'PRODUCTS' (Cost=1 Card=1 Bytes=27)
   8    7           INDEX (UNIQUE SCAN) OF 'SYS_C003127' (UNIQUE)
   9    2       VIEW OF 'VW_NSO_1' (Cost=77 Card=43285 Bytes=562705)
  10    9         FILTER
  11   10           HASH JOIN (Cost=77 Card=43285 Bytes=865700)
  12   11             TABLE ACCESS (FULL) OF 'ORDERS' (Cost=19 Card=3973 Bytes=47676)
  13   11             INDEX (FAST FULL SCAN) OF 'SYS_C003144' (UNIQUE)
                        (Cost=46 Card=108038 Bytes=864304)
  14    1     TABLE ACCESS (BY INDEX ROWID) OF 'PRODUCT_INVENTORY'
                (Cost=1 Card=5001 Bytes=35007)
  15   14       INDEX (UNIQUE SCAN) OF 'SYS_C003135' (UNIQUE)
```

13

```
Statistics
----------------------------------------------------------
          0  recursive calls
          0  db block gets
        795  consistent gets
        172  physical reads
          0  redo size
        557  bytes sent via SQL*Net to client
        499  bytes received via SQL*Net from client
          2  SQL*Net roundtrips to/from client
          0  sorts (memory)
          0  sorts (disk)
          3  rows processed
```

Quite a complex Explain Plan, isn't it? Don't let it intimidate you though! You need to see if there are unnecessary full table scans or any other costly operations that you can eliminate or reduce. Sometimes the answer is to rewrite the query, so look at how it is read step by step. You should read it from the inside out as follows:

1. Retrieves all rows from table SUPPLIERS.

2. Retrieves all the ROWIDs of the index SYS_C003130 of the PRODUCT SUPPLIER table.

3. A hash join is performed from two data sets, the SUPPLIERS and PRODUCTS tables. Oracle optimizer builds the hash table using the smaller of the two tables. It uses the statistics to identify the smaller table.

4. Retrieves a single ROWID from the index SYS_C003127 of the PRODUCTS table.

5. Retrieves rows from the PRODUCTS table through ROWID(s) returned by an index.

6. Joins the two data sets, one data set from the PRODUCTS table, and the other data set produced by the HASH JOIN in Step 3. The two joins are performed by iterating over the outer table, row set (the first child of the join) and, for each row, carrying out the steps of the inner row set (the second child). Corresponding pairs of rows are tested against the join condition specified in the query's WHERE clause.

7. Retrieves all rows from the ORDERS table.

8. Retrieves all of the ROWIDs of index SYS_C003144 of the ORDER_LINES table.

9. Performs a hash join of two sets of rows, one from the ORDERS table and the other from Step 8 (ORDER_LINES index). A hash table is built using the rows returned from the smaller set.

10. Performs filtration by accepting a set of rows from Step 9 and eliminating rows that are not needed.

11. Is the result of the subquery represented by the VIEW OF 'VW_NSO_1'. Oracle assigns a temporary view name to any inline view or subquery.

12. An anti-hash join is performed using two sets of rows, one from Step 6 and one from Step 11.

13. Retrieves a single ROWID from the index SYS_C003135 of the PRODUCT INVENTORY table.

14. Retrieves rows from the PRODUCT INVENTORY table through ROWID(s) returned by an index.

15. Performs a nested loop iterating the outer table with the inner table. These two tables are the results of Steps 12 and 14.

Figure 13-8 is a graphical representation of this Explain Plan, which was generated by the Top SQL utility of the Oracle Enterprise Manager, which was introduced in Chapter 12.

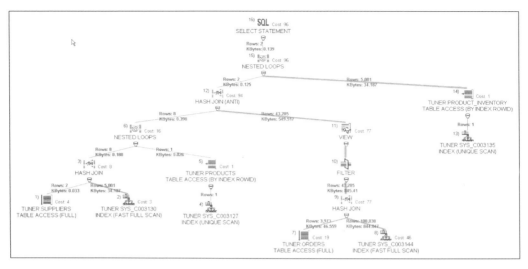

Figure 13-8   Execution plan generated by the Top SQL utility of Oracle Enterprise Manager

What can you do to reduce the cost of this operation from 96 to a cost closer to 1? You can look at the ORDER_DATE column in the ORDERS table in the subquery and the SUPPLIER_NAME column in SUPPLIERS. Neither column is indexed. You should, therefore, create an index and analyze it as in the statements that follow:

```
SQL> CREATE INDEX IDX_ORD_ORDER_DATE
  2      ON ORDERS(ORDER_DATE)
  3  /

Index created.

SQL> ANALYZE INDEX IDX_ORD_ORDER_DATE COMPUTE STATISTICS
  2  /

Index analyzed.

SQL> CREATE INDEX IDX_SUP_SUPPLIER_NAME
  2      ON SUPPLIERS(SUPPLIER_NAME)
  3  /

Index created.

SQL> ANALYZE INDEX IDX_SUP_SUPPLIER_NAME COMPUTE STATISTICS
  2  /

Index analyzed.
```

Now, rerun the query and examine the Explain Plan. As you can see, it did not improve:

13

```
Elapsed: 00:00:01.03

Execution Plan
-----------------------------------------------------------
   0        SELECT STATEMENT Optimizer=CHOOSE (Cost=97 Card=2 Bytes=142)
   1     0   NESTED LOOPS (Cost=97 Card=2 Bytes=142)
   2     1    HASH JOIN (ANTI) (Cost=95 Card=2 Bytes=128)
   3     2     NESTED LOOPS (Cost=17 Card=8 Bytes=408)
   4     3      NESTED LOOPS (Cost=9 Card=8 Bytes=192)
   5     4       TABLE ACCESS (BY INDEX ROWID) OF 'SUPPLIERS'
                  (Cost=3 Card=2 Bytes=34)
   6     5         INDEX (RANGE SCAN) OF 'IDX_SUP_SUPPLIER_NAME'
                    (NON-UNIQUE) (Cost=1 Card=2)
   7     4        INDEX (FAST FULL SCAN) OF 'SYS_C003130' (UNIQUE)
                   (Cost=3 Card=5001 Bytes=35007)
   8     3      TABLE ACCESS (BY INDEX ROWID) OF 'PRODUCTS'
                 (Cost=1 Card=1 Bytes=27)
   9     8        INDEX (UNIQUE SCAN) OF 'SYS_C003127' (UNIQUE)
  10     2     VIEW OF 'VW_NSO_1' (Cost=77 Card=43285 Bytes=562705)
  11    10      FILTER
  12    11       HASH JOIN (Cost=77 Card=43285 Bytes=865700)
  13    12        TABLE ACCESS (FULL) OF 'ORDERS'
                   (Cost=19 Card=3973 Bytes=47676)
  14    12         INDEX (FAST FULL SCAN) OF 'SYS_C003144' (UNIQUE)
                    (Cost=46 Card=108038 Bytes=864304)
  15     1   TABLE ACCESS (BY INDEX ROWID) OF 'PRODUCT_INVENTORY'
              (Cost=1 Card=5001 Bytes=35007)
  16    15    INDEX (UNIQUE SCAN) OF 'SYS_C003135' (UNIQUE)
```

You may also make one minor modification by changing the criteria with the (!=) operator to NOT EXISTS as shown in the following code segment. In general, NOT EXISTS performs better than anti-joins. As you can see, the cost is reduced to 91.

```
SQL> SELECT P.PRODUCT_NAME,
  2         PI.QTY_ON_HAND
  3    FROM PRODUCTS P,
  4         PRODUCT_INVENTORY PI,
  5         PRODUCT_SUPPLIER PS,
  6         SUPPLIERS S
  7   WHERE PI.PRODUCT_ID = P.PRODUCT_ID
  8     AND PS.PRODUCT_ID = P.PRODUCT_ID
  9     AND S.SUPPLIER_ID = PS.SUPPLIER_ID
 10     AND 'Lyon Inc.' = S.SUPPLIER_NAME
 11     AND PS.PRODUCT_ID = PI.PRODUCT_ID
 12     AND NOT EXISTS (SELECT 'X'
 13                       FROM ORDER_LINES OL,
 14                            ORDERS O
 15                      WHERE O.ORDER_ID = OL.ORDER_ID
 16                        AND O.ORDER_DATE BETWEEN '12-JUN-00' AND '12-JUN-02'
 17                        AND PS.PRODUCT_ID = PRODUCT_ID);

Execution Plan
----------------------------------------------------------
   0        SELECT STATEMENT Optimizer=CHOOSE (Cost=91 Card=1 Bytes=71)
   1    0     NESTED LOOPS (Cost=91 Card=1 Bytes=71)
   2    1       NESTED LOOPS (Cost=89 Card=2 Bytes=128)
   3    2         HASH JOIN (ANTI) (Cost=87 Card=2 Bytes=74)
   4    3           NESTED LOOPS (Cost=9 Card=8 Bytes=192)
   5    4             TABLE ACCESS (BY INDEX ROWID) OF 'SUPPLIERS' (Cost=3 Card=2 Bytes=34)
   6    5               INDEX (RANGE SCAN) OF 'IDX_SUP_SUPPLIER_NAME' (NON-UNIQUE) (Cost=1
                            Card=2)
   7    4             INDEX (FAST FULL SCAN) OF 'SYS_C003130' (UNIQUE) (Cost=3 Card=1 Bytes=7)
   8    3           VIEW OF 'VW_SQ_1' (Cost=77 Card=43285 Bytes=562705)
   9    8             FILTER
  10    9               HASH JOIN (Cost=77 Card=43285 Bytes=865700)
  11   10                 TABLE ACCESS (FULL) OF 'ORDERS' (Cost=19 Card=3973 Bytes=47676)
  12   10                 INDEX (FAST FULL SCAN) OF 'SYS_C003144' (UNIQUE) (Cost=46 Card=108038
                            Bytes=864304)
  13    2         TABLE ACCESS (BY INDEX ROWID) OF 'PRODUCTS' (Cost=1 Card=1 Bytes=27)
  14   13           INDEX (UNIQUE SCAN) OF 'SYS_C003127' (UNIQUE)
  15    1       TABLE ACCESS (BY INDEX ROWID) OF 'PRODUCT_INVENTORY' (Cost=1 Card=1 Bytes=7)
  16   15         INDEX (UNIQUE SCAN) OF 'SYS_C003135' (UNIQUE)
```

13

Run this with the RBO by setting the OPTIMIZER_GOAL to RULE. You can see from the timing and statistics that the rule-based method is slower and more resource costly despite using the indexes created earlier. The CBO did not use these indexes because it calculated that it would cost more to use the index. This is a real demonstration of the fact that indexes are sometimes not used because they may be a liability to performance rather than an improvement.

```
Elapsed: 00:00:04.06

Execution Plan
------------------------------------------------------------
   0          SELECT STATEMENT Optimizer=RULE
   1     0     FILTER
   2     1      NESTED LOOPS
   3     2       NESTED LOOPS
   4     3        NESTED LOOPS
   5     4         TABLE ACCESS (FULL) OF 'PRODUCT_SUPPLIER'
   6     4         TABLE ACCESS (BY INDEX ROWID) OF 'SUPPLIERS'
   7     6          INDEX (UNIQUE SCAN) OF 'SYS_C003111' (UNIQUE)
   8     3        TABLE ACCESS (BY INDEX ROWID) OF 'PRODUCTS'
   9     8          INDEX (UNIQUE SCAN) OF 'SYS_C003127' (UNIQUE)
  10     2       TABLE ACCESS (BY INDEX ROWID) OF 'PRODUCT_INVENTORY'
  11    10         INDEX (UNIQUE SCAN) OF 'SYS_C003135' (UNIQUE)
  12     1      TABLE ACCESS (BY INDEX ROWID) OF 'ORDER_LINES'
  13    12       NESTED LOOPS
  14    13        TABLE ACCESS (BY INDEX ROWID) OF 'ORDERS'
  15    14         INDEX (RANGE SCAN) OF 'IDX_ORD_ORDER_DATE'
                     (NON-UNIQUE)
  16    13        INDEX (RANGE SCAN) OF 'IDX_OL_ORDER_ID' (NON-UNIQUE)

Statistics
------------------------------------------------------------
        0  recursive calls
        0  db block gets
    54505  consistent gets
      560  physical reads
        0  redo size
      557  bytes sent via SQL*Net to client
      499  bytes received via SQL*Net from client
        2  SQL*Net roundtrips to/from client
        0  sorts (memory)
        0  sorts (disk)
        3  rows processed
```

Compare the PHYSICAL READS statistics obtained from CBO, which are 172, with RBO, which are 560. This tells you that RBO has consumed more I/O and is therefore a performance liability.

Query Example 3

In this example, you focus on query statistics. You trace a session using SQL Trace on a session issuing the same query twice, once in CHOOSE and another in RULE session for OPTIMIZER_GOAL. As a reminder of how to trace, here is an outline of the steps:

1. Log on as TUNER.

2. Log on in a different session as SYS.

3. Get SID, SERIAL#, and OS PROCESS ID for the TUNER session.

4. As SYS, use the DBMS_SYSTEM.SET_SQL_TRACE_IN_SESSION procedure to turn on tracing.

5. Log on as TUNER and set the session to a specific optimizer goal.

6. As TUNER, submit the following query:

```
SQL> SET HEAD OFF
SQL> SET PAGES 0
SQL> SET LINES 300
SQL> select /* SQL Trace */
  2          d.*, e.*, o.*, j.*, sm.*, pm.*, c.*
  3     from departments d, employees e, orders o,
  4          customers c, jobs j,  shipment_method sm, payment_method pm
  5    where d.department_name in ('Technology', 'Customer Service')
  6      and d.department_id = e.department_id
  7      and e.employee_id = c.sales_rep_id
  8      and e.employee_id = o.employee_id
  9      and e.job_id = j.job_id
 10      and c.customer_id = o.customer_id
 11      and o.shipment_method_id = sm.shipment_method_id
 12      and o.payment_method_id = pm.payment_method_id
 13   /
```

7. Turn off tracing.

8. Locate and format the trace file using the TKPROF utility.

Just before you run this query, analyze it. The number of table joins should be kept as low as possible, which means you should make sure that the query is using only necessary tables and that the query is retrieving only necessary data. So, if there is an opportunity to restrict certain rows, it is preferable and more efficient to narrow the search. This is similar to some Web site search engines that ask you to narrow your search when you enter a keyword and there are too many hits.

Going back to this example, you need to analyze the contents of the formatted trace file, as outlined in the following list, focusing more closely on statistics incurred by the query. Figure 13-9 shows the structure of the formatted trace file. The file is structured as follows:

- Header and file information followed by a statistics legend describing each statistics column

- Queries captured during the session; for each query there is:
  - Query text
  - Statistics table for executing the query
  - Execution plan (if the EXPLAIN option was used when formatting trace file)

- Summary statistics for the whole tracing session

13

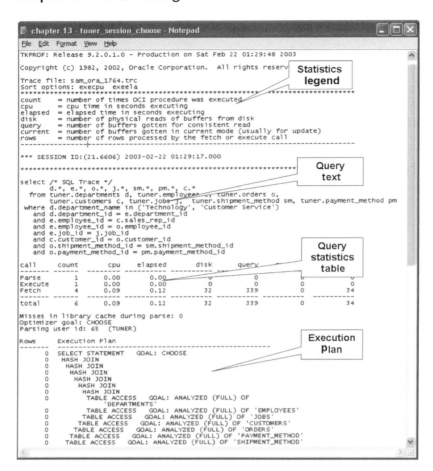

Figure 13-9   Formatted trace file generated by SQL Trace

The following is a partial listing of the formatted trace file showing the statistics and Explain Plan results of the CHOOSE optimizer goal. Here is a list of observations:

- The Oracle CBO did not use any index, even though all columns in the WHERE clause conditions have indexes on them.

- The Oracle optimizer performed the query using the hash join access method, which performs efficiently if the Optimizer correctly selects the smaller of the two joined tables to build the hash table.

- The query has a CPU cost of 0.09 seconds for a total number of rows and elapsed time of 0.12 seconds. This does not seem bad if the tables are large, but in this case they are small tables, and having a full table scan on each one of these table is costly.

- Number of I/Os (to the disk) is 32 again. For the number of fetched rows and the size of these tables, this is not acceptable.

```
call       count       cpu     elapsed       disk      query     current        rows
-------   ------   --------  ----------  ---------- ---------- ---------- ----------
Parse         1     0.00        0.00           0          0          0           0
Execute       1     0.00        0.00           0          0          0           0
Fetch         4     0.09        0.12          32        339          0          34
-------   ------   --------  ----------  ---------- ---------- ---------- ----------
total         6     0.09        0.12          32        339          0          34

Misses in library cache during parse: 0
Optimizer goal: CHOOSE
Parsing user id: 65   (TUNER)

Rows      Execution Plan
-------   ---------------------------------------------------------
     0    SELECT STATEMENT    GOAL: CHOOSE
     0     HASH JOIN
     0      HASH JOIN
     0       HASH JOIN
     0        HASH JOIN
     0         HASH JOIN
     0          HASH JOIN
     0            TABLE ACCESS    GOAL: ANALYZED (FULL) OF 'DEPARTMENTS'
     0            TABLE ACCESS    GOAL: ANALYZED (FULL) OF 'EMPLOYEES'
     0            TABLE ACCESS    GOAL: ANALYZED (FULL) OF 'JOBS'
     0           TABLE ACCESS    GOAL: ANALYZED (FULL) OF 'CUSTOMERS'
     0          TABLE ACCESS    GOAL: ANALYZED (FULL) OF 'ORDERS'
     0         TABLE ACCESS    GOAL: ANALYZED (FULL) OF 'PAYMENT_METHOD'
     0        TABLE ACCESS    GOAL: ANALYZED (FULL) OF 'SHIPMENT_METHOD'
```

The next listing is the results of tracing the same query but using a Rule-based Optimizer goal. Here is a list of observations:

- Oracle RBO used indexes for all tables.

- Even though indexes were used, the CPU cost and elapsed time went up from CBO.

- The number of I/O trips went down because data was cached in memory, which helps reduce I/O trips.

13

```
call       count      cpu    elapsed       disk      query    current       rows
-------    ------   --------  --------  ---------- ---------- ---------- ----------
Parse          1     0.00      0.00           0          0          0          0
Execute        1     0.00      0.00           0          0          0          0
Fetch          4     0.20      0.23          24      31000          0         34
-------    ------   --------  --------  ---------- ---------- ---------- ----------
total          6     0.20      0.23          24      31000          0         34

Misses in library cache during parse: 0
Optimizer goal: RULE
Parsing user id: 65   (TUNER)

Rows     Execution Plan
-------  ------------------------------------------------------
      0  SELECT STATEMENT    GOAL: RULE
      0   NESTED LOOPS
      0    NESTED LOOPS
      0     NESTED LOOPS
      0      NESTED LOOPS
      0       NESTED LOOPS
      0        NESTED LOOPS
      0         TABLE ACCESS    GOAL: ANALYZED (BY INDEX ROWID) OF 'PAYMENT_METHOD'
      0         TABLE ACCESS    GOAL: ANALYZED (BY INDEX ROWID) OF 'ORDERS'
      0          INDEX    GOAL: ANALYZED (RANGE SCAN) OF 'IDX_O_PAY_METHOD_ID' (NON-UNIQUE)
      0        TABLE ACCESS    GOAL: ANALYZED (BY INDEX ROWID) OF 'SHIPMENT_METHOD'
      0         INDEX    GOAL: ANALYZED (UNIQUE SCAN) OF 'SYS_C003113' (UNIQUE)
      0       TABLE ACCESS    GOAL: ANALYZED (BY INDEX ROWID) OF 'CUSTOMERS'
      0        INDEX    GOAL: ANALYZED (UNIQUE SCAN) OF 'SYS_C003139' (UNIQUE)
      0      TABLE ACCESS    GOAL: ANALYZED (BY INDEX ROWID) OF 'EMPLOYEES'
      0       INDEX    GOAL: ANALYZED (UNIQUE SCAN) OF 'SYS_C003119' (UNIQUE)
      0     TABLE ACCESS    GOAL: ANALYZED (BY INDEX ROWID) OF 'JOBS'
      0      INDEX    GOAL: ANALYZED (UNIQUE SCAN) OF 'SYS_C003117' (UNIQUE)
      0    TABLE ACCESS    GOAL: ANALYZED (BY INDEX ROWID) OF 'DEPARTMENTS'
      0     INDEX    GOAL: ANALYZED (UNIQUE SCAN) OF 'SYS_C003115' (UNIQUE)
```

What do you conclude from this example? Note that you should look at all the elements in the picture, which include the execution plan, statistics, purpose of the query, type of application, and resources, to name a few.

OPTIMIZER-RELATED PARAMETERS

This section presents initialization parameters that may influence the performance or behavior of the Oracle optimizer. These parameters are grouped into the following two categories: optimizer performance and optimizer behavior. Only the most important parameters are explained in this chapter; for more information, consult Oracle9i documentation.

- **Optimizer Performance**:
  - OPTIMIZER_DYNAMIC_SAMPLING
  - OPTIMIZER_FEATURES_ENABLE
  - OPTIMIZER_INDEX_CACHING

- OPTIMIZER_INDEX_COST_ADJ
- OPTIMIZER_MAX_PERMUTATIONS

- **Optimizer Behavior**:
  - CURSOR_SHARING
  - DB_FILE_MULTIBLOCK_READ_COUNT
  - HASH_AREA_SIZE
  - HASH_JOIN_ENABLED
  - PARTITION_VIEW_ENABLED
  - QUERY_REWRITE_ENABLED
  - SORT_AREA_SIZE
  - STAR_TRANSFORMATION_ENABLED

OPTIMIZER_FEATURES_ENABLE (Static) Parameter

With the release of every version of Oracle, the Oracle Optimizer changes and may behave differently. Because that could be a problem for existing applications, Oracle introduced a parameter that forces the optimizer to use certain Oracle optimizer behaviors. For example, if your database is upgraded from Oracle 8.1.7 to Oracle9*i*, you may not be sure how existing application queries behave with the new version and may not want to risk using the new version. Or you might not have time to analyze all queries under the new optimizer version. In any of these scenarios, you can set the OPTIMIZER_FEATURES_ENABLES parameter to one of these acceptable values: { 8.0.0 | 8.0.3 | 8.0.4 | 8.0.5 | 8.0.6 | 8.0.7 | 8.1.0 | 8.1.3 | 8.1.4 | 8.1.5 | 8.1.6 | 8.1.7 | 9.0.0 | 9.0.1 | 9.2.0 }.

13

OPTIMIZER_MAX_PERMUTATIONS (Dynamic for a Session)

Optimizer uses permutation of the tables for queries with joins. This parameter can be used to limit the number of permutations to reduce the time required to perform all these permutations.

OPTIMIZER_MODE (Static)

This parameter specifies the optimizer mode to be set for the whole instance.

OPTIMIZER HINTS

In many situations, you might mistakenly expect Oracle optimizer to execute a query in a specific way. Oracle optimizer is designed to execute queries in the most efficient way based on the statistical data available. To facilitate this efficiency, Oracle provides optimizer hints, which influences the Oracle optimizer. These hints are included in SQL statements to guide the optimizer's execution of the statements. There are over fifty hints that you can use, and they are grouped into seven categories, as shown in Figure 13-10. This section presents two hints from each category and shows you how to include hints in a query.

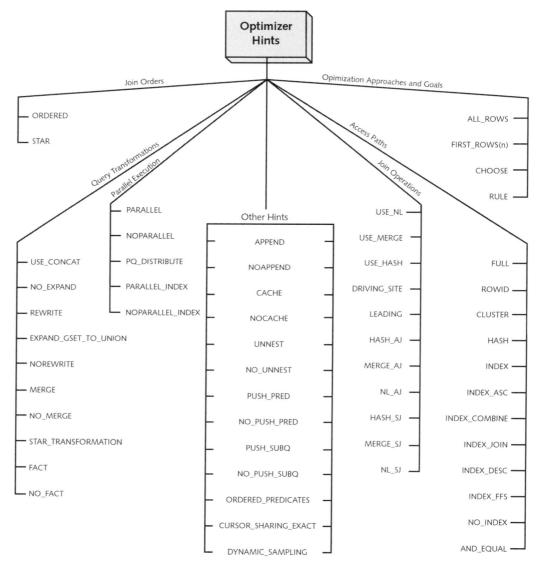

Figure 13-10   Oracle Optimizer Hints classified by function

So how do you include a hint in a query? You may have already seen some queries, which contain hints; if not, this is the method: a hint is included within an SQL comment following the SELECT keyword. You also need to add a plus sign (+) after the opening of the comment as shown in Figure 13-11.

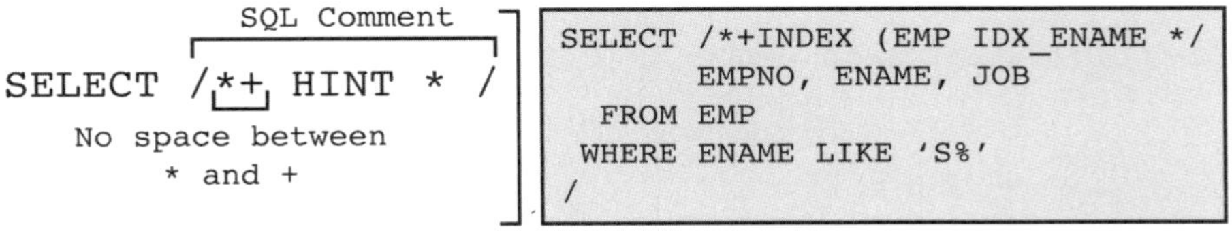

```
                  SQL Comment          SELECT /*+INDEX (EMP IDX_ENAME */
SELECT  /*+  HINT  *  /                       EMPNO, ENAME, JOB
       No space between                 FROM EMP
           * and +                     WHERE ENAME LIKE 'S%'
                                       /
```

Figure 13-11   Optimizer Hint syntax example

Join Orders Hints

This type of hint informs Oracle optimizer of the order of the tables to be joined.

ORDERED

The ORDERED hint tells the Oracle optimizer to execute the query based on the order of the tables listed in the FROM clause (from inside out). You may use this hint to influence the optimizer to choose as the driving table the one which has the fewest rows or is returning fewer rows than the other tables being joined. As you can see in the listing that follows, the first query uses CUSTOMERS as the driving table because it returns only one row, and it is then joined with ORDERS, which returns fewer rows than ORDER_LINES. In the second query, the tables in the FROM clause are reordered to show you that using ORDER_LINES as the driving table is not efficient. This is apparent from its cost, which went up from 12 to 361.

13

```
-- using ORDERED hint (Optimizer will use as driving table CUSTOMERS -> ORDERS -> ORDER_LINES)
SQL> SELECT /*+ ORDERED */
  2           O.ORDER_ID, C.FIRST_NAME, LAST_NAME, OL.TOTAL_AMOUNT
  3    FROM CUSTOMERS C, ORDERS O, ORDER_LINES OL
  4    WHERE C.CUSTOMER_ID = 121
  5      AND O.CUSTOMER_ID = C.CUSTOMER_ID
  6      AND O.ORDER_ID = OL.ORDER_ID
  7    /


Execution Plan
----------------------------------------------------------
   0          SELECT STATEMENT Optimizer=CHOOSE (Cost=12 Card=30 Bytes=1050)
   1     0     TABLE ACCESS (BY INDEX ROWID) OF 'ORDER_LINES' (Cost=2 Card=11 Bytes=88)
   2     1      NESTED LOOPS (Cost=12 Card=30 Bytes=1050)
   3     2       MERGE JOIN (CARTESIAN) (Cost=6 Card=3 Bytes=81)
   4     3        TABLE ACCESS (BY INDEX ROWID) OF 'CUSTOMERS' (Cost=2 Card=1 Bytes=20)
   5     4          INDEX (UNIQUE SCAN) OF 'SYS_C003139' (UNIQUE) (Cost=1 Card=4000)
   6     3         TABLE ACCESS (BY INDEX ROWID) OF 'ORDERS' (Cost=4 Card=3 Bytes=21)
   7     6           INDEX (RANGE SCAN) OF 'IDX_ORD_CUSTOMER' (NON-UNIQUE) (Cost=1 Card=3)
   8     2        INDEX (RANGE SCAN) OF 'SYS_C003144' (UNIQUE) (Cost=1 Card=11)

-- using ORDERED hint (Optimizer will use as driving table ORDER_LINES -> ORDERS -> CUSTOMERS)
SQL> SELECT /*+ ORDERED */
  2           O.ORDER_ID, C.FIRST_NAME, LAST_NAME, OL.TOTAL_AMOUNT
  3    FROM  ORDER_LINES OL, ORDERS O, CUSTOMERS C
  4    WHERE C.CUSTOMER_ID = 121
  5      AND O.CUSTOMER_ID = C.CUSTOMER_ID
  6      AND O.ORDER_ID = OL.ORDER_ID
  7    /


Execution Plan
----------------------------------------------------------
   0          SELECT STATEMENT Optimizer=CHOOSE (Cost=361 Card=30 Bytes=1050)
   1     0     MERGE JOIN (CARTESIAN) (Cost=361 Card=30 Bytes=1050)
   2     1      NESTED LOOPS (Cost=331 Card=30 Bytes=450)
   3     2       TABLE ACCESS (FULL) OF 'ORDER_LINES' (Cost=49 Card=108038 Bytes=864304)
   4     2       BITMAP CONVERSION (TO ROWIDS)
   5     4        BITMAP AND
   6     5         BITMAP CONVERSION (FROM ROWIDS)
   7     6          INDEX (RANGE SCAN) OF 'SYS_C003141' (UNIQUE)
   8     5         BITMAP CONVERSION (FROM ROWIDS)
   9     8          INDEX (RANGE SCAN) OF 'IDX_ORD_CUSTOMER' (NON-UNIQUE)
  10     1      BUFFER (SORT) (Cost=30 Card=1 Bytes=20)
  11    10       TABLE ACCESS (BY INDEX ROWID) OF 'CUSTOMERS' (Cost=1 Card=1 Bytes=20)
  12    11        INDEX (UNIQUE SCAN) OF 'SYS_C003139' (UNIQUE)
```

NOTE

The optimizer ignores hints if the hint has invalid syntax or if the table has an
alias in the SELECT statement and it is not used, for example:

```
SELECT /*+ INDEX(CUSTOMERS)  */
             . . .
      FROM CUSTOMERS C,
```

You should use the alias C instead of CUSTOMERS in the hint.

STAR

This hint is used in a star schema application, which is a data warehouse application. A star schema is used when you have a FACT table in the middle with several tables connected to it, looking like a star. Each connected table is called a DIMENSION. See Figure 13-12.

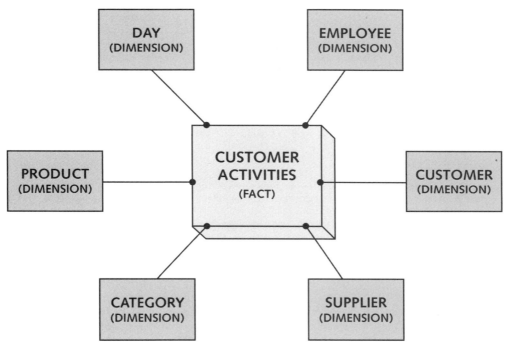

Figure 13-12   Example of a star schema data model

This hint tells the optimizer to use the FACT table last because the FACT table is usually the largest. There must be at least three tables in the JOIN statement.

Query Transformation Hints

This category contains hints related to executing the query in a different way to speed up the performance of the query.

USE_CONCAT

This hint tells the optimizer to convert the OR condition into a UNION ALL statement, combining the results of the first condition with the results of the second condition. The next example demonstrates how this hint reduces costs. The first query contains two conditions combined with an OR and the cost of this query is 19.

NOTE   The NO_EXPAND hint is the reverse of USE_CONCAT; it prevents concatenation.

```
-- No hint
SQL> SELECT ORDER_ID, ORDER_DATE
  2    FROM ORDERS
  3   WHERE ORDER_ID < 1000 OR ORDER_ID > 1000000
  4  /

Execution Plan
----------------------------------------------------------
   0      SELECT STATEMENT Optimizer=CHOOSE (Cost=19 Card=901 Bytes=9010)
   1    0   TABLE ACCESS (FULL) OF 'ORDERS' (Cost=19 Card=901 Bytes=9010)

-- add a hint USE_CONCAT cost is reduced to 7
SQL> SELECT /*+ USE_CONCAT */
  2          ORDER_ID, ORDER_DATE
  3    FROM ORDERS
  4   WHERE ORDER_ID < 1000 OR ORDER_ID > 1000000
  5  /

Execution Plan
----------------------------------------------------------
   0      SELECT STATEMENT Optimizer=CHOOSE (Cost=7 Card=46 Bytes=460)
   1    0   CONCATENATION
   2    1     TABLE ACCESS (BY INDEX ROWID) OF 'ORDERS' (Cost=4 Card=45 Bytes=450)
   3    2       INDEX (RANGE SCAN) OF 'SYS_C003141' (UNIQUE) (Cost=3 Card=45)
   4    1     TABLE ACCESS (BY INDEX ROWID) OF 'ORDERS' (Cost=4 Card=45 Bytes=450)
   5    4       INDEX (RANGE SCAN) OF 'SYS_C003141' (UNIQUE) (Cost=3 Card=45)
```

NOTE

The STAR_TRANSFORMATION hint is similar to the STAR hint, and the FACT hint tells the optimizer that the specified table should be treated as a FACT table.

Access Paths

Hints in this category notify the optimizer which access path to use to retrieve data.

FULL

This hint tells the optimizer to access the specified table with a full table scan (FTS):

```
SQL> SELECT /*+ FULL(EMPLOYEES) */
  2          FIRST_NAME, LAST_NAME
  3    FROM EMPLOYEES
  4   WHERE EMPLOYEE_ID = 1200
  5  /

Execution Plan
----------------------------------------------------------
   0      SELECT STATEMENT Optimizer=CHOOSE (Cost=2 Card=1 Bytes=19)
   1    0   TABLE ACCESS (FULL) OF 'EMPLOYEES' (Cost=2 Card=1 Bytes=19
```

INDEX

This hint tells the optimizer to use an index for the specified table to access data:

```
SQL> SELECT /*+ INDEX(CUSTOMERS IDX_CUS_CITY) */
  2          CUSTOMER_ID, FIRST_NAME, LAST_NAME
  3    FROM CUSTOMERS
  4   WHERE CITY = 'W%'
  5  /

Execution Plan
----------------------------------------------------------
   0      SELECT STATEMENT Optimizer=CHOOSE (Cost=13 Card=12 Bytes=372)
   1    0   TABLE ACCESS (BY INDEX ROWID) OF 'CUSTOMERS' (Cost=13 Card=12 Bytes=372)
   2    1     INDEX (RANGE SCAN) OF 'IDX_CUS_CITY' (NON-UNIQUE) (Cost=1 Card=12)
```

Parallel Executions

Hints in this category are used for parallel executions and for specifying the degree of parallelism.

PARALLEL

This hint tells the optimizer to execute the SQL statement in parallel using the specified concurrent servers. This hint has the following syntax:

```
/*+ PARALLEL ( table [{ , integer | , DEFAULT) | , } [ , integer | , DEFAULT ] ] ) */
```

The following example illustrates that a query without the PARALLEL hint has a higher cost than one with the PARALLEL hint:

13

```
-- No hint is included (cost 45)
SQL> SELECT C.FIRST_NAME CUS_FIRST, C.LAST_NAME CUS_LAST,
  2          S.SHIPMENT_DESCRIPTION, P.PAYMENT_DESCRIPTION,
  3          E.FIRST_NAME EMP_FIRST, E.LAST_NAME EMP_LAST
  4    FROM CUSTOMERS C, ORDERS O, EMPLOYEES E,
  5          SHIPMENT_METHOD S, PAYMENT_METHOD P
  6   WHERE O.CUSTOMER_ID = C.CUSTOMER_ID
  7     AND O.EMPLOYEE_ID = E.EMPLOYEE_ID
  8     AND O.SHIPMENT_METHOD_ID = S.SHIPMENT_METHOD_ID
  9     AND O.PAYMENT_METHOD_ID = P.PAYMENT_METHOD_ID
 10   /


Execution Plan
-----------------------------------------------------------
   0      SELECT STATEMENT Optimizer=CHOOSE (Cost=45 Card=9916 Bytes=694120)
   1    0   HASH JOIN (Cost=45 Card=9916 Bytes=694120)
   2    1    TABLE ACCESS (FULL) OF 'EMPLOYEES' (Cost=2 Card=294 Bytes=5586)
   3    1    HASH JOIN (Cost=42 Card=9916 Bytes=505716)
   4    3     TABLE ACCESS (FULL) OF 'SHIPMENT_METHOD' (Cost=2 Card=11 Bytes=99)
   5    3     HASH JOIN (Cost=39 Card=9916 Bytes=416472)
   6    5      TABLE ACCESS (FULL) OF 'CUSTOMERS' (Cost=13 Card=4000 Bytes=80000)
   7    5      HASH JOIN (Cost=22 Card=9916 Bytes=218152)
   8    7       TABLE ACCESS (FULL) OF 'PAYMENT_METHOD' (Cost=2 Card=9 Bytes=99)
   9    7       TABLE ACCESS (FULL) OF 'ORDERS' (Cost=19 Card=9916 Bytes=109076)

-- PARALLEL hint included using 4 concurrent servers (COST 24 down from 45)
SQL> SELECT /*+ PARALLEL(O,4) */
  2          C.FIRST_NAME CUS_FIRST, C.LAST_NAME CUS_LAST,
  3          S.SHIPMENT_DESCRIPTION, P.PAYMENT_DESCRIPTION,
  4          E.FIRST_NAME EMP_FIRST, E.LAST_NAME EMP_LAST
  5    FROM CUSTOMERS C, ORDERS O, EMPLOYEES E,
  6          SHIPMENT_METHOD S, PAYMENT_METHOD P
  7   WHERE O.CUSTOMER_ID = C.CUSTOMER_ID
  8     AND O.EMPLOYEE_ID = E.EMPLOYEE_ID
  9     AND O.SHIPMENT_METHOD_ID = S.SHIPMENT_METHOD_ID
 10     AND O.PAYMENT_METHOD_ID = P.PAYMENT_METHOD_ID
 11   /


Execution Plan
-----------------------------------------------------------
   0      SELECT STATEMENT Optimizer=CHOOSE (Cost=24 Card=9916 Bytes=694120)
   1    0   HASH JOIN* (Cost=24 Card=9916 Bytes=694120)                              :Q6005
   2    1    TABLE ACCESS* (FULL) OF 'CUSTOMERS' (Cost=13 Card=4000 Bytes=80000)      :Q6003
   3    1    HASH JOIN* (Cost=11 Card=9916 Bytes=495800)                             :Q6004
   4    3     TABLE ACCESS* (FULL) OF 'EMPLOYEES' (Cost=2 Card=294 Bytes=5586)        :Q6000
   5    3     HASH JOIN* (Cost=9 Card=9916 Bytes=307396)                             :Q6004
   6    5      TABLE ACCESS* (FULL) OF 'SHIPMENT_METHOD' (Cost=2 Card=11 Bytes=99)    :Q6001
   7    5      HASH JOIN* (Cost=7 Card=9916 Bytes=218152)                            :Q6004
   8    7       TABLE ACCESS* (FULL) OF 'PAYMENT_METHOD' (Cost=2 Card=9 Bytes=99)     :Q6002
   9    7       TABLE ACCESS* (FULL) OF 'ORDERS' (Cost=5 Card=9916 Bytes=109076)      :Q6004


  1 PARALLEL_TO_SERIAL           SELECT /*+ ORDERED NO_EXPAND USE_HASH(A2) SW
                                 AP_JOIN_INPUTS(A2) */ A2.C1,A2.C2,A1
  2 PARALLEL_FROM_SERIAL
  3 PARALLEL_TO_PARALLEL         SELECT /*+ ORDERED NO_EXPAND USE_HASH(A2) SW
                                 AP_JOIN_INPUTS(A2) */ A1.C3 C0,A2.C1
  4 PARALLEL_FROM_SERIAL
  5 PARALLEL_COMBINED_WITH_PARENT
  6 PARALLEL_FROM_SERIAL
  7 PARALLEL_COMBINED_WITH_PARENT
  8 PARALLEL_FROM_SERIAL
  9 PARALLEL_COMBINED_WITH_PARENT
```

PARALLEL_INDEX

This hint tells the optimizer the number of concurrent servers to be used to scan the range of a partitioned index. This hint has the following syntax:

```
/*+PARALLEL_INDEX ( table [index [, index]...] [{ , integer | , DEFAULT | , } [ , integer | ,
DEFAULT ]] ) */
```

Join Operations Hints

This category includes hints that direct the optimizer on how to join tables for queries with more than one table.

USE_HASH

This hint tells the optimizer to join each specified table using a hash join access path. The following is the syntax for this hint:

```
/*+ USE_HASH (table [table]...) */
```

The following is a demonstration of the USE_HASH hint. Notice that there is a slight improvement in the cost when the hint is added. You probably observed the order of the tables specified in the hint. "S" for SUPPLIERS was placed first because the number of rows returned from "S" is the least returned from all tables because of the condition in the WHERE clause. "PS" for PRODUCT_SUPPLIER is restricted by the number of rows returned by the SUPPLIER table.

13

```
-- No hint
SQL> SELECT P.PRODUCT_NAME, S.SUPPLIER_NAME
  2    FROM PRODUCTS P, PRODUCT_SUPPLIER PS, SUPPLIERS S
  3    WHERE P.PRODUCT_ID = PS.PRODUCT_ID
  4      AND PS.SUPPLIER_ID = S.SUPPLIER_ID
  5      AND S.CITY = 'West End'
  6    ORDER BY P.PRODUCT_NAME, S.SUPPLIER_NAME
  7   /

Execution Plan
----------------------------------------------------------
   0      SELECT STATEMENT Optimizer=CHOOSE (Cost=23 Card=16 Bytes=1024)
   1    0    SORT (ORDER BY) (Cost=23 Card=16 Bytes=1024)
   2    1      HASH JOIN (Cost=21 Card=16 Bytes=1024)
   3    2        TABLE ACCESS (BY INDEX ROWID) OF 'SUPPLIERS' (Cost=4 Card=3 Bytes=87)
   4    3          INDEX (RANGE SCAN) OF 'IDX_SUP_CITY' (NON-UNIQUE) (Cost=1 Card=333)
   5    2        HASH JOIN (Cost=16 Card=5001 Bytes=175035)
   6    5          INDEX (FAST FULL SCAN) OF 'SYS_C003130' (UNIQUE)
                        (Cost=3 Card=5001 Bytes=40008)
   7    5          TABLE ACCESS (FULL) OF 'PRODUCTS' (Cost=10 Card=5001 Bytes=135027)

-- with USE_HASH hint
SQL> SELECT /*+ USE_HASH(S,PS,P) */
  2          P.PRODUCT_NAME, S.SUPPLIER_NAME
  3    FROM PRODUCTS P, PRODUCT_SUPPLIER PS, SUPPLIERS S
  4    WHERE P.PRODUCT_ID = PS.PRODUCT_ID
  5      AND PS.SUPPLIER_ID = S.SUPPLIER_ID
  6      AND S.CITY = 'West End'
  7    ORDER BY P.PRODUCT_NAME, S.SUPPLIER_NAME
  8   /

Execution Plan
----------------------------------------------------------
   0      SELECT STATEMENT Optimizer=CHOOSE (Cost=21 Card=16 Bytes=1024)
   1    0    SORT (ORDER BY) (Cost=21 Card=16 Bytes=1024)
   2    1      HASH JOIN (Cost=19 Card=16 Bytes=1024)
   3    2        HASH JOIN (Cost=8 Card=16 Bytes=592)
   4    3          TABLE ACCESS (BY INDEX ROWID) OF 'SUPPLIERS' (Cost=4 Card=3 Bytes=87)
   5    4            INDEX (RANGE SCAN) OF 'IDX_SUP_CITY' (NON-UNIQUE) (Cost=1 Card=3)
   6    3          INDEX (FAST FULL SCAN) OF 'SYS_C003130' (UNIQUE)
                        (Cost=3 Card=5001 Bytes=40008)
   7    2        TABLE ACCESS (FULL) OF 'PRODUCTS' (Cost=10 Card=5001 Bytes=135027)
```

DRIVING SITE

This hint tells the optimizer to execute the query at the specified site. Consider the following scenario, as illustrated in Figure 13-13.

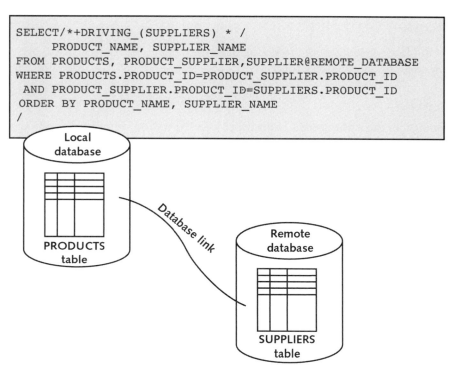

```
SELECT/*+DRIVING_(SUPPLIERS) * /
    PRODUCT_NAME, SUPPLIER_NAME
FROM PRODUCTS, PRODUCT_SUPPLIER,SUPPLIER@REMOTE_DATABASE
WHERE PRODUCTS.PRODUCT_ID=PRODUCT_SUPPLIER.PRODUCT_ID
 AND PRODUCT_SUPPLIER.PRODUCT_ID=SUPPLIERS.PRODUCT_ID
 ORDER BY PRODUCT_NAME, SUPPLIER_NAME
/
```

Figure 13-13   Example of a distributed database application

Suppose you have a distributed database application in which the tables of the application are located in two different locations. In this example, the PRODUCTS table resides locally in a database called LOCAL and the SUPPLIERS table resides in a remote database called REMOTE. The application is connected to LOCAL and must issue a simple query retrieving data from tables residing in both locations.

When you submit the query without a hint, it executes as follows:

1. Retrieves necessary rows from the SUPPLIERS table in the REMOTE database and sends them back to the LOCAL database.

2. Retrieves necessary rows from the PRODUCTS and PRODUCT_SUPPLIER tables in the LOCAL database.

3. Joins the results of the row sets locally in the LOCAL database, which implies that execution occurs at the LOCAL database.

When you include the hint DRIVING_SITE, however, the execution is as follows:

1. Retrieves necessary rows from the SUPPLIERS table in the REMOTE database.

2. Retrieves necessary rows from the PRODUCTS and PRODUCT_SUPPLIER tables in the LOCAL database and sends them to the REMOTE database.

3. Joins the results of the row sets remotely in the REMOTE database, which implies that execution occurs at REMOTE database.

Optimization Goal Hints

Hints in this category are used to set the optimizer goal to RBO or CBO as presented earlier in this chapter. See Figure 13-3.

ALL_ROWS

This hint tells the optimizer to choose a cost-based optimization goal and to determine the best way to retrieve all rows with minimal resource consumption:

```
SQL> SELECT /*+ ALL_ROWS */
  2          ORDER_ID, ORDER_DATE
  3    FROM ORDERS
  4   WHERE ORDER_DATE > '01-JAN-02'
  5  /

Execution Plan
----------------------------------------------------------
   0      SELECT STATEMENT Optimizer=HINT: ALL_ROWS (Cost=19 Card=1743 Bytes=17430)
   1    0   TABLE ACCESS (FULL) OF 'ORDERS' (Cost=19 Card=1743 Bytes=17430)
```

RULE

This hint tells the optimizer to use rule-based optimization as a goal to retrieve data:

```
SQL> SELECT /*+ RULE */
  2          ORDER_ID, ORDER_DATE
  3    FROM ORDERS
  4   WHERE ORDER_DATE > '01-JAN-02'
  5  /

Execution Plan
----------------------------------------------------------
   0      SELECT STATEMENT Optimizer=HINT: RULE
   1    0   TABLE ACCESS (BY INDEX ROWID) OF 'ORDERS'
   2    1     INDEX (RANGE SCAN) OF 'IDX_ORD_ORDER_DATE' (NON-UNIQUE)
```

Other Hints

Hints in this category cannot be associated with any specific operations and do not have common characteristics.

APPEND

This hint tells the optimizer to use a direct path when inserting a record to speed up the insert operation by bypassing the cache buffer and redo logs. Data is appended at the end of the table:

```
SQL> INSERT /*+ APPEND */ INTO TEST
  2      SELECT * FROM ORDER_LINES
  3  /
```

CURSOR_SHARING_EXACT

If the CURSOR_SHARING initialization parameter is set to FORCE or SIMILAR, this hint tells the optimizer to override the setting of EXACT. The EXACT setting tells the Oracle server to parse each submitted statement if the statement is not exactly the same text pattern.

```
SQL> SELECT /*+ CURSOR_SHARING_EXACT */
  2           PRODUCT_ID, PRODUCT_NAME
  3    FROM PRODUCTS
  4    WHERE PRODUCT_NAME LIKE 'P%'
  5  /
```

IDENTIFYING SQL QUERIES THAT CONSUME THE MOST RESOURCES

Harold had just arrived at work and as he was logging on to his machine, his manager, Bob, appeared at his desk. "Good morning, Harold," Bob said. Harold replied, "It does not seem so good! What's going on?" Bob said, "I thought you audited all queries and made sure all of them were optimized. The Data Center paged me and paged you. You must've missed it. It's about a report that is sucking up all the resources and everything is running as slowly as a snail." Harold looked at his pager, saw the alert, and said, "I really did optimize all queries. Here is the folder!" Bob did not believe him and after what had happened during the morning, doubted that the optimization had been done. As for Harold, he was not pleased that he was in his first compromising situation. Bob said, "I want you to investigate this further and after you're done, I need a report on my desk explaining in detail what happened. I'll have to explain this to the VP and our business partner."

Bob called Linda, another DBA on his team, briefed her about the problem, and asked her to investigate. Harold then signed onto the database to look at the query, specifically the execution plan. "There is nothing wrong," Harold murmured to himself. Then he looked at the statistics of the query causing the problem and his face turned pale. Can you guess why he was surprised?

Harold and Linda prepared their reports and met at Bob's office. "Go ahead, Linda, tell me what happened," Bob directed. Linda said, "In a nutshell, the query is not optimal and could be enhanced, but in general, because of the nature of the report retrieving data from large tables, it is slowing down more!" Bob looked fiercely at Harold and asked, "What about you? What did you come up with?" Harold explained, "First, I would like to confirm Linda's findings. Second, the query was optimized in the QA environment, which does not have the same amount of data as in production. I did my analysis in the QA environment and for the amount of data there, it was optimal. Third, as far as the staging environment, I could not run it there because the QA team was using the database for other functions and did not want any interference with their testing. Fourth, this is the only query I tested in QA. The rest were done in staging."

The moral of the story is that the amount of data being processed influences how the optimizer accesses data. Harold was a diligent DBA to analyze all queries in the staging environment except the one that caused the problem.

Now, go back to how this problematic query problem was detected. A tool that collects the top SQL queries that are consuming resources such as CPU and memory detected the problem. In this section, you revisit this topic and learn the important factors that you should look for to detect and collect the top 5, 10, or *n* SQL queries using the V$ performance view V$SQL and the Top SQL utility.

The important factor when it comes to detecting top SQL queries is statistics. As you already know, the V$SQL dynamic performance view contains SQL statements submitted to the database. It contains the SQL text as well as the execution statistical data of the statement. Table 13-3 presents columns for each category.

Table 13-3   Classification of V$SQL columns

Factor	Column or derived column
CPU consumption	■ CPU_TIME ■ CPU per execution = CPU_TIME/EXECUTIONS ■ ELAPSED_TIME ■ Elapsed time per execution = ELAPSED_TIME/EXECUTIONS
I/O (disk reads)	■ DISK_READS (column) ■ Disk reads per execution = DISK_READS/EXECUTIONS
MEMORY (buffer usage)	■ BUFFER_GETS ■ BUFFER_GETS per execution = BUFFER_GETS/EXECUTIONS ■ SHARABLE_MEM
PARSING	■ PARSE_CALLS (column) ■ EXECUTIONS (column) ■ Parsing per execution = PARSING/EXECUTION
SORTING	■ SORTS (column)
RETRIEVED ROWS	■ ROWS_PROCESSED (column) ■ Rows per execution = ROWS_PROCESSED/EXECUTIONS ■ FETCHES

The information in this table is derived from the online documentation that Oracle provides at the Oracle Technology Network site: *www.otn.oracle.com*.

To identify the five SQL queries that are consuming the most CPU time, you issue the following query:

```
SELECT *
  FROM (SELECT * FROM V$SQL ORDER BY CPU_TIME DESC) Q
 WHERE ROWNUM <= 5
```

What about the top ten SQL queries that have the most disk reads per execution? To identify them, you issue the following query:

```
SELECT *
  FROM (SELECT ROUND((DISK_READS/
                DECODE(EXECUTIONS, 0, -99999999, EXECUTIONS)))
                DISK_READS_PER_EXEC,
                V$SQL.*
          FROM V$SQL
         ORDER BY DISK_READS_PER_EXEC DESC) Q
 WHERE ROWNUM <= 10
```

If you like fancy colors and graphical screens, you can definitely use the Top SQL utility that comes with the Oracle Enterprise Manager Diagnostic Pack (see Chapter 12). This tool provides considerable functionality with which you can sort any statistics by a click of a button, and you can drill down on a query to view the full text of the query as well as the Explain Plan. Figure 13-14 illustrates the functionality of this tool.

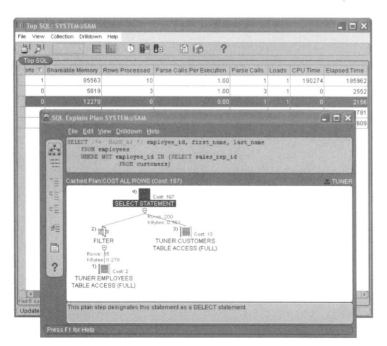

Figure 13-14   Oracle Enterprise Manager showing the main window and execution plan window of the Top SQL utility

UNDERSTANDING THE NEED FOR SQL STANDARDS

Why standards? What do they have to do with SQL tuning? You probably are asking yourself these questions. Frankly, the answer is that SQL standards do not enhance SQL performance, but not having them could degrade execution queries. Strange, isn't it! Standards provide consistency, and consistency leads to stability, that is, execution stability. The following true story illustrates this concept.

During five of the dot-com boom years, Danny worked as a DBA for a big company and then decided to climb on the consulting bandwagon. His first contract was with a midsize real estate company. He was hired to implement a new Web application that allowed users to query a database for houses. During his first two weeks, Danny took a survey of the database application functionality and requirements. Then he got very busy configuring the new database and carrying out other production preparations. The application went into production, and Danny was concerned about all aspects of the database performance. He monitored the database operation constantly the first two days and then he saw it! Four different statements that were retrieving the same data but were being parsed four times. He couldn't believe his eyes!

Danny went straight to his hiring manager and told him about his findings. He said, "I am not sure if there are more statements like this. I need to do a full audit of every query to find out more." When the manager asked him how serious the problem was, Danny replied, "Well, at this time it's not serious, but it could develop into a very big problem if we have more of these statements." The manager said, "The development team has so much on their plates. We'll tackle this problem later when they are less busy."

Three weeks went by and slowly but surely real estate brokers started to complain about how slow the database was, and very soon it became apparent to management that this was a problem that had to be dealt with immediately.

What was the problem? Because the submitted SQL statements were inconsistent, they were causing too much parsing. Why was this happening? Because there were no standards for writing SQL statements. So, each developer was using his own standards, some using lowercase for keys and some using uppercase, for example. The following sections present several standards issues that should be considered a part of the company's development standards.

Syntax Convention

All developers should follow the same conventions when writing SQL statements. Use of lowercase and uppercase must be consistent. One common SQL format is illustrated in the following query. As you can see, all SQL keywords are left justified and uppercase, whereas user code such as table names and column names are lowercase. However, it is much easier if you purchase a program that does SQL formatting.

```
SELECT c.customer_id, c.first_name, c.last_name
  FROM customers c,
       (SELECT supplier_id, supplier_name
          FROM suppliers
         WHERE city LIKE '%N') S
 WHERE c.city = s.city
```

Qualify Tables

You probably see the following practice almost everywhere: developers using synonyms rather than qualifying the table name with the table owner as in this example:

```
You should use
     SELECT * FROM tuner.customers
Rather than
     SELECT * FROM customers
This statement is using a public synonym pointing to TUNER.CUSTOMERS
```

Of course, it should be noted that the qualifying table owner will hard code all SQL statements to be used by the specified schema owner.

Table Aliasing

Table aliasing is the act of using a temporary synonym for a table in a SQL statement. You should use alias table names even if the column names specified in the SELECT statement are not common in the tables. For example, examine the code segment that follows:

```
-- Not recommended
SELECT FIRST_NAME || ' ' || LAST_NAME EMPLOYEE,
       DEPARTMENT_NAME DEPARTMENT
  FROM EMPLOYEES, DEPARTMENTS
 WHERE EMPLOYEES.DEPARTMENT_ID = DEPARTMENTS.DEPARTMENT_ID

-- Recommended
SELECT E.FIRST_NAME || ' ' || E.LAST_NAME EMPLOYEE,
       D.DEPARTMENT_NAME DEPARTMENT
  FROM EMPLOYEES E, DEPARTMENTS D
 WHERE E.DEPARTMENT_ID = D.DEPARTMENT_ID
```

By adding table aliasing you reduce the amount of typing. Even more important is column aliasing, which tells Oracle which table each column is coming from rather than wasting time determining the table to which it belongs.

Bind Variables

Using bind variables rather than literals reduces unnecessary parsing:

```
-- The following query is not recommended because it does
-- not use bind variables, instead it uses a date literal
SELECT ORDER_ID, CUSTOMER_ID, PAID
  FROM ORDERS
 WHERE ORDER_DATE = '01-JAN-00'  <-- date literal
/

-- The following query is recommended because it is using
-- a bind variable
SELECT ORDER_ID, CUSTOMER_ID, PAID
  FROM ORDERS
 WHERE ORDER_DATE = :ORD_DATE  <-- bind variable
/
```

As previously explained, not having standards could degrade the performance of the SQL statements. You are highly encouraged to develop SQL standards if your company does not employ them.

IMPROVING SQL STATEMENT EXECUTION

A senior DBA was hired to administer three main database applications. When she was interviewed, the manager told her, "When it comes to C++, I have highly qualified developers who can produce highly efficient code, but when it comes to SQL they are still learning. If you are hired, we will expect you to help in this area by tuning all SQL statements." The senior DBA replied, "I will definitely be an asset to your team and will apply all my knowledge to ensure that all SQL statements are optimal. Also, I will transfer my SQL expertise to your team by publishing a document with recommendations on how to improve SQL execution. By considering these recommendations, the developers can write better SQL."

Managers call this type of DBA a team player. She will not only complement the team with her SQL tuning expertise but will also impart knowledge! Transferring knowledge actually makes DBAs essential team players, gains them the respect of their managers and colleagues, and as a result, makes them indispensable assets to a team.

Outlined in the following list is a set of tips that you should consider when writing SQL statements. In most cases, these considerations enhance SQL execution. Also, you should remember that a tuned SQL statement is a statement that has been optimized by analyzing the execution plan of the query, not by looking at it and merely applying tips.

When writing a SQL statement, consider using one, all, or a combination of the following (sometimes you will use none):

- Record the time and cost before and after you improve a query.

- Record the time and cost before and after the execution plan of a query.

- Record the time and cost before and after you produce query statistics.

- Record the time and cost of actions you take to improve statement execution.

Analyze Tables and Indexes

On a regular basis, you should analyze tables, especially highly transactional tables, to provide the optimizer with all necessary statistical data to select the most efficient execution plan:

```
-- Deleting statistical data for ORDER_LINES table and its index
begin
   dbms_stats.delete_table_stats(ownname=> 'TUNER', tabname=> 'ORDER_LINES');
end;

begin
   dbms_stats.delete_index_stats(ownname=> 'TUNER', indname=> 'SYS_C003144', partname=> NULL);
end;

-- Query
SQL> SELECT PRODUCT_ID, ACTUAL_PRICE, DISCOUNT, QUANTITY, TOTAL_AMOUNT
  2     FROM ORDER_LINES
  3    WHERE ORDER_ID = 1543
  4   /

-- Before analyzing ORDER_LINES table and its indexes
Execution Plan
----------------------------------------------------------
   0      SELECT STATEMENT Optimizer=CHOOSE
   1    0    TABLE ACCESS (BY INDEX ROWID) OF 'ORDER_LINES'
   2    1      INDEX (RANGE SCAN) OF 'IDX_OL_ORDER_ID' (NON-UNIQUE)


-- After analyzing ORDER_LINES table and its indexes
Execution Plan
----------------------------------------------------------
   0      SELECT STATEMENT Optimizer=CHOOSE (Cost=2 Card=1080 Bytes=30240)
   1    0    TABLE ACCESS (BY INDEX ROWID) OF 'ORDER_LINES' (Cost=2 Card=1080 Bytes=30240)
   2    1      INDEX (RANGE SCAN) OF 'IDX_OL_ORDER_ID' (NON-UNIQUE) (Cost=1 Card=432)
```

13

You can see that the execution is quite different. First note that there are no cost statistics when the ORDER_LINES table had no statistics. Also note that the optimizer chose to execute the query using a rule-based access path when statistics were not found. So, this tells you that analyzing tables helps the optimizer to make better decisions in selecting an access path to retrieve data.

Creating Indexes

Columns used in the WHERE clause of the query should be indexed, especially if the table is large. In this example, notice that the cost was reduced from 49 to 16 when an index was added:

```
-- ORDER_LINES table does not have index on ACTUAL_PRICE column
SQL> SELECT ORDER_ID, PRODUCT_ID, ACTUAL_PRICE, QUANTITY, TOTAL_AMOUNT
  2    FROM ORDER_LINES
  3    WHERE ACTUAL_PRICE = 100
  4  /

-- Execution plan without index
Execution Plan
----------------------------------------------------------
   0      SELECT STATEMENT Optimizer=CHOOSE (Cost=49 Card=19 Bytes=342)
   1    0    TABLE ACCESS (FULL) OF 'ORDER_LINES' (Cost=49 Card=19 Bytes=342)

-- Creating and analyzing index on ACTUAL_PRICE
SQL> CREATE INDEX IDX_OL_ACTUAL_PRICE ON ORDER_LINES(ACTUAL_PRICE)
  2  /

Index created.

SQL> ANALYZE INDEX IDX_OL_ACTUAL_PRICE ESTIMATE STATISTICS SAMPLE 20 PERCENT
  2  /

Index analyzed.

-- Execution plan with index
Execution Plan
----------------------------------------------------------
   0      SELECT STATEMENT Optimizer=CHOOSE (Cost=16 Card=19 Bytes=342)
   1    0    TABLE ACCESS (BY INDEX ROWID) OF 'ORDER_LINES' (Cost=16 Card=19 Bytes=342)
   2    1      INDEX (RANGE SCAN) OF 'IDX_OL_ACTUAL_PRICE' (NON-UNIQUE)
```

Consider Creating Indexes on Foreign Keys

Most DBA experts highly recommend creating indexes on all foreign key columns, especially if the tables are large, as foreign keys are more often used to join related tables. In the following example, you have two very large tables, PRD and ORD. The ORD table has a column called PROD_ID, which is a foreign key to the PRD table. See what happens when you run the simplest query including a join of these two tables. As you can see, when an index was added on the FK column in the PRD table, the cost went down from 499 to 35.

```
-- No index exists on PROD_ID column which is FK in ORD table referencing PRD table
SQL> SELECT PRD.PROD_ID, ORD.QUANTITY_SOLD, ORD.AMOUNT_SOLD,
  2          PRD.PROD_NAME, PRD.PROD_LIST_PRICE
  3    FROM ORD, PRD
  4   WHERE PRD.PROD_ID = ORD.PROD_ID
  5     AND PRD.PROD_NAME = '1-Piece Cozy Horse Pajamas'
  6  /

3258 rows selected.

-- Execution plan without the index on FK column
Execution Plan
----------------------------------------------------------
   0      SELECT STATEMENT Optimizer=CHOOSE (Cost=499 Card=2666 Bytes=111972)
   1    0   HASH JOIN (Cost=499 Card=2666 Bytes=111972)
   2    1     TABLE ACCESS (BY INDEX ROWID) OF 'PRD' (Cost=9 Card=13 Bytes=429)
   3    2       INDEX (RANGE SCAN) OF 'IDX_PRD_NAME' (NON-UNIQUE) (Cost=1 Card=13)
   4    1     TABLE ACCESS (FULL) OF 'ORD' (Cost=481 Card=1016271 Bytes=9146439)

-- Creating an index on FK column in ORD table
SQL> CREATE INDEX IDX_ORD_PROD_ID ON ORD(PROD_ID)
  2  /

Index created.


-- Execution plan after the index on FK column
Execution Plan
----------------------------------------------------------
   0      SELECT STATEMENT Optimizer=CHOOSE (Cost=35 Card=2666 Bytes=111972)

   1    0   TABLE ACCESS (BY INDEX ROWID) OF 'ORD' (Cost=2 Card=202 Bytes=1818)

   2    1     NESTED LOOPS (Cost=35 Card=2666 Bytes=111972)
   3    2       TABLE ACCESS (BY INDEX ROWID) OF 'PRD' (Cost=9 Card=13 Bytes=429)
   4    3         INDEX (RANGE SCAN) OF 'IDX_PRD_NAME' (NON-UNIQUE) (Cost=1 Card=13)
   5    2       INDEX (RANGE SCAN) OF 'IDX_ORD_PROD_ID' (NON-UNIQUE) (Cost=1 Card=202)
```

13

Using Indexes for Small Tables

In this example, you see that an index on a small table is a liability. The query is a join of two tables, EMPLOYEES and JOBS, on column JOB_ID. In general, it is recommended that you create indexes on foreign keys, which, in this case, is the JOB_ID column in the EMPLOYEE table. In this example, the optimizer generated the same execution plan with the same cost of 5, whether or not an index on JOB_ID in EMPLOYEE table existed. When the optimizer was told to use an index via an INDEX hint, it produced a plan costing 44, which is much higher than before. This proves that using an index on small tables is a liability. Oracle can scan the whole table much faster than scanning the index to locate ROWID and retrieve the row from the table.

```
-- Index on JOB_ID in EMPLOYEES table does not exists
SQL> SELECT FIRST_NAME, LAST_NAME, JOB_DESCRIPTION
  2     FROM EMPLOYEES E,  JOBS J
  3   WHERE E.JOB_ID = J.JOB_ID
  4      AND J.JOB_ID BETWEEN 10 AND 50
  5  /


Execution Plan
----------------------------------------------------------
   0      SELECT STATEMENT Optimizer=CHOOSE (Cost=5 Card=69 Bytes=2484)
   1    0   HASH JOIN (Cost=5 Card=69 Bytes=2484)
   2    1     TABLE ACCESS (BY INDEX ROWID) OF 'JOBS' (Cost=2 Card=42 Bytes=756)
   3    2       INDEX (RANGE SCAN) OF 'SYS_C003117' (UNIQUE) (Cost=1 Card=42)
   4    1     TABLE ACCESS (FULL) OF 'EMPLOYEES' (Cost=2 Card=128 Bytes=2304)

-- Creating and analyzing index on JOB_ID in EMPLOYEES table
SQL> CREATE INDEX IDX_EMP_JOB_ID ON EMPLOYEES(JOB_ID)
  2  /

Index created.

SQL> ANALYZE INDEX IDX_EMP_JOB_ID ESTIMATE STATISTICS SAMPLE 20 PERCENT
  2  /

Index analyzed.

-- Execution plan after creating index, Optimizer chose not use index to retrieve data
Execution Plan
----------------------------------------------------------
   0      SELECT STATEMENT Optimizer=CHOOSE (Cost=5 Card=69 Bytes=2484)
   1    0   HASH JOIN (Cost=5 Card=69 Bytes=2484)
   2    1     TABLE ACCESS (BY INDEX ROWID) OF 'JOBS' (Cost=2 Card=42 Bytes=756)
   3    2       INDEX (RANGE SCAN) OF 'SYS_C003117' (UNIQUE) (Cost=1 Card=42)
   4    1     TABLE ACCESS (FULL) OF 'EMPLOYEES' (Cost=2 Card=128 Bytes=2304)

-- Query re-submitted with a HINT to use existing index on JOB_ID in EMPLOYEE table
SQL> SELECT /*+ INDEX(E IDX_EMP_JOB_ID) */
  2           FIRST_NAME, LAST_NAME, JOB_DESCRIPTION
  3     FROM EMPLOYEES E,  JOBS J
  4    WHERE E.JOB_ID = J.JOB_ID
  5      AND J.JOB_ID BETWEEN 10 AND 50
  6  /

-- Execution plan using index
Execution Plan
----------------------------------------------------------
   0      SELECT STATEMENT Optimizer=CHOOSE (Cost=44 Card=69 Bytes=2484)
   1    0   TABLE ACCESS (BY INDEX ROWID) OF 'EMPLOYEES' (Cost=1 Card=2 Bytes=36)
   2    1     NESTED LOOPS (Cost=44 Card=69 Bytes=2484)
   3    2       TABLE ACCESS (BY INDEX ROWID) OF 'JOBS' (Cost=2 Card=42 Bytes=756)
   4    3         INDEX (RANGE SCAN) OF 'SYS_C003117' (UNIQUE) (Cost=1 Card=42)
   5    2       INDEX (RANGE SCAN) OF 'IDX_EMP_JOB_ID' (NON-UNIQUE)
```

Using OR instead of UNION and Vice Versa

In many cases, you can substitute a UNION query with an OR statement and vice versa to improve execution of the query. For example, consider the following example:

```
-- statement with UNION (cost 62)
SQL> SELECT O.ORDER_ID, O.ORDER_DATE, O.PAID
  2    FROM ORDERS O, CUSTOMERS C
  3   WHERE O.CUSTOMER_ID = C.CUSTOMER_ID
  4     AND C.CITY = 'West End'
  5  UNION
  6  SELECT O.ORDER_ID, O.ORDER_DATE, O.PAID
  7    FROM ORDERS O, EMPLOYEES E
  8   WHERE O.EMPLOYEE_ID = E.EMPLOYEE_ID
  9     AND E.JOB_ID = 122
 10  /

Execution Plan
-----------------------------------------------------------
   0      SELECT STATEMENT Optimizer=CHOOSE (Cost=62 Card=762 Bytes=19380)
   1    0   SORT (UNIQUE) (Cost=62 Card=762 Bytes=19380)
   2    1     UNION-ALL
   3    2       HASH JOIN (Cost=33 Card=33 Bytes=1155)
   4    3         TABLE ACCESS (BY INDEX ROWID) OF 'CUSTOMERS' (Cost=13 Card=12 Bytes=192)
   5    4           INDEX (RANGE SCAN) OF 'IDX_CUS_CITY' (NON-UNIQUE) (Cost=1 Card=333)
   6    3         TABLE ACCESS (FULL) OF 'ORDERS' (Cost=19 Card=9916 Bytes=188404)
   7    2       HASH JOIN (Cost=22 Card=729 Bytes=18225)
   8    7         TABLE ACCESS (FULL) OF 'EMPLOYEES' (Cost=2 Card=3 Bytes=21)
   9    7         TABLE ACCESS (FULL) OF 'ORDERS' (Cost=19 Card=9916 Bytes=178488)


-- statement with OR producing same results as UNION statement (cost 39)
SQL> SELECT O.ORDER_ID, O.ORDER_DATE, O.PAID
  2    FROM ORDERS O, CUSTOMERS C, EMPLOYEES E
  3   WHERE O.CUSTOMER_ID = C.CUSTOMER_ID
  4     AND O.EMPLOYEE_ID = E.EMPLOYEE_ID
  5     AND (C.CITY = 'West End' OR E.JOB_ID = 122)
  6  /

Execution Plan
-----------------------------------------------------------
   0      SELECT STATEMENT Optimizer=CHOOSE (Cost=39 Card=137 Bytes=6302)
   1    0   HASH JOIN (Cost=39 Card=137 Bytes=6302)
   2    1     TABLE ACCESS (FULL) OF 'CUSTOMERS' (Cost=13 Card=4000 Bytes=64000)
   3    1     HASH JOIN (Cost=22 Card=9916 Bytes=297480)
   4    3       TABLE ACCESS (FULL) OF 'EMPLOYEES' (Cost=2 Card=294 Bytes=2058)
   5    3       TABLE ACCESS (FULL) OF 'ORDERS' (Cost=19 Card=9916 Bytes=228068)
```

13

Parallel Execution

As demonstrated earlier, parallel execution may tremendously enhance the performance of a SQL statement, especially when retrieving a large percentage of data from large tables, as shown in the following example:

```
-- No parallel execution
SQL> SELECT ORDER_ID, PRODUCT_ID, TOTAL_AMOUNT
  2    FROM ORDER_LINES OL
  3    ORDER BY 1, 2
  4  /

Execution Plan
----------------------------------------------------------
  0       SELECT STATEMENT Optimizer=CHOOSE (Cost=431 Card=108038 Bytes=1188418)
  1    0    SORT (ORDER BY) (Cost=431 Card=108038 Bytes=1188418)
  2    1      TABLE ACCESS (FULL) OF 'ORDER_LINES' (Cost=49 Card=108038 Bytes=1188418)

-- included a hint for parallel execution
SQL> SELECT /*+ PARALLEL(OL, 8) */
  2          ORDER_ID, PRODUCT_ID, TOTAL_AMOUNT
  3    FROM ORDER_LINES OL
  4    ORDER BY 1, 2
  5  /

Execution Plan
----------------------------------------------------------
  0       SELECT STATEMENT Optimizer=CHOOSE (Cost=66 Card=108038 Bytes=1188418)
  1    0    SORT* (ORDER BY) (Cost=66 Card=108038 Bytes=1188418)                    :Q15001
  2    1      TABLE ACCESS* (FULL) OF 'ORDER_LINES' (Cost=7 Card=108038 Bytes=1188418) :Q15000


  1 PARALLEL_TO_SERIAL          SELECT A1.C0 C0,A1.C1 C1,A1.C2 C2 FROM :Q150
                                00 A1 ORDER BY A1.C0,A1.C1


  2 PARALLEL_TO_PARALLEL        SELECT /*+ NO_EXPAND ROWID(A1) */ A1."ORDER_
                                ID" C0,A1."PRODUCT_ID" C1,A1."TOTAL_
```

Table Aliasing

As explained previously, it is recommended that you use **table aliasing**. Just follow these steps for a demonstration:

Step 1: As TUNER, issue the following statement that uses table aliasing:

```
SELECT /* NO TABLE ALIASING */
       FIRST_NAME || ' ' || LAST_NAME EMPLOYEE,
       DEPARTMENT_NAME DEPARTMENT
  FROM EMPLOYEES, DEPARTMENTS
 WHERE EMPLOYEES.DEPARTMENT_ID = DEPARTMENTS.DEPARTMENT_ID
```

Step 2: As TUNER, issue the following statement that does not use table aliasing:

```
SELECT /* WITH TABLE ALIASING */
       E.FIRST_NAME || ' ' || E.LAST_NAME EMPLOYEE,
       D.DEPARTMENT_NAME DEPARTMENT
  FROM EMPLOYEES E, DEPARTMENTS D
 WHERE E.DEPARTMENT_ID = D.DEPARTMENT_ID
```

Step 3: As SYSTEM, display ELAPSED_TIME for both queries using the following statement:

```
SQL> SELECT SQL_TEXT, ELAPSED_TIME
  2    FROM V$SQL
  3    WHERE SQL_TEXT LIKE '%TABLE ALIASING%'
  4    ORDER BY 1
  5  /

SQL_TEXT                             ELAPSED_TIME
----------------------------------- ------------
SELECT /* NO TABLE ALIASING */          10739
SELECT /* WITH TABLE ALIASING */        10563
```

As you can see, the elapsed time for the statement with table aliasing is less than the elapsed time for the table without table aliasing because Oracle does not need to do extra work to determine what columns belong to what table when table aliasing is omitted.

Using Table Join Instead of Simple Subqueries

Most simple subqueries in a SQL statement can be converted to a join table, which improves query execution. As you can see from the results in the following example, the cost went down from 5 to 3 when the SUBQUERY was converted to a table join:

13

```
-- Using SUB-QUERY
SQL> SELECT PRODUCT_ID, PRODUCT_NAME
  2    FROM PRODUCTS
  3   WHERE PRODUCT_ID IN (SELECT PRODUCT_ID
  4                          FROM PRODUCT_PRICES
  5                         WHERE LIST_PRICE = 10)
  6  /

Execution Plan
----------------------------------------------------------
   0        SELECT STATEMENT Optimizer=CHOOSE (Cost=5 Card=1 Bytes=37)
   1    0    NESTED LOOPS (Cost=5 Card=1 Bytes=37)
   2    1      SORT (UNIQUE)
   3    2        TABLE ACCESS (BY INDEX ROWID) OF 'PRODUCT_PRICES' (Cost=2 Card=1 Bytes=10)
   4    3          INDEX (RANGE SCAN) OF 'IDX_PRD_LIST_PRICE' (NON-UNIQUE) (Cost=1 Card=1)
   5    1      TABLE ACCESS (BY INDEX ROWID) OF 'PRODUCTS' (Cost=1 Card=1 Bytes=27)
   6    5        INDEX (UNIQUE SCAN) OF 'PK_PRO_PRODUCT_ID' (UNIQUE)


-- Converted SUB-QUERY to a table join
SQL> SELECT P.PRODUCT_ID, P.PRODUCT_NAME
  2    FROM PRODUCTS P, PRODUCT_PRICES PP
  3   WHERE P.PRODUCT_ID = PP.PRODUCT_ID
  4     AND PP.LIST_PRICE = 10
  5  /

Execution Plan
----------------------------------------------------------
   0        SELECT STATEMENT Optimizer=CHOOSE (Cost=3 Card=1 Bytes=37)
   1    0    NESTED LOOPS (Cost=3 Card=1 Bytes=37)
   2    1      TABLE ACCESS (BY INDEX ROWID) OF 'PRODUCT_PRICES' (Cost=2 Card=1 Bytes=10)
   3    2        INDEX (RANGE SCAN) OF 'IDX_PRD_LIST_PRICE' (NON-UNIQUE) (Cost=1 Card=1)
   4    1      TABLE ACCESS (BY INDEX ROWID) OF 'PRODUCTS' (Cost=1 Card=1 Bytes=27)
   5    4        INDEX (UNIQUE SCAN) OF 'PK_PRO_PRODUCT_ID' (UNIQUE)
```

Using the NOT EQUAL (!=) or NOT IN Operator Instead of NOT EXISTS Operator and Vice Versa

Here is another example. By rewriting the following query, replacing NOT EXISTS with NOT IN, the query improves dramatically:

```
-- using NOT EXISTS
SQL> SELECT product_id, product_name
  2    FROM products p
  3   WHERE NOT EXISTS (SELECT 'x'
  4                       FROM order_lines
  5                      where product_id = p.product_id
  6                        and total_amount < 100)
  7  /

Execution Plan
-------------------------------------------------------------
   0        SELECT STATEMENT Optimizer=CHOOSE (Cost=1260 Card=250 Bytes=6750)
   1     0    FILTER
   2     1      TABLE ACCESS (FULL) OF 'PRODUCTS' (Cost=10 Card=250 Bytes=6750)
   3     1      VIEW OF 'index$_join$_002' (Cost=5 Card=1 Bytes=10)
   4     3        HASH JOIN
   5     4          INDEX (RANGE SCAN) OF 'IDX_OL_PRODUCT_ID' (NON-UNIQUE)
                      (Cost=5 Card=1 Bytes=10)
   6     4          INDEX (RANGE SCAN) OF 'IDX_OL_TOTAL_AMOUNT' (NON-UNIQUE)
                      (Cost=5 Card=1 Bytes=10)

-- replacing NOT EXISTS with NOT IN
SQL> SELECT PRODUCT_ID, PRODUCT_NAME
  2    FROM PRODUCTS P
  3   WHERE PRODUCT_ID NOT IN (SELECT PRODUCT_ID
  4                              FROM ORDER_LINES
  5                             WHERE TOTAL_AMOUNT < 100)
  6  /

Execution Plan
-------------------------------------------------------------
   0        SELECT STATEMENT Optimizer=CHOOSE (Cost=36 Card=4980 Bytes=184260)
   1     0    HASH JOIN (ANTI) (Cost=36 Card=4980 Bytes=184260)
   2     1      TABLE ACCESS (FULL) OF 'PRODUCTS' (Cost=10 Card=5001 Bytes=135027)
   3     1      TABLE ACCESS (BY INDEX ROWID) OF 'ORDER_LINES' (Cost=23 Card=20 Bytes=200)
   4     3        INDEX (RANGE SCAN) OF 'IDX_OL_TOTAL_AMOUNT' (NON-UNIQUE) (Cost=2 Card=20)
```

13

Using Oracle Hints

Using Oracle hints is sometimes necessary, especially when the optimizer does not pick the right access path. You can enhance the performance of the query by providing a hint to influence the access path of the optimizer. Here is an example of how a hint improved the cost from 287 to 9 for a simple query:

```
-- no hint
SQL> SELECT EMPLOYEE_ID,
  2         FIRST_NAME || ' ' || LAST_NAME EMPLOYEE_NAME
  3    FROM EMPLOYEES
  4   WHERE EMPLOYEE_ID NOT IN (SELECT EMPLOYEE_ID
  5                               FROM ORDERS)
  6  /

Execution Plan
----------------------------------------------------------
   0      SELECT STATEMENT Optimizer=CHOOSE (Cost=287 Card=15 Bytes=285)
   1    0   FILTER
   2    1     TABLE ACCESS (FULL) OF 'EMPLOYEES' (Cost=2 Card=15 Bytes=285)
   3    1     TABLE ACCESS (FULL) OF 'ORDERS' (Cost=19 Card=496 Bytes=1984)

-- using a hint
SQL> SELECT /*+ INDEX_COMBINE(EMPLOYEES) */ EMPLOYEE_ID,
  2         FIRST_NAME || ' ' || LAST_NAME EMPLOYEE_NAME
  3    FROM EMPLOYEES
  4   WHERE EMPLOYEE_ID NOT IN (SELECT EMPLOYEE_ID
  5                               FROM ORDERS)
  6  /

Execution Plan
----------------------------------------------------------
   0      SELECT STATEMENT Optimizer=CHOOSE (Cost=9 Card=15 Bytes=285)
   1    0   TABLE ACCESS (BY INDEX ROWID) OF 'EMPLOYEES' (Cost=9 Card=15 Bytes=285)
   2    1     INDEX (FULL SCAN) OF 'SYS_C003119' (UNIQUE) (Cost=1 Card=15)
   3    2       TABLE ACCESS (FULL) OF 'ORDERS' (Cost=19 Card=496 Bytes=1984)
```

Using UNION ALL Instead of UNION

You already know that a UNION statement causes a sort to remove duplicates and a UNION ALL statement does not sort or remove duplicates:

```
-- Using UNION
SQL> SELECT FIRST_NAME, LAST_NAME
  2    FROM CUSTOMERS
  3    WHERE CITY = 'West End'
  4  UNION
  5  SELECT FIRST_NAME, LAST_NAME
  6    FROM EMPLOYEES
  7    WHERE DEPARTMENT_ID = 50
  8  /

Execution Plan
-----------------------------------------------------------
   0       SELECT STATEMENT Optimizer=CHOOSE (Cost=18 Card=16 Bytes=424)
   1    0    SORT (UNIQUE) (Cost=18 Card=16 Bytes=424)
   2    1      UNION-ALL
   3    2        TABLE ACCESS (FULL) OF 'CUSTOMERS' (Cost=13 Card=12 Bytes=276)
   4    2        TABLE ACCESS (BY INDEX ROWID) OF 'EMPLOYEES' (Cost=1 Card=4 Bytes=148)
   5    4          INDEX (RANGE SCAN) OF 'XIF12EMPLOYEES' (NON-UNIQUE) (Cost=1 Card=2)


-- Using UNION ALL
SQL> SELECT FIRST_NAME, LAST_NAME
  2    FROM CUSTOMERS
  3    WHERE CITY = 'West End'
  4  UNION ALL
  5  SELECT FIRST_NAME, LAST_NAME
  6    FROM EMPLOYEES
  7    WHERE DEPARTMENT_ID = 50
  8  /

Execution Plan
-----------------------------------------------------------
   0       SELECT STATEMENT Optimizer=CHOOSE (Cost=14 Card=16 Bytes=424)
   1    0    UNION-ALL
   2    1      TABLE ACCESS (FULL) OF 'CUSTOMERS' (Cost=13 Card=12 Bytes=276)
   3    1      TABLE ACCESS (BY INDEX ROWID) OF 'EMPLOYEES' (Cost=1 Card=4 Bytes=148)
   4    3        INDEX (RANGE SCAN) OF 'XIF12EMPLOYEES' (NON-UNIQUE) (Cost=1 Card=2)
```

13

The cost of the execution plan with UNION is 18, whereas the cost of UNION ALL is 14.

Using an Indexed Column When Counting Rows

In many situations, you need to count the number of rows for a table. Many developers are unaware that they can improve the performance of the simple COUNT statement by including an indexed column in the COUNT function.

The following COUNT statement was issued using the CUSTOMER_ID column that is not indexed. The cost returned for the statement is 19. But when the CUSTOMER_ID column is replaced with the ORDER_ID column that is indexed, you get a cost of 4. Quite a difference!

```
-- using CUSTOMER_ID column in the COUNT function which is not indexed
SQL> SELECT COUNT(CUSTOMER_ID)
  2      FROM ORDERS
  3  /


Elapsed: 00:00:00.04


Execution Plan
----------------------------------------------------------
   0       SELECT STATEMENT Optimizer=CHOOSE (Cost=19 Card=1 Bytes=4)
   1    0    SORT (AGGREGATE)
   2    1      TABLE ACCESS (FULL) OF 'ORDERS' (Cost=19 Card=9916 Bytes=39664)

-- using ORDER_ID column in the COUNT function which is indexed
SQL> SELECT COUNT(ORDER_ID)
  2      FROM ORDERS
  3  /


Elapsed: 00:00:00.03


Execution Plan
----------------------------------------------------------
   0       SELECT STATEMENT Optimizer=CHOOSE (Cost=4 Card=1)
   1    0    SORT (AGGREGATE)
   2    1      INDEX (FAST FULL SCAN) OF 'SYS_C003141' (UNIQUE) (Cost=4 Card=9916)
```

Rewriting Queries

Sometimes, even when you've used all the indexes, hints, and tips that you know, you can still enhance the execution of the query by simply rewriting it. As you can see, the new query, which produces the same results, reduced the cost tremendously from 1288 to 86.

```
-- All necessary indexes exists
SQL> SELECT CUSTOMER_ID,
  2           FIRST_NAME,
  3           LAST_NAME
  4    FROM DEPARTMENTS D,
  5           CUSTOMERS C
  6   WHERE D.CITY != C.CITY
  7  /

Execution Plan
----------------------------------------------------------
   0       SELECT STATEMENT Optimizer=CHOOSE (Cost=1288 Card=358990 Bytes=14718590)
   1    0    NESTED LOOPS (Cost=1288 Card=358990 Bytes=14718590)
   2    1      INDEX (FULL SCAN) OF 'IDX_DEP_CITY' (NON-UNIQUE) (Cost=1 Card=99 Bytes=990)
   3    1      TABLE ACCESS (FULL) OF 'CUSTOMERS' (Cost=13 Card=3626 Bytes=112406)


-- Query is rewritten producing same results
SQL> SELECT CUSTOMER_ID,
  2           FIRST_NAME,
  3           LAST_NAME
  4    FROM DEPARTMENTS D,
  5           CUSTOMERS C
  6   WHERE D.CITY < C.CITY
  7      OR D.CITY > C.CITY
  8  /

Execution Plan
----------------------------------------------------------
   0       SELECT STATEMENT Optimizer=CHOOSE (Cost=86 Card=20790 Bytes=852390)
   1    0    CONCATENATION
   2    1      MERGE JOIN (Cost=43 Card=990 Bytes=40590)
   3    2        SORT (JOIN) (Cost=1 Card=99 Bytes=990)
   4    3          INDEX (FULL SCAN) OF 'IDX_DEP_CITY' (NON-UNIQUE) (Cost=1 Card=99 Bytes=990)
   5    2        SORT (JOIN) (Cost=42 Card=4000 Bytes=124000)
   6    5          TABLE ACCESS (FULL) OF 'CUSTOMERS' (Cost=13 Card=4000 Bytes=124000)
   7    1      MERGE JOIN (Cost=43 Card=990 Bytes=40590)
   8    7        INDEX (FULL SCAN) OF 'IDX_DEP_CITY' (NON-UNIQUE) (Cost=1 Card=99 Bytes=990)
   9    7        FILTER
  10    9          SORT (JOIN)
  11   10            TABLE ACCESS (FULL) OF 'CUSTOMERS' (Cost=13 Card=4000 Bytes=124000)
```

Using Function-based Indexes

If you have a query with a WHERE clause containing a column that is indexed, but the column is part of an expression, the index will not be used. You need to create a function-based index to expedite data retrieval.

TIP

You need to grant the QUERY REWRITE system privilege to allow users to create a function-based index.

```
-- No function-based index
SQL> SELECT CUSTOMER_ID, FIRST_NAME, LAST_NAME
  2    FROM CUSTOMERS
  3   WHERE UPPER(LAST_NAME) LIKE 'SAM%'
  4  /

-- Explain plan no index
Execution Plan
----------------------------------------------------------
    0       SELECT STATEMENT Optimizer=CHOOSE (Cost=13 Card=200 Bytes=3400)
    1    0    TABLE ACCESS (FULL) OF 'CUSTOMERS' (Cost=13 Card=200 Bytes=3400)


-- Creating function-based index on UPPER(LAST_NAME) expression
SQL> CREATE INDEX IDX_CUS_UPP_LAST
  2      ON CUSTOMERS( UPPER(LAST_NAME) )
  3  /


-- Explain plan using function based index
Execution Plan
----------------------------------------------------------
    0       SELECT STATEMENT Optimizer=CHOOSE (Cost=10 Card=200 Bytes=3400)
    1    0    TABLE ACCESS (BY INDEX ROWID) OF 'CUSTOMERS' (Cost=10 Card=200 Bytes=3400)
    2    1      INDEX (RANGE SCAN) OF 'IDX_CUS_UPP_LAST' (NON-UNIQUE) (Cost=2 Card=36)
```

As you can see from the results of the execution plan, before creating a function-based index, the access to data was through a full table scan. After the index was created, the access path used the index, which reduced the cost from 13 to 10.

Using Bind Variables

As explained previously, there are advantages to using bind variables instead of literal values. The use of bind variables helps improve the performance of a SQL statement. Just follow these steps for a demonstration.

Step 1: As TUNER, issue the following the query:

```
SELECT /* PARSING_DEMO */
       FIRST_NAME, LAST_NAME
  FROM EMPLOYEES
 WHERE DEPARTMENT_ID = 10
/
```

Step 2: As TUNER, issue the same query changing the literal from 10 to 11:

```
SELECT /* PARSING_DEMO */
       FIRST_NAME, LAST_NAME
  FROM EMPLOYEES
 WHERE DEPARTMENT_ID = 11
/
```

Step 3: As TUNER, create a variable named DEPARTMENT and assign it a value of 20. Then issue the following modified query:

```
SQL> VARIABLE DEPARTMENT NUMBER
SQL> BEGIN
  2      :DEPARTMENT := 20;
  3  END;
  4  /

PL/SQL procedure successfully completed.

SQL> PRINT DEPARTMENT

DEPARTMENT
----------
        20

SQL> SELECT /* PARSING_DEMO */
  2          FIRST_NAME, LAST_NAME
  3    FROM EMPLOYEES
  4   WHERE DEPARTMENT_ID = :DEPARTMENT
  5  /
```

Step 4: As TUNER, issue the same query as in Step 3, but this time assign the value 21 to the variable DEPARTMENT.

```
SQL> BEGIN
  2      :DEPARTMENT := 21;
  3  END;
  4  /

PL/SQL procedure successfully completed.

SQL> PRINT DEPARTMENT

DEPARTMENT
----------
        21

SQL> SELECT /* PARSING */
  2          EMPLOYEE_ID, FIRST_NAME, LAST_NAME
  3    FROM EMPLOYEES
  4   WHERE DEPARTMENT_ID = :DEPARTMENT
  5  /
```

13

Step 5: As SYSTEM, issue the following query to retrieve the number of parsing calls for statements submitted by the TUNER session:

```
SQL> SELECT SQL_TEXT, PARSE_CALLS
  2     FROM V$SQL
  3     WHERE SQL_TEXT LIKE '%/* PARSING_DEMO */%'
  4     ORDER BY 1
  5  /

SQL_TEXT                                                                              PARSE_CALLS
-------------------------------------------------------------------------------       -----------
SELECT /* PARSING_DEMO */ FIRST_NAME, LAST_NAME FROM EMPLOYEES WHERE DEPARTMENT_ID = 10         1
SELECT /* PARSING_DEMO */ FIRST_NAME, LAST_NAME FROM EMPLOYEES WHERE DEPARTMENT_ID = 11         1
SELECT /* PARSING_DEMO */ FIRST_NAME, LAST_NAME FROM EMPLOYEES WHERE DEPARTMENT_ID = :DEPARTMENT 2
```

As you expected, the queries submitted in Steps 1 and 2 were parsed. However, when a bind variable was used, the same statement was used for both Steps 3 and 4.

PREVENTING SLOW SQL EXECUTION

How do you make sure a SQL statement is not the bottleneck of application performance? You do this by checking the following top 17 tips for avoiding problematic queries:

- **Cartesian product statement:** As a rule of thumb, if the FROM clause contains *n* tables, there should be at least *n*-1 conditions in the WHERE clause. Many times a Cartesian product is caused by an oversight, especially when writing a query that involves joining many tables.

- **Avoid full table scans on large tables:** When you are writing a query involving large tables:

  - Make sure that indexes exist on columns in the WHERE clause.

  - Analyze the query by looking at the Explain Plan and statistics.

  - When running the query the first time, limit the number of rows by adding AND ROWNUM < N (*N* any number of rows)

- **Use SQL standards and conventions to reduce parsing:** As explained earlier, standards and conventions prevent unnecessary parsing which can slow down execution of the query.

- **Lack of indexes:** Most of the time, the slow running of a query is caused by the lack of indexes on columns contained in the WHERE clause.

- **Avoid joining too many tables:** A query involving a join of many tables causes a slowdown because Oracle needs to get a record set from each table and then needs to join them using an access method. Usually, when many tables are necessary, you should think about materialized views to speed up performance. Having to join many tables could also be the result of over-normalizing. (Rather than normalizing the data model at 3NF, some over-achievers go to 4NF and even 5NF.)

- **Monitor V$SESSION_LONGOPS:** It is a good idea to monitor this dynamic performance view, which shows sessions that are running long operations. From this information, you can identify the queries and analyze them.

- **Using hints:** You should note that most of the time a hint performs differently when the query retrieves a large number of rows than when the query retrieves a few rows. Also, a hint may not be efficient when the number of rows in the table has changed.

- **Using the SHARED_CURSOR parameter:** This initialization parameter is helpful in reducing parsing, especially for statements that use literals or bind variables.

- **Rule-based optimizer goal:** In some situations, using a Rule-based Optimizer goal can produce better results than a Cost-based Optimizer goal. However, when you use a Rule-based Optimizer you should be sure to perform the following tasks:

  - Select the correct driving table. As explained earlier, RBO uses the order of the table in the FROM clause (from right to left) to determine the driving table.

  - Select the driving table with the smallest row set. In the example that follows, the driving table is DEP because it is the first table listed from right to left. The developer picked the DEP table as the driving table because it contains fewer rows than the EMP table.

  ```
  SELECT ...
  FROM EMP, DEP
  ```

- **Avoid unnecessary sorting:** In many instances developers perform sorting operations on the database by including the ORDER BY clause, UNION, and DISTINCT when they could avoid them by sorting on the application side.

- **Browned indexes:** Ensure that indexes are not browned because of deletions. You should monitor index browning and rebuild browned indexes. A browned index is an unbalanced index resulting from deletions.

- **Compound indexes:** Compound indexes with many columns should be carefully created especially if some of the individual columns in the compound index are used in a WHERE clause. Including columns in more than one index may influence the optimizer to select the wrong index.

- **Monitor query statistics:** You can always detect bad queries by identifying queries that are the top users of query statistics.

13

- **Use different tablespaces for tables and indexes:** Your objective as a DBA is to reduce I/O contention. It is good practice to place tables and their indexes in different tablespaces.

- **Table Partitioning:** Think about partitioning large tables and creating local indexes to prevent large table scans.

- **Use literals in the WHERE clause:** You should encourage the use of bind variables to avoid excessive parsing.

- **Outdated statistics**: The optimizer can pick the wrong access path to retrieve data if table and index statistics are out of date.

SQL ANALYSIS EXAMPLES

To supplement the analysis examples presented in this chapter, this section presents three different query analyses, as well as an analysis approach.

Approach

You can use the following steps to analyze and optimize a query:

1. Identify the query you want to analyze and make sure the query produces correct results.

2. Make sure all tables and indexes are analyzed.

3. Use real data on an environment that is similar to the production environment, and then generate an execution plan with statistics. You can use any one of these tools: AUTOTRACE, SQL Trace, or Oracle Enterprise Manager.

4. Determine the cost of the execution, and if it is not close to 1, proceed to Step 5. Remember, most queries may not be able to achieve a cost of 1, but you should try to get as close to 1 as possible.

5. Examine the access plan section of the execution plan to identify full table scans and join methods. If there is a full table scan on a large table, determine why. Most likely the cause is a missing index, an unanalyzed index, or use of the wrong index. Identify and compare join methods and determine if they can be improved.

6. Look at the execution statistics identifying any outrageous values.

In this section, you use this five-step approach to analyze three queries. But before you start, you analyze the whole TUNER schema to collect statistics:

```
begin
   dbms_stats.gather_schema_stats(ownname=> 'TUNER' , cascade=> TRUE);
end;
```

Query 1

The following is the Query 1 statement with an execution plan and statistics. Your first observation should be that the cost is 111, which could be high, so you need to look at access paths in the execution plan:

```
SQL> select /* Query1 */
  2          e.first_name, e.last_name, count(o.customer_id)
  3    from employees e, customers c, orders o
  4   where e.employee_id = c.sales_rep_id
  5     and c.customer_id = o.customer_id
  6   group by e.first_name, e.last_name
  7  /

8 rows selected.

Elapsed: 00:00:00.06

Execution Plan
----------------------------------------------------------
   0          SELECT STATEMENT Optimizer=CHOOSE (Cost=111 Card=9916 Bytes=327228)
   1     0   SORT (GROUP BY) (Cost=111 Card=9916 Bytes=327228)
   2     1     HASH JOIN (Cost=38 Card=9916 Bytes=327228)
   3     2       TABLE ACCESS (FULL) OF 'EMPLOYEES' (Cost=2 Card=294 Bytes=5586)
   4     2       HASH JOIN (Cost=35 Card=9916 Bytes=138824)
   5     4         TABLE ACCESS (FULL) OF 'CUSTOMERS' (Cost=13 Card=4000 Bytes=36000)
   6     4         TABLE ACCESS (FULL) OF 'ORDERS' (Cost=19 Card=9916 Bytes=49580)

Statistics
----------------------------------------------------------
          0  recursive calls
          0  db block gets
        308  consistent gets
        240  physical reads
         60  redo size
        709  bytes sent via SQL*Net to client
        499  bytes received via SQL*Net from client
          2  SQL*Net roundtrips to/from client
          1  sorts (memory)
          0  sorts (disk)
          8  rows processed
```

13

1. Looking at the execution plan, you can see that there are three full table scans. Notice that the scans for the ORDERS table are highest and this table is large, so modifying the access to its index may improve the cost. The modification would most likely involve creating an index on the CUSTOMER_ID column in the ORDERS table if does not exist. The table scans on the CUSTOMERS table may be acceptable since it is a considerably smaller table. The last full table scan, which is on the EMPLOYEES table, cannot be prevented since you are not restricting any rows from the table and you are using GROUP BY.

2. Looking at statistics, notice that retrieving data from all these tables resulted in many physical reads. This is fine if this query is part of a report and not part of OLTP module.

By creating an index on the CUSTOMER_ID column of the ORDERS tables, you bring down the cost from 19 to 4 as shown in the following listing of the execution plan. The cost fell from 111 to 96.

```
Execution Plan
----------------------------------------------------------
   0      SELECT STATEMENT Optimizer=CHOOSE (Cost=96 Card=9916 Bytes=327228)
   1    0   SORT (GROUP BY) (Cost=96 Card=9916 Bytes=327228)
   2    1     HASH JOIN (Cost=23 Card=9916 Bytes=327228)
   3    2       TABLE ACCESS (FULL) OF 'EMPLOYEES' (Cost=2 Card=294 Bytes=5586)
   4    2       HASH JOIN (Cost=20 Card=9916 Bytes=138824)
   5    4         TABLE ACCESS (FULL) OF 'CUSTOMERS' (Cost=13 Card=4000 Bytes=36000)

   6    4          INDEX (FAST FULL SCAN) OF 'IDX_ORD_CUSTOMER_ID' (NON-UNIQUE)
                       (Cost=4 Card=9916 Bytes=49580)
```

At this point you have to examine how the tables are joined. A hash join is usually very efficient especially if the hash table is composed of the smaller of the tables, which seems to be the case in this query. What else can you do? You can try to include different hints. This query is optimized.

Query 2

1. The following is the Query 2 statement with an execution plan and statistics:

```
SQL> select /* query2 */
  2          distinct c.city city
  3    from customers c, orders o
  4    where c.customer_id <> o.customer_id
  5      and o.order_date = '10-jun-02'
  6  /

Elapsed: 00:00:00.08

Execution Plan
----------------------------------------------------------
   0      SELECT STATEMENT Optimizer=CHOOSE (Cost=50 Card=324 Bytes=9396)
   1    0   SORT (UNIQUE) (Cost=50 Card=324 Bytes=9396)
   2    1     NESTED LOOPS (Cost=32 Card=4195 Bytes=121655)
   3    2       TABLE ACCESS (FULL) OF 'ORDERS' (Cost=19 Card=1 Bytes=13)
   4    2       TABLE ACCESS (FULL) OF 'CUSTOMERS' (Cost=13 Card=3999 Bytes=63984)

Statistics
----------------------------------------------------------
          0  recursive calls
          0  db block gets
        184  consistent gets
        143  physical reads
          0  redo size
        220  bytes sent via SQL*Net to client
        368  bytes received via SQL*Net from client
          1  SQL*Net roundtrips to/from client
          1  sorts (memory)
          0  sorts (disk)
          0  rows processed
```

2. The cost of this query is 50, most of which comes from two full table scans on ORDERS and CUSTOMERS. The full table scan on ORDERS is especially problematic when you have a WHERE clause restricting rows from the ORDERS table. You need to check if an index exists on the ORDER_DATE column. If so, you may want to find out if the cost is reduced if you add a hint to use the index. Also, you may want to consider rewriting the query to see if you can get better cost.

3. Execution statistics again tell you that there are many physical reads resulting from full table scans.

After checking indexes on the ORDERS tables, you see that there was no index on ORDER_DATE, so you create and analyze an index. Running the query again reduced the cost from 50 to 34. Is there room for more optimization? You can try rewriting the query.

```
Execution Plan
-----------------------------------------------------------
   0      SELECT STATEMENT Optimizer=CHOOSE (Cost=34 Card=324 Bytes=9396)
   1    0    SORT (UNIQUE) (Cost=34 Card=324 Bytes=9396)
   2    1      NESTED LOOPS (Cost=16 Card=4195 Bytes=121655)
   3    2        TABLE ACCESS (BY INDEX ROWID) OF 'ORDERS' (Cost=3 Card=1 Bytes=13)
   4    3          INDEX (RANGE SCAN) OF 'IDX_ORD_ORDER_DATE' (NON-UNIQUE) (Cost=1 Card=1)
   5    2        TABLE ACCESS (FULL) OF 'CUSTOMERS' (Cost=13 Card=3999 Bytes=63984)

Statistics
-----------------------------------------------------------
        0    recursive calls
        0    db block gets
        2    consistent gets
        0    physical reads
        0    redo size
      220    bytes sent via SQL*Net to client
      368    bytes received via SQL*Net from client
        1    SQL*Net roundtrips to/from client
        1    sorts (memory)
        0    sorts (disk)
        0    rows processed
```

After rewriting the query, you can see that the new query reduced the cost from 34 to 20, which seems to be optimal.

13

```
SQL> select distinct c.city city
  2     from customers c,
  3          orders o
  4    where (c.customer_id < o.customer_id
  5             OR c.customer_id > o.customer_id)
  6      and o.order_date = '10-jun-02'
  7   /

Elapsed: 00:00:00.03

Execution Plan
-----------------------------------------------------------
   0        SELECT STATEMENT Optimizer=CHOOSE (Cost=20 Card=324 Bytes=9396)
   1     0    SORT (UNIQUE) (Cost=20 Card=324 Bytes=9396)
   2     1      NESTED LOOPS (Cost=16 Card=409 Bytes=11861)
   3     2        TABLE ACCESS (BY INDEX ROWID) OF 'ORDERS' (Cost=3 Card=1 Bytes=13)
   4     3          INDEX (RANGE SCAN) OF 'IDX_ORD_ORDER_DATE' (NON-UNIQUE) (Cost=1 Card=1)
   5     2        TABLE ACCESS (FULL) OF 'CUSTOMERS' (Cost=13 Card=390 Bytes=6240)
```

Query 3

In this final example, you run the following query, which results in an execution plan and statistics that show that the query is optimal. Many hints were included to use an index as well as a different join method, but these could not reduce the cost to less than 15.

```
SQL> select /* Query3 */
  2          p.product_id, p.product_name,
  3          pi.qty_on_hand, pi.qty_on_order
  4     from products p, product_inventory pi
  5    where p.product_id = pi.product_id
  6      and pi.qty_on_hand < 3
  7   /

101 rows selected.

Elapsed: 00:00:00.04

Execution Plan
-----------------------------------------------------------
   0        SELECT STATEMENT Optimizer=CHOOSE (Cost=15 Card=102 Bytes=3774)
   1     0    HASH JOIN (Cost=15 Card=102 Bytes=3774)
   2     1      TABLE ACCESS (FULL) OF 'PRODUCT_INVENTORY' (Cost=4 Card=102 Bytes=1020)
   3     1      TABLE ACCESS (FULL) OF 'PRODUCTS' (Cost=10 Card=5001 Bytes=135027)
```

USING OUTLINES

A database developer took a two-day SQL course to learn how to write efficient queries. His first surprise was the instructor's explanation that Oracle has a program called the optimizer, which chooses how the SQL statement is executed. The second surprise was the news that one SQL statement can be rewritten to produce different response times at different times while still returning the same set of rows. The developer asked the instructor, "Are you telling me that if I write a SQL statement for a module in an application, and I test it and make sure that the response time is within the specification, there will come a day when it will not give me the response time? That's ridiculous!"

Yes, it would be ridiculous if Oracle did not support plan stability. You have already seen the parameter OPTIMIZER_FEATURES_ENABLE, which enables you to keep using the same version of the optimizer even when you upgrade to a new version of Oracle. In addition, Oracle has introduced the Outlines feature, which allows you to store the outline of an execution plan for a query in the database and use it indefinitely as long as there is no change in the query text.

NOTE You must grant the user the CREATE ANY OUTLINE privilege to allow the user to create outlines.

So how does it work? You write a query for a module, and then after you analyze and optimize the query, you store the outline execution plan for the query in the database. Then you issue the query. The optimizer uses the existing outline at all times. There are two methods to create outlines:

- **Automatically:** To have Oracle automatically generate an outline for every SQL statement submitted to the database, set the initialization parameter CRE-ATE_STORED_OUTLINES to TRUE (not recommended).

- **Manually:** By using the CREATE OUTLINE command, you can create an outline manually for any individual SQL statement.

NOTE Use the ALTER SYSTEM or ALTER SESSION statement to dynamically set CREATE_STORED_OUTLINES for an instance or a session.

13

Oracle Outlines supports categories to classify different stored outlines based on functionality or business requirements. For example, you may store all outlines for report queries within a category called REPORTING, and then you can enable all outlines for a specific session. Sounds easy? It is! You can simplify it even more by creating outlines for different scenarios.

Scenario 1

Suppose you work on optimizing a query, and you are satisfied with the execution plan and want to store this outline of the query. The following steps show how to do it.

Step 1: Analyze and optimize the query. In this case, consider the following as being optimized:

```
SQL> SELECT o.order_id, c.first_name, c.last_name, ol.total_amount
  2    FROM customers c, orders o, order_lines ol
  3   WHERE c.customer_id = 121
  4     AND o.customer_id = c.customer_id
  5     AND o.order_id = ol.order_id
  6     AND o.order_date = '01-jun-02'
  7  /
Elapsed: 00:00:00.00

Execution Plan
-------------------------------------------------------------
   0      SELECT STATEMENT Optimizer=CHOOSE (Cost=7 Card=1 Bytes=47)
   1    0   TABLE ACCESS (BY INDEX ROWID) OF 'ORDER_LINES' (Cost=2 Card=108038 Bytes=1080380)
   2    1     NESTED LOOPS (Cost=7 Card=1 Bytes=47)
   3    2       NESTED LOOPS (Cost=5 Card=1 Bytes=37)
   4    3         TABLE ACCESS (BY INDEX ROWID) OF 'CUSTOMERS' (Cost=2 Card=1 Bytes=20)
   5    4           INDEX (UNIQUE SCAN) OF 'SYS_C003139' (UNIQUE) (Cost=1 Card=4000)
   6    3         TABLE ACCESS (BY INDEX ROWID) OF 'ORDERS' (Cost=3 Card=1 Bytes=17)
   7    6           INDEX (RANGE SCAN) OF 'IDX_ORD_ORDER_DATE' (NON-UNIQUE) (Cost=1 Card=1)
   8    2       INDEX (RANGE SCAN) OF 'IDX_OL_ORDER_ID' (NON-UNIQUE) (Cost=1 Card=11)
```

Step 2: Create an outline for the query using the CREATE OUTLINE statement. Because you did not create a category for this outline, it is stored under the DEFAULT category.

```
SQL> CREATE OR REPLACE OUTLINE SCENARIO1 ON
  2      SELECT o.order_id, c.first_name, c.last_name, ol.total_amount
  3    FROM customers c, orders o, order_lines ol
  4   WHERE c.customer_id = 121
  5     AND o.customer_id = c.customer_id
  6     AND o.order_id = ol.order_id
  7     AND o.order_date = '01-jun-02'
  8  /

Outline created.
```

NOTE You can use the parameter USE_PRIVATE_OUTLINES to create a private outline that is seen only by the current session. This allows the user to edit and run outlines for the current session.

Step 3: If you want to enable this outline, you need to alter your session as in the statement that follows. As you can see, you have to use the parameter USE_STORED_OUTLINES to specify the outline category to be used. In this case you use the DEFAULT category.

```
SQL> ALTER SESSION SET USE_STORED_OUTLINES=DEFAULT
  2  /

Session altered.
```

Step 4: Issue the query for which you created the outline. Remember it has to be identical with the same text pattern literals and white spaces.

Step 5: Verify the creation of the outline and that it was used the last time you issued the query. As SYSTEM, view the contents of DBA_OUTLINES by issuing the following statement:

```
SQL> SELECT NAME, OWNER, CATEGORY, USED, SQL_TEXT
  2      FROM DBA_OUTLINES
  3  /

NAME        OWNER  CATEGORY  USED   SQL_TEXT
----------  -----  --------  -----  ----------------------------------------
SCENARIO1   TUNER  DEFAULT   USED   SELECT o.order_id, c.first_name, c.last_name
```

Scenario 2

In this scenario, you create an outline category called SCENARIO2_CATEGORY to store outlines for three queries automatically. Follow these steps:

Step 1: Analyze and optimize the desired queries. The following is a list of three queries to be used in this scenario:

```
SELECT E.FIRST_NAME || ' ' || E.LAST_NAME EMPLOYEE,
       D.DEPARTMENT_NAME DEPARTMENT
  FROM EMPLOYEES E, DEPARTMENTS D
 WHERE E.DEPARTMENT_ID = D.DEPARTMENT_ID
/

SELECT EMPLOYEE_ID,
       FIRST_NAME || ' ' || LAST_NAME EMPLOYEE_NAME
  FROM EMPLOYEES
 WHERE EMPLOYEE_ID NOT IN (SELECT EMPLOYEE_ID
                             FROM ORDERS)
/

SELECT EMPLOYEE_ID, COUNT(*) EMP_ORD_COUNT
  FROM ORDERS
 GROUP BY EMPLOYEE_ID
/
```

Step 2: Create a new outline category called SCENARIO2_CATEGORY using the parameter CREATE_STORED_OUTLINES in the following statement:

```
SQL> ALTER SESSION SET CREATE_STORED_OUTLINES=SCENARIO2_CATEGORY
  2  /

Session altered.
```

13

Step 3: Issue the queries as listed in Step 1.

Step 4: Turn off automatic outline creation:

```
SQL> ALTER SESSION SET CREATE_STORED_OUTLINES=FALSE
  2  /

Session altered.
```

Step 5: Verify creation of the outlines. Query the USER_OUTLINES view by issuing the following query:

```
SQL> SELECT NAME, CATEGORY, USED, SQL_TEXT
  2     FROM USER_OUTLINES
  3  /

NAME                             CATEGORY           USED   SQL_TEXT
-----------------------------    ----------------   ------ -----------------------------
SCENARIO1                        DEFAULT            USED   SELECT o.order_id, c.first_name,
SYS_OUTLINE_030226203020442      SCENARIO2_CATEGORY UNUSED SELECT E.FIRST_NAME || ' ' || E.LAST_
SYS_OUTLINE_030226203148599      SCENARIO2_CATEGORY UNUSED SELECT EMPLOYEE_ID,
SYS_OUTLINE_030226203156310      SCENARIO2_CATEGORY UNUSED SELECT EMPLOYEE_ID, COUNT(*) EMP_ORD_
```

Now, every time you turn on outlines for a session using DEFAULT or any stored category and you submit any query that stores an outline, the Optimizer uses the same execution plan, which guarantees plan stability.

NOTE
To use private outlines you must create the table that stores outline information in your schema. You can create this table using the DBMS_OUTLN_EDIT.CREATE_EDIT_TABLES procedure.

Scenario 3

Suppose you want to allow DEMO to create his own private outlines. Follow these steps:

Step 1: As SYSTEM, grant CREATE ANY OUTLINE system privilege to DEMO:

```
SQL> GRANT CREATE ANY OUTLINE TO DEMO
  2  /

Grant succeeded.
```

Step 2: As DEMO, create outline tables:

```
SQL> EXEC DBMS_OUTLN_EDIT.CREATE_EDIT_TABLES

PL/SQL procedure successfully completed.

SQL> SELECT * FROM TAB
  2  /

TNAME                               TABTYPE
-----------------------------       -------

OL$                                 TABLE
OL$HINTS                            TABLE
OL$NODES                            TABLE
```

NOTE

All public outlines are stored in the OUTLN schema.

Step 3: Create a private outline. You can also create a private outline from an existing public outline, but you must have the SELECT_CATALOG_ROLE role assigned to you to be able to do that. Also, you can use the DBMS_OUTLN_EDIT.REFRESH_PRIVATE_OUTLINE procedure to copy an existing public outline.

```
SQL> CREATE PRIVATE OUTLINE SCENARIO3 ON
  2      SELECT *
  3        FROM EMPLOYEE
  4        ORDER BY 1
  5  /

Outline created.

-- or you can create an outline from an existing public outline
-- DEMO must have SELECT_CATALOG_ROLE role
SQL> CREATE PRIVATE OUTLINE OUTLINE_COPY
  2      FROM SCENARIO1
  3  /

Outline created.

-- or using DBMS_OUTLN_EDIT
SQL> EXEC DBMS_OUTLN_EDIT.REFRESH_PRIVATE_OUTLINE('SYS_OUTLINE_030226203020442')

PL/SQL procedure successfully completed.
```

13

Scenario 4

Suppose you want to create an outline for a new category for one query, but you do not want to use SQL statements. In this case, you can use the Outline Management Tool included in Oracle Enterprise Manager.

 NOTE If the DEMO schema does not exist in your database, you can create it by issuing the following command from SQL*PlusSQL> @c:\oracle\ora92\rdbms\ admin\demo.sql.

Step 1: Start Outline Management from the Tuning Pack of the Oracle Enterprise Manager console as shown in Figure 13-15.

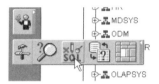

Figure 13-15   Oracle Enterprise Manager showing the Outline Management Tool button

Step 2: The main window of the Outline Management Tool is displayed. Click the **Create** button to create a new outline, as illustrated in Figure 13-16.

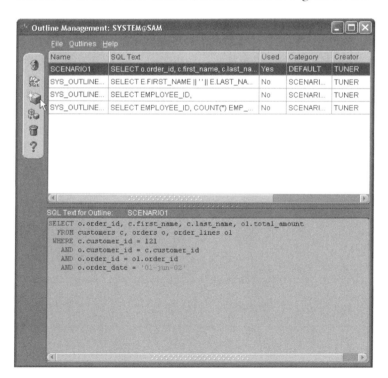

Figure 13-16   Main window of Oracle Enterprise Manager's Outline Management Tool

Step 3: An Outline window is displayed where you can enter the name of the outline category, the name of the outline, and outline details, as shown in Figure 13-17. From this editor you can maintain and edit existing outlines. For more details on this tool, consult Oracle Enterprise Manager documentation.

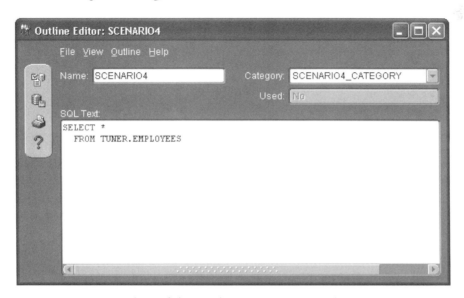

Figure 13-17   Window of the Outline Management Editor

To wrap up this section, review the following summary of all parameters, views, statements, and packages related to the outlines.

- Parameters
  - CREATE_STORED_OUTLINES
  - USED_STORED_OUTLINES

- Statements
  - CREATE OUTLINE
  - ALTER OUTLINE
  - DROP OUTLINE

- Views
  - DBA_OUTLINES
  - DBA_OUTLINE_HINTS
  - ALL_OUTLINES
  - ALL_OUTLINE_HINTS

13

- USER_OUTLINES
- USER_OUTLINE_HINTS

- Packages
  - DBMS_OUTLN
  - DBMS_OUTLN_EDIT
  - OUTLINE

CHAPTER SUMMARY

- Oracle optimizer is an algorithm that determines the most efficient way to execute a SQL statement and retrieve data.
- The OPTIMIZER_MODE initialization parameter can be configured for the whole system, whereas the OPTIMIZER_GOAL parameter sets the Optimizer mode for a session.
- The OPTIMIZER_GOAL is set by issuing ALTER SESSION, which impacts the current session only.
- The Rule-based Optimizer (RBO) determines the most efficient way to execute a SQL statement by using a set of rules and a ranking system.
- When evaluating a SQL statement, the Cost-based Optimizer (CBO) considers the consumption of all resources, number of rows retrieved, table size, row size, block size, and other factors.
- CBO generates all possible execution plans for a SQL statement by considering all available storage statistics and selecting the least expensive.
- An execution plan that has a cost of 1 (or near to 1) is considered optimal.
- The cost of a query is one of the indicators that tells you whether a query is efficient.
- The OPTIMIZER_FEATURES_ENABLE parameter forces the optimizer to use certain Oracle optimizer behaviors.
- To reduce the time required to perform permutations, the OPTIMIZER_MAX_PER-MUTATIONS parameter limits the number of permutations.
- The optimizer hints are included in a SQL statement to tell the optimizer how to influence the execution of a statement.
- The Outline feature allows you to store the outline of an execution plan for a query in the database and use it indefinitely as long as there is no change in the query text.
- Parameters used in this chapter include the following:
  - CREATE_STORED_OUTLINES
  - CURSOR_SHARING
  - DB_FILE_MULTIBLOCK_READ_COUNT

- HASH_AREA_SIZE
- HASH_JOIN_ENABLED
- OPTIMIZER_DYNAMIC_SAMPLING
- OPTIMIZER_FEATURES_ENABLE
- OPTIMIZER_GOAL
- OPTIMIZER_INDEX_CACHING
- OPTIMIZER_INDEX_COST_ADJ
- OPTIMIZER_MAX_PERMUTATIONS
- OPTIMIZER_MODE
- PARTITION_VIEW_ENABLED
- QUERY_REWRITE_ENABLED
- SORT_AREA_SIZE
- STAR_TRANSFORMATION_ENABLED
- USE_STORED_OUTLINES

❏ DBA views used in this chapter include the following:

- ALL_OUTLINES
- ALL_OUTLINE_HINTS
- DBA_OUTLINES
- DBA_OUTLINE_HINTS
- USER_OUTLINES
- USER_OUTLINE_HINTS

❏ Packages used in this chapter include the following:

- DBMS_OUTLN
- DBMS_OUTLN_EDIT
- OUTLINE

13

REVIEW QUESTIONS

1. To use optimizer hints, you can include /*+ HINT */ in a SQL statement. (True/False)

2. You set OPTIMIZER_MODE to COST to set the optimizer to the cost-based access method. (True/False)

3. Oracle recommends the use of the Cost-based Optimizer. (True/False)

4. The CBO can choose to execute a statement using either the rule-based or cost-based access method. (True/False)

5. The ALL_ROWS optimizer mode tells the optimizer to retrieve all rows at the same time. (True/False)

6. The FIRST_ROWS optimizer mode tells the optimizer to retrieve the first number of rows as fast as possible. (True/False)

7. A full table scan is always problematic and must be eliminated. (True/False)

8. The CBO Optimizer uses syntax and ranks if tables in the SQL statements are not analyzed. (True/False)

9. When analyzing SQL statements, you should look at the execution cost as well as execution statistics. (True/False)

10. In RBO, the optimizer chooses the table list from left-to-right as the driving table. (True/False)

11. Use the V$SQL dynamic performance view to identify problematic queries. (True/False)

12. A HASH JOIN builds a hash table out of the larger of two tables. (True/False)

13. Full table scans with indexes on a large table are problematic. (True/False)

14. Using SQL standards and conventions improves the performance of a query. (True/False)

15. You need to grant the REWRITE system privilege to allow users to create function-based indexes.

16. Write a query that identifies the top five queries for disk I/O per execution.

17. When would you use the hint FULL?

18. Analyze and explain the following execution plans:

```
-- BEFORE CREATING AN INDEX
SQL> SELECT SUPPLIER_NAME, PHONE, STATUS
  2    FROM SUPPLIERS
  3    WHERE SUPPLIER_NAME LIKE 'S%'
  4  /

Execution Plan
-----------------------------------------------------------
   0       SELECT STATEMENT Optimizer=CHOOSE (Cost=4 Card=41 Bytes=1066)
   1    0    TABLE ACCESS (FULL) OF 'SUPPLIERS' (Cost=4 Card=41 Bytes=1066)


-- CREATING AND ANALZYING INDEX
SQL> CREATE INDEX IDX_SUP_SUPPLIER_NAME ON SUPPLIERS(SUPPLIER_NAME)
  2  /

Index created.

SQL> ANALYZE INDEX IDX_SUP_SUPPLIER_NAME ESTIMATE STATISTICS SAMPLE 20 PERCENT
  2  /

Index analyzed.


-- AFTER CREATING AN INDEX
SQL> SELECT SUPPLIER_NAME, PHONE, STATUS
  2    FROM SUPPLIERS
  3    WHERE SUPPLIER_NAME LIKE 'S%'
  4  /

Execution Plan
-----------------------------------------------------------
   0       SELECT STATEMENT Optimizer=CHOOSE (Cost=4 Card=41 Bytes=1066)
   1    0    TABLE ACCESS (FULL) OF 'SUPPLIERS' (Cost=4 Card=41 Bytes=1066)
```

13

19. Provide an example of a situation in which you would use the INDEX_COMBINE hint.

EXAM REVIEW QUESTIONS: ORACLE9i PERFORMANCE TUNING (#1Z0-033)

1. Why would you analyze a table or index?

    a. To assist Oracle in determining the fastest method to access data

    b. Because statistical data is used by the Rule-based Optimizer to determine how to access data

    c. Because statistical data is used by the Cost-based Optimizer to determine how to access data

    d. Statistical data generated by the ANALYZE command is used by both CBO and RBO Optimizers.

2. Which parameter helps reduce statement parsing?

    a. CURSOR_SHARING

    b. CURSOR_SHARING_EXACT

    c. /*+ CURSOR_SHARING */

    d. /*+ CURSOR_SHARING_EXACT */

3. Which statement involves an optimized SQL query?

    a. A query that has an execution plan cost near 0 is considered optimized.

    b. A query that has an execution plan cost near 1 is considered optimized.

    c. A query that has an execution plan cost that is near 100 is considered optimized.

    d. None of the above

4. Which statement is true?

    a. The Cost-based Optimizer is driven by statistics and always selects the most efficient access path.

    b. The Rule-based Optimizer is driven by statistics and always selects the most efficient access path.

    c. The Cost-based Optimizer is driven by syntax and always selects the most efficient access path.

    d. The Rule-based Optimizer is driven by syntax and always selects the most efficient access path.

5. Which statement is true about RBO?

    a. RBO uses statistics as well as syntax to determine access paths to data.

    b. RBO uses statement syntax and ranks to determine access paths to data.

    c. RBO should not be used.

    d. RBO should be used only for previous versions of Oracle to ensure execution stability.

6. Which parameter would be used to set a session with the Rule-based Optimizer?

    a. /*+ RULE */

    b. OPTIMIZER_MODE

    c. OPTIMIZER_GOAL

    d. ALTER SESSION SET...

    e. RULE

7. What is the purpose of Outlines?

    a. It provides execution plan stability.

    b. It enables users to use the same execution plan.

    c. It enforces the optimizer to use the same Explain Plan.

    d. Users can select which outline category to use for executing SQL statements.

8. Which hint would be used to speed execution of a query?

    a. INDEX

    b. PARALLEL

    c. STAR

    d. CACHE

9. Which value is not valid for optimizer mode?

    a. CHOOSE

    b. RULE

    c. COST

    d. ALL_ROWS

    e. FIRST_ROWS

13

10. Outlines are stored in which of the following?

    a. SYSTEM schema

    b. OUTLINE schema

    c. OUTLN schema

    d. SYS schema

    e. Any schema

11. What action would you take to avoid a slow query?

    a. Eliminate full table scans.

    b. Use the UNION statement instead of UNION ALL.

    c. Replace simple subqueries with a join.

    d. Analyze and optimize queries.

12. Which hint is used to insert rows using the direct-path method?

    a. PARALLEL

    b. DIRECT

    c. APPEND

    d. CACHE

13. Which parameter can be used to tell the Oracle optimizer which optimizer version it should use?

    a. OPTIMIZER_VERSION_ENABLE

    b. OPTIMIZER_ENABLE_FEATURE

    c. OPTIMIZER_FEATURES_ENABLE

    d. OPTIMIZER_ENABLE_VERSION

14. Which statement does not cause a sort?

    a. DISTINCT

    b. UNION ALL

    c. GROUP BY

    d. ORDER BY

15. Which statement is true about generating outlines automatically?

    a. Set the CREATE_STORED_OUTLINES parameter to TRUE.

    b. Set the CREATE_STORED_OUTLINES parameter to FALSE.

    c. Set the USE_STORED_OUTLINES parameter to TRUE.

    d. Set the USE_STORED_OUTLINES parameter to FALSE.

HANDS-ON PROJECTS

**HANDS-ON
PROJECTS**

Please complete the projects provided below.

1. Reread the Performance Problem at the start of the chapter. Think of it in terms of the concepts you have learned in this chapter and answer the following questions. Can you help Conny by explaining the problem she is having? Can you optimize the query she is writing?

2. Optimize the following query if you think it is not optimized:

```
select C.CUSTOMER_ID, C.FIRST_NAME, C.LAST_NAME, O.ORD_AMT
 from CUSTOMERS C,
        (select O.CUSTOMER_ID, SUM(OL.TOTAL_AMOUNT) ORD_AMT
           from orders O, ORDER_LINES OL
          WHERE O.ORDER_ID = OL.ORDER_ID
          group by O.CUSTOMER_ID) O
 where C.CUSTOMER_id = o.CUSTOMER_id
   and C.CREDIT_LIMIT > O.ORD_AMT
 ORDER BY C.CUSTOMER_ID
 /
```

13

3. Is the following query optimal? If not, analyze it and optimize it.

```
SELECT P.PRODUCT_ID, P.PRODUCT_NAME,
       MM.MN_PRICE, MM.MX_PRICE
  FROM PRODUCTS P,
       (SELECT PRODUCT_ID,
               MIN(LIST_PRICE) MN_PRICE,
               MAX(LIST_PRICE) MX_PRICE
          FROM PRODUCT_PRICES
         GROUP BY PRODUCT_ID
       ) MM
 WHERE P.PRODUCT_ID = MM.PRODUCT_ID
   AND P.PRODUCT_ID IN (SELECT DISTINCT PRODUCT_ID
                          FROM ORDER_LINES)
 ORDER BY P.PRODUCT_ID
 /
```

4. This query produced the following execution plan. Analyze the results and recommend what you would do next.

```
SQL> SELECT DISTINCT C.CITY CITY
  2    FROM CUSTOMERS C
  3   WHERE NOT EXISTS (SELECT 'X'
  4                       FROM ORDERS
  5                      WHERE CUSTOMER_ID = C.CUSTOMER_ID)
  6  /

Execution Plan
----------------------------------------------------------
   0       SELECT STATEMENT Optimizer=CHOOSE (Cost=167 Card=152 Bytes=2432)
   1    0    SORT (UNIQUE) (Cost=15 Card=152 Bytes=2432)
   2    1      FILTER
   3    2        TABLE ACCESS (FULL) OF 'CUSTOMERS' (Cost=13 Card=200 Bytes=3200)
   4    2        INDEX (RANGE SCAN) OF 'IDX_ORD_CUSTOMER_ID' (NON-UNIQUE)
                   (Cost=1 Card=3 Bytes=15)
```

5. A developer on your team sent the following query and Explain Plan. He is asking you to interpret the results and recommend a course of action.

```
SQL> SELECT OL.ORDER_ID, OL.PRODUCT_ID, P.PRODUCT_NAME
  2    FROM ORDER_LINES OL, PRODUCTS P
  3   WHERE P.PRODUCT_ID = OL.PRODUCT_ID
  4     AND OL.TOTAL_AMOUNT > 1000
  5  /

Execution Plan
----------------------------------------------------------
   0       SELECT STATEMENT Optimizer=CHOOSE (Cost=87 Card=107833 Bytes=4097654)
   1    0    HASH JOIN (Cost=87 Card=107833 Bytes=4097654)
   2    1      TABLE ACCESS (FULL) OF 'PRODUCTS' (Cost=10 Card=5001 Bytes=135027)
   3    1      TABLE ACCESS (FULL) OF 'ORDER_LINES' (Cost=49 Card=107833 Bytes=1186163)
```

6. Find a hint from the Query Transformation category that will prevent concatenation for the following query:

```
SQL> SELECT
  2          ORDER_ID, ORDER_DATE
  3    FROM ORDERS
  4    WHERE ORDER_ID < 100 OR ORDER_ID > 10000
  5  /

Execution Plan
-------------------------------------------------------------
   0        SELECT STATEMENT Optimizer=CHOOSE (Cost=6 Card=16 Bytes=160)
   1    0     CONCATENATION
   2    1       TABLE ACCESS (BY INDEX ROWID) OF 'ORDERS' (Cost=3 Card=1 Bytes=10)
   3    2         INDEX (RANGE SCAN) OF 'SYS_C003141' (UNIQUE) (Cost=2 Card=1)
   4    1       TABLE ACCESS (BY INDEX ROWID) OF 'ORDERS' (Cost=3 Card=1 Bytes=10)
   5    4         INDEX (RANGE SCAN) OF 'SYS_C003141' (UNIQUE) (Cost=2 Card=1)
```

7. How can you improve the performance of this query?

```
SQL> SELECT /*+ USE_CONCAT */
  2          P.PRODUCT_ID, P.PRODUCT_NAME
  3    FROM PRODUCTS P
  4    WHERE P.PRODUCT_ID NOT IN (SELECT OL.PRODUCT_ID
  5                                 FROM ORDER_LINES OL)
  6  /

Execution Plan
-------------------------------------------------------------
   0        SELECT STATEMENT Optimizer=CHOOSE (Cost=75 Card=1090 Bytes=32700)
   1    0     HASH JOIN (ANTI) (Cost=75 Card=1090 Bytes=32700)
   2    1       TABLE ACCESS (FULL) OF 'PRODUCTS' (Cost=10 Card=5001 Bytes=135027)
   3    1       INDEX (FAST FULL SCAN) OF 'SYS_C003144' (UNIQUE)
                   (Cost=46 Card=108038 Bytes=324114)
```

13

8. Your boss asked you to assist her in a query she's working on. She said, "I think this query is optimal, what do you think?" Provide your analysis.

```
SELECT P.PRODUCT_ID, P.PRODUCT_NAME, PROD_SALE
  FROM PRODUCTS P,
       (SELECT PRODUCT_ID, SUM(TOTAL_AMOUNT) PROD_SALE
          FROM ORDER_LINES
         GROUP BY PRODUCT_ID
       ) OL
 WHERE P.PRODUCT_ID = OL.PRODUCT_ID
   AND PROD_SALE > 10000
 ORDER BY P.PRODUCT_ID
/
```

9. A DBA on your team dropped by for a little chat when he saw you working on a query. He said, "Pal, you definitely can do better than this!" What did he mean? What can you do?

```
select EMPLOYEE_ID, FIRST_NAME, LAST_NAME
  from EMPLOYEES
 WHERE EMPLOYEE_ID NOT IN (SELECT SALES_REP_ID
                                  FROM CUSTOMERS)
 /
```

10. As you were auditing the database for bad queries, you came across the following query. Why would you be concerned? Analyze it and outline your findings.

```
SELECT /*+ MERGE(O) */
       E.EMPLOYEE_ID, E.FIRST_NAME, E.LAST_NAME, O.NUM_SALES
  FROM EMPLOYEES E,
       (SELECT EMPLOYEE_ID, COUNT(*) NUM_SALES
          FROM ORDERS
         GROUP BY EMPLOYEE_ID
       ) O
 WHERE E.EMPLOYEE_ID = O.EMPLOYEE_ID
   AND O.NUM_SALES > 100
 ORDER BY EMPLOYEE_ID
 /
```

11. The following query and Explain Plan were e-mailed to you by a program that detects Top Queries.

a. Is this query problematic; if so, why?

b. Can you rewrite this query producing the same results and better cost?

```
SQL> SELECT PRODUCT_ID,
  2            PRODUCT_NAME
  3    FROM PRODUCTS P
  4   WHERE EXISTS (SELECT 'X'
  5                   FROM ORDER_LINES
  6                  WHERE PRODUCT_ID = P.PRODUCT_ID
  7                    AND TOTAL_AMOUNT < 100)
  8  /

Execution Plan
---------------------------------------------------------
   0       SELECT STATEMENT Optimizer=CHOOSE (Cost=36 Card=21 Bytes=777)
   1    0    HASH JOIN (SEMI) (Cost=36 Card=21 Bytes=777)
   2    1      TABLE ACCESS (FULL) OF 'PRODUCTS' (Cost=10 Card=5001 Bytes=135027)
   3    1      TABLE ACCESS (BY INDEX ROWID) OF 'ORDER_LINES' (Cost=23 Card=20 Bytes=200)
   4    3        INDEX (RANGE SCAN) OF 'IDX_OL_TOTAL_AMOUNT' (NON-UNIQUE)
                    (Cost=2 Card=20)
```

12. Analyze and optimize the following query:

```
select c.first_name, c.last_name, c.phone
  from orders o, customers c
 where c.customer_id = o.customer_id
   and order_id in (select order_id
                      from order_lines
                     group by order_id
                    having sum(tota_amount) = (select max(sum(total_amount))
                                                 from order_lines
                                                group by order_id))
```

13. Is the following query optimal? If not, what can you do to optimize it?

```
select s.shipment_description, count(*)
  from orders o, shipment_method s
 where o.shipment_method_id = s.shipment_method_id
 group by s.shipment_description
```

CASE PROJECTS

1. Trace My Session, Please!

You were hired as a DBA at Acme Company to administer an OLTP application in production. You got a call from one of the developers asking you to trace her session to
identify any bad queries or queries that can be optimized. Perform the following steps:

1. Set up a session for the developer (use the TUNER schema) and a session for
   yourself as a DBA.

2. Turn on tracing for the developer session.

13

3. The developer will submit the following queries:

```
--Query#1
SELECT P.PRODUCT_NAME, S.SUPPLIER_NAME,
       PI.DATE_ORDERED, PI.QTY_ON_ORDER
  FROM PRODUCTS P, PRODUCT_INVENTORY PI, SUPPLIERS S,
       PRODUCT_SUPPLIER PS
 WHERE P.PRODUCT_ID = PI.PRODUCT_ID
   AND P.PRODUCT_ID = PS.PRODUCT_ID
   AND PS.SUPPLIER_ID = S.SUPPLIER_ID
   AND PI.DELIVERY_DATE < (SELECT MIN(DELIVERY_DATE)
                             FROM PRODUCT_INVENTORY)
--Query#2
SELECT P.PRODUCT_NAME, S.SUPPLIER_NAME, PI.DATE_ORDERED,
       PI.QTY_ON_ORDER
  FROM PRODUCTS P, PRODUCT_INVENTORY PI, SUPPLIERS S,
       PRODUCT_SUPPLIER PS
 WHERE P.PRODUCT_ID = PI.PRODUCT_ID
   AND P.PRODUCT_ID = PS.PRODUCT_ID
   AND PS.SUPPLIER_ID = S.SUPPLIER_ID

--Query#3
SELECT *
  FROM categories, products, order_lines, orders
 WHERE ((products.product_id = order_lines.product_id)
        AND
        (orders.order_id = order_lines.order_id)
        AND
        (categories.cateogry_id = products.category_id))

--Query#4
SELECT *
  FROM categories, products, order_lines, orders
 WHERE ((products.product_id = order_lines.product_id)
        AND
        (orders.order_id = order_lines.order_id)
        AND (categories.cateogry_id = products.category_id))

--Query#3
SELECT FIRST_NAME, LAST_NAME
  FROM EMPLOYEES
 WHERE (FIRST_NAME, LAST_NAME) NOT IN (SELECT FIRST_NAME,
                                              LAST_NAME
                                         FROM CUSTOMERS)
```

4. Turn off tracing for the developer.

5. Generate a formatted trace file and analyze it to identify problematic queries, if any, and optimize them.

2.Top Queries, Please!

After you traced the developer's session in the first case project, your manager asked you
to get the top five queries for each of the following factors:

1. CPU consumption

2. Disk reads

3. Memory

4. Parsing

5. Sorting

13

14

OPTIMIZING APPLICATIONS

> **In this chapter you will:**
> - Learn effects on tuning and using different types of indexes
> - Monitor each type and variation of index to improve performance
> - Learn the characteristics of different types of tables
> - Partition tables using a variety of methods
> - Learn about the characteristics of different types of applications

This chapter covers the initial hands–on tuning of an application. During the design phase you should consider the different types of indexes and tables provided by Oracle that enhance your application's performance. Adjusting indexes and tables is important in later stages as well. When databases are in production and there are performance problems or issues, it is important to consider different indexing methods and data organization.

Learning the two main topics presented in this chapter will empower you to enhance the performance of a database application. The first topic is the effect on tuning of indexing, in which you learn the different types of indexes and their impact on performance. The second topic is organizing tables to enhance performance, in which you learn how to organize your data in different types of tables to enhance data retrieval and manageability. Finally, you are presented with a characteristics summary for various types of applications.

Performance Problem

This section outlines an actual performance problem. As you look it over, imagine yourself as the DBA who reported the problem and keep it in mind as you proceed through the chapter. The chapter presents concepts relevant to the problem. In the first Hands-on Project at the end of the chapter, you are asked to use the concepts you have learned to provide a solution, or partial solution, to this performance problem.

From: *Dennis Partings <mailto: dpartings@partitions.com>*

DATE: *14-Jun-03 12:23*

SUBJECT: *Explain this!!!*

RDBMS Version: *Oracle9i*

Is my DBA right?

I am running Oracle 9.x with a PeopleSoft HRMS implementation and using a reporting tool to generate reports. I am trying to speed up the process of extracting data from large tables and tables without indexes. Our DBA has recommended several methods. Here are some his recommendations:

a. *Extract only the necessary columns and rows from the permanent tables using nesting and/or joins.*

b. *Insert these rows into the temp table.*

c. *Create an index on the temp table.*

d. *Perform the main process using breaks and sorting against the temp table.*

e. *Truncate the temp table and drop the index.*

Dennis

EFFECT OF INDEXING ON TUNING

There are many horror stories about the misuse of indexes. Some cases are laughable and others disastrous. However, the story you are about to read is encouraging because it shows what a good DBA can accomplish.

A prominent retail department store used a customer care application to track customer transaction inquiries. Susan, a junior DBA, was hired when a new enhancement was about to be implemented in production. Her manager, Tina, assigned Susan to this project. Tina told Susan in her first weekly progress meeting that she wanted to make sure everything went smoothly with the project, because all the business managers were counting on it, and they were all anticipating the final enhancement. She told Susan to call on Brad, the DBA team leader, with any issues or concerns. Then she asked Susan to describe her plan.

Susan felt the pressure, albeit "good pressure," to deliver what she had promised. She proposed taking a full survey of the database to become familiar with the basic database configuration. Then, she would read all the documentation for the new module, revising all SQL and PL/SQL code used by the application. Finally, she would review any new database objects created for the new module and draft an implementation plan accordingly.

As Susan was reviewing all the queries, she came across full table scans on five new tables. Susan looked at the tables in the development database and found that they were small. Being a diligent DBA, Susan wrote a memo to the development team manager, copying the business manager, asking about the estimated growth on these tables and requesting more explanation of their use. She highlighted the two queries she found. The development manager thanked her for identifying the two queries and stressed that he understood her concerns. He wrote that the new tables were used heavily but would have slow growth according to Tommy, the Business Analyst. He didn't think it was a good idea to add indexes to these tables to eliminate full table scans, because the tables were small and rewriting the queries at that time was out of the question.

Susan went to Brad to consult with him on her plans and tell him that she wouldn't build any indexes on the tables because they were small. Brad agreed. Three weeks went by, and things were working fine and then, boom! Contrary to what business expected, these tables started to grow and performance degradation was evident. Susan was fully prepared because she had actually been monitoring the growth of these tables, and she decided to add the indexes after approval by her manager and the business manager. When the indexes had been added, she generated an execution plan and noticed that the cost of the query went down drastically.

Being a smart DBA, Susan's coherent action plan probably saved management and the development team from a serious performance problem and potential embarrassment. This true story demonstrates the importance of knowing when to use indexes.

Exactly what is an index? An **index** is a database object used by Oracle to speed up the retrieval of data from a table. Consider books, for example. Many books have indexes. If readers are looking for a specific topic, rather than browsing the whole book to find it, they can look in the index to locate specific references.

14

Like books, tables can have indexes for looking up the location of a row. An index is actually a table with two columns: one column is the value from the indexed table's column and the other column is the row location referred to as the ROWID. In Oracle, indexes should be used wisely and deemed necessary only when they will actually improve the performance of a query. Indexes should not be used arbitrarily simply because a column is used in a query. The following list shows, in order of priority, the situations for which you should consider creating indexes:

1. Large tables
2. Primary keys (automatically indexed)
3. Unique key columns (automatically indexed)
4. Foreign key columns
5. Column(s) used frequently in the WHERE clause on large tables

6. Columns used in ORDER BY or GROUP BY clauses

7. Queries that return less than 20 percent of the rows in the table

8. Columns that do not contain NULL values

Oracle offers two types of indexes with variations that are used for different purposes and situations. Figure 14-1 illustrates these two types—B*Tree and Bitmap Indexes. This figure shows that the B*Tree index is modeled after the binary tree data structure, in which each node has two entries: ROWID, which is the row's physical location, and the column value being indexed. The bitmap index is based on a matrix model. For each row, the bit is turned on to its matching value. For example, the column value for ROWB is PENDING, so the corresponding bit is turned on.

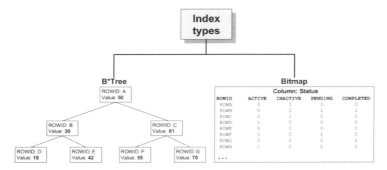

Figure 14-1 Oracle index types showing data structure for each type

Using the two basic types of indexes (B*Tree and Bitmap Indexes) and their options, you can create various types of indexes for different situations. The following is a list of the most common indexes that are presented in this chapter:

- B*Tree

- Composite

- Reverse

- Compressed

- Function-based

- Normal bitmap

A compressed index is a B★Tree index.

NOTE

B★Tree Indexes

A B★Tree index is a balanced binary tree index. It is sometimes referred to as a normal or simple index and is the most frequently used index type. The B★Tree index is composed of two columns: first, the ROWID, which is the location of the row, and second, the value of the column being indexed. You can administer index storage as you would with tables. B★Tree indexes are suitable for columns that have high cardinality, which means they are suitable for columns with many distinct values, and for application queries that retrieve a small number of rows, typically less than 20 percent of the total number of rows.

B★Tree indexes can have many variations, but the simplest form is the binary tree, which has a single column index with an index on that column. You typically find many B★Tree or normal indexes in most applications regardless of their type and purpose. Most developers and junior DBAs habitually index columns regardless of their use. You should question this practice, however, because despite all its benefits, an index has overhead that can become a liability. Each created index requires specific storage. In addition, every time the indexed column is updated (inserted, modified or deleted,) the index is updated. Also, frequent updates can require frequent maintenance such as reorganization and rebuilding of the index to reduce the adverse side effect of query performance degradation. In the following example, you create an index on the column CITY in the CUSTOMERS table because the column is used frequently in the WHERE condition.

```
CREATE INDEX IDX_CUS_CITY
  ON CUSTOMERS(CITY)
...
```

B★Tree indexes are not suited for columns with the following characteristics:

- Low cardinality (few distinct values)

- Frequent updates (every time a column is updated the index must be updated)

- Use with a function or an expression in the WHERE clause

Composite Index

A composite index is one type of B★Tree index and is composed of more than one column. The composite index is also referred to as a concatenated or compound index. This B★Tree composite index is used when you have frequent queries using two or more columns combined with an AND logical operator in a WHERE clause. For example, if you frequently retrieved a CUSTOMERS record using FIRST_NAME and LAST_NAME, you would create an index consisting of the two columns. Composite indexes are classified as normal indexes and have the same rules and criteria as normal indexes.

Because the order of columns in a composite index is important, be sure they are ordered for the most effective index performance. The following two criteria can be used as guidelines for ordering the columns:

14

- The leading column should be that most frequently used in queries.

- The leading column should be the most selective column, which means it has higher cardinality than the column that follows.

Let's take the example presented previously. You create the index with LAST_NAME as the leading column because it has higher cardinality than FIRST_NAME. If you make FIRST_NAME the leading column, and you submit a query looking for the name, George Ladd, there's a chance that more rows will be returned for George than for Ladd, and it will then be necessary to scan through those records to find Ladd. But if you use LAST_NAME as the leading column, fewer rows will be returned, which reduces the number of rows to scan through for George. The following statement creates this composite index using the order of the columns as specified:

```
CREATE INDEX IDX_CUS_LAST_FIRST
  ON CUSTOMERS(LAST_NAME, FIRST_NAME)
...
```

Composite indexes provide benefits in the following types of situations:

- Suppose you frequently have the following criteria in a WHERE clause: SHIP-MENT_METHOD_ID = 23 and SHIP_DATE = 'DD-MON-YYYY'. If you create an index for each column, both indexes will be read to search for the column value. But if you create one composite index for both columns, only one index is read, and that definitely requires less I/O than two indexes.

- Using the same criteria as the previous example, if you create a composite index, you will retrieve rows faster because you are eliminating all rows that do not have a SHIPMENT_METHOD_ID value of 23, and therefore you have reduced the number of rows to search for the SHIP_DATE.

Reverse indexes

Oracle supports another variation of an index type called the reverse index. In a reverse index the indexed column is actually reversed when it is indexed. For example if you have a column called ORDER_ID and its value in one row is 12345, Oracle reverses this value to 54321. You probably have a lingering question in your mind: What does the reverse option buy me? The main purpose of reverse option is to distribute index key values across different blocks in the index thus reducing block contention and eliminating index range scanning when retrieving values.

A reverse index is a B*Tree index.

To clarify this concept, examine an example of a reverse index in action. Suppose you already have a normal index on a column ORDER_ID in ORDERS. As you insert rows, the values for this column are 123, 124, 125, and 126. Because these numbers are so close, they are likely to fall into the same neighborhood (same block) when added to the index. But if you use the reverse option, these numbers become 321, 421, 521, and 621, which will probably be dispersed and spread out when they are added to the index.

NOTE

Only the value in the index is reversed; the value in the table remains constant.

The reverse index may reduce I/O contention but the reverse index has negative side effects. First, the major drawback is that when a query needs to retrieve several sequential values, the Optimizer makes a full table scan to retrieve these rows rather than an index range scan since the values are spread out. The second drawback is that there is a slight overhead for reversing the column value.

NOTE

You should not create a reverse index that is updated frequently.

The following is an example on how to create a reverse index on ORDER_ID in the ORDERS table

```
SQL> CREATE INDEX IDX_MY_ORDERS_ORDER_ID
  2      ON MY_ORDERS (ORDER_ID) REVERSE
  3  /

Index created.
```

14

NOTE

You may not alter an index after it is created to REVERSE/NOREVERSE by using the ALTER statement

```
SQL> ALTER INDEX SYS_C003141 REVERSE
  2  /
ALTER INDEX SYS_C003141 REVERSE
                *
ERROR at line 1:
ORA-14125: REVERSE/NOREVERSE may not be specified in this context
```

Skip Scan Index Functionality

You just learned about composite indexes and the importance of the order of the columns. Suppose you create a composite index on two columns, COL1 and COL2, with COL1 as the leading column. Every time you issue a query that references these two columns, this index will be used. Also, every time you issue a query referencing COL1, this index will be used. However, when only COL2 is referenced in the query, this index cannot be used. So, in many cases you will end up creating another index for COL2 or creating two separate indexes.

Oracle9*i* introduced the Skip Scan index feature, which enables the use of a composite index for queries that reference any column specified in the index, whether or not it's the leading column. Let's use an example to see how this feature works. Suppose you have a composite index consisting of two columns, COL1 and COL2. You issue a query that contains a WHERE clause referencing COL2. If Oracle Optimizer performs a Skip Scan, it will access the composite index once for each distinct value of column COL1, which is the leading column, and then scan through the returned rows for COL2.

The Oracle Optimizer evaluates whether the cost of a Skip Scan is less than a full table scan and executes the query accordingly. Skip Scan provides the following benefits:

- Reduces the number of indexes needed to support queries that reference indexed columns in the WHERE clause.

- Reduces storage required for each additional index.

- Improves performance of DML statements since fewer indexes will be updated.

- Reduces pressure on developers and DBAs to select the leading column correctly. However, you should always be diligent in creating composite indexes using the guidelines presented previously.

NOTE

The Skip Scan index feature is used most often on large tables with columns that are not high in cardinality.

You are probably asking yourself, "What do I need to do to take advantage of the Skip Scan feature?" The answer is that you do not need to do anything. As mentioned earlier, the Oracle Optimizer evaluates whether to use Skip Scan. But there is a little catch. You are at the mercy of the Oracle Optimizer, which means that the Optimizer might opt against using this feature because it costs more than full table scans. In that case, the query would be executed without using an index and that might increase the risk of degrading the per–formance of the query. The following steps illustrate the use of the Skip Scan feature.

Step #1: As TUNER, set AUTOTRACE on to generate an explain plan automatically:

```
SQL> SET AUTOTRACE TRACEONLY EXPLAIN
```

Step #2: Create a composite index on QUANTITY and DISCOUNT using QUANTITY as the leading column:

```
SQL> CREATE INDEX IDX_QUANTITY_DISCOUNT ON ORDER_LINES (QUANTITY, DISCOUNT)
  2  /

Index created.
```

Step #3: Issue a query referencing both columns in the WHERE clause. You'll see that the index that was just created is used.

```
SQL> SELECT *
  2    FROM ORDER_LINES
  3   WHERE QUANTITY = 50
  4     AND DISCOUNT = 12
  5  /

Execution Plan
----------------------------------------------------------
   0      SELECT STATEMENT Optimizer=CHOOSE (Cost=2 Card=56 Bytes=1400)
   1    0   TABLE ACCESS (BY INDEX ROWID) OF 'ORDER_LINES' (Cost=2 Card=56 Bytes=1400)
   2    1     INDEX (RANGE SCAN) OF 'IDX_QUANTITY_DISCOUNT' (NON-UNIQUE) (Cost=1 Card=56)
```

Step #4: Issue a query referencing only the leading column in the WHERE clause, QUANTITY. Notice that the index is used.

```
SQL> SELECT *
  2    FROM ORDER_LINES
  3   WHERE QUANTITY = 20
  4  /

Execution Plan
----------------------------------------------------------
   0      SELECT STATEMENT Optimizer=CHOOSE (Cost=37 Card=4502 Bytes=112550)
   1    0   TABLE ACCESS (BY INDEX ROWID) OF 'ORDER_LINES' (Cost=37 Card=4502 Bytes=112550)
   2    1     INDEX (RANGE SCAN) OF 'IDX_QUANTITY_DISCOUNT' (NON-UNIQUE) (Cost=3 Card=4502)
```

14

Step #5: Issue a query referencing the non-leading column, DISCOUNT. Notice that the Oracle Optimizer uses Skip Scan and an index.

```
SQL> SELECT *
  2    FROM ORDER_LINES
  3   WHERE DISCOUNT = 10
  4  /

Execution Plan
----------------------------------------------------------
   0      SELECT STATEMENT Optimizer=CHOOSE (Cost=35 Card=1350 Bytes=33750)
   1    0   TABLE ACCESS (BY INDEX ROWID) OF 'ORDER_LINES' (Cost=35 Card=1350 Bytes=33750)
   2    1     INDEX (SKIP SCAN) OF 'IDX_QUANTITY_DISCOUNT' (NON-UNIQUE) (Cost=25 Card=17)
```

Two observations can be made:

1. The Optimizer uses Skip Scan only it the table is large (millions of rows).

2. In the previous example, the Optimizer performed an index Skip Scan because the existing index had not been analyzed. If you analyzed the index, the Optimizer might perform a full table scan as shown in the following listing:

```
SQL> ANALYZE INDEX IDX_QUANTITY_DISCOUNT COMPUTE STATISTICS
  2  /

Index analyzed.
```

```
SQL> SELECT *
  2     FROM ORDER_LINES
  3   WHERE QUANTITY = 20
  4  /

Execution Plan
----------------------------------------------------------
   0       SELECT STATEMENT Optimizer=CHOOSE (Cost=49 Card=4502 Bytes=112550)
   1    0    TABLE ACCESS (FULL) OF 'ORDER_LINES' (Cost=49 Card=4502 Bytes=112550)
```

NOTE   Some DBA experts see few real benefits to the Skip Scan feature because the Oracle Optimizer decides when to use it and does not usually select the Skip Scan path.

Compressed Indexes

If you took a survey on how much of an application's storage is consumed by its indexes, you would find that on average the ratio is between 40 to 60 percent (that is, if developers and DBAs are reasonably wise at picking and creating indexes). Oracle provides an option to create a compressed index or rebuild an index by using the COMPRESS keyword. This mechanism provides an efficient way of storing duplicate values for a column and thereby reduces I/O. The COMPRESS keyword is usually followed by the number of key columns to be compressed.

For example, you have a composite index of four columns (COL1, COL2, COL3, and COL4) and you specify a compression clause as COMPRESS 3. This means that three key columns, from COL1 to COL3, will be compressed. In this case, valid compression levels are one to four.

Suppose you want to create a composite index (COL1 and COL2). If COL1 contains duplicate values and you want to compress this column, you can issue the following query:

```
CREATE INDEX index_name ON table_name(column list) COMPRESS n — where n is 1, 2, 3, … (columns)
/

Or

ALTER INDEX index_name REBUILD COMPRESS 1
/
```

The following is a list of the advantages of compressed indexes:

- Storage efficiency

- I/O efficiency since fewer blocks are read for a compressed index

- Less buffer cache consumption, which leads to less buffer thrashing

The following is a list of the disadvantages of compressed indexes:

- Consumption of more CPU resources because indexes require compression operations

- Slower query execution for tables that are not large

- Unsuitability for UNIQUE column values

Luckily, Oracle provides a way to determine if there will be savings in storage and if you will gain optimal levels of performance if you were to compress an index without physically compressing it. To make such a determination, follow these steps:

Step #1: Analyze the index using the VALIDATE statement:

```
SQL> VALIDATE INDEX IDX_ORD_PAID_STATUS
  2  /

Index analyzed.
```

Step #2: Issue the following query using the INDEX_STATS view. This view has two compression-related columns:

- OPT_CMPR_COUNT: indicates the optimal compression level that can be set to optimally save storage

- OPT_CMPR_PCTSAVE: indicates the optimal savings in storage if the index were compressed to OPT_CMPR_COUNT

```
SQL> SELECT NAME, OPT_CMPR_COUNT, OPT_CMPR_PCTSAVE
  2     FROM INDEX_STATS
  3  /

NAME                            OPT_CMPR_COUNT OPT_CMPR_PCTSAVE
------------------------------- -------------- ----------------
IDX_ORD_PAID_STATUS                          2               25
```

In this example, the query results indicate that if you rebuild the index using the compression clause, COMPRESS 2, you will save 25 percent of the currently consumed storage.

Function-based Indexes

The following conversation was overheard while Sue, a DBA, was eating lunch at the company cafeteria. "Do you know what I had to go through to rewrite the query I am working on?" Tarek asked. "What do you mean?" Bilal replied. "You know that anytime you use a column in an expression the index will not be used. So I had to figure out a way to rewrite the query so that it would not be part of an expression. Boy, this was a pain!" Bilal replied, "You must be kidding! Oracle has a function-based index which allows you to include the column in an expression." Tarek said, "Yes, I know, but the problem is that my company is not using Oracle! We are using..."

Yes, there are some database engines that do not support this feature, but you are not really concerned about those DBMSs. Not long ago, Oracle introduced the notion of a function-based index, which allows you to index a column that is part of an expression.

Let's look at this common scenario. Most applications offer an ad hoc, case-insensitive search on customer names. To make your search for LAST_NAME case-insensitive, you issue a query with the following condition in the WHERE clause: UPPER(LAST_NAME) = 'S%'. Oracle cannot use the index if it is not a function-based index. In other words, if LAST_NAME is indexed normally, the Optimizer will not use it because the column in the WHERE clause is part of an expression.

A function-based index is simply an index on a column(s) that is part of an expression. The following query illustrates how to create a function-based index. Notice that there is no keyword to indicate that this index is function based. The expression included in the column section of the CREATE INDEX statement notifies Oracle that the index is function based.

```
SQL> CREATE INDEX IDX_PP_PRICES
  2     ON PRODUCT_PRICES(PURCHASED_PRICE + MIN_PRICE)
  3  /

Index created.
```

You need to have the QUERY REWRITE system privilege to be able to create a function-based index; otherwise you will get an error as shown in the following listing:

```
SQL> CREATE INDEX IDX_PP_PRICES
  2      ON PRODUCT_PRICES(PURCHASED_PRICE + MIN_PRICE)
  3  /
   ON PRODUCT_PRICES(PURCHASED_PRICE + MIN_PRICE)
                                           *
ERROR at line 2:
ORA-01031: insufficient privileges
```

The following partial listing presents all the different types of indexes created by the user TUNER:

```
SQL> SELECT INDEX_NAME, INDEX_TYPE, COMPRESSION, UNIQUENESS
  2      FROM USER_INDEXES
  3  /

INDEX_NAME                      INDEX_TYPE                   COMPRESS UNIQUENES
------------------------------  ---------------------------  -------- ---------
IDX_CODES                       CLUSTER                      DISABLED UNIQUE
IDX_MY_ORDERS_ORDER_ID          NORMAL/REV                   DISABLED NONUNIQUE
IDX_OL_QTY_DSCT                 NORMAL                       ENABLED  NONUNIQUE
IDX_ORD_CUSTOMER_ID             NORMAL                       DISABLED NONUNIQUE
IDX_ORD_ORDER_DATE              NORMAL                       DISABLED NONUNIQUE
IDX_ORD_PAID_STATUS             NORMAL                       DISABLED NONUNIQUE
IDX_ORD_STATUS                  FUNCTION-BASED BITMAP        DISABLED NONUNIQUE
IDX_PI_QTY                      NORMAL                       DISABLED NONUNIQUE
IDX_PP_PRICES                   FUNCTION-BASED NORMAL        DISABLED NONUNIQUE
```

Of course, there are some restrictions on using function-based indexes as follows:

- Function-based indexes cannot use aggregate functions such as SUM or AVG as part of the expression.

- The expression at the time of index creation must have a deterministic value.

- If the expression is using a user-defined PL/SQL function and the function becomes invalid, the index is disabled.

- Functions used in the expression should not return NULL values.

- Columns used in the expression may not be of LOB data type.

- Columns used in the expression may not be part of a nested table.

14

Bitmap Indexes

A DBA contractor named Jimmy was hired by a small bank to administer 30 databases that were in development, QA, and production. The first three months, Jimmy spent his time responding to outstanding issues, development requests, routine database tasks, and getting familiar with the databases and their applications. Jimmy worked hard to stabilize his day-to-day tasks. He had time to look into each database in production to detect potential performance problems especially when one of the database developers mentioned that one database was performing sluggishly.

Jimmy went through his routine database health check and did not notice any major issues. But he did notice something strange about a large table with millions of rows and no fewer than 70 columns. Since this table belonged to a critical application, he looked for documentation on this application but found none. In particular, Jimmy was looking for the data model. So, using one of the tools he kept handy, he reverse-engineered the database to generate the data model. Voila! He started to look at the table to see if it was normalized. Jimmy was curious because of the number of columns, but everything seemed fine. The table could be normalized further but the gain would not be significant.

Jimmy did not stop there. He investigated the storage parameter configuration, and everything seemed to have been configured properly by the previous DBA. Then he looked at the indexes and wished he had not. He saw one composite index on 15 columns. He said to himself, "It cannot be—one index on 15 columns. Could it be that the query is using all these columns?" The next surprise was a bitmap index on two columns. He had learned that the application was an OLTP, which meant that it was highly active, and this table from the data model looked like a central table. He double-checked his findings before he called the lead developer of the application, Jessica. He introduced himself and told Jessica that he had found something peculiar about one index for table DAILY_ACTIVITIES. He asked if the table was DML active or if it was read-only and used for reporting. Jessica told him that the table was DML active and that transactions were recorded in the table. Jimmy was shocked and asked why the table was using a bitmap index. Jessica replied that the bitmap index was fine because the columns had a low number of distinct values, and bitmap indexes were suited for that. Jimmy said that they should meet to discuss the situation.

This story presents two problems. The first problem is the huge index on 15 columns, especially when the table is updated frequently. The second problem is that the index on two columns with high transaction activities is a bitmap index which violates one of the guidelines of bitmap indexes. Before you examine these problems, you need to understand what a bitmap index is.

A bitmap index uses a bit setting to indicate if a column value is set or not. Consider Figure 14-2 and note that the column STATUS can be only one of four possible values. For each row, the value 1 is set for the corresponding value. For example, ROWE is set for value COMPLETED.

Bitmap

Column: Status

ROWID	ACTIVE	INACTIVE	PENDING	COMPLETED
ROWA	0	1	0	0
ROWB	0	0	1	1
ROWC	0	1	0	0
ROWD	1	0	0	0
ROWE	0	0	0	1
ROWF	0	0	1	0
ROWG	0	0	0	1
ROWH	1	0	0	0

. . .

Figure 14-2 Bitmap index structure

When considering the use of a bitmap index on a column, there are two criteria that the column must meet, aside from the fact that the table that contains the column must be large:

1. The column must have low cardinality. This means that the number of distinct values in the column is in the range of 0.0001% for a large table that has more than one million rows, and 1% or less for a table that has one hundred thousands rows. Figure 14-3 illustrates the difference. For example, if you have a table with 1,000,000 rows, a column is considered to have low cardinality if the number of distinct values is less than 0.0001% of 1,000,000 rows = 100 values. This is a quick guideline to determine if a column has low cardinality.

2. The column and the table to which it belongs must not have transaction activities (updated).

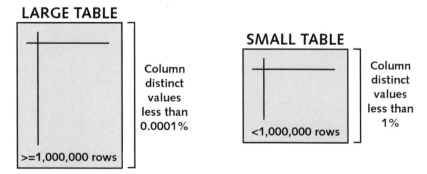

Figure 14-3 Low cardinality guidelines for columns

Going back to our story at the beginning of this section, remember that Jimmy was surprised that the index was the bitmap type because the indexed columns did not meet the two criteria. Every time the column is updated, the bitmap image must be updated, and that is expensive.

Here are some issues that you should keep in mind:

- Bitmap indexes usually consume less storage space than B*Tree indexes.

- Bitmap indexes are not considered by the Rule-based Optimizer.

- Bitmap indexes are more common in DSS applications than in OLTP applications.

- Bitmap indexes are suited for queries that use the OR condition in the WHERE clause.

- Bitmap indexes are not suited for tables with a high level of DML operations.

- If a bitmap index is created on a column that is updated frequently, not only is the cost high when remapping the image, but in addition, the table is locked during the operation, which will degrade the overall throughput of the database.

- It is not recommended to use bitmap indexes on columns with low cardinality such as a STATUS column with the possible values ACTIVE, INACTIVE, and UNKNOWN. Since the search will always return on third of the table, it might incur high overhead when using a bitmap index. The guideline says that you should not consider a bitmap index if more than one unique value represents more than 20 percent of the rows.

Here is an example of creating a bitmap index on the PAID column in an ORDERS table. As you can see, the creation of a bitmap index is similar to creating a normal index except you need to specify the keyword BITMAP.

```
SQL> CREATE BITMAP INDEX IDX_ORD_PAID
  2     ON ORDERS(PAID)
  3  /

Index created.
```

MONITORING INDEX USAGE

Kim is a developer who wants to be a DBA. She works for a small high tech company. She told the president of the company that everything was under control for delivering the company's application to its first and only client. The president of the company, Jack, was greatly concerned about the performance of the database because the application was real-time with no room for performance degradation.

Kim delivered and installed the application and everyone, except Jack, was excited. Even though he trusted Kim's development skills, he just did not have faith in the database. So he decided to hire a DBA expert, Helen, to do a quick survey of the database and application configuration. Jack said, "I really have confidence in Kim and know that she's doing her best, but this is our first client, and we cannot afford mistakes."

Helen spent five days reviewing the application and database as requested and wrote a report on her findings. In general, she gave the database a clean bill of health, but she had a couple of warnings about one database configuration and about the excessive use of indexes. Specifically, she told Jack, "I will write a couple of pages to give to Kim to monitor usage of the indexes. She should drop any index that is not used." Jack was very grateful and said, "Somehow I had the impression that most contractors come in, charge a lot of money, and leave without providing any added value, but you prove me wrong."

As you have guessed, Oracle provides a method to monitor index usage to ensure that indexes are not over-utilized and that you are not wasting space on unused indexes. The method involves the ALTER INDEX statement and the V$OBJECT_USAGE performance view. Returning to Helen—she probably wrote Kim the following steps to monitor index usage:

Step #1: As TUNER, open an **SQLsession** and mark it as **Session1**. Identify the index you want to monitor. You can get a full listing of the indexes by issuing the following query:

```
SQL> SELECT TABLE_NAME, INDEX_NAME
  2      FROM USER_INDEXES
  3    ORDER BY 1
  4  /

TABLE_NAME                         INDEX_NAME
-------------------------------    ----------------
CATEGORIES                         SYS_C003125
CODES                              IDX_CODES
CUSTOMERS                          SYS_C003139
DEPARTMENTS                        SYS_C003115
...
SALES_COMMISSION                   SYS_C003121
SHIPMENT_METHOD                    SYS_C003113
SUPPLIERS                          SYS_C003111
```

Step #2: If you want to monitor the index SYS_C003111 for the SUPPLIERS table, issue the following statement:

```
SQL> ALTER INDEX SYS_C003111 MONITORING USAGE
  2  /

Index altered.
```

14

Step #3: Issue the following query to determine if the index is being used. Notice that the column USED has a value NO, which means it is not used, and column MON, which is short for MONITORING, is set to YES.

```
SQL> SELECT * FROM V$OBJECT_USAGE
  2  /

INDEX_NAME                      TABLE_NAME                      MON USED START_MONITORING    END_MONITORING
------------------------------  ------------------------------  --- ---- ------------------  --------------
SYS_C003111                     SUPPLIERS                       YES NO   03/10/2002 16:24:41
```

An index is labeled as Not Used if it is not used as part of the execution plan to access data from the table.

NOTE

Step #4: Log on as TUNER to another session, mark it as Session 2, and issue the following query:

```
SQL> SELECT * FROM SUPPLIERS
  2    WHERE SUPPLIER_ID = 100
  3  /
```

Step #5: In Session 1, view the contents of the V$OBJECT_USAGE view. You will notice that the USED column has changed to YES, which means it was used.

```
SQL> SELECT * FROM V$OBJECT_USAGE
  2  /

INDEX_NAME                      TABLE_NAME                      MON USED START_MONITORING    END_MONITORING
------------------------------  ------------------------------  --- ---- ------------------  --------------
SYS_C003111                     SUPPLIERS                       YES YES  03/10/2002 16:24:41
```

Step #6: Turn off monitoring on index SYS_C003111. After you stop monitoring, see if END_MONITORING is populated with a timestamp. If so, the monitoring has ended.

```
SQL> ALTER INDEX SYS_C003111 NOMONITORING USAGE
  2  /

Index altered.

SQL> SELECT * FROM V$OBJECT_USAGE
  2  /

INDEX_NAME                      TABLE_NAME                      MON USED START_MONITORING    END_MONITORING
------------------------------  ------------------------------  --- ---- ------------------  --------------
SYS_C003111                     SUPPLIERS                       NO  YES  03/10/2002 16:24:41 03/10/2002 16:34:21
```

You should monitor all indexes for a full application cycle. That means that if it takes one week for an application to be fully utilized with all reports and functionality, you should monitor indexes for that period.

NOTE

Virtual Indexes

If you want virtual indexes, you're out of luck; there is no such thing in Oracle. However, the SQL Analyze tool, which is part of the Oracle Enterprise Manager Performance Pack, has a functionality called virtual index, which is a mechanism to determine if adding a new index on a table will enhance performance. Basically, the SQL Analyze tool creates a virtual index and quickly assesses whether the index will improve the performance of a query. This is helpful, and any little bit of help is good for a DBA. Open Oracle Enterprise Manager and follow these steps to see how it works:

Step #1: Using the Performance Pack toolbar, click the **SQL Analyze** button as shown in Figure 14-4.

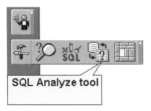

Figure 14-4   Oracle Enterprise Manager showing the SQL Analyze tool button

A dialog box displays asking you to log into the Oracle Management Server or to a standalone repository. Either way is fine; consult Oracle Enterprise Manager documentation for details on each option. In this case, log in using the TUNER account as shown in Figure 14-5.

Figure 14-5   SQL Analyze Login screen

Because this tool requires a repository, it performs more quickly if a repository exists. Otherwise it prompts you to create a repository as shown in Figure 14-6. When you click the Yes button, a progress screen displays as shown in Figure 14-7.

14

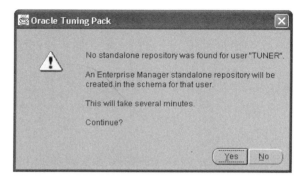

Figure 14-6 SQL Analyze repository creation

NOTE

To enable a user to create a repository, you must provide him with the following system privileges: EXECUTE ANY PROCEDURE, EXECUTE ANY TYPE, and SELECT ANY TABLE.

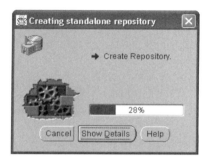

Figure 14-7 Repository creation progress screen

When the repository is fully created, the main screen displays, as shown in Figure 14-8.

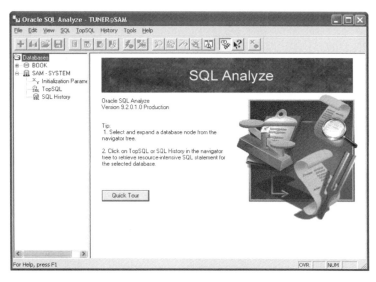

Figure 14-8   SQL Analyze tool main screen

This tool provides many different functions, but this section focuses on the virtual index functionality, so you should move on to the next step.

Step #2: From the SQL menu option, click **Create New SQL**, as shown in Figure 14-9. This enables the textbox in the right panel so that you can enter a query, as shown in Figure 14-10.

Figure 14-9   Create New SQL menu option

14

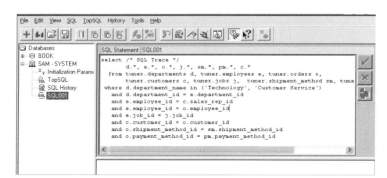

Figure 14-10   SQL Analyze tool showing SQL text panel

Step #3: Click the **Virtual Index Wizard** on the toolbar or select the **Menu option** from the Tools menu. A wizard window displays, as shown in Figure 14-11.

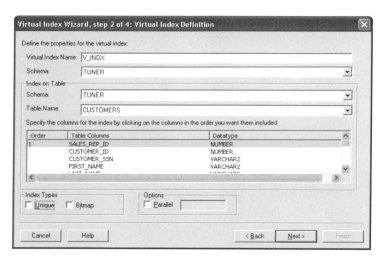

Figure 14-11   SQL Analyze Virtual Index Wizard, screen 2

Step #4: Suppose you decide to create a virtual index on the SALES_REP_ID column in the CUSTOMERS table to determine if it will improve the execution of the query. You will enter the values as shown in Figure 14-11, and then click the **Next** button. This takes you to the screen shown in Figure 14-12, where you select the type of access path.

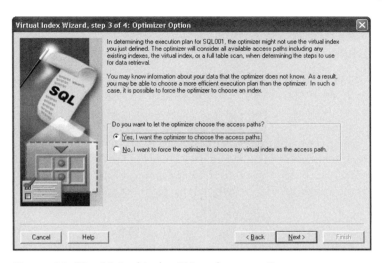

Figure 14-12   Virtual Index Wizard, screen 3

Step #5: Click the **Next** button and wait until the tool analyzes the new index and displays the assessment results. The results will look similar to Figure 14-13. Notice that the right bar on the graph shows that there would be no improvement if you created the index. You should also note that clicking the Show Comparison... button will display the explain plan for the query before and after the index is created.

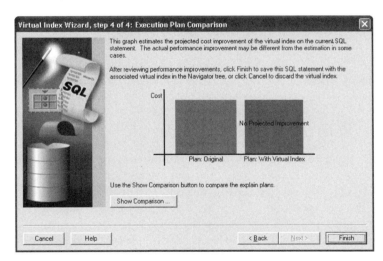

Figure 14-13   Virtual Index Wizard final screen

APPLICATION CONSIDERATIONS FOR TABLES

Mary, a junior DBA, had been working in a database group for a pharmaceutical company for six months since graduating from the DBA program at her local college. She was assigned administration of a new data warehouse database, which was under development. She had been taught to be involved in all phases of the database development life cycle, so she attended every design meeting and review. Everyone was impressed by her involvement and attentiveness. After six months of design and development, the application was ready for a pilot implementation. Mary reviewed the database configuration because she wanted to prove that she was a capable DBA on whom the team could count.

Three days before implementation, she met with the database architect, lead developer, and technical manager for the group to discuss several tables in the schema. Everyone wondered why she was holding this meeting, especially since the implementation was just around the corner. Mary announced that she wanted to use index-organized tables (IOT) for four tables that were prime candidates for that table type. Everyone was shocked and said that they had finished with the design and could not change any code. They declared that this was no time for experimenting. Mary told them to relax, that the changes were all on her end, and proceeded to explain IOT to them.

Mary had proven herself to be a stellar DBA. She had not confined her efforts to administration and routine issues. She had been involved and had recognized the fact that she had a situation in which she could implement IOTs. So what is the story about? Frankly, it is about applying your knowledge to implement the different types of tables called for. In this case, Mary knew the purpose of IOTs and used them in the right place, at the right time.

In this section, you focus on different types of tables available in Oracle and learn their characteristics. You are presented with three types of tables: index-organized tables, cluster-index tables, and partitioned tables.

Index-organized Table (IOT)

Although an index-organized table (IOT) is logically the same as a normal table, IOT significantly differs from a normal table in the physical organization of the data, as shown in Figure 14-14. A normal table is organized according to its primary key column. The table and the index of the primary key column are stored in separate data storage segments. Conversely, the index for an IOT is stored in the same data storage segment as the table. This reduces the storage consumed by the index. Although IOT reduces storage usage, it has several limitations, such as the number of indexes allowed in the segment.

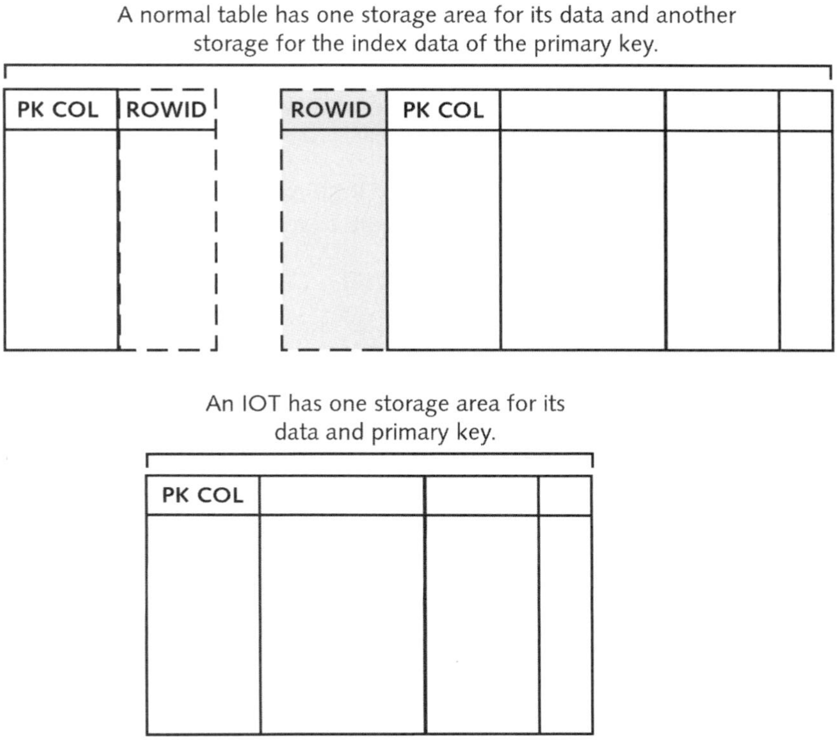

A normal table has one storage area for its data and another
storage for the index data of the primary key.

| PK COL | ROWID | ROWID | PK COL | | | |

An IOT has one storage area for its
data and primary key.

| PK COL | | | |

Figure 14-14   Index-organized table structure

IOTs are used primarily for situations in which most of the queries submitted will be searching on the primary key. The following list outlines IOT characteristics:

- The primary key must be specified.

- IOTs reduce I/O because one lookup is required to retrieve data through the primary key.

- The primary key index does not require an extra data storage segment. It is stored within the IOT structure.

- IOTs provide fast access to rows using primary key values.

- Data in index-organized tables is stored in the B*Tree structure based on the primary key, thereby saving disk space.

- You can define an "overflow" tablespace that will store the nonprimary key columns in case the primary tablespace is filled.

- Only one secondary index can be created.

- IOTs are good for queries using primary key values in the WHERE predicate but are inefficient for most ad hoc queries.

- As with a normal table, you can reorganize the table online, and you can use the MOVE command on an IOT.

- As with a normal table, you can replicate an IOT, add triggers to it, and apply constraints on its columns.

- As with a normal table, you can apply PARALLEL DML operations to an IOT, and you can apply a partitioning scheme to it.

Suppose you are asked to create an IOT called STATUS_CODES with the data structure presented in Table 14-1.

Table 14-1   STATUS_CODES table data structure

Column Name	Data Type
status_id	Number(4) (primary key)
status_code	Varchar2(10)
Status_desc	Varchar2(255)

Creating this IOT is quite simple; it requires issuing the following statement:

```
SQL> CREATE TABLE STATUS_CODES
  2  (
  3      STATUS_ID    NUMBER(4) PRIMARY KEY,
  4      STATUS_CODE  VARCHAR2(10),
  5      STATUS_DESC  VARCHAR2(255)
  6  )
  7  ORGANIZATION INDEX
  8  OVERFLOW TABLESPACE USERS
  9  /

Table created.

SQL> SELECT TABLE_NAME, IOT_NAME
  2    FROM USER_TABLES
  3   WHERE IOT_NAME IS NOT NULL
  4  /

TABLE_NAME                       IOT_NAME
------------------------------   ----------------
SYS_IOT_OVER_31992               STATUS_CODES
```

NOTE   The OVERFLOW TABLESPACE clause allows you to specify the tablespace to be used as storage when any column that is not the primary key value is updated and exceeds 20 percent of the block size

In previous versions of Oracle, IOTs were not allowed to create secondary indexes on any column other than the primary key. Oracle9i introduces the notion of mapping tables, which allow IOTs to create a secondary bitmap index on any column in the table. A mapping table is actually a bitmap position of the row address within the IOT. This mapping table is created when the MAPPING TABLE clause is included in the CREATE TABLE statement of the IOT. The next example creates an IOT with a mapping table.

```
SQL> CREATE TABLE IOT_MAPPING_TBL
  2  (
  3      NUM         NUMBER PRIMARY KEY,
  4      TEXT        VARCHAR2(20)
  5  )
  6  ORGANIZATION INDEX   -- THIS TO INDICATE THAT TABLE IS IOT
  7  MAPPING TABLE        -- THIS TO CREATE A MAPPING TABLE FOR THE ROW ADDRESSES OF THE IOT TABLE
  8  /

Table created.
```

 Like bitmap indexes, mapping tables incur high overhead on performance for high levels of DML activities.

NOTE

Cluster Tables

If you looked up the meaning of the word "cluster" in an English dictionary, you would find it defined as a grouping of similar things. This is exactly what it means in Oracle—a cluster is a grouping of tables. Tables are clustered together physically because they have a close relationship, typically a hierarchical relationship. Consider the classic examples of the DEPARTMENT/EMPLOYEE relationship and the ORDERS/ORDER_LINES relationship. Every department may have one or many employees, and every order may have one or many ORDER_LINES. Not only do these tables have a parent/child relationship, but in addition, most of the time data is retrieved from both tables through the same query. For tables with these two characteristics (a parent/child relationship and the ability to retrieve data through the same query), Oracle created the notion of cluster tables.

Figure 14-15 represents the structure of a two-table cluster. In this figure, you are looking at the classic example, DEPARTMENT and EMPLOYEE tables. If your application constantly retrieves employees for a specific department, a cluster structure will provide fast and efficient access to the data.

14

Department table

DEP_ID	DEP_NAME
100	Human Resources
200	Engineering
300	Sales
.	
.	
.	

Employee table

EMP_ID	DEP_NAME	. . .	DEP_ID
E100	Joe Doe	. . .	100
E200	John Smith	. . .	100
E300	Linda Kidrow	. . .	300
E600	Sam Clark	. . .	100
E212	Joe Blair	. . .	200
E312	Sid Nobel	. . .	300
E143	Jenny Joseph	. . .	100
E343	Sally Ball	. . .	300
E233	Danny Cry	. . .	300
E401	Bill Dean	. . .	200
E412	Samantha Dow	. . .	200

Clustered

Cluster table

Department: 100 - Human Resources

E100	Joe Doe	. . .
E200	John Smith	. . .
E600	Sam Clark	. . .
E143	Jenny Joseph	. . .

Department: 200 - Engineering

E212	Joe Blair	. . .
E401	Bill Dean	. . .
E412	Samantha Dow	. . .

Department: 300 - Sales

E300	Linda Kidrow	. . .
E312	Sid Nobel	. . .
E343	Sally Ball	. . .
E233	Danny Cry	. . .

Figure 14-15 Cluster table data structure

With the DEPARTMENT/EMPLOYEE example, use the following steps to cluster these two tables together.

Step #1: Log in as TUNER and create an index cluster for the two tables. This index cluster is usually the PRIMARY KEY/FOREIGN KEY column(s). In this case, the index cluster will be created on DEPARTMENT_ID.

```
SQL> CREATE CLUSTER DEPT_EMP_CLU
  2      (DEPARTMENT_ID NUMBER(2))
  3  /

Cluster created.
```

Step #2: Create tables that will be clustered in the DEPT_EMP_CLU cluster. See the following CREATE statements:

```
SQL> CREATE TABLE DEPT
  2  (
  3      DEPARTMENT_ID           NUMBER(2) PRIMARY KEY,
  4      DEPARTMENT_NAME         VARCHAR2(20),
  5      CITY                    VARCHAR2(30),
  6      STATE                   CHAR(2)
  7  )
  8  CLUSTER DEPT_EMP_CLU(DEPARTMENT_ID)
  9  /

Table created.

SQL> CREATE TABLE EMP
  2  (
  3      EMPLOYEE_ID             NUMBER(4) PRIMARY KEY,
  4      FIRST_NAME              VARCHAR2(20),
  5      LAST_NAME               VARCHAR2(20),
  6      SALARY                  NUMBER,
  7      DEPARTMENT_ID           NUMBER(2) REFERENCES DEPT(DEPARTMENT_ID)
  8  )
  9  CLUSTER DEPT_EMP_CLU(DEPARTMENT_ID)
 10  /

Table created.
```

14

Step #3: Create an index on DEPT_EMP_CLU.

```
SQL> CREATE INDEX IDX_DEPT_EMP_CLU ON CLUSTER DEPT_EMP_CLU
  2  /

Index created.
```

Step #4: Verify the creation of the cluster and tables by querying USER_TABLES and USER_CLUSTERS. Notice that the second query shows cluster type (index and hash).

```
SQL> SELECT TABLE_NAME, CLUSTER_NAME
  2    FROM USER_TABLES
  3    WHERE CLUSTER_NAME IS NOT NULL
  4  /

TABLE_NAME                          CLUSTER_NAME
-------------------------------     ---------------
DEPT                                DEPT_EMP_CLU
EMP                                 DEPT_EMP_CLU
...

SQL> SELECT CLUSTER_NAME, CLUSTER_TYPE
  2    FROM USER_CLUSTERS
  3  /

CLUSTER_NAME                        CLUST
-------------------------------     -----
CODES                               INDEX
DEPT_EMP_CLU                        INDEX
GRADES_CLUSTER                      HASH
STATUS_CODE                         INDEX
```

NOTE

Use data dictionary views DBA_CLUSTERS, DBA_CLUSTER_HASH_EXPRESSIONS and DBA_CLU_COLUMNS to view details on clusters created in the database.

What about cluster type? The cluster that you just created is type index, and is usually referred to as a cluster-index table. This type of cluster uses the indexed column values to cluster the tables together. In this case, DEPARTMENT_ID is the index column. This means that Oracle uses an index as a separate object, to locate values in the cluster. In Figure 14-16, you see two objects: the cluster table, which is the DEPT and EMP tables clustered together in one physical structure, and the cluster index, which is a normal index used to look up the ROWID for the DEPARTMENT_ID column. So in this case, every time you issue a statement looking for all employees in Department 200, the query will incur two I/Os: one to look up the rowid and another to fetch the rows.

Cluster index

ROWID	DEPARTMENT_ID
AAAHcvA...	100
AAAHcvB...	200
AAAHcvC...	300
.	
.	
.	

Cluster table

Department: 100 - Human Resources

E100	Joe Doe	...
E200	John Smith	...
E600	Sam Clark	...
E143	Jenny Joseph	...

Department: 200 - Engineering

E212	Joe Blair	...
E401	Bill Dean	...
E412	Samantha Dow	...

Department: 300 - Sales

E300	Linda Kidrow	...
E312	Sid Nobel	...
E343	Sally Ball	...
E233	Danny Cry	...

Figure 14-16   Cluster table and index example

As an alternative approach to this type of cluster (index cluster), Oracle provides a hash cluster, which uses a hash function to store and retrieve rows from the cluster without the need to use another cluster index object. If you issue the same query on a hash cluster, only one I/O is incurred, which is faster than a cluster index.

The following list outlines cluster considerations:

- When clusters are used, data is retrieved from two tables that have a parent/child relationship using a single query.

- Clusters facilitate quick access to data.

- A hash cluster is faster and more efficient than an index cluster.

- Clusters are not suited for high levels of activity for modifications of column values.

- Clusters are not suited for high levels of activity for inserts.

- In hash clusters, there is a possibility of hash key collisions especially if the table is constantly growing. In hash key collisions, the hash function generates the same key value for two different rows.

Table Partitioning

"John, what should I do about this table? It is growing and growing, and retrieving rows from it is becoming a problem," said Larry, a developer at a law firm. At the other end of the line, John told him that the solution was simple—partitioning the table. Larry went to the DBA and asked what she knew about table partitioning. He told her that the REGIS-TRATION_RECORDS table was getting out of hand and his friend, a DBA, recommended partitioning the table. Sue listened impatiently. She had discussed this specific problem with the developers but they had always said they would deal with it later. Sue told Larry she had warned the developers about the problem when she took over the database, mentioning specifically the rate the table was growing. She had requested a meeting to come up with a plan to partition this table. Larry told her that he and the other developers had been busy at that time, but that he now needed to hear more about partitioning.

As happens so often, Larry had waited until the problem could not be ignored and then reacted with urgency. The organizational structure of many environments puts tackling database problems low on the priority list of developers. As a passive DBA, Sue allowed database issues to slip from the top of the priority list. To be fair, it could be that her manager was not supportive of her decisions, or that she did not want to cause friction with the development team. Either way, the situation was not good. Larry's problem was a design issue from the beginning. Also, Larry's lack of knowledge about Oracle table partitioning caused him to make the wrong decision, and when he was told about it, he ignored the suggestion because it was not his idea or he was not familiar with the concept.

The performance problem caused by the growth of the table required immediate attention, and John recommended table partitioning. What would partitioning accomplish? In this section, you will be presented with a brief overview of table partitioning to provide you with some background information so that you can enhance applications whenever possible. Note that table partitioning is an advanced feature of Oracle, which is not covered extensively in this section.

Table partitioning is a method of dividing a table into physically separate parts while it remains logically one table. Each part of the table is referred to as a partition. Partitioning is ideal for very large tables. You can organize the data within the table into separate physical structures residing in the same or a different tablespace. This type of structure enhances data retrieval and makes data organization for historical purposes more efficient. See Figure 14-17 for an illustration.

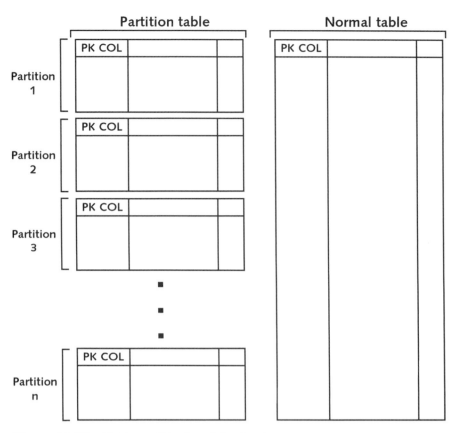

Figure 14-17   Table partitioning data structure

Implementing table partitioning provides several benefits which combine to improve your database application design and hence its performance. The following is the list of benefits:

- **Data management**: Table partitioning enables database administrators to manage a large amount of data in several physical partitions residing on different storage devices. This distributes I/O load, reduces contention, and enhances performance.

- **Data pruning**: Table partitioning is ideal for very large tables that need to keep data for historical purposes without impacting the speed of data retrieval.

- **Backup and recovery strategy**: Table partitioning enables you to implement backup strategies more easily because large tables are divided into smaller parts on different files.

- **Parallelism**: Table partitioning enables developers to execute queries and DML operations using the parallel option to enhance performance.

Oracle provides several types of partitioning, each with a specific purpose. The following list presents a description and example of each partitioning type.

- **List Partitioning**: This type of partitioning is based on a list of values for a column.

Example: Suppose you have a large table PROBLEM_TICKETS containing a column called STATUS which takes on one of four possible values: ACTIVE, INACTIVE, PENDING, or COMPLETED. You can partition this table using the list-partitioning method. This is how you would create the table:

```
SQL> CREATE TABLE PROBLEM_TICKETS
  2  (
  3      PROBLEM_ID        NUMBER,
  4      DESCRIPTION       VARCHAR2(2000),
  5      CUSTOMER_ID       NUMBER,
  6      DATE_ENTERED      DATE,
  7      STATUS            VARCHAR2(20)
  8  )
  9  PARTITION BY LIST ( STATUS )
 10  (
 11      PARTITION PROB_ACTIVE    VALUES ('ACTIVE')    TABLESPACE PROB_TS01,
 12      PARTITION PROB_INACTIVE  VALUES ('INACTIVE')  TABLESPACE PROB_TS02,
 13      PARTITION PROB_PENDING   VALUES ('PENDING')   TABLESPACE PROB_TS03,
 14      PARTITION PROB_COMPLETED VALUES ('COMPLETED') TABLESPACE PROB_TS04
 15  )
 16  /

Table created.
```

NOTE

You can view all partitions and subpartitions using the dictionary views DBA_TAB_PARTITIONS and DBA_TAB_SUBPARTITIONS.

- **Range partitioning**: This type of partitioning uses a range of values for a column, and this column is usually referred to as the partition key.

Example #1: Suppose the CUSTOMER table has 200,000 rows and you anticipate that it will grow to 800,000 rows. Being a proactive DBA, you decide to partition this table to improve query performance and reduce contention. So you select range partitioning to divide the table based on CUSTOMER_ID as the partition key. You can partition each range to hold a maximum of 1,000,000 rows, so you create partitions for CUSTOMER_ID values 0-100,000, 100,001-200,000, 200,001-300,000, and so on. The following CREATE statement demonstrates how to implement this example. Notice that each partition is contained within its own tablespace. In this case, you must create these tablespaces ahead of time.

```
SQL> CREATE TABLE CUSTOMER
  2  (
  3      CUSTOMER_ID      NUMBER,
  4      FIRST_NAME       VARCHAR2(30),
  5      LAST_NAME        VARCHAR2(30),
  6      PHONE            VARCHAR2(15),
  7      EMAIL            VARCHAR2(80),
  8      STATUS           CHAR(1)
  9  )
 10  PARTITION BY RANGE ( CUSTOMER_ID )
 11  (
 12      PARTITION CUS_PART01 VALUES LESS THAN ( 100000 ) TABLESPACE CUS_TS01,
 13      PARTITION CUS_PART02 VALUES LESS THAN ( 200000 ) TABLESPACE CUS_TS02,
 14      PARTITION CUS_PART03 VALUES LESS THAN ( 300000 ) TABLESPACE CUS_TS03,
 15      PARTITION CUS_PART04 VALUES LESS THAN ( 400000 ) TABLESPACE CUS_TS04,
 16      PARTITION CUS_PART05 VALUES LESS THAN ( 500000 ) TABLESPACE CUS_TS05,
 17      PARTITION CUS_PART06 VALUES LESS THAN ( 600000 ) TABLESPACE CUS_TS06,
 18      PARTITION CUS_PART07 VALUES LESS THAN ( 700000 ) TABLESPACE CUS_TS07,
 19      PARTITION CUS_PART08 VALUES LESS THAN ( 800000 ) TABLESPACE CUS_TS08
 20  )
 21  /

Table created.
```

Example #2: Suppose your business requirements for a database application call for ORDER_ACTIVITIES records to be available online for up to six months. Any record older than six months is archived and purged. In this case, you partition the table on ORDER_DATE by month. The following CREATE statement illustrates the implementation of this example:

```
SQL> CREATE TABLE ORDER_ACTIVITIES
  2  (
  3      ORDER_ID      NUMBER,
  4      ORDER_DATE    DATE,
  5      TOTAL_AMOUNT  NUMBER,
  6      CUSTOMER_ID   NUMBER,
  7      PAID          CHAR(1)
  8  )
  9  PARTITION BY RANGE ( ORDER_DATE )
 10  (
 11      PARTITION ORD_ACT_PART01 VALUES LESS THAN ( TO_DATE('01-MAY-2003', 'DD-MON-YYYY') ),
 12      PARTITION ORD_ACT_PART02 VALUES LESS THAN ( TO_DATE('01-JUN-2003', 'DD-MON-YYYY') ),
 13      PARTITION ORD_ACT_PART03 VALUES LESS THAN ( TO_DATE('01_JUL-2003', 'DD-MON-YYYY') )
 14  )
 15  /

Table created.
```

14

NOTE   Rows are automatically inserted into the proper partition based on the value of the partition key. If a partition does not exist for a specific value, an error is generated. In this case you need to create a new partition for this value.

- **Hash partitioning**: This type of partitioning uses a hash algorithm on a column value to determine what partition the row belongs to. This type is used when a column's values do not have any logical grouping to act as a key partition, or you do not know much about the key partition column's values. Oracle will try to distribute the rows among available partitions evenly.

Example: Suppose you decide to partition a table using the hash partitioning method using one of the columns in the table. The statement in the following code segment creates this table. As mentioned previously, you must create the tablespaces before you create the partition table.

```
SQL> CREATE TABLE HASH_PART_TBL
  2  (
  3     NUM        NUMBER,
  4     TEXT       VARCHAR2(80)
  5  )
  6  PARTITION BY HASH ( NUM )
  7  (
  8     PARTITION PART_01 TABLESPACE HASH01,
  9     PARTITION PART_02 TABLESPACE HASH01,
 10     PARTITION PART_03 TABLESPACE HASH01,
 11     PARTITION PART_04 TABLESPACE HASH01,
 12     PARTITION PART_05 TABLESPACE HASH01
 13  )
 14  /

Table created.
```

- **Composite-range-list partitioning**: This type of partitioning is a combination of range and list partitioning types. The table is partitioned by range first and then each partition is partitioned by the list partitioning method. A partition within a partition is referred to as a subpartition.

Example: Suppose you have a large table called ORDER_ACTIVITY containing customer orders. You decide to partition this table using range-list partitioning. The range partition is based on ORDER_DATE and the list partition is based on the PAID column. The following statement creates this table.

NOTE

Composite partitioning adds one more benefit to partitioning tables—partitioning granularity—regardless of the type of composite partitioning,

```
SQL> CREATE TABLE ORDER_ACTIVITY
  2  (
  3    ORDER_ID              NUMBER(5) NOT NULL,
  4    ORDER_DATE            DATE,
  5    CUSTOMER_ID           NUMBER(8),
  6    EMPLOYEE_ID           NUMBER(4),
  7    SHIP_DATE             DATE,
  8    SHIPMENT_METHOD_ID    NUMBER(2),
  9    PAYMENT_METHOD_ID     NUMBER(2),
 10    PAID                  CHAR(1),
 11    ORDER_STATUS          CHAR(1),
 12    COMMENTS              VARCHAR2(1024)
 13  )
 14  PARTITION BY RANGE (ORDER_DATE)
 15    SUBPARTITION BY LIST (PAID)
 16    SUBPARTITION TEMPLATE
 17    (
 18        SUBPARTITION SUB_PNO  VALUES ('N'),
 19        SUBPARTITION SUB_PYES VALUES ('Y')
 20    )
 21  (
 22    PARTITION PART_01  VALUES LESS THAN ( TO_DATE('01-JUN-2003', 'DD-MON-YYYY') ),
 23    PARTITION PART_02  VALUES LESS THAN ( TO_DATE('01-JUL-2003', 'DD-MON-YYYY') ),
 24    PARTITION PART_03  VALUES LESS THAN ( TO_DATE('01-AUG-2003', 'DD-MON-YYYY') )
 25  )
 26  /

Table created.
```

NOTE

You can apply partition methods on index-organized tables

- **Composite-range-hash partitioning**: This type of partitioning is a combination of range and hash partitioning types. The table is partitioned by range first and then each partition is partitioned by the hash partitioning method. The hash partitioning is referred to as a subpartition.

Example: Composite-range hash partitioning uses statements similar to the statements in the previous range-list example. The following statement creates a partition table on the PROD table using PRODUCT_ID as a range partition key and CATEGORY_ID as a hash partition key.

14

```
SQL> CREATE TABLE PROD
  2  (
  3    PRODUCT_ID      NUMBER NOT NULL,
  4    CATEGORY_ID     NUMBER,
  5    PRODUCT_NAME    VARCHAR2(80),
  6    PRODUCT_DESC    VARCHAR2(512),
  7    STATUS          CHAR(1),
  8    COMMENTS        VARCHAR2(1024)
  9  )
 10  PARTITION BY RANGE (PRODUCT_ID)
 11    SUBPARTITION BY HASH (CATEGORY_ID)
 12    SUBPARTITION TEMPLATE
 13    (
 14       SUBPARTITION SUB_01,
 15       SUBPARTITION SUB_02,
 16       SUBPARTITION SUB_03,
 17       SUBPARTITION SUB_04
 18    )
 19  (
 20    PARTITION PART_01  VALUES LESS THAN ( 500000 ),
 21    PARTITION PART_02  VALUES LESS THAN ( 5000000 ),
 22    PARTITION PART_03  VALUES LESS THAN ( 50000000 )
 23  )
 24  /

Table created.
```

As with a normal table, you can create indexes on a partitioned table to speed up row retrieval. Oracle provides three types of index partitioning:

- **Global partitioned index**: a partitioned index on a table that is either partitioned or not. A global partitioned index can only be partitioned using range partitioning.

- **Global nonpartitioned index**: a nonpartitioned index on a partitioned table.

- **Local index**: a partitioned index for a partitioned table. Each partition in the table will have a local index partition using the same method of partitioning and the same key partition column. Local indexes are considered to be faster than global partitioned indexes.

To wrap up this section on table partitioning, it is worth noting that most large databases (containing terabytes) with large tables (millions of rows) employ table partitioning. A database of that size that does not use partitioning is bound to have one or all of the following: data manageability problems, data retrieval performance problems, and backup and recovery implementation problems.

NOTE   You can select directly from a partition to expedite data retrieval and query performance by specifying the name of the partition from which rows should be retrieved. For an example, examine the following code segment:

```
SQL> SELECT *
  2    FROM PROD PARTITION (PART_01)
  3   WHERE PRODUCT_ID = 1
  4   /
```

Applications Characteristics

Cindy, a database expert, was hired as a contractor to help a development team design a new reporting application to be used by the marketing department to analyze products sold by the company. This company was a Java and Oracle workshop. Cindy knew less about Oracle than about other database management systems, but the development team respected her opinion and was excited to work with her.

Cindy and the team worked long hours discussing business requirements and spent endless days and nights brainstorming to come up with the most efficient design. Cindy's invaluable expertise complemented the development team's technical experience. She knew the nuts and bolts of many different types of applications as well as the factors that must be taken into account when designing those applications.

Being technically proficient in one area is not enough for a DBA. You should always broaden your experience by learning how different types of applications tick. As a head start, this short section presents a summarized list of characteristics for three types of applications.

Web Applications

- Must be accessible anytime from anywhere (high availability).

- Should be fast enough to respond to all requests within three seconds.

- Should be reliable with no chance of corrupting data as a result of the handling of the session (data integrity).

- Should perform session and connection pooling using an application server, which controls the number of resources tapped by users.

- Are highly scalable. This means that Web applications require a database management system and database design that can scale up to demand.

- Use a middle layer such as JDBC, ODBC, or database connectivity software to connect to the database.

- Take extra measures to authenticate users and ensure that users are legitimate.

14

OLTP Applications

- Handle high levels of activity in transaction operations.

- Handle high numbers of users, sessions, or connections.

- Receive queries that usually retrieve a small number of rows.

- Perform DML operations that usually affect a small number of rows.

- Have limited parallelism benefits.

- Store current data in an OLTP database.

- Store complete and detailed data in the OLTP database.

- Receive queries that are usually repetitive.

- Have database activity and behavior that are predictable.

- Are used by operators, clerks, and clients (users).

DSS Applications:

- Have limited or no transaction activities.

- Have a small number of users, sessions, or connections.

- Receive queries that usually retrieve a large number of rows.

- Receive queries that are usually complex.

- Receive a high numbers of queries that use aggregate functions.

- Have a high level of activity on temporary space due to sorting.

- Perform many full table scans.

- Have parallelism that benefits and enhances performance tremendously.

- Store historical data in a DSS database.

- Usually store summarized and aggregated data in a DSS database.

- Usually handle ad hoc queries.

- Have unpredictable database usage.

- Are used by middle and upper management.

- Refresh data periodically.

- Are used for reporting.

CHAPTER SUMMARY

❏ An index is a database object used by Oracle to speed up the retrieval of data from a table.

❏ Oracle offers two types of indexes with variations: B★Tree and bitmap.

❏ A B★Tree index is a balanced binary-tree index.

❏ A B★Tree index is sometimes referred to as a normal or simple index.

❏ The simplest form of a binary tree is the single column index, which is an index on one column.

❏ A composite index is composed of more than one column and is also referred to as a concatenated or compound index.

❏ The order of columns in the composite index is important. Therefore, DBAs need to make sure that columns are ordered so that the index is most effective: the leading column should be both the column most frequently used in queries and the most selective column.

❏ Skip Scan indexes enable the use of a composite index for queries that reference any column specified in the index, whether or not it's the leading column.

❏ Compressed indexes provide an efficient way of storing duplicate values for a column and thereby reduce I/O.

❏ A function-based index is simply an index on a column(s), which is part of an expression.

❏ QUERY REWRITE system privileges are necessary for creating a function-based index.

❏ A bitmap index uses a bit setting to indicate if a column value is set or not.

❏ For a bitmap index, two criteria that must be met: the column must have low cardinality values, and it can only receive very light DML operations.

❏ Oracle provides a method to monitor index usage to ensure that indexes are not over-utilized and space is not wasted on unused indexes. The method involves the ALTER INDEX statement and the V$OBJECT_USAGE performance view.

❏ The SQL Analyze tool in the Oracle Enterprise Manager Performance Pack has a function called virtual index, which is a mechanism to determine if adding a new index on a table to enhance performance of the query will be beneficial.

❏ Logically IOT is a normal table but it differs significantly from a normal table in the physical organization of the data.

❏ The index for an IOT is stored in the same data storage segment as the table, and this reduces the storage consumed by the index.

❏ A mapping table allows an IOT to create a secondary bitmap index on any column in the table.

❏ The clustering of tables is the grouping of two or more tables together in one physical structure.

14

❏ Table partitioning is a method of dividing a table into physically separate parts while the table logically remains one table.

❏ List partitioning is based on a list of values for a column.

❏ Range partitioning uses a range of values for a column, and this column is usually referred to as the partition key.

❏ Hash partitioning uses a hash algorithm on a column value to determine what partition the row belongs to.

❏ Composite-range-list partitioning is a combination of range and list partitioning.

❏ Composite-range-hash partitioning is a combination of range and hash partitioning.

❏ A global partitioned index is an index on a table that is either partitioned or not. This index can only be partitioned using range partitioning.

❏ A global nonpartitioned index is a nonpartitioned index on a partitioned table.

❏ A local index is a partitioned index for each partition in a partitioned table.

❏ Views used in this chapter include the following:

- USER_INDEXES

- USER_TABLES

- USER_CLUSTERS

- DBA_TAB_PARTITIONS

- DBA_TAB_SUBPARTITIONS

- V$OBJECT_USAGE

REVIEW QUESTIONS

1. Although B*Tree and bitmap indexes are different, they serve the same purpose. (True/False)

2. A bitmap index is more suited to reporting than to transactional applications. (True/False)

3. You cannot create compressed bitmap indexes. (True/False)

4. You should consider creating an index when a table is large and retrieving large numbers of rows. (True/False)

5. Use the hash partitioning method when column values do not have logical groupings. (True/False)

6. DBAs can view any index being monitored using V$OBJECT_USAGE. (True/False)

7. You should consider building a B*Tree index on a column that has high distinct values regardless of the type of the application. (True/False)

8. A Skip Scan index is a B*Tree index used to replace a composite index to discard column order. (True/False)

9. A bitmap index has low performance overhead when it is created on a table that is updated frequently. (True/False)

10. You can create a function-based index on any column in a table regardless of its data type. (True/False)

11. You can use the range-partitioning method on a column that can have four distinct values. (True/False)

12. One of the main advantages of table partitioning is data pruning. (True/False)

13. Databases must be able to scale up to the number of users for DSS applications. (True/False)

14. OLTP applications benefit a good deal from query and DML parallelism. (True/False)

15. List all the different types of indexes used in your database.

16. List all the different types of tables used in your database.

17. Describe a situation in which you would use a compressed index.

18. Describe a situation in which you would use an index-organized table and then create the table as a partitioned table.

19. Create a partitioned table with a local index for the following CLIENTS data structure, which is represented in Table 14-2. Justify the partitioning method you used.

Table 14-2   CLIENTS data structure

Column	Data Type
ID	NUMBER (PK)
FIRST_NAME	VARCHAR2(20)
LAST_NAME	VARCHAR2(20)
CITY	VARCHAR2(30)
PHONE	VARCHAR2(15)

14

20. Create a database table with two columns: the first column is called ID as a NUMBER data type; and the second column is called TEXT as a VARCHAR2(80) data type. Insert two rows and then try to convert it the table to an IOT outlining and justifying all the steps you take.

EXAM REVIEW QUESTIONS: ORACLE9i PERFORMANCE TUNING (#1Z0-033)

1. What type of a table would you use if you always join two tables together?

   a. normal

   b. IOT

   c. cluster

   d. partitioned

2. What type of a table would you use if you always use primary keys to retrieve data?

   a. normal

   b. IOT

   c. cluster

   d. partitioned

3. What type of an index would you use to speed retrieval of a row in a normal table?

   a. B*Tree index

   b. bitmap index

   c. B*Tree compressed index

   d. bitmap compressed index

4. What type of an index would you use in an OLTP database?

   a. B*Tree

   b. Bitmap

   c. Index-organized

   d. Cluster

   e. Local

5. What type of an index would you use in DSS database?

   a. B*Tree

   b. bitmap

   c. index-organized

   d. cluster

   e. local

6. In which situation would you use a function-based index?

   a. The column has a deterministic value.

   b. The column is part of an expression.

   c. The column is part of an aggregation function.

   d. Only if the column is a parameter in a user-defined PL/SQL function.

   e. None of the above.

7. Which criteria must be met to create Bitmap indexes? The column must
   _____. (Choose 2)

   a. have low distinct values

   b. have high distinct values

   c. have low DML operations

   d. not have low DML operations

8. You would use table partitioning when you have a large table _____.

   a. and you want to purge historical data periodically

   b. and you want to create bitmap indexes on it

   c. that needs to be backed up fast

   d. that processes many DML operations

9. Which of the following is not a valid partitioning method?

   a. Hash

   b. List

   c. Range

   d. List–hash

   e. Range–hash

10. Which clause would you issue with the ALTER INDEX statement to monitor
    index usage?

    a. MONITOR INDEX

    b. MONITOR USAGE

    c. MONITOR USE

    d. MONITOTING INDEX

    e. MONITORING USAGE

    f. MONITORING USE

14

11. Which statement is correct for creating an IOT?

    a. CREATE INDEX ORGANIZE TABLE IOT_TBL(...);

    b. CREATE ORGANIZED INDEX TABLE IOT_TBL(...);

    c. CREATE TABLE IOT_TBL (...) INDEX ORGANIZED;

    d. CREATE TABLE IOT_TBL (...) ORGANIZED INDEX;

    e. CREATE TABLE IOT_TBL (...) INDEX ORGANIZATION;

    f. CREATE TABLE IOT_TBL (...) ORGANIZATION INDEX;

12. Which system privilege do you need to create a function-based index?

    a. QUERY WRITE

    b. QUERY REWRITE

    c. REQUERY WRITE

    d. REQUERY REWRITE

    e. None of the above

13. Which of the following is not a DSS application?

    a. Reporting

    b. Batch-processing

    c. Data warehousing

    d. OLAP

    e. None of the above

    f. All of the above

14. Which index is not a valid variation of a B*Tree index?

    a. Normal

    b. Composite

    c. Reversed

    d. Compressed

    e. Skip scan

    f. None of the above

15. Which of the following is not a characteristic of an OLTP application?

    a. High activity on temporary space due to sorting

    b. High activity of transaction operations

    c. High number of users, sessions, or connections

    d. Small number of rows usually affected by DML operations

    e. Queries usually repetitive

HANDS-ON PROJECTS

**HANDS-ON
PROJECTS**

Please complete the projects provided below.

1. Reread the Performance Problem at the start of the chapter. Think of it in terms of the concepts you have learned in this chapter, analyze the problem, and provide a recommendation to the DBA.

2. You received a call from a developer who was implementing a new, small module for an existing application. The developer needed help on cluster tables. He told you he could not find help on this topic. He had three tables that fit the definition of a table cluster but could not find an example of the syntax for creating one. He asked you to e-mail him an example. Please do so.

3. Outline the steps necessary to create an example of clustering three tables.

4. List two advantages of table partitioning, and for each advantage produce an example outlining steps for implementing it.

5. You inherited a database after one of the DBAs in your team moved on to another job. You did a survey to get familiar with databases and noticed a large number of indexes. Outline the steps you would take to determine what indexes are not used so that you could drop them.

6. Consider the TUNER schema and identify tables that may be considered as IOT or cluster tables. Also, identify if there is a need to consider different types or variations of indexes.

7. Drop all indexes on the following two tables in the TUNER schema: ORDERS and ORDER_LINES. Using the Virtual Index Wizard in the Oracle Enterprise Manager SQL Analyze tool, analyze the following query:

```
SELECT O.ORDER_ID, O.ORDER_DATE, O.CUSTOMER_ID,
       OL.PRODUCT_ID, OL.QUANTITY, OL.TOTAL_AMOUNT
  FROM ORDERS O, ORDER_LINES OL
 WHERE O.ORDER_ID = OL.ORDER_ID
   AND O.SHIP_DATE = '12-JUN-2000'
/
```

14

8. Suppose the SUPPLIERS table in the TUNER schema is very large and you have decided to partition it. Identify a partition method and implement it. Justify your reasons for choosing any partition method.

9. Outline steps to demonstrate the Skip Scan index concept.

10. Identify a table in the TUNER schema for which you can implement a range-list composite partition.

CASE PROJECTS

CASE PROJECTS

1. Every Little Bit Helps—Databases

Jack, an Oracle DBA discussed the different types of tables available in Oracle with a developer named George. Jack told George that he wanted to be involved in the design of the application from the beginning so he could use different types of tables as appropriate. George asked how much performance could be improved by using different types of tables, so Jack agreed to show him.

1. Jack made sure timing was set in the SQL*Plus observing time consumed for each task. Jack also checked to make sure that the database had enough undo segments.

2. Jack created two tables—IOT_TBL and NORM_TBL—that had identical data structures as follows:

```
Name        PRIMARY KEY Type
--------    ----------- ------------
ID          YES         NUMBER
TEXT                    VARCHAR2(80)
```

3. He populated each table with 2,000,000 rows.

4. Then he set AUTOTRACE to TRACEONLY with the EXPLAIN option.

5. He issued a query on each of the two tables to retrieve a row with ID 23044. George then asked Jack to explain how the plan described each query.

6. Jack analyzed both tables and any indexes created specifically for these two tables.

7. Jack issued a query on each of the two tables to retrieve a row with ID 1230440. George asked if there was a difference in performance, and if so how and why. He asked Jack to explain why the execution plan was different than the execution plan in Step 5.

8. When George asked when Jack would use this type of table, Jack explained by giving a scenario on how this type of table is used.

9. George was fascinated when he saw that there was a difference in performance but said he didn't think a slight increase in performance speed would make much difference. Do you agree with him? Explain your answer.

2. Every Little Bit Helps—Partitions

George was so impressed when he saw the increase in performance caused in certain situations by IOT that he asked Jack about table partitioning and whether he could demonstrate how much faster a partitioned table works than a normal table. Jack was pleased to do so. First, he set the timing on and then worked through the following steps:

1. Jack created a new range partition table with the same structure as NORM_TBL and called it PART_TBL. He selected ID column as a partition key. Each partition would hold a maximum of 500,000 rows.

2. He populated the table with 2,000,000 rows.

3. Then he set AUTOTRACE to TRACEONLY with the EXPLAIN option.

4. He issued a query on each of the two tables to retrieve the row with ID 23044. George asked Jack to explain what the explain plan was saying for each query.

5. Jack analyzed both tables and any indexes created specifically for these two tables.

6. Then he issued a query on each of the two tables to retrieve the row with ID 1230440. George asked if there was a difference in performance and asked Jack to explain the difference in performance and why the execution plan was different than in Step 4.

7. Jack explained the differences in the execution plans generated in Steps 4 and 6.

8. Finally, Jack showed George how to directly retrieve rows from specific partitions.

9. Your assignment is to take the role of Jack and work through steps 1 through 8.

14

TUNING WORKSHOP AND STATISTIC COLLECTOR PROJECT

In this chapter you will:

♦ Practice tuning techniques by conducting a tuning workshop

♦ Use diagnostic queries to collect database statistics

This chapter is the culmination of your Oracle tuning studies in this book and gives you a chance to test your conceptual knowledge by implementing it in a real–world situation.

Throughout the previous chapters, you have learned valuable performance tuning concepts and techniques that enhance your ability to troubleshoot, diagnose, and optimize database performance. It is now time to take this knowledge and put it to work. This chapter serves two main objectives. The first objective is to practice what you've learned by conducting a tuning workshop, which encompasses all aspects of tuning approaches and methodologies. The second objective is to review all the diagnostic queries you learned and put them together in a project to collect statistics. Each objective requires some time to plan, prepare, and implement; therefore, you should set aside several periods of time to complete the project. To begin, put on your DBA hat and your white, Oracle wizard's robe, grab all your tools, get the documents and manuals that you need, turn your favorite music way up, and get ready to tune this engine!

TUNING WORKSHOP

The objective of this tuning workshop is to give you the experience that you would not be able to get unless you were working as a DBA in real life. The workshop is divided into two stages with each stage representing a different tuning methodology. The stages enable you to practice your analytical, diagnostic, and troubleshooting skills by solving tuning problems.

The Company

Six months ago, Acme Company created a new division specializing in various lines of products that would be either manufactured as a special edition or customized specifically for clients. This company has a customer base of 500,000 clients, a number estimated to grow by 100,000 a year. Acme Company sells about 100,000 different products and uses 1,000 different suppliers. The company has already sold about one million orders, and the marketing and sales team estimates that total will grow to about 25,000 orders a year.

The Application

You are dealing with an OLTP application, which is also used for reports. The application is used by 15 sales representatives, four customer care representatives, and three report writers during business hours, which are 7:00 a.m. to 7:00 p.m. on weekdays. The application has two types of frontends (client interfaces). The first frontend was developed using Visual Basic and is used for orders entered by sales representatives. The second frontend was developed using Java code and is used as a Web application for customer care. Through the company's Web site, customer care representatives retrieve miscellaneous information and enter comments. Another component of the application is a reporting component, which consists of both canned reports and ad hoc reports.

The Schema

You need to create a schema called WKSHP using the CHAPTER_15_USER.SQL script. You will be using this schema as the owner of the application for all performance sessions.

The Stages

As stated previously, there are two stages of this workshop, each with its own methodology for tuning. These two stages are called the reactive stage and the proactive stage, which are defined as follows:

- **Reactive stage:** In this stage you are playing the role of a reactive DBA who responds to problems only when they occur. Of course, this is an undesirable role, but it shows you what happens when a DBA fails to employ detective methods to prevent problems before they happen.

- **Proactive stage:** In this stage you are playing the proper role of a proactive DBA, thinking ahead to prevent problems by employing and utilizing all necessary tools and methods to ensure database performance is at an optimal level.

You should run scripts as they are and modify them only when you encounter Oracle errors. Some scripts may produce intentional errors.

Reactive Stage

In this stage of the tuning workshop, you are provided with an instance configuration and database configuration that you use to build the database. After building the database, you run scripts, which may or may not cause problems. You must determine if problems have occurred by monitoring the database performance.

Preparation Phase

In this phase, you build the database to the following list of specifications:

- **Instance configuration:** Use the file, CHAPTER_15_S01_INIT.TXT, which contains the list of modified initialization parameters you need to include in your INIT.ORA file.

- **Tablespace creation:** Use the script, CHAPTER_15_S01_TABLESPACE.SQL.

- **Schema creation:** Use the script, CHAPTER_15_S01_SCHEMA.SQL.

- **Data Loading:** Use the script, CHAPTER_15_s01_DATA.SQL, to load data for the schema.

- **Connect:** You should connect as WKSHP user to perform any of the performance sessions.

Production Phase

In this phase, you run a script for each performance session, and you diagnose and fix problems when necessary. For each performance session in this stage, you need to run dbSessions with 25 sessions for a period of three hours using CHAPTER_15_S01_DBSESSIONS_QUERIES.QRY.

Performance Session 1 (Storage Space)

1. Run the script, CHAPTER_15_S01_PS01_CHAIN.SQL.

2. Diagnose storage-related problems and fix them.

3. Outline observations or recommendations you have about the storage configuration.

Performance Session 2 (Memory)

1. Run the script, CHAPTER_15_S01_PS02_MEMORY.SQL.

15

2. Monitor memory and identify performance issues.

3. Diagnose and modify the memory configuration to enhance the performance of the database.

Performance Session 3 (Sorting)

1. Run the script, CHAPTER_15_S01_PS03_SORT.SQL.

2. Monitor the database and identify performance issues.

3. Fix performance problems or issues encountered in Step 2.

Performance Session 4 (Indexing)

1. Run the script, CHAPTER_15_S01_PS04_INDEX.SQL.

2. Monitor the database and identify performance issues.

3. Fix performance problems or issues encountered in Step 2.

Performance Session 5 (Query)

1. Run the script, CHAPTER_15_S01_PS05_QUERY.SQL.

2. Monitor the database and identify performance issues.

3. Fix performance problems or issues encountered in Step 2.

Proactive Stage

In this stage of the tuning workshop, you use the performance tuning methodology presented in this book to design data storage, configure an Oracle instance and database, and finally set up the tools necessary to detect database performance. Once these steps are accomplished, you put your database to the test by using the dbSessions tool to simulate sessions and user loads, and then you are asked to perform specific tasks while dbSessions is running. There are two phases in the proactive stage, the development and production phases.

Development Phase

In this phase your objective is to analyze the business requirements and make design decisions in configuring, building, and creating the database and the application schema. The following outline is a list of the tasks required to meet those overriding objectives.

For each phase in the performance tuning methodology, outline the tasks you must perform to implement the Acme database using the list that follows as a high-level outline of tasks:

- Tables and index design

- Table and index sizing

- Tablespace sizing and allocation

- Memory configuration

- Database configuration

- Application optimization

- Instance configuration

- Database creation

- Schema creation (use chapter_15_s02_schema.sql)

- Loading initial data (use chapter_15_s02_data.sql)

- Reporting queries

- Setup diagnostics and statistics tools for performance analysis

Production Phase

Now that the Oracle instance and database has been created and is ready for users, you should perform the following performance sessions in which each session is independent of the other:

Performance Session 1 (data retrieval)

1. Initiate dbSessions with 25 sessions for a period of three hours using chapter_15_s02_dbsessions_queries.qry.

2. Monitor the database and advice and performance issues.

3. For each identified performance issue in Step 2, provide a resolution, but do not implement it.

Performance Session 2 (transactions)

Open three different sessions to load and update data by using the following scripts: chapter_15_s02_ps01_load01.sql, chapter_15_s02_ps01_load02.sql, and chapter_15_s02_ps01_load03.sql. (*Do not look at the scripts.*)

1. Monitor the database for performance issues.

2. Outline how you would have loaded and updated data differently.

3. Open the scripts used in Step 1, review them, and advise management of major modifications you would have made to enhance performance.

Performance Session 3 (reporting)

1. Open two different sessions, and for each session run the following reports: chapter_15_s02_ps03_report01.sql and chapter_15_s02_ps03_report02.sql.

2. Get the query issued by each session and analyze each one.

3. Based on your analysis in Step 2, what would you do to improve the performance?

4. What would you recommend if more reports such as these were to be issued?

15

Performance Session 4 (stored procedures and triggers)

1. A new business requirement was added to audit all the data changes of the CUSTOMERS table. For auditing purposes, use the script, chapter_15_s02_ps04_audit01.sql to create an identical copy of the CUSTOMERS table and identical copies of related stored procedures and triggers.

2. Run the stored procedure that simulates data changes to the CUSTOMERS table.

3. As the stored procedure is running, identify performance problems.

4. Determine if the trigger is impacting performance. Provide an example of a situation in which the trigger may be a performance liability.

5. What conclusions and recommendations can you provide?

Performance Session 5 (Analysis)

1. From generated statistics, what can you conclude about your instance and database configuration?

2. Was there a need to modify this configuration, and if so why? How much modification was required for this stage compared to the reactive stage?

3. Is the performance tuning methodology helpful, and if so, explain why.

Final Thoughts

- Write a list of recommendations for enhancing future performance.

- Write a list of recommendations that you would have implemented, but could not because of resource or other limitations.

STATISTICS COLLECTOR PROJECT

Oracle provides a powerful package to collect database statistics called STATSPACK, but some DBAs feel constrained by the inflexible features of this package. Other third-party vendors provide fancy and sophisticated tools to collect statistics and perform other tuning tasks, but the price for these tools is hefty and sometimes unaffordable during tough times. An alternative method is to create your own statistics package and repository using PL/SQL code. In this section, you are presented with the full design specifications of a Statistics Collector project.

Purpose

Aside from the immediate benefits of the Statistics Collector project, which is collecting statistical data on databases for performance and diagnostic purposes, this project provides a quick overview of most of the performance indicators used to monitor the performance of a database. You will gain practical experience by setting up a repository and stored procedures to collect performance statistics. In this project, you write code to capture the data and store it in the repository. The emphasis is on determining the queries that can retrieve this data.

Description

The Statistics Collector is a tool that collects the statistical data of one or more databases that you want to monitor. The data collected is useful for several performance tasks such as diagnosing database configuration, planning capacity, and identifying problematic queries. This project involves the creation of the repository, development of the PL/SQL code, and scheduling jobs to collect data. The following is a list of components of the Statistics Collector with a brief description of each:

- **Repository:** Collection of tables and other database objects used to store statistical data

- **Stored PL/SQL Package:** PL/SQL code used to collect statistical data

- **Reporting:** Views and queries to retrieve performance data on the monitored database

- **Database links:** Configuration of database links to remotely collect statistical data

- **Job scheduling:** Use of the Oracle-supplied PL/SQL package, DBMS_JOB, or any other tool available to you

Architecture

Figure 15-1 illustrates the system architecture of the Statistics Collector. As you can see, the Statistics Collector schema may reside locally in any database. This schema owns the repository and code. The code will use database links to collect data from remote databases using the SYSTEM schema as a proxy user on the remote database, because it has all the required privileges to read dynamic performance views and data dictionary views. DBMS_JOB is used to schedule collection jobs.

15

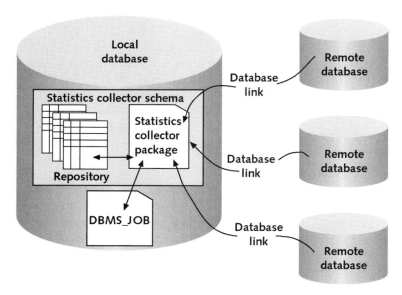

Figure 15-1   Architecture of the Statistics Collector

Data Model

Figure 15-2 presents the data model for the Statistics Collector project. It is composed of 10 entities. The main entity is SC_DATABASE, which holds generic data about each database from which you are interested in collecting data. SC_COLLECTION_JOB, another main entity, holds the collection timestamp and status of the job.

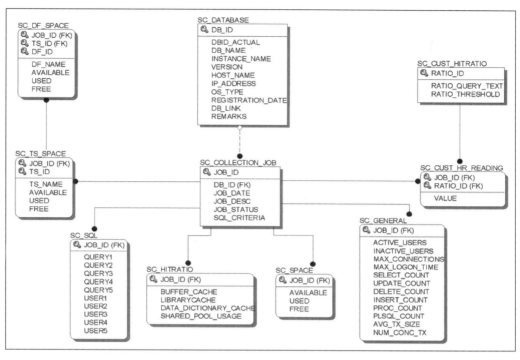

Figure 15-2   Data model of the Statistics Collector

Repository Physical Structure

This section provides the full physical data structure specification of the Statistics Collector repository.

SC_DATABASE table: This table holds generic data about the target database from which you want to collect statistics. You cannot collect statistics without registering a database in this table.

15

Column name	Data type	Description
DB_ID (Primary Key)	NUMBER	Identification number of the target database (The target database is the database from which you collect statistics)
DBID_ACTUAL	NUMBER	Actual database identification number obtained from V$DATABASE for the target database
DB_NAME	VARCHAR2(80)	Name of the target database obtained from V$DATABASE
INSTANCE_NAME	VARCHAR2(80)	Name of the target instance obtained from V$INSTANCE
VERSION	VARCHAR2(20)	Oracle version of the target database
HOST_NAME	VARCHAR2(80)	Name of the host machine hosting the target database

Column name	Data type	Description
IP_ADDRESS	VARCHAR2(15)	IP address of the host machine
OS_TYPE	VARCHAR2(80)	Operating system of the host machine (e.g., UNIX or Windows)
REGISTRATION_DATE	DATE	Date and time the target database was registered to collect statistics
DB_LINK	VARCHAR2(255)	Database link name to be used to connect to remote target database
REMARKS	VARCHAR2(4000)	DBA comments

SC_COLLECTION_JOB table: This table holds data about the statistics collection jobs for the target database.

Column name	Data type	Description
JOB_ID (Primary key)	NUMBER	Job identification number of collection job
DB_ID	NUMBER	Database identification number of the target database
JOB_DATE	DATE	Date and time of the collection job
JOB_DESC	VARCHAR2(255)	Job description of the collection
JOB_STATUS	CHAR(1)	Status of the job (Completed, broken, or pending)
SQL_CRITERIA	VARCHAR2(30)	Criteria used for SQL queries

SC_CUST_HITRATIO table: This table contains customized queries for retrieving the statistics that a DBA is interested in collecting from the target database.

Column name	Data type	Description
RATIO_ID (Primary key)	NUMBER	Ratio identification number of the customized hitratio query
RATIO_QUERY_TEXT	VARCHAR2(4000)	SQL query text for the ratio you are interested in collecting from the target database
RATIO_THRESHOLD	NUMBER	Threshold value for the ratio

SC_CUST_HR_READING table: This table contains the results of the customized query for the target database.

Column name	Data type	Description
JOB_ID (Primary key)	NUMBER	Job identification number of collection job
RATIO_ID (Primary key)	NUMBER	Ratio identification number of the customized hitratio query
VALUE	NUMBER	Result value of the customized hit ratio

SC_GENERAL table: This table holds generic statistical data collected from the target database.

Column name	Data type	Description
JOB_ID (Primary key)	NUMBER	Job identification number of collection job
ACTIVE_USERS	NUMBER	Number of active users at the time the collection job was issued
INACTIVE_USERS	NUMBER	Number of inactive users at the time the collection job was issued
MAX_CONNECTIONS	NUMBER	Maximum number of connections possible for a user
MAX_LOGON_TIME	NUMBER	Maximum logon time by a user regardless of session status
SELECT_COUNT	NUMBER	Number of active SELECT statements currently in librarycache
UPDATE_COUNT	NUMBER	Number of active UPDATE statements currently in librarycache
DELETE_COUNT	NUMBER	Number of active DELETE statements currently in librarycache
INSERT_COUNT	NUMBER	Number of active INSERT statements currently in librarycache
PROC_COUNT	NUMBER	Number of active named PL/SQL blocks currently in librarycache
PLSQL_COUNT	NUMBER	Number of active unnamed PL/SQL blocks currently in librarycache
AVG_TX_SIZE	NUMBER	Average transaction size
NUM_CONC_TX	NUMBER	Number of concurrent transactions

SC_SQL table: This table contains top queries on the target database using SQL_CRITERIA in SC_COLLECTION_JOB table.

Column name	Data type	Description
JOB_ID (Primary key)	NUMBER	Job identification number of collection job
QUERY1	VARCHAR2(4000)	SQL text for the #1 query consumption
QUERY2	VARCHAR2(4000)	SQL text for the #2 query consumption
QUERY3	VARCHAR2(4000)	SQL text for the #3 query consumption
QUERY4	VARCHAR2(4000)	SQL text for the #4 query consumption
QUERY5	VARCHAR2(4000)	SQL text for the #5 query consumption
USER1	VARCHAR2(30)	Username of the session issued #1 query
USER2	VARCHAR2(30)	Username of the session issued #2 query
USER3	VARCHAR2(30)	Username of the session issued #3 query

15

Column name	Data type	Description
USER4	VARCHAR2(30)	Username of the session issued #4 query
USER5	VARCHAR2(30)	Username of the session issued #5 query

SC_HITRATIO table: This table holds the memory hitratio collected from the target database.

Column name	Data type	Description
JOB_ID (Primary key)	NUMBER	Job identification number of collection job
BUFFER_CACHE	NUMBER	Buffer cache hitratio of the target database
LIBRARYCACHE	NUMBER	Librarycache hitratio of the target database
DATA_DICTIONARY_CACHE	NUMBER	Data dictionary cache hitratio of the target database
SHARED_POOL_USAGE	NUMBER	Shared pool usage ratio

SC_SPACE table: This table holds storage statistics of the target database.

Column name	Data type	Description
JOB_ID (Primary key)	NUMBER	Job identification number of collection job
AVAILABLE	NUMBER	Available storage from allocated space for the whole target database
USED	NUMBER	Used storage from allocated space for the whole target database
FREE	NUMBER	Free storage from allocated space for the whole target database

SC_TS_SPACE table: This table holds storage statistics for each tablespace in the target databa

Column name	Data type	Description
JOB_ID (Primary key)	NUMBER	Job identification number of collection job
TS_ID (Primary key)	NUMBER	Tablespace identification number belonging to target database
TS_NAME	VARCHAR2(30)	Tablespace name belonging to target database
AVAILABLE	NUMBER	Available storage from allocated space for the tablespace
USED	NUMBER	Used storage from allocated space for the tablespace
FREE	NUMBER	Free storage from allocated space for the tablespace

SC_DF_SPACE table: This table holds statistical data for each data file in the target database.

Column name	Data type	Description
JOB_ID (Primary key)	NUMBER	Job identification number of collection job
TS_ID (Primary key)	NUMBER	Tablespace identification number belonging to target database
DF_ID (Primary key)	NUMBER	Identification number of the data file belonging to the tablespace
DF_NAME	VARCHAR2(30)	Data file name belonging to target database
AVAILABLE	NUMBER	Available storage from allocated space for the data file
USED	NUMBER	Used storage from allocated space for the data file
FREE	NUMBER	Free storage from allocated space for the data file

Statistics Collector Stored Package

You will be creating a stored package called Statcol, which will have two main procedures and three functions:

```
FUNCTION REGISTER_DB(P_DBLINK VARCHAR2 DEFAULT 'LOCALHOST' ,

                     P_REMARKS VARCHAR2 DEFAULT NULL

                     ) RETURN NUMBER;

FUNCTION COLLECT(P_DBID NUMBER ) RETURN NUMBER;

FUNCTION COLLECT(P_DBNAME VARCHAR2) RETURN NUMBER;

PROCEDURE DELETE(P_JOBID NUMBER);

PROCEDURE PURGE_DB(P_DBID NUMBER);
```

FUNCTION REGISTER_DB: This function registers a database as a target database for collecting statistical data and returns the database identification number in the repository.

FUNCTION COLLECT: This function collects statistical data for a given target database identification number or name and stores the data in the repository. A collection job identification number is returned.

PROCEDURE DELETE: This procedure deletes the statistical data collected for a given collection job identification number.

PROCEDURE PURGE: This procedure purges all statistical data collected for a given database identification number.

Reporting

In this section, you will be developing basic reports to retrieve data collected.

- View, query, or SQL script to retrieve performance data for a specific database and specific time

- View, query, or SQL script to retrieve average performance data for a specific date for a specific database

- Other views, queries, or SQL scripts that would produce meaningful reports

Database Links

You need to set up a database link before registering a target database. The database link must use a FIXED USER configuration using SYSTEM or a user with DBA privileges who has access to all dynamic performance and data dictionary views on the remote database. The following is an example of creating a database link:

```
CREATE  DATABASE LINK PRD_SAM
    CONNECT TO SYSTEM IDENTIFIED BY password
      USING 'SAM'
```

Job Scheduling

You need to set up a job for each target database using the Oracle-supplied PL/SQL DBMS_JOB package. The job should execute at least twice a day but no more than four times a day. Use the following PL/SQL as a template to schedule a collection job:

```
VARIABLE jobno NUMBER;
BEGIN
   DBMS_JOB.SUBMIT(:jobno,
        'statcol.collect(12);', sysdate, 'sysdate + (3/(24*60))');
   COMMIT;
end;
/

PRINT jobno

EXEC DBMS_JOB.RUN(JOBNO);
```

Implementation Considerations

You may want to consider performing the following functions:

- Create a new schema just for the Statistics Collector.

- Create a tablespace specifically for the Statistics Collector.

- Create two separate SEQUENCES to generate DBID and JOBID.

- Consider monitoring storage space when you start collecting statistics. Initial storage space required is 50 MB.

- Consider table partitioning when applicable.

- Use the EXECUTE IMMEDIATE PL/SQL statement to create dynamic queries with PL/SQL blocks.

- You may need to set up a TNSNAME service for the target database.

- Test every database link you create before using it.

- Implement the Statistics Collector one module at a time.

A

ORACLE ARCHITECTURE OVERVIEW

Appendix A presents a quick overview of Oracle architecture and a summary reference guide on how to manage your Oracle instance. It is important to note that understanding the information in this appendix is essential for comprehending the material presented in this book.

Figure A-1 represents Oracle architecture, which consists of two structures: the logical structure is called the Oracle Instance and the physical structure is called the Oracle database. The Oracle Instance provides all the functionality of a database management system, and one of its main functions is to access data stored in the database.

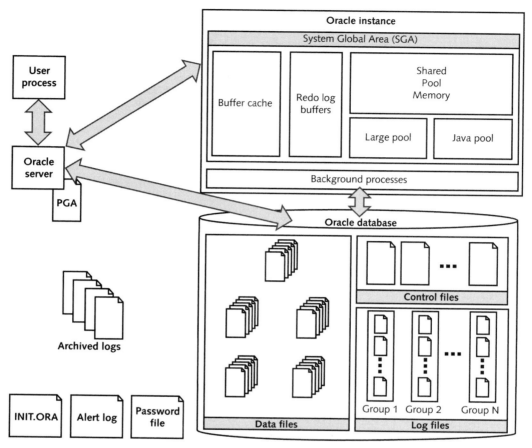

Figure A-1   Oracle architecture

The following is a brief description of each component outlined in the illustration and serves as a quick review of Oracle architecture.

ORACLE INSTANCE

The Oracle Instance consists of two components, the memory structure called the System Global Area and background processes.

System Global Area (SGA): Oracle background processes use the SGA memory structures as a buffer to facilitate and enhance the performance of Oracle operations. The SGA consists of the following:

- **Database buffer cache**: Part of the SGA memory structure. Stores the most frequently used data for fast access.

A

- **Redo log buffer**: Part of the SGA memory structure. It is controlled by the log writer (LGWR) background process and stores all transaction entries submitted to the database before they are written to redo logfiles.

- **Shared Pool Memory**: Part of the SGA memory structure. It is used to cache the most frequently used code and data definition structures to speed up the parsing process. There are two main parts of the Shared Pool Memory:

  - **Library cache**: Portion of the Shared Pool Memory used to cache the most frequent SQL statements and PL/SQL code.

  - **Data dictionary cache**: Portion of the Shared Pool Memory used to cache the definitions of the most frequently used database objects.

- **Java pool**: Part of the SGA memory structure used to cache Java code.

- **Large pool**: The large pool memory is an optional part of the SGA. It is used as a temporary placeholder for special programs and functionality such as the Recovery Manager (RMAN), Shared Server, and others.

Background processes: A background process is a small program residing in memory that performs a specific task. Oracle has several background processes which can be classified into two categories, main and other.

- **Main processes**: The following processes (except ARCn) are mandatory. But since most databases run in archivelog mode, the ARCn process is usually referred to as a main process.

  - **ARCn (Archiver)**: Reads the contents of the redo log file and writes it to a file called an archived log. This process runs only if the database is in ARCHIVELOG mode.

  - **CKPT (Checkpoint)**: Synchronizes all datafiles with system change numbers (SCNs).

  - **DBWR (Database writer)**: Writes the dirty block buffers to datafiles (n is 0-9).

  - **LGWR (Log writer)**: Writes all entries in the log buffer to redo log files.

  - **PMON (Process monitor)**: Monitors the status of other processes including user processes. PMON cleans up after defunct processes by releasing memory held by the defunct process.

  - **SMON (System monitor)**: Monitors and registers all events in the database to the alert file. Performs automatic recovery.

- **Other processes**: The following optional processes are usually initiated based on the Oracle Instance and database configuration:

  - **CJQ0 (Coordinator of job queue)**: Starts and monitors jobs in the JOB$ table. It executes jobs by starting a Jnnn process.

- **Dnnn (Dispatcher)**: Acts as a dispatcher routing user requests to different server background processes in shared server mode. (nnn is any number).

- **Jnnn (Job queue)**: Executes job requests issued by the CJQ0 background process (nnn is any number).

- **LCKn (LOCK)**: Manages instance resource requests and cross-instance call operations (n is any number).

- **LMD (Global enqueue service daemon)**: Handles remote resource requests and deadlock detection Global Enqueue Service (GES) requests.

- **LMON (Global enqueue service monitor)**: Monitors the entire cluster to manage global resources. Available in a real application cluster.

- **LMSn (Global cache service process)**: Handles remote messages for the Global Cache Service (GCS). Available with a Real Application Cluster (n is any number).

- **QMNn**: Available in a Real Application Cluster configuration. Responsible for managing resources and providing inter-instance resource control (n is any number).

- **RECO (Recoverer)**: Responsible for resolving pending distributed transactions due to transaction failure.

- **Snnn (Server)**: A server process is responsible for serving client requests assigned to it by a dispatcher process (nnn is any number).

- **SNPn (Snapshot)**: Initiated when replication is configured within the database to handle data refresh (n is any number).

Oracle Database

The Oracle database is considered the physical structure of Oracle and consists of Oracle datafiles and operating system datafiles. This physical structure is used for storing users' data and system data. The following is a list of all components of the Oracle Database:

- **Control file**: The control file is the heart of the database. If the control file is corrupted or lost, the whole database is unusable. Every database has at least one control file, which is usually multiplexed to minimize the risk of loss. This is a binary file (Oracle-formatted) created at the time of database creation and contains information about:

  - Database configuration

  - Names, locations, and sizes of datafiles created, as well as the names of tablespaces to which the files belong

  - Configuration, name, location, and size of redo log files

  - System change number

  - Backup and archiving history

A

- **Redo log file**: Contains all transactions submitted and applied to the database. It is used for database recovery and undo purposes. An Oracle database must have at least two redo log file groups.

- **Data files**: Binary, Oracle-formatted files. Data files can be classified as follows:

  - **System data files**: Contain system-related data such as data dictionary and dynamic performance views

  - **Temporary data files**: Temporary space used for storing data temporarily during sorting operations or index creation operations.

  - **Undo segments data files**: Store the before image until it is committed. Also support the functionality of rollback segments.

  - **Users' data files**: Store users' data.

- **Other Oracle Files**: These are operating system files and are classified as follows:

  - **INIT.ORA file**: The init.ora (initialization parameter) file is read once when the Oracle Instance is started. This file contains the setting of parameters to configure the logical structure (Instance) of Oracle. This file is also known as the PFILE or Parameter File.

  - **ALERT log file**: SMON registers all database-related events and errors, tracing information, detected deadlocks, and INIT.ORA parameter settings in this file.

  - **PASSWORD file**: This is an operating system binary file containing all Oracle users that have SYSDBA or SYSOPER system privileges. This file is created by the Oracle utility, ORAPWD.

  - **Archived log files**: Files that archive the contents of the redo logfiles. Generated by ARCn background process.

- **Oracle server**: Handles and executes all database requests submitted by a user process.

  - **Program global area (PGA)**: A memory structure that stores user session information. The PGA also sorts data, hash joins, and performs other program-related operations. It is created every time an Oracle server is initiated.

- **User process**: A client application process that submits database requests to the Oracle server and retrieves responses for the application from the Oracle server.

ORACLE INSTANCE MANAGEMENT

As a DBA, you can use Figure A-2 to help you manage an Oracle instance. The figure shows the statements that you must issue to move from one state to another as well as what data, data dictionary views, and performance dynamic views are accessible for each state. For example, if you decide to change the state of the database from CLOSED to OPEN, you use the STARTUP statement as shown in the grid below the pyramid.

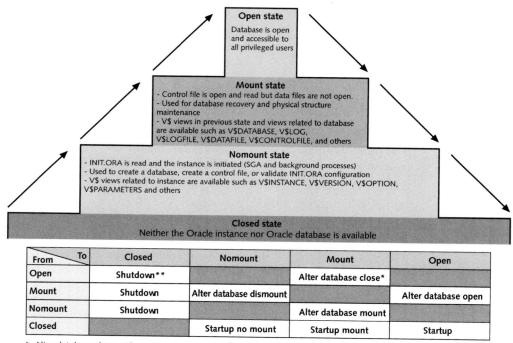

From \ To	Closed	Nomount	Mount	Open
Open	Shutdown**		Alter database close*	
Mount	Shutdown	Alter database dismount		Alter database open
Nomount	Shutdown		Alter database mount	
Closed		Startup no mount	Startup mount	Startup

* Alter database close: only permitted with no sessions connected
** Shutdown: disallows any new connections. The following are options that can be used:
> **Normal** (default): waits until all connected sessions are disconnected.
> **Immediate** (most used): rolls back all pending transactions and disconnect all sessions.
> **Transactional** (rarely used): waits until all pending transactions are committed and then disconnects all sessions.
> **Abort** (desperate measure): kills all connected sessions. A crash recovery is required when database is open.

Figure A-2   Pyramid Diagram of Oracle Instance Management

APPENDIX
B

DIAGNOSTICS QUERIES COLLECTION

Appendix B is designed as a quick reference guide to all the important queries presented in this book.

Buffer cache hitratio

```
COLUMN RATIO HEADING "Buffer Cache Hitratio" FORMAT A30
SELECT ROUND( (1 - (PHY.VALUE/(CUR.VALUE + CON.VALUE)))*100, 1)||'%' ratio
  FROM V$SYSSTAT PHY, V$SYSSTAT CUR, V$SYSSTAT CON
 WHERE PHY.NAME = 'physical reads'
   AND CUR.NAME = 'db block gets'
   AND CON.NAME = 'consistent gets';
```

Buffer cache hitratio per session

```
SELECT PHY.SID,
       S.USERNAME,
       1 - (PHY.VALUE)/(CUR.VALUE + CON.VALUE) BUFFER_HITRATIO
  FROM V$SESSTAT PHY, V$SESSTAT CUR, V$SESSTAT CON,
       V$STATNAME S1, V$STATNAME S2, V$STATNAME S3, V$SESSION S
 WHERE S1.NAME = 'physical reads'
   AND S2.NAME = 'db block gets'
   AND S3.NAME = 'consistent gets'
   AND PHY.STATISTIC# = S1.STATISTIC#
   AND CUR.STATISTIC# = S2.STATISTIC#
   AND CON.STATISTIC# = S3.STATISTIC#
   AND CUR.VALUE <> 0
   AND CON.VALUE <> 0
   AND PHY.SID = CUR.SID
   AND PHY.SID = CON.SID
   AND PHY.SID = S.SID
```

Buffer cache pool hitratio

```
SELECT NAME;
       BLOCK_SIZE,
       ROUND( (1 - (PHYSICAL_READS/(DB_BLOCK_GETS + CONSISTENT_GETS)))*100) || '%' ratio
  FROM V$BUFFER_POOL_STATISTICS
```

Cached objects and number of buffer blocks consumed

```
SELECT O.OWNER,
       O.OBJECT_TYPE,
       O.OBJECT_NAME,
       COUNT(*) buffers,
       ROUND((COUNT(*)/(SELECT COUNT(*)
                               FROM V$BH))*100) BUFFER_PERCENT
  FROM DBA_OBJECTS O, V$BH B
 WHERE O.OBJECT_ID = B.OBJD
   AND O.OWNER NOT IN ('SYS','SYSTEM')
 GROUP BY O.OWNER, O.OBJECT_TYPE, O.OBJECT_NAME
 ORDER BY 1, 2 DESC
```

Number of READ, DIRTY and FREE buffers

```
SELECT DECODE(DIRTY, 'Y', 'DIRTY BLOCK',
                'N', 'READ OR FREE',
                'TOTAL BUFFERS') STATUS,
       COUNT(*) BUFFERS
  FROM V$BH
 GROUP BY ROLLUP(DIRTY)
```

Number of buffers for each type of cache

```
SELECT DECODE(STATUS, 'free', 'Free: not currently in use',
                      'xcur', 'Locked: exclusive',
                      'scur', 'Locked: shared',
                      'cr',   'Consistent Read',
                      'read', 'Being read from disk',
                      'mrec', 'In media recovery mode',
                      'irec', 'In instance recovery mode',
                      'Total Buffers') STATUS,
       COUNT(*) BUFFERS
  FROM V$BH
 GROUP BY ROLLUP(STATUS)
```

Average size of redo entries

```
SELECT R.VALUE/E.VALUE "Average Size of Redo Entries"
  FROM V$SYSSTAT R, V$SYSSTAT E
 WHERE R.NAME = 'redo size'
   AND E.NAME = 'redo entries'
```

Log buffer entries and request ratio

```
SELECT (R.VALUE*5000)/E.VALUE "Redo Requests/Entries Ratio"
  FROM V$SYSSTAT R, V$SYSSTAT E
WHERE R.NAME = 'redo log space requests'
  AND E.NAME = 'redo entries'
```

Log buffer retries and entries ratio

```
SELECT R.VALUE/E.VALUE "Redo Retries/Entries Ratio"
  FROM V$SYSSTAT R, V$SYSSTAT E
WHERE R.NAME = 'redo buffer allocation retries'
  AND E.NAME = 'redo entries'
```

Librarycache reloads ratio

```
SELECT (RELOAD_COUNT/OBJECT_COUNT)*100 RELOADS_RATIO
  FROM (SELECT SUM(RELOADS) RELOAD_COUNT
          FROM V$LIBRARYCACHE),
        (SELECT COUNT(*) OBJECT_COUNT
          FROM V$DB_OBJECT_CACHE)
```

Librarycache invalidation ratio

```
SELECT (INVALIDATION_COUNT/OBJECT_COUNT)*100 INVALIDATION_RATIO
  FROM (SELECT SUM(RELOADS) INVALIDATION_COUNT
          FROM V$LIBRARYCACHE),
        (SELECT COUNT(*) OBJECT_COUNT
          FROM V$DB_OBJECT_CACHE)
```

Libararycache hitratio for each namespace

```
SELECT NAMESPACE, GETHITRATIO
  FROM V$LIBRARYCACHE
```

Overall librarycache hitratio

```
SELECT SUM(GETHITS)/SUM(GETS) LIBRARYCACHE_HIT_RATIO
  FROM V$LIBRARYCACHE
```

Librarycache reloads to pins ratio

```
SELECT SUM(RELOADS)/SUM(PINS)*100 RELAODS_PINS_RATIO
  FROM V$LIBRARYCACHE
```

Data dictionary getmisses

```
SELECT parameter,
       (SUM(GETMISSES)/SUM(GETS))*100 GETMISSES_RATIO
  FROM V$ROWCACHE
 WHERE gets > 0
 GROUP BY parameter
```

Shared pool memory usage ratio

```
SELECT (USED/VALUE)*100 SHARED_POOL_USAGE_RATIO
  FROM V$PARAMETER P,
       (SELECT SUM(BYTES) USED
          FROM V$SGASTAT
         WHERE POOL = 'shared pool'
           AND NAME <> 'free memory')
 WHERE P.NAME = 'shared_pool_size'
```

Shared pool free ratio

```
SELECT (S.BYTES/P.VALUE)*100 SHARED_POOL_FREE_RATIO
  FROM V$PARAMETER P, V$SGASTAT S
 WHERE S.POOL = 'shared pool'
   AND S.NAME = 'free memory'
   AND P.NAME = 'shared_pool_size'
```

Display all statements submitted by a user

```
SELECT SUBSTR(SQL_TEXT, 1, 40) SQL_TEXT,
       SHARABLE_MEM MEMORY,
       LOADS,
       EXECUTIONS EXEC,
       ROWS_PROCESSED ROWS,
       CPU_TIME CPU
  FROM V$SQLAREA
 WHERE PARSING_SCHEMA_ID = (SELECT USER_ID
                              FROM DBA_USERS
                             WHERE USERNAME = '&USER')
```

Display SQL statement executed or being executed by each session

```
SELECT USERNAME,
       SID,
       SERIAL#,
       OSUSER,
       TERMINAL,
       SUBSTR(SQL_TEXT, 1, 25) SQL_TEXT
  FROM V$SESSION, V$SQLAREA
 WHERE USERNAME NOT IN ('SYS', 'SYSTEM')
   AND USERNAME IS NOT NULL
   AND (SQL_ADDRESS = ADDRESS OR PREV_SQL_ADDR = ADDRESS)
```

Processes using and allocating the most PGA memory

```
SELECT DECODE(BACKGROUND,
              1, (SELECT NAME
                    FROM V$BGPROCESS
                   WHERE PADDR=P.ADDR),
              'USER') PROCESS,
       PGA_USED_MEM,
       PGA_ALLOC_MEM,
       PGA_MAX_MEM
  FROM V$PROCESS P
 ORDER BY 1
```

Percentage of allocated memory used

```
SELECT DECODE(BACKGROUND,
              1, 'BACKGROUND',
              'USER') PROCESSES,
       COUNT(*) PROCESSES_COUNT,
       round(SUM(PGA_USED_MEM)/
       SUM(PGA_ALLOC_MEM)*100) PGA_USED_ALLOC_PCT
  FROM V$PROCESS
 GROUP BY DECODE(BACKGROUND, 1, 'BACKGROUND', 'USER')
```

Top 5 queries using the most PGA memory

```
SELECT *
  FROM (SELECT U.USERNAME,
               SUBSTR(S.SQL_TEXT,1,40) SQL,
               SW.OPERATION_TYPE,
               SUM(SW.ESTIMATED_OPTIMAL_SIZE) OPTIMAL_SIZE
          FROM V$SQL S, V$SQL_WORKAREA SW, DBA_USERS U
         WHERE S.ADDRESS = SW.ADDRESS
           AND U.USER_ID = S.PARSING_SCHEMA_ID
           AND USERNAME NOT IN ('SYS','SYSTEM')
         GROUP BY U.USERNAME,
               SUBSTR(S.SQL_TEXT,1,40),
               SW.OPERATION_TYPE
         ORDER BY OPTIMAL_SIZE DESC)
 WHERE ROWNUM < 6
```

Top 20 queries with the most executions of all users

```
SELECT *
  FROM (SELECT U.USERNAME,
               SUBSTR(S.SQL_TEXT,1,30) SQL,
               SW.OPERATION_TYPE,
               SUM(SW.OPTIMAL_EXECUTIONS) OPT,
               SUM(SW.ONEPASS_EXECUTIONS) ONE,
               SUM(SW.MULTIPASSES_EXECUTIONS) MULTI
          FROM V$SQL S, V$SQL_WORKAREA SW, DBA_USERS U
         WHERE S.ADDRESS = SW.ADDRESS
           AND U.USER_ID = S.PARSING_SCHEMA_ID
         GROUP BY U.USERNAME,
               SUBSTR(S.SQL_TEXT,1,30),
               SW.OPERATION_TYPE
         ORDER BY OPT DESC)
 WHERE ROWNUM < 21
```

Sessions using temporary segments

```
SELECT S.USERNAME,
       SW.OPERATION_TYPE,
       SW.TABLESPACE,
       SW.TEMPSEG_SIZE/1024/1024 SIZE_IN_MB
  FROM V$SQL_WORKAREA_ACTIVE SW,
       V$SESSION S
 WHERE S.SID = SW.SID
```

Obtain the execution percentage for each type of Workarea

```
SELECT NAME WORKAREA_EXECUTION,
       ROUND(VALUE/
       ((SELECT SUM(VALUE)
            FROM V$SYSSTAT
          WHERE NAME LIKE '%workarea executions%'))*100) PCT
  FROM V$SYSSTAT
 WHERE NAME LIKE '%workarea executions%'
```

Display a percentage of the number of sorts performed on disk versus in memory for the whole system

```
SELECT DISK.VALUE DISK,
       MEM.VALUE MEMORY,
       ROUND((DISK.VALUE/MEM.VALUE)*100, 2) SORT_RATIO
  FROM V$SYSSTAT DISK, V$SYSSTAT MEM
 WHERE DISK.NAME = 'sorts (disk)'
   AND MEM.NAME  = 'sorts (memory)'
```

Display the sort ratio for all sessions

```
SELECT S.SID,
       S.USERNAME,
       S.PROGRAM,
       DISK.VALUE DISK,
       MEM.VALUE MEMORY,
       ROUND((DISK.VALUE/MEM.VALUE)*100, 2) SORT_RATIO
  FROM V$SESSTAT DISK,
       V$SESSTAT MEM,
       V$STATNAME N,
       V$SESSION S
 WHERE N.STATISTIC# = DISK.STATISTIC#
   AND N.STATISTIC# = MEM.STATISTIC#
   AND (N.NAME = 'sorts (disk)' OR N.NAME  = 'sorts (memory)')
   AND S.SID = DISK.SID
   AND S.SID = MEM.SID
   AND MEM.VALUE <> 0
```

Displays the number of commits and rollbacks made so far in the system

```
SELECT A.VALUE COMMITS,
       B.VALUE ROLLBACKS,
       A.VALUE + B.VALUE TOTAL
  FROM V$SYSSTAT A,
       V$SYSSTAT B
 WHERE A.NAME = 'USER COMMITS'
   AND B.NAME = 'USER ROLLBACKS'
```

Display the contention ratio for buffers that contain rollback segments

```
SELECT ((W1.COUNT+W2.COUNT+W3.COUNT+W4.COUNT)/
        (ST1.VALUE+ST2.VALUE))*100 RATIO
  FROM V$WAITSTAT W1,
       V$WAITSTAT W2,
       V$WAITSTAT W3,
       V$WAITSTAT W4,
       V$SYSSTAT ST1,
       V$SYSSTAT ST2
 WHERE W1.CLASS = 'system undo header'
   AND W2.CLASS = 'system undo block'
   AND W3.CLASS = 'undo header'
   AND W4.CLASS = 'undo block'
   AND ST1.NAME = 'db block gets'
   AND ST2.NAME = 'db block gets'
```

Display the time the longest transaction occurred and the amount of undo blocks it used

```
SELECT TO_CHAR(BEGIN_TIME, 'DD-MON-YYYY HH24:MI:SS') BEGIN_TIME,
       TO_CHAR(END_TIME, 'DD-MON-YYYY HH24:MI:SS') END_TIME,
       UNDOBLKS,
       TXNCOUNT,
       MAXCONCURRENCY
  FROM V$UNDOSTAT
 WHERE UNDOBLKS = (SELECT MAX(UNDOBLKS) FROM V$UNDOSTAT)
```

B

Display a graphic report showing tablespace usage

```
TTITLE 'Tablespace Usage Report|Values are expressed in MB'
COLUMN TABLESPACE FORMAT A30
COLUMN CHART FORMAT A15
SELECT FREE.TABLESPACE_NAME TABLESPACE,
       CEIL(TOT.TOTAL) TOTAL_SIZE,
       100 - CEIL( (FREE.FREE / TOT.TOTAL) * 100) PCT_USED,
       CEIL(FREE.FREE) FREE_SPACE,
       DATA_FILES,
       DECODE ((CEIL(10-(FREE.FREE / TOT.TOTAL) * 10)),
               0,'| .......... |',
               1,'| *......... |',
               2,'| **........ |',
               3,'| ***....... |',
               4,'| ****...... |',
               5,'| *****..... |',
               6,'| ******.... |',
               7,'| *******... |',
               8,'| ********.. |',
               9,'| *********. |',
              10,'| **DANGER** |') CHART
  FROM (SELECT TABLESPACE_NAME,
               CEIL(SUM(BYTES)/1048576) TOTAL ,
               COUNT(*) DATA_FILES
          FROM SYS.DBA_DATA_FILES
         GROUP BY TABLESPACE_NAME) TOT,
       (SELECT TABLESPACE_NAME,
               CEIL(SUM(BYTES)/1048576) FREE
          FROM SYS.DBA_FREE_SPACE
         GROUP BY TABLESPACE_NAME) FREE
 WHERE FREE.TABLESPACE_NAME = TOT.TABLESPACE_NAME
 ORDER BY PCT_USED
```

Displays data segments for tablespaces that don't have space to extend

```
SELECT S.OWNER,
       S.SEGMENT_TYPE,
       S.SEGMENT_NAME,
       S.TABLESPACE_NAME,
       S.NEXT_EXTENT/1024/1024 NEXT_EXTENT,
       TS.MAX_SPACE/1024/1024  MAX_SPACE
  FROM DBA_SEGMENTS S,
       (SELECT TABLESPACE_NAME,
               MAX(BYTES) MAX_SPACE
          FROM DBA_FREE_SPACE
         GROUP BY TABLESPACE_NAME) TS
 WHERE S.TABLESPACE_NAME = TS.TABLESPACE_NAME
   AND SEGMENT_TYPE IN ('TABLE',
                        'INDEX',
                        'CLUSTER',
                        'TABLE PARTITION',
                        'INDEX PARTITION')
   AND NEXT_EXTENT > MAX_SPACE
```

Generate a data file usage report

```
TTITLE 'Datafile Usage Report|Values are expressed in MB'
Column file_name format a50
set lines 120
set pages 9999
select file_name, total_size, used_size,
       total_size - used_size free_size
  from (select file_id, file_name, bytes/(1024*1024) total_size
          from dba_data_files) f,
       (select file_id,  sum(bytes)/(1024*1024) used_size
          from dba_free_space
         group by file_id) e
 where e.file_id=f.file_id
```

Obtain a ratio of the number of files being READ overloaded

```
SELECT ROUND((SELECT COUNT(*)
        FROM V$FILESTAT
       WHERE PHYRDS >= (SELECT AVG(PHYRDS)
                          FROM V$FILESTAT))/
       (SELECT COUNT(*) FROM V$DATAFILE) * 100)
       READS_RATIO
FROM DUAL
```

Detect WRITE overloaded files

```
SELECT ROUND((SELECT COUNT(*)
          FROM V$FILESTAT
          WHERE PHYWRTS >= (SELECT AVG(PHYWRTS)
                              FROM V$FILESTAT))/
        (SELECT COUNT(*) FROM V$DATAFILE) * 100)
       WRITES_RATIO
FROM DUAL
```

Display statistics for total reads and writes for each data file

```
SELECT DF.NAME FILE_NAME,
       FS.PHYRDS READS,
       FS.PHYWRTS WRITES
  FROM V$DATAFILE DF, V$FILESTAT FS
 WHERE DF.FILE#=FS.FILE#
```

Blockers and waiters

```
SELECT 'Blocker('||BW.HOLDING_SESSION||':'||SB.USERNAME||') - SQL: '||BQ.SQL_TEXT BLOCKERS,
       'Waiter ('||BW.WAITING_SESSION||':'||SW.USERNAME||') - SQL: '||SQ.SQL_TEXT WAITERS
  FROM DBA_WAITERS BW,
       V$SESSION SB,
       V$SESSION SW,
       V$SQLAREA BQ,
       V$SQLAREA SQ
 WHERE BW.HOLDING_SESSION = SB.SID
   AND BW.WAITING_SESSION = SW.SID
   AND SB.PREV_SQL_ADDR   = BQ.ADDRESS
   AND SW.SQL_ADDRESS     = SQ.ADDRESS
   AND BW.mode_HELD <> 'None'
```

Glossary

Automatic Space Management (ASM) — Eliminates the need for DBAs to manage free space. With ASM, Oracle ignores the PCTUSED, FREELISTS, and FREELIST GROUPS storage parameters.

BEGIN BACKUP status — A status used for open database backup. All tables within the tablespace are accessible. Although transactions on the tablespace are permitted, committed data are not written to the tablespace while in BEGIN BACKUP status.

bitmap merge area operation — An operation that results from a statement that is retrieving the rowid from two bitmap indexes that are merged into one.

blocking lock — A session that holds a lock on a row or an object and thereby prevents other sessions that are waiting to lock the row or the object.

buffer cache — An area in memory that stores the most frequently accessed Oracle data blocks.

cache hit — A cache hit occurs when data is cached and the Oracle server sends back the data requested without returning to the data files.

cache miss — A cache miss occurs when data is not cached and the Oracle server fetches the data from data files in the database based on an execution plan.

capacity planning — A method to plan and forecast proactively how much storage will be needed for the growth of all the databases in operation.

checkpoint — A method to commit data to a data file and timestamp it with time, date, and system change number.

COMPUTE STATISTICS method — When analyzing a table, you must specify whether you want Oracle to analyze every row in the table or only sample rows. To analyze every row in the table, you specify the COMPUTE STATISTICS method.

connect string — Information about the connection that tells Oracle the username, password and service name to be resolved.

contention — The competition between or among two or more processes for the same resources.

data dictionary cache — A major memory space of the shared pool that is used to store database object definitions temporarily.

data file — An Oracle-formatted file used to store system and user data.

data file allocation — Places data files across all mount points (disks) in the system based on data type and function, as well as disk configuration.

database statistics — Statistics that measure database operations, such as how fast a database reads data from a disk, to determine if database operations are optimal.

database tuning — An ongoing process to maintain the performance of the database at an optimal level based on attainable tuning goals.

DBWn (Database Writer) — A background process that can be tuned to enhance performance or reduce contention. This process performs the single function of writing dirty block buffers to data files and ensures that there are always free buffers in the database buffer cache memory.

DDL lock — A lock that Oracle automatically sets when a CREATE, TRUNCATE, or ALTER statement is issued to ensure that no transactions are submitted against the object during the execution of the statement.

deadlock — A deadlock occurs when two or more transactions are attempting and failing to process an object because it is locked.

dedicated server — A server that responds to a session request from a specified user.

dedicated server mode — When running in dedicated server mode, a server process serves requests for one specific user connection and session.

dictionary extent management — Oracle uses system tables to determine which extents are free and which are used.

dictionary-managed tablespace — Uses the system data dictionary to manage free space using PCTUSED parameter and FREELIST structure.

direct path method — Bypasses the cache buffer and loads data directly into the data file.

disk thrashing — Disk thrashing occurs when the operating system moves data from memory to disk temporarily and back to memory due to the small size of memory. The term *disk thrashing* is the symptom of high activity of I/O.

dispatcher process — A number of dispatcher processes form a dispatcher layer that acts as an interface between the user and Oracle.

DML lock — A lock that is acquired at the start of a transaction and released at the completion of the transaction.

enqueue — A data structure for locks that notifies Oracle of transactions waiting for a resource that is locked by another session.

ESTIMATE STATISTICS method — When analyzing a table, you must specify whether you want Oracle to analyze every row in the table or only sample rows. To analyze sample row in a table, specify the ESTIMATE STATISTICS method.

execution plan (explain plan) — A plan to retrieve data for a query.

extent — A physical and logical grouping of Oracle blocks.

FOR UPDATE clause — A clause of the SELECT statement that is used for reporting accuracy. The row selected is locked in the ROW SHARE lock mode.

full table scan — A data access method used by the Oracle Optimizer to scan every row in a table to retrieve data.

full table scan (FTS) — A function that occurs when the database server scans through a whole table to retrieve rows from a table

granule — A granule in Oracle9*i* is a memory unit.

hash-join area operation — An operation that joins a small- to medium-sized table to a large table in memory.

I/O activity — Reading from disk and writing to disk

I/O slave — An I/O slave is a process that works on behalf of the Database Writer to write dirty block bluffers to data files.

Java pool — Stores Java code used by user sessions.

large pool — Is a memory structure of the SGA, the large pool is used by programs such as EXP/IMP and RMAN.

least recent used (LRU) — Oracle uses the least recent used (LRU) structure and algorithm to determine which block is being used the least and flushes that block to release the memory it occupies. The major purpose of the LRU is to reduce disk I/O.

library cache — A major memory space of the shared pool that is used to cache SQL statements, PL/SQL blocks, and other object code used by an application.

local extent management — A method of retrieving information about the allocation of extents. It is called local, because, the information about extents is stored locally within the tablespace, where the extents reside.

locally managed tablespace (LMT) — Uses a bitmap image of free extents within the tablespace.

lock — A mechanism that protects a database object from being altered while it is being modified by other processes or users

logfile switch (log switch) — Occurs when the redo log file is filled or when an alter system switch logfile is issued.

Manual Space Management (MSM) — Makes DBAs responsible for administering free space using PCTFREE and FREELIST structures.

multi-pass execution — Performed when the workarea in PGA is too small to allocate memory for the current operation and requires multiple extra steps and passes to complete the operation.

one-pass execution — One-pass execution is performed when the workarea in PGA is not large enough to allocate memory for the current operation and requires one extra step or pass to complete the operation.

optimal execution — Optimal execution is performed when the workarea in the PGA is large enough to allocate memory for the current operation.

Oracle block — Each Oracle block is a multiple of operating system blocks, which can be 2 K, 4 K, 8 K, 16 K, or 32 K.

Oracle external file — A non-Oracle file that can be in any format.

Oracle Optimizer — An algorithm that determines the most efficient way to execute a SQL statement and retrieve data.

Oracle Outlines — Oracle Outlines supports categories to classify different stored outlines based on functionality or business requirements.

Parsing process — Tasks that ensure the validity of the statement as well as the validity of the selected columns and determine the best method to retrieve the data.

PCTFREE — Stands for percent free. A block option that specifies the percent of the block to be reserved as free for future row updates and block overhead growth. The default value is 10.

PCTINCREASE — Stands for percent increase. An extent option that tells Oracle to increase the next extent with the percentage specified by this value. The default value is 50. This is used as a fudge factor to accommodate data growth.

PCTUSED — Stands for percent used. A block option that specifies how much of the block is used before the block is added back to the free list, which contains a list of all free blocks. The default value is 40.

PGA advice — An Oracle9i feature that provides statistical data that helps DBAs to properly configure the PGA.

process — A process is a program that performs a specific task.

program global area (PGA) — The memory allocated from random access memory on the host machine where Oracle resides.

range scan — In a range scan, Oracle scans the rows of an object based on a range of values.

raw device — A disk that is not formatted and not managed by the operating system.

READ COMMITTED — If a DML statement is attempting to update data on an object that has been updated by another session and not committed (that is the statement is in a READ COMMITTED state) at any time during the session, the DML statement waits until the other session completes its transaction.

read consistency — The second function of an undo segment to be examined.

Real Application Cluster (RAC) — A new feature of the Oracle9*i* database system, which can distinguish Oracle databases from the databases of other vendors.

redo log buffer — A device that stores temporarily all transaction entries submitted to the database.

redundant array of inexpensive disks (RAID) (also known as redundant array of independent disks) — Protects data in case of disk media failure without any performance cost or compromise.

replication — Replication is an advanced feature of a database system that enables data objects to be replicated from one primary database to a secondary database

reserved shared pool — A contiguous memory area used when an application requires the loading and caching of a large stored procedure.

resource consumer group — A group of database users who are allocated a percentage of CPU usage based on user priorities.

response time — The time the database spends answering a query that is submitted by a user.

rollback segment — An undo segment that is used for storing rollback data. Also known as the BEFORE image.

row chaining — Occurs when a row is too big to fit in one block. In this case, Oracle keeps a portion of the row in the original block and the rest of the row is chained to another block.

row migration — Occurs when a row is updated and the size of the updated row becomes too large for the block in which it resides.

rowid — Stands for row identification and is the physical address of the row.

Rule-based Optimizer — Determines the most efficient way to execute the SQL statement using a set of rules and a ranking system. This optimizer evaluates the query using different execution paths to select the one that produces the lowest rank value.

scalability — The capability of a system to increase or decrease in size in response to the utilization load without impacting the performance of the system.

segment — A segment is a physical part of a database object such as table or index.

SELECT...FOR UPDATE clause — A clause that ensures that selected rows do not change while being read. The statement locks rows selected by the SELECT statement as well as all rows in the table that are in the ROW SHARE mode and thus effectively disallows any updates to the table.

server process — A number of server processes form a server layer. Each server process handles the user requests assigned by the dispatcher.

shared pool memory — Stores the most frequently submitted SQL statements and PL/SQL blocks to expedite the parsing process.

shared pool size advice — A feature that provides advisory statistics for the shared pool memory, specifically for its library cache portion.

shared server — An Oracle server mode in which many sessions share the same server.

shared server mode — When running in shared server mode, a process receives and responds to all requests submitted by the users.

statistical trend — A plot of several database measurements that shows the behavior of various database operations.

System Development Life Cycle (SDLC) — A structured methodology for building software application systems.

System Global Area (SGA) — The memory structure in which Oracle caches data that is retrieved for access, updates, submitted SQL statements, executed PL/SQL blocks, data dictionary definitions, and other cache mechanisms.

table allocation — Distributes tables among different application tablespaces.

table coalescing — The process of defragmenting tablespaces by combining contiguous small extents.

tablespace — A tablespace is a logical entity that serves as a logical container for physical data files, as well as a logical container for logical segments.

tablespace allocation — A design activity in which a database architect or administrator sizes and places data files in a manner compatible to OFA guidelines and recommendations to reduce I/O contention.

tablespace map — A physical layout of extents for each segment residing in the tablespace.

tablespace sizing — The process of computing the approximate size of a tablespace based on objects allocated or assigned to it.

tablespace sizing — Tablespace sizing is the process of computing an approximate size of a tablespace based on objects allocated or assigned to it.

temporary tablespace — A temporary space holder on a disk that you create when you need to perform a large sort operation and do not have enough space in memory to allocate to the PGA.

transportable tablespace — Tablespaces that can be moved and copied from one database to another.

tuning approach — A step-by-step process for optimizing database performance.

undo segment — When data has been changed but the change is not yet made permanent, Oracle retains the data that has been changed in a data file within a tablespace known as an undo segment so that it can be restored.

Index